KU-537-368

Brain Development and Cognition

LEEDS BECKETT UN

Leeds Metropolitan University

17 0346927 6

Brain Development and Cognition

A Reader

Second Edition

Mark H. Johnson,
Yuko Munakata,
and
Rick O. Gilmore

Blackwell
Publishers

© 1993 and 2002 by Blackwell Publishers Ltd
a Blackwell Publishing company

Editorial Offices:
108 Cowley Road, Oxford OX4 1JF, UK
Tel: +44 (0)1865 791100
350 Main Street, Malden, MA 02148-5018, USA
Tel: +1 781 388 8250

All rights reserved. No part of this publication may be reproduced, stored in
a retrieval system, or transmitted, in any form or by any means, electronic, mechanical,
photocopying, recording or otherwise, except as permitted by the UK Copyright, Designs
and Patents Act 1988, without the prior permission of the publisher.

First published 1993 by Basil Blackwell Ltd
Second edition published 2002 by Blackwell Publishers Ltd

Library of Congress Cataloging-in-Publication Data

Brain development and cognition : a reader / [edited by] Mark H. Johnson,
Yuko Munakata, and Rick O. Gilmore.—2nd ed.
p. ; cm.
Includes bibliographical references and index
ISBN 0-631-21736-3 (hardback : alk. paper)—ISBN 0-631-21737-1 (pb : alk. paper)
1. Cognitive neuroscience. 2. Cognition in children. 3. Brain—Growth.
4. Neuroplasticity. I. Johnson, Mark H. (Mark Henry), 1960– II. Munakata,
Yuko. III. Gilmore, Rick O.
[DNLM: 1. Brain—growth & development—Collected Works.
2. Cognition—physiology—Collected Works. 3. Neuronal Plasticity—Collected Works.
WL 300 B81238 2002
QP360.5 .B73 2002   612.8′2—dc21   2001052407

A catalogue record for this title is available from the British Library.

Set in 10 on 12pt Ehrhardt
by Kolam Information Services Private Ltd, Pondicherry, India
Printed and bound in Great Britain
by T. J. International,
Padstow, Cornwall

For further information on
Blackwell Publishers, visit our website:
www.blackwellpublishers.co.uk

LEEDS METROPOLITAN
UNIVERSITY
LEARNING CENTRE
1703469276
29. 11. 02
HI-D
CC- 34690 2 12.2002.
612·82 JOH

Contents

Contributors

Elizabeth A. Bates: University of California, San Diego, California

Daphne Bavelier: University of Rochester, Rochester, New York

James E. Black: University of Illinois, Urbana-Champaign, Illinois

Nancy Byl: University of California, San Francisco, California

Harry T. Chugani: Wayne State University, Detroit, Michigan

Adele Diamond: Eunice Kennedy Shriver Center, Waltham, Massachusetts

Jeffrey L. Elman: University of California, San Diego, California

Gilbert Gottlieb: University of North Carolina, Chapel Hill, North Carolina

William T. Greenough: University of Illinois, Urbana-Champaign, Illinois

Nancy L. Hayes: Robert Wood Johnson Medical School, Piscataway, New Jersey

Peter R. Huttenlocher: University of Chicago, Chicago, Illinois

William Jenkins: Scientific Learning Corporation, Oakland, California

Mark H. Johnson: Birkbeck, University of London, London, UK

Annette Karmiloff-Smith: Institute of Child Health, London, UK

Konrad Lorenz:* Max Plank Institute Fur Verhaltensphysiologie, Seewiesen, Germany

Peter Marler: University of California, Davis, California

John C. Mazziotta: University of California, Los Angeles School of Medicine, Los Angeles, California

Michael M. Merzenich: University of California, San Francisco, California

Steve Miller: Scientific Learning Corporation, Oakland, California

Charles A. Nelson: University of Minnesota, Minneapolis, Minnesota

Helen J. Neville: University of Oregon, Eugene, Oregon

Richard S. Nowakowski: Robert Wood Johnson Medical School, Piscataway, New Jersey

Dennis D. M. O'Leary: Salk Institute for Biological Studies, La Jolla, California

Randall C. O'Reilly: University of Colorado, Boulder, Colorado

Susan Oyama: City University of New York, New York

Bruce F. Pennington: University of Denver, Denver, Colorado

Michael E. Phelps: University of California, Los Angeles School of Medicine, Los Angeles, California

Jean Piaget:* University of Geneva, Geneva, Switzerland

Pasko Rakic: Yale University School of Medicine, New Haven, Connecticut

Judy Reilly: San Diego State University, San Diego, California

Carla J. Shatz: University of California, Berkeley, California

Joan Stiles: University of California, San Diego, California

Paula Tallal: Rutgers University, Newark, New Jersey

Donna Thal: San Diego State University, San Diego, California

Esther Thelen: Indiana University, Bloomington, Indiana

Doris A. Trauner: University of California, San Diego, California

Christopher S. Wallace: University of Illinois, Urbana-Champaign, Illinois

Beverly A. Wright: Northwestern University, Evanston, Illinois

Christian Xerri: University of Provence, Marseilles, France

*Deceased

Preface to First Edition

Several times in my scientific career I have felt pressure to classify myself as being either a "cognitive neuroscientist" or a "developmentalist". However, the more I considered which of these two I really was, the more I realized that the two enterprises are inextricably entwined. Indeed, I have come to the belief that significant progress in either field is crucially dependent upon its interaction with the other. This book represents an initial attempt to convince others that this might be the case.

The book was prepared with two types of reader in mind. The first type is students on courses in cognitive neuroscience and cognitive development. I hope this book will fill the gap that those of us who run such courses know to exist. The second type of reader I have in mind is the established researcher/teacher in cognitive science, neuroscience, or neuro-psychology who feels that he or she ought know something about the relation between the developing brain and mind. I hope these people find this a useful and stimulating reference volume.

I have no doubt that the particular choice of readings and new authors reflects my own particular biases, and that any other editor's selection would have been different. However, I have gone to some lengths to find out from others in the field what readings they would have chosen for a course on this topic. These consultations, and space limitations, have resulted in my making the difficult decision to drop some of my own personal favorites. Some of these have found their way into the further reading sections at the end of each of the part introductions. When the reactions to my current selection of readings began to vary from them being overall "too cognitive" to being overall "too neural", I realized that I must have got the balance about right! The best I can hope for is that readers familiar with the area will find that the selection includes at least the majority of those that they would have included.

The book would not have seen the light of day without at least two other people: first, Stephan Chambers of Basil Blackwell, with whom the idea for the book was originally born, and who nurtured it carefully from conception to publication; second, Leslie Tucker, whose cheerful application to the many chores associated with a book such as this never ceased to amaze me. Leslie also assisted indirectly by running my lab so efficiently that I have time to spend on projects such as this one. While Leslie labored in Pittsburgh, Judith Harvey and Pam Shahen did likewise in Blackwell's office in Oxford. Together they formed a formidable team.

Rarely can a prospective book have been given such a thorough testing bed as that provided by the students and postdocs who attended my fall 1991 "Brain Development and Cognition" course at Carnegie Mellon (Dan Appelquist, Maxwell Drain, Matt Isaak, Randy O'Reilly, Cathy Reed, Hermi Tabachnek, Shaun Vecera, Marcie Wallace and Gene Zilberstein). It was a joy to have such incisive and interested fellow travellers on my voyage of discovery.

Other people who provided advice on particular topics or readings were Jeri Janowsky, Annette Karmiloff-Smith, Yuko Munakata, and Joan Stiles. Thanks are also due to Bob Siegler and Annette Karmiloff-Smith who commented on the comprehensibility of my introductions to each of the sections. Needless to say, none of the above is in any way responsible for the views expressed in the final version.

Thanks are also due to the various publishers and authors who contributed to the book in ways big and small.

To my parents and sisters I owe thanks for putting up with my long absences, and neglect of family events, over the years.

Thanks are insufficient for Anoushka, who has brought so much that is good into my life.

Preface to Second Edition

In the years since the first edition of this Reader was published, the field of Developmental Cognitive Neuroscience has grown from embryo to infant. We hope that this updated and revised edition of the book will facilitate further growth from infant to adult. In the years intervening between editions of this Reader a number of other textbooks, readers, and handbooks have appeared with related titles and topics. We believe, however, that this Reader retains its unique niche combining as it does classic readings, updates on these papers, new contributions by top experts, as well as introductory text for each section. Like the first edition, we expect it to appeal as both a reference volume for researchers and teachers, and as a class book for undergraduate and postgraduate classes. The present edition of the Reader has also benefited from much "road testing" in the classroom, by both the editors and others. An additional feature designed to make this edition more useful to instructors is a web site. The site contains links to color figures from selected papers in the Reader, additional reference materials, and sample course syllabi, and will be updated regularly. The site can be found at http://blackwellpublishers.co.uk/johnson

Space limitations severely restricted the number of readings it was possible to include, and many of our personal favorites did not quite make it. These decisions were very hard, and the outcome was often decided by issues of overall balance and coverage, rather than the quality or importance of individual pieces. We believe this increasing competition for places within the Reader reflects well on the healthy development of our field.

The second edition of the Reader, like its predecessor, was dependent upon the work of many people. Once again, Leslie Tucker played a pivotal role in organizing and coordinating the volume, this time with the added complication of three editors on two continents. Monika Offerman also provided invaluable assistance. Many people at Blackwell Publishers, including Martin Davies, Phyllis Wentworth, Alison Dunnett, and Sarah Bird have helped from conception to production. Sincere thanks are also due to the authors who helped us reprint or modify existing material, or who prepared new chapters. We also wish to thank the many students that have provided us with feedback (good and bad!) on the previous edition and on contender papers for this edition.

Finally, we wish to thank our families, partners and friends for their patience during the preparation of the book. Without their support it would not have been possible.

Acknowledgments

1   Lorenz, K. (1965). Critique of the modern ethologists' attitude. From K. Lorenz, *Evolution and the Modification of Behavior*, chapter 5, pp. 29–48. Chicago: University of Chicago Press. Reprinted by kind permission;

2   Oyama, S. (2000). The problem of change. From S. Oyama, *The Ontogeny of Information: Developmental Systems and Evolution* (second edition), chapter 3, pp. 28–41. Durham, NC: Duke University Press. Copyright 2000. All rights reserved. Reprinted with permission;

3   Piaget, J. (1971). The epigenetic system and the development of cognitive functions. From J. Piaget, *Biology and Knowledge*, section 2, pp. 14–23. Edinburgh University Press and University of Chicago Press;

4   Gottlieb, G. (1992). From gene to organism: The developing individual as an emergent, interactional, hierarchical system. From G. Gottlieb, *Individual Development and Evolution: The Genesis of Novel Behavior*, chapter 13, pp. 158–72. New York: Oxford University Press. Copyright © 1991 by Oxford University Press. Used by permission of Oxford University Press, Inc.;

5   Nowakowski, R. S. and Hayes, N. L. (2001). General principles of CNS Development;

6   Rakic, P. (1998). Intrinsic and extrinsic determinants of neocortical parcellation: A radial unit model. From P. Rakic and W. Singer (eds.), *Neurobiology of Neocortex*, pp. 5–27. New York: John Wiley & Sons. Reproduced by permission of John Wiley & Sons Ltd;

7   Chugani, H. T., Phelps, M. E., and Mazziotta, J. C. (1987). Positron Emission Tomography study of human brain functional development. *Annals of Neurology* 22, pp. 487–97. Reprinted with permission;

8   Huttenlocher, P. R. (1990). Morphometric study of human cerebral cortex. *Neuropsychologia* 28, pp. 517–27. Reprinted with permission from Elsevier Science;

9   Johnson, M. H. (1995). The development of visual attention: A cognitive neuroscience perspective. From M. S. Gazzaniga (ed.), *The Cognitive Neurosciences*, pp. 735–47. Cambridge, MA: MIT Press. Reprinted with permission of MIT Press;

10 Nelson, C. A. (1995). The ontogeny of human memory: A cognitive neuroscience perspective. *Developmental Psychology* 31(5), pp. 723–8. Copyright © 1995 by the American Psychological Association. Reprinted with permission;

11   Greenough, W. T., Black, J. E., and Wallace, C. S. (1987). Experience and brain development. *Child Development* 58, pp. 539–59. Reprinted with permission of the Society for Research in Child Development;

12   O'Leary, D. D. M. (1989). Do cortical areas emerge from a protocortex? *Trends in the Neurosciences* 12, pp. 400–6. Reprinted with permission of Elsevier Science;

13   Shatz, C. J. (1996). Emergence of order in visual system development. *Proceedings of the National Academy of Sciences of the United States of America* 93(2), pp. 602–8. Republished with permission of the Proceedings of the National Academy of Sciences USA, 2101 Constitution Ave., NW, Washington, DC 20418. Reproduced by permission of the publisher via Copyright Clearance Center, Inc.;

14   Neville, H. J. and Bavelier, D. (1999). Specificity and plasticity in neurocognitive development in humans. From M. Gazzaniga (ed.), *The New Cognitive Neurosciences* (second edition), pp. 83–98. Cambridge, MA: MIT Press. Reprinted with permission of MIT Press;

15   Stiles, J., Bates, E. A., Thal, D., Trauner, D. A., and Reilly, J. (1998). Linguistic and spatial cognitive development in children with pre- and perinatal focal brain injury: A ten-year overview from the San Diego Longitudinal Project, *Advances in Infancy Research* 12, pp. 131–64. Norwood, NJ: Ablex; the chapter in the current volume is a shortened version of the original;

16   Merzenich, M. M., Wright, B. A., Jenkins, W., Xerri, C., Byl, N., Miller, S., and Tallal, P. (1996). Cortical plasticity underlying perceptual, motor, and cognitive skill development: Implications for neurorehabilitation. *Cold Spring Harbor Symposia on Quantitative Biology* 61, pp. 1–8. Reprinted with permission from Cold Spring Harbor Laboratory Press;

17   Marler, P. (1991). The instinct to learn. From S. Carey and R. Gelman (eds.), *The Epigenesis of Mind: Essays on Biology and Cognition*, pp. 37–66. Mahwah, NJ: Lawrence Erlbaum Associates;

18   Thelen, E. (1989). Self-organization in developmental processes: Can systems approaches work? In M. Gunnar and E. Thelen (eds.), *Systems and Development. The Minnesota Symposium on Child Psychology* 22, pp. 77–117. Mahwah, NJ: Lawrence Erlbaum Associates. Reprinted with permission from Lawrence Erlbaum Associates, Inc.;

19   Karmiloff-Smith, A. (1998). Development itself is the key to understanding developmental disorders. Reprinted from *Trends in Cognitive Science* 2(10), pp. 389–98, with permission from Elsevier Science;

20   O'Reilly, R. C. and Johnson, M. H. (1994). Object recognition and sensitive periods: A computational analysis of visual imprinting. *Neural Computation* 6, pp. 357–90;

21   Bates, E. A. and Elman, J. L. (2001). Connectionism and the study of change;

22   Diamond, A. (2001). A model system for studying the role of dopamine in prefrontal cortex during early development in humans;

23   Pennington, B. F. (2001). Genes and brain: Individual differences and human universals.

PART I

Perspectives on Development

Editors' Introduction to Part I

Few subjects in science have provoked such acrimonious and impassioned debate as development. These debates have often been centered on particular dichotomies, with each side characterizing the other's viewpoint as at an extreme end of the dichotomy, even though both may have been closer to the middle ground than their opponents would care to admit. Throughout the book, these dichotomies, such as nature versus nurture, and selection versus learning, will keep recurring in a variety of different contexts. We will discover that the same debates often rage simultaneously in the domains of neural, behavioral, and cognitive development. In Part I we begin by bringing some of these major issues out in the open in a number of writings by authors who have explicitly championed particular viewpoints on development.

The first two readings in this section put the case for and against the use of the nature versus nurture dichotomy (Lorenz for, and Oyama against). Although most researchers now agree that the study of development should be about unraveling the *interaction* between genetic specification and environmental influence, debates still rage about whether the role of experience is in structuring or organizing the mind/brain (Piaget), or whether its role is more that of a releaser of propensities already latent within the organism.

Lorenz defends the utility of the innate–learned dichotomy as a powerful tool for discovering important facts about development. The section reprinted is from a book written fairly late in his career and designed to answer the criticism of his earlier work, in which he argued for "innate" and "learned" components of behavior as being opposed and mutually exclusive. When it became clear from a number of experimental examples that the distinction between these two is often blurry, several critics (Lehrman (1953) perhaps foremost among them) argued that the search for purely "innate" behaviors was not only futile, but also misleading. Lorenz responds in the reprinted article by conceding that his earlier claims about the innate and learned being mutually exclusive were incorrect. "Learning" has to involve an innate component in two senses. First, a species has to be adapted to learn – it needs to have brain circuits that have been selected to be approximately plastic at certain points in development. The second sense in which innate information is important is that it often acts as a teacher, "the innate schoolmarm," for learning. This latter point re-emerges in Parts V and VI of this volume.

Lorenz refuses to yield with regard to the usefulness of the concept of the "innate" for two reasons. First, he argues that certain components of behavior are present without experience of the environment. In some cases, these systems have to be impervious to learning for them to be simultaneously efficient, fast acting, and relatively complex. Second, he argues that investigating the extent to which components of behavior are innate is the best, and may be the only, strategy for unpacking developmental processes scientifically.

The next reading, due to Susan Oyama, presents a very comprehensive attack on the nature/nurture dichotomy. Oyama attempts to show how even the implicit use of this dichotomy can mislead investigations of development. She argues that the nature/nurture dichotomy is partly the result of the scientific need to think in dichotomies, and partly the result of addressing the wrong question. She also maintains that the current scientific approaches to development are more deeply influenced by cultural traditions than we think. That is, both religion and science have looked for a source of prespecified instructions (information) outside the developmental process itself. While religion has attributed the emergence of structure or form to an outside creator, scientists have proposed that the source of prespecified instructions is to be found in the gene.

The first scientists interested in ontogeny hypothesized that a completely formed being existed within the "germ," either the egg or the sperm. In both varieties of the theory, the other partner's contribution was said merely to diffuse into the preformed being. Gradually, as scientific knowledge grew, the prespecifications for form became enclosed within the genetic material. In recent years, ever more elaborate metaphors have been devised as it becomes clear that the majority of genes cannot do the job of regulating development in isolation. The orchestration of development is now hypothesized to be controlled by "switching" genes, but these in turn are regulated by other "switching" genes, leading us, Oyama states, into an infinite regress. While there has been much debate between those concerned with whether the genes act as a blueprint, hypothesis generator, program, code, plan, or set of rules for development, no one has yet proposed that these views might *all* be wrong, she maintains.

Oyama believes that in understanding development we should be concerned more with change than with the steady state, with the process and not the phenotypic state at any point of time.

> Nativism and empiricism require each other as do warp and weft. What they share is the belief that information can pre-exist the processes that give rise to it. Yet information "in the genes" or "in the environment" is not biologically relevant until it participates in phenotypic processes. Once this happens, it becomes meaningful in the organism only as it is constituted by its developmental system. The result is not *more* information but *significant* information. (S. Oyama, *The Ontogeny of Information: Developmental Systems and Evolution*, second edition [Durham, NC: Duke University Press, 2000], pp. 15–16)

The difference between Oyama and Lorenz is brought out clearly, in one metaphor employed by the latter. Lorenz states it is not the bricks and mortar which regulate the building of a cathedral, but a pre-existing plan that has been devised by an architect. For Oyama, it is precisely the notion of a pre-existing plan that is misguided. When considering living forms, she argues that the "plan" is contained in each and every brick and piece of mortar.

What are the implications of these arguments for the study of cognitive development? Oyama urges us not to focus on constancy during development, since this inevitably leads us to look for an injection of pre-existing information from either the genes or the environment to account for changes. With few exceptions, this focus on constancy is a characteristic of models of cognitive development. This is partly because it is simply easier to describe particular stages in development than to account for the dynamic processes of change, and partly because of influential logical arguments such as those put forward by Jerry Fodor. Fodor argues, for example, that it is impossible to learn a language of thought whose predicates express extensions unexpressable in the previously available language. In Oyama's view, Fodor's arguments are based on a very static and stage-like conception of development. The emergence of a new language of thought should not be attributable to either learning or maturation (the latter of which Fodor settles for), bur rather should be seen as a product of the preceding developmental system. Despite the obsession of some of his followers with particular static *stages* of development, perhaps only in Jean Piaget's original writing is there the beginning of an attempt to address increases in significant information as part of the developmental process itself.

In the reprinted section from his volume *Biology and Knowledge*, Piaget discusses the notion of stages of development. While arguing for their usefulness if they are carefully defined, he also stresses that a stage is not a static phenomenon, but rather the temporarily balanced "dynamic equilibrium" of a variety of continually competing factors. Transition from one of these stages to the next is provoked by a disturbance of this equilibrium, a disequilibrium. Piaget argues for a particular kind of relation between one stage and the next, in which the previous stage is always crucial for the present one, without the present stage being in any sense contained within the previous one.

It is worth noting here that Piaget's conception of stages and the transitions between them is very different from the static "stages of development" notion criticized by Oyama. For Piaget, both the transitions and the stages are the products of dynamic interaction between a variety of factors, some related to the genes and others related to the environment. The transition phases occur when these competing factors become uneven, provoking disequilibrium. The conception is markedly different from the idea that either the genes or the environment push the organism from one stable static state to another. Indeed, Piaget sees the agenda for developmental psychology as

> to explain in detail how, in the field of knowledge as in that of organic epigenesis, this collaboration between the genome and the environment actually works – especially those details which concern autoregulations or progressive equilibrations which admit of the exclusion of both preformism and the notion of a reaction caused entirely by environment. (Piaget; p. 30, this volume)

Thus, Piaget distances himself from both nativists on the one hand, and empiricists on the other, suggesting that heredity opens up possibilities that have to be actualized by collaboration with the environment (see also Bates and Elman, Part VII).

Piaget presents us with a paradox: while there is no sense in which we can consider formal logical thinking to be specified in the genome, it is virtually always attained by a certain age in normal children, and always preceded by a certain sequence of earlier stages. He attempts to resolve this paradox by invoking a concept originally devised by the geneticist C. H. Waddington, that of necessary epigenetic routes or "chreods" (see Waddington, 1975, for further reading). Waddington proposed that development could be visualized in terms of an "epigenetic landscape" (see figure 1.1) in which processes tended to take only certain channels. Self-regulatory processes, such as "homeorhesis," ensure that the organism returns to its channel following small perturbations to the system (while very large perturbations can result in a quite different channel being taken). Thus, for the normal child, the same endpoint will be reached regardless of any small deviations that take place earlier. Piaget

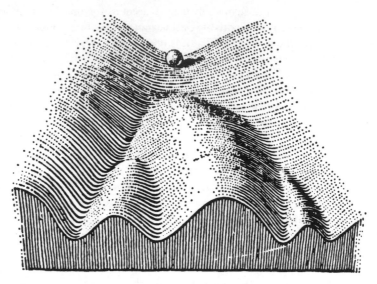

Figure 1.1   The epigenetic landscape. Reproduced from: C. H. Waddington, *The Evolution of an Evolutionist* (Edinburgh University Press, 1975) by kind permission.

also sees chreods as being important on the temporal dimension, processes of organization in particular domains have their own "time tally," rhythm, or schedule. Thus while some degree of acceleration can occur during some stages, the amount is limited.

The reading by Gottlieb takes up the theme of different epigenetic pathways during development. He begins by drawing an important contrast between *Predetermined epigenesis* and *Probabilistic epigenesis*. Predetermined epigenesis refers to a unidirectional causal path from genes to (brain) structural maturation to functional activity. In other words, it refers to arguments of the kind "when brain regions X matures, then function Y emerges . . ." By this view, the expression of genes and maturational processes are uninfluenced by function, activity, or experience. In contrast, probabilistic epigenesis refers to bidirectional reciprocal relations between genes, and (brain) structure and function. In other words, activity or function during development can influence processes down to the genetic level. Gottlieb discusses evidence consistent with the probabilistic epigenesis view, before going on to review the different roles that experience can play during ontogeny.

Gottlieb argues that experience can play at least three different roles in anatomical, physiological, and psychological development. First, it can serve a maintenance function by sustaining an already achieved state. Without experience, the state decays or reduces to an earlier form. Second, it can serve as facilitative function by speeding up the transition to the next developmental state. Finally, experience can have an inductive effect by bringing about a developmental change that would not otherwise happen. Examples of all three of these kinds of effects of experience can be found in readings in later sections of this book.

FURTHER READING

Boden, M. (1979). *Piaget*. London: Fontana. (A good psychological–philosophical introduction to Piaget's thinking.)

Braitenberg, V. (1984). *Vehicles: Experiments in Synthetic Psychology*. Cambridge, MA: MIT Press. (A wonderful collection of invented organisms that evolve ever more complex behaviors.)

Donaldson, M. (1978). *Children's Minds*. London: Fontana. (A basic psychological–experimental introduction to Piaget, with an excellent appendix outlining aspects of his theory.)

Gottlieb, G. (1996). *Synthesizing Nature–Nurture: Prenatal Roots of Instinctive Behavior*. Mahwah, NJ: Erlbaum. (An extended discussion of probabilistic epigenesis and experimental evidence for it.)

Johnson, M. H. and Morton, J. (1991). *Biology and Cognitive Development: The Case of Face Recognition*. Oxford: Blackwell. (Chapter 1 is relevant to the issues addressed in this part.)

Lehrman, D. S. (1953). A critique of Konrad Lorenz's theory of instinctive behavior. *Quarterly Review of Biology* 28, 337–63. (A prominent critique of Lorenz's early writing.)

Piatelli-Palmarini, M. (ed.). (1980). *Language and Learning. The Debate between Jean Piaget and Noam Chomsky*. London: Routledge & Kegan Paul. (A collection of position papers centered on the debates between Piaget and Chomsky at the Abbey de Royaumont conference.)

Siegler, R. S. (1996). *Emerging Minds: The Process of Change in Children's Thinking*. New York: Oxford. (A discussion of the dynamic nature of cognitive development in preschool and school-age children.)

Spelke, E. S. and Newport, E. L. (1997). Nativism, empiricism, and the development of knowledge. In R. M. Lerner (ed.), *Theoretical Models of Human Development* in W. Damon (series ed.), *Handbook of Child Psychology* (fifth edition). New York: Wiley.

Thompson, D. W. (1917 – abridged edition 1961). *On Growth and Form*. Cambridge: Cambridge University Press. (A classic introduction to fundamental issues surrounding development.)

Tinbergen, N. (1951). *The Study of Instinct*. Oxford: Clarendon Press. (The classic introduction to the ethological analysis of ontogeny.)

Waddington, C. H. (1975). *The Evolution of an Evolutionist*. Edinburgh: Edinburgh University Press. (A series of essays about evolution and ontogeny. Waddington's ideas on this topic greatly influenced Piaget and other constructivists.)

1

Critique of the Modern Ethologists' Attitude

Konrad Lorenz

What I propose to discuss here is mainly the assumptions already mentioned in the introduction: that "what we formerly called innate" and what we formerly called "learned" represent only the extreme ends of a continuum of insensibly graduated mixtures between the two, and that all behaviour, down to its smallest elements, owes its adaptedness to both processes. I think I can show that this assumption is not only bad strategy of research but completely unfounded and in all probability false.

In discussing the first behavioristic argument,[a] I have attempted to demonstrate the fallacy of treating the "innate" and the "learned" as opposed, mutually exclusive concepts. I tried to show that, while all learning is performed by mechanisms which do contain phylogenetically acquired information, no reasons exist for assuming that individually acquired information "enters into" every kind of phylogenetically adapted behaviour. For millions of years our planet has been inhabited by creatures possessing quite elaborate behaviour patterns which owed none of their adaptedness to any of the higher and typical forms of learning. We are certain that habituation and its counterpart, sensitization, are the only forms of adaptive modification of behaviour ever found in protozoa and in organisms with a diffuse nervous system. When, eons later, at a comparatively high level of neural organization, modifiability of behavior began to increase, a tremendous selection pressure must have been brought to bear on the development of mechanisms adaptively modifying individual behavior. The intensity of this pressure can be inferred from the omnipresence of its effect in all phyla of organisms which, independently of each other, have evolved a centralized nervous system.

Everything that has been said in criticism of the first behavioristic argument is a reason for not assuming an unlimited, diffuse mutual permeability and mixability of phylogenetic adaptation and learning. Only confirmed "preformationists" can doubt the fact that any specialized adaptive modifiability of behaviour, such as we find in vertebrates, arthropods, and cephalopods, can never be a product of chance, but has to be regarded as the function

a   The "first behavioristic argument" refers to the argument that the dissociation of behaviors into "innate" and "learned" components is not analytically valid since hitherto the only definition of "innate" is that which is not learned. (Editors' note.)

"Critique of the Modern Ethologists' Attitude" is an excerpt from: Konrad Lorenz, *Evolution and the Modification of Behavior* (University of Chicago Press, 1965, chapter 5, pp. 29–48) and is reprinted by kind permission.

of a nervous apparatus which is highly organized and which owes its origin, as all organization does, to the process of "pure induction" conducted by the evolution of every species. To assume diffuse permeability of phylogenetic adaptation and learning implies the assumption of an infinite number of such organizations, which is strictly contradicted by the hackneyed fact that there are, for each animal species, only limited numbers of highly specific stimulus situations that will act as reinforcements.

The notion that learning or any other change of behavior achieving survival value could possibly be the function of a non-specifically organized and programmed aggregation of neural elements, is absolutely untenable.

It is a matter of surprise and concern to me that this fallacy has been voiced in *Behaviour*[b] with great self-confidence and without arousing the least contradiction on the part of English-speaking ethologists. Ethology loses its character of a biological science if the fact is forgotten that adaptedness exists and needs an explanation. There is no hope of gaining greater "exactitude" by shedding biological knowledge and clinging to allegedly operational concepts. All conceptualizations employed in the scientific study of nature are fundamentally operational, and if the operations underlying the concepts used in phylogenetics are complicated and presuppose considerable knowledge, this furnishes no excuse for neglecting important and well-known facts. It is a great error to believe that "exactitude" can be gained by restricting research to one experimentally – and mentally – simple operation. The damage done by this type of procedure is best illustrated by Jensen's paper "Operationism and the Question 'Is This Behavior Learned or Innate?'" (1961).

Jensen argues in the following manner:

> The possibility of differences in behavior being neither innate (selected) nor learned (trained) but something else (produced by other operations) allows the separate classification of various types of operations or antecedent differences to which behavioral differences can be attributed. [A list of such operations, including food schedule, hormones, and even nervous system lesions, etc. follows.]

> Since behavioral differences may be attributed to effects and interactions of many factors, the original question can be rephrased in an unrestricted way. Instead of: "Is this behavior innate or learned?" we can ask: "What causes this difference in behavior?" So asked, the question becomes a matter for research instead of argument.

There is not and there cannot be any argument about the fact that the Kuenzers' (1962) young *Apistogramma* responded selectively to the configurational key stimulus of a yellow and black pattern by the specific activities of following the parent and that a mother *Apistogramma* is indeed striped black and yellow. Nor is it a matter of argument that a stickleback responds to the key stimulus "red below" by performing the motor patterns of rival fighting and that a male stickleback is indeed red on the ventral side. Only if we should forget these central facts of adaptedness, and only then, should we have to resort to the desperate strategy of research which Jensen recommends to us, unless we should prefer to give up as hopeless any further attempt to analyze behavior.

Non-adaptive differences in structure and behavior are of but secondary interest to the biologist, while they are the primary concern of the pathologist. A living organism is a very complicated and very finely balanced system, and there is precious little about it

b *Behaviour* is an international journal which publishes ethological studies of animal behaviour. (Editors' note.)

that cannot, at least on principle, be understood on the basis of phylogenetic adaptation and adaptive modification. Neither in an animal's body nor in its behavior are there many characters that may be changed by "other operations" without leading to destruction.

As students of behavior, we are not interested in ascertaining at random the innumerable factors that might lead to minute, just bearable differences of behavior bordering on the pathological. What we want to elucidate are the amazing facts of adaptedness. Life itself is a steady state of enormous general improbability and that which does need an explanation is the fact that organisms and species miraculously manage to stay alive. The answer to this question in respect to bodily structure as well as to behavior always hinges on the provenience of the information contained in and indispensable for the molding of the organism in such a way that it fits its environment and is able to cope with it. In the special case of our baby *Apistogramma* and of our male stickleback we want to know how the former can possess information on the external characteristics of its mother and how the latter can "know" what its rival looks like.

Instead of being faced, as Jensen's proposal would make it seem, with a Herculean task promising only uninteresting results, we have before us a program of practically feasible experiments which simply cannot fail to give interesting results one way or the other. All we have to do is to rear an animal, as perfectly as we can, under circumstances that withhold the particular information which we want to investigate. We need not bother about the innumerable factors which may cause "differences" in behavior as long as we are quite sure that they cannot possibly relay to the organism that particular information which we want to investigate. If our baby *Apistogrammas*, who have never seen an adult female of their species, selectively respond to a certain black and yellow pattern by following it and staying with it (as they would with their real mother) or if our stickleback responds to an object which is red below with the highly specific motor patterns used in fighting a rival, we are justified in asserting that the information which these fishes possess concerning these two objects is fully innate. In other words, the fish's genome must contain the blueprint of a perceptive apparatus which responds selectively to certain combinations and/or configurations of stimuli, and which relays the message "mother present" or "rival male present" to effector organizations equally adapted to dealing with this fact. That much we know, and this is, in my opinion, intensely interesting knowledge. Furthermore, it is knowledge which raises new questions.

First among these are the problems of ontogeny. It is a hackneyed fact that it is never more than just such a blueprint which is inherited and that between this inheritance and its final realization in bodily structures and functions lies the whole process of individual development of which experimental embryology (*Entwicklungsmechanik*) tries to gain causal understanding. This indeed is the truth contained in the statement that organs or behavior patterns must not be called innate. The experimental embryologists, while trying to gain insight into the physiological causality of development, have always acted on the knowledge that any structure which is elaborately adapted to functions and environmental givens to be faced only much later in individual life must be blueprinted in the genome. They also know that adaptive epigenetical regulation can only be expected on the basis of such information that one part of the embryo can receive from another. The ectoderm must have all the information about how to build a neural tube. What the ectoderm can "learn" from the organizer emanating from the chorda is only where to do so. If investigators never put this into words, it was because all this was a matter of course to all of them, but they certainly would not have gained the results they did had they allowed their approach to be narrowed by the attitude exemplified in Jensen's paper.

Any investigator of the ontogeny of animal behavior is well advised to begin with the time-honored procedure of first searching for whatever may be blueprinted by heredity. This is good strategy and not only for the simple reason that anatomy regularly begins with the investigation of the skeleton; in any system whose function consists of the interaction of many parts, the least changeable are the best point of departure, because their properties appear most often as causes and least often as effects in the interaction that is to be studied. An even better reason is that phylogenetically adapted structure represents, in the ontogeny of behavior, the indispensable prerequisite for guiding modification in the generally improbable direction of adaptedness. We cannot ever hope to understand any process of learning before we have grasped the hereditary teaching mechanism which contains this primary programming.

The emphasis which I am putting on the fact that we know about some indubitably inherited blueprints of motor patterns as well as of receptor organizations must not mislead anyone into thinking that I deem it unnecessary to investigate the ontogeny of behavior. The very opposite is true, particularly as far as receptor patterns (in other words, releasing mechanisms) are concerned. Among these, there is hardly one which, though indubitably based on innate information, is not rendered more selective by additional learning. A flashlike conditioning can take place at the very first function of a releasing mechanism and has to be taken into consideration in order to avoid the danger of mistaking what had actually been learned in the first experiment for innate information in later ones. In order to assess correctly the amount of innate information contained in a releasing mechanism, it is literally necessary to pull it to bits – no pun intended. The method of doing so will be discussed in the chapter on the deprivation experiment[c].

At present, one example is sufficient to illustrate the point. The behavior by which an inexperienced turkey hen responds to her first brood of chicks is dependent on a single phylogenetically adapted receptor mechanism. As Schleidt and Schleidt (1960) have conclusively shown, she treats every moving object within the nest as an enemy, unless it utters the specific note of the chick. A deaf hen invariably kills all of her own progeny immediately after hatching. A hen with normal hearing accepts and mothers any stuffed animal, if it is fitted with a small loudspeaker uttering the correct call notes. Under natural circumstances with a young turkey hen hatching her own young, the one phylogenetically adapted auditory reaction effects so rapid a conditioning of maternal responses to other stimuli emanating from the baby birds that after a few hours the unconditioned stimulus can be dispensed with and the mother is ready to brood the young even when they are silent. Nevertheless, the babies' call notes continue to enhance maternal activities.

The Schleidts did not succeed in finding an artificial substitute for the reinforcement of maternal behavior effected by the turkey chick's call note. Although it was possible with the utmost patience to sufficiently habituate some deaf hens to the presence of little chicks so that these were no longer killed on sight, it proved to be quite impossible to condition any deaf mother's maternal activities so as to respond to the babies. All that could be achieved was that the deaf birds behaved as if there were no chicks present, in spite of the fact that they were in exactly the right phase of their reproductive cycle and so tame that all kinds of manipulation were possible in the attempt to establish a contact between them and their progeny.

My point in telling about these highly interesting results is that they could never have been obtained by using the conceptualizations and methods proposed by Jensen. The

c   On page 89 of the book. (Editors' note.)

operation of withholding specific information underlying adaptedness is only one among literally millions of possible changes "causing differences in behavior," and the chances of finding the effective conditioning mechanism which the Schleidts found by these methods is correspondingly small.

No biologist in his right senses will forget that the blueprint contained in the genome requires innumerable environmental factors in order to be realized in the phenogeny of structures and functions. During his individual growth, the male stickleback may need water of sufficient oxygen content, copepods for food, light, detailed pictures on his retina, and millions of other conditions in order to enable him, as an adult, to respond selectively to the red belly of a rival. Whatever wonders phenogeny may perform, however, it cannot extract from these factors information which simply is not contained in them, namely, the information that a rival is red underneath.

We must be quite clear about what we call a "behavior element." If the Kuenzers' baby *Apistogrammas* responded selectively to a certain color configuration which roughly but sufficiently corresponds to the coloration of the mother they have to follow, we certainly must assume a nervous mechanism which, among innumerable other possible visual stimulus situations, selects this particular one and connects it with effector patterns phylogenetically adapted to keep the little family together. This mechanism is, of course, dependent on a structure built during ontogeny on the basis of a genetical blueprint. The whole function of specifically responding to the maternal color patterns involves functions other than that of this particular mechanism. Many of the processes which take place on the way from sensory stimulation to the response are less specific than the latter. Not only the processes of visual stimulation in the retina, but much more highly integrated functions, like those of perception (including depth perception, color constancy, and so on), are used in very many other responses and/or activities of the animal. Among these functions there may be some that require ontogenetically acquired information for their full development. Even the function of retinal elements requires "practice"; it is well known that retinal elements are subject to atrophy if not sufficiently used. The faculty of point discrimination, probably performed by the ganglion retinae, is lost to a large extent if not practiced, even if diffused light and unfocused images do impinge on the retina. If a person's vision is impaired for a long period by purely optical deficiencies of the eye, point discrimination remains seriously damaged even after correction of the optical apparatus, a state of affairs termed *amblyopsia ex anopsia* by oculists.

It is a matter of taste whether or not one chooses to call it learning when an activity is necessary to prevent atrophy and disintegration of a physiological mechanism, but it can be regarded as adaptive modification and it may well involve ontogenic acquisition of information. Much the same is true of the effector side of the reaction. Orientation mechanisms, motor patterns, etc. functioning in a stickleback fighting a rival or in an *Apistogramma* baby following its mother may also be elements of behavior that occur in other contexts as well. Among them, too, there may be some that need an inflow of individually acquired information for their full functional development.

These modifications adapting the less specific elements of a more specific response are indispensable requisites for the proper functioning of the latter. They must, therefore, never be forgotten or overlooked in our attempts to analyze this function. On principle, however, they are no obstacle to the solution of our fundamental question concerning the provenience of the information underlying each point of adaptedness in behavior. Nor do they represent a very serious source of error quantitatively. What may be overlooked is the effect of a little sensory adaptation making an afferent process a little more selective, or that of a little practice smoothing out a motor coordination. But there is little danger, with circumspect experimentation and with an experimenter knowing its pitfalls, that any process of true learning, particularly classical conditioning, might pass unnoticed.

It must not be thought that the learned prerequisites for the proper functioning of innate information are only made up of the primitive types of adaptive modification of behavior. True conditioning does figure among them. A good example of this is furnished by the copulatory response of some geese. Greylags (*Anser anser*), greater snow geese (*Anser hyperboreus atlanticus*), and probably many others possess perfectly good phylogenetic information about how a fellow member of the species behaves when inviting copulation, but they have to learn what a fellow member of the species looks like. The genetic information may be verbalized as follows: copulate with a conspecific who is lying low in the water and is stretched out along its surface. Hand-reared greylags, usually born in the first days of May, usually do not meet their human foster parents swimming in the water earlier than June (in our climate). They then regularly attempt to tread them. As a human swimmer is much longer than any goose and also is lying much lower in the water, he represents a supernormal object for the copulatory response of all those geese which regard him as a conspecific. Even in very young fledgling geese and also in females, which normally never show any copulatory movements, attempts to tread can reliably be released by this supernormal stimulation. These phenomena definitely are not a consequence of imprinting. The geese behaving thus remain otherwise quite normal in respect to their sexual objects and do not persist in trying to copulate with humans. Nor do they ever attempt copulation with any other randomly chosen object that happens to be elongated and lying low in the water. These configurational properties are effective as key stimuli only if they pertain to an object which the goslings have learned to know as a fellow member of their species, and this learning is achieved by all the many conditioning processes which attach the gosling to its parents and its siblings.

Much ontogenetically acquired adaptive modification of behavior may be involved in a functional whole, such as fighting a rival in the stickleback, following the mother in *Apistogramma*, or copulating with a conspecific in geese; however, it does not affect either the correctness or the justification of our statement that certain parts of the information which underlie the adaptedness of the whole and which can be ascertained by the deprivation experiment are indeed innate.

It is obviously this information alone to which we have a right to apply the term innate. We cannot, however, think of any way for this information to express itself in adapted behavior other than by the function of a neural structure. It is the distinctive property of this structure to select, from among innumerable other possible stimulus situations, the one which specifically elicits the response. This property definitely is a character of the species. The neural mechanism is an organ and not a character. A character in *The Oxford English Dictionary* is a "distinctive mark."

When some geneticists and, following them, many modern ethologists contend that characters must never be called innate, I have a suspicion that they are confounding the concepts of a character and of an organ. The latter, of course, really must not be called innate nor, indeed, must a behavior pattern. The formulation that it is not characters but differences between characters which may be described as innate is, in my opinion, an unsuccessful attempt to arrive at an operational definition. If we rear two or more organisms under identical conditions, any differences shown by them may be regarded as caused by differences in the genome. Theoretically this is all right, but I doubt whether the definition can be put into operation. If we rear a number of larval fish in the same tank under "identical conditions," for instance with very few larval crustacea present, the few fish which happen to catch these few nauplii will grow much faster than those that don't. How can we prevent, on principle, analogous sources of error? It seems to me that the opposite formulation is at least as workable: calling innate the similarities of characters developing under dissimilar rearing conditions. If we observe that all mallard drakes – and many other male dabbling ducks – whether reared in the wild or in captivity, by their own mothers or by a human keeper, under good or under highly unnatural conditions, perform the grunt-whistle in very nearly the same way, the breadth of variability being almost negligible in the confines of one species, our assertion that this similarity is innate, that is, based on genetical information, has at the very least the same likelihood of being correct as the opposite one, that dissimilarities in identically reared organisms are innate. It is, indeed, the similarity of individuals that tells the taxonomist what a species really is, and he was never mistaken in applying this indubitably genetical concept even in Linné's time.

Our question, "Whence does the organism derive the information underlying all adaptedness of behavior?" leads directly to more special and to more general questions. What rules ontogeny, in bodily as well as in behavioral development, is obviously the hereditary blueprint contained in the genome and not the environmental circumstances indispensable to its realization. It is not the bricks and the mortar which rule the building of a cathedral but a plan which has been conceived by an architect and which, of course, also depends on the solid causality of bricks and mortar for its realization. This plan must allow for a certain amount of adaptation that may become necessary during building; the soil may be looser on one side, necessitating compensatory strengthening of the fundaments. The phylogenetically adapted blueprint of the whole may rely on subordinate parts adaptively modifying each other. The prospective chorda exerts a very specific adaptively modifying effect on the neighboring ectoderm, causing it to form a neural tube in exactly the right place. The adaptive modification effected by one part on the other may even take the form of true learning. The gosling "knows innately" that it should copulate with a fellow member of the species stretching out low in the water, but it has to learn what a fellow member of the species is. Any such adaptive regulations, however, presuppose at the very least as much information contained in the genetical blueprint as any elements of little or no modifiability do. In other words, the apparatus which makes adaptive modifiability possible is genetically blueprinted itself, and it is in a very complicated form, particularly if it allows so much scope to regulations as we find in embryogeny.

Because all the causal chains of development begin with the hereditary information contained in the genome (and the plasma) of the egg, our first question concerning the ontogeny of an organism and its behavior is: "What is blueprinted in its genome?" The second is: "What are the causal chains which begin at the blueprints given in the genome and which end up, by devious and often highly regulative routes, by producing adapted structure ready to function?" We are fully aware that the processes of growth can be separated from those of behavior only by an injunctive definition permitting intermediates. We think, however, that the processes of individual learning is sufficiently distinct from other processes of adaptive modification, and particularly from those regulating structural growth, that we are justified in leaving, at least for the time being, to the care of the experimental embryologists all those questions which are concerned with the chains of physiological causation leading from the genome to the development of such neurosensory structures. These structures, like the releasing mechanism of the stickleback's rival fighting or like that of the turkey hen's response to the chick's call, demonstrably owe their specific adaptedness to information acquired in phylogeny and stored in genes.

Not being experimental embryologists but students of behavior, we begin our query, not at the beginning of the growth, but at the beginning of the function of such innate mechanisms. The modern English-speaking ethologists are generally agreed that the concept of the "innate" is valuable and valid only if defined as "not caused by modification." This cautious definition, although of course quite true as far as it goes, states only the less important side of the problem. The important one is that the phylogenetically adapted structures and their functions are what affect all adaptive modification. In regard to behavior, the innate is not only what is not learned, but what must be in existence before all individual learning in order to make learning possible. Thus, consciously paraphrasing Kant's definition of the *a priori*, we might define our concept of the innate.

This definition is truly operational, as can be seen in the Schleidts' and many other people's investigations. On the other hand, I defy anybody to put into practical operation the allegedly operational definition proposed by Jensen. Whoever tries it, will, with an overwhelming probability, die of old age before reaching publishable results. Hence the acceptance of this definition must discourage any investigation of the ontogeny of behavior.

Obviously it is the best strategy of research if, in our attempt to analyze the ontogeny of behavior, we first concentrate on the question: "What are the teaching mechanisms?" and second on the question: "What do they teach the animal?" In asking these questions, we may seem to neglect, at least for the time being, those "behavioral differences" which are "neither innate (selected) nor learned (trained) but something else (produced by other operations)." When we rear, in our experiments, an organism under circumstances which are calculated to withhold from it some specific information, we do our very best to avoid that kind of difference in behavior. In other words, we try to produce an individual whose genetical blueprints have been realized unscathed in the course of healthy phenogeny. Should we fail in this, we would incur the danger of mistaking some defects in our subject's behavior for the consequences of information withheld, while they really are the pathological results of stunted growth. This danger is very great if the investigator is not aware of it, if he does not know the system of actions of his subjects inside out, and if he does not possess what is called the "clinical eye." Otherwise, the danger is almost negligible.

Of course, the behavior of an otherwise perfectly healthy mandarin drake (*Aix galericulata L.*) whose sexual responses are fixated by the process of imprinting on mallard ducks (*Anas platyrhynchos L.*) is also indubitably pathological, particularly from the viewpoint of survival, as the bird is rendered permanently unable to reproduce. But not only do we know what behavioral system we have damaged in this mandarin by the intentional misinformation furnished to it at a critical stage of its ontogeny, but even if we did not know the previous history of the individual, we could still, with great certainty, deduce it from the symptoms.

In the present chapter, criticizing the assumption of a general and diffuse modifiability of phylogenetically adapted behavior mechanisms, I need only say that the enormous symptomatic difference between behavior defects caused by withholding information and defects "produced by other operations" is in itself extremely strong and convincing evidence against that assumption.

Finally, I want to discuss a speculative but, to me, rather convincing argument against assuming a diffuse modifiability of phylogenetically adapted behavior through learning. I have already said that with the increasing complication of an adapted system, the probability decreases that random change in any of its parts may produce anything but disadaptation. The power of the argument illustrated by the sports car is multiplied greatly when we consider really complicated neural systems, for instance, those performing real computations. Phylogenetic adaptation has created mechanisms of such subtle complication here that even a really brilliant physiological cyberneticist is barely able to gain a tolerably complete insight into their workings. After carefully reading and rereading Mittelstaedt's paper (1957) on the complex feedback mechanism enabling a mantid to aim a precise stroke at its prey, my own understanding of that mechanism is insufficient to permit sensible suggestions for its improvement. So I find it difficult to believe that the insect should be superior to myself in that respect, unless, of course, it possesses special built-in calibrating or adjusting mechanisms. I argue that this type of complicated neural mechanism must be highly refractory to random change by individual modification. The complexity and precision with which the processes of evolution have endowed these mechanisms would be destroyed immediately if individual modification by learning were allowed to tamper with them.

Even in man, computing mechanisms of this kind, particularly those of perception, are built in such a way as not to let learning "enter into" them. Although these mechanisms very often perform functions so closely analogous to rational operations that Brunswik (1957) termed them "ratio-morphous" processes, they stubbornly refuse to have anything to do with rational processes, least of all to let themselves be influenced by learning. As von Holst (1955, 1957) has shown, all so-called optical illusions, with very few exceptions, can be regarded as the results of ratio-morph operations which are caused to miscarry by the introduction of one erroneous "premise." From these, a perfectly logical computation draws a false conclusion. These mechanisms are not only inaccessible to self-observation but also refractory to learning.

If we consider learning as a specific function achieving a definite survival value, it appears as an entirely unfounded assumption that learning must necessarily "enter into" all other neurophysiological processes determining behavior. It is, however, by no means this theoretical consideration alone which causes us to reject that assumption; all experimental and observational evidence points that way. Not once has diffuse modifiability been demonstrated by experimentally changing arbitrarily chosen elements of phylogenetically adapted behavior mechanisms. On the other hand, innumerable observations and experiments tend to show that modifiability occurs, if at all, only in those preformed places where built-in learning mechanisms are phylogenetically programmed to perform just that function. How specifically these mechanisms are differentiated for one particular function is borne out by the fact that they are very often quite unable to modify any but one strictly determined system of behavior mechanisms. Honey bees can learn to use irregular forms, like those of trees or rocks, as landmarks by which to steer a course to and from the hive; but, they cannot, even by the most subtle conditioning technique, be taught to use these same forms as positive or negative signals indicating the presence or absence of food in a tray, as von Frisch (1914) has shown. As signals for food, bees can distinguish different forms only if they are geometrically regular, preferably radially symmetrical (Hertz, 1937).

In other words, the old and allegedly naïve theory of an "intercalation" of phylogenetically adapted and of individually modifiable behavior mechanisms, far from having been refuted by new facts, has proved to agree with them in a quite surprising manner. Scientists working on entirely different problems, such as the selectivity of innate releasing mechanisms, bird navigation, feedback mechanisms of aiming, circadian rhythms, etc. have one and all found that if modifiability existed at all, it was restricted to one particular link in the chain of neural processes determining behavior.

REFERENCES

Brunswik, E. (1957). Scope and Aspects of the Cognitive Problem. In J. S. Bruner et al., *Contemporary Approaches to Cognition*. Cambridge, MA: Harvard University Press.

Frisch, K., von. (1914). Der Farbensinn und Formensinn der Biene. *Zool. Jahrb*. 35, 1–188.

Hertz, M. (1937). Beitrag zum Farbensinn und Formensinn der Biene. *Z. vgl. Physiol*. 24, 413–21.

von Holst, E. (1955). Regelvorgänge in der optischen Wahrnehmung. *Rept, 5th Conf. Soc. Biol. Rythmn*, Stockholm.

von Holst, E. (1957). Aktive Leistung der menschlichen Gesichtswahrnehmung. *Studium Generale* 4, 231–43.

Jensen, D. D. (1961). Operationism and the Question "Is This Behavior Learned or Innate?" *Behaviour* 17, 1–8.

Kuenzer, E. and Kuenzer, P. (1962). Untersuchungen zur Brutpflege der Zwergcichliden *Apistogramma reitzigi* und *A. borrellii*. *Z. Tierpsychol*. 19, 56–83.

Mittelstaedt, H. (1957). Prey capture in Mantids. *Recent Advances in Invertebrate Physiology*. University of Oregon Publ., 51–57.

Schleidt, W. and Schleidt, M. (1960). Störung der Mutter-Kind-Beziehung bei Truthühnern durch Gehöverlust. *Behaviour* 16, 3–4.

2

The Problem of Change

Susan Oyama

In thinking about forms, we tend to focus on constancy rather than change – constancy of a character through time, in spite of turnover in constituent materials and shifting conditions, similarities among related individuals or members of a species, continuity across generations or among related species. In fact, though, change and variability are as basic to biological processes as uniformity. Change and variability are not the same thing, though they are associated in important ways, and they both pose difficult problems for the conception of the directive gene. We will consider change in an entity first; variability is the subject of the next chapter.

Embryogeny, as orderly, recurrent sequences of change, is the perfect synthesis of constancy and change. From day to day, sometimes from minute to minute, the entire system, increasingly intricate, changes – forms shift and disappear, lift and fold, divide and spread – yet each phase is largely predictable, at least in its outlines, as its end.[1]

Preformation, Epigenesis, and Golden Means

Students of development in the seventeenth, eighteenth, and nineteenth centuries discovered more astonishing complexity of change than had been previously imagined, and it was then that the preformationist and epigenetic views became engaged in an increasingly subtle dialectic, coalescing by the late nineteenth century to form what Oppenheim (1982, p. 37) describes as an essentially modern position: "transmission of a *predetermined* (or rather, a preorganized) germ plasm in the nucleus that in the course of ontogeny is expressed via cytoplasmic *epigenesis*." It will be recalled that Oppenheim uses "epigenesis" for progressive ontogenetic change. It is also important to bear in mind that the course of development was agreed by preformationists and epigeneticists alike to be predetermined in some sense; the question was how this was to be understood. Gould says:

> The solution to great arguments is usually close to the golden mean, and this debate is no exception. Modern genetics is about as midway as it could be between the extreme formulations of the eighteenth century. The preformationists were right in asserting that some preexistence is the only refuge from mysticism. But they were mistaken in postulating preformed structure, for we have discovered coded instructions. (It is scarcely

surprising that a world knowing nothing of the player piano – not to mention the computer program – should have neglected the storage of coded instructions.) The epigeneticists, on the other hand, were correct in insisting that the visual appearance of development is no mere illusion. (1977, p. 18)

I, on the other hand, tend to be skeptical of golden mean solutions, because when two great traditions battle for long periods, there is generally, along with their disagreements, some basic misapprehension that they share, and from which, therefore, they do not attempt to dissuade each other. Preformationism did offer a refuge from mysticism in the sense of vitalistic forces acting directly on development each time it occurred, but only at the price of postulating a one-time-only simultaneous creation of all things (and thus no need for real development). Though contemporary thought rejects nested bodies, it does not often balk at preformed targets and instructions. The preexistence that the preform-ationists, the epigeneticists, and current orthodoxy all agree upon is form, whether mini-aturized and encapsulated, re-created by a vitalistic force, or inscribed on a molecule. The corollary is that the preexisting form must be the "same" as the final one; for the preformationists both were concretely material, for the epigeneticists form was first disembodied, then embodied, and for most modern thinkers it is initially material but cryptic, then manifested in the phenotype. In fact, preformationism was not as naive as is often claimed; the important versions during biology's early years acknowledged differ-ences in the relative position and shape of encapsulated organs, agreeing that if the embryo were enlarged it would not look like a finished organism (Gould, 1977, p. 20; Oppenheim, 1982). This brings them closer both to their traditional opponents and to modern views.[2]

Though Gould states that the preformationists were in error in postulating preformed structure, there is really nothing problematic about this idea. What is misguided, not only about the preformationist belief but the modern version as well, is the assumption of *correspondence* between initial and final structures. The chromosomes are indeed highly structured, as are the cell organelles, the chemical substrates, and the extracellular environ-ment.

Emphasis on the structure in the genome without full acknowledgment of structure in the surround is common. Gould (1977, pp. 21–2) claims that the preformationist critique of epigenesis is still valid: if the egg is "truly unorganized, how could it yield such consistent complexity without a directing entelechy. It does so, and can only do so, because the information – not merely the raw material – needed to build this complexity already resides in the egg." Preformationists and epigeneticists agreed that a formless egg required form from without. Preformationists placed accomplished form inside the egg, while epigeneti-cists rejected this solution and instead posited an additional force. Gould appears to accept the vision of the formless egg and to place the entelechy-as-program inside. (See also Mayr, 1982, pp. 105–6.)

The situation is thus quite peculiar. What scientists say in some contexts is contradicted by what they say, know, and do in others. It is therefore difficult to grasp what is happening without following arguments or trains of thought quite closely, and this is one of my tasks in this book. In fact, no biologist seriously limits structure to the chromosomes; they sometimes sound as if they do because *they assign formative relevance only to the DNA, where the encoded representation of the phenotype (or of the instructions for building it) is thought to reside.* This is the error – along with the associated idea that unless such a representation exists, development cannot be structured – and it is a pervasive and fundamental error indeed.[3]

If matter and form are distinct, as one part of our classical tradition tells us, and matter is inert (recall Toulmin's argument about seventeenth-century thought [1967]), then both the emergence of form and change in that form must be explained. We tend to see the "biological" as that which has the power to effect change without being changed. Maturation, conceived causally rather than descriptively, is seen as a force bringing basic characters into being, without requiring, indeed, without permitting, more than minimal environmental influence (Oyama, 1982). Maturation in turn is seen as driven and guided by the genes, which "initiate and direct" development (Gesell, 1945, p. 19), which are potentially immortal (Williams, 1974, p. 24), and which, of course, are not generally altered by their cellular interactions. To continue the commonly agreed upon causal progression, the genes are formed by random variation and natural selection. Gatlin notes that "the words 'natural selection' play a role in the vocabulary of the evolutionary biologist similar to the word 'God' in ordinary language" (1972, p. 164), and Montalenti observes that natural selection is the biological *primum movens* (1974, p. 13). Just as traditional thought placed biological forms in the mind of God, so modern thought finds many ways of endowing the genes with ultimate formative power, a power bestowed by Nature over countless millennia.

"But wait," the exasperated reader cries, "everyone nowadays knows that development is a matter of interaction. You're beating a dead horse."

I reply, "I would like nothing better than to stop beating him,[4] but every time I think I am free of him he kicks me and does rude things to the intellectual and political environment. He seems to be a phantom horse with a thousand incarnations, and he gets more and more subtle each time around. Just look at the horselets, infrahorses, and metahorses described in this book. What we need here, to switch metaphors in midstream, is the stake-in-the-heart move, and the heart is the notion that some influences are more equal than others, that form – or its modern agent, information – exists before the interactions in which it appears and must be transmitted to the organism either through the genes or by the environment. This supports and requires just the conceptions of dual developmental processes that make up the nature–nurture complex. Compromises don't help because they don't alter this basic assumption."

Jacques Monod, who, with Jacob, presided over some of the most exciting developments in early molecular biology, describes in minute detail various macromolecular processes and their organizing functions. When he engages in straightforward description, the complexity and interdependence of causes are clear. When he interprets these processes in more general terms, however, an interesting thing occurs. He says, for example, that the genome "entirely defines" protein function, and asks if this is contradicted by the statement that the protein's three-dimensional structure has a "data content" that is "*richer* than the direct contribution made to the structure by the genome." His answer is that, because the three-dimensional, globular structure appears only under "strictly defined initial conditions," only one of all possible structures is realized. "Initial conditions hence enter among the items of information finally enclosed within the globular structure. Without specifying it, they contribute to the realization of a unique shape by eliminating all alternative structures, in this way proposing – or, rather, imposing – an unequivocal interpretation of a potentially equivocal message" (1971, p. 94). But if initial conditions select one folded structure among an array of possible ones, thus contributing to the unique shape, they *do* specify it, in cooperation with the linear structure. The particular globular shape results only when particular chains fold under particular conditions. Monod is forced, in his terms, to admit that the structure therefore "contains" more information than it would if such conditions were not critical. But his commitment to the power of the gene entirely to define leads him to withhold "specifying" power from the cellular environment. This is not due to idiosyncratic use of "specify"; elsewhere he makes much of the *specificity* of enzyme action – that is, the selective interaction with only one or two molecule types from many.

Earlier in the same book (p. 84), he asserts that he uses "epigenesis" for all structural and functional development, not in the old sense of the epigeneticists, who, in contrast to the preformationists, "believed in an *actual* enrichment of the initial genetic information." Since the eighteenth and nineteenth centuries lacked the contemporary notion of genetic information, one can only speculate on the precise meaning of this assertion, but in the light of Monod's general position it seems reasonable that he was distancing himself from any view that attributes real formative power to anything other than the gene. Again, in discussing the preformation-epigenesis dispute, he says:

> No preformed and complete structure preexisted anywhere; but the architectural plan for it was present in its very constituents. It can therefore come into being spontaneously and autonomously, without outside help and without the injection of additional information. The necessary information was present, but unexpressed, in the constituents. The epigenetic building of a structure is not a *creation;* it is a *revelation.* (1971, p. 7)

And, after another vivid description of development, he concludes, "The determining cause of the entire phenomenon, its source, is finally the genetic information represented by the sum of the polypeptide sequences, interpreted – or, to be more exact, screened – by the initial conditions" (p. 95). If by "initial conditions" he means only the intracellular environment when the molecular chain folds through the third dimension, he is excluding from this story all other nongenetic conditions, including substrates, intracellular machinery, factors influencing occurrence and rate of enzymatic action, as well as interactions at the tissue, organ, and organism levels that can, at best, be only partially explained by stereospecific interactions among molecules. Even if he includes these sources of specificity (and therefore of "information"), they evidently do not qualify as "determining causes" or "sources" of the phenomenon itself.

I dwell on Monod at length because he is a skilled and expressive writer; because it is difficult to question his credentials in molecular biology; because he has chosen to address issues beyond that field, such as ontogeny, evolution, and values; and because, given his standing as a scientist, he has unusual authority when he does so. He is thus in a powerful position to influence the thinking of his colleagues and of the general public, particularly because this conceptual ground is so well prepared.

In reviewing *Chance and Necessity*, Toulmin (1982, pp. 140–55) places Monod's thinking (and his rhetorical style) in the context of a French intellectual tradition that has been slow to relinquish progressivist ideas of evolution. Monod's emphasis on the role of the random in evolution and on the one-way flow of information from gene to protein is perhaps best understood in this light. Ravin (1977) points out that this latter notion of unidirectional transfer of information, Crick's "central dogma," is a denial of the inheritance of acquired characters. It is, however, unnecessary to deny nongenetic contributions to biological form in order to deny Lamarckian inheritance. As Toulmin points out in the review cited above, even randomness of variation is not essential to an anti-Lamarckian argument, though "decoupling" of variation from selection is.

One might argue that Monod is concerned not so much with the particulars of Lamarckian evolution (some of which Darwin did not himself reject) as with Lamarckianism as

emblematic of an unscientific vitalism. Not being above using "vitalistic" and "preforma-
tionistic" as terms of abuse myself, I would point out two things: First, both are descriptive
of particular kinds of attitudes and explanations, as well as of broad philosophical-theoret-
ical positions, and they can coexist within theories and within persons. Second, any
approach to biological processes that begins with inert raw materials requires a mindlike
force to fashion this matter into a functioning animal-machine. This approach is at odds
with what we know about physics and chemistry, including Monod's own findings about
the interactions of complex molecules. The implications of this view of development as
relevation will be elaborated in later chapters. At this point, however, lest it seem that I am
singling out a scholar whose primary field is not development, and in fact one who has
every reason to be particularly impressed with genetic functioning, let me point out that the
views described are not at all peculiar to Monod, or to molecular biologists. They exemplify
much thinking in biology and psychology. Indeed, if this were not so I would not be writing
this book.

Decades ago, a sensitive and sophisticated observer of human development made similar
statements about the causal primacy of the gene. In his much-quoted pronouncement,
Arnold Gesell declared that environmental factors "support, inflect, and specify, but they
do not engender the basic forms and sequences of ontogeny" (1954, p. 354; see discussion
in Oyama, 1982). Oppenheim (1982) has argued that Gesell sometimes belied his understanding of development in his efforts to counteract excessive emphasis on the environment. This seems correct and important to me; it is often the case that we must temper our
reading of documents with such historical perspective. As was the case with Monod's
polemic for scientific Darwinism and against mystical Lamarckianism, however, it is
important to distinguish justifiable implications from false ones. One of the problems
with these grand oppositions is that, while they may fuel investigation and theoretical
advance, by placing those activities in an erroneous context they make correct inference
improbable. Opponents tend to pay more attention to refuting each other's claims than to
examining the logical bases for those claims. By combatting environmental determinism
with special formative, engendering genetic causes, Gesell only legitimized the underlying
assumption that genetic and environmental causes could and should be distinguished in
this way. He thus helped perpetuate the empiricist-nativist opposition, when, as Oppenheim and I point out, his approach potentially transcended it.

It is the structure of the argument, finally, that intrigues and troubles. Almost three
hundred years ago, preformationists wondered whether the germ, the complete but inert
form, was in the sperm or the egg. Because fertilization was necessary to activate development, there were, as for Gesell and Monod, two necessary sets of interactants, neither
sufficient to produce the organism. Both influences were granted power to affect the
outcome (the parent who did not contribute the germ could still impart some qualities to
the offspring). The *basic* form, however, was contributed by only the egg or only the sperm,
depending on which camp one was in (Jacob, 1973, pp. 57–9).[5]

The assumption seems to be that change of the sort we see in developmental processes
must have a single, fundamental source; since such change is ordered and directional, the
problem becomes essentially that of the origin of form. Having defined an induced pattern
as one that is "imposed . . . by the immediate environment," Bonner comments that the
pattern resulting from embryological induction lies not in the inductor but "largely in the
stimulated tissues" (1974, pp. 221, 249). Much of the history of embryology has been
the chronicle of attempts to locate patterns in tissues or in chemicals (see Waddington,
1962, pp. 190–5, on patterns and prepatterns), just as that of the study of behavioral

development has frequently been an exercise in pronouncing patterns to be inborn or learned. The problem, of course, is that patterns as such don't exist anywhere before they are realized – constructed by reciprocal selection (or coaction – McClearn and DeFries, 1973, p. 311; and Oyama, 1981) in ontogeny.

Determination and Commitment

Yund and Germeraad follow standard procedure in declaring that development results from a "highly coordinated program of gene activity. The genome itself is the program. It must contain all the information for its own regulation." They admit, though, that little is known about the "branching" of the developmental program governing gene expression in multi-cellular organisms (1980, p. 317). They go on to describe cellular determination as "commit-ment" to a "particular branch of the developmental program" and outline the methods of investigating the time of determination by looking at subsequent differentiation of cells in vitro or after transplantation. Interestingly enough, they remark that the more sophisticated the manipulation, the fewer are the cases of completely stable, irreversible commitment. (See also Alberts et al., 1983, p. 835, who state that the crucial characteristic of determination is not irreversibility but heritability, defined as "self-perpetuating change of internal character that distinguishes it [the cell] and its progeny from other cells in the embryo and that commits these progeny to a specialized course of development." Note that "heritability" here refers not to genetic changes but to enduring alterations in cellular processes that distinguish the cell and its progeny from other cells. See also Margulis, 1981, pp. 164, 177, 224.) So dependent is commitment on the method of investigation and the particular question asked that its strict definition as stable cell fate has been abandoned. In its place is a conception in which a "separate decision, regardless of its stability, occurs at each branch in the program." One can say only that a cell is on a particular path at a particular time, and investigate the mechanisms and relative stability of the decision. Its developmental potential, say the authors, narrows with each decision (Yund and Germeraad, 1980, pp. 317–19). Surely this is not consistent with the idea that the cell's genetic program contains "infor-mation for its own regulation," but rather with an indeterminate process in time, whose regulation depends on conditions. "Decisions" are not written in the nucleus but are made on the basis of developmental contingency. It is no wonder that determination becomes largely a matter of methodology, since "decision" is merely an anthropomorphic locution for a consequence. Individuals may decide to become this or that, and resolutely commit themselves to a course of action. Cells change states or not, depending on their competence, which may change, and their surroundings, which may also change. Their "commitment" must therefore be assessed with respect to those considerations.

Under some circumstances, a peculiar phenomenon known as transdetermination may be observed. Transplanted imaginal disc tissue from the larva of the fly *Drosophila*, for example, usually behaves in a very "programmed" (i.e., predictable) manner, apparently being determined or committed very early in development to give rise to certain adult structures. It will sometimes, however, differentiate into structures characteristic of *other* discs. This new determined state can be propagated by serial cloning. Furthermore, transdetermination may occur repeatedly, with successive transplantations. The authors note that the ability to transdetermine depends on the developmental state of the cells, especially age, and on original position in the imaginal disc (Yund and Germeraad, 1980, pp. 333–5). Once again we observe that investigators' descriptions of actual phenomena give the lie to their general pronouncements on the nature of development. It is not even the case that each developmental decision narrows the cell's potential, any more than an individual's does; in transdetermination, potential seems to shift and *increase* in scope (Alberts et al., 1983, pp. 833–40).

Conceptually the problem of determination is parallel to that of the sensitive period as fixer of developmental fate. The behavioral notion of the sensitive period is in fact derived from the embryological one of critical period and tissue determination (Oyama, 1979). Detailed investigation in both cases reveals a phenomenon that is not absolute and definitive, but complex and relative, one that is much more consistent with the model of development being elaborated here than with any fixed program.

A corrective for a person who tends to think too much in terms of potters molding clay or of computers printing out messages might be the idea of campers raising and stabilizing a tent pole by pulling in opposite directions. Stability is dynamic, clearly depends on both participants, and may be maintained to the extent that variation from one or both directions can be compensated for. Attributing the general outcome to one camper and trivial details to the other would falsify the process. I hasten to add that I don't consider this an adequate metaphor for ontogeny, but rather an illustration of a fairly simple point about causation: that it is multiple, interdependent, and complex. Even the potter, in fact, does not command absolutely. An artisan respects the qualities and limits of the material as much as he or she does his or her own; much of artistry, in fact, lies in just this respect for, and sensitivity to, the medium and the developing form. Finally, a program, to be useful, must be responsive to its data; outcomes are jointly determined.

It would seem that polemics do not justify arguments of the Monod–Gesell type, which, being characterized by their structure, predate these two scientists and can be found on the environment side as well. They do not adequately represent the analytic reality that the author is attempting to convey. In fact, by misattributing the orderliness of these processes, they diminish the impact of the argument.

Change, then, is best thought of not as the result of a dose of form and animation from some causal agent, but rather as a system alteration jointly determined by contemporary influences and by the state of the system, which state represents the synthesis of earlier interactions. The functions of the gene or of any other influence can be understood only in relation to the system in which they are involved. The biological relevance of any influence, and therefore the very "information" it conveys, is jointly determined, frequently in a statistically interactive, not an additive, manner, by that influence and the system state it influences.

In mice, many cell types contain the same androgen receptor protein, but different types of cells respond to androgen stimulation by activating different genes (Paigen, 1980). The *Drosophila engrailed* mutation influences sex combs, bristles, or vein patterns, depending on the appendage. The authors who cite this research observe that organs seem not to have their own "subplans" but to use general mechanisms in specific ways (Leighton and Loomis, 1980, p. xvi). The impact of sensory stimuli is a joint function of the stimuli and the sensing organism; the "effective stimulus" is defined by the organism that is affected by it. That one creature's sensory meat is another's poison, or that the same stimulus may have different effects on the same organism at different times, does not render stimulation causally irrelevant or merely permissive (as opposed to formative). The concepts of motivation, personality, and maturation have been developed in part to address such contingency of stimulus effects. Similarly the gene controls by being controlled or selected, sometimes by other parts of the genome, and even regulatory genes regulate by being regulated (Kolata, 1984). One of the prime questions of developmental biology, in fact, is that of differential gene activation.

Causation is endlessly interlocked, and the biological "meaning" of changes depends on the level of analysis and the state of the whole. This perspective may make it more difficult to say with confidence what constitutes a "whole" or a "system" in any given case, but since the material of life is neither structureless nor inert, there is no need for animistic forces; form and control are defined in life processes, not the other way around. (See also Waddington, 1972, p. 111.)

In describing the nested feedback loops (which, by definition, involve reciprocal control) through which the environment influences developmental processes, Bonner declares the search for ultimate control factors to be futile, unless one conceives of ultimate control as that which

> comes from the power gained by repeated, successive life cycles. Only in this way can one achieve a vast array of complex, interacting events. Successive life cycles allow the accumulated information of millions of years to be used at a moment's notice. As far as control mechanisms go, there is no end: they go back to the beginning of life and are part of what we have called evolutionary development. The products of that control information are realized in each life cycle. (1974, pp. 156–7)

When Bonner asserts that life cycles may use "information" developed in previous cycles, he is referring primarily to cell products and structures already in place when a new sequence of ontogenetic differentiation begins. His discussion of nongenetic inheritance, in which "direct inheritance from one generation to the next is not restricted to the DNA of the genome, but many other substances and structures are built up from previous cell cycles" (p. 180), could readily be extended to include extracellular, even extraorganismic influences. The notion of life cycles as nested feedback loops (or at least nested sets of relationships) is a crucial one that deserves wider generalization to include not only pheromonal cycles in social insects, which Bonner considers to be the largest ontogenetic loop, but other essential ecological relationships as well, *even when they involve the inanimate world or other organisms.*

What we are moving toward is a conception of a developmental system, not as the reading off of a preexisting code, but as a complex of interacting influences, some inside the organism's skin, some external to it, and including its ecological niche in all its spatial and temporal aspects, *many of which are typically passed on in reproduction* either because they are in some way tied to the organism's (or its conspecifics') activities or characteristics or because they are stable features of the general environment. It is in this ontogenetic crucible that form appears and is transformed, not because it is immanent in some interactants and nourished by others, or because some interactants select from a range of forms present in others, but because any form is created by the precise activity of the system. Since even species-typical "programmed" form is not one but a near-infinite series in transition throughout the life cycle, each whole and functional in its own way, to refer to the type or the typical is also to refer to this series and the constant change that generates it.

If the genome, highly structured and integrated as it is, cannot by itself explain the products of ontogenetic change (the cognitive, planning function), can it at least be seen as the driving force (the causal, volitional, energetic function) of such change? Much is written about the genes initiating, engendering, and originating, and the idea of diminutive chemical engines powering biological processes is appealing. In fact, of course, a gene initiates a sequence of events *only if one chooses to begin analysis at that point*; it occupies no privileged energetic position outside the flux of physical interactions that constitutes the natural (and the artificial) world. A seed may remain dormant for years, and though plants frequently show this kind of developmental passivity,[6] it is observed among animals as well (Clutter, 1978). The seed "initiates" a period of growth when it is triggered by some change. Genes affect biological processes because they are reactive, and this reactivity is a prime characteristic of our world, at all levels of analysis, from the subatomic through the social to the astronomical. To describe biological processes as the product of exchanges of energy, matter, and information, while consistent with the temper of the times, is misleading in seeming to postulate a third, quasiphysical force at work in the world. Both the initiation and the course of biological change are functions of developmental systems, and there is no evidence that our notions of matter and energy exchanges, themselves admittedly evolving, are inadequate to describe them. Adding information to matter and energy is something like speaking of nations exchanging dollars, yen, and profits. The third term belongs on a different level. Not another form of currency, it describes a certain disposition and use of currencies. Just as time or information can, under certain circumstances, "be" money, matter and energy can sometimes "be" information.

It may be objected that this view of development as the result of changing and widely ramified systems is too complex and multiple, that its boundaries are too indistinct, potentially extending to anything and everything in the universe. Yet this is just the kind of world scientists show us. We can include only a few of its aspects in our models, and our choices can always be shown wrong. In fact, when we attempt to provide artificial conditions for proper development of captive animals, we are often forcefully reminded of the breadth and variety of linkages between biological processes and extraorganismic factors. When feeding or reproductive "instincts" fail in captivity, we are prompted to search for missing factors in the vital system, often without success. What is programmed, committed, or determined, switched or triggered, depends on external considerations that are as causally basic to the design of the phenomenon as internal factors, whether or not they are included in the design of the researcher, and however they are designated after the fact.

In living beings, no agent is needed to initiate sequences of change or to guide them to their proper goals. Matter, including living matter, is inherently reactive, and change, far from being an intrusion into some static natural order, is inevitable.

NOTES

1   Because ontogeny continues at least to the adult period – and, some would argue, through senescence to death (Bonner, 1974, pp. 167–8, for instance) – what is considered the "end" is somewhat arbitrary. Though the adult is traditionally seen to be the end of development, both in the sense of goal and in the sense of terminus, with everything else either an incomplete transition to, or a degeneration from, this basic form, a strong argument can be made that ontogenesis is continuous with the life cycle. Every stage is thus equally the "end" of development. Unlike a machine, which is generally useless until it is completely assembled, an organism "works" at all points in its development. For a view of development that places ends in genomes, this implies that not only the standard adult form but also every stage of life cycle must be "in" the genes. When norms of reaction or sets of potentials are thought of as being encoded, the genomic freight rapidly becomes prodigious.

2   Gasking distinguishes between preformationism as a *prediction* of what would be seen in the germ, especially if parts were hardened and made visible, and as an *explanation* of develop-

ment. It was the latter that was generally primary, and it was quite consistent with gradual appearance during embryogeny (1967, pp. 48–50).

3 These points become especially interesting and important in Gould's case, for unlike many of the other writers cited in these pages, he has been persistent in his opposition to various kinds of genetic determinism and alert to their consequences (1981, and numerous columns in the magazine *Natural History*, for instance). Over the last several years his writings on these issues have become steadily more "interactionist." Program metaphors seem to have dropped out, and in their place is an opposition between biological determinism as a "theory of limits" and "biological potentiality" "viewed as a range of capacity" (1984, p. 7). For reasons that will become clear later, this formulation unfortunately does not quite solve the problem. It neither distinguishes his position from those of the workers he criticizes (many of whom use an "interactionist" vocabulary of sorts and readily speak of *potential* rather than *fate*) nor, much the same thing, fully detaches him from the notion of fixed limits (often expressed, in fact, as biologically encoded potential). What are limits, in fact, but the boundaries of the range of capacity? (See S. Oyama, *The Ontogeny of Information: Developmental Systems and Evolution*, second edition [Durham, NC: Dule University Press, 2000], pp. 15–16.) Gould's eloquence and moral commitment are considerable; we will all benefit from his continued thinking about these matters.

4 In *The Ghost in the Machine*, Arthur Koestler gives a hierarchical systems account of ontogeny, phylogeny, and creativity, covering some of the problems treated here but in the service of a quite different aim. Having been accused of criticizing behaviorism once too often, he advocates the formation of the SPCDH, the Society for Prevention of Cruelty to Dead Horses (1967, p. 349). For an interesting treatment of Koestler's work, see the three reviews by Stephen Toulmin collected in Toulmin (1982).

5 It is perhaps significant that the arguments the preformationists had used against each other in the ovist-animalculist controversy were deployed in the mid-eighteenth century by Maupertuis against the preformationists themselves (Gasking, 1967, pp. 70–8).

6 "Active" and "passive," as should be clear from this discussion, do not generally characterize entities, but only signal focus on sources of perturbation and effects of perturbation, respectively.

REFERENCES

Alberts, B., Bray, D., Lewis, J., Raff, M., Roberts, K., and Watson, J. D. (1983). *Molecular Biology of the Cell*. New York: Garland.

Bonner, J. T. (1974). *On Development*. Cambridge, MA: Harvard University Press.

Clutter, M. E. (1978). *Dormancy and Developmental Arrest*. New York: Academic Press.

Gasking, E. (1967). *Investigations into Generation: 1651–1828*. Baltimore: Johns Hopkins University Press.

Gatlin, L. L. (1972). *Information Theory and the Living System*. New York: Columbia University Press.

Gesell, A. (1945). *The Embryology of Behavior*. Westport, Conn.: Greenwood Press.

Gesell, A. (1954). The ontogenesis of infant behavior. In L. Carmichael (ed.), *Manual of Child Psychology* (2nd edn.) (335–73). New York: Wiley.

Gould, S. J. (1977). *Ontogeny and Phylogeny*. Cambridge, MA: Harvard University Press/ Belknap Press.

Gould, S. J. (1981). *The Mismeasure of Man*. New York: Norton.

Gould, S. J. (1982). Darwinism and the expansion of evolutionary theory. *Science* 216, 380–7.

Gould, S. J. (August 12, 1984). Similarities between the sexes. *New York Times Book Review*, 7.

Jacob, F. (1973). *The Logic of Life: A history of heredity* (B. E. Spillman, trans.). New York: Pantheon Books. (Original work published 1970.)

Koestler, A. (1967). *The Ghost in the Machine*. New York: Macmillan.

Kolata, G. (1984). New clues to gene regulation. *Science* 224, 588–9.

Leighton, T. and Loomis, W. F. (1980). Introduction. In T. Leighton and W. F. Loomis (eds.), *The Molecular Genetics of Development* (xiii–xxiii). New York: Academic Press.

Margulis, L. (1981). *Symbiosis in Cell Evolution: Life and its environment on the early Earth*. San Francisco: Freeman.

Mayr, E. (1982). *The Growth of Biological Thought*. Cambridge, MA: Harvard University Press/ Belknap Press.

McClearn, G. E. and DeFries, J. C. (1973). *Introduction to Behavioral Genetics*. San Francisco: Freeman.

Monod, J. (1971). *Chance and Necessity* (A. Wainhouse, trans.). New York: Knopf.

Montalenti, G. (1974). From Aristotle to Democritus via Darwin. In F. J. Ayala and T. Dobzhansky (eds.), *Studies in the Philosophy of Biology* (3–19). Berkeley: University of California Press.

Oppenheim, R. W. (1982). Preformation and epigenesis in the origins of the nervous system and behavior: Issues, concepts, and their history. In P. P. G. Bateson and P. H. Klopfer (eds.), *Perspectives in Ethology* (Vol. 5) (1–100). New York: Plenum.

Oyama, S. (1979). The concept of the sensitive period in developmental studies. *Merrill-Palmer Quarterly* 25, 83–103.

Oyama, S. (1981). What does the phenocopy copy? *Psychological Reports* 48, 571–81.

Oyama, S. (1982). A reformulation of the concept of maturation. In P. P. G. Bateson and P. H. Klopfer (eds.), Perspectives in Ethology (Vol. 5) (101–31). New York: Plenum.

Paigen, K. (1980). Temporal genes and other developmental regulators in mammals. In T. Leighton and W. F. Loomis (eds.), *The Molecular Genetics of Development* (419–70). New York: Academic Press.

Ravin, A. W. (1977). The gene as catalyst; the gene as organism. In W. Coleman and C. Limoges (eds.), *Studies in History of Biology* (1–45). Baltimore: Johns Hopkins University Press.

Toulmin, S. (1967). Neuroscience and human understanding. In G. C. Quarton, T. Melnechuk, and F. O. Schmitt (eds.), *The Neurosciences: A study program* (822–32). New York: Rockefeller University Press.

Toulmin, S. (ed.) (1982). *The Return to Cosmology*. Berkeley: University of California Press.

Waddington, C. H. (1962). *New Patterns in Genetics and Development*. New York: Columbia University Press.

Waddington, C. H. (ed.) (1972). *Towards a Theoretical Biology* (Vol. 4). Edinburgh: Edinburgh University Press.

Williams, G. C. (1974). *Adaptation and Natural Selection*. Princeton: Princeton University Press.

Yund, M. A. and Germeraad, S. (1980). *Drosophila* development. In T. Leighton and W. F. Loomis (eds.), *The Molecular Genetics of Development* (237–360). New York: Academic Press.

3

The Epigenetic System and the Development of Cognitive Functions

Jean Piaget

1 Preformation and Epigenesis

The problem that has always arisen before one could tackle ontogenesis has been preformation or epigenesis. With the usual veering of fashion in the history of ideas, the tendency of many writers today is to return to the more or less strict preformation standpoint. Their grounds for this are that the chain or helical structure of the DNA or deoxyribonucleic acid molecule is susceptible of a combinatorial arrangement of its elements where "combinatorial" covers, by definition, the set of all possibilities. But if it is difficult, from the phylogenetic point of view, to conceive of man as preformed in bacterium or virus, it is every bit as hard to make out how, from the ontogenetic point of view, the main stages of "determination" or induction, and, most important, of the final functional "reintegration" of differentiated organs, could already be present in the initial stages of segmentation. Furthermore, Waddington has stated categorically that the idea of an entirely predetermined system in the DNA, however fashionable it may be at the moment, is just unacceptable in embryology.[a] At the symposium on this subject at Geneva in 1964, in the course of discussion about the regulations of development, he made a very profound comparison between epigenetic construction and a progression of geometric theorems in which each is rendered indispensable by the sum of those preceding it, though none is directly derived from the axioms underlying the original one.

The comparison of epigenesis with a progressive mathematical construction comes home to us all the more forcibly because the growth of elementary logico-mathematical operations during the ontogenesis of intelligence in a child raises the same problem of preformation or epigenetic construction as that which forms the basis of discussion about causal embryology.

We shall, indeed, find ourselves compelled to trace the origin of logico-mathematical operations back to an abstraction made from the general coordination of actions. On the one hand, such operations cannot possibly be based on the objects themselves, since abstraction

a   See Waddington (1975) – cited under Further reading in Editors' Introduction to Part I, p. 7.

"The Epigenetic System and the Development of Cognitive Functions" is an excerpt from: Jean Piaget, *Biology and Knowledge* (Edinburgh University Press and University of Chicago Press, 1971, section 2, pp. 14–23) and is reprinted by kind permission.

from objects can give rise only to non-necessitous statements (in the sense of deductive necessity) or, to put it more precisely, to judgements which are merely probable, whereas it is characteristic of logico-mathematical operations that they have an internal necessity attributable to their complete reversibility (and therefore not physical): for example, if $i = \sqrt{-1}$, then $i \times i = -1$. On the other hand, reunion, order, and interchangeable schemata are to be found in the general coordination of action, and these constitute the practical equivalent and even the motor equivalent of future interiorized operations.

If these elementary logico-mathematical operations are based on the coordination of actions, by means of reflective abstraction[b] drawn from sensorimotor schemata, do we have to conclude that the whole of mathematics is laid down in advance to our nervous system? Not only is this unthinkable, but the facts prove that logic itself, even in its most "natural" forms, is by no means innate in human beings in the sense that it exists at any age. Even the transitivity of equals or of cumulative differences ($A = C$ if $A = B$ and $B = C$, or $A < C$ if $A < B$ and $B < C$) is by no means obvious to a child of four to six years when he has to make a comparison between lengths and weights on first perceiving A and B simultaneously, next B and C, but not A and C (A subsequently being hidden and so presenting the problem).

The task of finding out about this transitivity raises all the main problems of epigenesis. Is this transitivity inherent in the genotype of the human species? If so, why does it not automatically come into play at about seven or eight years (and about nine or ten for weights)? Because, it will be said, new conditions are indispensable if the inherent virtual is later to become actual: for example, the intervention of regulatory genes or the collaboration of a number of genes not so far synergic (by reference to genetic or genic coadaptation, to use the currently accepted term). However, as these differentiated regulations are not made at any definite age in the particular case but may be accelerated or retarded according to conditions of exercise or acquired experience, they certainly exercise factors which are indirectly connected with environment.

Can it then be said that transitivity is utterly unconnected with the actions of the genome and solely dependent on phenotypic actions of the organism in relation to environment? In that case, how can it become "necessary" and generalizable? Because those actions which exert an influence on environment are influenced in their turn by the more generalized forms of internal coordinations of action? If that were so, would then generalized coordinations depend, in their turn, on the most common and deep-seated coordinations of the nervous system, which brings us back to the genome?

The evidence thus proves that the problem of preformation or epigenesis has nothing about it that appertains specially to organic embryogenesis, and it crops up in its most acute form every time we discuss the ontogenesis of cognitive functions. It may be objected that the problem is settled in advance, since the various aspects of intellectual behavior are phenotypic reactions and a phenotype is the result of interaction between the genotype and the environment. That is indisputable, but one still needs to explain in detail how, in the field of knowledge as in that of organic epigenesis, this collaboration between the genome and the environment actually works – especially those details which concern autoregulations or progressive equilibrations which admit of the exclusion of both preformism and the notion of a reaction caused entirely by environment.

---

b   Piaget defines "reflective abstraction" as the process of "reconstruction with new combinations, which allows for any operational structure at any previous stage or level to be integrated into a richer structure at a higher level" (section 20, part 4, p. 320 of *Biology and Knowledge*). (Editors' note.)

2   The Sequential Character of Stages

In this attempt at elucidation, the first step forward should be an examination of the sequential character of development. We call sequential a series of stages, each one of which is a necessary part of the whole and a necessary result of all the stages that precede it (except for the first one), as well as naturally leading on to the next stage (except for the last one). This seems to be the case with the embryogenesis of Metazoa, since the main stages constantly repeat themselves in the same order. However, no experiments have yet been done to control the impossibility of doing away with one stage, though these will doubtless be performed some day if someone succeeds in isolating processes which entail considerable speeding up or slowing down of the succession of stages. A further argument in favor of the sequential character and generality of the stages is the fact that, in mosaic-type embryos, namely at the initial level studied, those which have shown incomplete regeneration when separated from a blastomere reach a stage of partial control if the seed is split at the virgin egg stage (Ascidies de Dalcq).

Now this same problem about the sequential character of stages appears again in psychology in connection with the development of the cognitive functions. It is important to note that in this sphere the stages became increasingly clear and sequential in relation to controls that are better differentiated and of wider application.

Psychologists have relied too much on the notion of stage. Some speak as though it were nothing but a series of actions, not always, though "generally," in a constant order, and supposedly sharing a dominant characteristic, nothing more – which opens the door to arbitrary thinking. This is what Freud means by stages, for example, as far as the affective is concerned.

When it comes to intelligence, however, we use the term stage where the following conditions are fulfilled: first, where the series of actions is constant, independently of such speeding up or slowing down as may modify the middle range of chronological age[1] in terms of acquired experience and social environment (like individual aptitude); second, where each stage is determined not merely by a dominant property but by a whole structure which characterizes all further actions that belong to this stage; third, where these structures offer a process of integration such that each one is prepared by the preceding one and integrated into the one that follows. For example, without going into great detail about particular stages, three main periods can be seen in the case of operative intelligence:

A.   A sensorimotor period (from birth up to one and one-half to two years) during which sensorimotor schemata ranging up to acts of practical intelligence by means of immediate comprehension (using a stick or a piece of string, etc.) are established as well as practical substructures of future notions (permanent object schema, spatial displacement "group," sensorimotor causality, etc.).

B.   A period that begins when the semiotic function (language, game symbols, picture making) manifests itself and goes through the preparatory phase of preoperative representation (nonconservation, etc.). This ends not later than the eighth or ninth year with the setting up of operations which are called "concrete" because they still have a bearing on objects (classifying things, putting them in series, noting connections, understanding numbers).

C.   A period beginning at about the age of eleven or twelve which is characterized by propositional operations (implications, etc.) with their combinatorial quality and their possible transformations made by relation to a quaternary group – a combination of two elementary reversibility forms (inversion or negation and reciprocity).

A stage system of this kind (stages which can actually be even further differentiated into substages) makes up a sequential process: it is not possible to arrive at "concrete" operations without undergoing some sensorimotor preparation (which explains why, for example, blind people, having badly coordinated action schemata, may be retarded). It is also impossible to progress to propositional operations without support from previous concrete operations, etc. Thus, one is confronted with an epigenetic system whose stages may be characterized by fairly precise structures: coordination of sensorimotor schemata reaching certain invariables and an approximate reversibility (though in successive actions); "groupings" of concrete operations, that is, those elementary structures which are common to classifications and serializations, etc.; and combinatorial with a quaternary group at the third degree.[2]

By contrast, in the field of primary perceptions (or field effects) no comparable system of stages is to be found, and, as to behavior of medium complexity (perceptive activity in exploration, etc., and mental images), an intermediary situation is found halfway between an absence of stages and stages limited by their progressive integrations. Thus, everything seems to happen as though the more complex – in their organization and autoregulation systems – cognitive systems are, the more their formation is dependent on a sequential process comparable to a biological epigenesis.

3   Chreods

If a detailed study is to be made, that is, if the evolution of broad concepts or of particular operative structures is to be studied separately, then each one may give rise to its own respective stages in the midst of which is to be found the same sequential process. But the interesting thing about this point is that it presents us with differentiated channels, each one of which is nevertheless relatively even and follows its own course while still giving proof of varied interactions with the rest.

Waddington has suggested the name "chreods" (necessary routes) to describe developments particular to an organ or a part of an embryo, and he applies the term epigenetic system (or, epigenetic "scene") to the sum of the chreods, taken as being – to a greater or a lesser degree – channeled.[c] But the main interest of this idea is not just in the names he gives things (or in the symbolic patterns thereby presented to us, of channels, some wide, some narrow, that the processes must follow). It is, rather, in a new concept of equilibrium as something which is, as it were, kinematic and which, in determining such processes, is nevertheless quite distinct from homeostasis: there is a kind of "homeorhesis" when the formatory process, deviating from its course under outside influence, is brought back on course by the interplay of coercive compensations. In Waddington's opinion, such a mechanism is dependent upon a network of interactions rather than upon the action of individual genes; each group of genes is not even homeorhetic, and its return to a moral course or chreod presupposes, in this way, a complex interplay of regulations. It is true that some influence systematically exerted by the environment may eventually lead to lasting deviations in the chreod and to the consolidation of a new homeorhesis, but this is not the moment to raise such a problem. On the contrary, we would do better to emphasize the fact

---

c   See Editors' note a.

that the chreod and its homeorhesis do have a space–time aspect, not merely a space one. Differentiation in chreods is regulated in both time and space. The various channelings as well as the autocorrections which assure their homeorhetical equilibrium are under the control of a "time tally," which might well be described as a speed control for the processes of assimilation and organization. It is, then, only at the completion of development or at the completion of each structural achievement that homeorhesis gives place to homeostasis or functional equilibrium. In the latter case, the question naturally arises of determining the relationship between the two.

It is impossible to take note of such a picture without immediately thinking of the far-reaching analogies it has with the development of schemata or ideas in the intelligence, and with that of operational structures.

To put the matter in a familiar way, let us begin by noting that these analogies are very far from being universally accepted; very rarely have I been able, in America, to expound any aspect of my stage theory without being asked, "How can you speed up this development?" And that excellent psychologist, J. Bruner, has gone so far as to state that you can teach anything to any child at any age if only you set about it the right way. My answer to this is in the form of two questions: first, would it ever be possible to make the theory of relativity or even the simple handling of propositional or hypothetico-deductive operations comprehensible to a four-year-old? And, second, why does a human baby not discover the continued presence of something that he sees you hide beneath a screen until he reaches the age of nine months and upward, whereas kittens (in a study made by H. Gruber when he discovered the same preliminary stages in them as in us) do so at three months, even though they make no further progress in coordinating successive positions?

The truth, it seems to me, is that every notional or operational construction implies some optimum length of time, the expression of the most favorable transformation or assimilation speeds. This is because such a construction contains a certain number of necessary stages whose itinerary is the equivalent of a "chreod." In the sphere of the mind, where social influences are added to factors of physical experience (material environment), deviations easily occur, and short circuits too. Thus, the natural way for the mind to attain the concept of whole numbers consists of syntheses of inclusion of classes and the sequence of transitive asymmetrical relationships, in spite of the fact that the latter two systems develop along partly independent lines. Now the natural structure of the number concept can be modified in various ways. First of all, as is done by many parents, it can be taught the child verbally – ten to twenty, etc. But this only modifies the child's comprehension very slightly; we are constantly coming across subjects of four to five years old who will deny the equality of two piles of objects, even though they have counted what is in each pile as being perhaps seven or ten, because the way the objects were arranged in space or subdivided into small groups was changed each time. In such cases, outside influences, such as counting out loud, only produce a slight deviation leading back to the "chreod" at the four- to five-year-old level, for lack of any means of assimilation at higher levels. In other cases, a genuine acceleration can be set up, but only at one point (for example, in experiments where transfers are made one at a time in succession, thus facilitating, by repetition of the same actions, the synthesis of inclusions and the serial order).[3] This local synthesis is not necessarily followed by comprehension, nor will it guarantee retention of the number in transfer experiments between groups of objects arranged differently on different planes.

Briefly, intellectual growth contains its own rhythm and its "chreods" just as physical growth does. This is not, of course, to say that the best teaching methods, by which we mean the most "active" ones, cannot, to a certain extent, speed up the critical ages dealt with so far, but this speeding up cannot be indefinitely continued.

4   Maturation and Environment

The epigenesis of the cognitive functions, like any other, does, in fact, presuppose an increasingly close collaboration between the factors of environment and the genome, the former increasing in importance the larger the subject grows.

The factors relative to the genome are certainly not to be left out of account, in spite of what some scholars, empirically oriented, have said about all knowledge being drawn from outside experience. At this stage of our knowledge, these factors certainly cannot be tested in detail, but the best indication that they do intervene is the fact that the maturation of the nervous system is continuous right up to the age of fifteen or sixteen years. This, of course, in no way implies that ready-made knowledge is written into the nervous system from the outset in the way that "innate ideas" are, and, even if this idea proves acceptable in the case of certain instincts, there does not seem to be any similar phenomenon where human knowledge is concerned. On the contrary, heredity and maturation open up new possibilities in the human child, possibilities quite unknown to lower types of animal but which still have to be actualized by collaboration with the environment. These possibilities, for all they are opened up in stages, are nonetheless essentially functional (having no preformed structures) in that they represent a progressive power of coordination; but this very power is what makes possible the general coordinations of action on which logico-mathematical operations are based, which is why the continuous maturation of the nervous system that goes on until fifteen or sixteen years is a factor by no means to be ignored.

Such maturation does not, moreover, depend solely on the genome. But it does depend on that among other things (with the intervention of exercise factors, etc.), and, in general terms, it is admitted today that every phenotypic growth (including, therefore, cognitive functions in general) is the product of close interreactions between the genome and the environment.

The analysis of this collaboration remains, it is true, very complex and has scarcely been touched on so far. At this point we might begin by referring to an idea for which we are indebted, once more, to Waddington. This time it dates back to the work he did in 1932 on the phenomena of induction in the embryos of hens and ducks, to the idea of "competence," or the physiological state of a tissue, which permits it to react in a specific way to given stimuli. Competence is naturally subject to time conditions such as we talked about earlier, and a tissue may be competent at one particular phase without having been so previously or even remaining so afterward.

Surely no one can fail to see the analogy between this notion in relation to the embryonic mechanism and the facts brought out by experiments in the field of learning in logico-mathematical operations. The work of such people as Inhelder, Sinclair, and Bovet opened this up. When mechanisms favorable to the acquisition of knowledge are thus presented (for example, retaining the idea that there is the same amount of liquid when changing it from one vessel to another of a different shape), the results are utterly different according to the stage of the child's development, and the particular presentation which causes one subject to learn more quickly about a constant quantity will leave another utterly unmoved. The explanation of this again lies in the fact that sensitivity to stimuli (not only perceptual stimuli but in some cases those which set up a reasoning process) is a function of such assimilation schemata as are available to the subject. In this case, then, "competence" is a particular instance of what we call cognitive "assimilation," but assimilation schemata are built up by the interplay among the subject's powers of coordination and by the data of experience and environment.

To put it briefly, the epigenetic process which is the basis of intellectual operations is rather closely comparable to embryological epigenesis and the organic formation of phenotypes. Of course, the part played by environment is much larger, since the essential function of knowledge is to make contact with environment. To the effects of physical environment we must add those of social environment (for the individual genome is always the reflection of multiple crossbreedings and of a fairly broad range of "population"). But the essential question does not concern the quantitative sum of the respective influences exerted by endogenitive and external factors; rather, it has to do with qualitative analogies, and from that point of view it seems obvious that internal coordinations of the necessary and constant type, which make possible the integration of exterior cognitive aliment, give rise to the same biological problem of collaboration between the genome and the environment as do all the other forms of organization which occur in the course of development.

NOTES

1   In psychology the distinction is always made between chronological and mental age.

2   This sequential character of the stages of intelligence certainly seems to prove the necessity of an endogenic factor in nervous maturation, but by no means excludes either the intervention of the environment (experience) or, more particularly, the interaction of environment and maturation at the center of a process of equilibration or progressive autoregulation.

3   In this case, it was the putting of beads, simultaneously, one in each hand, into transparent bottles. See Inhelder and Piaget, *La formation des raisonnements récurrentiels*, Etudes d'épistémologie génétique, 17 (Presses Universitaires de France, 1963), chapter 2.

4

From Gene to Organism: The Developing Individual as an Emergent, Interactional, Hierarchical System

Gilbert Gottlieb

The historically correct definition of epigenesis – the emergence of new structures and functions during the course of individual development – did not specify, even in a general way, how these emergent properties come into existence. Thus, there was still room for preformation-like thinking about development, which I (Gottlieb, 1970) earlier labeled the predetermined conception of epigenesis, in contrast to a probabilistic conception (see table 4.1 for details). That epigenetic development is probabilistically determined by active interactions among its constituent parts is now so well accepted that epigenesis itself is sometimes defined as the interactionist approach to the study of individual development (e.g., Dewsbury, 1978; Johnston, 1987). That is a fitting tribute to the career-long labors of Zing-Yang Kuo (1976), T. C. Schneirla (1961), and Daniel S. Lehrman (1970), the principal champions of the interaction idea in the field of psychology, particularly as it applies to the study of behavioral and psychological development. Thus, it seems appropriate to offer a new definition of epigenesis that includes not only the idea of the emergence of new properties but also the idea that the emergent properties arise through reciprocal interactions (coactions) among already existing constituents. Somewhat more formally expressed, the new definition of epigenesis would say that *individual development is characterized by an increase of complexity of organization – i.e., the emergence of new structural and functional properties and competencies – at all levels of analysis* (molecular, subcellular, cellular, organismic) *as a consequence of horizontal and vertical coactions among its parts, including organism–environment coactions.* Horizontal coactions are those that occur at the same level (gene–gene, cell–cell, tissue–tissue, organism–organism), whereas vertical coactions occur at different levels (gene–cytoplasm, cell–tissue, behavioral activity–nervous system) and are reciprocal, meaning that they can influence each other in either direction, from lower to higher, or from higher to lower, levels of the developing system. For example, the sensory experience of a developing organism affects the differentiation of its nerve cells, such that the more experience the more differentiation and the less experience the less differentiation. (For example, enhanced activity or experience during individual development causes more elaborate branching of dendrites and more synaptic contacts among nerve cells in the brain [Greenough and Juraska, 1979.])[1] Reciprocally, the more highly differentiated nervous system permits a greater degree of behavioral competency and the less differentiated nervous system permits a lesser degree of behavioral competency. Thus, the essence of the probabilistic conception of epigenesis is the bidirectionality of structure–function relationships, as depicted in table 4.1. It is important to note that this hierarchical, reciprocal, coactive definition of epigenesis holds for anatomy and physiology (cf. the embryologist P. D. Nieuwkoop's definition in Gerhart, 1987), as well as for behavior and psychological functioning. The traffic is bidirectional, neither exclusively bottom–up or top–down. The embryologists Ludwig von Bertalanffy (1933–62) and Paul Weiss (1939–69), and the geneticist Sewall Wright (1968) have long been championing such a systems view for developmental genetics and developmental biology. The systems view in developmental psychology is exemplified by approaches and theories that have been called ecological (Bronfenbrenner, 1979), transactional (Dewey and Bentley, 1949; Sameroff, 1983), contextual (Lerner and Kaufman, 1985), interactive (Johnston, 1987; Magnusson, 1988), probabilistic epigenetic (Gottlieb, 1970), individual–socioecological (Valsiner, 1987), structural–behavioral (Horowitz, 1987), and, most globally speaking, interdisciplinary developmental science (Cairns, 1979).

Table 4.1   Two Versions of Epigenetic Development

Predetermined Epigenesis
Unidirectional Structure-Function Development

Genetic Activity → Structural Maturation → Function, Activity, or Experience (DNA → RNA → Protein)

Probabilistic Epigenesis
Bidirectional Structure-Function Development

Genetic Activity ↔ Structural Maturation ↔ Function, Activity, or Experience (DNA ↔ RNA ↔ Protein)

As applied to the nervous system, structural maturation refers to neurophysiological and neuroanatomical development, principally the structure and function of nerve cells and their synaptic interconnections. The unidirectional structure-function view assumes that genetic activity gives rise to structural maturation that then leads to function in a nonreciprocal fashion, whereas the bidirectional view holds that there are constructive reciprocal relations between genetic activity, maturation, and function. In the unidirectional view, the activity of genes and the maturational process are pictured as relatively encapsulated or insulated so that they are uninfluenced by feedback from the maturation process or function, whereas the bidirectional view assumes that genetic activity and maturation are affected by function, activity, or experience. The bidirectional or probabilistic view calls for arrows going back to genetic activity to indicate feedback serving as signals for the turning off and turning on of DNA to manufacture protein. The usual view calls for genetic activity to be regulated by the genetic system itself in a strictly feedforward manner. That the feedback (actually, feeddown) view is correct is evidenced by the experimental results of Zamenhof and van Marthens, Uphouse and Bonner, and Grouse et al. reviewed in this chapter.

Note: Throughout this work I have presented DNA → RNA → protein pathway in an oversimplified manner that, although it seems appropriate for the present purpose, does disregard the fact that a number of crucial events intervene between RNA and protein formation. In fact, according to Pritchard (1986), dozens of known factors intervene between RNA activity and protein formation! Thus, it is an oversimplification to imply that DNA and RNA alone produce specific proteins – other factors (e.g., cytoplasm) contribute to the specificity of the protein.

Figure 4.1   Clockwise from upper left: Zing-Yang Kuo (1898–1970), T. C. Schneirla (1902–68), and Daniel S. Lehrman (1919–72), principal champions of the interactionist viewpoint in psychological and behavior development.

Developmental Causality (Coaction)

Behavioral (or organic or neural) outcomes of development are a consequence of *at least* (at minimum) *two* specific components of coaction (e.g., person–person, organism–organism, organism–environment, cell–cell, nucleus–cytoplasm, sensory stimulation–sensory system, activity–motor behavior). The cause of development – what makes development happen – is the relationship of the two components, not the components themselves. Genes in themselves cannot cause development any more than stimulation in itself can cause development. When we speak of coaction as being at the heart of developmental analysis or causality what we mean is that we need to specify some relationship between at least two components of the developmental system. The concept used most frequently to designate coactions at the organismic level of functioning is *experience:* experience is thus a relational term. As documented elsewhere (Gottlieb, 1976a, 1976b), experience can play at least three different roles in anatomical, physiological, and behavioral development (figure 4.2). It can be necessary to sustain already achieved states of affairs (*maintenance function*), it can temporally regulate when a feature appears during development (*facilitative function*), and it can be necessary to bring about a state of affairs that would not appear unless the experience occurred (*inductive function*).

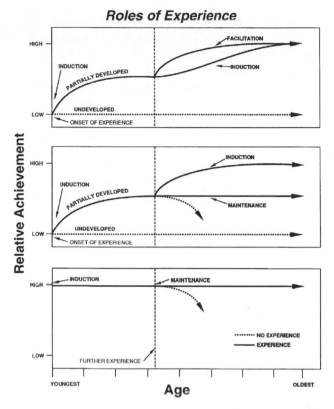

Figure 4.2 Three roles that experience plays in the development of anatomy, physiology, and behavior.

Since first defining and formulating the various roles of experience in 1976, it has become apparent that interactive *activity* of some kind (e.g., activity-dependent regulation of gene expression) is a usual part of development at all levels from the subcellular to the organismic, so I have here (figure 4.2) modified the early scheme to reflect that eventuality. (See note 1 to this chapter for a more precise definition of intrinsic experience.) While this scheme is not exhaustive, it does call attention to the various roles that experience (interactive activity) can play in both intrinsic relations (inside the organism) and extrinsic ones (organism–organism or organism–environment relations), as Bateson (1983) and others have pointed out. In this scheme experience is defined as interactive activity, whether it is analyzed under or outside the skin of the organism, or, preferably, both under (say at the cellular level) and outside which can now be realized in research in developmental neurobiology. The techniques at hand make such thoroughgoing analyses quite feasible, especially in multidisciplinary research settings where investigators can pool their skills from the most molar levels (culture, society) to the most molecular levels of analysis. Such a multidisciplinary developmental systems approach is described and discussed in the first section of the January 1991 issue of *Developmental Psychology*, and one hopes it will become more commonplace in the years to come.

Since developing systems are by definition always changing in some way, statements of developmental causality must also include a *temporal* dimension describing when the experience occurred. For example, one of the earliest findings of experimental embry-ology had to do with the differences in outcome according to the time during early development when tissue was transplanted. When tissue from the head region of the embryo was transplanted to the embryo's back, if the transplantation occurred early in development the tissue differentiated according to its new surround (i.e., it differentiated into back tissue), whereas, if the transplant occurred later in development the tissue differentiated according to its previous surround so that, for example, a third eye might appear on the back of the embryo. These transplantation experiments demonstrated not only the import of time but also showed the essentially coactional nature of embryonic development.

Significance of Coaction for Individual Development

The early formulation by August Weismann of the role of the hereditary material (what came to be called genes) in individual development held that different parts of the genome or genic system caused the differentiation of the different parts of the developing organism, so there were thought to be genes for eyes, genes for legs, genes for toes, and so forth. Hans Driesch's experiment, in which he separated the first two cells of a sea urchin's development and obtained a fully formed sea urchin from each of the cells, showed that each cell contained a complete complement of genes. This means that each cell is capable of developing into any part of the body, a competency that was called *equipotentiality* or *pluripotency* in the jargon of the early history of experimental embryology and *totipotency* and *multipotentiality* in today's terms (e.g., DiBerardino, 1988). Each cell does not develop into just any part of the body even though it has the capability of doing so. Each cell develops in accordance with its surround, so cells at the anterior pole of the embryo develop into parts of the head, cells at the posterior pole develop into parts of the tail end of the body, cells in the foremost lateral region of the embryo develop into forelimbs, cells in the hindmost lateral region develop hindlimbs, the dorsal area of the embryo develops into the back, and so on. Although we do not know what actually causes cells to differentiate appropriately according to their surround, we do know that it is the cell's interaction with its surround, including other cells in that same area, that causes the cell to differentiate appropriately. The actual role of genes (DNA) is not to produce an arm or a leg or fingers, but to produce protein (through the coactions inherent in the formula DNA ↔ RNA ↔ protein). The protein produced by the DNA–RNA–cytoplasm coaction then differentiates according to coactions with other cells in its surround. Thus, differentiation occurs according to coactions *above the level of DNA–RNA coaction* (i.e., at the supragenetic level). The DNA–RNA coaction produces protein and that protein subsequently differen-tiates according to where it finds itself in the three-dimensional space of the embryo (the anterior-posterior, lateral, and dorsal-ventral spatial dimensions), plus the temporal dimension alluded to earlier. Thus it is the coactions during each phase of embryonic development that somehow, by means not yet understood, eventually produce a mature organism.[2]

Another demonstration that genes merely produce protein and not mature traits comes from an ingenious experiment by J. B. Gurdon (1968). If genes (DNA) in the nucleus of a cell did produce specific traits (e.g., an intestinal cell), then, should it prove possible to recover the nucleus from such a cell it would be missing that part of its genetic complement because those genes would have been used up in creating the intestinal cell. By way of proving that idea wrong, Gurdon recovered the nucleus from an intestinal cell of a tadpole and inserted that nucleus into an early embryonic (blastula) cell whose nucleus had been removed. Such nuclear transfers yield entirely normal and fertile adult male and female toads, thus proving that the differentiation of a cell does not require any loss whatsoever of genetic material and that differentiation occurs above the level of the genes after the genes, in coaction with RNA and cytoplasm, have manufactured the protein that is an essential building block of all cells in the body. When certain scientists refer to behavior or any other aspect of organismic structure or function as being "genetically determined" they are not mindful of the fact that genes synthesize protein and not fully developed features of the organism. And, as experiments on the early development of the nervous system have demonstrated, the amount of protein synthesis is regulated by neural activity itself, once again demonstrating the bidirectionality and coaction of influences during individual development (Born and Rubel, 1988).

The Hierarchical Systems View

Much has been written about the holistic or systems nature of individual development. In fact, there is no other way to envisage the manner in which development must occur if a harmoniously functioning, fully integrated organism is to be its product. In earlier chapters, figures were reproduced from the writings of the geneticist Sewall Wright (Figure 10–5 in Chapter 10) and the embryologist Paul Weiss (Figure 12–2 in Chapter 12), which portray well the major components of the developing individual as an emergent, coactional, hierarchical system. So far we have dealt with the concepts of emergence and coaction as they pertain to the development of individuals. The notion of hierarchy, as it applies to individual development, simply means that coactions occur vertically as well as horizontally in all developmental systems. All the parts of the system are capable of influencing all the other parts of the system, however indirectly that influence may manifest itself. Consonant with Sewall Wright's and Paul Weiss's depiction of the developmental system, the organismic hierarchy proceeds from the lowest level, that of the genome or DNA in the nucleus, to the nucleus in the cytoplasm in the cell, to the cell in a tissue, to the tissue in an organ, the organ in an organ system, the organ system in an organism, the organism in an environment of other organisms and physical features, the environment in an ecosystem, and so on back down through the hierarchical developmental system (review by Grene, 1987). A fascinating example of the environment-to-gene hierarchical pathway is the finding that the genes that respond to heat shock in fruitfly larvae are more apt to do so if the to-be-shocked larvae have been kept at warm temperatures rather than cold ones. The characteristic heat-shock proteins that these "heat-shock genes" produce are less evident in cold-reared larvae (Singh and Lakhotin, 1988). Another dramatic developmental effect traversing the many levels from the environment back to the cytoplasm of the cell is shown by the experiments of Victor Jollos in the 1930s and Mae-Wan Ho in the 1980s. In Ho's experiment (reviewed in Chapter 12), an extraorganismic environmental event such as a brief period of exposure to ether occurring at a particular time in embryonic development can alter the cytoplasm of the cell in such a way that a different pattern of protein is produced that eventually results in a second set of wings (an abnormal "bithorax" condition) in place of the halteres (balancing organs) on the body of an otherwise normal fruitfly. Obviously, it is very likely that "signals" have been altered at various levels of the developmental hierarchy to achieve such an outcome. (Two excellent texts that describe the many different kinds of coactions that are a necessary and normal part of embryonic development are D. J. Pritchard's [1986] *Foundations of Developmental Genetics* and N. K. Wessells's [1977] *Tissue Interactions and Development.*)

It happens that when the cytoplasm of the cell is altered, as in the experiments of Jollos and Ho, the effect is transgenerational such that the untreated daughters of the treated mothers continue for a number of generations to produce bithorax offspring and do so even when mated with males from untreated lines. Such a result has evolutionary as well as developmental significance, which, to this date, has been little exploited because the neo-Darwinian, modern synthesis does not yet have a role in evolution for anything but changes in genes and gene frequencies in evolution: epigenetic development above the level of the genes has not yet been incorporated into the modern synthesis (Futuyma, 1988; Løvtrup, 1987).[3] (In the next chapter, I will describe more fully the idea that the first step in the evolutionary pathway may sometimes not involve a genetic change or mutation.)

Another remarkable organism–environment coaction occurs routinely in coral reef fish. These fish live in spatially well-defined, social groups in which there are many females and few males. When a male dies or is otherwise removed from the group, one of the females initiates a sex reversal over a period of about two days in which she develops the coloration, behavior, and gonadal physiology and anatomy of a fully functioning male (Shapiro, 1981). Such sex reversals keep the sex ratios about the same in social groups of coral reef fish. Apparently, it is the higher ranking females that are the first to change their sex and that inhibits sex reversal in lower ranking females in the group. Sex reversal in coral reef fish provides an excellent example of the vertical dimension of developmental causality.

The completely reciprocal or bidirectional nature of the vertical or hierarchical organization of individual development is nowhere more apparent than the responsiveness of cellular or nuclear DNA itself to events originating in the external environment of the organism. The major theoretical point of this monograph is that the genes are part of the developmental system in the same sense as other components (cell, tissue, organism), so genes must be susceptible to influence from other levels during the process of individual development. DNA produces protein, cells are composed of protein, so there must be a high correlation between the *size* of cells, amount of protein, and quantity of DNA, and there must also be a high correlation between the *number* of cells, amount of protein, and quantity of DNA, and so there is (Cavalier-Smith, 1985; Mirsky and Ris, 1951). For our behavioral–psychological purposes, it is most interesting to focus on the developing brain, where we do indeed find the expected correlation among size and/or number of brain cells, amount of protein, and quantity of DNA (Zamenhof and van Marthens, 1978, 1979).

Table 4.2 Sequence complexities of visual cortex RNAs

Group	No. of Separate RNA Preparations	No. of Hybridization Reactions at $ER_0t = 211300$	RNA Complexity as Percentage of uDNA
Unsutured	5	18	11.77 ± 0.59
Sutured	5	10	8.69 ± 0.19
Repeat-sutured	4	8	9.22 ± 0.86

From Grouse et al. (1979).

From the present point of view, it is significant that cell size, if not cell number, in the developing rodent and chick brain is responsive to two sorts of environmental input: nutrition and sensorimotor experience. Undernutrition and "supernutrition" produce newborn rats and chicks with lower and higher quantities of cerebral DNA respectively (Zamenhof and van Marthens, 1978, 1979). Similar cerebral consequences are produced by extreme variations (social isolation, environmental enrichment) in sensorimotor experience during the postnatal period (Rosenzweig and Bennett, 1978).

Since the route from DNA to protein is through the mediation of RNA (DNA $\to$ RNA $\to$ protein), it is significant for the present theoretical viewpoint that social isolation and environmental enrichment produce alterations in the complexity (or diversity) of RNA sequences in the brains of rodents. (RNA complexity or diversity refers to the total number of nucleotides of individual RNA molecules.) A specific example of a change in RNA complexity as a consequence of normal and deprived visual experience is shown in table 4.2. When the eyelids of kittens are sutured closed so they cannot receive visual stimulation, they show less RNA complexity in the visual cortex of the brain compared to normal (unsutured) kittens (Grouse et al., 1979). In general, environmental enrichment produces an increase in the complexity of expression of RNA sequences, whereas social isolation and environmental deprivation result in a significantly reduced degree of RNA complexity (Grouse et al., 1980; Uphouse and Bonner, 1975). These experientially produced alterations in RNA diversity are specific to the brain. When other organs are examined (e.g., liver), no such changes are found.

Nonlinear Causality

Because of the emergent nature of epigenetic development, another important feature of developmental systems is that causality is often not "linear" or straightforward. In developmental systems the coaction of X and Y often produces W rather than more of X or Y, or some variant of X or Y. Another, perhaps clearer, way to express this same idea is to say that developmental causality is often not obvious. In my own research, for example, I found that mallard duck embryos had to hear their own vocalizations prior to hatching if they were to show their usual highly specific behavioral response to the mallard maternal assembly call after hatching. If the mallard duck embryo was deprived of hearing its own or sib vocalizations, it lost its species-specific perceptual specificity and became as responsive to the maternal assembly calls of other species as to the mallard hen's call. To the human ear, the embryo's vocalizations sound nothing like the maternal call. It turned out, however, that there are certain rather abstract acoustic ingredients in the embryonic vocalizations that correspond to critical acoustic features that identify the mallard hen's assembly call. In the absence of experiencing those ingredients, the mallard duckling's auditory perceptual system is not completely "tuned" to those features in the mallard hen's call and they respond to the calls of other species that resemble the mallard in these acoustic dimensions. The intricacy of the developmental causal network revealed in these experiments proved to be striking. Not only must the duckling experience the vocalizations as an embryo (the experience is ineffective after hatching), the embryo must experience *embryonic* vocalizations. That is, the embryonic vocalizations change after hatching and no longer contain the proper ingredients to tune the embryo to the maternal cell (Gottlieb, 1985).

Prenatal nonlinear causality is also nonobvious because the information, outside of experimental laboratory contexts, is usually not available to us. For example, the rate of adult sexual development is retarded in female gerbils that were adjacent to a male fetus during gestation (Clark and Galef, 1988). To further compound the nonobvious, the daughters of late-maturing females are themselves retarded in that respect – a transgenerational effect!

In a very different example of nonobvious and nonlinear developmental causality, Cierpial and McCarty (1987) found that the so-called spontaneously hypertensive (SHR) rat strain employed as an animal model of human hypertension is made hypertensive by coacting with their mothers after birth. When SHR rat pups are suckled and reared by normal rat mothers after birth they do not develop hypertension. It appears that there is a "hyperactive" component in SHR mothers' maternal behavior that causes SHR pups to develop hypertension (Myers, Brunelli, Shair, Squire, and Hofer, 1989; Myers, Brunelli, Squire, Shindeldecker, and Hofer, 1989). The highly specific coactional nature of the development of hypertension in SHR rats is shown by the fact that normotensive rats do not develop hypertension when they are suckled and reared by SHR mothers. Thus, although SHR rat pups differ in some way from normal rat pups, the development of hypertension in them nonetheless requires an interaction with their mother; it is not an inevitable outcome of the fact that they are genetically, physiologically, and/or anatomically different from normal rat pups. This is a good example of the *relational* aspect of the definition of experience and developmental causality offered earlier in this chapter. The cause of the hypertension in the SHR rat strain is not in the SHR rat pups or in the SHR mothers but in the nursing relationship between the SHR rat pups and their mother.

Another example of a nonlinear and nonobvious developmental experience undergirding species-typical behavioral development is Wallman's (1979) demonstration that if chicks are not permitted to see their toes during the first two days after hatching, they do not eat or pick up mealworms as chicks normally do. Instead, the chicks stare at the mealworms. Wallman suggests that many features of the usual rearing environment of infants may offer experiences that are necessary for the expression of species-typical behavior.

The Unresolved Problem of Differentiation

The nonlinear, emergent, coactional nature of individual development is well exemplified by the phenomenon of *differentiation*, whereby a new kind of organization comes into being by the coaction of preexisting parts. If genes directly caused parts of the embryo rather than producing protein, there would be less of a problem in understanding differentiation. Since the route from gene to mature structure or organism is not straightforward, differentiation poses a significant intellectual puzzle, as recognized as early as 1962 by Ephrussi (1979), among others. The problem of differentiation also involves our limited understanding of the role of genes in development; what else, if anything, might genes do than produce protein?

It has been recognized since the time of Driesch's earth-shaking experiments demonstrating the genetic equipotentiality of all cells of the organism that the chief problem of understanding development was that of understanding why originally equipotential cells actually do become different in the course of development, i.e., how is it they differentiate into cells that form the tissues of very different organ systems. The problem of understanding development thus became the problem of understanding cellular differentiation. We still do not understand differentiation today, and it is quite telling of the immense difficulty of the problem that today's theory of differentiation is very much like the necessarily vaguer theories put forth by E. B. Wilson in 1896 and T. H. Morgan in 1934 (reviewed in Davidson, 1986), that ultimate or eventual cellular differentiation is influenced by an earlier coaction between the genetic material in the nucleus of the cell with particular regions of the cytoplasm of the cell. Some of the vagueness has been removed in recent years by the actual determination of regional differences in the cytoplasm (extensively reviewed by Davidson, 1986). Thus, the undifferentiated protein resulting from locale or regional differences of nucleo–cytoplasmic coaction is biochemically distinct, which, in some as yet unknown way, influences or biases its future course of development. For example, protein with the same or similar biochemical makeups may stay together during cellular migration during early development and thus eventually come to form a certain part of the organism by the three-dimensional spatial field considerations of the embryo mentioned earlier in this chapter. Although the actual means or mechanisms by which some cells become one part of the organism and others become another part are still unresolved, we do have a name for the essential coactions that cause cells to differentiate: they are called embryonic *inductions*. The nonlinear hallmark of developmental causality is well exemplified by embryonic induction, in which one kind of cell (*A*) coacting with a second kind of cell (*B*) produces a third kind of cell (*C*). For example, if left in place, cells in the upper one-third of an early frog embryo differentiate into nerve cells; if removed from that region, those same cells can become skin cells. Equipotentiality and the critical role of spatial position in determining differentiation in the embryo is well captured in a quotation from the autobiography of Hans Spemann, the principal discoverer of the phenomenon of embryonic induction: "We are standing and walking with parts of our body which could have been used for thinking if they had been developed in another position in the embryo" (translated by B. K. Hall, 1988, p. 174). It might have been even more striking – and equally correct – if Spemann had elected to say, "We are sitting with parts of our body which could have been used for thinking..."!

Even if we do not yet have a complete understanding of differentiation, the facts at our disposal show us that epigenetic development is correctly characterized as an emergent, coactional, hierarchical system that results in increasingly complex organization. It remains now to use that conceptual framework to fashion a developmentally based view of evolutionary change.

NOTES

1   In 1976 I (Gottlieb, 1976a, b) defined experience in such a way as to include spontaneous activity generated within the nervous system as well as evoked activity arising from sensory stimulation originating in the organism's environment. Since that time it has been shown that spontaneous as well as evoked activity does play an important role in the normal neuroanatomical development of the brain (e.g., Born and Rubel, 1988; Shatz and Stryker, 1988). The brain develops abnormally (deficiently) when normal spontaneous or evoked activity is curtailed by experimental means. This area of research is coming to the forefront in developmental neuroscience under the rubric *activity-dependent regulation of gene expression*, a concept that meshes extremely well with the view of the mechanisms of individual development expressed in the present work (review in Changeux and Konishi, 1987). The contribution of factors "upstream" from the genes is also being recognized by the "new look" in developmental neuroscience (e.g., Edelman, 1988).

2   With the realization that Weismann's notion that specific genes give rise to specific parts of the body is erroneous, various biologists have been working on hierarchically organized

field-theory approaches to an understanding of individual morphological development. Among the current workers are Goodwin (1984), Hall (1988), and Oster, Odell, and Alberch, (1980). It is curious that some ostensible field theorists such as Wolpert (1971, 1982) still hold that the morphological development of the individual is somehow preprogrammed in the genes. So, when I say "the realization that Weismann's view is erroneous," it is obvious that the implications of that statement are not unequivocally understood by all developmental biologists, even if they happen to be working on field theories of individual development!

3   It is especially noteworthy that someone like Futuyma acknowledges the lack of developmental thinking in the neo-Darwinian concept of evolution, because he is firmly identified with the population-genetic tradition that undergirds the modern synthesis. On the other hand, Futuyma seems to see no substantive difference or change in the neo-Darwinian synthesis resulting from an inclusion of developmental considerations: "The need for a theory of development ... is evident, but at this point, the need for a new evolutionary paradigm is not" (Futuyma, 1988, p. 221). Other biologists do not agree with Futuyma; they try to show why a new evolutionary paradigm *is* necessary when individual development is taken into account (Ho and Saunders, 1984; Ho and Fox, 1988). In Chapter 14 (of the original publication) I try to show what differences accrue to evolutionary thinking when developmental behavioral and psychological concerns are placed in the forefront.

REFERENCES

Bateson, P. G. (1983). Genes, environment, and the development of behaviour. In T. R. Halliday and P. J. B. Slater (eds.), *Animal Behaviour*, vol. 3. *Genes, development, and learning*. Oxford: Blackwell.

von Bertalanffy, L. (1962). *Modern Theories of Development: An introduction to theoretical biology*. New York: Harper. (Originally published in German in 1933.)

Born, D. E. and Rubel, E. W. (1988). Afferent influences on brain stem auditory nuclei of the chicken: Presynaptic action potentials regulate protein synthesis in nucleus magnocellularis neurons. *Journal of Neuroscience* 8, 901–19.

Bronfenbrenner, U. (1979). *The Ecology of Human Development: Experiments by nature and design*. Cambridge, MA: Harvard University Press.

Cairns, R. B. (1979). *Social Development: The origins and plasticity of interchanges*. San Francisco: W. H. Freeman.

Cavalier-Smith, T. (1985). Cell volume and the evolution of eukaryote genome size. In T. Cavalier-Smith (ed.), *The Evolution of Genome Size*. Chichester, England: Wiley.

Changeux, J.-P. and Konishi, M. (eds.) (1987). *The Neural and Molecular Bases of Learning*. Chichester, England: Wiley.

Cierpial, M. A. and McCarty, R. (1987). Hypertension in SHR rats: Contribution of maternal environment. *American Journal of Physiology* 253, 980–4.

Clark, N. M. and Galef, B. G. (1988). Effects of uterine position on rate of sexual development in female mongolian gerbils. *Physiology and Behavior* 42, 15–18.

Darwin, C. (1859). *On the Origin of Species*. (A facsimile of the 1st edition, published by Harvard University Press in 1964.)

Darwin, E. (1794). *Zoonomia; or the laws of organic life*. London: Johnson.

Davidson, E. H. (1986). *Gene Activity in Early Development*. Orlando, Florida: Academic Press.

Dewey, J. and Bentley, A. F. (1949). *Knowing and the Known*. Boston: Beacon.

Dewsbury, D. A. (1978). *Comparative Animal Behavior*. New York: McGraw-Hill.

DiBerardino, M. A. (1988). Genomic multipotentiality of differentiated somatic cells. In G. Eguchi, T. S. Okada, Saxén (eds.), *Regulatory Mechanisms in Developmental Processes*. Ireland: Elsevier.

Driesch, H. (1908/1929). *The Science and Philosophy of the Organism*. London: A. & C. Black. (The 2nd abridged edition was used in the present work.)

Edelman, G. M. (1988). *Topobiology*. New York: Basic Books.

Ephrussi, B. (1979). Mendelism and the new genetics. *Somatic Cell Genetics* 5, 681–95.

Futuyma, D. J. (1988). *Sturm und Drang* and the evolutionary synthesis. *Evolution* 42, 217–26.

Gerhart, J. C. (1987). The epigenetic nature of vertebrate development: An interview of Pieter D. Nieuwkoop on the occasion of his 70th birthday. *Development* 101, 653–7.

Goodwin, B. C. (1984). A relational or field theory of reproduction and its evolutionary implications. In M.-W. Ho and P. T. Saunders (eds.), *Beyond neo-Darwinism: An introduction to the new evolutionary paradigm*. London: Academic Press.

Gottlieb, G. (1970). Conceptions of prenatal behavior. In L. R. Aronson et al. (eds.), *Development and Evolution of Behavior*. San Francisco: W. H. Freeman.

Gottlieb, G. (1976a). The roles of experience in the development of behavior and the nervous system. In G. Gottlieb (ed.), *Neural and Behavioral Specificity*. New York: Academic Press.

Gottlieb, G. (1976b). Conceptions of prenatal development: Behavioral embryology. *Psychological Review* 83, 215–34.

Gottlieb, G. (1985). Development of species identification in ducklings: XI. Embryonic critical period for species typical perception in the hatchling. *Animal Behaviour* 33, 225–33.

Greenough, W. T. and Juraska, J. M. (1979). Experience-induced changes in brain fine structure: Their behavioral implications. In M. E. Hahn, C. Jensen, and B. C. Dudek (eds.), *Development and Evolution of Brain Size*. New York: Academic Press.

Grene, M. (1987). Hierarchies in biology. *American Scientist* 75, 504–10.

Grouse, L. D., Schrier, B. K., and Nelson, P. G. (1979). Effect of visual experience on gene expression during the development of stimulus specificity in cat brain. *Experimental Neurology* 64, 354–9.

Grouse, L. D., Schrier, B. K., Letendre, C. H., and Nelson, P. G. (1980). RNA sequence complexity in central nervous system development and plasticity. *Current Topics in Developmental Biology* 16, 381–97.

Gurdon, J. B. (1968). Transplanted nuclei and cell differentiation. *Scientific American* 219, 24–35.

Hall, B. K. (1988). The embryonic development of bone. *American Scientist* 76, 174–81.

Ho, M.-W. (1984). Environment and heredity in development and evolution. In M.-W. Ho and P. T. Saunders (eds.), *Beyond neo-Darwinism: An introduction to the new evolutionary paradigm*. London: Academic Press.

Ho, M.-W. and Fox, S. W. (eds.) (1988). *Evolutionary Processes and Metaphors*. New York: Wiley.

Ho, M.-W. and Saunders, P. T. (eds.) (1984). *Beyond neo-Darwinism: An introduction to the new evolutionary paradigm*. London: Academic Press.

Horowitz, F. D. (1987). *Exploring Developmental Theories: Toward a structural/behavioral model of development*. Hillsdale, New Jersey: Erlbaum.

Johnston, T. D. (1987). The persistence of dichotomies in the study of behavioral development. *Developmental Review* 7, 149–82.

Jollos, V. (1934). Inherited changes produced by heat treatment in *Drosophila melanogaster*. *Genetics* 16, 476–94.

Kuo, Z.-Y. (1976). *The Dynamics of Behavior Development: An epigenetic view* (enlarged edn.). New York: Plenum Press.

Lehrman, D. S. (1970). Semantic and conceptual issues in the nature–nurture problem. In L. R. Aronson, D. S. Lehrman, E. Tobach, and J. S. Rosenblatt (eds.), *Development and Evolution of Behavior*. San Francisco, California: W. H. Freeman.

Lerner, R. M. and Kaufman, M. B. (1985). The concept of development in contextualism. *Developmental Review* 5, 309–33.

Lovtrup, S. (1987). *Darwinism: Refutation of a myth*. Beckenham, Kent, England: Croom Helm.

Magnusson, D. (1988). *Individual Development from an Interactional Perspective: A longitudinal study*. Hillsdale, New Jersey: Erlbaum.

Mirsky, A. E. and Ris, H. (1951). The desoxyribonucleic acid content of animal cells and its evolutionary significance. *Journal of General Physiology* 34, 451–62.

Morgan, T. H. (1934). *Embryology and Genetics*. Westport, Connecticut: Greenwood.

Myers, M. M. Brunelli, S. A., Shair, H. N., Squire, J. M., and Hofer, M. A. (1989). Relationships between maternal behavior of SHR and WKY dams and adult blood pressures of cross-fostered F_1 pups. *Developmental Psychobiology* 22, 55–67.

Myers, M. M., Brunelli, S. A., Squire, J. M., Shindeldecker, R. D., and Hofer, M. A. (1989). Maternal behavior of SHR rats and its relationship to offspring blood pressures. *Developmental Psychobiology* 22, 29–53.

Oster, G., Odell, G. and Alberch, P. (1980). Mechanics, morphogenesis, and evolution. *Lectures on Mathematics in the Life Sciences* 13, 165–255.

Pritchard, D. J. (1986). *Foundations of Developmental Genetics*. London and Philadelphia: Taylor and Francis.

Rosenzweig, M. R. and Bennett, E. L. (1978). Experiential influences on brain anatomy and brain chemistry in rodents. In G. Gottlieb (ed.), *Early Influences*. New York: Academic Press.

Sameroff, A. J. (1983). Developmental systems: Contexts and evolution. In P. H. Mussen (ed.), *Handbook of Child Psychology* (vol. 1): W. Kessen (ed.), *History, theory, and methods*. New York: Wiley.

Schneirla, T. C. (1961). Instinctive behavior, maturation – experience and development. In B. Kaplan and S. Wapner (eds.), *Perspectives in Psychological Theory – Essays in honor of Heinz Werner*. New York: International Universities Press.

Shapiro, D. Y. (1981). Serial female sex changes after simultaneous removal of males from social groups of a coral reef fish. *Science* 209, 1136–7.

Shatz, C. J. and Stryker, M. P. (1988). Prenatal tetrodotoxin infusion blocks segregation of retinogeniculate afferents. *Science* 242, 87–9.

Singh, A. K. and Lakhotin, S. C. (1988). Effect of low-temperature rearing on heat shock protein synthesis and heat sensitivity in *Drosophila melanogaster*. *Developmental Genetics* 9, 193–201.

Uphouse, L. L. and Bonner, J. T. (1975). Preliminary evidence for the effects of environmental complexity on hybridization of rat brain RNA to rat unique DNA. *Developmental Psychobiology* 8, 171–8.

Valsiner, J. (1987). *Culture and the Development of Children's Action*. Chichester, England: Wiley.

Wallman, J. (1979). A minimal visual restriction experiment: Preventing chicks from seeing their feet affects later responses to mealworms. *Developmental Psychobiology* 12, 391–7.

Weismann, A. (1894). *The Effect of External Influences upon Development*. London: Henry Frowde.

Weiss, P. (1959). Cellular dynamics. *Reviews of Modern Physics* 31, 11–20.

Wessells, N. K. (1977). *Tissue Interactions and Development*. Menlo Park, California: W. A. Benjamin.

Wolpert, L. (1971). Positional information and pattern formation. *Current Topics in Developmental Biology* 6, 183–224.

Wolpert, L. and Stein, W. D. (1982). Evolution and development. In H. C. Plotkin (ed.), *Learning, Development, and Culture: Essays in evolutionary epistemology*. London: Wiley.

Wright, S. (1968). *Evolution and the Genetics of Populations*, vol. 1: *Genetic and biometric foundations*. Chicago: University of Chicago Press.

Zamenhof, S. and van Marthens, E. (1978). Nutritional influences on prenatal brain development. In G. Gottlieb (ed.), *Early Influences*. New York: Academic Press.

Zamenhof, S. and van Marthens, E. (1979). Brain weight, brain chemical content, and their early manipulation. In M. E. Hahn, C. Jensen, and B. C. Dudek (eds.), *Development and Evolution of Brain Size*. New York: Academic Press.

PART II

Brain Maturation

Editors' Introduction to Part II

One of the earliest roots of developmental psychology in the United States was the study of how brain maturation gives rise to motor development. During the behaviorist era, this approach fell out of favor, and the infant was viewed as more of a *tabula rasa*, albeit one containing some powerful learning algorithms. As mentioned earlier, part of the purpose of this book is to redress the balance, and to enquire more closely into the relation between the developing brain and cognitive change. To do this, however, we need to review what is known about the pre- and postnatal development of the brain. In this and the following part, we focus on intrinsic determinants of developmental change. In contrast to this, Parts IV and V focus on the influence of external experience on neural and cognitive development.

Developmental neurobiology is a large and rapidly growing field of enquiry, at least as large as cognitive development. The articles that are contained in this part only present a tiny proportion of what is known. However, they serve to illustrate that brain development is not a uniform process. There are variations not only in the timing of development between brain regions, but also between aspects of neuronal development within a brain region. Some of the conclusions for this part may be summarized as follows:

1 Different regions of the brain develop at different times and rates (Nowakowski and Hayes; Chugani et al.; Huttenlocher).
2 Different progressive and regressive events in neurogenesis often occur at different times within any given region (Nowakowski and Hayes; Rakic; Huttenlocher).
3 Many (but not all) markers of neurogenesis show an "inside-out" pattern of growth within the cerebral cortex, but the opposite pattern in other regions of the brain (Rakic; Huttenlocher).
4 Major regressive events occur during postnatal brain development (Nowakowski and Hayes; Chugani et al.; Huttenlocher).

In the first reading of this part, Nowakowski and Hayes review studies of the development of the brain from its earliest embryonic stages to around the time of birth. They distinguish between "the *when*, the *where*, and the *what*" questions. The "when" question can be further divided into issues surrounding the *absolute* time frame, and issues surrounding the *relative* timing of events. With regard to the latter they point out that development is a sequential cascade of events where a particular event can affect those that follow it, but not those that precede it. One example of this concerns the relative numbers of certain types of cells generated for the cerebellar cortex, a part of the brain involved in coordinating major behavior. Cell types that are generated slightly earlier in development (Purkinje cells) appear to have a role in regulating the number of cells of a different type generated slightly later in development (granule cells), but not vice versa. Thus, data on the relative timing of developmental events can be crucial in unravelling causal relations in development.

The importance of "where" questions is illustrated by Nowakowski and Hayes's discussion of the importance of the three dimensions of the neural tube (length, circumference, and radial dimensions), the first manifestation of what will subsequently become the brain in the vertebrate embryo (see figure 5.3 in Nowakowski and Hayes's chapter). The major divisions of the nervous system are produced along the longitudinal dimension of the neural tube, with one end becoming the spinal cord and the other forebrain. Differentiation along another dimension of the neural tube gives rise to many of the laminar structures found within vertebrate brains.

The cerebral cortex, like some other brain regions, is highly structured in both the radial and laminar planes. In the radial plane, functionally organized "columns" form, while in the laminar plane layers with particular cell types and connectivity patterns form. Nowakowski and Hayes also consider evidence relating to the "what" question. That is, how do cells differentiate into types and gain their specific connectivity patterns? In some brain regions, cells reach their final destination by being passively pushed away from the proliferative zone by more recently generated cells. This results in an "outside to inside" pattern developing, with the most developed cells being furthest away from the site of origination. In more distinctly layered structures, such as the cerebral cortex, the opposite pattern is found: the most recently generated cells migrate past their older relatives, resulting in the cells closest to the proliferative zone (the deeper layers – 5 and 6 – of the mammalian cortex) being first to develop. Some computational consequences of this characteristic "inside to outside" pattern of growth are investigated in Part III (Johnson). The cells migrate by a mechanism that may help to create the radial structure of the cortex: they become attached to a radial glial fibre that acts like a climbing rope to guide them to their appropriate location. This mechanism is discussed in more detail by its main proponent, Pasko Rakic, in the next reading.

Rakic's "radial unit model" of neocortical parcellation gives an account of how both the radial and the laminar structure of the mammalian cerebral neocortex arise. The columnar organization of the cerebral cortex is determined by the fact that each proliferative unit gives rise to about 100 neurons that all migrate up the same radial glial fibre, with the latest born travelling furthest, and past their older relatives (resulting in the inside-out pattern of growth mentioned earlier). Rakic speculates that regulatory genes, known as homeobox genes, may be involved in parcellating the proliferative zone into a basic protomap of cortical cytoarchitectonic areas. The scaffolding provided by the radial glial fibres simply enables the translation of this 2D map from one location to another. While the general boundaries between cortical areas may be partly regulated by genetic control, Rakic also discusses evidence that thalamic inputs adjust the relative sizes of these areas in a use-dependent way (see also the reading by O'Leary in Part IV). That is, competitive interactions between thalamic inputs to the cortex may determine the number of proliferative units that are devoted to that input. While there is as yet, no strong evidence that this fetal vertical organization maps directly onto the functional cortical columns found in the adult, it is possible that they correspond in some respects.

With regard to the laminar structure of the cerebral cortex, Rakic explores the possibility that cells only differentiate once they have reached their appropriate vertical location. By this account, certain genes would be expressed according to the local biochemical environment at certain distances from the proliferative zone. But, since we know that in the adult cortex different cell types appear within the same layer, this cannot be the whole explanation. Furthermore, Rakic cites some recent evidence that cells begin to differentiate before they reach their final vertical location.

For example, in the genetic mutation "reeler" mice, cells that acquire inappropriate laminar positions within the cortex still differentiate into neuronal types according to their time of origin rather than the types that would normally be expected at their new location. This implies that the information required for differentiation is present at cell birth at the proliferative zone, rather than it being dependent upon vertical spatial location.

Rakic also discusses the role of genetic regulation in species differences. He points out that a single round of additional symmetric cell division at the proliferative unit formation stage would double the number of ontogenetic columns, and hence the area of cortex. In contrast, an additional single round of division at the latest stage from the proliferative zone, would only increase the six layers of a column by one cell (about 1 percent). With this in mind he points out that there is very little variation between mammalian species in the layering of the cortex, while the total surface area of the cortex varies by a factor of 100 or more between different species.

Chugani and colleagues report the results of a positron emission tomography (PET) study of the functional development of the human brain. Owing to the potential hazards of the procedure, the study is based on data from children who had to undergo PET scanning for clinical reasons. This study yielded two main conclusions. The first is that particular regions of the brain develop at different times and rates. Thus, while the sensorimotor cortex and some subcortical regions showed high levels of activation from birth, frontal regions did not show a maturational rise in glucose metabolism until six to eight months of age. The second, and perhaps more surprising, observation is that the absolute rates of glucose metabolism rise postnatally until they *exceed* adult levels, before returning to adult levels by about nine years of age. For most cerebral cortical regions the levels reached are about double those found in the adult. Of several reasons that the authors give for this developmental pattern of glucose uptake, possibly the most attractive is that it corresponds to the overproduction of synapses known to occur in many primate brain regions. The topic of exuberant connectivity is taken up at the neuroanatomical level in the next reading.

Huttenlocher focuses on quantitative neuroanatomical evidence from two comparatively well studied regions of the human brain – the primary visual cortex and a part of the prefrontal cortex. In both regions, the density of synapses (contact points between neurones) shows a characteristic increase during childhood to levels about twice that found in the adults. This is then followed by a period of synaptic loss. Huttenlocher suggests that this initial over-production of synapses may have an important role in the apparent plasticity of the young brain.

The inside-out pattern of cortical growth described earlier for neurons is also apparent in the growth of dendrites and dentritic trees. For example, while the mean total length of dendrites for pyramidal cells of layer III of the human primary visual cortex is only 30 percent of the maximum at birth, in layer V (a deeper layer) it is already 60 percent of the maximum. Interestingly this inside-out pattern of growth is not evident in the later occurring rise and fall in synaptic density. For this measure, there are no clear differences between cerebral layers. Consistent with the PET findings of Chugani and colleagues,

Huttenlocher reports clear evidence of a difference in the timing of postnatal neuroanatom-ical events between the primary visual cortex and the frontal cortex, with the latter reaching the same developmental landmarks considerably later in postnatal life than the former.

FURTHER READING

General introduction to neurobiology

Kandel, E. R., Schwartz, J. H., and Jessell, T. M. (2000). *Principles of Neural Science (4th edition)*. New York: McGraw-Hill. (Classic and comprehensive textbook on neuroscience geared toward advanced students.)

Bear, M. F., Connors, B. W., and Paradiso, M. A. (2001). *Neuroscience. Exploring the Brain* (2nd edition). Baltimore, MD: Lippincott, Williams & Wilkins. (Text geared toward beginning students.)

Zigmond, M. J., Bloom, F. E., Landis, S. C., and Squire, L. R. (eds.) (1998). *Fundamental Neuroscience*. San Diego: Academic Press. (Advanced text.)

Introductions to neural development

Brown, M. C., Hopkins, W. G., and Keynes, R. J. (1991). *Essentials of Neural Development*. Cambridge: Cambridge University Press. (A useful short introduction to neural develop-ment.)

Purves, D. (1988). *Body and Brain: a Trophic Theory of Neural Connections*. Cambridge, MA: Harvard University Press. (Explores the evidence and implications of trophic theories of neural development.)

Purves, D. and Lichtman, J. W. (1985). *Principles of Neural Development*. Sunderland, MA: Sinauer Associates. (An excellent comprehensive introduction to developmental neurobiol-ogy.)

Webb, S. J., Monk, C. S., and Nelson, C. A. (in press). Mechanisms of postnatal neurobiological development: Implications for human development. *Developmental Neuropsychology*. (Review of postnatal changes in human brain anatomy.)

Others

Allman, J. M. (1999). *Evolving Brains*. New York: W. H. Freeman & Co. (Highly readable discussion of brain evolution across species.)

Conel, J. L. (1939–67). *The Postnatal Development of the Human Cerebral Cortex. Volumes I–VIII*. Cambridge, MA: Harvard University Press. (The original volumes describe in detail the postnatal growth of the human cortex. It remains an excellent reference source despite being written before more recent quantitative techniques in neuroanatomy.)

Huttenlocher, P. R. and Dabholkar, A. S. (1997). Regional differences in synaptogenesis in human cerebral cortex. *Journal of Comparative Neurology* 387, 167–78. (Evidence regarding patterns of synapse formation and loss in auditory and frontal cortex.)

5

General Principles of CNS Development

Richard S. Nowakowski *and* Nancy L. Hayes

The human central nervous system (CNS) is the most complex organ in the body, and the processes involved in its development are commensurately complex. A basic understanding of these processes is an essential part of understanding how disruptions of development that result in changes in the "hardware" that occur as cells make and become the adult brain can be related to changes in the function of the adult brain. Thus, the current goal in this field is directed toward understanding the contributions of processes *intrinsic* to the CNS, such as genes, cell–cell interactions, etc., relative to the contributions of influences from *extrinsic* sources, such as behavioral experience, trauma, nutrition, hormonal states, etc. In other words, the issue is not whether nature or nurture is the major contributor but rather how each contributes to the development of specific structures and areas. For the developing CNS, this analysis continues on a variety of levels ranging from the level of the organism (influences intrinsic to the organism vs. influences from the environment), through the level of the organ (influences intrinsic to the brain vs. influences from elsewhere in the body), through the level of a given structure (influences intrinsic to one brain structure vs. influences from other parts of the brain), to the level of interactions between cells (influences intrinsic to a single cell vs. influences on that cell from other cells).

The links between development and behavioral pathologies or behavioral capacities exhibited by adults or during behavioral development are not easy to establish. However, these links can be easier to understand through the windows of one or more of the basic developmental processes of cell proliferation, cell migration, cell differentiation or cell death. Thus, in order to arrive at an understanding of how a modification in a developmental process exerts its influence on a particular behavior, it is necessary to understand where the developmental process is being modified (e.g., which kinds of cells and in which part of the brain), how the structure (e.g., the "wiring", etc.) of the mature brain will be changed, and also how the structural changes that are produced will change the ability of the brain to process the information it confronts during a complex behavioral task (for reviews see Nowakowski, 1987; Nowakowski and Hayes, 1999). Therefore, in this review, the relationship between the basic organization of the embryonic CNS and the adult CNS will be described in order to provide a simplified set of principles for understanding the complex anatomy of the adult brain. Also, the special embryological mechanisms that are involved in generating the diversity that characterizes the adult CNS will be reviewed in order to provide a set of concepts to aid in understanding the variety of complex processes occurring during

CNS development. Finally, included in this discussion will be examples describing how modifications of the normal development of the CNS by traumatic injury, by environmental and experiential influences, and by genetic variation may affect and modify the development of the CNS and thereby influence the resultant structure and function of the adult CNS. It cannot be emphasized too strongly that the kind of modifications resulting from any particular intervention are directly related to: (1) **what** is happening in the developing CNS at the time that the intervention occurs, and (2) **which** cell types and developmental processes are affected by the intervention.

The Problem and its Magnitude

The magnitude of this problem is at least partially reflected in the facts that there are between 10 and 20 billion (i.e., approximately 10^{10}) neurons in the cerebral cortex alone of an adult human brain and 5–10 times as many glial cells (Blinkov and Glezer, 1968). Although the glial cells certainly contribute in important ways (Kuffler et al., 1984), it is the diversity in shape, form, and interconnections of the neurons that is ultimately responsible for the ability of the CNS to process information, and any changes in the properties of neurons will alter function. For this reason, the "life history" of the neurons of the CNS is the focal point for understanding CNS development because the neurons are the components that are "assembled" into an information processing network that controls function. In particular, it is important to define the common features, influences, and capabilities of the differentiating neurons of the CNS and to elucidate sets of "principles" or "rules" that make understanding the diversity of a complex system easier. Each division and subdivision of the brain has its own characteristic structure and function. Thus, the problem faced by the neuroembryologist is to try to understand: (1) how this tremendous diversity in form is generated, and (2) how each portion of the CNS is integrated into the whole to produce a functional entity. These issues must be addressed not only in terms of relatively gross changes in the architecture of the developing CNS but also in terms of the "behavior" of its cellular constituents and of changes in gene expression within the cells. Another reflection of the importance of these issues is that the recent advances in molecular genetics have identified numerous genes that are expressed in the developing brain and that control CNS development. These advances have in the past few years dramatically changed our understanding of CNS development and the relationship of genetics to normal and abnormal development. This progress will certainly accelerate in the future and the basis of this progress is a firm foundation of the understanding of normal development.

The Basic Questions

The assembly of the brain from its component parts can be conceptualized using a simple metaphor, i.e., the building of a house. The parallels are: (1) the genome serves as the blueprint for the brain, (2) the neurons and glia serve as the bricks and mortar, lumber, etc., and (3) axons, dendrites and synaptic connections among neurons serve as the wiring for electricity, telephone, etc. Just as in the construction of a house, events and processes must occur in a particular sequence and at particular times. Thus, a framework for understanding CNS development is provided by a set of simple questions: when? where? what? Although answers to these questions provide a reasonably complete description of the phenomena underlying CNS development, they do not come simply because there are multiple and simultaneously occurring processes that must be considered. Furthermore, another "simple" question: *how?* needs to be posed. How are processes during CNS development controlled? How do cells and cellular interactions influence the fate of other cells? How is gene expression controlled? How does the maturation of one region of the CNS affect the maturation of other regions of the CNS?. In the following paragraphs these four simple questions, *when?*, *where?*, *what?*, and *how?* will be used to describe the major issues in understanding the development of the CNS.

"When?": A Question of Time and Timing

In a developmental sense there are two aspects of "when" – the absolute time that an event occurs and the time relative to other events. The absolute time frame of development for both humans and most experimental animals is usually measured as days (or some other convenient unit) after conception and days after birth. For the staging of human embryos and fetus's gestation is generally measured from the time of occurrence of the last menstrual period rather than from the day of conception. With this method human gestation is considered to be 40 weeks long (even though the conceptus is only present for 38 weeks), and the gestation period of humans is generally divided into trimesters each lasting about 13 weeks. The staging system for human embryos and fetuses (Olivier and Pineau, 1961) relies upon easily measurable features such as greatest length (GL) or crown-to-rump length (CRL). It is of great significance that the development of the human CNS is not confined to the gestational period. For example, during the intrauterine period the brain grows from nothing to about 350 g (Blinkov and Glezer, 1968). During this period, most of the neurons of the CNS are produced (see below). However, after birth the brain continues to grow, reaching a size of about 1350 g at 20 years of age (Blinkov and Glezer, 1968). Most of the postnatal growth occurs within the first three or four years after birth (Blinkov and Glezer, 1968), but changes in myelination (Yakovlev, 1967) and in other measures (e.g., cortical surface area, numbers of glial cells, etc.) continue to be apparent even 70 to 80 years after birth (Blinkov and Glezer, 1968). This review focuses on the early prenatal periods of CNS development, and it should be emphasized that the time of birth is NOT correlated with most measures of the maturity of the CNS. This means that events occurring prenatally in some species may occur postnatally in another species. For example, for the maturation of the cerebral cortex in rats and mice most of the cells destined to comprise the cerebral cortex are generated during the second half of gestation, ending only a few days before birth (Angevine, 1965; Berry and Rogers, 1965; Miller, 1985), whereas in monkeys and humans these same events are completed about the time of the end of the second trimester, well before birth (Rakic, 1974; Rakic, 1975b; Kostovic and Rakic, 1980).

The *relative timing* or sequence of occurrence of events is a second critical component of "when." The general principle is that development occurs as a cascade of events and that any one event *may* influence those that follow it but not those that precede it. Thus, knowledge of the order of occurrence of developmental events can provide information about the presence or absence of a causal relationship between the two events. Relative timing can be thought of as a simple cascade of events, such as A → B → C (figure 5.1a). If event A occurs before event B, then it is possible for A to influence B but *not* for B to influence A (figure 5.1b). In addition, events that occur simultaneously can influence each other (figure 5.1c). Thus, although additional evidence other than relative timing is needed

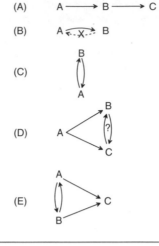

INCREASING DEVELOPMENTAL AGE

Figure 5.1   Examples of how events during development influence each other in different ways. A. Events which follow each other in a sequence can be causally related. B. A late-occurring event cannot influence an earlier occurring event. C. Two events occurring at the same time can influence each other. D. One early-occurring event can influence two (or more) later occurring events which may or may not influence each other. E. One event may be dependent on the interaction of two (or more) earlier occurring events.

to establish if events are in a cascade, rather than simply in sequence, relative timing can be used to eliminate events from a cascade. In other words, just because A precedes B and C this does not necessarily mean that A influences either B or C. In addition, cascades are not necessarily simple and/or direct; one early-occurring event can influence more than one later-occurring event which may or may not interact (figure 5.1d), or two early-occurring events might need to interact in order for some later event to occur (figure 5.1e). In general, the earlier during development that a particular event occurs the greater is its *potential* influence on subsequently occurring events and the greater the likelihood that it will have a greater effect on the adult structure than the disruption of a later occurring event. For example, if A is the production of neurons and B is the subsequently occurring process of neuronal cell death, then both events A and B influence the total *number* of neurons in the adult animal. Additional events (e.g., C, D, etc.) could also affect neuron number but *only events occurring prior to or during* the time that event A occurs could affect neuron number by affecting cell proliferation. It is, perhaps, useful to emphasize that a large number of "events" influence the development of any given region of the nervous system and even of any given cell type and that it is the summation of these events which produces the mature functioning whole. In addition, there may be interaction between and among various regions of the brain.

A potentially important use for the knowledge of *when* something occurs is to corroborate and/or eliminate possible biological bases for behavioral critical periods. For example, Greer, Diamond and Tang (1982) have shown that an enriched behavioral experience during the developmental period can increase cell number in the adult rat neocortex. It is known that the cells comprising the adult neocortex are generated *before* this critical period. This knowledge definitively eliminates an influence on cell proliferation as being responsible; the likely mechanism is, therefore, a reduction in cell death (i.e., hypothanasia) (Hollyday and Hamburger, 1976). Cell death is a normal aspect of CNS development and is found in most regions (Oppenheim, 1991) including the neocortex (Finlay and Slattery, 1983; Thomaidou et al., 1997; Verney et al., 2000). More recent experiments have shown that behavioral experience can modify *both* cell proliferation and decreased cell death, i.e., increased survival, in the dentate gyrus (Kempermann et al., 1997b; Kempermann et al., 1998), a structure in which cell proliferation continues even in the adult rodent (Kempermann et al., 1997a). Knowledge of the time that something occurs is also important when assessing the possible trauma of events such as the development of a tumor (Gilles, 1985), malnutrition (Smart, 1991; Morgane et al., 1993) or exposure to alcohol (Luo and Miller, 1998) or radiation (Otake and Schull, 1984). For the last example mentioned, a particularly striking relationship has been shown between mental retardation in children who were exposed *in utero* to the high radiation levels associated with the atomic bombs dropped on Hiroshima and Nagasaki and the *gestational age* of the children at the time of the exposure. Otake and Schull (1984) showed that during a critical period lasting from the 8th to the 15th week of gestation the risk of developing mental retardation later in life was directly proportional to the dose of radiation received. However, for embryos exposed before the 8th week there was no risk of developing mental retardation, and for embryos exposed after the 15th week, the risk of developing mental retardation was less than one-fifth that of the risk associated with the critical period. The time of occurrence of this critical period allowed Otake and Schull (1984) to hypothesize that the proliferation and migration of neurons destined for the cerebral cortex were severely compromised by the radiation (see below for a description of these processes).

"Where?": The Three Dimensions of the Neural Tube

Where in the CNS a particular event occurs is defined by regional variation in development that delineates subdivisions. Thus: (1) developmental subdivisions precede and presage functional subdivisions, and (2) it is easier to understand the organization of the adult CNS once the organization of the simpler, developing CNS is understood. The three dimensions of the CNS are defined in the neural tube, the end result of the process of neurulation which marks the earliest appearance of the CNS in the embryo (figure 5.2a–c). The neural tube, like any other tube, has three dimensions: a longitudinal dimension or length, a circumferential or tangential dimension, and a radial or laminar dimension (figure 5.2d). During subsequent development the cavity of the neural tube becomes the ventricles of the brain and the central canal of the spinal cord. Differentiation of the wall of the neural tube along these three dimensions is a useful way to conceptualize the primitive organization of the mammalian CNS (figure 5.2d). Along the length of the neural tube the major divisions of the nervous system are produced; around its circumference functionally distinct subdivisions within each division arise; and along the radial dimension the wall of the neural tube develops laminae or layers that are distinct for each subdivision.

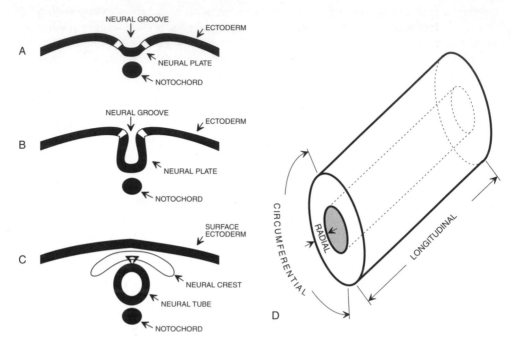

Figure 5.2   Neurulation: The process of neurulation begins at the end of the third week after conception. During the next few days, the outer surface of the embryo (or ectoderm) folds in upon itself to form the neural tube. **A**. At the beginning of neurulation a shallow groove appears to mark the position of the neural plate (**A**). **B**. Subsequently, the groove deepens and (as seen in **C**) the lateral edges of the neural plate fuse to become the neural tube. A small group of cells just lateral to the edge of the neural plate and some cells from the dorsal-most portion of the neural tube (arrows in **C** become the neural crest). **C**. The neural tube is the forerunner of the central nervous system (i.e., the brain and spinal cord), whereas the neural crest cells produce most of the peripheral nervous system. Together the neural tube and the neural crest are often referred to as the neuroectoderm. **D**. Once closed the neural tube, just like any other tube, can be considered to have three dimensions: length or a longitudinal dimension, a circumferential or tangential dimension, and a radial dimension. Differentiation of the neural tube along these three dimensions is a useful way to conceptualize the primitive organization of the mammalian CNS. See the text for further details.

Differentiation along the longitudinal dimension

Already at the time of neurulation the head and tail ends of the embryo have been determined, and, in fact, neurulation proceeds at different rates in the different parts of the neuraxis. Eventually, about 50 percent of the tail or caudal end of the neural tube becomes the spinal cord which is organized segmentally, i.e., it is organized in repeated units called segments each of which is associated with the sensory and motor innervation of a small part of the body. The head or cephalic portions of the neural tube become the brain. Most of the head or cephalic portion of the neural tube acquires a suprasegmental organization, which means: (1) that its organization does not repeat, and (2) that a substantial portion of its innervation and output is not devoted to or derived from a single body segment but rather to providing input to and receiving output from the segmental parts of the nervous system. It should be noted that the brainstem (i.e., the adult medulla, pons and midbrain), which develops from intermediate portions of the neural tube, acquires a pattern of organization which is in part segmental (i.e., the motor and sensory components of the cranial nerves) and in part suprasegmental. The molecular basis of the segmental organization of the brainstem and spinal cord has been shown to lie, in part, in the segmentally restricted expression of numerous genes from the Hox, Pax, engrailed and other gene families (Lumsden and Krumlauf, 1996; Studer et al., 1996; Rubinstein and Shimamura, 1997; Araki and Naka-mura, 1999; Lee and Jessell, 1999; Barrow et al., 2000).

In humans, the cephalic portions of the neural tube grow tremendously, and this disproportionate growth tube is referred to as "encephalization". Even before the closure of the neural tube is complete, the cephalic neural tube differentiates into three primary vesicles (i.e., "bulges") that form from its wall (see figure 5.3). From rostral-to-caudal (i.e., from front-to-back, literally "beak-to-tail") these vesicles are: (1) the prosencephalon or forebrain, (2) the mesencephalon or midbrain, and (3) the rhombencephalon or hindbrain (table 5.1). Subsequently, the prosencephalon becomes subdivided into the telencephalon and the diencephalon, and the rhombencephalon becomes subdivided into the metencephalon and myelencephalon, thereby forming *five* secondary vesicles. In the human embryo, these five secondary vesicles are already recognizable at the 5th week of gestation (Hoch-stetter, 1919). Thus, at a very early stage in development the major structural subdivisions of the adult brain are defined by these vesicles. In fact, their names are used to refer to parts of the adult brain. Examples of major adult structures derived from each of these secondary vesicles are: (1) the cortex is derived from the telencephalon, (2) the thalamus and hypothalamus are derived from the diencephalon, (3) the midbrain is derived from the

Table 5.1 The "Encephalons"

prosencephalon:	"Forebrain"	=	*proso*, forward + *enkephalos*
telencephalon:	"Endbrain"	=	*telos*, end + *enkephalos*
diencephalon:	"Throughbrain"	=	*dia*, through or across + *enkephalos* (Many ascending and descending pathways cross or pass through the diencephalon on their way to or from the telencephalon.)
mesencephalon:	"Midbrain"	=	*mesos*, middle + *enkephalos*
rhombencephalon:	"Rhombic-brain"	=	*rhombos*, rhombic + *enkephalos* (At this level of the brain, the ventricle is shaped like a rhombus.)
metencephalon:	"Afterbrain"	=	*meta*, after or post + *enkephalos*
myelencephalon:	"Medulla"	=	*myelos*, marrow + *enkephalos* (The spinal cord is the "marrow" of the vertebral column and the medulla is the spinal-most portion of the brain.)

At first, the names of the subdivisions of the embryonic brain seem formidable, but an examination of their root meanings facilitates becoming comfortable with their usage. In all cases, the second part of the name is derived from the Greek word *enkephalos* (*en*, in + *kephalos*, head). Each prefix has a similarly descriptive root that is derived either from its relative position in the neural tube or some other salient feature. See figure 5.3.

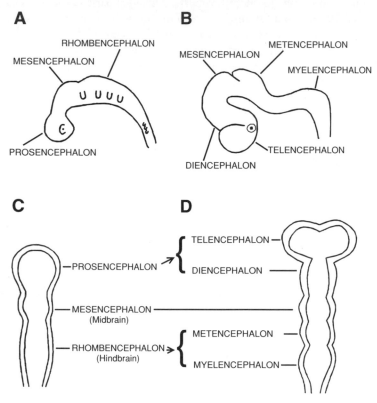

Figure 5.3   Longitudinal Differential of the Neural Tube: **A**. A drawing of a lateral view of the brain of a four week old human embryo. This is only shortly after neurulation and already the three primary brain vesicles (the prosencephalon, mesencephalon and rhombencephalon) are present. **B**. A stretched out and cut away dorsal view of the four week old brain as seen in **A**. **C**. A drawing of a lateral view of the brain of a five week old human embryo. At this age the prosencephalon has become divided into the telencephalon and diencephalon and the rhomben-cephalon has become divided into the metencephalon and myelencephalon. **D**. A stretched out and cut away dorsal view of the five week old brain as seen in **C**.

mesencephalon, (4) the pons and cerebellum are derived from the metencephalon, and (5) the medulla is derived from the myelencephalon.

 Developmental *errors* in neural tube closure and in the subsequent longitudinal parcella-tion of the nervous system lead to profound disturbances of the nervous system. The closure of the neural tube begins in the vicinity of the future medulla and pons and moves downward and upward from there (sort of like a zipper). Thus, the two most common places for the failure of the neural tube to close are at its two ends, i.e., in the spinal cord and prosencephalon (Friede, 1989). When the neural tube fails to close at the caudal end, a severe form of spina bifida known as rachischisis occurs. In rachischisis, the spinal cord, the vertebrae and the overlying skin are malformed such that the central canal of the spinal cord (i.e., the cavity of the neural tube) is open (Friede, 1989). As a result this malformation is detectable by ultrasonography and/or by measurement of serum alpha-fetoprotein (Bell and Gosden, 1978). Rachischisis is the result of a very early failure of neural tube closure; later closures result in less deleterious forms of spina bifida (Friede, 1989). Similar malformations occurring at the rostral end of the neural tube result in anencephaly which is a malformation in which the derivatives of the prosencephalon do not form (Friede, 1989). Genetic analysis indicates that Pax and Patch genes may be partly responsible for some forms of spina bifida and anencephaly (Payne et al., 1997; Joosten et al., 1998).

Differentiation in the circumferential or tangential dimension

Specializations also develop *circumferentially* around the neural tube (i.e., *tangential* to its surface (figure 5.4). The significance of this circumferential differentiation is that: (1) it

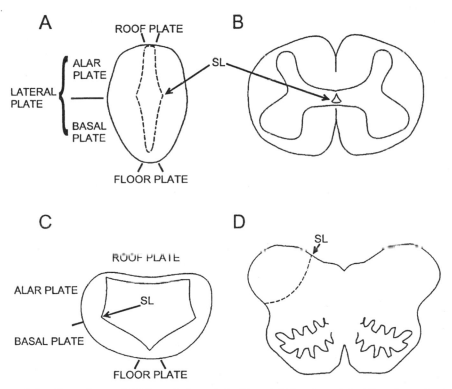

Figure 5.4 Circumferential Differentiation of the Neural Tube: **A** and **B**. The circumferential zones or "plates" are best seen in the developing spinal cord, where there are four of them: a floor plate, two paired lateral plates and a roof plate. Each lateral plate is usually divided at the sulcus limitans into a basal plate and an alar plate, which become the motor and sensory portions of the spinal gray, respectively. The names of these plates are derived from their position around the tube (alar is derived from the Latin word *ala*, wing). **C** and **D**. In the medulla, the roof plate becomes wide and attenuated and displaces the alar and basal plates laterally. Nevertheless, the sulcus limitans continues to mark the border between the basal and alar plates, and, in the adult, the morphological relationship between the sensory and motor derivatives of these two plates is similar to that found in the spinal cord except that they are displaced laterally by the extension of the roof plate, and, thus, their relationship shifts from dorsoventral in the spinal cord to mediolateral in the medulla.

precedes the *functional* organization of the CNS into sensory and motor subdivisions and other functional subdivisions, and (2) it reflects developmental processes that extend beyond the borders of any single longitudinal subdivision. These specializations are most easily described for the future spinal cord which can be divided into four circumferentially defined zones or "plates" (Kingsbury, 1922): the floor plate, paired lateral plates, and the roof plate (figure 5.4a). Each lateral plate is usually divided into a basal plate and an alar plate. The adult spinal cord is derived primarily from the alar and basal plates, which become the dorsal and ventral horns of the spinal cord, respectively. The pattern formation underlying the circumferential divisions of the spinal cord occurs early during development, concomitant with neurulation. The first step is the induction of neural tube formation by signals arising from the notochord and other mesodermal structures (figure 5.4a). Chief among these signals is a molecule called "sonic hedgehog" (shh) that induces the formation of the floor plate and initiates a cascade of events that acts to assign a "ventral" fate to the cells of the floor and basal plates (Tanabe and Jessell, 1996; Dodd et al., 1998; Lee and Jessell, 1999). As the neural tube closes other signaling factors are secreted by the cells of the overlying ectoderm that is first lateral to the neural plate and then overlies the neural tube (figure 5.4a–c). These factors include members of the bone morphogenetic protein family (the "BMPs") which act on the roof plate (and may also be propagated by it) and the adjacent portions of the alar plate to induce a cascade of responses that leads to the specification of "dorsal" fates in these cells and their progeny (Lee and Jessell, 1999). It seems that induction by signaling factors arising both ventrally and dorsally is essential for normal spinal cord development (Tanabe and Jessell, 1996; Lee and Jessell, 1999) which is an example of an interaction of a cascade in which distinct early events must both occur and interact for normal development to occur (figure 5.1e).

The same four circumferential subdivisions can be identified in the lower brainstem (figure 5.4c), and, despite the fact that the roof and floor plates distort the shape of the neural tube, the relationship of sensory and motor functions to the structures derived from alar and basal plates is retained (figure 5.4d). In addition, signaling by both ventrally and dorsally derived factors continues to play a role in specifying the fates of neurons in the brainstem including the cerebellum and midbrain (Lee and Jessell, 1999). In contrast, in the prosencephalic derivatives, it is difficult to define the extension of the alar, basal, roof and floor plates (Johnston, 1902; His, 1904; Schulte et al., 1915; Kingsbury, 1922). However, differentiation in the tangential dimension is still obvious in these regions. For example, in the diencephalon, His (1904) defined three sulci that divide the wall of the diencephalon into four zones that become the epithalamus, dorsal thalamus, ventral thalamus and the hypothalamus, respectively (Miura, 1933; Kuhlenbeck, 1973; Sidman and Rakic, 1982). Similarly, in the telencephalon, the archicortex is derived from the medial wall of the lateral hemisphere, the neocortex from the dorsolateral wall, and the paleocortex from the lateral wall of the hemisphere (Polyakov, 1949; Kuhlenbeck, 1977; Sidman and Rakic, 1982). The molecular and cellular interactions that produce these tangential zones is beginning to be revealed by molecular and genetic analysis (Lumsden and Krumlauf, 1996; Rubinstein and Shimamura, 1997; Lee and Jessell, 1999). Indeed, it has been proposed that the combination of molecular markers of longitudinal and tangential subdivisions of the neural tube divide the wall of the neural tube into a grid-like pattern of domains that define a grid-like pattern of fates (Rubinstein and Shimamura, 1997). Disruptions of this grid could underlie specific developmental diseases such as autism (Rodier et al., 1996; Rodier, 2000).

Differentiation in the radial or laminar dimension

From the description outlined above, it should be clear that the different areas of the CNS are discernible very early during development and that differentiation of the neural tube along its length and circumference defines its basic organizational plan. However, further refinement in the structure occurs before the CNS can be considered to be mature. For the most part, this additional differentiation consists of a series of changes in the radial dimension to produce a variety of laminar schemes. *What* is happening to produce this variety of lamination patterns is discussed in the following section.

What?: Cellular Actions and Interactions during Development

The question "what is happening in a particular part of the developing CNS at a particular time?" can best be answered in terms of cellular processes. At the simplest level of analysis, there are four of these processes to consider: cell proliferation, cell migration, cell differentiation, and, for some cells, cell death. The "life history" of any single neuron or glial cell can be traced by considering each of these processes as a developmental "step" through which each cell passes. Thus, these steps represent a cascade of developmental events of which the earliest occurring ones may influence the subsequently occurring ones, but the later occurring ones cannot influence the earlier occurring ones. In addition, as will become clear in the descriptions that follow, cell proliferation, cell migration, cell differentiation and sometimes cell death occur simultaneously in any given subdivision of the developing CNS. This is simply because different cells in the population are passing through different portions of their life histories at any given time. For this reason, in order to complete the description of CNS development in cellular terms, it is necessary to add the additional concept of intercellular interactions as a way for one cell to influence the fate of another cell. Intercellular interactions can occur between cells in the same state of maturation, e.g., one differentiating cell can influence another, or between cells of different levels of maturation, e.g., a migrating cell can interact with a differentiated cell. In the following paragraphs the processes and events associated with cell proliferation, cell migration, cell differentiation and cell death are described. Emphasis will be placed on these processes as they apply to neurons, and, in general, the opportunities for intercellular interactions will only be pointed out when especially good examples are known.

Cell proliferation

Most of the neurons of the adult CNS are produced during the prenatal period (Nowakowski, 1987). In the wall of the neural tube proliferating cells are found surrounding the lumen of the tube (see figure 5.5). With only a few exceptions, most of the cells of the CNS are produced by one of two proliferative zones adjacent to the future ventricular system. The first of these two zones to appear is the "ventricular zone" (Boulder Committee, 1970) which is a pseudostratified columnar epithelium (for explanation see figure 5.5). In some parts of the developing CNS, the ventricular zone is the only proliferative zone to appear, and, thus, it is reasonable to assume that it produces all of the cell types (figure 5.5a–e). In other parts of the developing CNS, however, a second proliferative zone appears

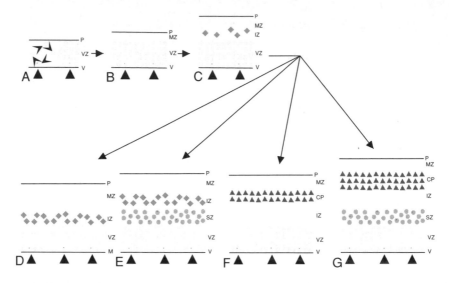

Figure 5.5　Radial Differentiation of the Neural Tube: **A**, **B**, and **C** are schematic diagrams of the early stages of the radial differentiation of the neural tube through which every part of the CNS passes. **D**, **E**, **F**, and **G** are schematic diagrams of various options for the later stages of the radial differentiation of the neural tube. Each of these options is characteristic of a different part of the neural tube. **A**. At the time of closure of the neural tube its wall consists of a population of proliferating cells organized into a pseudostratified columnar epithelium, known as the ventricular zone (VZ). In this proliferative zone the nuclei of the cells are stratified, but each cell has processes that contact the ventricular (V) and pial (P) surfaces of the neural tube. As diagrammed on the right hand side of the drawing, mitosis occurs at the pial surface, and during the cell cycle the nucleus of each cell moves to a different level. DNA synthesis, for example, occurs in the outer half of the ventricular zone. This to-and-fro movement of the cell nuclei is known as interkinetic nuclear migration, and means that all cells, even though they are apparently at different levels, are part of the proliferative population. **B**. The next zone to appear during the radial differentiation of the neural tube is the marginal zone (MZ) which is an almost cell-free zone between the ventricular zone and the pial surface. **C**. The intermediate zone (IZ), which contains the first postmitotic cells in the nervous system, is the next to form. This zone is located between the ventricular zone and the marginal zone. **D**. In some parts of the neural tube, such as the spinal cord, the postmitotic cells derived from the ventricular zone aggregate and mature in a densely populated intermediate zone. **E**. In some areas, such as the dorsal thalamus, a second proliferative zone, the subventricular zone (SVZ), is formed between the ventricular zone and the intermediate zone. In the subventricular zone, interkinetic nuclear migration does not occur, instead mitotic figures are found scattered throughout the thickness of the zone. (DNA synthesis also occurs throughout the thickness of the subventricular zone.) The postmitotic cells derived from both the ventricular and subventricular zones aggregate and mature in a densely populated intermediate zone. (Note, however, that any cells derived from the ventricular zone must cross the subventricular zone.) **F**. In the hippocampus, the postmitotic cells derived from the ventricular zone migrate across a sparsely-populated intermediate zone to form a cortical plate. **G**. In the cerebral cortex, postmitotic cells derived from both the ventricular and subventricular zones migrate across a sparsely-populated intermediate zone to form a cortical plate. Abbreviations: V: Ventricular surface; VZ: Ventricular Zone; SZ: Subventricular Zone; IZ: Intermediate Zone; CP, Cortical Plate; MZ, Marginal Zone; P, Pial surface.

(figure 5.5f–g). This second zone, known as the subventricular zone, differs in several ways from the ventricular zone (figure 5.5). It is attractive to speculate that the subventricular zone is a phylogenetically recently acquired specialization. For example, the hippocampus is classified as an archicortical (i.e., "old" cortex) structure and the neurons of its major subdivisions (areas CA1, CA2 and CA3) are all derived from the ventricular zone (Nowakowski and Rakic, 1981). In contrast, in the neocortex (i.e., "new" cortex) the subventricular zone is substantial and, although it is unlikely to contribute large numbers of neurons to the neocortex (Takahashi et al., 1995b), it produces glial cells and also neurons in other parts of the telencephalon (Goldman, 1995; Garcia-Verdugo et al., 1998). A similar contrast occurs in the developing diencephalon in which the hypothalamus lacks a subventricular zone whereas other diencephalic subdivisions have both ventricular and subventricular zones (Rakic, 1977). These differences in the proliferative zones are present even as the first neurons are being produced (Nowakowski and Rakic, 1981) indicating that one level of functional differentiation, the development of the major subdivisions of the CNS, is well underway even at a very early stage (in humans this would be occurring during the second month of gestation).

The proliferating cells of the ventricular zone comprise a proliferative ventricular epithelium (PVE) which is pseudostratified. This means that although the nuclei appear to be at different levels each cell maintains attachments to both the ventricular and pial surfaces. The nuclei of the PVE move up-and-down, i.e., ab- and adventricularly, as they move through the cell cycle (Sauer, 1936; Sidman, 1970). At the beginning of the cell cycle, i.e., just as the cell leaves M and enters G1, the nucleus of a PVE cell is located at the ventricular surface (figure 5.6). As the cell moves through G1 and enters S it moves away from the ventricular surface reaching its maximum distance as it enters S (Takahashi et al., 1993; Takahashi et al., 1996a; Hayes and Nowakowski, 2000). During G2 the nucleus moves rapidly towards the ventricular surface, and the cell divides during M at the ventricular surface (figure 5.6). With each pass through the cell cycle the cell must decide whether or not it will continue to proliferate, re-enter the S phase or stop proliferating to become a postmitotic neuron (a Q cell) and migrate out of the ventricular zone towards its final destination. Analyses of the cell cycle for the PVE in developing mouse neocortex have shown that during a 6 day period when neurons are being produced the cell cycle progressively lengthens from about 8 hours to about 20 hours (Caviness et al., 1995; Takahashi et al., 1995a; Takahashi et al., 1995b; Takahashi et al., 1996b; Takahashi et al., 1997). Thus, during this 6 day period the nuclei of the PVE make 11 round trips through the cell cycle. In addition, at each pass through the cell cycle the population produces an ever increasing proportion of "Q" cells, i.e., postmitotic neurons (figure 5.6) (Caviness et al., 1995; Takahashi et al., 1997). The cell cycle is longer in primates (Kornack and Rakic, 1998), and in the human the comparable period of time during which neurons are produced is much longer, about 120 days (Caviness et al., 1995). From this it has been estimated that about 34–35 cell cycles would be required to make all of the neurons of the human neocortex (Caviness et al., 1995).

The subventricular zone cells, in contrast, neither maintain an attachment to the ventricular or pial surfaces nor do their nuclei move as they move through the cell cycle (Sidman, 1970). In the neocortical proliferative zones the length of the cell cycle of the ventricular and subventricular zones is similar (Takahashi et al., 1995b). The contributions of the subventricular zone to the adult brain is important (Doetsch et al., 1997; Doetsch et al., 1999) and most of the glia are produced there (Goldman, 1995). In addition, in some areas a significant number of neurons are also produced in the subventricular zone (Garcia-Verdugo et al., 1998).

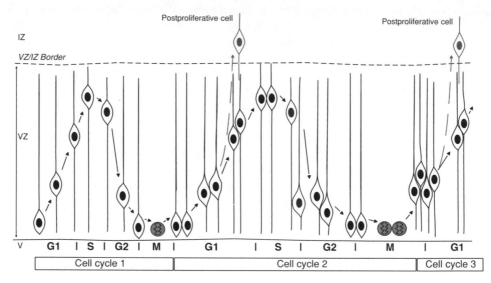

Figure 5.6   The Cell Cycle in the Ventricular Zone of the Developing CNS: This schematic diagram illustrates the up-and-down movement of the nuclei of the cells comprising the proliferative ventricular epithelium of the ventricular zone (VZ). With each pass through the cell cycle the nucleus of a single cell moves from its starting position at the ventricular surface at the beginning of G1 to the border of the VZ where it enters S. During G2, the nucleus again moves down to the ventricular surface where it enters M and divides to form 2 cells. With each pass through the cell cycle some postmitotic neurons are produced. The postmitotic neurons migrate away from the VZ to produce the structures of the adult brain (in this case, the cerebral neocortex). During the production of the neocortex in the mouse, the cell cycle lengthens with each cell cycle and there are a total of 11 cell cycles.

Cell migration influences ultimate cell position

As illustrated in figure 5.5, cell proliferation occurs in different locations than the ultimate destination of the neurons. Thus, postmitotic young neurons must move from the site of their proliferation to their final position. There are two essentially different ways that cells make this movement. In some parts of the developing nervous system as the postmitotic neurons leave the proliferative population they move only a very short distance from the border of the proliferative zone. Subsequently, these neurons are displaced outward away from the proliferative zone by newly produced cells (see figure 5.7). Since this type of cell movement requires minimal active locomotor activity by the migrating cell it is considered to be a *passive cell displacement.* In the areas where passive cell displacement occurs, the neurons that are generated earliest are located farthest away from the proliferative zone and subsequently generated neurons are found at levels progressively closer to the proliferative zone (figure 5.7). This correlation between the distribution of neurons and their time of origin is referred to as an "outside-to-inside" spatiotemporal gradient, where outside and inside are defined with respect to the position of the cells in reference to the proliferative zone. (It should be noted, however, that the presence of an outside-to-inside spatiotemporal gradient does not necessarily imply that the neurons moved only by passive displacement.) Areas in which an outside-to-inside spatiotemporal pattern is present include the thalamus

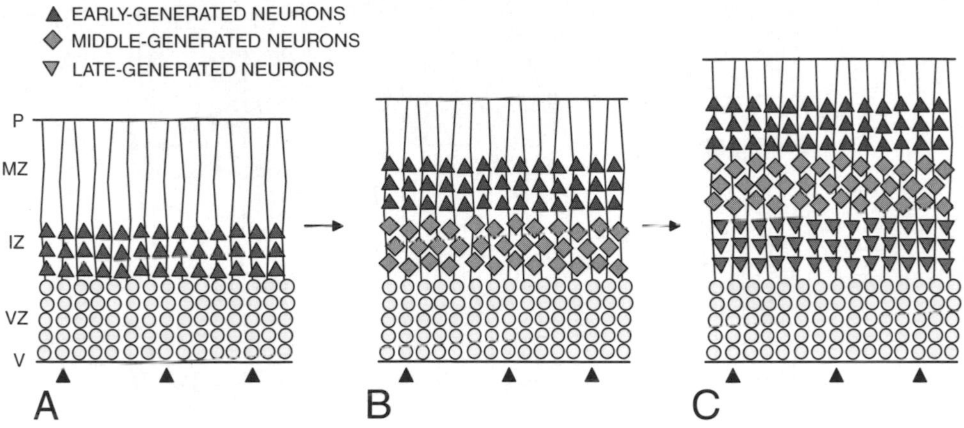

▲ EARLY-GENERATED NEURONS
◆ MIDDLE-GENERATED NEURONS
▽ LATE-GENERATED NEURONS

Figure 5.7 Cell Movement by Passive Displacement: Some cells leave the proliferative zones and move only a short distance from the outer edge of the zone. Subsequently, these cells are displaced outward away from the proliferative zone by newly produced cells. This sequence of events is illustrated in diagrams **A** through **C**. In **A**, the first neurons to leave the ventricular zone are shown as triangles. In **B**, the next neurons to form (shown as diamonds) move away from the ventricular zone displacing the earlier generated ones outward. Finally, in **C**, the last neurons to form (shown as inverted triangles) move away from the ventricular zone and displace both populations of earlier generated neurons. This sequence of events results in a specific distribution of neurons generally known as an outside-to-inside spatiotemporal gradient. Abbreviations: V: Ventricular surface; VZ: Ventricular Zone; IZ: Intermediate Zone; CP, Cortical Plate; MZ, Marginal Zone; P, Pial surface.

(Angevine, 1970; Rakic, 1977; Altman and Bayer, 1979), hypothalamus (Ifft, 1972), spinal cord (Nornes and Das, 1974), the retina (Sidman, 1961; Walsh et al., 1983), the dentate gyrus of the hippocampal formation (Angevine, 1965; Nowakowski and Rakic, 1981; Bayer et al., 1982; Wyss and Sripanidkulchai, 1985), and many regions of the brainstem (Taber-Pierce, 1972; Altman and Bayer, 1981).

In many other parts of the developing nervous system the migrating cells play a much more active role in reaching their final position. In these cases the young neurons move a much greater distance, and the earliest neurons to be generated are bypassed by the progressively later generated neurons (figure 5.8). This requires the active participation of the migrating cell itself in its own displacement. This active process is generally referred to as *neuronal migration* (Sidman and Rakic, 1973). When the migrating young neuron bypasses the previously generated cells, the result is an "inside-to-outside" spatiotemporal gradient (figure 5.8). This pattern is found in most portions of the cerebral cortex (Angevine and Sidman, 1961; Angevine, 1965; Hinds, 1968; Rakic, 1975b; Rakic and Nowakowski, 1981; Caviness, 1982; Wyss and Sripanidkulchai, 1985) and in several subcortical areas (Cooper and Rakic, 1981; Hickey and Hitchcock, 1984). What these areas have in common is that they are all *well-laminated* structures (which means that they are divided up into tangentially-oriented layers that run *parallel* with the surface of the proliferative zone). Structures which are formed by an outside-to-inside spatiotemporal gradient (see previous paragraph) tend not to exhibit such well-laminated structure. In other words, the inside-to-outside *vs* outside-to-inside pattern of distribution of neurons is

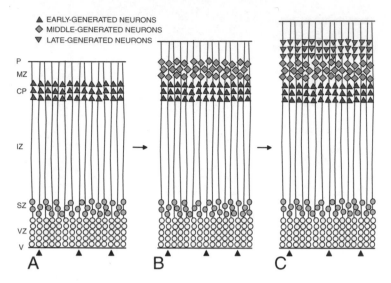

Figure 5.8   Cell Movement by Active Migration: In many parts of the developing nervous system cells leaving the proliferative population move a considerable distance from the proliferative zone. For example, in the cerebral cortex, the later generated cells bypass the earlier generated cells and take up a position even more distant from the proliferative zone. In **A**, the first neurons to leave the proliferative zones are shown as triangles. These cells form a cortical plate between the intermediate and the marginal zones. In **B**, the next neurons to form (shown as diamonds) leave the proliferative zones, migrate across the intermediate zone and *past* the previously generated cells to the top of the cortical plate. In **C**, the final neurons to reach the cortical plate are shown as inverted triangles. These cells have also migrated across the intermediate zone and *past* the previously generated cells to the top of the cortical plate. This sequence of events results in a specific distribution of neurons generally known as an inside-to-outside spatiotemporal gradient. Abbreviations: V: Ventricular surface; VZ: Ventricular Zone; SZ: Subventricular Zone; IZ: Intermediate Zone; CP, Cortical Plate; MZ, Marginal Zone; P, Pial surface.

correlated with the eventual organization of the region of the CNS to which the migrating neurons will eventually belong.

How do migrating neurons "know" how to reach their final destination? A partial answer was provided by Rakic who discovered that migrating neurons in the developing cerebral and cerebellar cortex use radial glial fibers as guides during their migration (Rakic, 1971; Rakic, 1972). This finding has since been confirmed for other parts of the cerebral cortex and it is now widely accepted that during the development of the cerebral cortex young neurons are intimately apposed to radially aligned glial fibers that provide guidance (Rakic, 1972; Nowakowski and Rakic, 1979; Rakic et al., 1994). This interaction of migrating young neurons with radial glial fibers is one of the best documented examples of cell interactions in the developing CNS. The process of neuronal migration consists of at least three phases (figure 5.9; for reviews see Nowakowski, 1986; Rakic et al., 1994; Hatten, 1999). First, a young neuron *starts* its migration. During this phase a cell in the proliferating population makes the transition from neuroblast to young neuron, becomes apposed to a radial glial fiber and establishes an axis of polarity away from the ventricular surface. In the second or locomotory phase, a young neuron propels itself along the surface of the radial glial cell,

Stages of Neuronal Migration

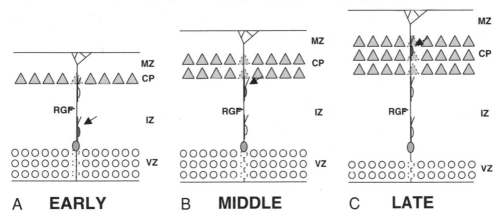

A   **EARLY**   B   **MIDDLE**   C   **LATE**

Figure 5.9 Interaction between Migrating Neurons and Radial Glial Cells: As a young neuron moves from its site of origin in the proliferative zone to its final position in the cortical plate it is guided by a radially aligned glial cell. In this figure the movement of a young neuron is depicted by a darkened cell (marked by an arrow) in each of the three drawings. This migratory process can be divided into three phases. Initially (A), a young neuron leaves the proliferative population, becomes apposed to a radial glial fiber, and acquires a polarity directed towards the pial surface (P). Next (B), it must traverse the intermediate zone (IZ); while doing this it maintains its apposition to the radial glial fiber and its polarity. Finally (C), as it reaches the top of the cortical plate, it stops its forward progress, loses it apposition to the radial glial fiber, and reorganizes its polarity in order to become a mature neuron. Disruption of any of these three steps could lead to neuronal heterotopias. Abbreviations: V: Ventricular surface; VZ: Ventricular Zone; SZ: Subventricular Zone; IZ: Intermediate Zone; CP, Cortical Plate; MZ, Marginal Zone; P, Pial surface

while maintaining its apposition to the radial fiber and its axis of polarity. Finally, in the third phase of its migration, a young neuron "recognizes" that it has reached its final destination and stops its migration. During this phase the migrating neuron detaches from the radial glial fiber and the young neuron can continue to differentiate. Also, as a result of this detachment the surface of the radial glial fiber is made available for the guidance of subsequently generated neurons that migrate past those that were previously generated (Pinto-Lord et al., 1982). The analysis of neuronal migration in normal and mutant mice and also in human pathological conditions indicates that there are specific molecules which mediate the contact of migrating neurons with radial glial fibers (Hatten, 1999). In addition, guidance may involve ion channels (Komuro and Rakic, 1998b; Komuro and Rakic, 1998a) and adhesive interactions may also be mediated in part by specific cell surface related molecules, e.g., integrins (Anton and Kreidberg, 1999). Key information about the nature of the signal(s) for detaching from the radial glial fiber has come from the analysis of mutant mice and, in particular, from the reeler mutant mouse which has an "inverted" cortex reflecting abnormalities in neuronal migration (Caviness and Sidman, 1973; Pinto-Lord et al., 1982). Recently, "reelin", the cell surface molecule that is mutated in reeler, has been identified (Curran and D'Arcangelo, 1998; Lambert de Rouvroit and Goffinet, 1998) and its cellular roles in providing a "stopping signal" are beginning to be elucidated

(Alvarez-Dolado et al., 1999; D'Arcangelo et al., 1999; Rice and Curran, 1999; Trommsdorff et al., 1999).

If neuronal migration is disrupted, an *abnormality in cell position results*. When this happens the neurons are said to be heterotopic or ectopic (Rakic, 1975a). In humans, the best studied examples are in the cerebral cortex, where defects in neuronal migration have been associated with a variety of syndromes and diseases ranging from behavioral disorders to extremely severe mental retardation and failure to thrive (for reviews see Rakic, 1975a; Barth, 1987; Dobyns and Truwit, 1995; Pearlman et al., 1998; Reiner and Sapir, 1998). Behavioral disorders that have been associated with a disruption of neuronal migration include some forms of schizophrenia (Arnold and Trojanowski, 1996; Chua and Murray, 1996), dyslexia (Galaburda and Kemper, 1979; Peterson, 1995), and autism (Peterson, 1995; Bailey et al., 1998; Kemper and Bauman, 1998).

Cell differentiation is the final complication

Once a neuron or glial cell has left the proliferative population and reached its final position it enters the final phase in its life history, i.e., its differentiation. During its differentiation each neuron grows out its axon and its dendrites. In many cases the axon grows a long distance over a complicated terrain before reaching its final target. The dendrites grow out and form their characteristic pattern of arborization for the particular cell class. Each differentiating neuron also must express the specific enzymes it requires in order to produce the neurotransmitter(s) it will use. Also, each postsynaptic site must express the receptors it needs to receive input from its presynaptic partner. Simultaneous with the acquisition of mature properties by the neurons, the glial cells are also differentiating into oligodendrocytes that make myelin and astrocytes that perform other functions (Lillien and Raff, 1990; Goldman, 1995; Raff et al., 1998). For example, in humans the myelination of most pathways in the CNS continues long after birth (for review see Richardson, 1982), and, in fact, the classical work by Flechsig (1920) on myelination in the developing human cerebral cortex provided the basis of the traditional classification of cortical areas into primary, secondary, and association areas. Many aspects of cell differentiation in the CNS are beyond the scope of this review, and, for this reason, the discussion below will be confined to the limited issue of the transient connections made by some axons.

The growth of axons in the CNS involves the extension of a process from the cell body to a target or postsynaptic cell. Each growing axon must find its way through a complicated terrain to its target area and once there it must select the appropriate target cell and even the appropriate part of the dendritic tree in order to make its synapses. It is likely that the growing axon makes use of a variety of mechanisms to find its way to its final target (Goodman, 1996; Tessier-Lavigne and Goodman, 1996). Interestingly, in many parts of the developing CNS the growing axons do not grow directly to their final targets, but instead grow "exuberantly" such that they transiently innervate areas and cells that they do not normally contact in the adult. Two types of transient connections are made (see figure 5.10): divergent and convergent. Divergence means that one neuron (or population of neurons) innervates more cells (or a greater area) than it normally does in the adult (figure 5.10a). During development the extra collaterals of the divergently projecting population are eliminated such that the projection area is reduced to its adult size (figure 5.10a'). Convergence means that several neurons (or populations of neurons) innervate one target neuron (or area) (figure 5.10b), which in the adult is innervated by only one of these

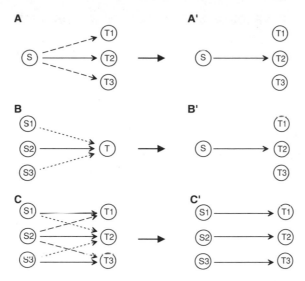

Figure 5.10 There are two types of exuberant projections which occur during the development of the CNS. In A, the transient *divergence* of a single source of axons is illustrated. In this case, the circle represents a single source of axons (a cell or population of cells) that projects to an area broader than its eventual adult distribution. Subsequently, some portion of the projection is withdrawn (through a variety of mechanisms) to produce the adult pattern (**A′**). In **B**, the transient *convergence* of projections from more than one source (i.e., from more than one cell or a population of cells) all terminating on a single target is illustrated. In this case, the projections from some of the sources are lost in order to establish the adult pattern (**B′**). In **C**, the simultaneous presence of both transient divergence and convergence is illustrated. In this case, both types of exuberant projections have to be lost in order to establish the adult pattern of connections (**C′**).

neurons (or populations) (figure 5.10b′). These two types of transient projections are *not* mutually exclusive and it is possible that both could be found within a single population of cells (figure 5.10c). In this case, both the divergent and convergent projections would have to be eliminated in order to establish the adult pattern of connections (figure 5.10c′).

Cell Death and Transient Connections

The elimination of transient connections involves two distinctly different regressive phenomena: (1) removal by a retraction of the collaterals of the neuron's axon or by a shrinking of the terminal arborization of the axon, and (2) removal through selective cell death such that the neurons that are "unsuccessful" in establishing projections to their normal adult territory die. Both of these mechanisms of elimination are known to occur. For example, during the development of the cerebral cortex pyramidal neurons in the visual cortex send collaterals to targets, such as the spinal cord, which they do not ordinarily innervate in the adult animal. As the animal matures, some of the collaterals of these cells are lost, whereas other collaterals persist (O'Leary and Stanfield, 1985; Stanfield and O'Leary, 1985b; Stanfield and O'Leary, 1985a). The refinement of point-to-point connections to the visual cortex from the lateral geniculate nucleus also involves reorganization of the input (Wiesel,

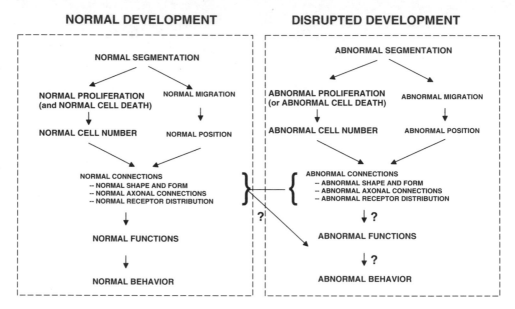

Figure 5.11 Schematic diagram of the cascade of events associated with normal and disrupted migration in the developing CNS. The diagram on the left shows the normal sequence of events, and the diagram on the right shows the disrupted sequence. Even if disruption of migration occurs in only one part of the CNS, the connections between the abnormally positioned neurons and their normally positioned counterparts may be affected, and abnormal functions and behavior may result.

1982). In many other parts of the CNS neuron death also contributes to the elimination of divergently projecting collaterals (Cowan et al., 1984; O'Leary, 1987; Oppenheim, 1991; Burek and Oppenheim, 1996). Thus, it is of great interest (and some irony) that an important set of processes during the development of the nervous system, which is generally thought of as being a series of *progressive* events, are *regressive* events involving the retraction of axons and the death of cells. There is no doubt, however, that cell death is an important developmental feature because "knockout" mice with mutant genes that prevent cell death have severe developmental abnormalities in the CNS (Kuida et al., 1998; Haydar et al., 1999; Roth et al., 2000).

The Effects of Abnormal Development

"How" are cell proliferation, cell migration and cell differentiation controlled? As discussed in the introduction to this paper, the simple answers are that they are each controlled by processes intrinsic to the cell or by processes extrinsic to the cell, i.e., by cell–cell interactions, by interactions of cells with hormones, etc. How do abnormalities in development affect the adult CNS and behavior? The answers to this question are less clear, but abnormalities in neural tube segmentation, cell proliferation, migration or in cell death clearly produce changes in the connections of the neurons of the adult brain. For example, abnormalities in CNS segmentation could lead to missing subdivisions or changes in the identity of subdivisions and in disorders in which either cell proliferation or neuronal migration is disrupted in some way; either fewer neurons or abnormally positioned neurons result. These events occur relatively early during developmental cascade (figure 5.1), and, thus, are likely to have further impact on CNS organization. The neurons of the affected regions will almost certainly not make normal connections, setting up a cascade of abnormalities as connections are formed, and, as a result, normal functional competence will not be achieved (figure 5.11). These changes in connections could involve both the regions in which the primary disruption occurs and also relatively distant regions that receive connections from or send connections to the affected regions (figure 5.11). The same sorts of cascade of consequences will occur whenever subsequent development operates on an abnormal substrate.

REFERENCES

Altman J. and Bayer S. A. (1979). Development of the diencephalon in the rat. V. Thymidine-radiographic observations on internuclear and intranuclear gradients in the thalamus. *Journal of Comparative Neurology* 188, 473–500.

Altman J. and Bayer S. A. (1981). Development of the brain stem in the rat. V. Thymidine-radiographic study of the time of origin of neurons in the midbrain tegmentum. *Journal of Comparative Neurology* 198, 677–716.

Alvarez-Dolado M., Ruiz M., Del Rio J. A., Alcantara S., Burgaya F., Sheldon M., Nakajima K., Bernal J., Howell B. W., Curran T., Soriano E., and Munoz A. (1999). Thyroid hormone regulates reelin and dab1 expression during brain development. *J. Neurosci.* 19, 6979–93.

Angevine J. B. J. (1965). Time of neuron origin in the hippocampal region: an autoradiographic study in the mouse. *Experimental Neurology Supplement* 2, 1–71.

Angevine J. B. J. (1970). Time of neuron origin in the diencephalon of the mouse. An autoradiographic study. *Journal of Comparative Neurology* 139, 129–88.

Angevine J. B. J. and Sidman R. L. (1961). Autoradiographic study of cell migration during histogenesis of cerebral cortex in the mouse. *Nature* 192, 766–8.

Anton E. S. and Kreidberg J. A. (1999). Distinct functions of a3 and av integrin receptors in neuronal migration and laminar organization of the cerebral cortex. *Neuron* 22, 277–89.

Araki I. and Nakamura H. (1999). Engrailed Defines the position of dorsal di-mesencephalic boundary by repressing diencephalic fate. *Development* 126, 5127–35.

Arnold S. E. and Trojanowski J. Q. (1996). Recent advances in defining the neuropathology of schizophrenia. *Acta Neuropathol. (Berl.)* 92, 217–31.

Bailey A., Luthert P., Dean A., Harding B., Janota I., Montgomery M., Rutter M., and Lantos P. (1998). A clinicopathological study of autism. *Brain* 121, 889–905.

Barrow J. R., Stadler H. S., and Capecchi M. R. (2000). Roles of Hoxa1 and Hoxa2 in patterning the early hindbrain of the mouse. *Development* 127, 933–44.

Barth P. G. (1987). Disorders of neuronal migration. *Can. J. Neurol. Sci.* 14, 1–16.

Bayer S. A., Yackel J. W., and Puri P. S. (1982). Neurons in the rat dentate gyrus granular layer substantially increase during juvenile and adult life. *Science* 216, 890–2.

Bell J. E. and Gosden C. M. (1978). Central nervous system abnormalities – contrasting patterns in early and late pregnancy. *Clinical Genetics* 13, 387–96.

Berry M. and Rogers A. W. (1965). The migration of neuroblasts in the developing cerebral cortex. *Journal of Anatomy* 99, 691–709.

Blinkov S. M. and Glezer I. I. (1968). *The Human Brain in Figures and Tables: A Quantitative Handbook*. New York: Plenum Press.

Boulder Committee (1970). Embryonic vertebrate central nervous system: revised terminology. *Anatomical Record* 166, 257–62.

Burek M. J. and Oppenheim R. W. (1996). Programmed cell death in the developing nervous system. *Brain Pathology* 6, 427–46.

Caviness V., Takahashi T., and Nowakowski R. (1995). Numbers, time and neocortical neuronogenesis: a general developmental and evolutionary model. *Trends in Neuroscience* 18, 379–83.

Caviness V. S., Jr. (1982). Neocortical histogenesis in normal and reeler mice: a developmental study based upon [3H]thymidine autoradiography. *Developmental Brain Research* 4, 293–302.

Caviness V. S. Jr. and Sidman R. L. (1973). Time of origin of corresponding cell classes in the cerebral cortex of normal and reeler mutant mice: an autoradiographic analysis. *Journal of Comparative Neurology* 148, 141–51.

Chua S. E. and Murray R. M. (1996). The neurodevelopmental theory of schizophrenia: evidence concerning structure and neuropsychology. *Ann. Med.* 28, 547–55.

Cooper M. L. and Rakic P. (1981). Neurogenetic gradients in the superior and inferior colliculi of the rhesus monkey. *J. Comp. Neurol.* 202, 309–34.

Cowan W. M., Fawcett J. W., O'Leary D. D., and Stanfield B. B. (1984). Regressive events in neurogenesis. *Science* 225, 1258–65.

Curran T. and D'Arcangelo G. (1998). Role of reelin in the control of brain development. *Brain Research Reviews* 26, 285–94.

D'Arcangelo G., Homayouni R., Keshvara L., Rice D. S., Sheldon M., and Curran T. (1999). Reelin is a ligand for lipoprotein receptors. *Neuron* 24, 471–9.

Dobyns W. B. and Truwit C. L. (1995). Lissencephaly and other malformations of cortical development: 1995 update. *Neuropediatrics* 26, 132–47.

Dodd J., Jessell T. M., and Placzek M. (1998). The When and Where of Floor Plate Induction. *Science* 282, 1654–7.

Doetsch F., Caille I., Lim D. A., Garcia-Verdugo J. M., and Alvarez-Buylla A. (1999). Subventricular zone astrocytes are neural stem cells in the adult mammalian brain. *Cell* 97, 703–16.

Doetsch F., Garcia-Verdugo J. M., and Alvarez-Buylla A. (1997). Cellular composition and three-dimensional organization of the subventricular germinal zone in the adult mammalian brain. *J. Neurosci.* 17, 5046–61.

Finlay B. L. and Slattery M. (1983). Local differences in the amount of early cell death in neocortex predict adult local specializations. *Science* 219, 1349–51.

Flechsig P. (1920). *Anatomie des menschlichen Gehirns und Ruckenmarks auf myelogenetischer Grundlage.* Leipzig: Georg Thieme.

Friede R. L. (1989). *Developmental Neuropathology*, 2nd edition. New York: Springer-Verlag.

Galaburda A. M. and Kemper T. L. (1979). Cytoarchitectonic abnormalities in developmental dyslexia: a case study. *Annals of Neurology* 6, 94–100.

Garcia-Verdugo J. M., Doetsch F., Wichterle H., Lim D. A., and Alvarez-Buylla A. (1998). Architecture and cell types of the adult subventricular zone: in search of the stem cells. *Journal of Neurobiology* 36, 234–48.

Gilles F. H. (1985). Classifications of childhood brain tumors. *Cancer* 56, 1850–7.

Goldman J. E. (1995). Lineage, migration, and fate determination of postnatal subventricular zone cells in the mammalian CNS. *J. Neurooncol.* 24, 61–4.

Goodman C. S. (1996). Mechanisms and molecules that control growth cone guidance. *Annual Reviews of Neuroscience* 19, 341–77.

Greer E. R., Diamond M. C., and Tang J. M. (1982). Environmental enrichment in Brattleboro rats: brain morphology. *Annals of the New York Academy of Sciences* 394, 749–52.

Hatten M. E. (1999). Central Nervous System Neuronal Migration. *Annual Reviews of Neuroscience* 22, 511–39.

Haydar T. F., Kuan C. Y., Flavell R. A., and Rakic P. (1999). The role of cell death in regulating the size and shape of the mammalian forebrain. *Cereb. Cortex* 9, 621–6.

Hayes N. L. and Nowakowski R. S. (2000). Exploiting the dynamics of S-phase tracers in developing brain: interkinetic nuclear migration for cells entering vs leaving the S-phase. *Developmental Neuroscience* 22, in press.

Hickey T. L. and Hitchcock P. F. (1984). Genesis of neurons in the dorsal lateral geniculate nucleus of the cat. *J. Comp. Neurol.* 228, 186–99.

Hinds J. W. (1968). Autoradiographic study of histogenesis in the mouse olfactory bulb. I. Time of origin of neurons and neuroglia. *Journal of Comparative Neurology* 134, 287–304.

His W. (1904). *Die Entwicklung des Menschlichen Gehirns wahrend der ersten Monate.* Leipzig: von S. Hirzel.

Hochstetter F. (1919). *Beitrage zur Entwicklungsgeschichte des menschlichen Gehirns.* Leipzig Wien: Deuticke.

Hollyday M. and Hamburger V. (1976). Reduction of the naturally occurring motor neuron loss by enlargement of the periphery. *Journal of Comparative Neurology* 170, 311–20.

Ifft J. D. (1972). An autoradiographic study of the time of final division of neurons in the rat hypothalamic nuclei. *Journal of Comparative Neurology* 144, 193–204.

Johnston J. B. (1902). An attempt to define the primitive functional divisions of the central nervous system. *Journal of Comparative Neurology* 12, 87–106.

Joosten P. H. Hol F. A., van Beersum S. E., Peters H., Hamel B. C., Afink G. B., van Zoelen E. J., and Mariman E. C. (1998). Altered regulation of platelet-derived growth factor receptor-alpha gene-transcription in vitro by spina bifida-associated mutant Pax1 proteins. *Proc. Natl. Acad. Sci. USA* 95, 14459–63.

Kemper T. L. and Bauman M. (1998). Neuropathology of infantile autism. *Journal of Neuropathology and Experimental Neurology* 57, 645–52.

Kempermann G., Brandon E. P., and Gage F. H. (1998). Environmental stimulation of 129/SvJ mice causes increased cell proliferation and neurogenesis in the adult dentate gyrus. *Current Biology* 8, 939–42.

Kempermann G., Kuhn H. G., and Gage F. H. (1997a). Genetic influence on neurogenesis in the dentate gyrus of adult mice. *Proceedings of the National Academy of Science USA* 94, 10409–14.

Kempermann G., Kuhn H. G., and Gage F. H. (1997b). More hippocampal neurons in adult mice living in an enriched environment. *Nature* 386, 493–5.

Kingsbury B. F. (1922). The fundamental plan of the vertebrate brain. *Journal of Comparative Neurology* 34, 461–91.

Komuro H. and Rakic P. (1998a). Distinct modes of neuronal migration in different domains of developing cerebellar cortex. *Journal of Neuroscience* 18, 1478–90.

Komuro H. and Rakic P. (1998b). Orchestration of neuronal migration by activity of ion channels, neurotransmitter receptors, and intracellular Ca2+ fluctuations. *Journal of Neurobiology* 37, 110–30.

Kornack D. R. and Rakic P. (1998). Changes in cell-cycle kinetics during the development and evolution of primate neocortex. *Proceedings of the National Academy of Science USA* 95, 1242–6.

Kostovic I. and Rakic P. (1980). Cytology and time of origin of interstitial neurons in the white matter in infant and adult human and monkey telencephalon. *Journal of Neurocytology* 9, 219–42.

Kuffler S. W., Nicholls J. G., and Martin A. R. (1984). *From Neuron to Brain: A Cellular Approach to the Function of the Nervous System.* Second Edition. Sunderland, Massachusetts: Sinauer Associates, Inc.

Kuhlenbeck H. (1973). *The Central Nervous System of Vertebrates:* Vol. 3, Pt. 2. *Overall morphological pattern.* Basel: Karger.

Kuhlenbeck H. (1977). *The Central Nervous System of Vertebrates:* Vol. 5, Pt. 1. *Derivatives of the prosencephalon: Diencephalon and telencephalon.* Basel: Karger.

Kuida K., Haydar T. F., Kuan C. Y., Gu Y., Taya C., Karasuyama H., Su M. S., Rakic P., and Flavell R. A. (1998). Reduced apoptosis and cytochrome c-mediated caspase activation in mice lacking caspase 9. *Cell* 94, 325–37.

Lambert de Rouvroit C. and Goffinet A. M. (1998). The reeler mouse as a model of brain development. *Advances in Anatomy, Embryology and Cell Biology* 150, 1–106.

Lee K. J. and Jessell T. M. (1999). The specification of dorsal cell fates in the vertebrate central nervous system. *Annual Revews of Neuroscience* 22, 261–94.

Lillien L. E. and Raff M. C. (1990). Differentiation signals in the CNS: type-2 astrocyte development in vitro as a model system. *Neuron* 5, 111–19.

Lumsden A. and Krumlauf R. (1996). Patterning the vertebrate neuraxis. *Science* 274, 1109–15.

Luo J. and Miller M. W. (1998). Growth factor-mediated neural proliferation: target of ethanol toxicity. *Brain Research Reviews* 27, 157–67.

Miller M. W. (1985). Cogeneration of retrogradely labeled corticocortical projection and GABA-immunoreactive local circuit neurons in cerebral cortex. *Brain Research* 355, 187–92.

Miura R. (1933). Über die differenzierung der Grundbestandteile im Zwischenhirn des Kaninchens. *Anatomische Anzeiger* 77, 1–65.

Morgane P. J., Austin-LaFrance R., Bronzino J., Tonkiss J., Diaz-Cintra S., Cintra L., Kemper T., and Galler J. R. (1993). Prenatal malnutrition and development of the brain. *Neuroscience and Biobehavioral Reviews* 17, 91–128.

Nornes H. O. and Das G. D. (1974). Temporal patterns of neurons in spinal cord of rat. I. An autoradiographic study – Time and sites of origin and migration and settling patterns of neuroblasts. *Brain Research* 73, 121–38.

Nowakowski R. S. (1986). Neuronal Migration in the Hippocampal Lamination Defect (Hld) Mutant Mouse. In: *Cellular and Molecular Control of Direct Cell Interactions* (Marthy H. J., ed.), pp. 133–54. New York: Plenum Press.

Nowakowski R. S. (1987). Basic concepts of CNS development. *Child Development* 58, 568–95.

Nowakowski R. S. and Hayes N. L. (1999). CNS development: an overview. *Dev. Psychopathol.* 11, 395–417.

Nowakowski R. S. and Rakic P. (1979). The mode of migration of neurons to the hippocampus: a Golgi and electron microscopic analysis in foetal rhesus monkey. *Journal of Neurocytology* 8, 697–718.

Nowakowski R. S. and Rakic P. (1981). The site of origin and route and rate of migration of neurons to the hippocampal region of the rhesus monkey. *Journal of Comparative Neurology* 196, 129–54.

O'Leary D. D. (1987). Remodelling of early axonal projections through the selective elimination of neurons and long axon collaterals. *Ciba Foundation Symposium* 126, 113–42.

O'Leary D. D. and Stanfield B. B. (1985). Occipital cortical neurons with transient pyramidal tract axons extend and maintain collaterals to subcortical but not intracortical targets. *Brain Research* 336, 326–33.

Olivier G. and Pineau H. (1961). Horizons de Streeter et age embryonaire. *Bull. Ass. Anat.* (Nancy) 47e, 573–6.

Oppenheim R. W. (1991). Cell death during development of the nervous system. In: *Annual Review of Neuroscience* (Cowan W. M., Shooter E. M., Stevens C. F., and Thompson R. F., eds.), pp. 453–501. Palo Alto: Annual Reviews, Inc.

Otake M. and Schull W. J. (1984). In utero exposure to A-bomb radiation and mental retardation; a reassessment. *British Journal of Radiology* 57, 409–14.

Payne J., Shibasaki F., and Mercola M. (1997). Spina bifida occulta in homozygous Patch mouse embryos. *Dev. Dyn.* 209, 105–16.

Pearlman A. L., Faust P. L., Hatten M. E., and Brunstrom J. E. (1998). New directions for neuronal migration. *Current Opinions in Neurobiology* 8, 45–54.

Peterson B. S. (1995). Neuroimaging in child and adolescent neuropsychiatric disorders. *Journal of the American Academy of Child and Adolescent Psychiatry* 34, 1560–76.

Pinto-Lord M. C., Evrard P., and Caviness V. S. J. (1982). Obstructed neuronal migration along radial glial fibers in the neocortex of the reeler mouse: A Golgi-EM analysis. *Developmental Brain Research* 4, 379–93.

Polyakov G. I. (1949). Strukturnaya organizatsiya kory boljshogo mozga cheloveka po dannym razvitiya ee v ontogeneze. In: *Tsitoarkhitektonika Kory Bojshogo Mozga Cheloveka* (Sarkisov S. A., Filimonov I. N., and Preobrazhenskaya N. S., eds.), pp. 33–92. Moscow: Medgiz.

Raff M. C., Durand B., and Gao F. B. (1998). Cell number control and timing in animal development: the oligodendrocyte cell lineage. *International Journal of Developmental Biology* 42, 263–7.

Rakic P. (1971). Neuron–glia relationship during granule cell migration in developing cerebellar cortex. A Golgi and electron microscopic study in macacus rhesus. *Journal of Comparative Neurology* 141, 283–312.

Rakic P. (1972). Mode of cell migration to the superficial layers of fetal monkey neocortex. *Journal of Comparative Neurology* 145, 61–84.

Rakic P. (1974). Neurons in rhesus monkey visual cortex: systematic relation between time of origin and eventual disposition. *Science* 183, 425–7.

Rakic P. (1975a). Cell migration and neuronal ectopias in the brain. *Birth Defects Original Article Series* 11, 95–129.

Rakic P. (1975b). Timing of major ontogenetic events in the visual cortex of the rhesus monkey. In: *Brain Mechanisms in Mental Retardation* (Buchwald N. A. and Brazier M. A. B., eds.), pp. 3–40. New York: Academic Press.

Rakic P. (1977). Genesis of the dorsal lateral geniculate nucleus in the rhesus monkey: site and time of origin, kinetics of proliferation, routes of migration and pattern of distribution of neurons. *Journal of Comparative Neurology* 176, 23–52.

Rakic P., Cameron R. S., and Komuro H. (1994). Recognition, adhesion, transmembrane signaling and cell motility in guided neuronal migration. *Current Opinions in Neurobiology* 4, 63–9.

Rakic P. and Nowakowski R. S. (1981). The time of origin of neurons in the hippocampal region of the rhesus monkey. *Journal of Comparative Neurology* 196, 99–128.

Reiner O. and Sapir T. (1998). Abnormal cortical development; towards elucidation of the LIS1 gene product function (review). *International Journal of Molecular Medicine* 1, 849–53.

Rice D. S. and Curran T. (1999). Mutant mice with scrambled brains: understanding the signaling pathways that control cell positioning in the CNS. *Genes Dev.* 13, 2758–73.

Richardson E. P., Jr. (1982). Myelination in the human central nervous system. In: *Histology and Histopathology of the Nervous System* (Adams Ward, ed.), pp. 146–73. Springfield, Illinois: C. C. Thomas.

Rodier P. M. (2000). The early origins of autism. *Sci. Am.* 282, 56–63.

Rodier P. M., Ingram J. L., Tisdale B., Nelson S., and Romano J. (1996). Embryological origin for autism: developmental anomalies of the cranial nerve motor nuclei. *J. Comp. Neurol.* 370, 247–61.

Roth K. A., Kuan C., Haydar T. F., D'Sa-Eipper C., Shindler K. S., Zheng T. S., Kuida K., Flavell R. A., and Rakic P. (2000). Epistatic and independent functions of caspase-3 and Bcl-X(L) in developmental programmed cell death. *Proc. Natl. Acad. Sci. USA* 97, 466–71.

Rubinstein J. L. R. and Shimamura K. (1997). Regulation of patterning and differentiation in the embryonic vertebrate forebrain. In: *Molecular and Cellular Approaches to Neural Development* (Cowan W. M., Jessell T. M., and Zipursky S. L., eds.), pp. 356–90. New York: Oxford University Press.

Sauer F. C. (1936). The interkinetic migration of embryonic epithelial nuclei. *J. Morphol.* 60, 1–11.

Schulte H., von W. and Tilney F. (1915). Development of the neuraxis in the domestic cat to the stage of twenty-one somites. *Annals of the New York Academy of Science* 24, 319–46.

Sidman R. L. (1961). Histogenesis of mouse retina studied with thymidine-H3. In: *Structure of the Eye*, pp. 487–506. New York: Academic Press.

Sidman R. L. (1970). Autoradiographic methods and principles for study of the nervous system with thymidine-H3. In: *Contemporary Research Methods in Neuroanatomy* (Nauta W. J. H. and Ebbesson S. O. E., eds.), pp. 252–74. New York: Springer.

Sidman R. L. and Rakic P. (1973). Neuronal migration with special reference to developing human brain: a review. *Brain Research* 62, 1–35.

Sidman R. L. and Rakic P. (1982). Development of the human central nervous system. In: *Histology and Histopathology of the Nervous System* (Haymaker W. and Adams R. D., eds.), pp. 3–145. Springfield: Charles C. Thomas.

Smart J. L. (1991). Critical periods in brain development. *Ciba Found. Symposium* 156, 109–24.

Stanfield B. B. and O'Leary D. D. (1985a). Fetal occipital cortical neurones transplanted to the rostral cortex can extend and maintain a pyramidal tract axon. *Nature* 313, 135–7.

Stanfield B. B. and O'Leary D. D. (1985b). The transient corticospinal projection from the occipital cortex during the postnatal development of the rat. *Journal of Comparative Neurology* 238, 236–48.

Studer M., Lumsden A., Ariza-McNaughton L., Bradley A., and Krumlauf R. (1996). Altered segment identity and abnormal migration of motor neurons in mice lacking Hoxb-1. *Nature* 384, 630–4.

Taber-Pierce E. (1972). Time of origin of neurons in the brain stem of the mouse. *Progress in Brain Research* 40, 53–66.

Takahashi T., Nowakowski R. S., and Caviness V. S., Jr. (1993). Cell cycle parameters and patterns of nuclear movement in the neocortical proliferative zone of the fetal mouse. *J. Neurosci.* 13, 820–33.

Takahashi T., Nowakowski R. S., and Caviness V. S., Jr. (1995a). The cell cycle of the pseudostratified ventricular epithelium of the embryonic murine cerebral wall. *J. Neurosci.* 15, 6046–57.

Takahashi T., Nowakowski R. S., and Caviness V. S., Jr. (1995b). Early ontogeny of the secondary proliferative population of the embryonic murine cerebral wall. *J. Neurosci.* 15, 6058–68.

Takahashi T., Nowakowski R. S., and Caviness V. S., Jr. (1996a). Interkinetic and migratory behavior of a cohort of neocortical neurons arising in the early embryonic murine cerebral wall. *Journal of Neuroscience* 16, 5762–76.

Takahashi T., Nowakowski R. S., and Caviness V. S., Jr. (1996b). The leaving or Q fraction of the murine cerebral proliferative epithelium: a general model of neocortical neuronogenesis. *J. Neurosci.* 16, 6183–96.

Takahashi T., Nowakowski R. S., and Caviness V. S., Jr. (1997). The mathematics of neocortical neuronogenesis. *Developmental Neuroscience* 19, 17–22.

Tanabe Y. and Jessell T. M. (1996). Diversity and pattern in the developing spinal cord [published erratum appears in *Science* 1997 Apr. 4; 276(5309), 21]. *Science* 274, 1115–23.

Tessier-Lavigne M. and Goodman C. S. (1996). The molecular biology of axon guidance. *Science* 274, 1123–33.

Thomaidou D., Mione M. C., Cavanagh J. F., and Parnavelas J. G. (1997). Apoptosis and its relation to the cell cycle in the developing cerebral cortex. *Journal of Neuroscience* 17, 1075–85.

Trommsdorff M., Gotthardt M., Hiesberger T., Shelton J., Stockinger W., Nimpf J., Hammer R. E., Richardson J. A., and Herz J. (1999). Reeler/Disabled-like disruption of neuronal migration in knockout mice lacking the VLDL receptor and ApoE receptor 2. *Cell* 97, 689–701.

Verney C., Takahashi T., Bhide P. G., Nowakowski R. S., and Caviness Jr. V. S. (2000). Independent controls for neocortical neuron production and histogenetic cell death [In Process Citation]. *Dev. Neurosci.* 22, 125–38.

Walsh C., Polley E. H., Hickey T. L., and Guillery R. W. (1983). Generation of cat retinal ganglion cells in relation to central pathways. *Nature* 302, 611–14.

Wiesel T. N. (1982). Postnatal development of the visual cortex and the influence of environment. *Nature* 299, 583–91.

Wyss J. M. and Sripanidkulchai B. (1985). An autoradiographic analysis of the time of origin of neurons in the hypothalamus of the cat. *Brain Research* 353, 89–98.

Yakovlev P. I. and Lecours A. R. (1967). The myelogenetic cycles of regional maturation of the brain. In: *Regional Development of Brain in Early Life* (Minkowski A., ed.), pp. 3–70. Oxford: Blackwell Science.

6

Intrinsic and Extrinsic Determinants of Neocortical Parcellation: A Radial Unit Model

Pasko Rakic

Introduction

In this chapter, I will review some developmental principles and several lines of evidence in support of the radial unit model of neocortical ontogeny and phylogeny. This model, which involves the kinetics of cell proliferation, neuronal migration, competitive interactions, and selective cell elimination, has implications for understanding the genetic and epigenetic regulation of neocortical parcellation during development, and provides a new view on the pathogenesis of certain cortical malformations in man.

I will draw background information mostly from the analysis of cortical development in rhesus monkeys, which has become accessible to experimental analysis with modern methods including axonal tracing, electron microscopy, immunocytochemistry, *in situ* hybridization, receptor binding, and ^{3}H-thymidine autoradiography. Advances made in techniques of neurosurgery on the fetal cerebrum *in utero* make experimental manipulations that were traditionally limited to avain and amphibian embryos possible in large mammals (Rakic and Goldman-Rakic, 1985). The size of the monkey's cerebrum during the second half of gestation and the presence of visible morphological landmarks at its surface allow precise localization for excision of specific cortical areas, while protracted development provides high temporal resolution of cellular events. Finally, the similarity between man and monkey of the convoluted cerebral surface and of distinct boundaries between major cytoarchitectonic fields enables comparison between findings obtained from animal research and findings from normal and pathological human autopsy specimens.

I will concentrate on the formation of cytoarchitectonic areas during ontogenetic and phylogenetic development. A comparison of cytoarchitectonic maps in various species reveals four important points relevant to the proposed developmental model. First, the neocortex expands enormously during phylogeny (e.g. the surface of rat's neocortex is less than 1 percent of a monkey's and 0.1 percent of a human's). Second, all cytoarchitectonic areas do not expand equally (e.g. striate cortex occupies only 3 percent of the cerebral

"Intrinsic and Extrinsic Determinants of Neocortical Parcellation: a Radial Unit Model" first appeared in *Neurobiology of Neocortex*, edited by P. Rakic and W. Singer (John Wiley & Sons, 1988, pp. 5–27), © S. Bernhard, Dahlem Konferenzen, 1988, and is reprinted by kind permission.

surface in humans but more than 15 percent of the cerebral surface in monkeys). Third, new cytoarchitectonic areas become introduced during evolution (e.g. monkeys do not have Broca's area). Fourth, there are large interspecies variations in the sizes of cortical areas, as well as differences between the hemispheres of the same individual (e.g. the auditory cortex may be three times larger on the left side in right-handed humans).

How are differences in cortical parcellation between species and individuals generated? Is the number of neurons in each cytoarchitectonic area genetically determined? Do environmental factors and functional activity play any role? If so, when does the capacity for structural change stop? To answer some of these questions, we first must know when and where cortical neurons are generated and how they assume their positions within the cortex. Then we have to determine whether their fate can be experimentally manipulated.

Origin of Cortical Neurons

Classical histological studies suggested that the majority of cortical neurons in man are generated outside of the cortex itself, probably well before birth (Sidman and Rakic, 1973). However, only the introduction of the DNA labeling method using ^{3}H-thymidine provided sufficiently precise data on the onset and end of corticogenesis. For example, analysis of a series of adult rhesus monkeys that were exposed to ^{3}H-thymidine during various pre- and postnatal stages revealed that all cortical neurons in this species are generated during the middle of gestation (Rakic, 1974; Rakic and Goldman-Rakic, 1982). The first cortical neurons arise around the 40th embryonic day (E40); the last at a more variable time. Thus, corticogenesis in the cingulate cortex stops at E70; in the striate cortex at E100. No neocortical neurons are produced during the last two prenatal months nor at any time after birth, which in rhesus monkeys occurs around E165 (Rakic, 1985). This contrasts with reports of neurogenesis in the cortex of mature rodents (Kaplan, 1981). Comparative cytological analysis indicates that in humans, with a normal gestation of about E265, the first cortical neurons are also generated around E40, and their production is complete by E125 (Rakic, 1978). Thus, unlike rodents, where the last neocortical neurons are produced close to or shortly after birth (Angevine and Sidman, 1961; Berry and Rogers, 1965; Smart and Smart, 1982), primates including man acquire their full complement of neurons by midgestation.

The high proportion of mitotic figures at the ventricular surface suggested to the early neuroanatomists that most cortical neurons might be produced there (His, 1904; Ramon y Cajal, 1911). Again, the direct evidence for this conclusion came from ^{3}H-thymidine autoradiographic analysis. A series of monkey embryos sacrificed within two hours after injection of isotope showed that all neurons of the neocortex are produced in the proliferative zone near the cerebral ventricle (Rakic, 1978; Rakic and Goldman-Rakic, 1982). Therefore, cortical neurons must migrate to the cortex after their last mitotic division. Golgi, electron microscopic, autoradiographic, and immunocytochemical analyses have revealed that both neuronal and glial cells coexist in the proliferative zone from the onset of corticogenesis (Levitt et al., 1983; Rakic, 1972b; Schmechel and Rakic, 1979). The point relevant to the proposed radial unit model of cortical development is that interaction between glial fibers and postmitotic neurons has to be taken into account when considering mechanisms of neuronal migration and cortical parcellation (Rakic, 1972b).

Neurons Migrate Along Radial Glial Grids

Although the most massive migration of neurons in primates occurs during the rapid and differential growth of the cerebral wall that causes buckling of its surface, postmitotic neurons nevertheless find their way through the intricate cellular lattice of the intermediate and subplate zones. Electron microscopic studies revealed that the pathways of migrating cells are established by a guidance mechanism that depends on interaction with the shafts of radial glial cells that stretch across the developing telencephalic wall (Rakic, 1972b). Therefore, the migrational pattern of these neurons is imposed by the shape and nature of non-neuronal scaffolding, which is provided by the fascicles of radial glial fibers. This scaffolding is particularly prominent during a period of about two months when most radial glial cells do not divide (Schmechel and Rakic, 1979). Possible cellular and molecular mechanisms underlying the translocation of migrating cells and their guidance to the cortex have been reviewed elsewhere, and several candidate molecules have been tested *in vitro* (Edelman, 1983; Hatten and Mason, 1986; Lindner et al., 1983). Here, I will focus only on the significance of the glial scaffolding for columnar compartmentalization of the neocortex as it relates to the radial unit hypothesis.

Migrating neurons in the large primate cerebrum have to pass through a long and often tortuous pathway across the intermediate zone and, at later stages, across the subplate zone before arriving at their proper destination (figure 6.1). The intermediate zone increases in thickness by the addition of axonal fascicles of various origins. After most of these axons acquire their myelin sheet, this zone is transformed into the subcortical white matter. The transient subplate zone, which is situated below the developing cortical plate, consists of early generated interstitial neurons dispersed among incoming thalamic afferents (Kostovic and Rakic, 1980; Rakic, 1977; Rakic and Goldman-Rakic, 1982; Shatz and Luskin, 1986) and, at later stages, among corticocortical afferents as well (Goldman-Rakic, 1981; Rakic and Goldman-Rakic, 1982). It has been suggested that the subplate zone might be a waiting compartment where afferent fibers make temporary contacts with interstitial cells and migrating neurons before their entry into the cortex (Rakic, 1977). We do not yet understand the nature of these contacts or their significance, although the presence of synapses, neurotransmitters, and neuromodulators, indicates neuronal interaction (Chun et al., 1987; Kostovic and Rakic, 1980).

The proliferative zone can be regarded as a mosaic of proliferative units, each of which provides about one hundred generations of neurons that follow the same radial glial pathway (figure 6.1). The cohorts of genealogically related cells finally end up in the cortical plate stacked one above the other in the form of ontogenetic columns (Rakic, 1974, 1978; Rakic and Goldman-Rakic, 1982). Confinement of several generations of postmitotic cells to a common glial guide may serve to divide the cerebral wall into radial units that extend from the proliferative units across the migratory intermediate zone to the ontogenetic columns in the cortex (figure 6.1). The number of proliferative units, therefore, determines the number of ontogenetic columns (Rakic, 1978). A set of regulatory genes analogous to the homeotic genes, which govern segmental differentiation in drosophila (Lewis, 1978; Morata and Lawrence, 1977; Scott, 1984), may parcellate proliferative units within the ventricular zone into a proto-map of basic cytoarchitectonic areas. The radial glial scaffolding simply enables translation of such a map from the ventricular zone to the expanding cortical plate. The use of the term "proto-map" in this context implies that a given site (proliferative unit) of the ventricular zone generates neurons that form

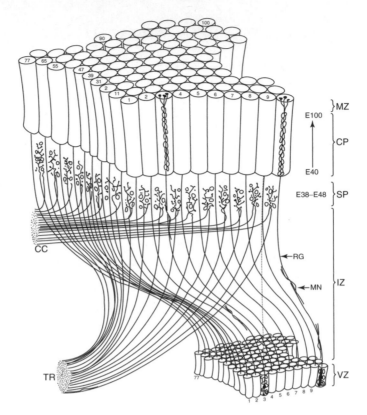

Figure 6.1   The relationship between a small patch of the proliferative, ventricular zone (VZ) and its corresponding area within the cortical plate (CP) in the developing cerebrum. Although the cerebral surface in primates expands during prenatal development, resulting in a shift between the VZ and CP, ontogenetic columns (outlined by cylinders) remain attached to the corresponding proliferative units by the grid of radial glial fibers. All cortical neurons produced between E40 and E100 by a given proliferative unit migrate in succession along the same radial glial guides (RG) and form a single ontogenetic column. Each migrating neuron (MN) traverses the intermediate (IZ) and subplate (SP) zones that contain "waiting" terminals of thalamic radiation (TR) and corticocortical afferents (CC). After entering the cortical plate, each MN bypasses deeper-lying earlier generated neurons and assumes the most superficial position at the interphase between the CP and marginal zone (MZ). As a result, the set of proliferative units 1–100 produce a set of ontogenetic columns 1–100 in the same relative position to each other. Glial scaffolding prevents a mismatch between proliferative unit 3 and ontogenetic column 9 (dashed line). According to the radial unit model, the tangential coordinates of cortical neurons are determined by the position of their ancestors at the ventricle, while their radial positions are determined by the time of genesis and rate of neuronal migration. Thus, the basic topography and/or modality is specified by the spatial distribution of proliferative units, while the neuronal phenotypes within units are specified by time. Modified from Rakic (1978, 1982).

area-specific ontogenetic columns. After the number of proliferative units is established, homeotic genes may turn on another set of genes that determine individual phenotypes of cells produced in each proliferative unit. Therefore, this hypothesis is based on the assumption that (a) within the ventricular zone some proliferative cells have been committed to differentiate into a particular cortical area; and (b) cells produced within an ontogenetic column are genealogically related (Rakic, 1972b, 1978, 1988; Rakic and Goldman-Rakic, 1982). Thus, the complex three-dimensional organization of the adult cortex can be explained by genetic specification as well as spatial and temporal gradients originating from the two-dimensional map of the proliferative zone (figure 6.1).

Laminar Position and Phenotype of Neurons Are Time-Specific

As suspected from the examination of Golgi impregnated tissue (Koelliker, 1896; Ramon y Cajal, 1911; Vignal, 1888) and proven by ^{3}H-thymidine autoradiography in a variety of species (Angevine and Sidman, 1961; Berry and Rogers, 1965; Luskin and Shatz, 1985; Rakic, 1974; Smart and Smart, 1982), neurons destined for deeper cortical layers are generated earliest and are bypassed by those of the more superficial layers. The relationship between the time of neuronal origin and their laminar position, referred to as an "inside-out" gradient of neurogenesis, is particularly sharp in primates where each injection of ^{3}H-thymidine labels a highly selective sample of cortical neurons (Rakic, 1974). This gradient is present throughout the entire cortex, although simultaneously generated neurons destined for various areas display small differences in their laminar position (Rakic, 1974, 1978; Rakic and Goldman-Rakic, 1982; Sidman and Rakic, 1973; Smart and Smart, 1982). The inside-out gradient is characteristic of the mammalian telencephalon, since in reptiles telencephalic neurons settle in an opposite (outside-in) gradient (Goffinet et al., 1986).

On a given day, one area may receive pyramidal cells of layer V, while on the next day it may receive stellate neurons of layer IV. On the other hand, both types of neurons within one layer can be generated simultaneously. It remains possible that different phenotypes of the same ontogenetic column may originate from two or more clones situated in the single proliferative unit (Rakic, 1978; Rakic and Goldman-Rakic, 1982). At present, we are not able to follow the lineage of cortical neurons as has been done for neurons in some simple invertebrates, but we can determine when they become committed to their phenotypes.

Several lines of evidence suggest that a neuron's fate may be determined before the cell assumes its final position. First, in reeler mutant mice, cells that acquire inappropriate laminar positions within the cortex nevertheless differentiate into neuronal types corresponding to the time of their origin rather than the types expected in their new location (Caviness and Rakic, 1978). Second, neurons that remain close to their origin near the ventricular surface due to X-irradiation, which prevents their migration, assume their appropriate phenotype and also establish appropriate efferent connections (Jensen and Killackey, 1984). Third, ventricular cells transplanted into a host's proliferative zone migrate to the positions and assume morphological characteristics similar to those of normal cortical neurons with the same birthdates (McConnell, 1985, 1987). Finally, a subset of callosal neurons destined for layer III in the monkey fetus sends its axons to the opposite hemisphere before entering the cortical plate (Schwartz and Goldman-Rakic, 1986). These findings collectively suggest that the basic properties of neurons such as their morphology and/or prospective synaptic contacts may be specified early, i.e. determined before cells reach their final positions. A similar conclusion has been drawn for the neuronal classes of the cerebellar cortex (granule cells, interneurons of the molecular layer, and Purkinje cells), which originate from different precursors (Rakic, 1972a). More recently, it has been suggested that all Purkinje cells arise from a few clones established early in the proliferative zones (Herrup, 1986). It should be emphasized, however, that determination of the basic types of neurons (e.g. pyramidal versus stellate) does not address the larger issue of their areal specificity (e.g. area 17 versus area 18), or modal specificity (e.g. visual versus auditory). Knowing how and when neurons differentiate into certain types does not tell us how they find their areal and laminar positions, what controls their number, or how they become an integral part of the cortex as a whole.

Fetal Cortex Consists of Ontogenetic Columns

According to the radial unit hypothesis, proliferative units should have corresponding ontogenetic columns in the cortex (Rakic, 1978). In monkey embryos at midgestation, each ontogenetic column may contain between 80 and 120 neurons stacked on top of one another, separated by intercolumnar spaces. In some areas like the cingulate cortex, where neurogenesis lasts about one month, ontogenetic columns have fewer neurons, whereas the visual cortex, which is produced over almost two months, has columns with a higher number of neurons (Rakic, submitted). However, final numbers of neurons within the columns may be subsequently modified by differential cell death (Finlay and Slattery, 1983).

The total number of proliferative units and the number of units subserving specific cytoarchitectonic areas vary between species and among individuals of the same species. We estimate that in the fetal monkey, the number of proliferative units in the cerebral ventricular zone and the number of ontogenetic columns in the cortical plate may be in the vicinity of 15 to 20 million. In humans, the number is probably ten times higher, while in the rat, probably ten times smaller. The number of ontogenetic columns comprising various areas has not been precisely determined in any species, but it is likely that the average striate cortex in a rhesus monkey contains between 2.5 and 3 million (Rakic, unpublished). These numbers are rough approximations complicated by large individual variations. Subsequent neuronal growth, elaboration of dendrites, ingrowth of afferents, formation of synapses, and proliferation of glial cells distort the initially simple radial organization. Although in most areas the fetal type of radial organization disappears by the time the cortical plate acquires its horizontal lamination, its vestiges can still be discerned in some areas, even in an adult.

Columnar deployment of neurons in the adult neocortex was recognized over fifty years ago (Lorente de No, 1938), but most subsequent research focused on its laminar organization. It was Mountcastle (1957) who established the functional significance of radial organization in the cerebral cortex by discovering that all neurons within a single column respond to the same stimulus. His work revealed that the cortex can be conceived of as a mosaic of interrelated cellular columns concerned with one specific modality (touch, pressure, joint movement, etc.) and with a single point (receptive field) at the periphery (Mountcastle, 1957, 1979). Projections from a given thalamic nucleus or from its parts may terminate in the form of stripes that innervate arrays of ontogenetic columns arranged as "colonnades", or parallel rows of columns (Eccles, 1984; Mountcastle, 1979; Szentagothai, 1978). Similar functional or anatomical columns have been observed in other sensory areas (Hubel and Wiesel, 1977; Jones et al., 1975; Jones, 1981) as well as in association cortex (Goldman and Nauta, 1977; Goldman-Rakic and Schwartz, 1982). However, the present article is not concerned with the columnar terminal fields of thalamic or corticocortical connections. Rather, it is focused on the cohorts of genealogically related neurons that may provide the developmental basis for the columnar organization of neurons and their function in the adult cortex (Rakic, 1978).

Cortex Expands Mainly by Addition of Radial Units

There is little doubt that the neocortical mantle enlarges during evolution by unequal growth of existing cytoarchitectonic areas and by the addition of new ones (e.g. Brodmann, 1909; Ebbesson, 1980; Kaas, 1987; Sanides, 1972). This is accomplished by the addition of ontogenetic columns, which in turn are produced by the proliferative units in the ventricular zone. The hypothesis consistent with our findings is that cells of the proliferative units arise mainly by symmetrical cell divisions, while later they produce cortical cells mainly by asymmetrical divisions. The number of units in each individual, therefore, must be determined early, before the onset of neurogenesis. A single additional round of symmetrical cell divisions at the stage of unit formation would double their number as well as the number of ontogenetic columns that they subsequently produce. Conversely, the number of neurons within the ontogenetic columns depends on the rate of cell production by asymmetrical division in the proliferative units. An additional cell division would increase the number of neurons within a given ontogenetic column by only one. Indeed, the number of cells in ontogenetic columns, reflected in the thickness of the cortex, changes relatively little during evolution (Rockel et al., 1980). It may not be coincidental that the size of the columnated afferent terminal fields in the cortex is relatively constant, even in species with large differences in the cerebral surface (Bugbee and Goldman-Rakic, 1983). Although an increase in the number of ontogenetic columns explains the expansion of the cortical surface as a whole, it does not address the issue of a differential increase in the surface of various cytoarchitectonic areas.

Two basic cellular mechanisms, or their combination, could account for differential expansion of cytoarchitectonic fields. According to one hypothesis, the areal specificity of cortical neurons is rigidly determined within the ventricular zone (i.e. the number of proliferative units devoted to each area is fixed). The differential increase in the number of units producing area-specific columns can be regulated at early embryonic stages by homeosis, meaning the "assumption of one member of a metric series of the form to another member of the series" (Bateson, 1894). More recently, genes that regulate such developmental changes, the so-called homeotic genes, have been demonstrated in a variety of species (Gehring, 1985; Lewis, 1978; Scott, 1984). It is likely that such master genes, at later stages, control production of neuronal phenotypes within the proliferative units, thereby generating variations on the common neural pattern in ontogenetic columns subserving individual cytoarchitectonic areas. Therefore, regulatory genes may preserve an evolutionary component and provide instruction both for duplication and for changes in the mosaic of proliferative units at the ventricular surface.

An alternative possibility is that the real positions and modal specificity of neurons are not determined in the proliferative units, and that their phenotype and function are decided later by the type of input they receive from the periphery via the thalamus (Creutzfeldt, 1977; Mountcastle, 1957). Although this hypothesis provides a logical and attractive explanation for the diversification of cytoarchitectonic areas, it is difficult to reconcile it with a variety of evidence indicating that the information from the receptors of the periphery cannot be the sole determinant of cortical areas. For example, the basic pattern of geniculocortical connections is present not only before the formation of contacts with the retinal receptors (Nishimura and Rakic, 1986), but they develop appropriate topography and are maintained in the absence of both eyes (Olivaria and van Sluyters, 1984; Rakic, 1988; Rakic and Williams, 1986). Results of these and other studies, some of which are reviewed in preceding sections, indicate that certain areal markers must be present in the cortical plate independently of input from the periphery.

There is a third possibility which combines features from both above-mentioned hypotheses and is compatible with most of the available information. According to the radial unit model, proliferation units produce area-specific ontogenetic columns, but their final number devoted to a given area can be adjusted downward by a complex input/ output relationship. This model would be in general accord with the theories of selective stabilization (Changeux and Danchin, 1976), neuronal group selection (Edelman and Finkel, 1984), and competitive elimination (Rakic, 1986), which were proposed to explain the fine tuning of synaptic connections within a given system. We are now at a point where the various hypotheses proposed for cortical parcellation can be experimentally tested.

Experimental Manipulation of Cytoarchitectonic Areas

To distinguish between mechanisms of cortical parcellation discussed in the preceding section, a number of axons in a specific thalamocortical or corticocortical system should be altered at early embryonic stages and the effect on cortical areas examined. We have recently found that binocular enucleation performed on monkey embryos in the first half of gestation provides a useful test of the role thalamic afferents may play in the regulation of cytoarchitectonic fields. When enucleation is performed around E60, after all neurons of the lateral geniculate nucleus have been generated, but prior to ingrowth of their axons into the developing cortical plate (Rakic, 1977), this thalamic nucleus comes to contain less than one-half of the neurons present in the age-matched controls (Rakic, submitted; Rakic and Williams 1986; Rakic, unpublished). The occipital lobe in enucleated animals displays dramatic changes in the pattern of convolutions but has topographically well-defined residual connections with the diminished lateral geniculate nucleus. Since geniculocortical axons project to the striate cortex in a predictable manner (figure 6.2A), the presence of fewer fibers during corticogenesis could affect the size of the primary visual cortex in at least three ways: (a) the number and height of the ontogenetic columns may remain the same as in controls, resulting in dilution of geniculocortical afferents (figure 6.2B); (b) the number of columns devoted to area 17 could remain the same, but their height may be diminished by the process of second order transneuronal degeneration (figure 6.2C); (c) the number of ontogenetic columns can be reduced, while their height (i.e. the number of cells in each column) remains the same (figure 6.2D).

The results support the model illustrated in figure 6.2D. The striate cortex in enucleates was well-defined by a sharp border with the adjacent area, indicating that a morphological distinction between them develops in the absence of any information from the retina. Most unexpectedly, the thickness of the striate cortex and its characteristic complement of layers and sublayers was within the normal range (Rakic, 1988; Rakic and Williams, 1986). However, most importantly, the area of the striate cortex in enucleates was less than half the size it was in the age-matched controls. Thus, despite the absence of retinal input to the lateral geniculate nucleus and the severely reduced number of geniculocortical afferents, the striate cortex had the normal number of neurons per layer and per ontogenetic column, while the total number of neurons in the area and its surface was diminished in proportion to the loss of geniculate neurons (Rakic, 1988; Rakic and Williams, 1986; Rakic, unpublished). The method of this reduction is not understood, and our working hypotheses are

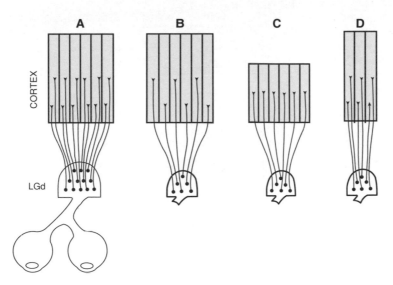

Figure 6.2 Schematic of the possible consequences of diminished afferent input to the visual cortex from the dorsal lateral geniculate nucleus (LGd) in animals binocularly enucleated at early embryonic stages. The normal numerical relationship between geniculocortical projections and ontogenetic columns in the cortex schematically illustrated in A can be altered in three basic ways (B, C, D), discussed in the text.

illustrated in figure 6.3: the striate cortex (area 17) can simply lose a number of ontogenetic columns, diminishing the total size of the cortex (figure 6.3B). Alternatively, the prestriate cortex (area 18), which normally receives input from the adjacent thalamic nucleus (pulvinar) and from the other parietal and temporal cortices, could take over some of the territory from area 17 (figure 6.3C). Finally, a number of columns that were specified for area 17 (X in figure 6.3D) could, in the absence of normal afferents, receive input from the pulvinar and other cortical areas, thus becoming a new cytoarchitectonic area that is genetically striate (area 17) and connectionally prestriate (area 18). Our preliminary data favor the last hypothesis (figure 6.3D), but additional experiments need to be done.

So far, results obtained from our experiments are in harmony with the observation that the human left cerebral hemisphere with a larger auditory cortex also has a larger medial geniculate nucleus (Eidelberg and Galaburda, 1982). Finally, it may be relevant to mention that the laminar distribution of major neurotransmitter receptors within the striate area in early enucleated monkeys retains the appropriate pattern (Rakic et al., 1987), and that synaptic density within each layer, as revealed by quantitative electron microscopy, develops within the normal range (Bourgeois and Rakic, 1987). Thus, our data demonstrate that the number of specific thalamic afferents affects the final number of ontogenetic columns in the corresponding cortical area, but does not alter the number of neurons within each ontogenetic column or their phenotype.

Thalamic regulation may be only part of a more complex interactive process that occurs during development and parcellation of the neocortex. Prenatal resection of the fetal cortex, which eliminates or decreases specific corticocortical input to the subplate at early stages, has a profound effect on the gyral pattern and anatomy of the other, unoperated areas on both sides (Goldman-Rakic, 1980; Goldman-Rakic and Rakic, 1984; Rakic, 1988). On the

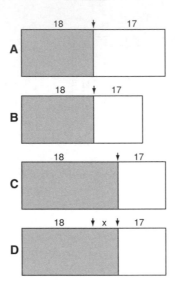

Figure 6.3 Schematic of the relationship between the striate (area 17) and prestriate (area 18) cortex in a normal animal (A) and the possible mechanisms responsible for the reduction of area 17 in binocular enucleates (B–D): the striate cortex can be diminished by differential cell death due to diminished input (B); encroachment of area 18 into its territory (C); or by formation of a new area (X), which is genetically striate but receives input characteristic for area 18 (D). Further explanation in the text.

basis of experiments in other systems, one can predict that multiple inputs to a given cytoarchitectonic area could have an effect on its final size. For example, we have found that initially overproduced retinogeniculate axons compete for their territory and for their survival (Rakic, 1981; Rakic and Riley, 1983). This can be demonstrated by early monocular enucleation, as graphically presented in figure 6.4A–C. In this series of experiments we found that by midgestation, about 3 million axons originating from each eye terminate in an overlapping manner in the lateral geniculate nucleus, but that their number diminished during the period of segregation to about 1.2 million. However, if one eye is removed at the stage of retinogeniculate overlap, the remaining eye retains a larger number of ganglion cells and their axons than it otherwise would, but this number is still smaller than the sum of two normal eyes (Rakic and Riley, 1983).

Our preliminary data indicate that the same general principle of competitive elimination may apply for cortical areas that share some common synaptic targets during development (figure 6.4D, E). For example, unilateral resection of the occipital cortex at midgestational periods results in an enlarged inferior parietal lobule on the side of the lesion (Goldman-Rakic and Rakic, 1984; Rakic, unpublished). One hypothesis to explain this dramatic result is that supernumerary cells in the parietal lobe may survive in the absence of competition with projections from the occipital lobe in the subcortical structures, or in the other cortical areas with which they share common synaptic targets (Figure 6.4D, E). Another hypothesis is that input from the remaining areas spreads to the territories normally occupied by the removed region. In cortical ablation experiments and in thalamic reduction experiments (described above), ontogenetic columns genetically specified for one area receive afferents characteristic of another area. As a result, we may have experimentally created a new

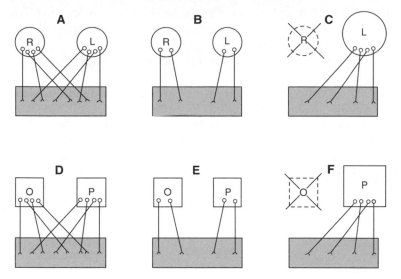

Figure 6.4 Diagrammatic representation of the model of competitive interaction between structures with supernumerary projections that share common synaptic targets (shaded boxes). A, Projections from the right (R) and left (L) eye to the brain are initially overproduced and intermixed. B, These projections become segregated by competitive elimination during normal development. C, Removal of the competition from one eye at the critical period results in retention of a larger number of neurons and axons in the remaining eye. Views D–F are diagrammatic representations of the similar type of competitive interaction that may occur between neurons of the occipital (O) and parietal cortex (P) which share a common synaptic target during embryogenesis. Further explanation in the text.

cytoarchitectonic area that could contain different synaptoarchitecture. This is an important goal of future research as it may hold a key to understanding how new cytoarchitectonic areas may be introduced during evolution.

Reorganization of Cortical Representation Within Areas

Development and modifiability of the cortical representation is related, but is a somewhat different issue since it involves the intra-areal changes in maps (within a single area), rather than inter-areal changes (between different areas). Nevertheless, the results of intercortical manipulation in nonhuman primates are in general agreement with the "intracortical principles of magnification", according to which more densely innervated parts of the periphery have a larger representation in the somatosensory (Woolsey et al., 1942), visual (Daniel and Whitteridge, 1961), and auditory (Suga and Jen, 1976) areas. For example, in the trigeminal system in rodents, the number of sensory axons innervating a given vibrissal follicle and the size of the corresponding barrel in the cortex are closely correlated (Lee and Woolsey, 1975; van der Loos, 1979). Manipulation of the size of trigeminal innervation by a neonatal lesion in neighboring follicles or by selective inbreeding of mice with an "extra" whisker indicate that the "size of the somatory map and of its parts, while relating to the number of nerve fibers innervating the corresponding sensory periphery, is not an invariable function of it" (Welker and van der Loos, 1986). Recently, it has been shown that the forepaw and hindpaw representations in the somatosensory map also can be changed by damage to the periphery in newborn rodents (Dawson and, Killackey 1987; Seo and Ito, 1987). Likewise, peripheral nerve injury in developing rats changes the representational pattern in the motor cortex (Danoghue and Sanes, 1987).

Physiologically defined shifts in the borders of somatosensory representations have also been demonstrated in adult monkeys and cats. For example, peripheral nerve transection or digit amputation in adult primates (Merzenich et al., 1983) alters the borders between areas representing these digits. Likewise, in adult cats elimination of thalamic input to the motor cortex results in the reorganization of corticocortical projections (Asanuma et al., 1985). Although no anatomical substrate has thus far been demonstrated for these changes, they indicate considerable competitive interaction among various cortical connections in the adult cortex. Data from such a heterogeneous set of experimental results obtained by different methods in various species are not easily comparable and are still far from being conclusive. Nevertheless, they support the notion that, although areal specificity and representation of the periphery may be already indicated at the time of cell production within the proliferative zone, the final number of ontogenetic columns devoted to a given receptive field or area may be to some extent regulated by competitive interaction among participating neurons.

Radial Unit Model Can Explain the Pattern of Some Human Cortical Malformations

Another source of evidence supporting the radial unit hypothesis comes from the pattern of major cortical malformations in humans. Among abnormalities of the cortical mantle caused by defective proliferation and/or migration of cortical neurons, lissencephaly and polymicrogyria are the most prominent (reviewed in Volpe, 1981). There are several variations of these two basic types of malformations but in general, lissencephalic brains have a smooth cerebral surface, diminished total area, and approximately normal cortical thickness, whereas polymicrogyria is characterized by a highly convoluted cerebrum with nearly normal surface area, and thin cortex (Richman et al., 1974; Volpe, 1981). Since the etiology of these two malformations is a mystery, their classification in the past has been based on the appearance of the cortex at the time of death.

These types of cortical malformation can now be classified into two major categories on the basis of developmental mechanisms outlined by the radial unit hypothesis. The first category consists of malformations in which the number of ontogenetic columns in the cortex is diminished, while the number of neurons within each ontogenetic column remains relatively normal. The second category consists of malformations in which the number of ontogenetic columns in the cortex remains normal, while the number of neurons within each column is diminished. Although most malformations predominantly display features of one or the other of these two categories, some are a mixture of both types.

It can be expected that the first category is the result of an early defect that occurs at the time when proliferative units are being formed within the cerebral ventricular zone. The defect in this case should precede the onset of neurogenesis and therefore probably occurs in humans within the first seven weeks of gestation. Once the number of proliferative units in the ventricular zone has been established, each unit produces the usual number of neurons that form ontogenetic columns of normal height. As a result, the cortex has normal thickness but a smaller surface.

The defect in the second category of malformations begins after the normal number of proliferative units have been established. This defect should, therefore, occur after the seventh week of gestation, and should not greatly affect the number of ontogenetic columns. However, it can be expected that it affects the number of neurons produced within each proliferative unit. As a result, ontogenetic columns should have fewer neurons and consequently a thinner cortex. It should be emphasized that a smaller number of cells in the ontogenetic columns could be the result of low production in the proliferative unit, subsequent cell death, or a failure of their migration. In the latter case, some cortical neurons may survive in ectopic positions within the white matter, as frequently occurs in polymicrogyric brains (Volpe, 1981). Although the proposed classification of cortical malformations does not address the issue of their primary etiology, it suggests possible developmental mechanisms and delineates the timing and sequence of cellular events. The pattern of cortical malformations, on the other hand, supports the radial unit hypothesis by exposing the possible consequences of defects occurring during the stages when proliferative units or columns are forming.

Unsolved Questions and Future Prospects

The *radial unit model* can explain how the immense cellular mass of the neocortex disperses so that postmitotic cells generated near the cerebral ventricle find their final laminar and regional positions in appropriate cytoarchitectonic areas with species-specific and individual-specific differences in their size. This model assumes that cortical areas are the end-product of genetic information that can be modified by epigenetic variables. Advances in genetic and experimental manipulation of cortical development provide an opportunity to examine the validity of the radial unit model of cortical parcellation, and to determine the role of intrinsic and extrinsic factors in regulating the size of cytoarchitectonic areas. Furthermore, the fact that the radial unit model is consistent with the observed pattern of cortical abnormalities in major cortical malformations allows its validation at the genetic level.

Although the proposed model and its experimental testing have settled some issues, it has also led to a new set of questions. For example, we have learned that the number of radial columns devoted to the striate area can be altered by manipulation of the input it receives, but we do not understand the mechanisms involved in this regulatory process (figure 6.3). We do not even have some rather basic facts. For example, is the area of the striate cortex in early enucleates diminished by differential neuronal elimination, or by a shifting of the adjacent peristriate area into the territory normally occupied by the striate columns? If the latter possibility is the case, should this region be considered an enlarged area 18, or a new type of cortex which has input appropriate for area 18, but ontogenetic columns appropriate for area 17? What is the pattern of connectivity and what is the function of this artificially formed cortical area? What is the best research strategy to mark the embryonic site of the prospective areal borders before afferents invade the cortical plate and cytoarchitectonic characteristics emerge? Modern methods and research strategies using a combination of prenatal neurosurgery, transgenetic animals, cDNA and mRNA probes, or retrovirus-mediated gene transfer to label and to follow the progeny of neuronal clones from the site of their origin in the proliferative units to their final positions in the ontogenetic columns promise to provide further testing of the radial unit model of cortical development.

ACKNOWLEDGMENTS

This work from the author's laboratory was supported by grants NS14841, EY02593, and Program Project NS22807.

REFERENCES

Allman, J. (1986). Maps in context: some analogies between visual cortical and genetic maps. In *Matters of Intelligence*, ed. L. Vaina, pp. 347–70. Holland: Reidel.

Angevine, J. B. Jr. and Sidman, R. L. (1961). Autoradiographic study of cell migration during histogenesis of cerebral cortex in the mouse. *Nature* 192: 766–8.

Asanuma, H., Kosar, E., Tsukuhora, N., and Robinson, H. (1985). Modification of the projection from the sensory cortex to the motor cortex following the elimination of thalamic projections to the motor cortex in cat. *Brain Res.* 345: 79–86.

Bateson, W. (1894). *Materials for the Study of Variation Treated with Especial Regard to Discontinuity in the Origin of the Species.* London: Macmillan.

Berry, M. and Rogers, A. W. (1965). The migration of neuroblasts in the developing cortex. *J. Anat.* 99: 691–709.

Bourgeois, J.-P. and Rakic, P. (1987). Distribution, density and ultrastructure of synapses in the visual cortex in monkeys devoid of retinal input from early embryonic stages. *Soc. Neurosci. Abst.* 13: 1044.

Brodmann, K. (1909). *Lokalisationslehre der Grosshirnrinde in ihren Principien dargestellt auf Grund des Zellenbaue.* Leipzig: Barth.

Bugbee, N. M. and Goldman-Rakic, P. S. (1983). Columnar organization of corticocortical projections in squirrel and rhesus monkeys: similarity of column width in species differing in cortical volume. *J. Comp. Neurol.* 220: 355–64.

Caviness, V. S. Jr. and Rakic, P. (1978). Mechanisms of cortical development: a view from mutations in mice. *Ann. Rev. Neurosci.* 1: 297–326.

Changeux, J.-P. and Danchin, A. (1976). Selective stabilization of developing synapses as a mechanism for the specialization of neural network. *Nature* 264: 705–12.

Chun, J. J., Nakamura, M. J., and Shatz, C. J. (1987). Transient cells of the developing mammalian telencephalon are peptide-immunoreactive neurons. *Nature* 325: 617–20.

Creutzfeldt, O. D. (1977). Generality of the functional structure of the neocortex. *Naturwissenschaften* 64: 507–17.

Daniel, P. M. and Whitteridge, D. (1961). The representation of the visual field on the cerebral cortex in monkeys. *J. Physiol.* 159: 203–21.

Danoghue, J. P. and Sanes, J. N. (1987). Peripheral nerve injury in developing rats reorganizes representation pattern in motor cortex. *Proc. Natl Acad. Sci. USA* 84: 1123–6.

Dawson, D. R. and Killackey, H. P. (1987). The organization and mutability of the forepaw and hindpaw representations in the somatosensory cortex of the neonatal rat. *J. Comp. Neurol.* 256: 246–56.

Ebbesson, S. O. E. (1980). The parcellation theory and its relation to interspecific variability in brain organization, evolutionary and ontogenetic development, and neuronal plasticity. *Cell Tissue Res.* 213: 179–212.

Eccles, J. C. (1984). The cerebral neocortex. A theory of its operation. In *Cerebral Cortex, vol. 2,* eds E. G. Jones and A. Peters, pp. 1–36. New York: Plenum.

Edelman, G. M. (1983). Cell adhesion molecules. *Science* 219: 450–57.

Edelman, G. M. and Finkel, L. H. (1984). Neuronal group selection in the cerebral cortex. In *Dynamic Aspects of Neocortical Function*, eds G. M. Edelman, E. W. Gall, and W. M. Cowan, pp. 653–94. New York: Wiley & Sons.

Eidelberg, D. and Galaburda, A. M. (1982). Symmetry and asymmetry in the human posterior thalamus. *Arch. Neurol.* 39: 325–32.

Finlay, B. L. and Slattery, M. (1983). Local differences in the amount of early cell death in neocortex predict adult local specialization. *Science* 219: 1349–51.

Gehring, W. J. (1985). The homeobox: a key to the understanding of development. *Cell* 40: 3–5.

Goffinet, A. M., Doumierie, C., Langerwerf, B., and Pieau, C. (1986). Neurogenesis in reptilian cortical structures: ^{3}H-thymidine autoradiographic analysis. *J. Comp. Neurol.* 243: 106–16.

Goldman, P. S. and Nauta, W. J. H. (1977). Columnar organization of association and motor cortex: autoradiographic evidence for cortico-cortical and commissural columns in the frontal lobe of the newborn rhesus monkey. *Brain Res.* 122: 369–85.

Goldman-Rakic, P. S. (1980). Morphological consequences of prenatal injury to the primate brain. *Prog. Brain Res.* 53: 3–19.

Goldman-Rakic, P. S. (1981). Development and plasticity of primate frontal association cortex. In *The Organization of the Cerebral Cortex*, eds F. O. Schmitt, F. G. Worden, S. G. Dennis, and G. Adelman, pp. 69–97. Cambridge, MA: MIT Press.

Goldman-Rakic, P. S. and Rakic, P. (1984). Experimental modification of gyral patterns. In *Cerebral Dominance: The Biological Foundation*, eds N. Geschwind and A. M. Galaburda, pp. 179–92. Cambridge, MA: Harvard Univ. Press.

Goldman-Rakic, P. S. and Schwartz, M. L. (1982). Interdigitation of contralateral and ipsilateral columnar projections to frontal association cortex in primates. *Science* 216: 755–7.

Hatten, M. E. and Mason, C. A. (1986). Neuron-astroglia interactions in vitro and in vivo. *Trends Neurosci.* 9: 168–74.

Herrup, K. (1986). Cell lineage relationship in the development of the mammalian central nervous system: role of cell lineage in control of cerebellar Purkinje cell number. *Dev. Biol.* 115: 148–54.

His, W. (1904). *Die Entwicklung des menschlichen Gehirns während der ersten Monate.* Leipzig: Hirzel.

Hubel, D. H. and Wiesel, T. N. (1977). Ferrier lecture. Functional architecture of macaque monkey visual cortex. *Proc. R. Soc. Lond. B.* 198: 1–59.

Jensen, K. F. and Killackey, H. P. (1984). Subcortical projections from ectopic neocortical neurons. *Proc. Natl Acad. Sci. USA* 81: 964–8.

Jones, E. G. (1981). Anatomy of cerebral cortex: columnar input-output organization. In *The Organization of the Cerebral Cortex*, eds F. O. Schmitt, F. G. Warden, G. Adelman, and S. G. Dennis, pp. 199–235. Cambridge, MA: MIT Press.

Jones, E. G., Burton, H., and Porter, R. (1975). Commissural and cortico-cortical "columns" in the somatic sensory cortex of primates. *Science* 190: 572–4.

Kaas, J. H. (1987). The organization and evolution of neocortex. In *Higher Brain Functions*, ed. S. P. Wise.

Kaplan, M. S. (1981). Neurogenesis in the 3-month-old rat visual cortex. *J. Comp. Neurol.* 195: 323–38.

Koelliker, A. (1896). *Handbuch der Gewebelehre des Menschen. Vol. 2, Nervensystem des Menschen und der Thiere.* Leipzig: W. Engelmann.

Kostovic, I. and Rakic, P. (1980). Cytology and time of origin of interstitial neurons in the white matter in infant and adult human and monkey telencephalon. *J. Neurocytol.* 9: 219–42.

Lee, K. J. and Woolsey, T. A. (1975). A proportional relationship between peripheral innervation density and cortical neuron number in the somatosensory system of the mouse. *Brain Res.* 99: 349–53.

Levitt, P., Cooper, M. L., and Rakic, P. (1983). Early divergence and changing proportions of neuronal and glial precursor cells in the primate cerebral ventricular zone. *Dev. Biol.* 96: 472–84.

Lewis, E. B. (1978). A gene complex controlling segmentation in *Drosophila*. *Nature* 276: 565–70.

Lindner, J., Rathjen, F. G., and Schachner, M. (1983). LI mono- and polyclonal antibodies modify cell migration in early postnatal mouse cerebellum. *Nature* 305: 427–30.

Lorente de No, R. (1938). Architectonic structure of the cerebral cortex. In *Physiology of the Nervous System*, ed. J. F. Fulton, pp. 291–339. London: Oxford Univ. Press.

Luskin, M. B. and Shatz, C. J. (1985). Neurogenesis of the cat's primary visual cortex. *J. Comp. Neurol.* 242: 611–31.

McConnell, S. K. (1985). Migration and differentiation of cerebral cortical neurons after transplantation into brain of ferrets. *Science* 229: 1268–71.

McConnell, S. K. (1987). Fates of transplanted visual cortical neurons. Thesis. Cambridge, MA: Harvard Univ.

Merzenich, M. M., Kaas, J. H., Wall, J., Nelson, R. J., Sur, M., and Fellman, D. J. (1983). Topographic reorganization of somatosensory cortical areas 3b and 1 in adult monkeys following restricted deafferentiation. *Neurosci.* 8: 33–55.

Morata, G. and Lawrence, A. (1977). Homeotic genes, compartments and cell determination in *Drosophila*. *Nature* 265: 211–16.

Mountcastle, V. B. (1957). Modality and topographic properties of single neurons of cat's somatic sensory cortex. *J. Neurophysiol.* 20: 408–34.

Mountcastle, V. B. (1979). An organizing principle for cerebral function: the unit module and the distributed system. In *The Neurosciences: Fourth Study Program*, eds F. O. Schmitt and F. G. Worden, pp. 21–42. Cambridge, MA: MIT Press.

Nishimura, Y. and Rakic, P. (1986). Development of the rhesus monkey retina. II. Three dimensional analysis of microcircuitry in the inner plexiform layer. *J. Comp. Neurol.* 241: 420–34.

Olivaria, J. and van Sluyters, R. C. (1984). Callosal connections of the posterior neocortex in normal-eyed, congenitally anophthalmic, and neonatally enucleated mice. *J. Comp. Neurol.* 230: 249–68.

Rakic, P. (1972a). Extrinsic cytological determinants of basket and stellate cell dendritic pattern in the cerebellar molecular layer. *J. Comp. Neurol.* 146: 335–54.

Rakic, P. (1972b). Mode of cell migration to the superficial layers of fetal monkey neocortex. *J. Comp. Neurol.* 145: 61–84.

Rakic, P. (1974). Neurons in rhesus monkey visual cortex: systematic relation between time of origin and eventual disposition. *Science* 183: 425–7.

Rakic, P. (1977). Prenatal development of the visual system in the rhesus monkey. *Phil. Trans. R. Soc. Lond. B* 278: 245–60.

Rakic, P. (1978). Neuronal migration and contact guidance in primate telencephalon. *Postgrad. Med. J.* 54: 25–40.

Rakic, P. (1981). Development of visual centers in primate brain depends on binocular competition before birth. *Science* 214: 928–31.

Rakic, P. (1985). Limits of neurogenesis in primates. *Science* 227: 154–6.

Rakic, P. (1986). Mechanisms of ocular dominance segregation in the lateral geniculate nucleus: competitive elimination hypothesis. *Trends Neurosci.* 9: 11–15.

Rakic, P. (1988). Specification of neocortical areas: radial unit hypothesis. *Science*, in press.

Rakic, P. and Goldman-Rakic, P. S. (1982). Development and modifiability of the cerebral cortex. *Neurosci. Res. Prog. Bull.* (Edited volume for MIT Press, Cambridge, MA) 20: 429–611.

Rakic, P. and Goldman-Rakic, P. S. (1985). Use of fetal neurosurgery for experimental studies of structural and functional brain development in nonhuman primates. In *Prenatal Neurology and Neurosurgery*, eds R. A. Thompson and J. R. Green, pp. 1–15. New York: Spectrum Press.

Rakic, P., Kritzer, M., and Gallager, D. (1987). Distribution of major neurotransmitter receptors in visual cortex of monkeys deprived of retinal input from early embryonic stages. *Soc. Neurosci. Abst.* 13: 358.

Rakic, P. and Riley, K. P. (1983). Regulation of axon number in primate optic nerve by binocular competition. *Nature* 305: 135–7.

Rakic, P. and Williams, R. W. (1986). Thalamic regulation of cortical parcellation: an experimental perturbation of the striate cortex in rhesus monkeys. *Soc. Neurosci. Abst.* 12: 1499.

Ramon y Cajal, S. (1911). *Histologie du Système Nerveux de l'Homme et des Vertèbres. Reprinted by Consejo Superior de Investigaciones Científicas*. Paris: Maloine.

Richman, D. P., Stewart, R. M., and Caviness, V. S. Jr. (1974). Cerebral microgyria in a 27 week fetus: an architectonic and topographic analysis. *J. Neuropath. Exp. Neur.* 33: 374–84.

Rockel, A. J., Hiorns, R. W., and Powell, T. P. S. (1980). The basic uniformity in structure of the neocortex. *Brain* 103: 221–44.

Rose, J. E. and Woolsey, C. N. (1949). The relations of thalamic connections, cellular structure and evocable electrical activity in the auditory region of the cat. *J. Comp. Neurol.* 91: 441–66.

Sanides, F. (1972). Representation in the cerebral cortex and its areal lamination patterns. In *Structure and Function of Nervous Tissue, vol. 5*, ed. G. H. Bourne, pp. 329–453. New York: Raven.

Schmechel, D. E. and Rakic, P. (1979). Arrested proliferation of radial glial cells during midgestation in rhesus monkey. *Nature* 277: 303–5.

Schwartz, M. L. and Goldman-Rakic, P. S. (1986). Some callosal neurons of the fetal monkey frontal cortex have axons in the contralateral hemisphere prior to the completion of migration. *Soc. Neurosci. Abst.* 12: 1211.

Scott, M. P. (1984). Homeotic gene transcripts in the neural tissue of insects. *Trends Neurosci.* 7: 221–3.

Seo, M. L. and Ito, M. (1987). Reorganization of rat vibrissa barrelfield as studied by cortical lesioning on different postnatal days. *Exp. Brain. Res.* 65: 251–60.

Shatz, C. J. and Luskin, M. B. (1986). The relationship between the geniculocortical afferents and their cortical target cells during development of the cat's primary visual cortex. *J. Neurosci.* 6: 3655–68.

Sidman, R. L. and Rakic, P. (1973). Neuronal migration, with special reference to developing human brain: a review. *Brain Res.* 62: 1–35.

Smart, I. H. M. and McSherry, G. M. (1982). Growth patterns in the lateral wall of the mouse telencephalon: II. Histological changes during and subsequent to the period of isocortical neuron production. *J. Anat.* 134: 415–42.

Smart, I. H. and Smart, M. (1982). Growth patterns in the lateral wall of the mouse telencephalon: I. Autoradiographic studies of the histogenesis of the isocortex and adjacent areas. *J. Anat.* 134: 273–98.

Suga, N. and Jen, P. H.-S. (1976). Disproportionate tonotopic representation for processing species-specific CF-FM sonar signals in the mustached auditory cortex. *Science* 194: 542–4.

Szentagothai, J. (1978). The neuronal network of the cerebral cortex: a functional interpretation. *Proc. R. Soc. Lond. B* 201: 219–48.

van der Loos, H. (1979). The development of topographical equivalences in the brain. In *Neural Growth and Differentiation*, eds. E. Meisami and M. A. B. Braizer, pp. 331–6. New York: Raven Press.

Vignal, W. (1888). Recherches sur le développement des éléments des couches corticales du cerveau et du cervelet chez l'homme et les mammifères. *Arch. Physiol. Norm. Path. (Paris) Ser. IV* 2: 228–54.

Volpe, J. J. (1981). *Neurology of the Newborn*. Philadelphia: Saunders.

Welker, E. and van der Loos, H. (1986). Quantitative correlation between barrelfield size and the sensory innervation of the whisker pad: a comparative study in six strains of mice bred for different patterns of mystacial vibrissae. *J. Neurosci.* 6: 3355–73.

Woolsey, C. N., Marshall, W. H., and Bard, P. (1942). Representation of cutaneous tactile sensibility in the cerebral cortex of the monkey as indicated by evoked potentials. *Bull. Johns Hopk. Hosp.* 70: 399–441.

7

Positron Emission Tomography Study of Human Brain Functional Development

Harry T. Chugani, Michael E. Phelps *and* John C. Mazziotta

During development, the brain undergoes the sequential anatomical, functional, and organizational changes necessary to support the complex adaptive behavior of a fully mature normal individual. The delineation of developmental changes occuring in different brain regions would provide a means of relating various behavioral phenomena to maturation of specific brain structures, thereby enhancing our understanding of structure–function relationships in both normal and disease states.

One approach to the study of these relationships has been to measure regional substrate utilization at different stages of cerebral maturation. Since the principal brain substrates for energy production are glucose and oxygen, the determination of their regional alterations would provide a measure of the local energy requirement for maintenance processes and functional activity. This approach has been used in the study of brain–behavior relationships in various animal models [1, 18, 31], and has generated important concepts in our understanding of brain function. Alternatively, because of the close relationship between local cerebral blood flow (lCBF) and local cerebral metabolic rate under normal conditions [54], an indirect assessment of local functional activity can also be obtained by the measurement of lCBF during development [4, 29, 30, 43].

The development of positron emission tomography (PET) [47], which employs tracer kinetic measurements of compounds labelled with positron-emitting isotopes [48, 49], has enabled us to apply directly the regional substrate utilization approach in studying human brain development. Using 2-deoxy-2{^{18}F}fluoro-D-glucose (FDG) and PET, we have measured local cerebral metabolic rates for glucose (lCMRGlc) in infants and children during postnatal brain development.

In an earlier communication [6], we used relative measures of lCMRGlc to determine the temporal relationship of human functional development during the first 18 months of life. These studies demonstrated that the order of functional development, from the relatively earlier maturation of phylogenetically older brain structures to the later maturation of newer structures, is in general agreement with behavioral, neurophysiological, and anatomical alterations known to accompany infant development. We now report absolute values of lCMRGlc for different brain regions from birth to adolescence and compare them with normal adult values.

"Positron Emission Tomography Study of Human Brain Functional Development" first appeared in *Annals of Neurology* 22 (1987), pp. 487–97, and is reprinted by kind permission.

Table 7.1 Patient summary

Age, Sex	Clinical information	Laboratory data	Medication on day of study	Period of follow-up after onset of neurological event
5 days, M	42 weeks gestation; mild fetal distress; Apgar scores 2 at 1 minute, 8 at 5 minutes; seizures on days 1 and 2	EEG multifocal spikes, CT scan normal	Phenobarbital	24 months
5 weeks, M	Tonic seizures at age 4 weeks	EEG normal, CT scan normal	Phenobarbital	16 months
8 weeks, F	Onset of myoclonic jerks at age 2 weeks	EEG normal, CT scan normal	None	4 months
13.5 weeks, F	Asymptomatic, left facial port-wine nevus (? Sturge–Weber syndrome)	EEG normal, CT scan normal	None	22 months
4 months, M	Normal birth; one seizure on day 1, none since	EEG normal, CT scan normal	Phenobarbital	17 months
6.25 months, F	Onset of seizures at age 5 months	EEG normal, CT and MRI scans normal	Phenobarbital	3 months
7.6 months, M	Opsoclonus and myoclonus developed at age 6.5 months, responded well to adrenocorticotropic hormone	EEG paroxysmal generalized spike and wave activity, CT scan normal	Phenobarbital, clonazepam	22 months
1 year, F	Asymptomatic, left facial port-wine nevus (? Sturge–Weber syndrome)	EEG normal, CT scan normal	None	32 months
1.5 years, F	Glaucoma OS, bilateral facial port-wine nevi (? Sturge–Weber syndrome)	EEG normal	None	36 months
1.5 years, M	Glaucoma OD, right facial port-wine nevus (? Sturge–Weber syndrome)	EEG normal, CT scan normal	None	27 months
1.6 years, M	Onset of apneic episodes at age 9 months	EEG normal, CT scan normal	None	18 months
3.5 years, F	Onset of seizures at age 1.5 years	EEG normal, CT scan normal	Carbamazepine	26 months
3.7 years, F	Complex febrile seizures	EEG normal	Phenobarbital	43 months
5.7 years, F	Onset of rolandic epilepsy at age 2.5 years	EEG right centrotemporal spike-wave discharges, CT scan normal	Carbamazepine	4 years

Continued overleaf

Table 7.1 Continued

6.7 years, M	Episodic generalized paresthesias (? seizures)	EEG normal, CT and MRI scans normal	None	11 months
6.8 years, M	Visual hallucinations beginning at age 5.5 years	EEG normal, CT and MRI scans normal	Carbamazepine, clorazepate	18 months
7 years, F	2 grand mal seizures at age 5 years	EEG normal, CT scan normal	Carbamazepine	34 months
7.1 years, F	A single nocturnal seizure at age 7 years	EEG infrequent right centrotemporal spike-wave discharges, CT scan normal	Carbamazepine	5 months
7.2 years, M	15 episodes of tunnel vision at age 7 years	EEG normal, CT and MRI scans normal	None	18 months
7.5 years, F	Onset of complex partial seizures at age 6 years	EEG occasional generalized spike-wave discharges, CT and MRI scans normal	Phenobarbital carbamazepine	24 months
8.4 years, M	Rolandic seizures beginning at age 5 years	EEG left centrotemporal spikes, CT scan normal	Phenobarbital	4 years
8.5 years, M	Hypoplastic kidneys, on chronic ambulatory peritoneal dialysis; febrile seizures in infancy (? myoclonic seizures at age 6 years)	EEG generalized irregular spike-wave activity only during sleep, CT scan normal	Clonazepam	32 months
8.6 years, M	Hemolytic–uremic syndrome at age 8 years with convulsion in acute phase	EEG normal, CT scan normal	None	9 months
9.3 years, M	Onset of complex partial seizures at age 9 months, infrequent episodes	EEG normal, CT scan normal	Carbamazepine	7 months
9.5 years, F	Asymptomatic, left facial port-wine nevus (? Sturge–Weber syndrome)	EEG normal, CT scan normal	None	10 years
9.8 years, M	Onset of left simple partial motor seizures at age 3 years	EEG right paracentral spikes, CT and MRI scans normal	Carbamazepine, phenytoin	6 years
12 years, F	Onset of complex partial seizures at age 2 years, infrequent episodes	EEG normal, CT scan normal	Carbamazepine	10 years
13.5 years, M	Onset of complex partial seizures at age 10 years, infrequent episodes	EEG normal, CT scan normal	Carbamazepine	3 years
15.1 years, M	Onset of seizures with migraine at age 11 years	EEG normal, CT scan normal	None	4 years

M = male; F = female; EEG = electroencephalogram; CT = computed tomography; MRI = magnetic resonance imaging; OS = left eye; OD = right eye.

Materials and Methods

Patient population

We have retrospectively selected 29 subjects from over 100 infants and children studied with FDG-PET at UCLA School of Medicine since 1983. Clinical summaries of these 29 children are provided in Table 7.1. Of the 29 individuals, 24 were selected from our research protocol designed to evaluate the role of PET in seizures and epilepsy. Each had suffered transient neurological events not significantly altering neurological development on close follow-up. Informed consent was obtained in all cases. The remaining five subjects were asymptomatic, but because they had facial capillary nevi they were evaluated with FDG-PET for possible Sturge–Weber syndrome. The parents of each of these five subjects were anxious to accept any noninvasive procedure with potential diagnostic value. FDG-PET did not disclose any hemispheric asymmetry of lCMRGlc in any one of these five patients. We believe that these 29 children are reasonably representative of normal children and provide an opportunity to measure lCMRGlc changes during normal brain development, since entirely normal children cannot be studied with PET for ethical reasons. Indeed, the older children in this subpopulation were all attending school and performing well in classes for normal children. Of the infants studied, none had been born prematurely and all continue to develop normally. There were 16 males and 13 females, and their ages ranged from five days to 15.1 years at the time of study. Although 18 of the 29 subjects were taking daily anticonvulsants at the time of PET, none displayed sedation or other side-effects.

PET procedure

All studies were performed in accordance with the policies of the UCLA Human Subject Protection Committee. Subjects were fasted (except for water) for 4 hours prior to PET. One hour prior to the study, golden disk electrodes were applied to the patient's scalp for later electroencephalographic (EEG) monitoring. Then a venous catheter was inserted in a hand vein for blood collection. The blood was arterialized by placing the hand into a water chamber heated to 44°C [48]. Radial arterial catheters were used in three subjects.

FDG (0.143 mCi/kg) was administered intravenously as a pulse at a different site from the catheter, and serial blood samples were collected to determine plasma FDG and glucose concentrations as described elsewhere [48]. In infants younger than two years, microtechniques were employed to minimize total blood collected (5 ml). The dose of FDG was approximately 25 percent lower than that used in adults, and in children results in a whole body radiation exposure of approximately 300 mrads. The dose to the brain is about 500 mrads (as compared to 1–3 rads in X-ray computed tomography).

EEG activity was monitored, and the children were closely observed for seizure activity. The EEG recordings were also useful in the early detection of drowsiness in some children. When a child became drowsy, as evidenced by diminishing amplitude and slowing of EEG activity, he or she was gently tapped on the shoulder to be kept awake and alert. Other than this occasional stimulus, all visual, auditory, and other sensory stimuli were minimized by dimming the lights and discouraging talking and other forms of interaction. Patients' eyes and ears were open during the study.

Forty minutes after FDG injection scanning of the brain was initiated using the NeuroECAT positron tomograph (CTI, Knoxville, TN) with a spatial resolution of 8.4 mm in the plane of section and a 12.4 mm slice thickness [19]. A head holder minimized head movement during scanning [38]. To confirm true axial positioning two rectilinear images (anteroposterior and lateral views) were obtained prior to generating a standard set of 12 tomographic images parallel to the canthomeatal line.

Data analysis

Patterns of lCMRGlc on the PET images were initially assessed by inspection. Then the images were displayed on a display monitor, and regions of interest were drawn for different brain structures using anatomical atlases, patients' CT scans, and standard lCMRGlc functional maps as references [39]. Using the operational equation of Sokoloff and associates [55] as modified by Phelps and associates [48] and Huang and associates [21], lCMRGlc for the different brain regions was then calculated and expressed in μmol/min/ 100 gm. Whenever a brain region appeared on more than one tomographic level, the lCMRGlc value used for that region was a bilateral average (weighted by area) of the values for each tomographic plane where that region appeared. The lumped constant and rate constants employed were those measured previously for normal young adults [21, 48].

The anatomical distribution and absolute values of lCMRGlc in the children were compared to those of adults studied under similar conditions. The latter group consisted of seven young healthy volunteers (aged 19–30 years; mean age 24.4 years; five males, two females) whose detailed neurological and psychological examinations disclosed no abnormalities.

Results

The PET images revealed several distinct patterns of lCMRGlc in the first year of life (figure 7.1) as described below. Although the anatomical distribution of lCMRGlc by one year of age was similar to that of adults, absolute values of lCMRGlc were lower than adult rates (figure 7.2 and table 7.2). Adult rates were reached by approximately two years of age; however, lCMRGlc for all regions measured continued to increase, and by three to four years attained values that exceeded those of adults by a factor of approximately 2 (see table 7.2). These high values of lCMRGlc were maintained until approximately 9 years of age, when they began to decline, and reached adult rates again by the end of the second decade. Although this general pattern of maturational rise and decline of lCMRGlc was seen in all brain regions studied, there were individual differences in the rates of maturation among structures as described below.

Statistical analysis of these data consisted of multiple *t*-tests between age groups for each structure using the Bonferroni adjustment for multiple testing. An acceptance criterion of $p < 0.05$ or better was employed for statistical significance. Although mean lCMRGlc values at one to two years were higher than those from birth to 1 year for all structures (see table 7.2), the differences were not statistically significant at the 5 percent level except for frontal cortex because of the use of multiple testing adjustment. Differences between the birth to one year and three to eight years groups were statistically significant for all structures measured ($p < 0.01$). Differences between the 3 to 8 years and 9 to 15 years

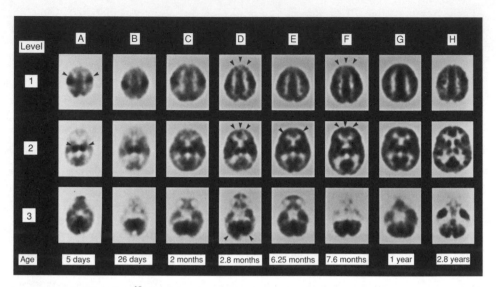

Figure 7.1 2-Deoxy-2$\{^{18}F\}$ fluoro-D-glucose (FDG)-positron emission tomography (PET) images illustrating developmental changes in local cerebral metabolic rates for glucose (lCMRGlc) in the normal human infant with increasing age, as compared to lCMRGlc of the adult (image sizes not on same scale). Level 1 is a superior section, at the level of the cingulate gyrus. Level 2 is more inferior, at the level of caudate, putamen, and thalamus. Level 3 is an inferior section of the brain, at the level of cerebellum and inferior portion of the temporal lobes. Gray scale is proportional to lCMRGlc with black being highest. Images from all subjects are not shown on the same absolute gray scale of lCMRGlc: instead, images of each subject are shown with the full grey scale to maximize grey scale display of lCMRGlc at each age. Changes in absolute lCMRGlc with age appear in figure 7.2 and table 7.2. In each image, the anterior portion of the brain is at the top of the image and the left side of the brain is at the left of the image. (A) In the five-day-old, lCMRGlc is highest in sensorimotor cortex, thalamus, cerebellar vermis (arrows), and brainstem (not shown). (B,C,D) lCMRGlc gradually increases in parietal, temporal, and calcarine cortices: basal ganglia: and cerebellar cortex (arrows), particularly during the second and third months. (E) In the frontal cortex, lCMRGlc increases first in the lateral prefrontal regions by approximately six months. (F) By approximately eight months, lCMRGlc also increases in the medial aspects of the frontal cortex (arrows), as well as the dorsolateral occipital cortex. (G) By one year, the lCMRGlc pattern resembles that of adults (H).

groups were statistically significant ($p < 0.05$) for all structures except the caudate and lenticular nuclei, brainstem, and cerebellum. Comparisons with the adult group were significantly different for the 3 to 8 and 9 to 15 years age groups, except for brainstem and cerebellum (cerebellum showed a significant difference for the 3 to 8 years age group only). Finally, comparisons between adult and 1 to 2 years age groups were not statistically significant throughout.

Cerebral cortex

In the neonatal period (less than 4 weeks of age), the most prominent area of metabolic activity in the cerebral cortex was the primary sensorimotor area (see figure 7.1 A). The

Table 7.2 Local cerebral metabolic rates for glucose[a] (lCMRGlc) in mol/min/100 gm and as a ratio[b] to adult rates for selected brain regions during development

Structure	Birth–1 year (n = 7)		1–2 years (n = 4)		3–8 years (n = 12)		9–15 years (n = 6)		Adult 19–30 years (n = 7)
	lCMRGlc	Ratio	lCMRGlc	Ratio	lCMRGlc	Ratio	lCMRGlc	Ratio	lCMRGlc
Cerebral hemisphere	20.35 ± 1.81	0.84	27.36 ± 3.23	1.13	48.07 ± 1.68	1.98	39.23 ± 0.79	1.62	24.27 ± 1.09
Cerebral cortex									
Frontal cortex	19.68 ± 1.83	0.73	29.65 ± 3.65	1.09	54.01 ± 1.82	1.99	44.59 ± 1.21	1.64	27.11 ± 1.26
Parietal cortex	20.23 ± 1.90	0.84	28.76 ± 3.54	1.19	53.98 ± 1.66	2.24	43.10 ± 1.50	1.78	24.15 ± 1.40
Temporal cortex	20.00 ± 1.60	0.83	28.64 ± 4.27	1.19	48.94 ± 1.69	2.04	40.05 ± 1.31	1.67	23.98 ± 1.15
Occipital cortex	20.54 ± 1.92	0.76	30.39 ± 3.50	1.16	56.35 ± 2.11	2.10	45.66 ± 0.78	1.70	26.85 ± 1.09
Calcarine cortex	22.07 ± 2.20	0.72	32.39 ± 3.55	1.06	61.01 ± 2.22	1.99	50.45 ± 0.35	1.65	30.59 ± 1.15
Sensorimotor cortex	22.17 ± 1.93	0.93	29.73 ± 3.72	1.25	52.85 ± 1.75	2.22	42.04 ± 1.52	1.76	23.83 ± 1.30
Anterior cingulate cortex	20.53 ± 1.85	0.69	29.61 ± 3.20	0.99	55.08 ± 1.88	1.85	45.36 ± 1.01	1.52	29.79 ± 1.33
Transverse temporal cortex	25.47 ± 2.44	0.86	34.00 ± 4.38	1.14	57.25 ± 2.10	1.92	47.00 ± 1.41	1.57	29.86 ± 1.33
Basal ganglia and thalamus									
Caudate (head)	22.95 ± 2.67	0.71	28.77 ± 3.67	0.89	48.86 ± 1.96	1.52	44.76 ± 0.83	1.39	32.20 ± 1.34
Lenticular nuclei	26.42 ± 2.70	0.79	32.36 ± 4.02	0.97	53.08 ± 1.98	1.58	48.15 ± 0.96	1.44	33.50 ± 1.27
Thalamus	27.15 ± 2.97	0.84	29.48 ± 2.95	0.92	49.54 ± 1.71	1.54	43.81 ± 0.28	1.36	32.19 ± 1.96
Cerebellum									
Cerebellar cortex	17.59 ± 1.02	0.93	19.50 ± 2.50	1.03	32.28 ± 1.56	1.71	27.38 ± 0.75	1.45	18.85 ± 0.86
Brainstem	18.63 ± 1.44	0.89	21.17 ± 1.80	1.01	30.74 ± 2.75	1.46	30.61 ± 2.68	1.45	21.04 ± 1.12

a Mean ± SEM
b Ratio to mean adult lCMRGlc

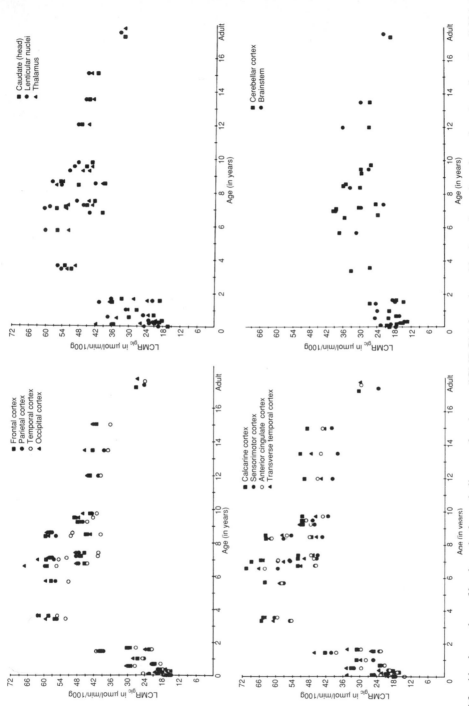

Figure 7.2 Absolute values of local cerebral metabolic rates for glucose (lCMRGlc) for selected brain regions plotted as a function of age for all 29 infants and children, and corresponding adult values. In the infants and children, points represent individual values of lCMRGlc: in adults, points are mean values from seven subjects, in which the size of the symbols equals the standard error of the mean (also see table 7.2). (A, B) Selected regions of cerebral cortex; (C) basal ganglia and thalamus: (D) cerebellar cortex and brainstem.

remaining cerebral cortical regions had comparatively lower lCMRGlc. By approximately 4 weeks, lCMRGlc in parietal cortex had increased only slightly (see figure 7.1B), and by approximately the second postnatal month, lCMRGlc had slightly increased in calcarine and temporal cortices also (see figure 7.1C). Considerable maturational rises in lCMRGlc were seen in the anterior parietal, temporal, and calcarine cortices by approximately three months postnally (see figure 7.1D). However, most of the frontal cortex, as well as dorsolateral occipital (visual association) cortical regions, was slower to display a developmental increase. Although lCMRGlc in frontal cortex, particularly the lateral prefrontal regions, had increased slightly by 6 months (see figure 7.1E), both frontal and visual-association cortical lCMRGlc continued to rise considerably during the next several months (see figure 7.1F, G). By one year, the lCMRGlc pattern resembled that in adults (see figure 7.1G, H).

As depicted in table 7.2 mean lCMRGlc for cerebral cortical regions in the first year of life ranged from 65 to 86 percent of the corresponding adult values. The lCMRGlc for the sensorimotor cortex, which was the earliest cortical region to display its maturational rise, was the closest to the adult rates during the first year compared to other cortical structures. After the first year, the maturational curves for all cerebral cortical regions displayed a similar pattern (see figure 7.2A, B). Between 3 and 8 years, mean lCMRGlc for most cerebral cortical regions were 190–226 percent of corresponding adult values. As a whole, cerebral cortical structures underwent the highest proportional increase in lCMRGlc over their mature rates when compared to other portions of the brain.

Basal ganglia and thalamus

The basal ganglia and thalamus displayed developmental increases in lCMRGlc earlier than most areas of the cerebral cortex (see figures 7.1A–C, 7.2C). The thalamus was one of the earliest structures to show a maturational rise in lCMRGlc and was prominently active even in the five-day-old infant (see figure 7.1A). Indeed, mean lCMRGlc for the thalamus was already 84 percent of its adult rates during the first year; for lenticular nuclei it was 75 percent and for caudate nuclei 69 percent. Although peak values of lCMRGlc attained by the basal ganglia and thalamus during childhood exceeded those of corresponding structures in the adult, the magnitude of increase (155 to 162 percent) was less than that of cerebral cortex (see table 7.2).

Cerebellum

During the first year, lCMRGlc for the ccrebellum as a whole was closer to adult rates than any other portion of the brain (see table 7.2). Within the cerebellum, however, a heterogeneous pattern of maturation was observed. The centrally located, phylogenetically older portion (vermis) of the cerebellum was the first to display a maturational rise (see figure 7.1A, B), showing relatively high lCMRGlc as early as five days of age. The cerebellar hemispheres, or ncocerebellum, had comparatively lower lCMRGlc in the neonatal period, and only displayed a maturational rise in lCMRGlc by the third postnatal month (see figure 7.1D). During childhood, peak values of lCMRGlc in the cerebellum were approximately 175 percent of adult rates for this structure (see table 7.2).

Brainstem

The maturational pattern of the brainstem was similar to that of the cerebellum in that rates were relatively advanced at birth. During the first year, mean lCMRGlc for brainstem was approximately 82 percent of mature rates, and subsequent peak values were approximately 170 percent of corresponding adult values (see table 7.2).

Discussion

Methodological issues

Although approximately two-thirds of the subjects in this study were taking anticonvulsants daily, sedative effects were not seen. Nevertheless, in PET studies of adult intractable epileptics taking multiple anticonvulsants, lCMRGlc in cerebral cortex increased by a mean of 37 percent after withdrawal of phenobarbital or primidone [58], and a mean of 13 percent after withdrawal of phenytoin [57]. It seems unlikely that our findings were significantly affected by anticonvulsant use, since subjects of all ages were taking drugs at the time of PET and drug effects on lCMRGlc, if they occurred, would tend to be random.

A second methodological issue in our study involves the use of rate constants from normal young adults for calculating lCMRGlc in children. This has relatively little impact on the absolute values of lCMRGlc, because the rate constants appear with terms in the equation that contain exponentials to a negative power multiplied by time. Thus, at the late times after measurement these factors are small, and variations in the exact values of the rate constants cause only small errors over the range of calculated lCMRGlc values in this study [21, 22, 48, 55].

Earlier studies of cerebral blood flow and substrate utilization during development

Prior to the development of PET, there had been no adequate noninvasive method to study changes of local substrate utilization in the developing human brain. Nevertheless, in their studies of cerebral blood flow and oxygen utilization, Kennedy and Sokoloff [32] demonstrated that the average global cerebral blood flow in nine normal children (aged three to 11 years) was approximately 1.8 times that of normal young adults. Similarly, average cerebral oxygen utilization was approximately 1.3 times higher in children than in adults.

The subsequent development of autoradiographic techniques for measuring lCBF [33, 52] and lCMRGlc [55] in laboratory animals enabled substrate utilization to be determined in individual anatomical structures during cerebral maturation. These previous investigations have suggested that during different stages of development cerebral structures with relatively high lCBF or lCMRGlc in general determine the predominant behavioral pattern at the particular stage [1, 4, 29–31, 43]. For example, using [14C]2-deoxyglucose autoradiography, Kennedy and associates [31] found lCMRGlc in neonatal monkeys to be lower than adult rates in structures above the midbrain, particularly striate and the inferior temporal cortex. In contrast, lCMRGlc in neonatal auditory and somatosensory cortical areas were similar to mature rates, and neonatal thalamic rates were also relatively high when compared to other structures. These findings supported the concept that, in general, a rise in metabolic rate of a particular structure marks the time of its contribution to the animal's behavior. In the case of the monkey, structures with the highest lCMRGlc in the neonatal period dominated the behavior at that age [31].

Correlation between lCMRGlc and behavior during human development

Our data on the patterns of lCMRGlc in human neonates are congruous with the thesis that there is a relationship between a metabolic increase within neuroanatomical structures and the emergence of corresponding function. Neonatal behavior is primarily dominated by subcortical brain structure activity. Intrinsic brainstem reflexes, such as the Moro, root, and grasp reflexes, are prominent. Visuomotor function is present only in rudimentary form [60], and cortical function is mostly limited to primary sensory and motor areas. The prominent metabolic activity in sensorimotor cortex (see figure 7.1A) is also consistent with its relatively early morphological maturation compared to other cortical areas [51].

An interesting finding in the neonatal PET images is the relatively low lCMRGlc in the striatum compared to the more functionally mature thalamus (see figure 7.1A, B). This lCMRGlc relationship is also seen in adults with Huntington's disease [35]. Since normal newborn infants manifest nonpurposeful limb movements similar to those seen in Huntington's disease, the mechanism of chorea may be related to a functional imbalance in the interaction among striatum, thalamus, and cerebral cortex. Pathological chorea may result from striatal loss of function, whereas newborn physiological chorea occurs prior to emergence of significant lCMRGlc in the striatum and much of the cerebral cortex. It would, therefore, be of interest to determine whether a similar relationship in lCMRGlc among these structures exists in other clinical entities where chorea is a prominent feature.

By approximately three months, when striatal lCMRGlc has approached that of thalamus (see figure 7.1D), nonpurposeful limb movements have been replaced by more coordinated reaching movements. During this time, lCMRGlc has also increased in structures important for visuospatial and visuo-sensorimotor integration, such as parietal cortex, primary visual (calcarine) cortex, and cerebellar hemispheres. Indeed, infants between two and three months of age often open their hands during forward extension of the arm while visually fixing on an object as a preparatory maneuver to manipulate the object [59]. The increasingly sophisticated nature of these reaching movements is consistent with the notion that, whereas visual function in newborns may be mediated by phylogenetically older (subcortical) visual structures, the primary visual (calcarine) cortex begins to play a more important role in visual function by two to three months [3]. The lCMRGlc in the visual association areas, however, remains relatively low during this period, a finding consistent with the delayed anatomical maturation of the dorsolateral occipital cortex compared to calcarine cortex [51].

Another behavioral hallmark of two to four month-old infants is the attenuation and gradual disappearance of intrinsic brainstem reflexes, presumably as a result of increasing cortical influence [2, 45]. Since the frontal cortex remains relatively hypometabolic compared to parietal, temporal, and calcarine cortices during this time (see figure 7.1C, D), cortical suppression of brainstem reflexes (assuming this to be the mechanism) is probably not exclusively the result of frontal cortical input. These primitive newborn reflexes are also often seen in demented individuals suffering from Alzheimer's disease [46], where PET has demonstrated the early decrease of parietal, prior to frontal lobe, metabolism [9,

15, 34]. Therefore, the concept of *frontal release signs*, a phrase often used to denote the emergence of primitive reflexes in both demented and normal elderly individuals, may be more accurately referred to as *cortical release signs*.

The EEG, another measure of cerebral cortical activity, also undergoes considerable maturation during the second and third postnatal months. During this time, newborn EEG patterns, such as trace alternant, frontal rhythmic delta, and frontal sharp transients, disappear, and the precursors of alpha rhythm appear [28]. Thus, it is not surprising that increases of lCMRGlc in cerebral cortical structures should occur during this period of cortical maturation as evidenced by dramatic EEG changes.

By eight months postnatally, lCMRGlc had increased in dorsolateral occipital cortex and much of the frontal cortex (see figure 7.1F). These increases coincide with the appearance of higher cortical and cognitive function [27]. The infant now shows a more sophisticated interaction with his or her surroundings and exhibits the phenomenon of stranger anxiety [12]. In addition, the infant improves his or her performance on the delayed response task, a commonly used neuropsychological paradigm for evaluating prefrontal lobe integrity [16, 17]. Together, these changes in the skills of the infant imply increasing function in the prefrontal cortex. Neuroanatomically, this stage is accompanied by an expansion of dendritic fields [53] and an increase in capillary density [8] of human frontal cortex.

Possible causes of high lCMRGlc during development

Although by eight to 12 months of age the anatomical distribution of lCMRGlc seen with PET qualitatively resembled that of young adults, and by two years absolute lCMRGlc for most structures were similar to those of adults, brain development was far from complete. In virtually all brain regions measured, lCMRGlc continued to increase, although to varying degrees depending upon the specific structures, reaching very high values compared to adults. Only during the second decade did lCMRGlc decline to approximate adult values (see figure 7.2). Evidence in support of these high metabolic rates during childhood was first reported by Kennedy and Sokoloff [32] some 30 years ago in a study alluded to earlier in this discussion.

There are a number of possible explanations for the high energy demands of the brain during development. First, there is now ample evidence in humans [51] and in other species [10, 36, 44] that during development the brain produces a vast excess of neurons, synapses, and dendritic spines. For example, the phenomenon of polyneuronal innervation, where synaptic targets receive innervation from more neurons during development than will remain in the adult, has been well documented (reviewed in [50]). The overproduction of neurons and their synaptic contacts is biologically advantageous in reducing the genetic load that would otherwise be required for specifically programming the enormous numbers of synaptic contacts in the nervous system [5, 25]. Many neurons subsequently die, and there is a regression of dendritic spines and synapses [7]. This form of cell death occurs early in development – by two years of age in humans [51] – but the loss of synaptic elements is a more protracted process. For example, the concentration of synaptic contacts in both human frontal [23] and visual [24] cortices of children up to 11 years old exceeds those of corresponding regions in adults. Specifically, at age seven years, when the child's brain is almost identical in size and weight to that of the adult, average synaptic density in frontal cortex is about 1.4 times the adult value [23].

The biological rules governing regression of neuroanatomical elements are poorly understood, but these phenomena are believed to account, at least in part, for nervous system plasticity [11]. The concept that there are mechanisms that act to retain those pathways in which patterns of external stimuli induce activity and eliminate potential connections not so activated has been termed *functional validation* by Jacobson [25], and *selective stabilization* by Changeux and Danchin [5]. This process would account for the contribution of early experience of the developing individual toward the final neuroanatomical composition and neurophysiological representation within the nervous system. This notion is supported by data from animal studies [13, 40, 41, 56, 61].

Our finding of higher lCMRGlc in children compared to adults is consistent with the excessive numbers of dendritic processes and synapses in childhood, since these elements account for most of the glucose utilized [26, 37, 42]. Therefore, the large surface area of an excess number of processes might lead to high resting glucose metabolic rates for maintenance of membrane potentials. As the density of processes diminishes, lCMRGlc also decreases to approach adult levels.

A second cause for high lCMRGlc in the developing brain may be excessive fuel expenditure by oligodendroglia during myelination, which continues, in the human brain, throughout the first decade of life [20, 62], and undergoes remodelling throughout life [14]. Conversely, incomplete myelination of brain pathways may result in suboptimal conduction efficiency, thus requiring greater energy expenditure. The relative contributions of these possible mechanisms in accounting for the high lCMRGlc in the developing brain can only be speculated. Since myelin remodelling is a slow process, it is unlikely to contribute significantly to immediate energy expenditure in the brain. Nevertheless, it is possible that all of these factors, and perhaps others, collectively account for the high lCMRGlc in the developing brain.

Conclusion

Our findings support the commonly accepted view that brain maturation in humans proceeds at least into the second decade of life. This study illustrates the potentially powerful approach PET provides in the study of human brain development. PET has opened a new window on our understanding of neuroanatomical correlation with brain function and behavior. Since both the anatomical distribution and absolute values of lCMRGlc in children are age dependent, the precise mapping of these maturational changes in the normally developing brain is a prerequisite to PET studies of abnormal brain development in children ranging from various learning disabilities to severe psychomotor retardation. Finally, by establishing changes in lCMRGlc during normal development, it will be possible to use PET in the study of central nervous system plasticity in children with early brain injury and other disease processes.

ACKNOWLEDGMENTS

Supported by Department of Energy contract No DE-AC03-SF7600012 and by USPHS grants nos 5R01-MH37916-04 and 2P01-NS15654-06. Dr Chugani is the recipient of Teacher-Investigator Developmental Award 1-K07-NS00886-03, and Dr Mazziotta is the recipient of Teacher-Investigator Developmental Award 1-K07-NS00588-05-NSBA from the National Institute of Neurological and Communicative Diseases and Stroke.

We thank Drs C. Kennedy, P. Phelps, P. Nelson, P. Huttenlocher, F. Gilles, D. Holtzman, L. Sokoloff, and C. Smith for helpful comments, and Ms Marybeth Literarus for typing the manuscript. The support and assistance of the UCLA Pediatrics housestaff are greatly appreciated.

REFERENCES

1   Abrams R. M., Ito M., Frisinger J. E., et al. Local cerebral glucose utilization in fetal and neonatal sheep. *Am. J. Physiol.* 246:R608–R618, 1984.

2   Andre-Thomas C. Y. and Saint-Anne Dargassies S. *The Neurological Examination of the Infant*. London, Medical Advisory Committee of the National Spastics Society, 1960.

3   Bronson G. The postnatal growth of visual capacity. *Child Dev.* 45:873–90, 1974.

4   Cavazzuti M. and Duffy T. E. Regulation of local cerebral blood flow in normal and hypoxic newborn dogs. *Ann. Neurol.* 11:247–57, 1982.

5   Changeux J.-P. and Danchin A. Selective stabilization of developing synapses as a mechanism for the specification of neuronal networks. *Nature* 264:705–12, 1976.

6   Chugani H. T. and Phelps M. E. Maturational changes in cerebral function in infants determined by [18]FDG positron emission tomography. *Science* 231:840–3, 1986.

7   Cowan W. M., Fawcett J. W., O'Leary D. D. M., and Stanfield B. B. Regressive events in neurogenesis. *Science* 225:1258–65, 1984.

8   Diemer K. Capillarisation and oxygen supply of the brain. In Lubbers D. W., Luft U. C., Thews G., and Witzleb E. (eds): *Oxygen Transport in Blood and Tissue*. Stuttgart, Thieme Inc. 1968, pp. 118–23.

9   Duara R., Grady C., Haxby J., et al. Positron emission tomography in Alzheimer's disease. *Neurology* 36:879–87, 1986.

10 Duffy C. J. and Rakic P. Differentiation of granule cell dendrites in the dentate gyrus of the rhesus monkey: a quantitative Golgi study. *J. Comp. Neurol.* 214:224–37, 1983.

11 Easter S. S. Jr, Purves D., Rakic P., and Spitzer N. C. The changing view of neural specificity. *Science* 230:507–11, 1985.

12 Emde R. N., Gaensbauer T. J., and Harmon R. J. *Emotional Expression in Infancy: A behavioral study*, vol. 10. New York, University Press, 1976.

13 Fiala B. A., Joyce J. N., and Greenough W. T. Environmental complexity modulates growth of granule cell dendrites in developing but not adult hippocampus of rats. *Exp. Neurol.* 59:372–83, 1978.

14 Fishman M. A., Agrawal H. C., Alexander A., et al. Biochemical maturation of human central nervous system myelin. *J. Neurochem.* 24:689–94, 1975.

15 Frackowiak R. S. J., Pozzilli C., Legg N. J., et al. Regional cerebral oxygen supply and utilization in dementia. A clinical and physiological study with oxygen-15 and positron emission tomography. *Brain* 104:753–78, 1981.

16 Fuster J. M. Behavioral electrophysiology of the prefrontal cortex. *Trends Neurosci.* 7:408–14, 1984.

17 Goldman-Rakic P. S. The frontal lobes: uncharted provinces of the brain. *Trends Neurosci.* 7:425–9, 1984.

18 Himwich H. E. and Fazekas J. F. Comparative studies of the metabolism of the brain in infant and adult dogs. *Am. J. Physiol.* 132:454–9, 1941.

19 Hottman E. J., Phelps M. E., and Huang S. C. Performance evaluation of a positron tomograph designed for brain imaging. *J. Nucl. Med.* 24:245–57, 1983.

20 Holland B. A., Haas D. K., Norman D., et al: MRI of normal brain maturation. *AJNR* 7:201–8, 1986.

21 Huang S. C., Phelps M. E., Hoffman E. J., et al. Noninvasive determination of local cerebral metabolic rate of glucose in man. *Am. J. Physiol.* 238:E69–E82, 1980.

22 Huang S. C., Phelps M. E., Hoffman E. J., and Kuhl D. E. Error sensitivity of fluorodeoxyglucose method for measurement of cerebral metabolic rate of glucose. *J. Cereb. Blood Flow Metab.* 1:391–401, 1981.

23 Huttenlocher P. R. Synaptic density in human frontal cortex – developmental changes and effects of aging. *Brain Res.* 163:195–205, 1979.

24 Huttenlocher P. R., de Courten C., Gary L. J., and van der Loos H. Synaptogenesis in human visual cortex – evidence for synapse elimination during normal development. *Neurosci. Lett.* 33:247–52, 1982.

25 Jacobson M. and Abrahams R. M. *Developmental Neurobiology*, 2nd edn. New York, Plenum, 1978, pp. 302–7.

26 Kadekaro M., Crane A. M., and Sokoloff L. Differential effects of electrical stimulation of sciatic nerve on metabolic activity in spinal cord and dorsal root ganglion in the rat. *Proc. Natl. Acad. Sci. USA* 82:6010–13, 1985.

27 Kagan J. Do infants think? *Scientific American* 226:74–82, 1972.

28 Kellaway P. An orderly approach to visual analysis: parameters of the normal EEG in adults and children. In Klass D. W., Daly D. D. (eds): *Current practice of clinical electro-encephalography.* New York, Raven, 1979, pp. 69 147.

29 Kennedy C., Grave G. D., Jehle J. W., and Sokoloff L. Blood flow to white matter during maturation of the brain. *Neurology* 20:613–18, 1970.

30 Kennedy C., Grave G. D., Jehle J. W., and Sokoloff L. Changes in blood flow in the component structures of the dog brain during postnatal maturation. *J. Neurochem.* 19:2423–33, 1972.

31 Kennedy C., Sakurada O., Shinohara M., and Miyaoka M. Local cerebral glucose utilization in the newborn macaque monkey. *Ann. Neurol.* 12:333–40, 1982.

32 Kennedy C. and Sokoloff L. An adaptation of the nitrous oxide method to the study of the cerebral circulation in children; normal values for cerebral blood flow and cerebral metabolic rate in childhood. *J. Clin. Invest.* 36:1130–7, 1957.

33 Kety S. S. Measurement of local blood flow by the exchange of an inert, diffusible substance. *Methods Med. Res.* 8:228–36, 1960.

34 Kuhl D. E., Metter E. J., and Riege W. H. Patterns of cerebral glucose utilization in depression, multiple infarct dementia, and Alzheimer's disease. In Sokoloff L. (ed.): *Brain imaging and brain function.* New York, Raven, 1985, pp. 211–26.

35 Kuhl D. E., Phelps M. E., Markham C. H., et al. Cerebral metabolism and atrophy in Huntington's disease determined by 18-FDG and computed tomographic scan. *Ann. Neurol.* 12:425–34, 1982.

36 Lund J. S., Boothe R. G., and Lund R. D. Development of neurons in the visual cortex (area 17) of the monkey (Macaca nemestrina): a Golgi study from fetal day 127 to postnatal maturity. *J. Comp. Neurol.* 176:149–88, 1977.

37 Mata M., Fink D. J., Gainer H., et al. Activity-dependent energy metabolism in rat posterior pituitary primarily reflects sodium pump activity. *J. Neurochem.* 34:213–15, 1980.

38 Mazziotta J. C., Phelps M. E., Meadors A. K., et al. Anatomical localization schemes for use in positron computed tomography using a specially designed head holder. *J. Comput. Assist. Tomogr.* 6:848–53, 1982.

39 Mazziotta J. C., Phelps M. E., Plummer D., et al. Optimization and standardization of anatomical data in neuro-behavioral investigations using positron computed tomography. *J. Cereb. Blood Flow Metab.* 3(Suppl 1):S266–S267, 1983.

40 Mistretta C. M. and Bradley R. M. Effects of early sensory experience on brain and behavioral development. In Gottlieb G. (ed.): *Studies on the development of behavior and the nervous system, vol. 4. Early influences.* New York, Academic Press, 1978. pp. 215–47.

41 Mollgaard K., Diamond M. C., Bennett E. L., et al. Quantitative synaptic changes with differential experience in rat brain. *Int. J. Neurosci.* 2:113–28, 1971.

42 Nudo R. J. and Masterton R. B. Stimulation-induced [14C]2-deoxy-glucose labeling of synaptic activity in the central auditory system. *J. Comp. Neurol.* 245:553–65, 1986.

43 Ohata M., Sundaram U., Fredericks W. R., et al. Regional cerebral blood flow during development and ageing of the rat brain. *Brain* 104:319–32, 1981.

44 Oppenheim R. W. Naturally occurring cell death during neural development. *Trends Neurosci.* 8:487–93, 1985.

45 Parmelee A. H. Jr and Sigman M. D. Perinatal brain development and behavior. In Haith M. and Campos J. (eds): *Biology and infancy, vol. II*, New York, Wiley, 1983, pp. 95–155.

46 Paulson G. and Gottlieb G. Development reflexes: the reappearance of fetal and neonatal reflexes in aged patients. *Brain* 91:37–52, 1968.

47 Phelps M. E., Hoffman E. J., Mullani N. A., and Ter-Pogossian M. M. Application of annihilation coincidence detection to transaxial reconstruction tomography. *J. Nucl. Med.* 16:210–24, 1975.

48 Phelps M. E., Huang S. C., Hoffman E. J., et al. Tomographic measurement of local cerebral glucose metabolic rate in humans with (F-18)2-Fluoro-2-deoxyglucose: validation of method. *Ann. Neurol.* 6:371–88, 1979.

49 Phelps M. E. and Mazziotta J. C. Positron emission tomography: human brain function and biochemistry. *Science* 228:799–809, 1985.

50 Purves D. and Lichtman J. W. Elimination of synapses in the developing nervous system. *Science* 210:153–7, 1980.

51 Rabinowicz T. The differentiate maturation of the human cerebral cortex. In Falkner F. and Tanner J. M. (eds): *Human growth, vol 3, Neurobiology and nutrition.* New York, Plenum, 1979, pp. 97–123.

52 Sakurada O., Kennedy C., Jehle J., et al. Measurement of local cerebral blood flow with iodo[14C]antipyrine. *Am. J. Physiol.* 234:H59–H66, 1978.

53 Schade J. P. and van Groenigen W. B. Structural organization of the human cerebral cortex. *Acta. Anat.* 47:74–111, 1961.

54 Sokoloff L. Localization of functional activity in the central nervous system by measurement of glucose utilization with radioactive deoxyglucose. *J. Cereb. Blood Flow Metab.* 1:7–36, 1981.

55 Sokoloff L., Reivich M., Kennedy C., et al. The (14-C) deoxyglucose method for the measurement of local cerebral glucose utilization: theory, procedure, and normal values in the conscious and anesthetized albino rat. *J. Neurochem.* 28:897–916, 1977.

56 Spinelli D. N., Jensen F. E., and di Prisco G. V. Early experience effect on dendritic branching in normally reared kittens. *Exp. Neurol.* 68:1–11, 1980.

57 Theodore W. H., Bairamian D., Newmark M. E., et al. Effect of phenytoin on human cerebral glucose metabolism. *J. Cereb. Blood Flow Metab.* 6:315–20, 1986.

58 Theodore W. H., DiChiro G., Margolin R., et al. Barbiturates reduce human cerebral glucose metabolism. *Neurology* 36:60–4, 1986.

59 Von Hofsten C. Developmental changes in the organization of prereaching movements. *Dev. Psychobiol.* 20:378–88, 1984.

60 Von Hofsten C. Eye–hand coordination in the newborn. *Dev. Psychol.* 18:450–61, 1982.

61 Wiesel T. N. and Hubel D. H. Effects of visual deprivation on morphology and physiology of cells in the cat's lateral geniculate body. *J. Neurophysiol.* 26:978–93, 1963.

62 Yakovlev P. I. and Lecours A. R. The myelogenetic cycles of regional maturation of the brain. In Minkowski A. (ed.): *Regional development of the brain in early life.* Philadelphia, Davis Co, 1967, pp. 3–70.

8

Morphometric Study of Human Cerebral Cortex Development

Peter R. Huttenlocher

Introduction

Recent morphometric studies of human cerebral cortex during development provide interesting insights into the anatomical substrate of emerging cortical functions in the infant and child. They give evidence for a dynamic, changing system, at least into the late childhood years, an age at which cortical structure had been thought to be relatively stable. The quantitative approach has been especially productive in the area of synaptogenesis. However, quantitative data on cortical volume, neuronal number, and dendritic growth also have yielded important findings.

As yet, there has been little attempt to correlate developmental changes in these different components of the neuropil.[a] Extensive data are now available for specific cortical areas, especially for primary visual cortex. These make it possible to obtain a fairly comprehensive picture of the changes that occur in cortical neurons during pre- and postnatal development. The present report is concerned with an analysis of extant data, emphasizing those in visual cortex, comparing them to findings in frontal cortex and stressing relationships between dendritic and synaptic growth.

Volume of Visual Cortex (Area 17)

Most quantitative morphologic data are obtained in terms of densities, i.e. number of structure per unit volume. For these to be meaningful, they have to be correlated with the total volume of the tissue. This is especially important during early development, when volume expansion of brain is an important factor. Measurements of volume of most cortical regions are difficult if not impossible, due to the fact that structural changes from one area to the other tend to be subtle, and transitions gradual. The primary visual cortex (area 17) forms a notable exception. It is clearly demarcated by its characteristic anatomy, with a very

---

a   Neuropil refers to the mass of interwoven dendrites and axons within which the nerve cell-bodies of the brain are embedded. (Editors' note.)

Reprinted with permission from Huttenlocher "Morphometric Study of Human Cerebral Cortex Development" from *Neuropsychologia* (1990, Pergamon Plc) pp. 517–27.

Table 8.1 Volume, neuronal density, and total number of neurons in striate cortex (area 17) at various ages

Age	Volume (mm^3)	Neurons/mm^3 ($\times 10^4$)	Total neurons ($\times 10^7$)
28 wk GA	230	61.9	14.2
Newborn	920	9.6	8.8
6 days	1270	9.4	11.9
2 wk	1330	10.9[a]	14.5
2 mon.	2720	5.2	14.1
4 mon.	3800	3.5	13.5
19 mon.	4170	3.0	12.5
$3\frac{9}{12}$ yr	4430	3.1	13.7
5 yr	4310	2.5[a]	10.8
11 yr	3620	2.5	9.1
13 yr	3620	2.9[a]	10.5
26 yr	3790	3.6	14.6
71 yr	3850	4.2	16.2

The cortical volume and neuronal density data are not corrected for tissue shrinkage, since the neuronal density values published by Leuba and Garey [26] do not contain such corrections. Readers interested in volume data corrected for tissue shrinkage are referred to ref. [23].

[a] No neuronal density value was available for the exact age. Values for the nearest available ages are shown.

large granular layer, transsected by a prominent bundle of fibers, the stria of Gennari. Measurements of volume of area 17 during development have been made by Huttenlocher et al. [22, 23] and by Sauer et al. [37]. The two studies show similar findings, i.e. rapid expansion of cortical volume during fetal life and during the first four postnatal months. During late childhood there is a small but statistically significant contraction in cortical volume. The values used for the present calculations of total number of neurons (table 8.1)

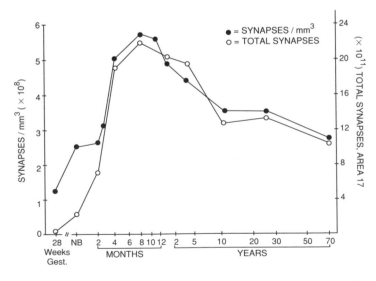

Figure 8.1 Synaptic density and total synapses in visual cortex as a function of age.

and synapses (figure 8.1) are those published by Huttenlocher et al. [22, 23]. Some of the other quantitative data analyzed in this report, including synapse counts and counts of neuronal number, were carried out on the same brains. Tissue shrinkage or swelling during the agonal period and during fixation and embedding therefore is apt to be approximately the same for the volume and synaptic and neuronal density data, making it possible to examine relationships between them.

The very early growth of visual cortex, with maximum volume reached at about age four months, is somewhat surprising when one considers the size of the brain as a whole, which at four months is only about half that of the adult. It is likely that cortical association areas, especially frontal cortex, grow more slowly. Much of the later gain in brain weight may also be related to myelination of subcortical white matter which continues throughout the childhood years [47]. The slight decrease in volume of visual cortex observed during late childhood may reflect certain regressive changes in cerebral cortex that occur late in development, and that are subsequently detailed.

Neuronal Number in Visual Cortex

Extensive data on the density of neurons in visual cortex during development have recently been reported by Leuba and Garey [26]. These data are especially useful for comparisons of synaptic and neuronal numbers during development (see below), since many of the cell counts were on semithin sections fixed in glutaraldehyde and embedded in Spurr's medium, with adjacent, identically prepared blocks of tissue used for synapse quantitation [22, 23]. Values obtained at ages when cortical volume measurements were also available are listed in table 8.1. The density of neurons decreases markedly during fetal and early postnatal development, from about 62×10^4 neurons per mm^3 at 28 weeks gestational age to about 4×10^4 in the adult. These values become meaningful only when they are related to cortical volume. Comparison with volume data for visual cortex shows that total neuronal number remains constant through the life span, at least from gestational age (GA) 28 weeks to about age 70 years (table 8.1). By GA 28 weeks all cortical neurons have arrived at the cortical plate where they are densely crowded together. The decrease in packing density observed during development appears to be entirely secondary to expansion of the volume of cortex, which in turn is related to the growth of axons, dendrites, and glia. The data provide no evidence that cortical neurons are lost during normal development or during the adult years. The total numbers of neurons in visual cortex in different brains show fluctuations from about 9 to 16×10^7 which are not age related. Some of this variability may be related to inaccuracies in cell counts and volume measurements. It may also reflect normal variations in brain size. It is well known that the human brain can be organized into normal functioning units over a fairly large range in brain size, with total brain weight ranging from about 1 000 to 1 800 g in normal adults.

Dendritic Development in Visual Cortex

Human cortical neurons are characterized by great complexity and length of dendritic arborizations. The function of cerebral cortex is thought to be closely linked to dendritic morphology. Stunted growth of cortical dendrites has been found in some forms of mental retardation [20, 42]. Defective morphology of dendritic spines – the specialized regions on dendrites in which many synaptic contacts are located – has also been reported in brains from the mentally retarded [29, 30, 34, 35].

Several aspects of dendritic development have been quantitated in human cerebral cortex, including dendritic spine formation, dendritic length, and complexity of branching patterns. Michel and Garey [31] examined the density of spines on apical dendrites[b] of pyramidal neurons in layer III of visual cortex (area 17). They found that the mean number of dendritic spines[c] increases to a maximum of about 79 per 50 μm of dendritic length at about age five months. It declines thereafter, and the adult value of about 50 spines/50 μm is reached by age 21 months. These data *per se* do not provide information as to whether there is actual loss of spines – and hence presumably of synapses related to spines – after age five months, or whether the decrease in spine density is related to progressive elongation of dendrites, the number of spines per neuron remaining constant. Data published by Becker et al. [4] show that progressive elongation of dendrites occurs between ages 5 and 21 months. These authors obtained measurements of total dendritic length of pyramidal neurons in layers III and V of area 17. Total length of apical dendrites in layer III, the structures studied by Michel and Garey, increased from about 800 μm at age five months to 1 400 μm at age 24 months. The increase in dendritic length is very close to the figure that would have been predicted on the assumption that the decrease in dendritic spine density that occurs during the same period is due to increase in dendritic length alone. The combined data therefore do not provide evidence for actual loss of spines.

The study of Becker et al. [4] suggests that the time course of dendritic growth varies in different cortical layers. The dendritic trees of pyramidal cells in layer V grow earlier than those in layer III. The mean total length of dendrites for pyramidal cells in layer III is only about 30 percent of the maximum at birth, while in layer V it is already about 60 percent of maximum. In addition, a higher degree of dendritic branching was observed in layer V neurons at birth than in layer III neurons. Dendritic development appears to reflect differences in the time course of neurogenesis in general. The birth of neurons and neuronal migration in the lower layers of cortex precede these events in the upper layers, in what is referred to as the inside-out pattern of cortical development [41]. A pattern of earlier dendritic development in the lower cortical layers has also been reported in human motor cortex [28].

The study of Becker et al. [4] provides no evidence for regressive changes in dendritic development. There appears to be no significant overall pruning of dendrites on cortical neurons as development progresses, at least up to age seven years. Elongation of dendrites on pyramidal neurons in visual cortex appears to end by about age 18 months, and dendritic length shows no significant change between that age and seven years. The study leaves unanswered whether changes in dendritic length occur after seven years, the oldest age examined by these authors.

Synaptogenesis in Visual Cortex

Dendritic geometry of neurons relates to function of the system through cellular interactions that occur along the dendritic membranes at synapses. Data on synaptogenesis in

---

b   Apical dendrites are the prominent leading dendrites which extend from the top of pyramidal cell bodies toward the upper layers of the cortex. (Editors' note.)

c   Dendritic spines are small protuberances on the surface of dendrites upon which is a synapse. (Editors' note.)

area 17 are available for all cortical layers, from GA 28 weeks to the adult [22, 23]. Synaptic profiles are detectable already in the fetal brain at GA 28 weeks, but synaptic density at that stage is low, about 1×10^8 synapses per mm³ of tissue, or 1/3 of the adult value. Synaptic density increases during late fetal life and in early infancy. A sudden spurt occurs between ages two and four months, when synaptic density almost doubles. After age one year synaptic density begins to decline to an adult value about 60 percent of the maximum, which is reached by age 11 years (figure 8.1). Analysis of synaptic density by cortical layers does not show an inside-out pattern of development, i.e. synaptogenesis in the lower cortical layers does not precede that in the upper ones. This has also been noted by Rakic et al. in the monkey [36]. In humans, there is some difference between layers, with a trend toward later synaptogenesis in the lower layers: in layer V maximum synaptic density is reached by age 11 months, and in layer VI by 19 months, while density in layer III is maximum already at four months. In visual cortex, synaptogenesis in regions concerned with processing of afferent inputs appears to lead that in efferent systems.

Availability of synaptic density and volume data on the same brains has made it possible to calculate the approximate total number of synapses in area 17 at various ages (figure 8.1). Only about 1 percent of the maximum are present at GA 28 weeks, and about 10 percent at birth. The maximum is reached at postnatal age eight months. Subsequently, there is a decrease to 50–60 percent of maximum, which is reached by age 11 years. The data indicate a very significant loss of synapses during postnatal development of cerebral cortex.

Several derived values can be calculated from extant data on synaptic density, neuronal density, and dendritic length. The average calculated number of synapses per neuron at various ages is given in figure 8.2. This value reaches a maximum of over 15 000 at age eight months and declines to about 10 000 in the adult, for area 17 as a whole. It is lower for layer IVc, as would be expected from the fact that small neurons predominate in this cortical layer.

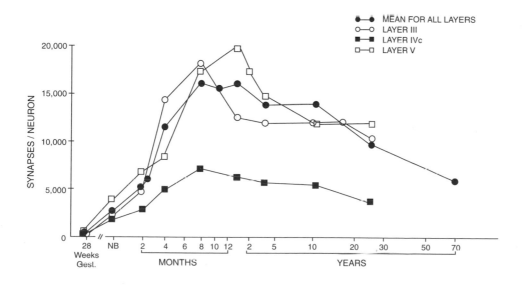

Figure 8.2 Mean number of synapses per neuron in visual cortex as a whole and in selected cortical layers as a function of age.

The average number of synapses per micron of dendritic length also declines during childhood. These values have been calculated, using data for total dendritic length in layers III and V provided by Becker et al. [4], and synaptic density and neuronal density values for the same layers, obtained from Huttenlocher and de Courten [23] and Leuba and Garey [26]. The results are shown in figure 8.3. The findings appear to differ between the two cortical layers, with greater crowding of synapses on dendrites during development of layer III than of layer V. Maximum density of synapses on dendrites is reached earlier in layer III, at about age eight months, *vs* about 18 months in layer V. However, the values calculated at age seven years are almost identical for the two cortical layers. These derived values are very gross approximations, since the calculations include the incorrect assumptions that all synapses are axodendritic, and that all neurons in layers III and V are pyramidal cells. However, the errors introduced by these assumptions are likely to remain constant across age, and are unlikely to affect the age-related trends indicated in figure 8.3.

Frontal Cortex

Available information on the development of cortical areas other than 17 in humans is limited. The only other area for which combined data on neuronal number, synaptic density and dendritic development are available is the middle frontal gyrus. The findings in frontal cortex form an interesting contrast to those in visual cortex, in that they indicate different developmental schedules in the two cortical areas. In frontal cortex, neuronal density in layer III at birth is about $100\,000/mm^3$, similar to that in area 17. The subsequent decline in density is slower. While neuronal density in visual cortex reaches the adult value by about postnatal age five months, in frontal cortex it is still 55 percent above adult mean at age two years, and 10 percent above adult mean at seven years. No volume data are available for frontal cortex, and it is therefore unknown whether the decrease in density is related to expansion of cortex or to neuronal loss. The adult value for neuronal density in layer III of middle frontal gyrus is about $13\,000/mm^3$ [19, 38].

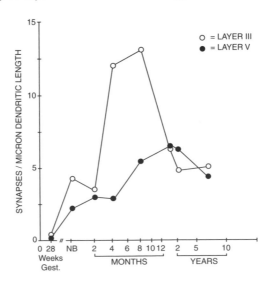

Figure 8.3 Estimate of distribution of synapses on dendrites as a function of age.

Published values for motor cortex vary from about 10 000 to 26 000 neurons/mm^3. Values for both of these frontal regions are considerably smaller than that for visual cortex, which is about 40 000 for layer III [12, 26, 39].

Dendritic development in middle frontal gyrus also progresses considerably more slowly than in visual cortex. In area 17, the total dendritic length of pyramidal neurons approaches the adult value by age four months in layer V and by 18 months in layer III [4]. In contrast, dendritic length in layer III of middle frontal gyrus is only about 50 percent of the adult at age two years [38].

By age two years, mean total dendritic length of pyramidal neurons in layer III of middle frontal gyrus is already more than twice that of visual cortex. This, as well as the lower density of neurons, undoubtedly reflects the greater complexity and size of pyramidal neurons in the frontal areas. In general, a decrease in density of cortical neurons has been observed as one progresses from simpler to more complex cortical systems, both within a species and phylogenetically [12, 18, 32, 39, 40, 44]. The limited available data also suggest that growth of some neural elements, especially dendrites, continues for a longer period of time in frontal cortex. Buell and Coleman [6, 7] have found that dendritic elongation continues even in old age, where it may provide compensation for neuronal loss.

Synaptic density data during development of middle frontal gyrus are available for layer III only [21]. They show a slower postnatal increase in synaptic density than in visual cortex. Maximum density is reached at about age one year, *vs* age four months in visual cortex. Subsequently, synaptic density declines, but again more slowly than in visual cortex. The decrease in synaptic density does not become evident until after age seven years, at which age synaptic density in visual cortex is already near the adult value, i.e. at about 60 percent of maximum. Synaptic density in frontal cortex is at adult level by age 16 years. The synaptic density data therefore show regional differences in the time course of cortical synaptogenesis in the human. In that respect, synaptogenesis in human brain appears to differ from that in the monkey, where concurrent overproduction of synapses in diverse regions of cerebral cortex has been found [36]. Available data indicate that synaptic density in adult frontal cortex exceeds that in visual cortex. Cragg [12, 13], who obtained synapse quantitations in motor and visual cortex in the same brains, found synaptic density in area 4 to be about 50 percent greater than in area 17.

Calculated values derived from neuronal density, dendritic length and synaptic density figures in frontal cortex show trends similar to those in visual cortex, but with a slower time course. The number of synapses per neuron appears to decrease between late childhood and age 16 years. The number of synapses per micron of dendritic length also decreases, the adult value being about 50 percent of the value obtained at age two years. It is not possible to be certain that actual loss of synapses occurs during development of middle frontal gyrus, since no volume data are available. However, the fact that synaptic density declines after neuronal density has stabilized, i.e. after age seven years, suggests that loss of synapses does occur, similar in extent but later in age than in visual cortex.

Discussion

The quantitative anatomy approach to cortical development has clear limitations which need to be spelled out in order to put the present data into proper perspective. Development is an ongoing, dynamic process. The anatomical method is a static one, providing a glimpse of only one point in time for any given case. In the human, the material that is available for study may be affected by such uncontrollable events as effects of the agonal illness on the tissue and postmortem changes [45]. Even at best, the quantitative method gives only mean values. Growth and regressive changes may occur at the same time and may balance each other, in which case quantitation would show no change at all, and would suggest a static rather than a dynamic system. This may well be the case in the adult brain. It is quite likely that new synapses are constantly formed and old connections disappear, a phenomenon that is not reflected in the data on total synapse number in adults, which show little evidence of change. Finally, the anatomical methods are tedious, and they require the availability of samples of brain tissue. Both of these factors make it impractical to study the large number of subjects that would be required for the statistical analyses needed for the detection of small changes.

Nevertheless, important information has resulted from morphometric analysis of cerebral cortex. Some widely held notions have been put in question. For example, programmed neuronal death, i.e., the normal loss of neurons during development [11], is often assumed to be a universal developmental event. In fact, the extant developmental data show no evidence that neuronal death is important during development of the largest and most complex aggregate of neurons, the human cerebral cortex. Interestingly, this could not have been predicted from animal studies. In the mouse, a 30 percent loss of cortical neurons has been shown during development [18, 19]. A smaller neuronal loss, about 15 percent, has been reported between birth and adulthood in area 17 in the monkey [32]. The data suggest that programmed cell death may be more important in less complex neural systems. It is generally accepted that programmed cell death relates to the failure of developing neurons to find targets for innervation. Target finding may be easier in systems of great complexity, such as human cerebral cortex, where potential targets are available on large populations of nearby neurons.

The data for synapse elimination during cortical development show phylogenetic changes which are opposite those for programmed neuronal death. In rodents, there is little evidence for overproduction of synapses. Aghajanian and Bloom [1] found that synaptic density in the rat brain reaches a maximum at about postnatal day 35, which is less than 10 percent greater than the adult value. More definite evidence for synapse elimination has been found in the kitten, where the maximum, about 50 percent above the adult value, is reached at about age 36 days [14]. The findings in the monkey resemble those in humans, with synaptic density values during infancy (age six months) that are 75–95 percent above the adult value [32, 36].

It therefore appears that synapse elimination in cerebral cortex becomes a more important developmental event as the complexity of the system increases. This result conforms to expectations that derive from a theory concerning synaptogenesis proposed by Changeux [8, 9]. It is argued that genetic determination of synaptogenesis in complex systems is incomplete, the genome being insufficient in size to allow for specification of all synaptic connections. "The genetic program directs the proper interaction between main categories of neurons. During development within a category several contacts form at the same site; in other words a significant... redundancy... of the connections exists" [8]. These early synaptic contacts are viewed as being labile (synaptic plasticity). Some connections are stabilized by being incorporated into functioning systems either through the establishment of intrinsic neuronal circuits or through afferent activity transmitted from sense organs. The stabilized synaptic contacts persist, while labile contacts that fail to be incorporated into functioning units regress. The theory thus implies overproduction of synaptic contacts during development, followed by synapse elimination. Recent computer simulations of nerve nets provide evidence that randomly connected systems can develop considerable organization in terms of strength of internal connections and output, provided that they are subjected to non-random input [15].

The anatomical findings in humans are consistent with Changeux's theory, and they also provide data as to the ages at which synapses are most numerous, as well as the time course of their regression. The postnatal occurrence of these events is of particular interest. It suggests that the anatomical changes may be directly related to the development of cortical functions, including learning, memory and language.

Parallels between the anatomical changes and functional development are easily discernible in visual cortex, since the functions of this cortical region are well understood. Relatively few synaptic connections (about 10 percent of the maximum) are found at birth, a time when visual alertness is as yet very low and visual fixation and following are just beginning to be demonstrable. The rapid burst in synaptogenesis at age four months correlates well with a sudden increase in visual alertness at about that time. Binocular interactions, which are clearly dependent on cortical rather than primarily retinal or lateral geniculate function, first appear between ages four and five months. These include stereopsis, stereoacuity, equalization of the optokinetic nystagmus to nasotemporal and temporonasal motion, and binocular summation of the light reflex [5, 17, 43]. Clinical observations confirm the importance of afferent input for the formation of functional connections during this period. Strabismic amblyopia, i.e. blindness in the squinting eye, and amblyopia due to absence of formed visual inputs, as occurs in congenital cataract, have been observed to occur at this age [16, 25, 27].

Synaptic density — and hence presumably the number of unspecified or labile synaptic contacts – continues to be high in visual cortex until at least age four years. Functionally, this correlates with persistence of plasticity in the visual system. Most notably, strabismic amblyopia can be reversed during this time, provided that the good eye is occluded and the child is forced to use the squinting eye [2, 3].

The persistence of large numbers of labile synapses may provide the anatomical substrate for neural plasticity in the child [24]. If so, then one would expect plasticity to persist later in middle frontal gyrus, where synapse elimination does not begin until about age seven years. Unfortunately, we have no clear information about the functions of this cortical area. However, it is known that plasticity for some functions persists into late childhood. An example is the ability to recover language functions after large dominant hemisphere lesions. This appears to persist until at least age eight years [46] and appears to depend on changes in the functional organization of the non-dominant hemisphere.

The presence of large numbers of synaptic contacts during postnatal development probably influences cortical function in ways other than through imparting plasticity to the system. Available evidence suggests that at least some of the exuberant synapses may be active rather than silent. This evidence derives from studies of cerebral metabolism. Cerebral metabolic rate is closely linked to the synaptic activity of cortical neurons. Developmental data show a remarkable parallel between synaptic density and cerebral metabolic rate as determined by positron emission tomography [10]. The metabolic rate in human cerebral cortex rises rapidly during the first postnatal years, remains above adult levels throughout childhood, and declines to adult values during adolescence. These changes show a rough parallel to the age-related variations in synaptic density observed in frontal cortex, but they correlate less well with changes in synaptic density in primary visual cortex. It may well be that area 17 has an unusual, early developmental schedule that differs from that of most other cortical regions.

The presence of excess synaptic activity may well have certain negative effects on brain function in the child. Activity in large pools of unspecified synapses may to some extent interfere with cortical processing. It may account for the well-known high susceptibility of the young child to seizures. The high metabolic demand of immature brain also may make it more susceptible to damage related to deficiency of metabolic substrates, including oxygen. Many components of the complex interactions between structure and function in developing cerebral cortex are as yet unknown. Newer methodologies, including *in vivo* imaging techniques [10] and computerized quantitation [33], are likely to bring significant future advances in this field.

REFERENCES

1   Aghajanian, G. K. and Bloom, F. E. The formation of synaptic junctions in developing rat brain: a quantitative electron microscopic study. *Brain Res.* 6, 716–27, 1967.

2   Assaf, A. A. The sensitive period: transfer of fixation after occlusion for strabismic amblyopia. *Br. J. Ophthalmol.* 66, 64–70, 1982.

3   Awaya, S., Miyake, Y., Imaizumi, Y., Shoise, Y., Kanda, T., and Komuro, K. Amblyopia in man, suggestive of stimulus deprivation amblyopia. *Jpn. J. Ophthalmol.* 17, 69–82, 1973.

4   Becker, L. E., Armstrong, D. L., Chan, F., and Wood, M. M. Dendritic development in human occipital cortical neurons. *Devl. Brain Res.* 13, 117–24, 1984.

5   Birch, E. E. and Held, R. The development of binocular summation in human infants. *Invest. Ophthalmol. Vis. Sci.* 14, 1103–7, 1983.

6   Buell, S. J. and Coleman, P. D. Dendritic growth in the aged human brain and failure of growth in senile dementia. *Science* 206, 854–6, 1979.

7   Buell, S. J. and Coleman, P. D. Quantitative evidence for selective dendritic growth in normal human aging but not in senile dementia. *Brain Res.* 214, 23–41, 1981.

8   Changeux, J.-P. and Danchin, A. Selective stabilization of developing synapses as a mechanism for the specification of neuronal networks. *Nature* 264, 705–12, 1976.

9   Changeux, J.-P., Heidmann, T., and Patte, P. Learning by selection. In *The Biology of Learning*, P. Marler and H. S. Terrace (eds.), pp. 115–37. Springer-Verlag, New York, 1984.

10 Chugani, H. T., Phelps, M. E., and Mazziotta, J. C. Positron emission tomography study of human brain functional development. *Ann. Neural.* 22, 487–97, 1987.

11 Cowan, W. M. Neuronal death as a regulative mechanism in the control of cell number in the nervous system. In *Development and Aging in the Nervous System*, M. Rockstein (ed.), pp. 19–41. Academic Press, New York, 1973.

12 Cragg, B. G. The density of synapses and neurons in the motor and visual areas of the cerebral cortex. *J. Anat.* 101, 639–54, 1967.

13 Cragg, B. G. The density of synapses and neurons in normal, mentally defective and aging human brains. *Brain* 98, 81–90, 1975.

14 Cragg, B. G. The development of synapses in the visual system of the cat. *J. Comp. Neurol.* 160, 147–66, 1975.

15 Edelman, G. M. *Neural Darwinism. The Theory of Neuronal Group Selection*. Basic Books, New York, 1987.

16 Gelbert, S. S., Hoyt, C. S., Jastrebski, G., and Marg, E. Long-term visual results in bilateral congenital cataracts. *Am. J. Ophthalmol.* 93, 615–21, 1982.

17 Held, R., Birch, E., and Gwiazda, J. Stereoacuity of human infants. *Proc. Natl Acad. Sci. USA* 77, 5572–4, 1980.

18 Heumann, D., Leuba, G., and Rabinowicz, T. Postnatal development of the mouse cerebral neocortex. IV. Evolution of the total cortical volume, of the population of neurons and glial cells. *J. Hirnforsch.* 19, 385–93, 1978.

19 Heumann, D. and Leuba, G. Neuronal death in the development and aging of the cerebral cortex of the mouse. *Neuropath. Appl. Neurobiol.* 9, 297–311, 1983.

20 Huttenlocher, P. R. Dendritic development in neocortex of children with mental defect and infantile spasms. *Neurology* 24, 203–10, 1974.

21 Huttenlocher, P. R. Synaptic density in human frontal cortex. Developmental changes and effects of aging. *Brain Res.* 163, 195–205, 1979.

22 Huttenlocher, P. R., De Courten, C., Garey, L. G., and Van Der Loos, H. Synaptogenesis in human visual cortex – evidence for synapse elimination during normal development. *Neurosci. Lett.* 33, 247–52, 1982.

23 Huttenlocher, P. R. and De Courten, C. The development of synapses in striate cortex of man. *Hum. Neurobiol.* 6, 1–9, 1987.

24 Huttenlocher, P. R. Synapse elimination and plasticity in developing human cerebral cortex. *Am. J. Mental Deficiency* 88, 488–96, 1984.

25 Jacobsen, S. G., Mohindra, I., and Held, R. Age of onset of amblyopia in infants with esotropia. *Doc. Ophthal. Proc. Ser.*, Vol. 30. L. Maffei (ed.), pp. 210–16. Dr W. Junk, Publishers, The Hague, 1981.

26 Leuba, G. and Garey, L. J. Evolution of neuronal numerical density in the developing and aging human visual cortex. *Hum. Neurobiol.* 6, 11–18, 1987.

27 Lewis, T. L., Maurer, D., and Brent, H. P. Effect on perceptual development of visual deprivation during infancy, *Br. J. Ophthalmol.* 70, 214–20, 1986.

28 Marin-Padilla, M. Prenatal and early postnatal ontogenesis of the human motor cortex: a Golgi study. I. The sequential development of the cortical layers. *Brain Res.* 23, 167–83, 1970.

29 Marin-Padilla, M. Structural abnormalities of the cerebral cortex in human chromosomal aberrations. A Golgi study. *Brain Res.* 44, 625–9, 1972.

30 Marin-Padilla, M. Pyramidal cell abnormalities in the motor cortex of a child with Down's syndrome. A Golgi study. *J. Comp. Neurol.* 167, 63–82, 1976.

31 Michel, A. E. and Garey, L. J. The development of dendritic spines in the human visual cortex. *Hum. Neurobiol.* 3, 223–7, 1984.

32 O'Kusky, J. and Colonnier, M. Postnatal changes in the number of neurons and synapses in the visual cortex (A17) of the macaque monkey. *J. Comp. Neurol.* 210, 291–6, 1982.

33 Paldino, A. M. and Purpura, D. P. Quantitative analysis of the spatial distribution of axonal and dendritic terminals of hippocampal pyramidal neurons in immature human brain. *Expl. Neurol.* 64, 604–19, 1979.

34 Purpura, D. P. Dendritic spine "dysgenesis" and mental retardation. *Science* 186, 1126–8, 1974.

35 Purpura, D. P. Normal and aberrant neuronal development in the cerebral cortex of human fetus and young infants. In *Brain Mechanisms in Mental Retardation*. N. A. Buchwald and M. A. B. Brazier (eds.), pp. 141–69. Academic Press, New York, 1975.

36 Rakic, P., Bourgeois, J.-P., Eckenhoff, M. F., Zecevic, M., and Golman-Rakic, P. S. Concurrent overproduction of synapses in diverse regions of primate cerebral cortex. *Science* 232, 232–4, 1986.

37 Sauer, N., Kammaradt. G., Krauthausen, I., Kretschmann, H.-T., Lange, H. W., and Wingert, F. Qualitative and quantitative development of the visual cortex in man. *J. Comp. Neurol.* 214, 441–50, 1983.

38 Schade, J. P. and Van Groenigen, W. B. Structural organization of the human cerebral cortex. I. Maturation of the middle frontal gyrus. *Acta Anat.* 47, 74–111, 1961.

39   Shariff, G. A. Cell counts in the primate cerebral cortex. *J. Comp. Neurol.* 98, 381–400, 1953.

40   Sholl, D. A. A comparative study of the neuronal packing density in the cerebral cortex. *J. Anat.* 93, 143–58. 1959.

41   Sidman, R. L. and Rakic, P. Neuronal migration, with special reference to developing human brain: a review. *Brain Res.* 62, 1–35, 1973.

42   Takashima, S., Becker, L. E., Armstrong, D. A., and Chan, F. Abnormal neuronal development in the visual cortex of the human fetus and infant with Down's syndrome. A quantitative and qualitative Golgi study. *Brain Res.* 225, 1–21, 1981.

43   Teller, D. Y. Scotopic vision, color vision and stereopsis in infants. *Curr. Eye Res.* 2, 199–210, 1983.

44   Tower, D. B. Structural and functional organization of mammalian cerebral cortex: the correlation of neurone density with brain size. *J. Comp. Neurol.* 101, 19–51, 1954.

45   Williams, R. S., Ferrante, R. J., and Caviness, V. S. The rapid Golgi method in clinical neuropathology: the morphologic consequences of suboptimal fixation. *J. Neuropath. Exp. Neurol.* 37, 13–33, 1978.

46   Woods, B. T. and Teuber, H. L. Changing patterns of childhood aphasia, *Ann. Neurol.* 3, 273–80, 1978.

47   Yakovlev, P. I. and Lecours, A.-R. The myelogenetic cycles of regional maturation of the brain. In *Regional Development of the Brain in Early Life*, A. Minkowsky (ed.), pp. 3–70. Blackwell, Oxford, 1967.

PART III

Brain Maturation and Cognition

Editors' Introduction to Part III

Perhaps the most obvious way to relate brain development and cognition is to attribute the onset of a certain cognitive ability to the maturation of underlying neural circuitry. Part III presents two papers, by Johnson and Nelson, that take this kind of approach. Although this type of argument has commonly been applied to the onset of an ability, it may also be applied to the termination of an ability (e.g., in sensitive periods, as discussed by Lorenz in Part I, Marler in Part V, and O'Reilly and Johnson in Part VI). The variations on this general claim usually take one of the following forms: (a) sequences of brain maturation are used to predict the sequence of development of certain cognitive abilities (as evidenced in the paper by Johnson); (b) specific neural developments at a certain age are posited to give rise to a specific computational advance at that same age (as evidenced in the paper by Nelson).

The paper by Johnson uses evidence about patterns of postnatal brain growth to make predictions about the sequence of development in visual attention and orienting. Johnson discusses both overt orienting (head and eye movements that shift gaze) and covert shifts of attention (independent of head and eye movements). In the case of overt orienting, Johnson makes three neuroanatomical observations: (a) the primary visual cortex is the main gateway to several pathways that underlie components of visual attention and orienting; (b) primary visual cortex, like other areas of cortex, has a layer-specific pattern of connectivity to these other neural structures and pathways; and (c) some measures of postnatal cortical growth show a layer-specific pattern of development from deeper layers to more superficial ones (as we saw in Part II). These facts support inferences regarding the development of cortical pathways, such as the earlier development of the visual pathway involving the middle temporal area relative to the pathway involving the frontal eye fields. These pathways underlie particular components of visual orienting and attention, supporting predictions about sequences of development at the cognitive level, such as smooth visual tracking preceding anticipatory eye movements. Johnson reviews a large amount of evidence on the development of visual orienting in human infants to provide support for the predicted sequences.

In the case of covert shifts of attention, Johnson focuses on the effects of facilitation (faster responding to a stimulus appearing in a covertly attended location) and inhibition of return (IOR, slower responding to a stimulus appearing in a covertly attended location). Facilitation generally occurs when a target stimulus appears soon after the offset of the cue that shifts attention, whereas IOR occurs with longer latencies between cue and target. Covert shifts of attention appear to involve the parietal lobe, and IOR requires the superior colliculus. Again, Johnson uses sequences of development of such neural structures to predict sequences of development at the behavioral level, in terms of facilitation and IOR, and reviews relevant evidence.

Nelson takes the first of the two approaches outlined above, reviewing neural developments posited to give rise to advances in distinct types of memory at particular ages. Nelson discusses many distinctions made in the memory literature, including explicit versus implicit, procedural learning and conditioning, and working memory. He suggests that the early development of the striatum may support infants' success in procedural learning tasks in the first few months of life, and the early development of the cerebellum may support conditioning in young infants. Explicit memory may emerge somewhat later (between 6 and 12 months) due to the development of temporal lobe structures, following the development of a preexplicit memory dependent on the hippocampus. Working memory may also begin to develop within the 6–12 month period, due to developments in the prefrontal cortex (see the Diamond reading in Part VII for a thorough discussion of the role of dopamine in this process). Nelson notes that all of these forms of memory may continue to develop for many months and years.

Nelson emphasizes at the outset that there are multiple caveats to exploring the relation between brain development and memory development. For example, because the brain works as an integrated system, the brain structures outlined above do not subserve their purported functions alone, but rather as parts of complex circuits. As a result, the interpretation of behaviors following lesions can be quite difficult. Further, caution must be taken in comparing the behaviors of human infants and adults and other species. We note that even within the infant literature, there is controversy over the interpretation of performance in various tasks and the implications for memory development (cf. Rovee-Collier's (1997) analysis of the development of implicit and explicit memory, Diamond's (1991) work on the effects of hippocampal maturation, and Munakata's (1998) discussion of working memory development). Resolving these controversies may be a useful step in understanding distinct types of memory and their neural substrates.

FURTHER READING

Atkinson, J. (1984). Human visual development over the first six months of life: A review and a hypothesis. *Human Neurobiology* 3: 61–74. (A comprehensive review of the development of vision and its neural basis.)

Bachevalier, J. and Mishkin, M. (1984). An early and a late developing system for learning and retention in infant monkeys. *Behavioral Neuroscience* 98: 770–8.

Bates, E., Thal, D., et al. (1992). Early language development and its neural correlates. *Handbook of Neuropsychology*. I. Rapin and S. Segalowitz (eds.). Amsterdam: Elsevier. Vol 6: *Child Neurology*. (A review of neurodevelopmental correlates of language acquisition.)

Bronson, G. W. (1974). The postnatal growth of visual capacity. *Child Development* 45: 873–90. (The now classic original statement proposing that the development of visually guided behavior in the human infant can be viewed in terms of a transition from subcortical to cortical processing.)

Carey, S. (1980). Maturational factors in human development. *Biological Studies of Mental Processes*. D. Caplan. Cambridge, MA: MIT Press: 1–7. (An introduction to some of the issues about the relation between brain development and cognitive development.)

Carey, S. and Diamond, R. (1980). Maturational determination of the developmental course of face encoding. *Biological Studies of Mental Processes*. Cambridge, MA: MIT Press. (Evidence for a maturationally determined "dip" in face recognition abilities around the time of puberty.)

Dehaene, S. and Changeux, J. P. (1989). A simple model of prefrontal cortex function in delayed-response tasks. *Journal of Cognitive Neuroscience* 1(3): 244–61.

Diamond, A. (1991). Neuropsychological insights into the meaning of object concept development. *The Epigenesis of Mind: Essays on Biology and Cognition*. S. Carey and R. Gelman. Hillsdale, NJ: Lawrence Erlbaum Associates: 67–110.

Goldman-Rakic, P. S. (1987). Development of cortical circuitry and cognitive function. *Child Development* 58: 601–22. (A review of the possible effects of prefrontal cortex maturation on cognition.)

Goldman-Rakic, P. S. and Isseroff, A., et al. (1983). The neurobiology of cognitive development. *Handbook of Child Psychology: Biology and Infancy Development*. P. Mussen (ed.). New York: Wiley: 281–334. (A comprehensive overview of the relation between the anatomical development of the cortex, especially the prefrontal cortex, and some aspects of behavioral development.)

Held, R. (1985). Binocular vision: Behavioral and neuronal development. *Neonate Cognition: Beyond the Blooming, Buzzing Confusion*. J. Mehler and R. Fox (eds.). Hillsdale, NJ: Lawrence Erlbaum.

Johnson, M. H. (1990). Cortical maturation and the development of visual attention in early infancy. *Journal of Cognitive Neuroscience* 2(2): 81–95.

Muir, D. W. and Clifton, R. K., et al. (1989). The development of a human auditory localization response: A U-shaped function. *Canadian Journal of Psychology* 43: 199–216. (A review of experiments indicating that auditory orienting in the human infant goes through a similar subcortical to cortical shift to that described in the visual system.)

Munakata, Y. (1998). Infant perseveration and implications for object permanence theories: A PDP Model of the A-not-B task. *Developmental Science* 1(2): 161–84.

Nelson, C. A. (1995). The ontogeny of human memory: A cognitive neuroscience perspective. *Developmental Psychology* 31(5): 723–38.

Newport, E. L. (1990). Maturational constraints on language learning. *Cognitive Science* 14: 11–28. (Argues for maturational constraints of language acquisition.)

Rovee-Collier, C. (1997). Dissociations in Infant Memory: Rethinking the Development of Implicit and Explicit Memory. *Psychological Review* 104: 467–98.

Witelson, S. F. (1987). Neurobiological aspects of language in children. *Child Development* 58: 653–8. (Explores some parallels between aspects of brain and language development.)

9

The Development of Visual Attention: A Cognitive Neuroscience Perspective

Mark H. Johnson

Neuropsychological studies with adult patients examine the effects on cognition of the loss of certain neural systems or structures, while work with other species allows us to analyze brain–cognitive relations in simpler, and more tractable, neural systems. Development can be used as a method for studying the relation between neural systems and cognition in a way that complements the use of patient or animal data, for in developmental studies we can examine the effects of the addition of new neural systems to the simpler form of the human brain found in the newborn infant.

In recent years, it has become evident that there are multiple pathways involved in the control of eye movements and visual attention in adults (e.g., Schiller, 1985; Posner and Petersen, 1990) (figure 9.1). Given the obvious difficulty in analyzing the complex combinations of hierarchical and parallel systems found in the adult, investigating the sequential development of these pathways and the construction of interacting brain systems during ontogeny may be informative (see Johnson, 1990, 1994a). Further, properly directed attention during infancy plays a vital role in ensuring the normal development of other cognitive functions, such as face recognition (Johnson and Morton, 1991; Johnson, 1992). In this chapter, I review studies on the ontogeny of both overt and covert aspects of visual orienting and suggest some ways that this infant data can shed light on the neural basis of visual attention.

Although our understanding of visual attention and orienting in adults is far from complete, a number of distinctions have been proposed that will be helpful in reviewing the ontogeny of attention (figure 9.2). Eye movements that shift gaze from one location to another may be referred to as *overt* orienting. In contrast, shifts of visual attention between spatial locations or objects that occur independently of eye and head movements are referred to as *covert* (Posner, 1980). Only in the past few years have studies designed to detect covert shifts of attention in infancy been performed, and the extent to which these covert processes in infants resemble those in adults requires further research.

A further distinction in the adult literature is that between *endogenous* and *exogenous* cuing of visual orienting (Klein, Kingstone, and Pontefract, 1992). Exogenously driven saccades are often short-latency and reflexive and are triggered by stimuli that appear within the visual field. In contrast, endogenously driven saccades are commonly of longer latency and are described as *intentional* or *volitional*. A common experimental procedure for

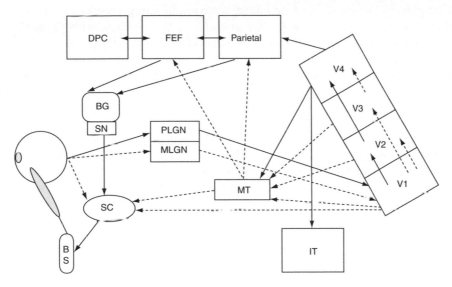

Figure 9.1 A diagram representing some of the main neural pathways and structures involved in visual orienting and attention. Solid lines indicate primarily parvocellular input, whereas the dashed arrows represent magnocellular input. V1–V4, visual cortex; FEF, frontal eye fields; DPC, dorsolateral prefrontal cortex; BG, basal ganglia; SN, substantia nigra; MLGN, PLGN, lateral geniculate, magno and parvo portions; MT, middle temporal area; IT, inferotemporal cortex; SC, superior colliculus; BS, brain stem. Bold lines indicate mixed input. (Courtesy of Rick Gilmore.)

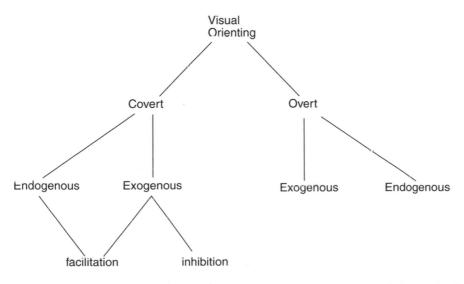

Figure 9.2 Diagram representing some dissociations between components of visual orienting and attention. See text for further explanation.

studying exogenous cuing involves a brief cue stimulus being presented in a particular spatial location. This cue serves to draw attention to that location, with the result that subjects are (initially) faster to respond to targets that appear in the same place. In an endogenous cuing experiment, a centrally presented arrow pointing to the right or left, an auditory cue, or a verbal instruction to look in a certain direction is used to direct attention. In this chapter, we will see how the ontogeny of visually guided behavior over the first few months of life can be partly viewed as a transition from exogenous to endogenous control of orienting.

A challenge facing all those interested in the neural basis of visual orienting and attention is to understand the mapping between the various neural pathways implicated in these processes (see figure 9.1) and the distinctions revealed by cognitive studies (see figure 9.2). As we shall see, the study of development offers a unique perspective on this mapping.

Overt Visual Orienting in Early Infancy

Bronson (1974, 1982) argued that visually guided behavior in the newborn human infant is controlled primarily by means of the subcortical retinocollicular pathway and that it is only by approximately 2 or 3 months of age that the locus of control switches to cortical pathways. The development of visually guided behavior can thus be viewed as a shift from subcortical to cortical processing. The claim that the primary visual pathway is not fully functioning until 2 or 3 months of postnatal age has been supported by a variety of electrophysiological, neuroanatomical, and behavioral studies (for reviews, see Atkinson, 1984, and Johnson, 1990). However, two factors have led to criticism of Bronson's original proposals. First, more recent neurophysiological knowledge about the visual pathways of the mammalian brain has led to reconsideration of the original two-pathways account. For example, it is now known that there are several comparatively independent cortical streams of processing held to have differing information-processing functions. Furthermore, our understanding of the integrative abilities of the superior colliculus has greatly increased in recent years. Thus, both Atkinson (1984) and Johnson (1990) have argued that the original cortical–subcortical dichotomy for the ontogeny of visual processing may inadequately capture the complexity of the transition. Second, the striking perceptual abilities of the very young infant in some tasks have led many psychologists to question the notion of the "decorticate" newborn (e.g., Slater, Morison, and Somers, 1988; Bushnell, Sai, and Mullin, 1989).

As a result of these considerations, Johnson (1990) suggested a specific hypothesis about the partial cortical functioning of newborns and its expansion over the first 6 months of life. This hypothesis accounts for changes in the development of overt visual orienting over the first few months of life, in terms of the maturation of several cortical pathways. These pathways were derived from proposals initially introduced to account for adult primate electrophysiological and lesion data related to oculomotor control (Schiller, 1985) and are as follows:

1   A direct pathway from the retina to the superior colliculus, involved in rapid input-driven (exogenous) eye movements toward simple, easily discriminable stimuli and fed mainly by the temporal visual field.

2 A cortical pathway that goes to the superior colliculus both directly from the primary visual cortex and also via the middle temporal area (MT). This pathway is largely driven by the broadband or magnocellular stream.

3 A cortical pathway that combines both broadband and color-opponent streams of processing in the frontal eye fields (FEFs) and that is involved in the detailed and complex analysis of visual stimuli, such as the temporal sequencing of eye movements within complex arrays and anticipatory saccades.

4 A final pathway for the control of eye movements involving tonic inhibition of the colliculus via the substantia nigra and basal ganglia.

Schiller (1985) proposed that the fourth pathway ensures that the activity of the colliculus can be regulated. More recent findings suggest that this oculomotor pathway forms an integrated system with the FEF and parietal lobes (e.g., Alexander, DeLong, and Strick, 1986) and that it plays some role in regulating subcortical processing by these cortical structures.

Johnson (1990) proposed that the characteristics of visually guided behavior of the infant at particular ages is determined by which of these pathways is functional, and which of these pathways is functional is influenced by the developmental state of the primary visual cortex. The basis of this claim at the neuroanatomical level lies in three sets of observations: (i) The primary visual cortex is the major (though not exclusive) gateway for input to the three cortical pathways (2, 3, 4) (Schiller, 1985); (ii) the primary visual cortex shows a postnatal continuation of the prenatal inside-out pattern of growth of the cortex, with the deeper layers (5 and 6) showing greater dendritic branching, length, and extent of myelinization than more superficial layers (2 and 3) near the time of birth (e.g., Purpura, 1975; Rabinowicz, 1979; Becker et al., 1984; Huttenlocher, 1990); and (iii) there is a restricted pattern of inputs and outputs from the primary visual cortex (e.g., the efferents to V2 depart from the upper layers; see, for example, Rockland and Pandya, 1979, and Burkhalter and Bernardo, 1989).

Johnson (1990) reasoned that if more superficial layers of the primary visual cortex are comparatively less developed than deeper layers in terms of the extent of dendritic growth, then projections from the superficial layers may be weaker, or even nonfunctional, at a stage when projections from the deeper layers are strong. This hypothesized relative restriction on projection patterns yielded the prediction that output from V1 to pathway 2 should be stronger than the projection to pathway 3 at early stages of development. Such a prediction from cellular development has implications for information processing: The functions subserved by pathway 2 involving structure MT should appear earlier in development than those of pathway 3 involving the FEF. Employing this logic, Johnson (1990) attempted to account for characteristics of the visually guided behavior of the infant in terms of the sequential development of pathways underlying visual orienting. This sequential development is a dynamic process, but a number of phases may be characterized.

It should be stressed that the phases described in the following sections are not meant to be rigid or sudden-onset stages of development. Rather they are to be viewed as snapshots along a dynamic and constantly changing path. Similarly, the strong predictions from Johnson's (1990) account concern the *sequence* of development within an individual infant rather than the exact ages of group effects. In general, the transitions described next can be characterized as a shift from exogenous or automatic eye movement control to a more predictive system influenced by endogenous factors (see Johnson, 1994b).

The newborn

As mentioned previously, evidence from measures of the extent of dendritic arborization and myelinization suggest the hypothesis that only the deeper layers of the primary visual cortex are capable of supporting organized information-processing activity in the human newborn. Because the majority of feedforward intracortical projections depart from outside the deeper layers (5 and 6), some of the cortical orienting pathways (those involving MT and the FEFs) may be receiving only weak or disorganized input at this stage. Nonetheless, evidence from various sources, such as visually evoked potentials, indicate that information from the eye is entering the primary visual cortex in the newborn. Thus, while agreeing with Bronson's (1974) proposal that *most* of the newborn's visual behavior can be accounted for in terms of processing in the subcortical pathway, Johnson (1990) argued that there is *some* information processing occurring in the deeper cortical layers at birth.

There are a number of characteristics of newborn visually guided behavior consistent with predominantly subcortical control. Among these are saccadic pursuit tracking of moving stimuli, preferential orienting to the temporal field, and the externality effect.

Saccadic pursuit tracking of moving stimuli

Aslin (1981) reports that tracking in very early infancy has two characteristics. The first is that the eye movements follow the stimulus in a saccadic or steplike manner, as opposed to the smooth pursuit found in adults and older infants. The second characteristic is that the eye movements always lag behind the movement of the stimulus rather than predicting its trajectory. Therefore, when a newborn infant visually tracks a moving stimulus, it could be described as performing a series of separate reorientations. Such behavior is consistent with collicular control of orienting (see Johnson, 1990, for details).

Preferential orienting to the temporal field

Newborns much more readily orient toward stimuli in the temporal, as opposed to the nasal, visual field (e.g., Lewis, Maurer, and Milewski, 1979). Posner and Rothbart (1980) suggest that midbrain structures such as the colliculus can be driven most readily by temporal field input. This proposal has been confirmed in studies of adult blindsight patients by Rafal and coworkers (1990), who established that distractor stimuli placed in the temporal "blind field" had an effect on orienting into the good field, whereas distractor stimuli in the nasal blind field did not. Recent evidence from studies of infants with complete hemispherectomy indicate that the subcortical (collicular) pathway is capable of supporting saccades toward a peripheral stimulus in the cortically blind field (Braddick et al., 1992).

The externality effect

Infants in the first few months of life do not attend to stationary pattern elements within a larger frame or pattern (e.g., Maurer and Young, 1983) unless these elements are moving (Bushnell, 1979). Although a variety of explanations have been proposed to account for this phenomenon (e.g., Aslin and Smith, 1988), Johnson (1990) proposed that part of the explanation could involve a collicular mechanism attempting to shift the retinal image of the largest frame or pattern elements into the foveal field.

Bearing in mind that the majority of visuomotor functions in the newborn are likely to be primarily subcortical, we should note that evidence for pattern recognition (Slater,

Morison, and Rose, 1982) and orientation discrimination (Atkinson et al., 1988; Slater, Morison, and Somers, 1988) are indicative of at least some cortical functioning.

One month of age

Between 1 and 3 months of age, infants show obligatory attention (Stechler and Latz, 1966): That is, they have great difficulty in disengaging their gaze from a stimulus in order to saccade elsewhere. Although this phenomenon remains poorly understood, Johnson (1990) suggests that it is due to the development of tonic inhibition of the colliculus via the substantia nigra (pathway 4). This as yet unregulated tonic inhibition of the colliculus has the consequence that stimuli impinging on the peripheral visual field no longer elicit an automatic exogenous saccade as readily as in newborns. An alternative account of obligatory attention was proposed by Posner and Rothbart (1980), who suggest that it is only after development of the parietal lobes that the infant has the ability to disengage from stimuli. Thus, the end of obligatory attention marks the onset of covert attention abilities in the infant (see next section). Whichever of these accounts of obligatory attention proves to be correct, the failure to disengage may be object-centered rather than dependent on spatial location (see Johnson, 1994a).

Two months of age

Although their eye movements still lag behind the movement of the stimulus, infants at approximately 2 months of age begin to demonstrate periods of smooth visual tracking. Furthermore, they become more sensitive to stimuli placed in the nasal visual field (Aslin, 1981) and become sensitive to coherent motion (R. Spitz, personal communication, 1992). Johnson (1990) proposed that the onset of these behaviors coincides with the functioning of the pathway involving structure MT. The enabling of this route of eye movement control may provide the cortical magnocellular stream with the ability to regulate activity in the superior colliculus.

More than 3 months of age

After approximately 3 months of age, the pathway involving the FEFs may gain in strength due to further dendritic growth and myelinization within the upper layers of the primary visual cortex. These cellular level developments may greatly increase the infant's ability to make anticipatory eye movements and to learn sequences of looking patterns. Further, with regard to the visual tracking of a moving object, not only do infants now show periods of smooth tracking, but their eye movements often predict the movement of the stimulus in an anticipatory manner. A number of experiments by Haith and colleagues (1988) have demonstrated that anticipatory eye movements can be readily elicited from infants by this age. Haith exposed $3\frac{1}{2}$-month-old infants to a series of picture slides that appeared either on the right or on the left side of the infant. These stimuli were presented either in an alternating sequence with a fixed interstimulus interval (ISI) or with an irregular alternation pattern and ISI. The regular alternation pattern produced more stimulus anticipations, and reaction times to make an eye movement were reliably faster than in the irregular series. Haith (1988) concluded from these results that infants of this age are able to develop expectancies for noncontrollable spatiotemporal events. Canfield and Haith (1991) tested 2- and 3-month-old infants in a similar experiment that included more complex sequences (such as left–left–right, left–left–right). They failed to find significant effects with 2-month-olds, but 3-month-olds appeared able to acquire at least some of the more complex sequences. Furthermore, if the acquired sequence was changed to another sequence, infants of 3 months made errors consistent with having acquired the first sequence (Arehart and Haith, 1991).

Evidence for Covert Shifts of Visual Attention in Early Infancy

In adults, covert attention may be directed to a spatial location by a very briefly presented visual stimulus. Although subjects do not make a saccade to this stimulus, they are faster to report (often by means of a button press) the appearance of a target stimulus in the cued location than in another location. We may therefore infer that a covert shift of attention to the cued location facilitates subsequent detection at the location.

With infants, we are limited to indirect methods of studying covert shifts of attention. Furthermore, we have the problem that infants do not accept verbal instruction and are poor at motor responses readily elicited from adults (e.g., a button press). One motor response that can be readily elicited even from very young infants is eye movement (overt orienting). Thus, in most of the experiments reported here, measures of overt orienting are used to study covert shifts of attention. This can be done by examining the influence of a cue stimulus, to which infants do not make an eye movement, on their subsequent saccades toward target stimuli. This approach has also been taken in some adult studies purporting to measure shifts of covert attention (e.g., Maylor, 1985; Shephard, Findlay, and Hockey, 1986). Of course, this does not mean that covert shifts of attention are not involved in tasks in which the infant makes a saccade toward the cue, merely that it is more difficult to establish that this is so.

Whereas processes of covert attention develop throughout the school-age years (e.g., Enns and Brodeur, 1989; Tipper et al., 1989), I will focus on developments in the first 6–8 months of life, as these can more readily be associated with the development of neural pathways and structures and are thus more relevant for a cognitive neuroscientific perspective.

Exogenously cued covert shifts of attention

One way in which evidence for covert attention has been provided in adults is by studying the effect on detection of cueing saccades to a particular spatial location. A briefly presented cue serves to draw covert attention to the location, resulting in the subsequent facilitation of detection of targets at that location (Posner and Cohen, 1980; Maylor, 1985). Whereas *facilitation* of detection and responses to a covertly attended location occurs if the target stimulus appears very shortly after the cue offset, *inhibition* of saccades toward that location occurs with longer latencies between cue and target. This latter phenomenon, referred to as *inhibition of return* (Posner et al., 1985), may reflect an evolutionarily important mechanism for preventing attention from returning to a spatial location that has very recently been processed. In adults, facilitation is observed reliably when targets appeared at the cued location within approximately 150 ms of the cue, whereas targets that appear between 300 and 1300 ms after a peripheral (exogenous) cue result in longer detection latencies (e.g., Posner and Cohen, 1980, 1984; Maylor, 1985).

After incurring lesions to the posterior parietal lobe, adults show severe neglect of the contralateral visual field. According to Posner and colleagues (Posner 1988; Posner and Petersen, 1990), this neglect is due to damage to the posterior attention network, a brain circuit that includes not only the posterior parietal lobe but also the pulvinar and superior colliculus (see figure 9.1 for all but the pulvinar). Damage to this circuit is postulated to impair subjects' ability to shift covert attention to a cued spatial location. The involvement of these regions in shifts of visual attention has been confirmed by positron emission tomography (PET) studies. Both neuroanatomical (Conel, 1939–1967) and PET (Chugani, Phelps, and Mazziotta, 1987) evidence from the human infant indicate that the parietal lobe is undergoing substantive and rapid development between 3 and 6 months after birth. The question arises, therefore, as to whether infants become capable of covert shifts of attention during this time.

Hood and Atkinson (1991; see also Hood, 1995) reported that 6-month-old infants displayed faster reaction times (RTs) to make a saccade to a target when it appeared immediately after a brief (100-ms) cue stimulus, whereas a group of 3-month-olds did not. Johnson (1993a, 1994b) employed a similar procedure in which a brief (100-ms) cue was presented on one of two side screens before bilateral targets were presented either 100 or 600 ms later. He reasoned that the 200-ms stimulus onset asynchrony (SOA) may be short enough to produce facilitation, whereas the long SOA trials should result in preferential orienting toward the opposite side (inhibition of return). From figure 9.3, it can be seen that there was no significant difference in the RT to make a saccade to the cued or opposite target between the long and the short ISI trials for a group of 2-month-old infants. However, in a 4-month-old group of infants, a significant facilitation of RTs was noted

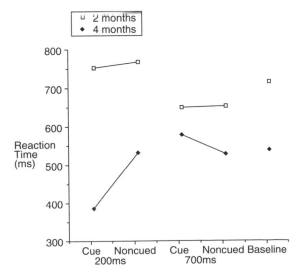

Figure 9.3 The mean median reaction time of groups of 2- and 4-month-old infants to respond to cued targets, opposite targets, and no-cue baseline trials, following either a short (200 ms) or long (700 ms) stimulus onset asynchrony. (Data from Johnson, 1993a.)

when making a saccade toward the cued target: At the short ISI, these infants showed a faster RT toward the cued target, whereas at the long ISI, they were slower to respond to the cued target (inhibition). A similar result was found with the direction of saccade (cued or opposite target) data (Johnson, 1993a).

Similar experiments run with slightly older infants indicate that covert shifts of attention may get faster between 4 and 8 months of age. Whereas 4-month-olds show clear facilitation when a target is presented 200 ms after the onset of a cue, 6- and 8-month-olds, like adults, show equivalent facilitation only if the target is presented less than 150 ms after cue onset (Johnson, 1993a, b). At present, it remains an open question whether the facilitation produced by the cue in these experiments is the result of direct priming of the eye movement system or whether the eye movements are following an independent covert shift of attention. However, the finding that 4-month-old infants show facilitation to a cue even when it predicts the presentation of a target in the opposite direction (normally also necessitating an eye movement in the opposite direction) is more consistent with the theory that facilitation effects are due to drawing covert attention to the location (Johnson, Posner, and Rothbart, 1994).

While facilitation of responding to a cued spatial location may depend on the functioning of the parietal lobe, inhibition of return (IOR) has been more closely associated with the functioning of the superior colliculus. For example, supranuclear palsy, a progressive disease that affects the colliculus, selectively reduces IOR (Posner et al., 1985). Because midbrain structures such as the superior colliculus are believed to be well developed at the time of birth (Bronson, 1974; Atkinson, 1984; Chugani, Phelps, and Mazziotta, 1987; Johnson, 1990), we would expect that IOR should be present from around the time of birth in the human infant.

IOR can be studied in infants following either overt or covert shifts of attention, according to whether or not the infant is allowed to make a saccade toward the cue stimulus. Clohessy and colleagues (1991) studied IOR following overt orienting. Infants sat in front of three monitor screens on which colorful dynamic stimuli were presented. At the start of each trial, an attractive fixation stimulus appeared on the central screen. Once the infant had fixated on this stimulus, a cue stimulus was presented on one of the two side monitor screens. When the infant had made a saccade toward the cue, it was turned off, following which the infant returned its gaze to the center screen before an identical target stimulus was presented bilaterally on both side screens. Infants of 3 months of age showed no significant preferential orienting to the bilateral targets as a result of the cue, but infants of 6 months of age made saccades more frequently toward the side opposite that on which the cue had appeared. The authors argued that this preferential orienting toward the opposite side from the cue is indicative of IOR and its development between 3 and 6 months of age.

More recent experiments suggest that the age when IOR can first be demonstrated may depend on the size of the visual angle between the central fixation point and the cue or target. Harman, Posner, and Rothbart (1994) reasoned that if infants have to make several saccades to a target at 30° eccentricity, then they will not show IOR at the target destination. This is because in adult studies, IOR has been linked to saccade planning (Rafal et al., 1989). A target at only 10° eccentricity, however, can easily be reached in one saccade in the very young infant, and thus IOR should be observed. In accordance with their prediction, Harman, Posner, and Rothbart (1994) found evidence of IOR in 3-month-old infants at 10° but not at 30°. Although it is possible that IOR might be found at still younger ages (Valenza et al., 1992), Harman and colleagues suggest that its developmental onset probably is linked to the maturation of cortical structures involved in the development of programmed eye movements, namely the FEFs.

To date, evidence for IOR following covert shifts of attention has been detected only in infants of 4 months and older. Hood and Atkinson (1991) used a short cue duration (100 ms) to ensure that the infants did not make a saccade toward this stimulus. Thus, any effects of the cue presentation on subsequent saccades to the target could be attributed to a covert shift of attention during the cue presentation. Six-month-old infants showed IOR under these conditions, but a group of 3-month-old infants did not. Hood (1995) reports an experiment similar to that of Hood and Atkinson (1991) but with an improved method that allows, among other things, more accurate assessment of RTs to make a saccade toward the target. In this experiment, a group of 6-month-olds were exposed to a longer-duration cue (180 ms) before immediately being presented with a single target on either the ipsilateral or the contralateral side. This procedure resulted in a clear difference in mean RT to orient toward the target, depending on whether it appeared in the same spatial location as the cue. Using methods similar to those of Hood and colleagues, Johnson (1993b, 1994b) studied IOR after covert orienting in 2-, 4-, 6-, and 8-month-old infants and confirmed that the phenomenon was present only in the older age groups (for 2- and 4-month-old RT data, see figure 9.3). Because all these studies used peripheral cues and targets that were more than 10° from fixation, the conclusion that infants younger than 4 months do not show IOR under these circumstances must remain preliminary.

The pattern of results obtained with infants after covert and overt orienting suggests one of two possibilities about the neural basis of IOR: (1) that, in addition to the colliculus, IOR involves cortical structures such as the FEF, which become sufficiently mature 3–4 months after birth, or (2) that covert shifts of attention require cortical structures that are not functional until 3–4 months of age, and thus IOR after covert shifts of attention cannot be demonstrated until this age. The second of these possibilities predicts that IOR after overt orienting will be present in the first few months of life and perhaps even from birth. A recent report claims to find IOR in newborns after overt orienting (Valenza et al., 1992). If this preliminary evidence from newborns can be replicated, then the infant data suggest that IOR after overt orienting is exclusively dependent on subcortical structures and that cortical structures are involved only after covert shifts of attention.

Endogenously cued covert shifts of attention

The direction of attention in response to verbal, symbolic, or memorized cues is referred to as *endogenously driven orienting*. Whereas the endogenous direction of attention undoubtedly involves many of the same structures and circuits as play a role in orienting to exogeneous cues, recent PET evidence indicates additional involvement of the prefrontal cortex when endogenous cues are used (Deiber et al., 1991; Frith et al., 1991; Corbetta et al., 1993).

Most adult studies of endogenously cued shifts of attention have involved the use of verbal or symbolic cues (such as an arrow), but with infants we have to rely on memory as the source of endogenous cuing. This has been done in several laboratories by rewarding infants for making a saccade in a particular direction after presentation of an auditory or visual cue (e.g., de Schonen and Bry, 1987; Colombo et al., 1990; Johnson, Posner, and Rothbart, 1991).

One example of such a study was conducted by Johnson, Posner, and Rothbart (1991), who attempted to train infants to use a stimulus presented in a central location as a cue to predict the peripheral location (right or left of center) at which an attractive target stimulus would subsequently appear. This experiment is similar, in some respects, to studies in adults in which attention is cued to a peripheral location by means of a central (endogenous) cue such as an arrow. Groups of 2-, 3-, and 4-month-old infants were exposed to a number of training trials in which there was a contingent relation between which of two cue stimuli were presented on the central monitor and the location (right or left of center) at which an attractive target stimulus was subsequently presented. After a number of such training trials, we occasionally presented test trials in which the target appeared on both of the side monitors, regardless of which central stimulus preceded it. In these test trials, we measured whether the infants looked more toward the cued location than toward the opposite location. Whereas 2- and 3-month-old infants looked equally frequently to the cued and opposite sides, the group of 4-month-olds looked significantly more often toward the cued location. This result, taken together with a similar finding in an earlier study (de Schonen and Bry, 1987), is consistent with endogenously cued shifts of attention being present in 4-month-old infants.

Several other tasks recently conducted with infants are consistent with an increasing prefrontal cortex endogenous control over shifts of attention and saccades at approximately 4 months of age. For example, Funahashi, Bruce, and Goldman-Rakic (1989, 1990) have devised an oculomotor delayed response task to study the properties of neurons in the dorsolateral prefrontal cortex of macaque monkeys. In this task, the monkey plans a saccade toward a particular spatial location but has to wait for a period (usually between 2 and 5 seconds) before actually executing the saccade. Single-unit recording in the macaque indicates that some cells in the dorsolateral prefrontal cortex code for the direction of the saccade during the delay. Furthermore, reversible microlesions to the area result in selective amnesia for saccades to a localized part of the visual field. A recent PET study on human subjects has confirmed the involvement of prefrontal cortex (and parietal cortex) in this task (Jonides et al., 1993).

Gilmore and Johnson (1994) devised an infant version of the oculomotor delayed response task. The results obtained to date indicate that 6-month-old human infants can perform delayed saccades successfully with delays of up to at least 5 seconds, suggesting some influence of the prefrontal cortex on eye movement control by this age. As an aside, these findings with infants are relevant to claims that the dorsolateral prefrontal cortex is not sufficiently developed to support tasks that require both inhibition and working memory until approximately 10 months (e.g., Diamond, 1991) and may be consistent with a more graded account of the development of these abilities (see Munakata et al., 1994).

Another way in which the development of endogenous control can be studied is to investigate the extent to which endogenous factors can override or inhibit the influence of exogenous cues. One task that opposes the influence of exogenous and endogenous cues is the so-called antisaccade task (Hallett, 1978). In an antisaccade task, subjects are instructed not to make a saccade toward a stimulus but rather to saccade in the opposite direction where a second stimulus is subsequently presented: That is, subjects have to inhibit a spontaneous, automatic, eye movement toward a stimulus and direct their saccade in the opposite direction. Guitton, Buchtel, and Douglas (1985) reported that while normal subjects and patients with temporal lobe damage could do this easily, patients with frontal lobe damage, and especially those with damage around the FEF, were severely impaired.

That is, the frontal lobe patients had difficulty suppressing the automatic saccades toward the first stimulus.

Clearly, one cannot give verbal instructions to a young infant to make a saccade in a direction opposite from the location in which the first stimulus appears. However, we can motivate the infant to want to look at a second (target) stimulus more than at the first (cue) stimulus. This can be achieved by making the second stimulus more dynamic and colorful than the first. Thus, over a series of trials, an infant may learn to withhold a saccade to the first stimulus in order to anticipate the appearance of the second stimulus on the opposite side of center.

Preliminary evidence has been obtained for a steady decrease in the extent of orienting toward the first (cue) stimulus over a number of training trials in 4-month-old infants (from an initial level of more than 80 percent to a level of less than 50 percent) (see Johnson, 1994b). Although this preliminary finding needs to be replicated and extended with a larger sample, the large number of trials in which infants made a saccade straight from the fixation point to the second (target) stimulus in the later stages of the experiment indicates that endogenous control can influence responses to exogenous cues.

Another manifestation of the endogenous control of attention concerns so-called sustained attention. *Sustained attention* is the ability of subjects to maintain the direction of their attention toward a stimulus even in the presence of distractors. Richards (1989a, b) has developed a heart rate marker for sustained attention in infants. The heart rate-defined period of sustained attention usually lasts for between 5 and 15 seconds after the onset of a complex stimulus. Figure 9.4 illustrates the heart rate-defined periods of sustained attention delineated by Richards and Casey (1991).

To investigate the effect of sustained attention on the response to exogenous cues, Richards (1989a, b) used an interrupted stimulus method in which a peripheral stimulus (a flashing light) is presented while the infant is gazing at a central stimulus (a television screen with a complex visual pattern). By varying the length of time between the onset of

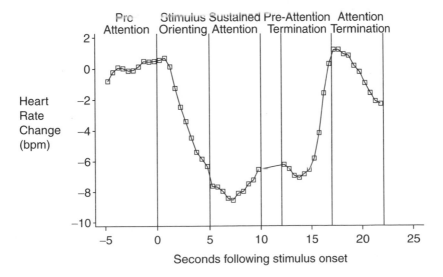

Figure 9.4 The heart rate-defined phases of sustained attention. (From Richards, J. E. and Casey, B. J. (1991). Heart rate variability during attention phases in young infants. *Psychophysiology* 24, 744. Reprinted with permission of Cambridge University Press.)

the television image and the onset of the peripheral stimulus, he was able to present the peripheral stimulus either within the period of sustained covert attention or outside it. Richards found that during the periods when heart rate was decreased (sustained endogenous attention), it took twice as long for the infant to shift its gaze toward the peripheral stimulus as when heart rate had returned to prestimulus levels (attention termination). Furthermore, those saccades that are made to a peripheral stimulus during sustained attention are less accurate than normal and involve multiple hypometric saccades, characteristics of collicular-generated saccades (Richards, 1991). Thus, the lack of distractibility during periods of sustained attention is likely to be due to cortically mediated pathways inhibiting collicular mechanisms.

If we assume that the cortically mediated pathways responsible for the regulation of collicular saccades are in the frontal cortex, then we should expect there to be no clearly definable period of sustained attention in infants younger than approximately 4 months. Concordant with this suggestion, Richards (1989a) reports that the clearly defined differences in distractibility in relation to heart rate were not found, or were at least very slight, in a group of infants 8 weeks of age.

Cortical control of attentional shifts and the oculomotor circuit

Three regions of cortex have been identified as being important for shifts of attention: The FEFs are linked to the endogenous control of eye movements, the parietal cortex to covert shifts of attention, and the prefrontal cortex to endogenous control involving delays. Clearly, it would be simple-minded to believe that the functions of these three structures are completely independent of one another. It would also be misleading to describe the onset of functioning in these structures as an all-or-none phenomenon. It is much more likely that their functioning develops in a more collaborative and graded manner. This being likely, it is interesting to note that there are a number of closed-loop circuits that project down from the cortex to the basal ganglia before returning to one of the cortical regions from which it originated (for review, see Alexander, DeLong, and Strick, 1986). One of these pathways is referred to commonly as the *oculomotor circuit*, due to evidence from neurophysiological studies of its involvement in eye movements. It has been proposed that this circuit is crucial for voluntary saccades (Alexander, DeLong, and Strick, 1986). It receives projections from the FEF, parietal cortex, and dorsolateral prefrontal cortex. After passing through a number of subcortical structures such as the caudate and portions of the substantia nigra (which is crucial for tonic inhibition of the colliculus), it returns to the FEF. An attractive possibility is that the oculomotor circuit develops as an integrated whole, giving rise to many of the transitions observed in both overt and covert orienting at approximately 4 months of age.

Conclusions and Future Directions

In this chapter, I have traced the hierarchical development of neural pathways underlying components of visual orienting and attention. These neural developments were reflected in a general trend at the behavioral level: The control of saccades passed from being driven mainly by exogenous stimuli to being largely under the control of endogenous factors such as memory. This trend is seen in a variety of tasks, including those in which the infant learns to predict the spatial location at which a target will appear. We have also seen how developmental data can complement data from other sources and even help to resolve controversies about the neural basis of attention in adults.

At least three directions for future research are evident at this point: preattentive parsing of the visual field, the study of infants with brain damage, and neuroimaging studies. Rovee-Collier, Hankins, and Bhatt (1992) have begun work on the first of these issues, preattentive processing, by demonstrating that 3-month-olds show some similar "pop-out" effects to those observed in adults. Interestingly, while their 3-month-old subjects appeared to parse the visual field in a way similar to adults in the presence of one target, they did not show evidence of focused attention when presented with multiple target stimuli within an array. From the viewpoint developed in this chapter, we would expect such focused attention to be present from 4 months of age. Furthermore, it is possible that phenomena such as the externality effect observed over the first month or so of life may reflect the inability of infants to segment the visual field in the same way as do adults.

A number of laboratories have begun to apply visual attention tasks such as those discussed in this chapter to infants with focal or diffuse brain damage (e.g., Braddick et al., 1992; Ross, Tesman, and Nass, 1992). Such investigations not only will allow us to test theories about the relation between the developing brain and attention but may also prove to be of clinical and diagnostic value. Finally, noninvasive neuroimaging methods such as high-density event-related potentials are likely to be powerful tools for unraveling the relation between the development of the brain and this aspect of cognition.

ACKNOWLEDGMENTS

I wish to thank Mike Posner, Rick Gilmore and Jeff Shrager for comments on drafts of this chapter, and Leslie Tucker and Kathy Sutton for their assistance with some experiments described as well as with preparation of the manuscript. Financial assistance was provided by National Science Foundation grant DBS-9120433 and the Carnegie Mellon faculty development fund.

REFERENCES

Alexander, G. E., M. R. DeLong, and P. L. Strick (1986). Parallel organization of functionally segregated circuits linking basal ganglia and cortex. *Annu. Rev. Neurosci.* 9:357–82.

Arehart, D. M. and M. M. Haith (1991). Evidence for visual expectation violations in 13-week old infants. *Abstracts of the Society for Research in Child Development volume 8.*

Aslin, R. N. (1981). Development of smooth pursuit in human infants. In *Eye Movements: Cognition and Visual Perception*, D. F. Fisher, R. A. Monty, and J. W. Senders, eds. Hillsdale, N.J.: Erlbaum, pp. 31–51.

Aslin, R. N. and L. B. Smith (1988). Perceptual development. *Annu. Rev. Psychol.* 39:435–73.

Atkinson, J. (1984). Human visual development over the first six months of life: A review and a hypothesis. *Hum. Neurobiol.* 3:61–74.

Atkinson, J., B. Hood, J. Wattam-Bell, S. Anker, and J. Tricklebank (1988). Development of orientation discrimination in infants. *Perception* 17:587–95.

Becker, L. E., D. L. Armstrong, F. Chan, and M. M. Wood (1984). Dendritic development on human occipital cortex neurones. *Brain Res.* 315:117–24.

Braddick, O. J., J. Atkinson, B. Hood, W. Harkness, G. Jackson, and F. Vargha-Khadem (1992). Possible blindsight in infants lacking one cerebral hemisphere. *Nature* 360:461–3.

Bronson, G. W. (1974). The postnatal growth of visual capacity. *Child Dev.* 45:873–90.

Bronson, G. W. (1982). Structure, status and characteristics of the nervous system at birth. In *Psychobiology of the Human Newborn*, P. Stratton, ed. Chichester: Wiley.

Burkhalter, A. and K. L. Bernardo (1989). Organization of corticocortical connections in human visual cortex. *Proc. Natl. Acad. Sci.* 86:1071–5.

Bushnell, I. W. R. (1979). Modification of the externality effect in young infants. *J. Exp. Child Psychol.* 28:111–229.

Bushnell, I. W. R., F. Sai, and J. Mullin (1989). Neonatal recognition of the mother's face. *Br. J. Dev. Psychol.* 7:3–15.

Canfield, R. L. and M. M. Haith (1991). Young infants' visual expectations for symmetric and asymmetric stimulus sequences. *Dev. Psychol.* 27:198–208.

Chugani, H. T., M. E. Phelps, and J. C. Mazziotta (1987). Positron emission tomography study of human brain functional development. *Ann. Neurol.* 22:487–97.

Clohessy, A. B., M. I. Posner, M. K. Rothbart, and S. Vecera (1991). The development of inhibition of return in early infancy. *J. Cogn. Neurosci.* 3:346–57.

Colombo, J., D. W. Mitchell, J. T. Coldren, and J. D. Atwater (1990). Discrimination learning during the first year: Stimulus and positional cues. *J. Exp. Psychol. [Learn. Mem. Cogn.]* 16:98–109.

Conel, J. L. (1939–1967). *The Postnatal Development of the Human Cerebral Cortex*, vols. 1–8. Cambridge, Mass.: Harvard University Press.

Corbetta, M., F. M. Miezin, G. L. Shulman, and S. E. Petersen (1993). A PET study of visuospatial attention. *F. Neurosci.* 13:1202–26.

Deiber, M. P., R. E. Passingham, J. G. Colebatch, K. J. Friston, P. D. Nixon, and R. S. J. Frackowiak (1991). Cortical areas and the selection of movement: A study with positron emission tomography. *Exp. Brain Res.* 84:393–402.

De Schonen, S. and I. Bry (1987). Interhemispheric communication of visual learning: A developmental study in 3–6 month old infants. *Neuropsychologia* 25:73–83.

Diamond, A. (1991). Neuropsychological insights into the meaning of object concept development. In *The Epigenesis of Mind: Essays on Biology and Cognition*, S. Carey and R. Gelman, eds. Hillsdale, N.J.: Erlbaum.

Enns, J. T. and D. A. Brodeur (1989). A developmental study of covert orienting to peripheral visual cues. *J. Exp. Child Psychol.* 48:171–89.

Frith, C. D., K. Friston, P. F. Liddle, and R. S. J. Frackowiak (1991). Willed action and the prefrontal cortex in man: A study with PET. *Proc. R. Soc. Lond.* 244:241–6.

Funahashi, S., C. J. Bruce, and P. S. Goldman-Rakic (1989). Mnemonic coding of visual space in the monkey's dorsolateral prefrontal cortex. *J. Neurophysiol.* 61:331–49.

Funahashi, S., C. J. Bruce, and P. S. Goldman-Rakic (1990). Visuospatial coding in primate prefrontal neurons revealed by oculomotor paradigms. *J. Neurophysiol.* 63(4):814–31.

Gilmore, R. and M. H. Johnson (1994). Six month olds' performance in versions of the oculomotor delayed response task. *Infant Behavior and Development* (ICIS Abstracts).

Guitton, H. A., H. A. Buchtel, and R. M. Douglas (1985). Frontal lobe lesions in man cause difficulties in suppressing reflexive glances and in generating goal-directed saccades. *Exp. Brain Res.* 58:455–72.

Haith, M. M., C. Hazan, and G. S. Goodman (1983). Expectation and anticipation of dynamic visual events by 3.5-month-old babies. *Child Dev.* 59:467–79.

Hallett, P. E. (1978). Primary and secondary saccades to goals defined by instructions. *Vision Res.* 18:1279–96.

Harman, C., M. I. Posner, M. K. Rothbart, and L. Thomas-Thrapp (1994). Development of orienting to locations and objects in human infants. *Can. J. Psychol.* 48(2):301–18.

Hood, B. M. (1993). Inhibition of return produced by covert shifts of visual attention in 6-month old infants. *Infant Behav. Dev.* 16:245–54.

Hood, B. M. (1995). Shifts of visual attention in the infant: A neuroscientific approach. In *Advance in Infancy Research*. C. Rovee-Collien and L. Lipsett, eds. Norwood, N.J.: Allex. Vol. 9, pp. 163–216.

Hood, B. and J. Atkinson (1991). Shifting covert attention in infants. *Abstracts of the Society for Research in Child Development*, Vol. 8.

Huttenlocher, P. (1990). Morphometric study of human cerebral cortex development. *Neuropsychologia* 28:517–27.

Johnson, M. H. (1990). Cortical maturation and the development of visual attention in early infancy. *J. Cogn. Neurosci.* 2:81–95.

Johnson, M. H. (1992). Cognition and development: Four contentions about the role of visual attention. In *Cognitive Science and Clinical Disorders*, D. J. Stein and J. E. Young, eds. San Diego: Academic Press, pp. 43–60.

Johnson, M. H. (1993a). Evidence for covert shifts of attention in early infancy. Manuscript submitted for publication.

Johnson, M. H. (1993b). The temporal dynamics of shifting visual attention during early infancy. Manuscript submitted for publication.

Johnson, M. H. (1994a). Dissociating components of visual attention. A neurodevelopmental approach. In *The Neural Basis of High-Level Vision*, M. J. Farah and G. Radcliffe, eds. Hillsdale, N.J.: Erlbaum, pp. 241–68.

Johnson, M. H. (1994b). Visual attention and the control of eye movements in early infancy. In *Attention and Performance: XV. Conscious and Nonconscious Information Processing*, C. Umilta, and M. Moscovitch, eds. Cambridge, Mass.: MIT Press, pp. 291–310.

Johnson, M. H. and J. Morton (1991). *Biology and Cognitive Development: The Case of Face Recognition*. Oxford: Blackwell.

Johnson, M. H., M. I. Posner, and M. K. Rothbart (1991). Components of visual orienting in early infancy: Contingency learning, anticipatory looking, and disengaging. *J. Cogn. Neurosci.* 3:335–44.

Johnson, M. H., M. I. Posner, and M. K. Rothbart (1994). Facilitation of saccades toward a covertly attended location in early infancy. *Psychol. Sci.* 5:90–3.

Jonides, J., E. E. Smith, R. A. Koeppe, E. Awh, S. Minoshima, and M. A. Mintun (1993). Spatial working memory in humans as revealed by PET. *Nature* 363:623–5.

Klein, R. M., A. Kingstone, and A. Pontefract (1992). Orienting of visual attention. In *Eye Movements and Visual Cognition: Scene Perception and Reading*, K. Rayner, ed. New York: Springer-Verlag.

Lewis, T. L., D. Maurer, and A. Milewski (1979). The development of nasal field detection in young infants. *Diss. Abstr. Int.* 41B:1547.

Maurer, D. and R. E. Young (1983). The scanning of compound figures by young infants. *J. Exp. Child Psychol.* 35:437–48.

Maylor, E. A. (1985). Facilitatory and inhibitory components of orienting in visual space. In *Attention and Performance*, vol. 11, M. I. Posner and O. M. Marin, eds. Hillsdale, N.J.: Erlbaum.

Munakata, Y., J. L. McClelland, M. H. Johnson, and R. S. Siegler (1994). Rethinking object permanence: Do the ends justify the means-ends? *Infant Behavior and Development* (ICIS Abstracts).

Posner, M. I. (1980). Orienting of attention. *Q. F. Exp. Psychol.* 32:3–25.

Posner, M. I. (1988). Localization of cognitive functions in the human brain. *Science* 240:1627–31.

Posner, M. I. and Y. Cohen (1980). Attention and the control of movements. In *Tutorials in Motor Behavior*, G. E. Stelmach and J. Requin, eds. Amsterdam: North Holland, pp. 243–58.

Posner, M. I. and Y. Cohen (1984). Components of visual orienting. In *Attention and Performance*, H. Bouma and D. G. Bouwhis, eds. Hillsdale, N.J.: Erlbaum.

Posner, M. I. and S. E. Petersen (1990). The attention system of the human brain. *Annu. Rev. Neurosci.* 13:25–42.

Posner, M. I., R. D. Rafal, L. S. Choate, and J. Vaughan (1985). Inhibition of return: Neural basis and function. *Cogn. Neuropsychol.* 2:211–28.

Posner, M. I. and M. K. Rothbart (1980). The development of attentional mechanisms. In *Nebraska Symposium on Motivation*, J. H. Flower, ed. Lincoln, Neb.: University of Nebraska Press.

Purpura, D. P. (1975). Normal and aberrant neuronal development in the cerebral cortex of human fetus and young infant. In *Brain Mechanisms of Mental Retardation*, N. A. Buchwald and M. A. B. Brazier, eds. New York: Academic Press.

Rabinowicz, T. (1979). The different maturation of the human cerebral cortex. In *Human Growth: 3. Neurobiology and Nutrition*, F. Falkner and J. M. Tanner, eds. New York: Plenum.

Rafal, R. D., P. A. Calabresi, C. W. Brennan, and T. K. Sciolto (1989). Saccade preparation inhibits reorienting to recently attended locations. *J. Exp. Psychol. [Hum. Percept. Perform.]* 15:673–85.

Rafal, R., J. Smith, J. Krantz, A. Cohen, and C. Brennan (1990). Extrageniculate vision in hemianopic humans: Saccade inhibition by signals in the blind field. *Science* 250:1507–18.

Richards, J. E. (1989a). Sustained visual attention in 8-week old infants. *Infant Behav. Dev.* 12:425–36.

Richards, J. E. (1989b). Development and stability of HR–defined, visual sustained attention in 14, 20, and 26 week old infants. *Psychophysiology* 26:422–30.

Richards, J. E. (1991). Infant eye movements during peripheral visual stimulus localization as a function of central stimulus attention status. *Psychophysiology* 28:S4.

Richards, J. E. and B. J. Casey (1991). Heart rate variability during attention phases in young infants. *Psychophysiology* 28:43–53.

Rockland and Pandya (1979). Laminar origins and terminations of cortical connections of the occipital lobe in the rhesus monkey. *Brain Res.* 179:3–20.

Ross, G., P. Auld, J. Tesman, and R. Nass (1992). Effects of subependymal and mild intraventricular lesions on visual attention and memory in premature infants. *Dev. Psychol.* 28(6):1067–74.

Rovee-Collier, C., E. Hankins, and R. Bhatt (1992). Textons, visual pop-out effects, and object recognition in infancy. *J. Exp. Psychol. [Gen.]* 121:435–45.

Schiller, P. H. (1985). A model for the generation of visually guided saccadic eye movements. In *Models of the Visual Cortex*, D. Rose and V. G. Dobson, eds. Chicester, Engl.: Wiley.

Shephard, M., J. M. Findlay, and R. J. Hockey (1986). The relationship between eye movements and spatial attention. *Q. J. Exp. Psychol.* 38A:475–91.

Slater, A. M., V. Morison, and D. Rose (1982). Perception of shape by the new-born baby. *Br. J. Dev. Psychol.* 1:135–42.

Slater, A. M., V. Morison, and M. Somers (1988). Orientation discrimination and cortical function in the human newborn. *Perception* 17:597–602.

Stechler, G. and E. Latz (1966). Some observations on attention and arousal in the human infant. *J. Am. Acad. Child Psychiatry* 5:517–25.

Tipper, S., T. Bourque, S. H. Anderson, and J. C. Brehaut (1989). Mechanisms of attention: A developmental study. *J. Exp. Child Psychol.* 48:353–78.

Valenza, E., F. Simion, C. Umilta, and E. Paiusco (1992). Inhibition of return in newborn infants. Unpublished manuscript, University of Padua, Italy.

10

The Ontogeny of Human Memory: A Cognitive Neuroscience Perspective

Charles A. Nelson

Although attempts to understand human memory and its neural bases have captured the imagination of scientists and philosophers for well over a century (Dunn, 1845; Ebbinghaus, 1885a, 1885b; Korsakoff, 1889, cited in Schacter, 1987), progress in studying this problem has arguably been the greatest over the past decade. Many of the gains that have been made can be attributed to improvements in in vivo imaging of the human brain and conducting comparative work with nonhuman primates (Mishkin and Appenzeller, 1987; Petri and Mishkin, 1994; Squire, 1986, 1987, 1992). Relatively ignored, however, has been the study of this problem in the context of development. By drawing on research from developmental psychology, basic neuroscience, and cognitive neuroscience, I will attempt to integrate information across these domains to provide a model that accounts for the development of mature memory function.

This article begins with a theoretical overview of adult memory and the neural substrates presumed to underlie adult memory. The goal of this section is to provide a conceptual framework for considering the developmental literature. The study of the adult, however, may prove a poor model for the study of development, because the methods used to study the adult often do not generalize to the study of the infant or young child. Accordingly, greater emphasis is placed on relating what is currently known about the development of the brain to what is known about infant memory. This discussion is complemented by also considering the cognitive neuroscience literature on brain–memory relations in the developing nonhuman primate. This latter literature proves critical to the main thesis of this article, as in many instances the paradigms used to study the human infant have been identical to those used to study the infant monkey (see table 10.1 for examples). On the basis of these integrative reviews, it is proposed that the foundation on which adult memory is assembled is initially fractionated into several different "types" of memory, each of which is subserved by a different neural system. Over the first year or so of life, subsequent developments in the brain result in a form of "cognitive pruning," ultimately resulting in the adult configuration of memory.

Adult Models of Memory Function

Although not completely adhered to by all (e.g., Roediger, 1984; Roediger, Rajaram, and Srivas, 1990), a prevailing view in adult cognitive psychology and neuropsychology is that

Table 10.1 Tasks Used to Study Memory Development in the Human and the
Monkey (Infancy Period)

Task	Human	Monkey
Delayed nonmatch to sample	x	x
Visual paired comparison	x	x
Habituation	x	
A-not-B/delayed response	x	x
Sequencing and deferred imitation	x	
Cross-modal recognition memory	x	x
Visual expectancies	x	
Conditioning	x	

memory is not a unitary trait. It has been proposed by a number of investigators, for example, that there may be two types of memory. Although the nomenclature used to describe these types has varied (for discussions and reviews, see Schacter and Tulving, 1994; Sherry and Schacter, 1987), for purpose of this review, the terms *explicit* and *implicit* memory are used. Explicit memory is usually taken to refer to memory that can be stated explicitly or declared, that can be brought to mind as an image or proposition in the absence of ongoing perceptual support, and/or of which one is consciously aware. Implicit memory is often taken to reflect a constellation of abilities, such as the acquisition of motor or cognitive skills, classical conditioning, and priming. In addition, it is memory of which one is generally not consciously aware (see Squire, 1986, 1987). The distinctions between these types of memory can be based on psychological dissociations (e.g., Tulving, 1985). For example, implicit memory is revealed when exposure to a stimulus affects performance on a task that does not require the subject to explicitly remember that stimulus (e.g., Graf and Schacter, 1985). These distinctions can also be made on the basis of neurological findings. For example, studies of disease or surgical ablation in the human adult (e.g., Milner, Corkin, and Teuber, 1968; Scoville and Milner, 1957), lesions performed in animals (e.g., Mishkin and Appenzeller, 1987; Mishkin and Delacour, 1975; Petri and Mishkin, 1994), and increasingly, imaging studies using positron emission tomography (PET; e.g., Squire et al., 1992; Squire and Zola-Morgan, 1991) or event-related potentials (ERPs; e.g., Paller, 1990; Paller and Kutas, 1992) reveal that structures that lie in the medial temporal lobe (e.g., hippocampus and entorhinal cortex) appear to support performance on tasks of explicit memory. In contrast, structures that lie in the cerebellum (for conditioning; see Thompson, 1986, 1991), extrastriate occipital cortex and inferior temporal cortex (for visual word form priming; see Biederman and Cooper, 1991, 1992; Petersen, Fox, Posner, Mintun, and Raichle, 1990), and striatum (for procedural learning; see Saint-Cyr, Taylor, and Lang, 1988) have been implicated in performance on tasks of implicit memory (for a general discussion, see Squire, 1994).

Caveats to a Neural Basis of Memory

Review of much of the above research and the work on development may imply that there is an isomorphic relation between brain structure and function. This is not strictly the case, however, as the brain works as an integrated system. For example, although the hippocampus contributes disproportionately to performance on explicit memory tasks, the hippocampus is part of a complex circuit that receives inputs and outputs to and from a number of local and distal structures. Thus, the mapping of structure to function is likely not as rigid as may be implied in the text. A second caveat pertains to the interpretation of lesion data. A number of investigators have reported that bilateral lesions of certain temporal lobe structures impair explicit memory. However, lesioning a certain area of the brain may also affect the working of an entire circuit, not just the structure itself. A third caveat involves the use of standard infant-testing paradigms with adult humans or monkeys. Although this approach of comparing subjects of different ages or species has its advantages, it can also be problematic, as it is virtually impossible to know if the adult human or monkey is using the same processes as the infant would when approaching the same task.

These three caveats are important to keep in mind while reviewing the literature on the neural bases of memory. They reflect the fact that the relation between brain structure and brain function is an imperfect science. As the tools of the cognitive neuroscientist become more refined and sophisticated, the ability to study the neural bases of cognitive development will be vastly improved.

With this background and these caveats in mind, the remainder of the article is organized topically around task. Reviewed first are a number of tasks that appear to depend on medial temporal lobe structures and that collectively reflect different aspects of explicit memory. This is followed by a discussion of tasks that depend on prefrontal cortex and that reflect working-memory capacity. Tasks that depend on the striatum and reflect a form of procedural learning (a type of implicit memory) are reviewed next, followed by a discussion of tasks that depend on the cerebellum and brain stem and that reflect conditioning (perhaps another type of implicit memory). A number of proposals are then put forth that relate these early forms of memory to adult memory.

Tasks That Might Depend on the Hippocampus

Delayed nonmatch to sample

The delayed nonmatch to sample (DNMS) task has long been thought of as a prototypical test of memory in the nonhuman primate (e.g., Mishkin and Delacour, 1975). The task is as follows. The animal is presented with a sample object. When this object is removed, a food reward is revealed. The animal is then presented with the sample object and a novel object. Reaching for the novel object is rewarded with food. In this manner, the animal must acquire a general rule that the novel object is the correct object. On each trial, new stimuli serve as sample and comparison (i.e., trial-unique procedure). Once the animal has learned to reach for the novel object (i.e., has learned the nonmatching rule) as indexed by a high level of performance (e.g., 90 percent criterion), the demand on memory can be increased by imposing greater delays between presentation of the sample and test objects.

Studies with nonhuman primates have demonstrated that it is not until 4 months that infant monkeys even begin to learn the DNMS task, and it is not until 1 year that adult performance is approached (Bachevalier and Mishkin, 1984). Overman and colleagues (Overman, Bachevalier, Turner, and Peuster, 1992) have recently contrasted monkey performance to that of human infants. They reported that 12–15-month-old human infants require extensive training to perform the DNMS task (no infants did so until 15 months), with considerably less training necessary by the time infants are between 18 and 32 months old. However, even the oldest children in this study (45–81 months) were significantly worse than adults (Overman et al., 1992). When one imposes a 4:1 ratio of monkey years to human years (J. Bachevalier and V. Gunderson, personal communication, September 1993), these human data correspond well with the monkey data.

The late development of adultlike DNMS performance in the monkey was surprising in light of how well infant monkeys do on a task of concurrent object discrimination. Here, animals are presented with pairs of objects, and over repeated daily trials, they are required to select consistently one member of the pair. Three-month-old animals that took 720 trials to learn DNMS took only 16 trials to attain the same level of 90 percent correct on the concurrent object discrimination task (see Overman et al., 1992).

As discussed by Overman, Bachevalier, Sewell, and Drew (1993), the high level of performance obtained on the object discrimination task suggests that the failure to behave similarly on the DNMS task is not due to problems in perception, reaching, motivation, or associating a stimulus with a response. Thus (see Bachevalier and Mishkin, 1984), delayed maturation on the DNMS task may reflect the (relatively) late development of visual recognition memory.

This account has recently been called into question. A study conducted by Diamond (1992; also see a preliminary report in Diamond, 1990) indicated that if human infants are required only to look at the novel object and not reach for it, adultlike performance on the DNMS task is obtained by 6–12 months. This report has recently been replicated by Overman et al. (1993), who administered the standard DNMS task to four groups of human infants (10–15 months, 18–20 months, 22–38 months, and 45–107 months) and to adults. Visual fixations were recorded on each DNMS trial. Overman et al. reported that, in all age groups, longer looking was obtained to the novel as opposed to the familiar stimulus. On the basis of these results (and those of Diamond, 1992), it seems reasonable to conclude that adult performance on the DNMS task must require more than visual recognition memory, as even the youngest infants in this study discriminated the novel from familiar stimulus. It remains uncertain what other ability is being tapped. One possibility may be that the strong tendency to prefer novelty (until the second or third year of life) artificially inflates performance of the younger infants, fundamentally altering the task demands. A second possibility (Diamond, 1994) is the infant's ability to resist interference. Providing a reward for displacing the sample stimulus during the familiarization phase may distract the infant from shifting his or her attention from the sample to the novel stimulus during the test phase.[1]

These recent behavioral observations regarding DNMS performance also conform to the results of studies examining the neural bases of DNMS performance. Mishkin, Malamut, and Bachevalier (1984) had initially demonstrated that lesions of the medial temporal lobe (hippocampus, amygdala, and the rhinal cortex comprising the entorhinal and perirhinal cortices) impaired performance on the DNMS task. This finding has also been found to be true in rats, with more recent work pointing to the rhinal cortex as

1   *Editors' Note*: Diamond et al. (1999) demonstrated the importance of a third factor: the ability to understand the relation between a stimulus and a reward. When the DNMS task was simplified such that the reward was directly linked to the stimulus (with velcro), children succeeded much earlier than in the typical task.

playing a particularly important role in DNMS performance (Mumby and Pinel, 1994). Because of the late onset of adultlike DNMS performance, it had therefore been assumed that these structures mature late. However, several observations call this assumption into question. First, Bachevalier and colleagues (Bachevalier, 1990; Bachevalier, Hagger, and Mishkin, 1991; Bachevalier and Mishkin, 1992) have demonstrated that the DNMS task may depend on the inferior temporal regions TE and TEO, not just the hippocampus. They have reported that neonatal (early) lesions or adult (late) lesions of the hippocampus, amygdala, and surrounding tissue (i.e., an H | A+ lesion) both significantly reduce adult performance. However, only late lesions of area TE impaired performance on the DNMS task, whereas early lesions had no effect. These findings would suggest that (a) the DNMS task (at least the conventional reaching version) may well depend additionally on cortical area TE, as well as on subcortical limbic areas such as the hippocampus (this point is elaborated later), and (b) the relatively "late" acquisition of adultlike performance on DNMS is due to delayed maturation of area TE, not immaturity of the hippocampus and rhinal cortex (i.e., it is not until 4 months that monkeys begin to learn this task and 12 months when they attain adult levels of proficiency; human infants begin to learn the task at about 1.5 years of age, although they are still not performing as well as adults by 4+ years of age).

One final point to consider in this discussion is the increasing evidence that in the primate (human and nonhuman), the hippocampus matures relatively early in postnatal life. For example, the distribution of muscarinic receptors (receptors for acetylcholine) in the monkey limbic cortex are adultlike at birth, in contrast to those in the cortex, which mature later (O'Neil, Friedman, Bachevalier, and Ungerleider, 1986). The volume of human limbic cortex and the size of surrounding limbic structures (e.g., hippocampus) rapidly become adultlike in the second half of the first year of life (Kretschmann, Kammradt, Krauthausen, Sauer, and Wingert, 1986). In addition, the subiculum (which links the entorhinal cortex with the hippocampus) and the hippocampus proper mature relatively early in human postnatal development (Humphrey, 1966). The entorhinal cortex (which is the structural gateway between the hippocampus and the cortex) has already begun to form synapses and to express neurotransmitters by mid-gestation in the monkey and may already have begun to form extrinsic connections (Berger and Alvarez, 1994; Berger, Alvarez, and Goldman-Rakic, 1993); it is also the area that shows the most advanced areal differentiation in the cortex in the human – an event that occurs by the 10th prenatal week (Kostovic, Pentanjek, and Judas, 1990). Furthermore, dendritic development in the hippocampus precedes that in the visual cortex (Paldino and Purpura, 1979), a structure known to be quite functional by the second half of the first year of life (see Aslin, 1987, for a review of human behavioral data; see Bourgeois and Rakic, 1993, for a discussion of nonhuman primate physiological data). Finally, metabolic activity in the temporal lobes increases substantially by 3 postnatal months and precedes that of prefrontal cortex by several months (Chugani, 1994; Chugani and Phelps, 1986). The only area functionally related to the hippocampus that appears to have somewhat protracted postnatal development is in the area of the dentate, where adult levels of synapses are not attained until 10 months in the monkey (corresponding to approximately 3–4 years in the human; see Eckenhoff and Rakic, 1991).

Collectively, these data support the conclusion that the human and nonhuman primate hippocampus and surrounding structures (excluding the dentate) mature early in life. Thus, the late development of DNMS performance is unlikely to be due to delayed hippocampal development.

Visual paired-comparison task

This procedure was originally developed by Fantz (1956) as a method of examining early perceptual function. However, it quickly blossomed into a major tool of those studying early memory and has been a mainstay ever since.

Fantz (1956) discovered that infants had a proclivity to respond to novel stimuli; that is, when given a choice between a familiar stimulus and a novel stimulus, infants older than 2–3 months would "prefer" (i.e., look longer at) the latter. What determined whether a stimulus was novel or familiar was accomplished by providing the infant with previous experience with one of them. Thus, infants would typically be shown a pair of identical stimuli for some period of study (e.g., 60 s), followed by a test phase. During the test phase, the familiar stimulus would appear on one side of the screen, and the novel stimulus (i.e., a stimulus not previously seen) would appear on the other side. To offset side preferences, two such trials would typically be given, counterbalancing the side on which the novel stimulus was presented. Trained observers, unaware of the stimuli being presented, recorded corneal reflections from the infants' eyes, thereby objectively determining which of the stimuli the infant fixated more.

There are many variants of the visual paired-comparison procedure, including (a) varying the length of the familiarization period, (b) exposing infants to a range of stimuli during the familiarization period (e.g., each trial might consist of the same face in different orientations), (c) using novel and familiar stimuli that vary along only one or two dimensions versus many dimensions, and (d) imposing a delay between familiarization and test. In nearly all cases, however, the observation that infants prefer to look at a novel stimulus more than a familiar stimulus has been interpreted by most investigators as evidence of recognition memory. Such evidence has most reliably been obtained in infants older than 2–3 months (for a discussion, see Fagan, 1990), although novelty preferences after a 2-min delay have recently been reported in 3-day-old infants (Pascalis and de Schonen, 1994). The longest delay that human infants appear able to tolerate has been 48 hr for abstract patterns and 2 weeks for faces (Fagan, 1970, 1973). In addition, although not exhaustively studied, infant pig-tailed macaques have been shown to tolerate a delay of 24 hr in an identical visual paradigm (Gunderson and Swartz, 1985).

Similar to the visual paired-comparison paradigm, the habituation procedure permits one to infer recognition memory from infant preferences for novel stimuli. Infants are presented with a single stimulus repeatedly until their looking declines to some predetermined value (e.g., a typical criterion of habituation would be that infants have two consecutive looks that are 50 percent shorter than their first one or two looks). After the infant has habituated, a novel stimulus is presented. If the infant's looking recovers (i.e., dishabituates), it is assumed that he or she has identified this stimulus as novel or, more parsimoniously, has determined that this is not the familiar stimulus (for a discussion, see Bornstein, 1985).

Like the visual paired-comparison procedure, there are many variants of the habituation procedure, including (a) using different criterial values, (b) imposing a delay between habituation and test, and (c) exposing infants to a category of stimuli (e.g., different male faces) and examining whether infants generalize their looking to a new exemplar of the old category (e.g., a previously unseen male face) and discriminate this category from a new category (e.g., female faces). In general, however, longer looking to the novel stimulus compared with the familiar stimulus has been interpreted as evidence of recognition memory. Such evidence has been obtained in infants just a few days old (e.g., Slater, 1995). Infants are typically able to remember the familiar stimulus for periods of time ranging from 24 to 48 hr. In the auditory modality, Swain, Zelazo, and Clifton (1993) reported that newborns (1–2 days old) are able to recognize a word after a delay of 24 hr.

Neural Basis of Novelty Preferences

There are data from both nonhuman primates and from humans that suggest that novelty preferences (at least as examined in the visual paired-comparison procedure) are mediated by the hippocampus and surrounding structures. Bachevalier, Brickson, and Hagger (1993) presented 5-, 15-, and 30-day-old infant monkeys and adult monkeys with pairs of identical stimuli for 30 s. A 10-s delay then ensued, followed by two 5-s test trials. Bachevalier et al. reported that monkeys older than 15 days of age showed robust novelty preferences. However, if the amygdala and hippocampus were removed bilaterally, such preferences failed to obtain. In addition, lesions of area TE in infancy have no effect on visual paired-comparison performance, although lesioning this same area in the adult will effectively yield a severe impairment in task performance (J. Bachevalier and L. Ungerleider, personal communication, May 1993). From these results, one may conclude that the hippocampus and surrounding tissue likely support novelty preferences, at least in the infancy period. However, as may be the case for DNMS performance, area TE may contribute to novelty preferences in the juvenile or adult monkey.

McKee and Squire (1993) tested elderly participants (*M* age = 63 years) using a procedure that was nearly identical to that used by Bachevalier et al. (1993). Pairs of identical stimuli were initially presented (familiarization phase), followed by 5-s test trials containing pairs of familiar and novel stimuli. Duration of looking was monitored and recorded. McKee and Squire reported that neurologically normal adults showed novelty preferences after delays as long as several hours. However, adults suffering from bilateral damage to the hippocampal formation or diencephalic regions only showed such preferences when the delay between familiarization and test was less than 1 s; when such delays exceeded 2 min, no such preferences were evident. Collectively, these studies demonstrate that intact temporal and limbic lobe structures are responsible for novelty preferences (at least as evaluated in the visual paired-comparison procedure) and that such structures become operational in the monkey by approximately 15 days of life.

Does Dependence on the Hippocampus Make a Task "Explicit"?

It is important to question whether dependence on the hippocampus and related limbic structures is sufficient evidence to argue that tasks that depend on these structures therefore reflect explicit memory. As is demonstrated below, such a conclusion may be premature.

If the visual paired-comparison task reflects explicit memory, one must account for why infants do not demonstrate evidence of recognition or recall memory until the second half of the first year of life when tested in other, presumably explicitlike tasks.

Cross-modal recognition memory

A task that has proven to be somewhat more difficult for the infant than visual recognition memory is cross-modal recognition memory. Here, infants are familiarized to a stimulus in one sense modality, without benefit of experience gained through other modalities. They are then presented with the familiar stimulus and a novel stimulus (singly or in pairs) in a different modality. For example, in the more commonly used procedure, an infant might be allowed to feel an object (e.g., wooden block) without being allowed to see it. The infant is then presented with a picture of the object they initially felt, along with a picture of a novel object. Longer looking at the picture of the novel object is taken to imply recognition of the familiar object. For infants to be successful on this task, they must encode the familiar stimulus in one modality, transfer the representation of this stimulus to a second modality, retain this representation in memory (for whatever delay ensues between familiarization and test), and then discriminate the familiar and novel objects.

Much of the behavioral work using this paradigm has been conducted by Rose, Ruff, and colleagues (for a review, see Rose and Ruff, 1989). A general finding has been that it is not until 6 to 8 months of age that infants become successful on this task; that is, that they consistently prefer the novel stimulus over the familiar stimulus. The fact that performance on this task develops later than on unimodal (e.g., visual) recognition memory tasks may suggest that (a) additional limbic structures may be required for forming cross-modal associations and (b) tasks that require more than simple novelty preferences may not be within the infant's behavioral repertoire until after the first 6 months or so, when additional neural development has occurred.

A likely candidate for the involvement of limbic structures in addition to the hippocampus is the amygdala. For example, Murray and Mishkin (1985) reported that bilateral lesions of the amygdala impair the ability to make cross-modal associations. This suggests that when cross-modal recognition is required, involvement of both the amygdala and hippocampus are necessary – the latter structure for mediating novelty preferences and the former for drawing cross-modal associations (and possibly also memory). (It may be, however, that the amygdala and surrounding cortex mediate stimulus–stimulus associations more generally and not just cross-modal associations; see Murray and Gaffan, 1994, for a discussion.)

Although it has been impossible to examine directly amygdala and hippocampal involvement in cross-modal recognition memory in the human infant, there are indirect data that support the assertion that these structures do underlie these tasks. Nelson, Henschel, and Collins (1993) allowed 8-month-old infants to feel an object for 60 s, without benefit of seeing the object. Cortical event-related potentials (ERPs) were then recorded as the infants were presented with alternating pictures of the familiar object and a novel object. In previous studies (for a review, see Nelson, 1994), a baseline response invoked by a familiar stimulus and a positive slow-wave response invoked by a novel stimulus had been interpreted to reflect, respectively, the recognition of a familiar event and the updating of working memory for a partially encoded event. In the Nelson et al. (1993) study, this same pattern was observed; specifically, the picture of the object to which infants had been familiarized haptically invoked a baseline response, whereas the picture of the novel object invoked a positive slow-wave response. Although it is difficult to ascertain with certainty the neural substrate responsible for generating the observed ERPs, the data point to involvement of the limbic structures responsible for recognition memory and for cross-modal (or stimulus–stimulus) associations.

Collectively, the human infant ERP data, coupled with the data from nonhuman primates, suggest that cross-modal recognition memory depends on limbic structures in addition to the hippocampus and requires more than simple novelty preferences. Thus, simple novelty preferences (presumably mediated by the hippocampus) may not reflect the end state of mature explicit memory.

Memory for event sequences and deferred imitation

A second task that might be thought of as reflecting a form of explicit memory is memory for event sequences. Here, infants are shown a sequence of events (generally 2–5 steps long) involving real objects and are "asked" to reproduce this event sequence either immediately or after some delay (e.g., a doll is undressed, put in a bathtub, washed, dried, and reclothed). Work by Bauer (e.g., Bauer, 1992), Mandler (e.g., Mandler, 1990), and Meltzoff (e.g., Meltzoff, 1990) has demonstrated that by approximately 9 to 12 months, infants are able to observe an event or sequence of events acted out by the investigator and, at some later date, reproduce this sequence. The delay tolerated between initial observation of the sequence and subsequent reproduction of the sequence varies as a function of age. For example, Bauer and colleagues (Bauer, Hertsgaard, and Dow, 1994) have recently demonstrated that 16- to 18-month-old infants are able to remember this sequence for as long as 8 months; 12-month-olds can also remember the sample sequence, but the effects are less robust.

Recent work with human adults has examined the neural bases underlying these types of tasks. McDonough, Mandler, McKee, and Squire (1994) tested neurologically normal controls and amnesic adults (3 with confirmed [by magnetic resonance image] or presumed [by etiology] damage to the hippocampal formation and 4 with confirmed [by computed tomography] damage to the diencephalic region) using a paradigm virtually identical to that used with infants. Participants (*M* age = 66.7 years for adults with amnesia, 66.4 years for controls) were shown a series of eight different action sequences on one day and, on the next day, were tested under two conditions: either instructed to imitate the previously seen sequences or simply observed to see if they did so spontaneously. As is the case with infant studies, both causal and arbitrary sequences were used. McDonough et al. reported that only the control participants were able to reproduce the sequences and did so under both instructed and uninstructed conditions. In contrast, the participants with amnesia failed to reproduce the sequences in either condition. This pattern of findings suggests that performance on the sequencing task depends on an intact hippocampal or diencephalic region.

Collectively, the data from the cross-modal recognition and event memory tasks point to a different time frame of development compared with tasks that require simple novelty preferences. Although all of the tasks reviewed in this section require the hippocampus or the cortex surrounding the hippocampus, it appears that the type of memory evaluated in these last two tasks may differ from that evaluated by the visual paired-comparison and habituation procedures. This could be the result of a number of factors, including the necessity for structures other than the hippocampus to be involved and for abilities other than simple novelty preferences to be involved.

One way to reconcile the apparent differences in age of onset between these tasks and those cited earlier is to propose that memory processes that are dependent on the hippocampus early in life differ qualitatively from those observed later in the first year. Indeed, it has been proposed (Nelson, 1994; Nelson and Collins, 1991; Webster, Ungerleider, and Bachevalier, 1991b) that novelty preferences early in life may be reflexive or obligatory in nature, and thus this form of memory differs qualitatively from that observed in tasks like DNMS. Recent evidence using cortical ERPs supports this assumption (see Nelson and Collins, 1991, 1992). For example, ERPs were used to disentangle how often a stimulus was presented from whether that stimulus was novel or familiar. Infants were presented with two faces equally often, for 10 trials each, with the aim to familiarize infants to two events. Infants were then presented with three classes of events. On 60 percent of the trials, one of the faces seen during familiarization was presented (*frequent-familiar* event). On a random 20 percent of the trials, the other familiarization face was presented (*infrequent-familiar* event). Finally, on each of the remaining 20 percent of the trials (12 in all), a different face was presented (*infrequent-novel* events). If infants had fully encoded both events during familiarization, then one might expect them to respond equivalently to these same two faces presented during test and distinguish these faces from the novel faces. What in fact was found, however, was that, at 4 months, infants failed to distinguish among the three classes of events. At 6 months, they appeared to respond both to how often the stimuli were presented (i.e., they distinguished between familiar stimuli presented frequently vs. infrequently) and to whether the stimuli had been seen before (they distinguished between the familiar stimulus and the novel stimuli). At 8 months, infants' ERPs only distinguished between the novel and familiar events; event frequency was no longer a factor in their ERP response. The shift in performance noted across these three age groups suggested that the so-called novelty reaction in infants younger than 6 months may in fact be an obligatory response to infrequently presented events. It is only by approximately 8 months that infants ignore event frequency and attend instead to whether a stimulus is novel or familiar.

These findings suggest that novelty preferences, at least until 6–8 months of life, may be reflex-like in nature. Memory inferred from novelty preferences, despite being dependent on hippocampal or related structures, may thus differ qualitatively from memory as evaluated in the DNMS task.

It has recently been reported that, in the monkey, adult levels of glucose utilization are not obtained in area TE until approximately 4 months of age, the age at which infants first begin to succeed on the DNMS task (Bachevalier et al., 1991). In contrast, the hippocampus appears to be functionally developed within the first month or so of life. This suggests that whatever role TE plays in novelty preferences does not emerge until 4 months in the monkey and nearly a year in the human. It has also been reported (Webster, Ungerleider, and Bachevalier, 1991a) that in unlesioned monkeys, a transient projection is observed from area TEO to the lateral basal nucleus of the amygdala; this projection is retracted later in development and is not present in the adult. However, when area TE is removed during the neonatal period (i.e., between 8 and 23 days of age), this normally transient projection is seen in the adult. In addition, projections from area TEO to the dorsal part of the lateral nucleus of the amygdala, which are normally transient and disappear in the adult, tend to expand into the zone normally occupied by terminals from area TE when TE is lesioned in infancy. It has been speculated that the sparing in DNMS performance that has been noted with early TE lesions may be due to the retention of these early transient projections (Webster et al., 1991a). Similarly, the presence of these transient projections early in life in the intact animal, followed by their regression, may account for some forms of medial temporal lobe-dependent memory to precede other forms, for example, visual paired comparison versus DNMS.

Summary

The argument being put forth is that there may be two types of memory processes in the infant. One is an early form that depends predominantly on the medial temporal lobe (hippocampus in particular) and results in preferences for novelty that are reflexive in nature. This form accounts for performance on any task that involves a novelty preference but for which task demands (e.g., familiarization and test stimuli presented in a single modality) or delays are minimal (e.g., seconds vs. minutes, hours, or weeks). Some time between 6 and 12 months, this early form is supplanted and modified by a second form, which depends on cortical structures (e.g., area TE) as well as further elaboration of structures in the hippocampal formation (e.g., dentate). This latter form is likely responsible for the emergence of function in cross-modal recognition memory tasks, sequencing and deferred imitation tasks, and the DNMS task.

Tasks That Might Depend on Prefrontal Cortex

The tasks to be discussed in this section have in common their dependence on working-memory capacity. *Working memory* is defined as the ability to hold information on-line until some action can be initiated (for discussions, see Baddeley, 1986, 1992; Goldman-Rakic, 1987; Moscovitch, 1992). Working memory differs most from other forms of memory discussed. For example, in tasks of preexplicit or explicit memory, infants may be asked to hold information in memory for relatively extended periods of time (e.g., minutes, hours, or days). In addition, the infant is not required to do anything with this information other than eventually recognize that they had seen something at some previous point in time (the exception may be in deferred imitation tasks, in which infants must reproduce a sequence of events experienced at some previous point in time). In contrast, in the tasks described in this section, infants must typically hold information in memory for brief periods of time (e.g., seconds); in addition, they must use the contents of their memory in some way, such as to retrieve a hidden object.

Piagetian A-not-B task

This task, as originally conceived by Piaget (Piaget, 1952), was designed to examine the infant's concept of object permanence. An object would be hidden at one location (A), and the infant would be allowed to retrieve it. After the object was successfully retrieved, the same object would again be placed in location A and then moved to location B (generally adjacent to location A). Infants younger than approximately 8 or so months would consistently fail to retrieve the object at location B. As age increases, so does the ability to reach successfully for the object at location B; however, if a delay is imposed between hiding the object at B and permitting the infant to reach, performance declines (i.e., infants reach to A instead of to B). In a longitudinal study conducted by Diamond (1985), it was reported that 8-month-olds were able to tolerate a delay of only 1 or 2 s between hiding and retrieval, whereas by 12–13 months this delay could be increased to nearly 10 s before the infants made the "A-not-B" error (i.e., reaching incorrectly at A instead of correctly at B; note, however, that other investigators have reported that relatively few 12-month-olds can tolerate delays of 10 s and that it may not be until approximately 15 months that such a delay can be tolerated; see Bell and Fox, 1992; Matthews, Ellis, and Nelson, 1994).

Delayed response task

A close analog to the A–not–B task that has been used with nonhuman primates for nearly 60 years is the *delayed response* (DR) task (Jacobsen, 1936). Here the animal is presented with two wells, one of which is baited. As the animal watches, the bait is moved from one well to the other. A delay then ensues, after which the baited and nonbaited wells are presented again. Reaching to the latter constitutes incorrect performance. Recent work has demonstrated that these tasks are comparable in the demands they place on memory and that the developmental course of both the A–not–B and DR tasks is similar in both human and nonhuman primate infants (Diamond and Doar, 1989).

Neural bases of A–not–B and DR performance

It has been known for some time that the dorsolateral prefrontal cortex is involved in spatial working memory, that is, the ability to remember the location of a hidden object long enough to attempt to retrieve that object. For example, lesions of the adult dorsolateral prefrontal cortex profoundly impair performance on the DR task, and similar lesions also affect performance on the Piagetian A–not–B task (Diamond and Goldman-Rakic, 1989). Adult lesions (in the monkey) of parietal cortex or lesions of the hippocampus, amygdala, and surrounding cortex (H+A+ lesions) do not affect performance on A–not–B tasks, unless the delay between hiding and retrieval begins to exceed 15–30 s (Diamond, Zola-Morgan, and Squire, 1989). From this work follows the suggestion that structures in the medial temporal and parietal lobes are not involved in the A–not–B and DR tasks, whereas the dorsolateral prefrontal cortex is involved in these tasks.

It should be noted that Goldman-Rakic and colleagues (Wilson, O'Scalaidhe, and Goldman-Rakic, 1993) have recently reported an anatomical dissociation between spatial working memory and object working memory. Specifically, whereas the former ability is mediated by neurons that lie in the dorsolateral prefrontal cortex, the ability to remember the object itself is mediated by neurons in the inferior prefrontal convexity.[2] In addition, object working memory may not be specific to the inferior convexity of the prefrontal cortex, as other investigators have reported a similar phenomenon involving the inferior temporal (IT) cortex (see Miller and Desimone, 1994).[3]

Goldman-Rakic and colleagues (e.g., Goldman, 1971) investigated the role of the dorsolateral prefrontal cortex in DR performance in infant monkeys. It was initially demonstrated that neonatal lesions of the dorsolateral prefrontal cortex had little effect on performance during the later infancy period (i.e., 8 months). More recently, however,

2   *Editors' Note*: More recent evidence suggests that the anatomical dissociation between spatial and object working memory may be an artifact of independent training on tasks that tap these two components (Rao, Rainer, and Miller, 1997).
3   *Editors' Note*: Relative to the working memory associated with prefrontal cortex, memory in posterior cortical areas is more susceptible to interference from other stimuli, both in IT as shown by Miller and Desimone, and in parietal cortex (Steinmetz et al., 1994).

Diamond and Goldman-Rakic (see Diamond, 1990) demonstrated that when lesions are done later in the infancy period (4 $\frac{1}{2}$ months) and testing follows soon thereafter (1 month later), DR and A-not-B performance are deleteriously affected. Although this finding would suggest that this region of the brain is functional early in monkey life and mediates performance on these tasks, one must keep in mind that Goldman (Goldman-Rakic, 1985) has proposed that other, more developmentally mature structures in the general prefrontal circuitry might subserve performance on these tasks during infancy. For example, Goldman and Rosvold (1972) demonstrated that lesions of the anterodorsal sector of the caudate performed in infancy (48–65 days) or adulthood impair DR performance; other candidate structures might also include the orbital prefrontal cortex and the mediodorsal nucleus (Goldman, 1971; Goldman and Rosvold, 1972). Only later in life (after 12–16 months) will dorsolateral prefrontal cortex subsume control.

One reason for proposing that the dorsolateral prefrontal cortex may not be involved in A-not-B or DR performance until the end of the infancy period comes from the human data on the development of prefrontal cortex in general. First, it has been reported that adult levels of synapses are not obtained until adolescence; before this, there is an over-abundance of synapses, which peaks at about 6 years and gradually declines over the next 10 years or so (Huttenlocher, 1979, 1990; for a review, see Huttenlocher, 1994). Second, myelination in the prefrontal cortex is very delayed, continuing through adolescence and beyond (Jernigan, Trauner, Hesselink, and Tallal, 1991; Yakovlev and LeCours, 1967). Third, PET studies have indicated that metabolic activity in the frontal cortex lags behind all other cortical regions, only approaching adult values by 1 year and continuing to develop over the next decade or more (Chugani, 1994; Chugani and Phelps, 1986).

Overall, a parsimonious interpretation of the data from the A-not-B and DR tasks is that some general aspect of the dorsolateral prefrontal circuitry probably mediates task performance during the first year of life. Unfortunately, it is not clear whether it is the prefrontal cortex per se, deeper structures within this circuitry (e.g., caudate), or the linking up of this set of structures that are primarily responsible for task performance. In addition, because the A-not-B and DR tasks require much more than working memory, it is difficult to disentangle the memory requirements from the nonmemory requirements. For example, in addition to remembering the location of the hidden object, infants may also need to (a) learn to associate a reward with a correct response, (b) coordinate action sequences, and (c) inhibit a prepotent response. Thus, it is not clear whether the delayed maturation of the A-not-B and DR tasks is due to changes in the structures underlying the ability to hold a representation in memory or the structures responsible for the other abilities required in these tasks. Recent work from Baillargeon's laboratory (see Baillargeon, 1993, for a discussion) casts doubt on the first hypothesis.

Baillargeon and colleagues (e.g., Baillargeon, 1993; Baillargeon, DeVos, and Graber, 1989; Baillargeon and Graber, 1988) have developed a task whereby infants' looking times are used to index their memory for the location of a hidden object. Here, an infant might observe an object being hidden in a possible versus impossible location (e.g., behind a block of wood that obscures its view vs. disappearing completely in a seemingly improbable way, such as dropping through a hole in the table that is occluded by a block of wood). Longer looking at the impossible event/location is used to infer location memory. In a series of studies, Baillargeon and colleagues have demonstrated that infants as young as 8 months can remember the location of a hidden object for as long as 70 s. These data would suggest, then, that working-memory capacity is quite well developed by the time infants are merely beginning to remember the location of the hidden object in the A-not-B or DR task.

The neural bases of this performance, however, are unclear. There is no evidence that has attributed working-memory capacity to the caudate or other striatal structures. These structures appear to possess a reasonable degree of functional maturation in the first half of the first year of human life and this would argue against their involvement in the infant's ability to tolerate increasingly long delays in the A-not-B and DR tasks. If dorsolateral prefrontal cortex is involved in spatial working memory, then Baillargeon et al.'s data would argue against the hypothesis that development of this structure is responsible for infants' tolerating increasingly long delays in the A-not-B and DR tasks. What seems most likely is the coordination of a set of structures that subserve the ability to use working memory to coordinate a series of behaviors (see Moscovitch, 1992, for a discussion of working *with* memory). These behaviors most likely include the following: knowing where the object was and where the object was not; inhibiting an incorrect response when memory for the correct response begins to decay; knowledge that objects continue to exist when no longer in sight; possibly, knowledge about the properties of the object itself; and, in the case of the DR task, learning to associate a reward with a particular location. It would appear that dorsolateral prefrontal cortex is sufficiently developed by 6–12 months of age to support the working-memory requirements imposed by the A-not-B and DR tasks. However, to coordinate the use of working memory in the context of the other requirements imposed by these tasks awaits the development of a coordinated set of structures involving (at the least) the dorsolateral and orbito prefrontal cortices, the mediodorsal nucleus, and the anterodorsal caudate nucleus.

Tasks That May Depend on the Striatum

Haith and colleagues have developed a paradigm that permits one to examine the infant's ability to form expectations about future events (for a review, see Haith, Wentworth, and Canfield, 1993). Here, infants' eye movements are recorded as they fixate a series of lights that, when lit in succession, create a certain pattern. Infants' visual reaction times to anticipating the next light in the sequence are recorded through corneal photography. The critical questions are (a) does the infant correctly anticipate the next light in the sequence and (b) do the infant's reaction times decline when the sequence changes? It has been consistently demonstrated that infants as young as 3.5 months will rapidly "learn" the sequence of lights as indexed by anticipating the next light in the sequence (as evidenced by reduced reaction times); when the learned pattern is interrupted, reaction time increases, suggesting that the infant recognized the change in sequence (Haith, Hazan, and Goodman, 1988; Wentworth and Haith, 1992). Thus far, there are no data that address how long infants retain information about the pattern.

Unfortunately, there are no data describing the neural bases underlying this task. A possible analogue, however, might include a method used by Knopman and Nissen (Knopman, 1991; Knopman and Nissen, 1987) to examine procedural memory, a type of memory that has been thought to depend on the striatum. Participants were presented with a series of lights. There were four lights in a row, and 10 rows altogether. One light in each row came on, and the participant was required to push a key corresponding to each light. The sequence of 10 lights made a pattern, and after the 10th light came on, the sequence began anew. Elderly adults with Alzheimer's disease (AD) and healthy elderly controls served as participants. Both groups of participants showed decreased reaction times as the 10-light sequence emerged, and both groups showed increased reaction times when the sequence of lights was unexpectedly changed. These data suggest that both groups learned the sequence; however, only the control participants professed awareness (as indexed verbally) that a sequence of lights had been presented and, subsequently, that the sequence had been changed.

The significance of this work is that the AD patients were selectively impaired on the explicit memory aspects of the task (i.e., awareness of the pattern) but unimpaired on the procedural memory aspects (i.e., learning as inferred from reaction times). On the basis of formal diagnosis (for discussions, see Pearson, Esiri, Hiorns, Wilcock, and Powell, 1985; Proctor et al., 1988), it was assumed that the AD patients suffered from neuropathology that was disproportionately restricted to the medial temporal lobes. It therefore seemed reasonable to conclude that this region of the brain was not involved in task performance. Determining which precise region or regions were involved is a bit more difficult, although a reasonable hypothesis is that in this task, as in other procedural memory tasks, an intact striatum is required. Given that the AD patients suffered no known pathology to these structures, it was assumed that the normative procedural learning that was observed was due to intact striatal structures. Thus, it may be that an intact striatum made possible the procedural learning that was evidenced by comparable task performance in both groups, but medial temporal lobe impairment in the AD group prevented these participants from possessing explicit knowledge of the lights' sequence.

The similarity between the infant paradigm and that used with adults by Knopman and Nissen (1987) suggests that the performance on the former task did not depend on temporal lobe structures but may well have depended on striatal structures. Although relatively little is known about the development of the human striatum, in general, the structures that constitute the basal ganglia (caudate, putamen, globus pallidus, subthalamic nucleus, and substantia nigra) are differentiated at birth. The striatum in particular (which consists of the caudate and putamen) is the first of the telencephalic structures to begin myelinating. Within the basal ganglia, the inner segment of the globus pallidus is well myelinated by the eighth postnatal month, although the outer segment does not reach adult levels of myelin until beyond the first postnatal year (for a discussion, see Sidman and Rakic, 1982). This latter observation is in agreement with metabolic studies. For example, Chugani and colleagues (Chugani, 1994; Chugani and Phelps, 1986; Chugani, Phelps, and Mazziotta, 1987) have reported that the basal ganglia display increases in metabolic activity earlier than most regions of the cortex. On the basis of these data, it seems reasonable to propose that the striatum may support performance in the visual expectancy paradigm and, as such, may reflect a form of procedural learning akin to that in the adult.

Tasks That Do Not Depend on the Medial Temporal Lobe, Striatum, or Prefrontal Cortices but That May Depend on the Cerebellum and the Olivary–Cerebellar Complex

Instrumental conditioning

Sucking behavior. DeCasper and colleagues (DeCasper and Fifer, 1980; DeCasper and Spence, 1986, 1991) have conducted a series of studies using nonnutritive sucking designed to examine newborn infants' recognition of their mother's voice. Infants are allowed to suck on a nonnutritive nipple until a baseline suck rate (e.g., how hard or how often the infant sucks) is established. At this point, different auditory stimuli are presented coincident with sucking. Some of these stimuli are presumed to be familiar to the infant, whereas others are not. The goal is to establish whether the infant's sucking behavior can be modified by the presentation of a particular stimulus. If it can, memory for this stimulus is then inferred.

In brief, from this work, it has been demonstrated that infants within a day or two of being born not only recognize their mother's voice (e.g., DeCasper and Fifer, 1980), but they can also distinguish between a story the mother had read outloud during the last weeks of pregnancy (i.e., a familiar story) from a novel story (e.g., DeCasper and Spence, 1986; for an elaboration, see DeCasper and Spence, 1991). For example, DeCasper and colleagues have reported a differential effect on sucking by the mother's voice or by the voice of their mother reading a familiar nursery rhyme in comparison with the voice of a stranger or the voice of the mother reading an unfamiliar nursery rhyme. The presumed basis of this finding is that infants profited from prenatal experience of hearing the mother's voice, and then recognized this voice at birth.

Leg-kick conditioning. The other method by which memory is inferred from instrumental behavior concerns conditioned leg kicking. This procedure has been extensively developed by Rovee-Collier and colleagues (for recent reviews, see Rovee-Collier, 1990; Rovee-Collier and Fagen, 1981; Rovee-Collier and Hayne, 1987). Here, infants are positioned on their backs in a crib, with a mobile suspended above them. After obtaining some baseline level of kicking (in which there is no contingency between leg kicking and mobile movement), a ribbon is attached to the mobile at one end and to the infant's leg at the other. Infants as young as 3 months readily draw the association between their leg movement and the movement of the mobile, and the highly reinforcing properties of the mobile's movement generally result in a substantial increase of leg kicking in relation to baseline. In one variation of this procedure, a test phase generally follows this reinforcement phase, with delays between the two phases that vary by minutes, days, or weeks. Here, infants are simply presented with the nonmoving mobile and testing for recognition (i.e., do they demonstrate memory of the mobile as evinced by leg kicking?). In a second variation of this procedure, a brief period of reinstatement (e.g., simply showing the infant the mobile) is provided after some interval (again, minutes, days, or weeks), with testing generally following the next day. Thus, training might occur on Day 1, reinstatement on Day 13, and testing on Day 14. The goal of this variation is to examine whether long-term retention can be improved by providing the infant with a reminder.

The utility of this procedure has been extensively explored, and many variants have been used. These include (a) varying the context of training and test, (b) requiring a discrimination test, (c) examining the role of reinstatement (see earlier), and (d) varying the retention interval. The results in nearly all cases are robust; infants as young as 3 months show evidence of learning and recognition after intervals as long as 2–4 weeks, with more robust effects (i.e., lengthier intervals) found when reinstatement is administered (e.g., Rovee-Collier and Hayne, 1987). This memory is often highly specific and context-bound, however. For example, Fagen, Rovee-Collier, and Kaplan (1976) reported that 3-month-old infants' retention after a 24-hr delay declined appreciably if the test mobile varied from the training mobile by more than one object (i.e., more than one additional element had been added to the mobile). However, as the retention interval increases, retention again improves, suggesting that as time passes infants begin to forget the details of the original training session (for a discussion, see Rovee-Collier, 1990). Similarly, Butler (1986; also see Butler and Rovee-Collier, 1989) reported that changing the crib bumper will eliminate retention after a 3-day delay, whereas testing the infant with the same crib bumper yields excellent retention. These last two findings suggest that during the initial training phase, infants encode not only the details of the stimulus (which seem to be forgotten over time) but also many aspects of the more general context of the training environment (which appear to be retained).

Although this task differs procedurally from those discussed earlier, it and most of these other procedures all evaluate visual recognition memory; that is, infants are being asked to discriminate one mobile from another on the basis of visual features. However, where this procedure appears to differ from the others is that, through leg-kick conditioning, infants appear capable of showing fairly long-term memory, even when as young as 3 months; recall that in the visual paired-comparison and habituation procedures, information is rarely retained by more than days. Three possibilities must be considered in accounting for this difference. First, in contrast to the other methods discussed previously, in leg-kick conditioning the actual encoding of the stimulus is embedded in the context of motor activity (similar, perhaps, to skill learning in implicit memory paradigms). Second, infants in the leg-kick paradigm are provided with relatively lengthy exposures to the stimulus, far longer than are typically provided in the visual recognition paradigms discussed earlier. Finally, the reactivation paradigm bears some similarity to priming; that is, a brief reexposure to the test stimulus facilitates recognition. Collectively, these differences suggest, but do not prove, that the type of memory being evaluated using conditioned leg kicking bears similarity to studies of implicit memory and clearly differs from that evaluated using nonconditioning procedures, such as the visual paired-comparison procedure, despite the commonality of evaluating visual recognition memory.

Neural bases of instrumental conditioning

It is extraordinarily difficult to ascertain the neural bases of these forms of memory, as these procedures have not been used with adult humans or with monkeys. A possible analogy to Rovee-Collier's (e.g., Rovee-Collier and Fagen, 1981; Rovee-Collier and Hayne, 1987) work might be the instrumentally conditioned limb flexion response. In this procedure, animals (often cats) are first conditioned to associate a tone (conditioned stimulus; CS) with a shock (unconditioned stimulus; UCS) applied to the leg. They must then learn to flex their leg during the time the CS is presented before the CS terminates in the UCS; that is, to move their leg before being shocked. For example, Voneida and colleagues (e.g., Voneida, Christie, Bogdanski, and Chopko, 1990) demonstrated that lesions in the olivary–cerebellar complex of the cat result in severe loss of the response. The lesions resulting in the greatest loss involved damage to the rostral parts of the dorsal and medial accessory olivary nuclei (which receives inputs from the forelimb spinal cord and cerebral cortical areas). In contrast, rostralmedial olivary lesions had little effect on behavior.

A direct comparison between the instrumental conditioned response studied by Rovee-Collier and colleagues (e.g., Rovee-Collier, 1990) and the limb flexion response described may not be entirely appropriate. The limb-flexion response involves aversive conditioning, whereas the leg-kick response (presumably) involves positive reinforcement. Nevertheless, it may be possible that in the former procedure, portions of the olivary–cerebellar complex are involved, at least insofar as learning the task. The critical components of this complex likely include cerebellar Purkinje cells, which receive input from the contralateral inferior olivary complex through the climbing fibers and from the mossy fibers, which transmit a wide range of sensory input. Thus, the underlying neuroanatomy includes the cerebellum and certain deep nuclei of the brain stem. This latter argument is bolstered by reports that lesions of certain cerebellar nuclei can block acquisition of some forms of motor learning, such as the eye-blink conditioned response (e.g., Steinmetz, Lavond, Ikovich, Logan, and Thompson, 1992), and aversive signaled barpress learning (e.g., Steinmetz, Logue, and Miller, 1993). These speculations should not be wholly surprising given what is involved in performing this task (i.e., reinforcing a limb movement).

Classical conditioning

Despite the prominence of classical conditioning in the behavioral neuroscience literature, there has been relatively little work done in this context with human infants. Two historical examples should suffice. Marquis (1931) demonstrated that newborns could be conditioned to suck when a sound was presented if this sound was first associated with the presentation of milk. Wickens and Wickens (1940) demonstrated conditioned foot withdrawal to a buzzer by associating the buzzer with foot shock. These early studies, coupled with many subsequent studies (for a review, see Rosenblith, 1992), have determined that infants can, in fact, be conditioned. Of particular relevance to the goals of the present article is the small literature on the conditioned eye-blink response. As is done with animals, participants are initially presented with a tone (CS). Shortly thereafter (although still coincident with the tone), a puff of air is presented to the eye (UCS). This combination results in a blink (unconditioned response). After a certain number of trials has elapsed, the CS alone results in a blink (conditioned response). Although this paradigm has been used little in the past 20 years, a brief synopsis of this literature would suggest that the conditioned eye-blink response appears to develop between 10 and 30 days in the human (see Lipsitt, 1990).

Neural bases of classical conditioning

Animal studies.   The conditioned eye-blink response has been extensively studied in the adult rabbit by Thompson and others (for a review, see Woodruff-Pak, Logan, and Thompson, 1990); unfortunately, comparable work has not been done at the beginning of the life span. In general, the neural circuitry involved in eye-blink conditioning has been well worked out. It has been demonstrated that the cerebellum and its associated brainstem circuitry are responsible for acquisition (for a discussion, see Woodruff-Pak and Thompson, 1988). The general hypothesis put forth by Thompson, Woodruff-Pak, and colleagues has been that the CS activates mossy fibers of the cerebellum, whereas the UCS activates climbing fibers. Cerebellar Purkinje cells (with contributions, perhaps, from stellate and basket cells) are the most likely candidates. Finally, although the cerebellum is responsible for acquisition of the eye-blink response, the hippocampus may be involved in the storage process. For example, activity in the CA1 region increases within trials early in the acquisition phase, but only when learning is occurring.

Human data.   There are a handful of studies examining the conditioned eye-blink response in the human. For example, Daum, Schugens, et al. (1993) reported that patients with cerebellar pathology (e.g., due to ischemic lesions) or who had undergone surgical resection of the cerebellum demonstrated a severe impairment in acquiring the conditioned eye-blink response. It is interesting to note, however, that all patients were aware of the reinforcement contingencies. In a parallel fashion, Woodruff-Pak (1993) reported that patient H.M., who had undergone a bilateral resection of the temporal lobes (see Milner et al., 1968; Scoville and Milner, 1957), could acquire the conditioned eye-blink response, although in certain situations acquisition was delayed, possibly due to atrophy of the cerebellar vermis and hemispheres (for a discussion, see Woodruff-Pak, 1993, p. 923), although he was not aware of having done so.[4] Collectively, then, it would appear that the human literature is in agreement with the animal literature: Specifically, acquiring the conditioned eye-blink response requires the cerebellum and does not require medial temporal lobe structures.

Thus far, it has been argued that instrumental conditioning involves the cerebellum and certain deep nuclei of the brain stem and that acquisition of the conditioned eye-blink response requires the cerebellum. Are there data to support the assertion that these structures and nuclei are sufficiently mature early in life to support such conditioning?

In general, little is known about the development of either the cerebellum or deep nuclei. It is known that prenatal development of the cerebellum lags behind that of the cortex by several weeks (see Kandel, Schwartz, and Jessell, 1991). Nevertheless, PET studies have revealed that glucose activity (a metric of energy metabolism and perhaps a corollary of synapse formation) in the cerebellum during the first postnatal year of life more closely approximates adult values than virtually any other region of the brain (Chugani, 1994; Chugani and Phelps, 1986). Portions of the superior and inferior cerebellar peduncles and the decussation of the superior cerebellum peduncles are developed at birth. More important, myelination patterns of the entire cerebellum appear adultlike by 3 postnatal months (Barkovich, Kjos, Jackson, and Norman, 1988). Thus, although the development of the cerebellum initially (i.e., prenatally) lags behind that of the cortex, rapid development appears to occur toward the end of the last part of gestation and the first part of postnatal life. These general findings may possibly account for the high motor learning potential and conditionability of the young infant.

Ontogeny of Memory Revisited

This article began with an exposition of the adult classification of memory. It was argued that there are at least two major types of memory, explicit and implicit, and that each type depends on different neural circuits. Based on an examination of the demands each of these tasks makes on memory and the development of the neural circuitry associated with each of these tasks, it was proposed that several types of memory are evident over the first 1–2 years of life.

Perhaps the clearest examples from the developmental psychology literature of what might be considered explicit memory in the adult include the following: tasks in which infants must reproduce sequences of events after some intervening delay (and with no practice); cross-modal recognition memory tasks, in which infants must represent an object in one modality, transfer this representation to a second modality, and then distinguish between a familiar and an unfamiliar object; and the DNMS task, in which infants must choose a novel object over a familiar object after some intervening delay. In all of these cases, the form of memory represented by these tasks emerges somewhere between 8 and

---

4   *Author's note*: It had earlier been pointed out that the hippocampus may be required for retaining the conditioned eye-blink response. Although H.M. has no hippocampus and appears to retain this response after a period of weeks, his may not be the best case to evaluate this proposal. Specifically, in animals, the bilateral resection of the hippocampus typically immediately precedes or follows training and testing. In H.M.'s case, his hippocampus was removed 38 years earlier. Thus, one cannot rule out some recovery of function over this period of time.

approximately 15–18 months of life (when memory is fully mature is not known). It was also concluded that the memory requirements of these tasks were, depending on the length of the delay, limbic- and cortical-dependent.

Based in part on animal lesion studies and in part on a componential analysis of particular tasks, it was proposed further that any task that depended solely on novelty preferences was also limbic-dependent. However, because these tasks did not require infants to dissociate how often events were presented (i.e., frequently vs. rarely) from memory information (i.e., whether events were novel or familiar), and because these tasks appear to rely exclusively on the hippocampus and not on cortical areas (e.g., area TE), these represented an earlier, possibly more "primitive" form of memory. Nevertheless, because these tasks share with the explicit memory tasks a similar (albeit not identical) neural circuitry, they might best be construed as a precursor to explicit memory – perhaps *preexplicit* memory might be accurate. The transition from *preexplicit* to *explicit* memory likely occurs after approximately 8 months of life. The further development and elaboration of explicit memory, however, transpires over the next several years. At the neural level, such change will likely be due to further developments in the hippocampal formation (e.g., dentate) and the temporal cortex (e.g., area TE); at the cognitive level, the emergence of language, and later, the development and use of strategies (Kail, 1990), will likely facilitate additional development.

The type of memory required for performance in the A-not-B and DR tasks is likely working memory (although working memory is not the only ability required in these tasks). Given the evidence that the working-memory requirements imposed by these tasks are well within the limits of an 8- to 12-month-old infant, then the relatively protracted development of performance in the A-not-B and DR tasks must not be due to improvements in working memory per se. Rather, it seems likely that such improvement is due to gains made in other areas. However, if spatial working memory is mediated by dorsolateral prefrontal cortex, and if this region undergoes considerable development well beyond the infancy period, then what makes possible the reasonable working memory possessed by the 8-month-old? Similarly, if dorsolateral prefrontal cortex continues to mature beyond the first 2 years of life, how is it that 8- to 12-month-old infants tolerate even minor delays (e.g., 5 s) in the A-not-B and DR tasks? The answer to the first question might be that the portions of dorsolateral prefrontal cortex that deal with working memory develop between 6 and 12 months. However, dorsolateral prefrontal cortex makes possible more than working memory; it likely also coordinates action schemes in concert with other structures in the general prefrontal circuitry. It is this development that likely emerges after a year or two of age – that is, further elaboration of the dorsolateral prefrontal cortex specifically and the prefrontal circuitry generally. What mediates A-not-B and DR performance before this? Very possibly the limited working-memory capacity of dorsolateral prefrontal cortex in conjunction with the caudate. This argument, then, would have it that the other abilities required of these tasks are subserved by the caudate early in life, and later in life are taken over by the dorsolateral prefrontal cortex, which serves to regulate the various structures in the general prefrontal circuitry. Unfortunately, it is not clear at what point adult or adultlike capacity is obtained, again, primarily because the tasks used to evaluate infants versus adults and monkeys versus humans differ so dramatically.

The visual expectancy paradigm was characterized as reflecting procedural memory. This adult classification was based on similarity to tasks used with adults, in whom striatal structures are thought to mediate task performance and in whom the temporal lobe (cf. Knopman and Nissen, 1987) and cerebellum are thought not to be involved (e.g., cerebellar lesions seem not to affect procedural learning in the adult human; see Daum, Ackermann, et al., 1993).

Finally, memory tasks that require conditioning (be it leg kick or eye blink) seem to depend on the cerebellum and deep nuclei of the brain stem for acquisition, and possibly the hippocampus for retrieval and maintenance (particularly in the case of leg-kick conditioning, in which visual recognition memory is required). Although memory is clearly demonstrated in these tasks, their main agenda is to demonstrate learning. In addition, some aspects of the leg-kick conditioning paradigm resemble perceptual priming (i.e., those involving reinstatement), in that a brief exposure to the previously learned stimulus facilitates recognition. Collectively, the neuroscience evidence available to date, coupled with an examination of the task demands, suggests that these tasks represent a qualitatively different form of memory than those construed as explicit or preexplicit. Whether they represent a form of implicit memory (as they likely would in the adult) or represent a completely separate behavioral–neural system is unclear.

Given the nature of the task demands and the relative maturity of the associated neural circuitry underlying both conditioning and procedural learning, it would seem reasonable to propose that less subsequent development would be evident here than in forms of explicit memory. In these former cases, memory appears early in life and, at least in the case of conditioning, remains robust for at least the next several months.

Conclusion

It has been proposed that memory likely dependent on the striatum (procedural memory), on the cerebellar–olivary complex and possibly the hippocampus (conditioning), and on portions of the limbic system (preexplicit memory) develops within the first few months of life. Between 6 and 12 months, preexplicit memory may be supplanted by a more adultlike form of temporal lobe memory (explicit memory). Finally, memory dependent on the prefrontal circuitry (working memory) also develops in this general age span. Although all of these forms of memory may continue to develop through the ensuing months and years of life, it is likely changes in explicit memory that undergo the greatest transformation. However, tasks that require the infant to use working memory in some capacity will also be seen to improve over the next few years of life.

ACKNOWLEDGMENTS

Research and manuscript preparation were made possible in part by grants from the National Institute of Mental Health (Grant MH46860) and the National Institute of Neurological Disorders and Stroke (Grant NS32976), and by a single-quarter leave made possible by the University of Minnesota.

I owe my gratitude to a number of individuals who have helped shape my thinking on the subject of infant memory, either by way of electronic or verbal communication (Jocelyne Bachevalier and Adele Diamond) or by reading this article (Patricia Bauer, Virginia Gunderson, Olivier Pascalis, and Susan Rose). A debt of thanks is also extended to the present and past members of my Developmental Cognitive Neuroscience Laboratory (University of Minnesota) and the members of the MacArthur Network on Psychopathology and Development (David Kupfer, Chair), who have all made good sounding boards, and to William Greenough and Paul Chapman for their assistance in clarifying my thinking on the neurobiology of conditioning.

Correspondence concerning this article should be addressed to Charles A. Nelson, Institute of Child Development, University of Minnesota, 51 East River Road, Minneapolis, Minnesota 55455.

Electronic mail may be sent via Internet to CANELSON@VX.CIS.UMN.EDU.

REFERENCES

Aslin, R. N. (1987). Visual and auditory development in infancy. In J. D. Osofsky (ed.), *Handbook of Infant Development* (2nd edn., pp. 5–97). New York: Wiley.

Bachevalier, J. (1990). Ontogenetic development of habit and memory formation in primates. In A. Diamond (ed.), *Development and Neural Bases of Higher Cognitive Functions* (pp. 457–84). New York: New York Academy of Sciences Press.

Bachevalier, J. (1992). Cortical versus limbic immaturity: Relationship to infantile amnesia. In M. R. Gunnar and C. A. Nelson (eds.), *Minnesota Symposia on Child Psychology: Developmental neuroscience* (Vol. 24, pp. 129–53). Hillsdale, NJ: Erlbaum.

Bachevalier, J., Brickson, M., and Hagger, C. (1993). Limbic-dependent recognition memory in monkeys develops early in infancy. *Neuro Report* 4, 77–80.

Bachevalier, J., Hagger, C., and Mishkin, M. (1991). Functional maturation of the occipito-temporal pathway in infant rhesus monkeys. In N. A. Lassen, D. H. Ingvar, M. E. Raiche, and L. Friberg (eds.), *Brain work and Mental Activity* (pp. 231–40). Copenhagen, Denmark: Munksgaard.

Bachevalier, J. and Mishkin, M. (1984). An early and a late developing system for learning and retention in infant monkeys. *Behavioral Neuroscience* 98, 770–8.

Bachevalier, J. and Mishkin, M. (1992). *Dissociation of the effects of neonatal inferior temporal cortical versus limbic lesions on visual recognition in 10-month-old rhesus monkeys.* Manuscript submitted for publication.

Baddeley, A. D. (1986). *Working Memory*. Oxford: Oxford University Press.

Baddeley, A. D. (1992). Working memory. *Science* 255, 556–9.

Baillargeon, R. (1993). The object concept revisited: New directions in the investigation of infants' physical knowledge. In C. E. Granrud (ed.), *Visual Perception and Cognition in Infancy: Carnegie-Mellon Symposia on Cognition* (Vol. 23, pp. 265–315). Hillsdale, NJ: Erlbaum.

Baillargeon, R., DeVos, J., and Graber, M. (1989). Location memory in 8-month-old infants in a non-search AB task: Further evidence. *Cognitive Development* 4, 345–67.

Baillargeon, R. and Graber, M. (1988). Evidence of location memory in 8-month-old infants in a nonsearch AB task. *Developmental Psychology* 24, 502–11.

Barkovich, A. J., Kjos, B. O., Jackson, D. E., and Norman, D. (1988). Normal maturation of the neonatal and infant brain: MR imaging at 1.5 T. *Neuroradiology* 166, 173–80.

Bauer, P. J. (1992). Holding it all together: How enabling relations facilitate young children's event recall. *Cognitive Development* 7, 1–28.

Bauer, P. J., Hertsgaard, L. A., and Dow, G. A. (1994). After 8 months have passed: Long-term recall of events by 1- and 2-year-old children. *Memory* 2, 353–82.

Bell, M. A. and Fox, N. A. (1992). The relations between frontal brain electrical activity and cognitive development during infancy. *Child Development* 63, 1142–63.

Berger, B. and Alvarez, C. (1994). Neurochemical development of the hippocampal region in the fetal rhesus monkey: II. Immunocyto-chemistry of peptides, calcium-binding proteins, DARPP-32, and monoamine innervation in the entorhinal cortex by the end of gestation. *Hippocampus* 4, 85–114.

Berger, B., Alvarez, C., and Goldman-Rakic, P. S. (1993). Neurochemical development of the hippocampal region in the fetal rhesus monkey: I. Early appearance of peptides, calcium-binding proteins, DARPP-32, and monoamine innervation in the entorhinal cortex during the first half of gestation (E47 to E90). *Hippocampus* 3, 279–305.

Biederman, I. and Cooper, E. E. (1991). Evidence for complete translational and reflectional invariance in visual object priming. *Perception* 20, 585–93.

Biederman, I. and Cooper, E. E. (1992). Size invariance in visual object priming. *Journal of Experimental Psychology: Human Perception and Performance* 18, 121–33.

Bornstein, M. H. (1985). Habituation as a measure of visual information processing in human infants: Summary, systematization, and synthesis. In G. Gottlieb and N. A. Krasnegor (eds.), *The Measurement of Audition and Vision in the First Year of Postnatal Life: A methodological overview* (pp. 253–300). Norwood, NJ: Ablex.

Bourgeois, J.-P. and Rakic, P. (1993). Changes in synaptic density in the primary visual cortex of the macaque monkey from fetal to adult stage. *Journal of Neuroscience* 13, 2801–20.

Butler, J. (1986). *A contextual hierarchy in infant memory*. Unpublished master's thesis, Rutgers University.

Butler, J. and Rovee-Collier, C. (1989). Contextual gating of memory retrieval. *Developmental Psychobiology* 22, 533–52.

Chugani, H. T. (1994). Development of regional brain glucose metabolism in relation to behavior and plasticity. In G. Dawson and K. Fischer (eds.), *Human Behavior and the Developing Brain* (pp. 153–75). New York: Guilford Press.

Chugani, H. T. and Phelps, M. E. (1986). Maturational changes in cerebral function in infants determined by [18]FDG positron emission tomography. *Science* 231, 840–3.

Chugani, H. T., Phelps, M. E., and Mazziotta, J. C. (1987). Positron emission tomography study of human brain functional development. *Annals of Neurology* 22, 487–97.

Daum, I., Ackermann, H., Schugens, M. M., Reimold, C., Dichgans, J., and Birbaumer, N. (1993). The cerebellum and cognitive functions in humans. *Behavioral Neuroscience* 107, 411–19.

Daum, I., Schugens, M. M., Ackermann, H., Lutzenberger, W., Dichgans, J., and Birbaumer, N. (1993). Classical conditioning after cerebellar lesions in humans. *Behavioral Neuroscience* 107, 748–56.

DeCasper, A. J. and Fifer, W. P. (1980). Of human bonding: Newborns prefer their mother's voices. *Science* 208, 1174–6.

DeCasper, A. J. and Spence, M. J. (1986). Prenatal maternal speech influences newborns' perception of speech sounds. *Infant Behavior and Development* 9, 133–50.

DeCasper, A. J. and Spence, M. J. (1991). Auditory mediated behavior during the perinatal period: A cognitive view. In M. J. S. Weiss and P. R. Zelazo (eds.), *Newborn Attention: Biological constraints and the influence of experience* (pp. 142–76). Norwood, NJ: Ablex.

Diamond, A. (1985). Development of the ability to use recall to guide action, as indicated by infants' performance on AB. *Child Development* 56, 868–83.

Diamond, A. (1990). The development and neural bases of memory functions as indexed by the AB and delayed response tasks in human infants and infant monkeys. In A. Diamond (ed.), *Development and Neural Bases of Higher Cognitive Functions* (pp. 267–317). New York: New York Academy of Sciences Press.

Diamond, A. (1992). *Recognition memory assessed by looking vs. reaching: Infants' performance on the visual paired comparison and delayed non-matching to sample tasks* (IRCS Report No. 92–11). Philadelphia: University of Pennsylvania, Department of Psychology.

Diamond, A. (1994). *Young children's performance on a task sensitive to the memory functions of the medial temporal lobe in adults, the delayed nonmatching to sample task*. Manuscript submitted for publication.

Diamond, A. and Doar, B. (1989). The performance of human infants on a measure of frontal cortex function, the delayed response task. *Developmental Psychobiology* 22, 271–94.

Diamond, A. and Goldman-Rakic, P. S. (1989). Comparison of human infants and rhesus monkeys on Piaget's AB task: Evidence for dependence on dorsolateral prefrontal cortex. *Experimental Brain Research* 74, 24–40.

Diamond, A., Zola-Morgan, S., and Squire, L. R. (1989). Successful performance by monkeys with lesions of the hippocampal formation on AB and object retrieval, two tasks that mark developmental changes in human infants. *Behavioral Neuroscience* 103, 526–37.

Dunn, R. (1845). Case of suspension of the mental faculties. *Lancet* 2, 588–90.

Ebbinghaus, H. (1885a). *Memory: A contribution to experimental psychology*. New York: Dover.

Ebbinghaus, H. (1885b). *Uber das Gedächtnis* [Memory]. Leipzig, Germany: Duncker and Humblot.

Eckenhoff, M. F. and Rakic, P. (1991). A quantitative analysis of synaptogenesis in the molecular layer of the dentate gyrus in the rhesus monkey. *Developmental Brain Research* 64, 129–35.

Fagan, J. F., III (1970). Memory in the infant. *Journal of Experimental Child Psychology* 9, 217–26.

Fagan, J. F., III (1973). Infants' delayed recognition memory and forgetting. *Journal of Experimental Child Psychology* 16, 424–50.

Fagan, J. F., III (1990). The paired-comparison paradigm and infant intelligence. In A. Diamond (ed.), *Development and Neural Bases of Higher Cognitive Functions* (pp. 337–64). New York: New York Academy of Sciences Press.

Fagen, J. W., Rovee-Collier, C. K., and Kaplan, M. G. (1976). Psychophysical scaling of stimulus similarity in 3-month-old infants and adults. *Journal of Experimental Child Psychology* 22, 272–81.

Fantz, R. L. (1956). A method for studying early visual development. *Perceptual and Motor Skills* 6, 13–15.

Goldman, P. S. (1971). Functional development of the prefrontal cortex in early life and the problem of neuronal plasticity. *Experimental Neurology* 32, 366–87.

Goldman, P. S. and Rosvold, H. E. (1972). The effects of selective caudate lesions in infant and juvenile rhesus monkeys. *Brain Research* 43, 53–66.

Goldman-Rakic, P. S. (1985). Toward a neurobiology of cognitive development. In J. Mahler (ed.), *Neonate Cognition* (pp. 285–306). Hillsdale, NJ: Erlbaum.

Goldman-Rakic, P. S. (1987). Circuitry of the prefrontal cortex and the regulation of behavior by representational knowledge. In F. Plum and V. Mountcastle (eds.), *Handbook of Physiology: I. The nervous system: Higher functions of the brain* (Vol. 5, pp. 373–417). Bethesda, MD: American Physiological Society.

Graf, P. and Schacter, D. L. (1985). Implicit and explicit memory for new associations in normal and amnesic subjects. *Journal of Experimental Psychology: Learning, Memory, and Cognition* 11, 501–18.

Gunderson, V. M. and Swartz, K. B. (1985). Visual recognition in infant pigtailed macaques after a 24-hour delay. *American Journal of Primatology* 8, 259–64.

Haith, M. M., Hazan, C., and Goodman, G. S. (1988). Expectation and anticipation of dynamic visual events by 3.5-month-old infants. *Child Development* 59, 467.

Haith, M. M., Wentworth, N., and Canfield, R. L. (1993). The formation of expectations in early infancy. In C. Rovee-Collier and L. P. Lipsitt (eds.), *Advances in Infancy Research* (pp. 251–97). Norwood, NJ: Ablex.

Humphrey, T. (1966). The development of the human hippocampal formation correlated with some aspects of its phylogenetic history. In S. Hassler (ed.), *Evolution of the Forebrain* (pp. 104–16). Stuttgart, Germany: Thieme.

Huttenlocher, P. R. (1979). Synaptic density in human frontal cortex: Developmental changes and effects of aging. *Brain Research* 163, 195–205.

Huttenlocher, P. R. (1990). Morphometric study of human cerebral cortex development. *Neuropsychologia* 28, 517–27.

Huttenlocher, P. R. (1994). Synaptogenesis, synapse elimination, and neural plasticity in human cerebral cortex. In C. A. Nelson (ed.), *Threats to Optimal Development: Integrating biological, psychological, and social risk factors: Minnesota symposium on child psychology* (Vol. 27, pp. 35–54). Hillsdale, NJ: Erlbaum.

Jacobsen, C. F. (1936). Studies of cerebral function in primates. *Comparative Psychology Monographs* 13, 1–68.

Jernigan, T. L., Trauner, D. A., Hesselink, J. R., and Tallal, P. A. (1991). Maturation of human cerebrum observed in vivo during adolescence. *Brain* 114, 2037–49.

Kail, R. (1990). *The Development of Memory in Children* (3rd edn.). New York: Freeman.

Kandel, E., Schwartz, J. H., and Jessell, T. M. (1991). *Principles of Neural Science* (3rd edn.). New York: Elsevier.

Knopman, D. S. (1991). Long-term retention of implicitly acquired learning in patients with Alzheimer's disease. *Journal of Clinical and Experimental Neuropsychology* 13, 880–94.

Knopman, D. S. and Nissen, M. J. (1987). Implicit learning in patients with probable Alzheimer's disease. *Neurology* 37, 784–8.

Korsakoff, S. S. (1889). Etude médico-psychologue sur une forme des maladies de la mémoire [Medical-psychological study of a form of diseases of memory]. *Revue Philosophique* 28, 501–30.

Kostovic, I., Pentanjek, Z., and Judas, M. (1990). The earliest areal differentiation of the human cerebral cortex: Entorhinal area. *Society for Neuroscience Abstract* 16, 846.

Kretschmann, J.-J., Kammradt, G., Krauthausen, I., Sauer, B., and Wingert, F. (1986). Growth of the hippocampal formation in man. *Bibliotheca Anatomica* 28, 27–52.

Lipsitt, L. P. (1990). Learning processes in the human newborn: Sensitization, habituation, and classical conditioning. In A. Diamond (ed.), *Development and Neural Bases of Higher Cognitive Functions* (pp. 113–27). New York: New York Academy of Sciences Press.

Mandler, J. M. (1990). Recall of events by preverbal children. In A. Diamond (ed.), *Development and Neural Bases of Higher Cognitive Functions* (pp. 485–516). New York: New York Academy of Sciences Press.

Marquis, D. (1931). Can conditioned responses be established in the newborn infant? *Journal of Genetic Psychology* 39, 479–90.

Matthews, A., Ellis, A. E., and Nelson, C. A. (1994). *Developmental relations in the behavioral neuropsychology of object permanence: Implications for brain development.* Manuscript submitted for publication.

McDonough, L., Mandler, J. M., McKee, R. D., and Squire, L. R. (1994). *What amnesic patients forget that infants remember: The deferred imitation task as a nonverbal measure of declarative memory.* Manuscript submitted for publication.

McKee, R. D. and Squire, L. R. (1993). On the development of declarative memory. *Journal of Experimental Psychology: Learning, Memory, and Cognition* 19, 397–404.

Meltzoff, A. (1990). Towards a developmental cognitive science: The implications of cross-modal matching and imitation for the development of representation and memory in infancy. In A. Diamond (ed.), *Development and Neural Bases of Higher Cognitive Functions* (pp. 1–37). New York: New York Academy of Sciences Press.

Miller, E. K. and Desimone, R. (1994). Parallel neuronal mechanisms for short-term memory. *Science* 263, 520–2.

Milner, B., Corkin, S., and Teuber, H.-L. (1968). Further analysis of the hippocampal amnesic syndrome: A 14 year follow-up study of H.M. *Neuropsychologia* 6, 215–34.

Mishkin, M. and Appenzeller, T. (1987). The anatomy of memory. *Scientific American* 256, 2–11.

Mishkin, M. and Delacour, J. (1975). An analysis of short-term visual memory in the monkey. *Journal of Experimental Psychology: Animal Behavior Processes* 1, 326–34.

Mishkin, M., Malamut, B., and Bachevalier, J. (1984). Memories and habits: Two neural systems. In G. Lynch, J. L. McGaugh, and N. M. Weinberger (eds.), *Neurobiology of learning and memory* (pp. 65–77). New York: Guilford Press.

Moscovitch, M. (1992). Memory and working-with-memory: A component process model based on modules and central systems. *Journal of Cognitive Neuroscience* 4, 257–67.

Mumby, D. G. and Pinel, J. P. J. (1994). Rhinal cortex lesions and object recognition in rats. *Behavioral Neuroscience* 108, 11–18.

Murray, E. A. and Gaffan, D. (1994). Removal of the amygdala plus subjacent cortex disrupts the retention of both intramodal and cross-modal associative memories in monkeys. *Behavioral Neuroscience* 108, 494–500.

Murray, E. A. and Mishkin, M. (1985). Amygdalectomy impairs cross-modal association in monkeys. *Science* 228, 604–6.

Nelson, C. A. (1994). Neural correlates of recognition memory in the first postnatal year of life. In G. Dawson and K. Fischer (eds.), *Human Development and the Developing Brain* (pp. 269–313). New York: Guilford Press.

Nelson, C. A. and Collins, P. F. (1991). Event-related potential and looking time analysis of infants' responses to familiar and novel events: Implications for visual recognition memory. *Developmental Psychology* 27, 50–8.

Nelson, C. A. and Collins, P. F. (1992). Neural and behavioral correlates of recognition memory in 4- and 8-month-old infants. *Brain and Cognition* 19, 105–21.

Nelson, C. A., Henschel, M., and Collins, P. F. (1993). Neural correlates of cross-modal recognition memory in 8-month-old infants. *Developmental Psychology* 29, 411–20.

O'Neil, J. B., Friedman, D. P., Bachevalier, J., and Ungerleider, L. G. (1986). Distribution of muscarinic receptors in the brain of a newborn rhesus monkey. *Society for Neuroscience Abstracts* 12, 809.

Overman, W. H., Bachevalier, J., Sewell, F., and Drew, J. (1993). A comparison of children's performance on two recognition memory tasks: Delayed nonmatch-to-sample vs. visual paired-comparison. *Developmental Psychobiology* 26, 345–57.

Overman, W., Bachevalier, J., Turner, M., and Peuster, A. (1992). Object recognition versus object discrimination: Comparison between human infants and infant monkeys. *Behavioral Neuroscience* 106, 15–29.

Paldino, A. M. and Purpura, D. P. (1979). Branching patterns of hippocampal neurons of human fetus during dendritic differentiation. *Experimental Neurology* 64, 620–31.

Paller, K. A. (1990). Recall and stem-completion priming have different electrophysiological correlates and are modified differentially by directed forgetting. *Journal of Experimental Psychology: Learning, Memory, and Cognition* 16, 1021–32.

Paller, K. A. and Kutas, M. (1992). Brain potentials during memory retrieval provide neurophysiological support for the distinction between conscious recollection and priming. *Journal of Cognitive Neuroscience* 4, 375–91.

Pascalis, O. and de Schonen, S. (1994). Recognition memory in 3–4 day old human neonates. *NeuroReport* 5, 1721–4.

Pearson, R. C. A., Esiri, M. M., Hiorns, R. W., Wilcock, G. K., and Powell, T. P. S. (1985). Anatomical correlates of the distribution of the pathological changes in the neocortex of Alzheimer's disease. *Proceedings of the National Academy of Sciences USA* 82, 4531–4.

Petersen, S. E., Fox, P. T., Posner, M. I., Mintun, M., and Raichle, M. E. (1990). Positron emission tomographic studies of the processing of single words. *Journal of Cognitive Neuroscience* 1, 153–70.

Petri, H. L. and Mishkin, M. (1994). Behaviorism, cognition, and the neuropsychology of memory. *American Scientist* 82, 30–7.

Piaget, J. (1952). *The Origins of Intelligence in Children*. New York: International Universities Press.

Proctor, A. W., Lowe, S. L., Palmer, A. M., Franceis, P., Esiri, M. M., Stratmann, G. C., Najlerahim, A., Patel, A. J., Hunt, A., and Bowen, D. M. (1988). Topographic distribution of neurochemical changes in Alzheimer's disease. *Journal of the Neurological Sciences* 84, 125–40.

Roediger, H. L., III (1984). Does current evidence from dissociation experiments favor the episodic/semantic distinction? *Behavioral and Brain Sciences* 7, 252–4.

Roediger, H. L., III, Rajaram, S., and Srivivas, K. (1990). Specifying criteria for postulating memory systems. In A. Diamond (ed.), *The Development and Neural Bases of Higher Cognitive Functions* (pp. 572–95). New York: New York Academy of Sciences Press.

Rose, S. A. and Ruff, H. A. (1989). Cross-modal abilities in human infants. In J. D. Osofsky (ed.), *Handbook of Infant Development* (pp. 318 62). New York: Wiley.

Rosenblith, J. F. (1992). *In the Beginning* (2nd cdn.). Newbury Park, CA: Sage.

Rovee-Collier, C. (1990). The "memory system" of prelinguistic infants. In A. Diamond (ed.), *Development and Neural Bases of Higher Cognitive Functions* (pp. 517–42). New York: New York Academy of Sciences Press.

Rovee-Collier, C. K. and Fagen, J. W. (1981). The retrieval of memory in early infancy. In L. P. Lipsitt and C. K. Rovee-Collier (eds.), *Advances in Infancy Research* (Vol. 1, pp. 225–54). Norwood, NJ: Ablex.

Rovee-Collier, C. and Hayne, H. (1987). Reactivation of infant memory: Implications for cognitive development. In H. W. Reese (ed.), *Advances in Child Development and Behavior* (Vol. 20, pp. 185–238). New York: Academic Press.

Saint-Cyr, J. A., Taylor, A. E., and Lang, A. E. (1988). Procedural learning and neostriatal dysfunction in man. *Brain* 111, 941–59.

Schacter, D. L. (1987). Implicit memory: History and current status. *Journal of Experimental Psychology: Learning, Memory, and Cognition* 13, 501–18.

Schacter, D. L. and Tulving, E. (1994). What are the memory systems of 1994? In D. L. Schacter and E. Tulving (eds.), *Memory Systems 1994* (pp. 1–38) Cambridge, MA: MIT Press.

Scoville, W. B. and Milner, B. (1957). Loss of recent memory after bilateral hippocampal lesions. *Journal of Neurology, Neurosurgery, and Psychiatry* 20, 11–21.

Sherry, F. and Schacter, D. L. (1987). The evolution of multiple memory-systems. *Psychological Review* 94, 439–54.

Sidman, R. L. and Rakic, P. (1982). Development of the human central nervous system. In W. Haymaker and R. D. Adams (eds.), *Histology and Histopathology of the Nervous System* (pp. 3–145). Springfield, IL: Charles C. Thomas.

Slater, A. (1995). Visual perception and memory at birth. *Advances in Infancy Research* 9, 107–62.

Squire, L. R. (1986). Mechanisms of memory. *Science* 232, 1612–19.

Squire, L. R. (1987). *Memory and Brain*. New York: Oxford Press.

Squire, L. R. (1992). Declarative and non-declarative memory: Multiple brain systems supporting learning and memory. *Journal of Cognitive Neuroscience* 4, 232–43.

Squire, L. R. (1994). Declarative and nondeclarative memory: Multiple brain systems supporting learning and memory. In D. L. Schacter and E. Tulving (eds.), *Memory Systems 1994* (pp. 203–31). Cambridge, MA: MIT Press.

Squire, L. R., Ojemann, J. G., Miezin, F. M., Petersen, S. E., Videen, T. O., and Raichle, M. E. (1992). Activation of the hippocampus in normal humans: A functional anatomical study of memory. *Proceedings of the National Academy of Sciences USA* 89, 1837–41.

Squire, L. R. and Zola-Morgan, S. (1991). The medial temporal lobe memory system. *Science* 253, 1380–6.

Steinmetz, J. E., Lavond, D. G., Ikovich, D., Logan, C. G., and Thompson, R. F. (1992). Disruption of classical eyelid conditioning after cerebellar lesions: Damage to a memory trace system or a simple performance deficit? *Journal of Neuroscience* 12, 4403–26.

Steinmetz, J. E., Logue, S. F., and Miller, D. P. (1993). Using signaled barpressing tasks to study the neural substrates of appetitive and aversive learning in rats: Behavioral manipulations and cerebellar lesions. *Behavioral Neuroscience* 107, 941–54.

Swain, I. U., Zelazo, P. R., and Clifton, R. K. (1993). Newborn infants' memory for speech sounds retained over 24 hours. *Developmental Psychology* 29, 312–23.

Thompson, R. F. (1986). The neurobiology of learning and memory. *Science* 233, 941–7.

Thompson, R. F. (1991). Neural mechanisms of classical conditioning in mammals. In J. R. Krebs and G. Horn (eds.), *Behavioural and Neural Aspects of Learning and Memory* (pp. 63–72). Oxford, England: Clarendon Press.

Tulving, E. (1985). How many memory systems are there? *American Psychologist* 40, 385–98.

Voneida, T. J., Christie, D., Bogdanski, R., and Chopko, B. (1990). Changes in instrumentally and classically conditioned limb-flexion responses following inferior olivary lesions and olivocerebellar tractotomy in the cat. *Journal of Neuroscience* 10, 3583–93.

Webster, M. J., Ungerleider, L. G., and Bachevalier, J. (1991a). Connections of inferior temporal areas TE and TEO with medial temporal-lobe structures in infant and adult monkeys. *Journal of Neuroscience* 11, 1095–116.

Webster, M. J., Ungerleider, L. G., and Bachevalier, J. (1991b). Lesions of inferior temporal area TE in infant monkeys alter cortico-amygdalar projections. *Developmental Neuroscience* 2, 769–72.

Wentworth, N. and Haith, M. M. (1992). Event-specific expectations of 2- and 3-month-old infants. *Developmental Psychology* 28, 842–50.

Wickens, D. D. and Wickens, C. (1940). A study of conditioning in the neonate. *Journal of Experimental Psychology* 25, 94–102.

Wilson, F. A. W., O'Scalaidhe, S. P., and Goldman-Rakic, P. S. (1993). Dissociation of object and spatial processing domains in primate prefrontal cortex. *Science* 260, 1955–8.

Woodruff-Pak, D. S. (1993). Eyeblink classical conditioning in H.M.: Delay and trace paradigms. *Behavioral Neuroscience* 107, 911–25.

Woodruff-Pak, D. S., Logan, C. G., and Thompson, R. F. (1990). In A. Diamond (ed.), *Development and Neural Bases of Higher Cognitive Functions* (pp. 150–78). New York: New York Academy of Sciences Press.

Woodruff-Pak, D. S. and Thompson, R. F. (1988). Cerebellar correlates of classical conditioning across the life span. In P. B. Baltes, R. M. Lerner, and D. M. Featherman (eds.), *Life-span Development and Behavior* (Vol. 9, pp. 1–37). Hillsdale, NJ: Erlbaum.

Yakovlev, P. I. and LeCours, A.-R. (1967). The myelogenetic cycles of regional maturation of the brain. In A. Minkowski (ed.), *Regional Development of the Brain in Early Life* (pp. 3–70). Oxford: Blackwell Scientific.

PART IV

Brain Plasticity

Editors' Introduction to Part IV

A confusion is often made between the level of explanation for a developmental change, cognitive or neural, and the extent to which that change is attributable to experience rather than maturation. Thus, evidence that a change at the behavioral level is due to developments at the neural level is often taken as evidence for that change being due to maturation. The readings in this section should dispel this myth, and reveal how open to the effects of experience some aspects of brain development are. It is also important to realize that this plasticity in the brain goes down to the expression of genes themselves. In other words, development involves probabilistic epigenesis (see Gottlieb, Part I). To the biologist this is no surprise. Ever since the time of Ramon y Cajal (1911) it has been believed that information is encoded in the brain by changes in the contacts between neurons. As any biologist knows, constructive changes in the structure of neuronal elements requires the production of their building blocks, proteins, and the instruction to the cell to produce proteins comes from the genes. Thus, to the biologist, the notion that information storage in the brain requires gene expression is obvious. To the developmental psychologist, used to thinking in terms of learning as being distinct from maturation, by contrast, the fact that learning involves the expression of genes may be somewhat surprising. While it had been known for some time that gene expression is influenced by temporal, locational, and biochemical factors such as those alluded to by Rakic in Part II, recent experiments have indicated that specific postnatal sensory experience, such as exposure to patterned light, can also play a role in regulating gene expression (see, for example, writings by Black and colleagues in suggestions for further reading).

In Part I, Oyama described why we need to move beyond the nature–nurture dichotomy. But, there is a problem in doing this. Discarding this dichotomy results in the loss of one of the most powerful analytic tools in development. How are we then to unpack developmental processes? One possible way out of this impasse is to analyse development in terms of components of environmental influence. This is the approach taken by Greenough and colleagues. The reading is concerned with the effects of experience on neuroanatomical measures of neuronal structure in the cortex. After reviewing a series of studies on the effects of rearing rats in impoverished as opposed to comparatively enriched environments, these authors propose a distinction between two types of information storage in the brain induced by the environment. The first, *experience-expectant* information storage, refers to changes induced by aspects of the environment that are common to all species members.

For example, the developing visual system will almost always be exposed to patterned light. There is no need for the genes to code for every detail of a complex nervous system when certain aspects of the environment can be sure to help in sculpting connectivity. Greenough et al. propose that this class of information storage is commonly associated with a particular form of neuronal change: the selective loss of synapses (such as that reviewed by Hutten-locher in Part II). The second type of information incorporated by the brain from the environment is referred to as *experience-dependent*. This refers to information absorbed from the environment that is, or can be, unique to the individual. Examples of such information include learning about characteristics of particular conspecifics, or acquiring a particular vocabulary. The authors present some evidence in support of their claim that this type of information storage involves the generation of new synaptic connections, possibly even in the adult.

The dissociation discussed by Greenough and colleagues is similar to one proposed independently by Johnson and Morton (1991). These authors proposed a way out of the interactionist impasse outlined earlier by clearly separating out classes of environmental influence on phenotypes. Instead of the dichotomy being reduced to the necessity or otherwise of environmental input, Johnson and Morton put forward a framework which, like Greenough and colleagues, distinguishes between the various levels of environmental input. There are at least three levels at which "environment" interacts with genotype. First, there is the environment within the genetic material. The location of a gene in the genetic material will determine when it is expressed, and with which other genes. Second, there is the local biochemical environment, which can either act with gene products, or act upon the gene itself. Third, there is the interaction between the product of the first two levels and the world outside the organism. It is only this latter level of environmental influence that is directly relevant to those interested in cognitive development. Johnson and Morton invoked the phrase *internal* environment for the first two levels of environmental influence, and *external* environment for the third. At the level of the external environmental input they proposed another distinction, that between the *species-typical environment* (STE) (roughly equivalent to experience-expectant information storage) and the *individual-specific environment* (ISE) (roughly equivalent to experience-dependent storage). For example, while being exposed to spoken language would be an aspect of the human STE, being exposed to English, rather than French, in early childhood would be an aspect of the ISE.

One difference between the Johnson and Morton analysis and that discussed by Green-ough and colleagues is that the latter see their categories of experience-expectant and experience-dependant as being forms of information storage in the brain, with the one form of experience giving rise to different synaptic mechanisms from the other. This means that any single aspect of experience would give rise to one or the other class of neuronal change. In contrast, in the Johnson and Morton account, it is quite possible for some aspects of the environment to act as both STE and ISE for the same species. For example, the language input to a human child provides both STE and ISE. Language input itself is species-typical, and any language input will serve to develop the language-specific struc-tures of the brain. In this sense, all languages are equivalent. At the same time, the particular language we hear as an infant is part of the ISE. Such an analysis can be carried further by identifying particular aspects of the grammar that are part of the STE. Note that even if certain aspects of grammar turn out to be universal to all cultures, this does not mean that they are "genetic." It does imply, however, that it is part of the environment that the developing human brain can expect to encounter.

The next reading (O'Leary) addresses the issue of plasticity with regard to one particular mammalian brain structure, the cerebral cortex. This structure appears to be considerably more open to influence by sensory experience than any other region of the mammalian brain. In order to understand further the extent to which this structure is organized by sensory input, we may divide cortical differentiation into three types (see also Sur et al., 1990): first, *radial specification* (differentiation into different cortical areas); second, the development of *external connections* with both subcortical and other cortical structures; and third, the development of the *internal microcircuitry* within the cortex.

The first of these, the laminar structure of the cortex, deviates very little with varying sensory experience. Both from one area of cortex to another, and across species, the characteristic six-layered structure of the cortex seems to be maintained, with each layer possessing particular cell types and the same general patterns of connectivity. In experiments where the thalamic (sensory) input to an area of cortex is drastically reduced, the six-layered structure of the cortex is still maintained, despite corresponding reductions in the area of cortex innervated by those inputs. For example, a reduction of 50 percent in the thalamic input to the primary visual cortex results in a 50 percent reduction in the size of this structure — area 18 (V2) now occupies much of the area of cortex which was previously V1 (see figure 12.3 from O'Leary). Despite this reduction in its size, the depth of the remaining V1 is identical to that found normally, and all six layers with their corresponding neuron types are present. Thus, as discussed in the reading by Rakic in Part II, it appears that the radial structure of the cortex is extremely robust, and not open to influence by sensory factors.

The story with regard to the external connections of the cortex is a little different. O'Leary describes some experimental manipulations in which visual input is rerouted to the primary auditory or somatosensory cortices. Not only does the visual input find its way to these primary cortices and innervate them, but these cortices then develop at least some of the information processing properties normally found in the primary visual cortex. For example, in the ferret, visual input can be induced to innervate the auditory cortex. Such rewiring results not only in cells in the auditory cortex being sensitive to visual input, but also in some of them becoming orientation selective, direction selective, and even binocular (see also Sur et al., 1990). Furthermore, the auditory cortex sometimes develops a two-dimensional map of visual space, very different from the normal one-dimensional tonotopic map found in the auditory cortex. Thus, the nature of the thalamic afferents to a region of cortex appears to determine to some extent the nature of the representations that it deals with, and presumably therefore some aspects of its internal microcircuitry.

With regard to the outputs, or efferents, from the cortex to subcortical regions, O'Leary describes experiments involving the transplantation of cortex from one region to another. These experiments lead to the conclusion that the regional location of a developing piece of cortex is the most important determiner of its subsequent subcortical projections. For example, visual cortical neurones which are transplanted into the motor region of a newborn rat develop, and permanently retain, projections to subcortical regions characteristic of motor, and not visual, cortex (see figure 12.4 from O'Leary). Outputs to subcortical regions, therefore, also appear to depend on location within the cortex as a whole, rather than the origins of the developing piece of cortex. In conclusion, the findings described by O'Leary strongly suggest that the cortex is composed of basic building blocks (those described in the reading by Rakic in Part II), which are somewhat equipotential. If the location of any unit within the whole is changed early in development, this unit will develop inputs, outputs, and cortico–cortico connections quite appropriate for the region within which it finds itself. Furthermore, it may also perform, at least to some extent, information-processing functions appropriate for that location.

The third reading (Shatz) cautions us not to presume that brain structures which are sensitive to patterned neural activity require stimulation from the external environment. Shatz describes how the initial projections from ganglion cells in the retinae from both eyes connect broadly throughout the target lateral geniculate nucleus (LGN) in the thalamus. The adult-like pattern of connectivity, in which LGN cells respond only to input from one eye or the other, emerges prenatally, before patterned light falls on the retina. At the same time, the formation of eye-specific layers is dependent on activity in the retina – blocking the propagation of action potentials to the LGN abolishes the development of eye-specific layers. This apparent paradox is resolved by an elegant series of studies showing that the ganglion cells of the retina generate waves of action potentials spontaneously in the absence of input from the light-sensitive photoreceptors. Indeed, the waves of activity occur before the photoreceptors have matured sufficiently to respond to light stimulation.

How do the spontaneous waves of activity in the retina induce the formation of eye-specific layers in the LGN? Shatz argues that ganglion cell inputs compete for functional synapses at the LGN, by means of an activity-dependent learning mechanism in which correlated or synchronous inputs cause synapses with target LGN cells to increase in strength. More than 50 years ago, Hebb (1949) proposed the existence of synapses that would increase in strength whenever activity in the presynaptic and postsynaptic cells occurred simultaneously. There is now ample evidence for Hebbian-type synapses that undergo long-term potentiation (LTP), or synaptic strengthening, in many areas of the nervous system, including the hippocampus and cerebral cortex. Moreover, this type of learning mechanism is widely used to simulate processes of learning and plasticity (see O'Reilly and Johnson, in Part VII for one example). In the LGN, Shatz demonstrates that synapses between ganglion cells and LGN neurons undergo LTP, and that the synaptic strengthening can be prevented by chemicals which block LTP in other areas of the brain. Thus, Shatz and colleagues appear to have identified a plausible mechanism for activity-related plasticity in the LGN.

Shatz also describes how an activity-dependent mechanism could cause the eye-specific layers in the LGN to form in such a regular and precise way. Specifically, the random waves of spontaneous activity cause ganglion cells within one eye to fire in a more correlated fashion than those in the other eye. The relative difference in correlations causes recipient cells in the LGN to strengthen synapses with inputs from one or the other eye. A similar idea underlies computational models of the formation of ocular dominance columns in primary visual cortex (Miller, Keller, and Stryker, 1989; for recent reviews of this work see Swindale, 1996; Erwin et al., 1995).

Shatz speculates that intrinsic activity may play an important role in shaping connectivity in other areas of the brain, including the cerebral cortex. If so, then spontaneous patterns of activity may provide another mechanism, beyond regularities in the external environment, for achieving a high precision of connectivity in the brain but without the need for detailed genetic specification.

FURTHER READING

Black, I. B., et al. (1984). Neurotransmitter plasticity at the molecular level. *Science* 225, 1266–70.
Black, I. B. (1991). *Information in the Brain: A Molecular Perspective*. Cambridge, MA: Bradford Books/MIT Press.

Erwin, E., Obermayer, K., and Schulten, K. (1995). Models of orientation and ocular dominance columns in the visual cortex: A critical comparison. *Neural Computation* 7, 425–68. (Examines the utility of computational simulations of various properties of neurons in primary visual cortex.)

Hebb, D. O., (1949). *The Organization of Behavior*. New York: Wiley. (Classic neuropsychological text with a prescient description of a form of simple learning.)

Jenkins, W. M., Merzenich, M. M., and Recanzone, G. (1990). Neocortical representational dynamics in adult primates: Implications for neuropsychology. *Neuropsychologia* 28, 573–84. (Reviews studies concerned with representational plasticity in the adult primate brain.)

Johnson, M. H. (1997). *Developmental Cognitive Neuroscience*. Oxford: Blackwell. (Chapter 2 discusses evidence on cortical plasticity.)

Johnson, M. H. and Morton, J. (1991). *Biology and Cognitive Development: The Case of Face Recognition*. Oxford: Blackwell. (Chapter 1 is relevant to the issues addressed in this section.)

Killackey, H. P. (1990). Neocortical expansion: an attempt toward relating phylogeny and ontogeny. *Journal of Cognitive Neuroscience* 2, 1–17. (Argues that both phylogenetic and ontogenetic development can be understood in terms of the addition of cortical "units.")

Kolb, B. (1989). Brain development, plasticity, and behavior. *American Psychologist* 44.

Knudsen, E. I. (1998). Capacity for plasticity in the adult owl auditory system expanded by juvenile experience. *Science* 279, 1531–3. (Evidence that the effects of some forms of plasticity induced early in life persist into adulthood.)

Knudsen, E. I. and Brainard, M. S. (1995). Creating a unified representation of visual and auditory space in the brain. *Annual Review of Neuroscience* 18, 19–43. (Summary of evidence concerning the coordination of visual and auditory information about spatial location by means of postnatal changes in brain connectivity.)

Miller, K. D., Keller, J. B., and Stryker, M. P. (1989). Ocular dominance column development: Analysis and simulation. *Science* 245, 605–15.

Rauschecker, J. P. and Marler, P. (eds.) (1987). *Imprinting and Cortical Plasticity: Comparative Aspects of Sensitive Periods*. New York: John Wiley & Sons. (A useful and well-edited collection of chapters about cortical plasticity and sensitive periods in a variety of species and contexts.)

Schoups, A. and Black, I. B. (1991). Visual experience specifically regulates synaptic molecules in rat visual cortex. *Journal of Cognitive Neuroscience* 3, 252–7. (Further evidence that visual experience can affect gene expression.)

Sharma, J., Angelucci, A., and Sur, M. (2000). Induction of visual orientation modules in auditory cortex. *Nature* 404, 841. (Evidence for the capacity of neurons in auditory cortex to develop functional properties characteristic of visual cortex under some conditions.)

Swindale, N. V. (1996). The development of topography in the visual cortex: A review of models. *Network: Computation in Neural Systems* 7, 161–247. (Review of computational models that simulate the development of ocular dominance and orientation columns in primary visual cortex.)

Sur, M., Pallas, S. L., and Roe, A. W. (1990). Cross-modal plasticity in cortical development: differentiation and specification of sensory neocortex. *Trends in the Neurosciences* 13, 227–33. (A review of the authors' work on "rewiring" the inputs to regions of cortex.)

11

Experience and Brain Development

William T. Greenough, James E. Black, *and* Christopher S. Wallace

What is the Meaning of Infancy? What is the meaning of the fact that man is born into the world more helpless than any other creature, and needs for a much longer season than any other living thing the tender care and wise counsel of his elders?

(John Fiske, 1883/1909, p. 1)

The extended period of infancy reflects the importance of incorporating enormous amounts of information into the brain. It has been estimated that, even within the much smaller brain of the rat, perhaps a quarter of a million connections between nerve cells are formed each second during the first month of postnatal development (Schüz, 1978). These connections, at least those that persist, comprise the combination of intrinsic and experiential information, recorded in neural circuitry, upon which behavior is based. Although research has demonstrated substantial effects of experience on brain connections, we do not yet understand just how the infant's brain is specialized to organize and incorporate experience, or the ways in which the infant may program its own experience. However, biological research using animals has helped outline basic mechanisms whereby experience affects the brain, and has provided a new view of how the brain may adapt to different types of experience.

Such studies of animal development have suggested a fundamentally different view of what have been called "sensitive-period" or "critical-period" phenomena. The traditional concept has been likened by Bateson (1979) to the brief opening of a window, with experience influencing development only while the window is open. A window for visual development in kittens, for example, might open at the time the eyes first open, and close a few weeks later. Although the term "sensitive period" is a useful label for such a process, it does little to explain the underlying mechanisms. We propose a new classification based on the type of information that is stored and the brain mechanisms used to store it. This approach allows consideration of the evolutionary origins of a process, its adaptive value for the individual, the required timing and character of experience, and the organism's potentially active role in obtaining appropriate experience for itself.

"Experience and Brain Development" first appeared in *Child Development* 58 (1987), pp. 539–59, and is reprinted by kind permission.

We propose that mammalian brain development relies upon two different categories of plasticity for the storage of environmentally originating information. The first of these probably underlies many sensitive- or critical-period phenomena. This process, which we term *experience-expectant*, is designed to utilize the sort of environmental information that is ubiquitous and has been so throughout much of the evolutionary history of the species. Since the normal environment reliably provides all species members with certain experiences, such as seeing contrast borders, many mammalian species have evolved neural mechanisms that take advantage of such experiences to shape developing sensory and motor systems. An important component of the neural processes underlying experience-expectant information storage appears to be the intrinsically governed generation of an excess of synaptic connections among neurons, with experiential input subsequently determining which of them survive. The second type of plasticity, which we call *experience-dependent*, is involved in the storage of information that is unique to the individual. Mammals in particular have evolved nervous systems that can take advantage of such information, as of sources of food and haven, and individual survival depends upon it to a very great extent. Since such experience will differ in both timing and character among individuals, the nervous system must be ready to incorporate the information when it becomes available. An important aspect of the mechanism underlying experience-dependent information storage appears to be the generation of new synaptic connections in response to the occurrence of a to-be-remembered event.

Sensitive Periods in Sensory-System Development: Experience-expectant Information Storage

That there are sensitive periods during which experience manipulations profoundly affect sensory-system development in mammals is well known, and this will be reviewed only briefly here. For more extensive reviews, the reader is referred to Mitchell and Timney (1984) or Movshon and Van Sluyters (1981). The vast majority of data regarding experience effects on sensory development have come from studies of the visual system. However, to the extent that other modalities have been examined, relatively similar results have been obtained (Clopton and Winfield, 1976; Feng and Rogowski, 1980; Meisami, 1975). The visual manipulations range from total pattern deprivation (bilateral eyelid suture or dark rearing) to selective deprivation (e.g. of certain contours or of movement). Monocular deprivation in species with binocularly overlapping visual fields and binocular depth perception is a special case that will be discussed separately. Each of these manipulations interferes with an experience that otherwise would be common to the young of the species.

Behavior

Total pattern deprivation may occasionally involve interpretational problems, since dark rearing can disturb endocrine rhythms, parental behavior, and feeding (Eayrs and Ireland, 1950; Mos, 1976) and can damage the retinae of some species (Rasch et al., 1961), and eyelid suture can lengthen the optical axis of the eye, causing nearsightedness (Wiesel and Raviola, 1977). Nonetheless, an extensive literature demonstrates that behavioral deficits resulting from total pattern deprivation arise primarily from impairment of visual information processing by the brain. In rats, for example, Tees (1979) has noted that particular aspects of visual discrimination tasks, such as the relation among elements within the stimulus, rather than task difficulty *per se* (measured as number of trials required for learning), are sensitive indicators of visual deprivation induced impairment. Moreover, visually deprived rats are not impaired on similarly complex tasks involving nonvisual modalities (Tees and Cartwright, 1972). A human parallel to this process is the impaired vision of the surgically corrected congenital cataract patients of Senden (1960). For at least two weeks, such patients could discriminate forms such as squares and triangles only by counting their corners. In general, total deprivation effects become less reversible by later visual experience with longer periods of deprivation (Crabtree and Riesen, 1979; Timney et al., 1980). This may result in part because deprived animals tend increasingly to rely on nonvisual cues (Fox, 1966), but it certainly reflects impairment of visual processing ability as well.

Physiology

Deficits at the neurophysiological level parallel, and presumably underlie, the behavioral impairments. The neurophysiological deficits described to date probably relate more closely to differences in acuity than to ones in complex aspects of form and pattern perception – the latter processes having not yet been understood at the neurophysiological level. What have been studied are the stimuli that best activate single neurons in the visual system, recognizing generally that such neurons are merely components of a quite complicated circuit. In kittens at the time the eyes open, somewhat less than half of primary visual cortex neurons respond selectively to the orientation or direction of movement of a stimulus (Blakemore and Van Sluyters, 1975; Buisseret and Imbert, 1976). Over several weeks in normal light, virtually all cells gain orientation sensitivity, and there is a general tendency for cells to become much more selective to specific orientations as well. In the absence of patterned visual stimulation, visual cortex neurons gradually lose responsiveness to stimulus orientation. As with behavior, the degree to which recovery toward normal physiological responsiveness can be achieved with exposure to patterned stimulation declines as deprivation is prolonged (Cynader et al., 1976). Moreover, the recovered animal, if it has binocularly overlapping vision, is quite different from the normal: about half of its neurons never recover, and the ability to orient to stimuli across the midline is lost from both eyes (Sherman, 1973, 1977).

More selective effects have been obtained with selective forms of deprivation. In the most extensively studied paradigm, animals have been reared such that their visual experience is limited to a pattern of lines at a particular (usually horizontal or vertical) orientation. Initial neurophysiological studies indicated that visual cortex neurons fired strongly when the animal saw lines at angles close to those of the rearing stimuli (Hirsch and Spinelli, 1970). Later work has qualified these findings to some extent (e.g. Gordon et al., 1979; Leventhal and Hirsch, 1975), but the essential details remain intact. As expected, these animals were also better at resolving lines at those same angles in behavioral tasks (e.g. Blasdel et al., 1977; Corrigan and Carpenter, 1979). Similar results have been obtained for cortical neurons sensitive to direction of stimulus movement. Cynader and Chernenko (1976), for example, deprived cats of visual movement perception by rearing them in a stroboscopic environment. Because the flashes of light were very brief, these cats saw the world as a series of "still pictures" rather than one of continuous movement. In these animals, cells sensitive to movement were much less frequently found. Thus cells in visual cortex were impaired in responding to specific stimulus characteristics that were missing from the rearing environment. A behavioral parallel to this in humans has been suggested by a persistent reduction in acuity, even while wearing glasses, if astigmatism went uncorrected in childhood (Mitchell et al., 1973).

Morphology

Total pattern deprivation has pronounced effects on central visual structures, and particularly upon the visual cortex. Most nerve cell connections in the visual cortex occur on spines (see figure 11.1). There are fewer of these spines on dendrites of neurons in visually deprived animals (Fifkova, 1968, 1970; Rothblat and Schwartz, 1979; Valverde, 1971). This indicates that the nerve cells of visually deprived animals make fewer interconnections. While later exposure to light can reverse differences to some extent, at least in dark-reared mice (Valverde, 1971), significant differences persist (Ruiz-Marcos and Valverde, 1969). Reduction in the overall amount of dendrite has also been reported for visual cortex neurons following dark rearing in some species, again indicating fewer connections among neurons (Coleman and Riesen, 1968; Valverde, 1970). Finally, an overall measure of synaptic connectivity, the number of synapses per visual cortex nerve cell, was lower in visually deprived than in normal cats (Cragg, 1975a; Winfield, 1981). A straightforward interpretation is that the complexity of the visual cortex "wiring diagram" is reduced in animals deprived of visual experience during early postnatal sensitive periods.

While the results will not be detailed here, differences in the morphology of subcortical visual structures (see figure 11.1) have also been reported following visual deprivation (e.g. Fifkova, 1979; for review, see Globus, 1975). Overstimulation (constant lighting), a procedure that eventually damages the rat retina, has been reported to increase spine frequency on neurons above that seen with normal diurnal lighting in the lateral geniculate nucleus (Parnavelas et al., 1973) and also in the visual cortex (Parnavelas and Globus, 1976). These findings indicate that many brain structures may be affected simultaneously by experience.

Particularly interesting morphological results have been reported in a selective visual experience paradigm. Coleman et al. (1981) studied the orientation of dendrites of visual cortex neurons in cats raised with their visual experience limited to either horizontal or vertical lines, as described above. They found that the outer dendrites were oriented at about 90° from each other in the two groups, a result that could correspond to the visual cortex neurons selectively modifying their dendrites such that they responded to the exposure orientation. Tieman and Hirsch (1982) similarly reported approximately perpendicularly oriented visual cortex dendrites in vertical and horizontal stripe reared cats. These studies indicate that the pattern of connections among visual cortex neurons, not merely the number of connections, is influenced by visual experience during early development.

Expected experience

An important question is *why* there are experience-expectant or sensitive periods in sensory development. On the surface, it may not seem to make much evolutionary sense to have designed an organism that will be forever impaired in its sensory performance if the proper sorts of experiences do not occur at relatively specific developmental time points. The offsetting advantage appears to be that sensory systems can develop much greater

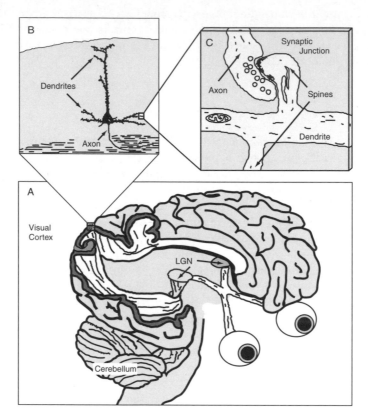

Figure 11.1 **A,** A human brain, with much of the right hemisphere removed and many subcortical structures omitted to reveal a simplified view of the visual system. Visual information travels from the retina to visual cortex via the lateral geniculate nucleus (LGN). As fibers from the retina pass back toward the LGN, some of them cross to the other side, reflecting the general principle that a sensory input originating on one side of the body is processed by brain structures in the hemisphere on the opposite side. Fibers from each retina which receive light from the *right* half of the visual field project to visual cortex on the *left* hemisphere. Hence, the visual cortex in the left hemisphere "sees" only the right half of the world, through both eyes. Within visual cortex, inputs from each eye are organized into adjacent bands called "ocular dominance columns." **B,** A section of visual cortex showing a neuron, as would be seen through a light microscope. Visual cortex, which is approximately 2 mm thick in a two year old infant, is actually much more densely packed with neurons and their interconnecting fibers than is depicted by this figure. A neuron in visual cortex might receive, depending on cell type, 10 000–30 000 synaptic inputs to its dendrites, most of which will occur on spines. At this level of magnification, spines appear as tiny dots along the dendrites. **C,** Detail of a portion of dendrite containing a synapse between an axon terminal (distinguished by the presence of spheres called vesicles) and a dendritic spine, a small projection from the dendrite trunk. For perspective, note that spines are somewhat less than 1/1 000 of a millimeter wide. Thus, to see a synapse requires the resolving power of an electron microscope.

performance capabilities by taking advantage of experiences that can be expected to be available in the environment of all young animals. Thus many species seem to have evolved such that the genes need only roughly outline the pattern of neural connectivity in a sensory system, leaving the more specific details to be determined through the organism's interactions with its environment.

The way in which this finer tuning of both sensory and motor systems is often accomplished has provided us with some real insight into the circumstances that may give rise to sensitive-period phenomena. Studies of a number of developing sensory systems as well as of peripheral connections in the autonomic and skeletal musculature systems have indicated that synapses are overproduced in early development (Boothe et al., 1979; Brown et al., 1976; Brunjes et al., 1982; Cragg, 1975b; Purves and Lichtman, 1980). Similar findings have been described in the human visual and frontal cortex (Huttenlocher, 1979; Huttenlocher et al., 1982). As development proceeds, the extra synapses are lost, such that the final wiring diagram consists of those synapses that remain. Two examples serve to illustrate how a refined pattern can emerge from relatively more chaotic beginnings through selective retention of synapses: synapse elimination at the neuromuscular junction and ocular dominance column (see figure 11.1 caption) formation in the visual cortex.

Motor neurons in the spinal cord connect with fibers of skeletal muscle. While a specific spinal location projects to each muscle, the pattern is quite different in the newborn rat from that in the adult. Brown et al. (1976) reported an overlapping pattern in the newborn rat, such that individual motor neurons connect to several muscle fibers, and each muscle fiber receives connections from several motor neurons. During the first two weeks after birth, these overlapping multiple connections disappear, as all but one of the synapses on each muscle fiber drop out. Brown et al. (1976) suggest that a selection process occurs that involves competition between the various neurons innervating a muscle fiber, leaving behind a one-to-one pattern. Precisely what leads to competitive success is not known, but at least some experiments have suggested that neuronal activity is a necessary part of the process (Gouze et al., 1983, O'Brien et al., 1978; Thompson et al., 1979). The important point is that, if the proper connections are selectively retained (or if improper ones are selectively eliminated), a highly ordered pattern can emerge from a much less organized one by the loss of synaptic connections (Changeux and Danchin, 1977).

The development of ocular dominance columns in mammals with binocularly overlapping visual systems provides an example of a similar selection process in the central nervous system. In species such as cats or monkeys, closure of one eye during a relatively brief postnatal sensitive period causes a severe visual impairment when the eye is later reopened (Wiesel and Hubel, 1963). The effect is far more pronounced and lasting than that seen with binocular deprivation (Wiesel and Hubel, 1965). At the neurophysiological level, the deprived eye loses most of its ability to control the activity of visual cortex neurons, while the open eye correspondingly gains in control. Thus it appears that the deprived eye becomes functionally disconnected from visual cortex neurons. LeVay et al. (1980) have shown that the monocular deprivation effect involves a competitive process in which connections actually are lost in the visual cortex. In the binocular regions of normal adult monkey visual cortex, inputs from the two eyes terminate in alternating bands termed "columns" which are about 400 micrometers wide. In monkeys in which one eye has been closed during development, the bands are still present, but those arising from the deprived eye are much narrower than normal, and those arising from the open eye are correspondingly wider. LeVay et al. (1980), studying the development of these bands, found that axons from the two eyes initially have overlapping terminal fields (figure 11.2), such that distinct columns are not present. In normal development, the terminal fields of axons from both eyes gradually and simultaneously regress, such that the sharply defined ocular dominance bands of the adult emerge. When one eye is deprived, its terminals regress more than normally, whereas those of the open eye retain a larger part of initial dually innervated territory, thus generating the alternating pattern of narrow and wide bands. This work, along with supportive evidence (e.g. Guillery, 1972), points to the view that a competition process occurs in the visual cortex, in which inputs from experienced eyes are advantaged. Hypotheses regarding the neural bases of the advantage have proposed that actively firing synapses are more likely to be preserved, or that synchronous firing of the presynaptic terminal and the postsynaptic neuron may stabilize the synapse (see e.g. Singer, 1986), a process similar to that proposed by Hebb (1949).

These two examples illustrate a major point. In both cases, during a relatively restricted period, an *expected experience* (motor activity or visual stimulation) participates in the organization of a detailed neural pattern. The neural manifestation of expectation or sensitivity appears to be the production of an excess number of synapses, a subset of which will be selectively preserved by experience-generated neural activity. If the normal pattern of experience occurs, a normal pattern of neural organization results. If an abnormal pattern of experience occurs, an abnormal neural organization pattern will occur. We do not, of course, know that similar processes underlie all phenomena proposed to involve sensitive periods, and we shall see below that other factors may be involved in the determination of sensitive periods. Nonetheless, it seems clear that the production of more synapses than can eventually survive, combined with an experience-based selection

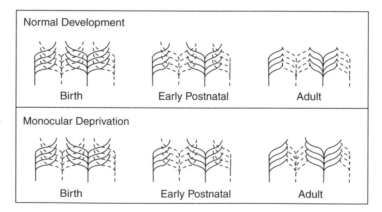

Figure 11.2 Schematic depiction of ocular dominance column development in monkeys reared normally or monocularly deprived. The left panels represent the substantial overlap of the axonal branches from the two eyes at birth. In normal development (top), the competitive interactions result in equal pruning back of axons from each eye in the adult (right panels). After monocular deprivation, however, axons from the nondeprived eye (solid lines) retain more branches, while the axons from the deprived eye (dashed lines) retain fewer branches. (From Greenough, W. T. and Schwark, H. D. (1984). Age-related aspects of experience effects upon brain structure. In R. D. Emde and R. J. Harmon (eds.), *Continuities and Discontinuities in Development*, p. 82. Hillsdale, NJ: Plenum. Reprinted with permission of Kluwer Academic/ Plenum Publishers.)

process, is a central aspect of the sensitive-period phenomena that have been most extensively studied. Because the developing mammal's experience has been predictable throughout the evolutionary history of the species, the species has come to count on or expect its occurrence in the developmental process. We refer to this as *experience-expectant* information storage.

Schüz (1978), comparing altricial (born underdeveloped) with precocial species, has similarly noted that the overproduction of synapses might be an indication of readiness for expected experience. With its eyes open and able to move about, the precocial guinea pig's cerebral cortex shows many more dendritic spines at birth than that of the newborn mouse, which is born in a relatively altricial state. However, at the time the mouse's eyes open, about two weeks after birth, its cortical neurons have developed a density of spines comparable to that of the newborn guinea pig. Thus spines matured at the time the animal became able to actively explore the environment.

Control of experience-expectant processes

The character or quality of expected experiences may also play a role in determining the length of time that the developing nervous system remains sensitive to their effects. For example, since success in competition and consequent elimination of alternative neural patterns is promoted by experience-based neural activity, a relative reduction in that activity may prolong the competition process. Cynader and Mitchell (1980) found that kittens dark reared until six, eight, or ten months remained highly sensitive to monocular deprivation effects. This is in contrast to light-reared kittens, in which peak sensitivity to monocular deprivation normally occurs within the first two months of life, and negligible effects of monocular deprivation are seen in kittens reared normally if deprivation begins after three or four months (Hubel and Wiesel, 1970; Olson and Freeman, 1978). Relatively small amounts of normal visual experience appear to set in motion processes that can protect the organism against later deprivation (Mower et al., 1983).

The character of experience may not be the only factor regulating the temporal aspects of sensitive periods. Kasamatsu and Pettigrew (1976) initially proposed that the chemical neurotransmitter norepinephrine regulated sensitivity to monocular deprivation. They found that treatment with 6-hydroxydopamine, which reduces brain norepinephrine, prevented the shift in control of visual cortex neurons from the deprived eye in cats that were monocularly deprived during the sensitive period. If norepinephrine was replaced by local administration into visual cortex, however, the ocular dominance shift did occur in 6-hydroxydopamine-treated cats (Pettigrew and Kasamatsu, 1978). More recent work (Bear and Singer, 1986) has suggested that two neurotransmitters, norepinephrine and acetyl-choline, may be involved in regulating developmental sensitivity of the visual cortex. There have also been some reports that drugs that interfere with norepinephrine action reduce or prevent the brain and behavioral effects of environmental complexity that are discussed in a later section of this article (Mirmiran and Uylings, 1983; O'Shea et al., 1983; Pearlman, 1983). These results suggest that neurotransmitters such as norepinephrine and acetylcholine may be involved in initiating or maintaining neuronal sensitivity to experience, a role consistent with the term "neuromodulator," often applied to norepinephrine. Parallel reports of noradrenergic regulation of adult memory storage processes (e.g. Gold, 1984) suggest the possibility of a quite general role for norepinephrine systems in the governance of plastic neural processes.

On the "Chalkboard" metaphor

An important question involves the extent to which developing sensory systems merely follow the pattern imposed upon them by sensory experience, in the manner of a "blank slate," as opposed to selectively utilizing or actively creating information in experience. At the level of the neuron, an equivalent question is whether all input promotes similar structural change. It is clear that sensory systems have strong predispositions at the time of birth; for example, the initial stages of the binocular segregation process precede eye opening in the monkey visual cortex (LeVay et al., 1980), and oriented receptive fields are present to some extent at birth (Blakemore and Van Sluyters, 1975) and certain orientations appear to be more predisposed to arise in the absence of appropriate input in the cat (Leventhal and Hirsch, 1975). The rudimentary neural organization imposes order on its input. A phenomenon that may illustrate this is the apparent compensatory change that has been reported in intact modalities' central representations with damage to or deprivation of other modalities. For example, the auditory cortex increases in size in visually deprived or blinded animals (Gyllensten et al., 1966; Ryugo et al., 1975). Since auditory stimulation is equivalent in deprived and sighted animals, the size increase must depend upon some aspect of the increased reliance upon audition that becomes necessary in the absence of visual input. That is, the brain's differential use of the same auditory information determines the information's effect on brain structure. It is but a small extension of this idea to note that individual differences could be preserved even in the face of identical environmental experience.

Possible human behavioral reflections of neural predispositions to select and organize experience are also evident. For example, infants may have "hard-wired" capacities for categorical perception of phonemes (Eimas, 1975) and syntactic structure (Chomsky, 1980). The infant's behavioral and affective responses to caretaker speech can make the social interaction highly rewarding for both participants, perhaps even encouraging a phonetic adjustment to match the perceptual limitations of the infant (Fernald, 1984). An innate predisposition of the infant to smile and make noises, if it exists, could serve the infant by shaping the caretaker's speech toward an optimal form of linguistic input. Thelen (1980) has suggested that kicking and other behaviors, while serving as neural foundations of mature motor systems, can also help the infant control experience (e.g. as in communicating distress or pleasure). From this perspective, the infant may often pick and choose from an experiential smorgasbord available during development. In fact, we suspect that some types of "expected" experience may rely largely on the infant to produce them.

Early sensory-system development: summary

The primary quality of experience effects in early sensory-system development that sets them apart from many later developmental processes, as well as from adult learning and memory, is the degree to which they are age dependent and subsequently irreversible. At the behavioral level, a relevant human example may be the loss of perceived phonemic boundaries present in infants if the language to which they are exposed does not utilize them (Werker and Tees, 1984). At the neural level, the irreversibility appears to arise in at least some cases because a set of synapses has become committed to a particular pattern of organization, while synapses that could have subserved alternative patterns have been lost.

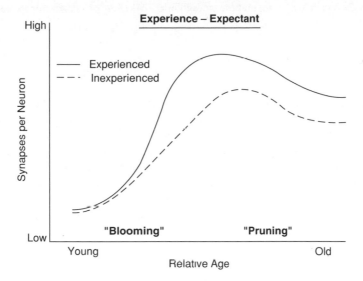

Figure 11.3 Schematic diagram of synapse overproduction ("blooming") and deletion ("pruning"; Schneider, 1981) during an experience-expectant process. (From Black and Greenough, 1986, vol. 4, p. 28; copyright 1986 by Lawrence Erlbaum Associates; reprinted by permission.)

A process seen in the brain that may underlie this is a rapid peaking of synapse numbers, followed by the loss of a significant proportion of them, as shown in figure 11.3. The rate and extent of commitment of synapses may be regulated by both the quality of experience and intrinsic factors such as broadly acting neurochemical systems. In at least some cases, it seems clear that central system organization is not merely "painted" on the brain by experience, since both the quality of information and the way in which it is used can affect the rate of pattern formation as well as the character of the pattern.

Experience-dependent Information Storage in Later Development and Adulthood

Many of the effects of experience upon behavioral development do not appear to exhibit the relatively strict age-dependent character associated with early sensory system development. One reason for this may be that a species cannot count on certain important experiences to occur at particular points in the lifespan. Another is that much of the information that an animal or human must acquire during development or adulthood is unique to its own particular environment: information about the physical characteristics of the surroundings, the social system and the roles of specific individuals, and, in humans, the details of one's language(s) and other formally specified cognitive capacities. It is not clear *a priori* whether the brain mechanisms involved in storing these kinds of information are the same as those used for experience-expectant processes, although evolution tends to produce new adaptations (such as the unique plasticity of the mammalian brain) by modifying existing systems, as opposed to creating entirely new ones. We will review some of what is known about these more nature categories of information storage and will then return to our consideration of neural mechanisms.

The environmental complexity paradigm

The research that has perhaps taught us the most about mechanisms of cognitive development in animals utilizes variations in the physical and social complexity of the rearing environment. This line of research began with Hebb's (1949) rearing of rats as pets in his home for comparison with laboratory-reared animals, but most researchers have adopted less life-disrupting laboratory versions of Hebb's home. Most commonly, two or all of the following three conditions have been employed. (1) *Environmental complexity* (EC) animals are housed in groups of about a dozen in large cages filled with various objects with which the animals are free to play and explore. Often the animals are given additional daily exposure to a maze or a toy-filled field. In our work and most others', the play objects are changed and rearranged daily. (2) *Social cage* (SC) animals are housed in pairs or small groups in standard laboratory cages, without objects beyond food and water containers. (3) *Individual cage* (IC) animals are housed alone in similar or identical laboratory cages. The term "enriched condition" has been used to describe what we call environmental complexity, but we prefer the latter to emphasize that these conditions represent an incomplete attempt to mimic some aspects of the wild environment and should be considered "enriched" only in comparison to the humdrum life of the typical laboratory animal.

Behavior.   Since Hebb's (1949) initial demonstration that home-reared rats were superior to laboratory-reared rats at learning a series of complex maze patterns, a large number of experiments have confirmed that rats and mice reared in complex environments are generally superior on complex, appetitive tasks. A significant number of experiments have been directed at particular behavioral characteristics that differentiate EC from SC and IC animals, and it seems safe to conclude that no single explanation, such as differential emotional reactivity, better use of extra-maze cues, or differential visual ability, can account for the pattern of behavioral differences that have been reported (Greenough et al., 1972; Krech et al., 1962; Ravizza and Herschberger, 1966; see Greenough, 1976, for review). All of these may play a role under certain circumstances, of course (Brown, 1968; Hymovitch, 1952; Myers and Fox, 1963), but the differences appear to be quite general, extending even to models of Piagetian volume-conservation tasks (Thinus-Blanc, 1981), such that the most likely explanation (if not the most satisfying in specificity) may well be that the groups differ in the amount of stored knowledge upon which they can draw in novel situations.

It appears that active interaction with the environment is necessary for the animal to extract very much appropriate information. Not only do the EC and SC conditions differ little with regard to the average intensity of energy impinging upon most sensory modalities, but merely making visual experience of a complex environment available to animals otherwise unable to interact with it has little behavioral effect. Forgays and Forgays (1952), for example, found little benefit to maze performance of having been housed in small cages within the EC environment. Similar results have been reported with regard to some of the brain effects of EC rearing that are described below (Ferchmin et al., 1975).

Morphology.   Following initial reports that several regions of the cerebral cortex were heavier and thicker in EC than in IC rats (Bennett et al., 1964) and had larger neuronal cell bodies and more glial (i.e. supportive) cells (Diamond, 1967; Diamond et al., 1972), detailed studies began to indicate probable differences in the number of synaptic connections. Differences in the amount of dendrite per neuron, that is, the amount of surface available for synaptic connections, of up to 20 percent were reported in the upper visual cortex of rats reared in EC versus IC environments from weaning to late adolescence (Greenough and Volkmar, 1973; Holloway, 1966). Values for SC rats were intermediate, although generally closer to those of IC rats, in the Greenough and Volkmar study, and this has tended to be the case in other experiments in which such a group has been included. Small differences in the frequency of postsynaptic spines (see figure 11.1) favoring EC rats were also reported (Globus et al., 1973), suggesting that synapses were not merely spaced farther apart on the longer dendrites of the EC rats. A direct demonstration that EC rats exceeded IC rats in synapses per neuron in upper visual cortex by 20–25 percent (Turner and Greenough, 1985) led us to consider what similar extremes might result if all neurons in the human brain were equally plastic. The difference of about 2 000 synapses per neuron in the rat would translate into many trillions of synapses on the 100–200 billion neurons of the human brain!

While EC–IC differences (in male rats) are greatest in the occipital, or visual, region of the cerebral cortex, they occur in other neocortical regions as well, including those associated with audition and somesthesis and also regions somewhat functionally comparable to the human frontal cortex (Greenough et al., 1973; Rosenzweig et al., 1972; Uylings et al., 1978). Differences in dendritic field size following similar differential rearing have also been reported in subcortical regions such as the rat hippocampal formation and monkey and rat cerebellum (Floeter and Greenough, 1979; Juraska et al., 1985; Pysh and Weiss, 1979), suggesting that this later plasticity is not a phenomenon unique to regions like cerebral cortex that are most prominent in mammals. A surprising finding is that different patterns of EC–IC differences in visual cortex and hippocampus are found in males and females (Juraska, 1984; Juraska et al., 1985). Males show greater differences across environmental extremes in the visual cortex, whereas females show greater differences in some regions of the hippocampus. Although the behavioral significance of this is still under investigation, it suggests that very similar experiences may have different effects on individually different brains.

Adult brain morphology

Until relatively recently, it was widely assumed that, except for certain cases of response to brain damage, the brain acquired all of the synapses it was going to have during development, and that further plastic change was probably accomplished through modification of the strength of preexisting connections. While some morphological and electrophysiological data suggest that changes in the strength of existing connections may occur in response to experience manipulations (see Greenough and Chang, 1985, for review), it has now become quite clear that new connections may arise as a result of differential housing conditions and other manipulations throughout much, if not all, of the life of the rat, and presumably of other higher mammals as well. Bennett et al. (1964) had actually reported quite early that cortical weight differences induced by EC versus IC housing occurred in adult rats, but over a decade passed before reports appeared that dendritic field size was affected by these conditions in both young adult (Juraska et al., 1980; Uylings et al., 1978) and middle-aged (Green et al., 1983) rats. While direct measurements of synapses per neuron have yet to be reported in adults under these conditions, the correspondence between dendritic field and synapse-per-neuron measures in younger animals (Greenough and Volkmar, 1973; Juraska, 1984; Turner and Greenough, 1985) gives us considerable confidence that the increase in adult postsynaptic surface is paralleled by an increase in synapse numbers. While not all neuron types affected by postweaning exposure to differential environmental complexity may be affected by these environments in adult animals, there is little question at this point that the cerebral cortex, and also the cerebellar cortex (Greenough et al., 1986), retain the capacity to form new synaptic connections in response to new experiences.

Effects of training on adult brain morphology

There has not yet been a specific demonstration of what might be represented by the changes in synaptic connections brought about by differential environmental complexity, nor are the details of the relationships between brain structure and behavioral performance very clear. If we follow the rather hazy terminology of "accumulated knowledge" used above, then one might suggest that these changes have something to do with storing (and/or accessing) that knowledge. A simple view of nearly a century ago (Ramon y Cajal, 1893; Tanzi, 1893), which has been embellished by the more detailed theorizing of Hebb (1949) and many others, is that memory, in both the very broad and the psychologically more specific sense, might be encoded in the functional pattern of connections between neurons. While demonstrating unequivocally the involvement of brain phenomena in learning or memory has been a difficult process for a variety of reasons, it is possible to perform experiments the outcomes of which would be either compatible or incompatible with such an interpretation. For example, if the changes in synaptic organization that occur in complex environments are involved in storage of information from the experience, then we might be able to detect similar morphological changes in animals trained on specific learning tasks.

Since the experience of training probably provides a more limited range of information than that available in the complex environment, we might expect the morphological effects of training to be more limited (and harder to detect). In the first experiment of this sort, young adult rats were trained on a changing series of patterns in the Hebb–Williams maze (the maze Hebb used in the initial test of home-reared rats) over a period of about 25 days (Greenough et al., 1979). In the visual cortex of the trained animals, two types of neurons had more dendrite than in nontrained animals, while a third type was unaffected. The unaffected type was one that had been altered in previous EC studies. Thus training affected a measure related to synaptic connectivity, and the effects were more localized and specific than were those of the complex environment experience.

In a similar experiment, Bennett et al. (1979) exposed weanling rats to a changing series of mazes in their rearing cages for 30 days. The visual cortices of these animals were heavier than those of rats kept in IC cages for the same period. Rats housed with an unchanging simple maze pattern were intermediate between these groups, suggesting that the information available in the changing-maze patterns was an important aspect of their results.

A problem in the interpretation of these results and, in fact, in the interpretation of the environmental complexity findings as well, is the possibility that brain effects might arise from stress, sensory stimulation, motor activity, or other nonspecific consequences of the training procedure, rather than from the information acquired through training. This problem is, of course, not trivial, and it has been one of the major difficulties in a long history of previous experiments designed to elucidate the molecular biological underpinnings of the memory process (see Dunn, 1980; Greenough and Maier, 1972; Rose, 1981, for perspectives on this work). No single experiment (and maybe no set of experiments) can rule out all alternatives, but the involvement of generally acting factors such as hormonal or metabolic consequences of a training procedure can be examined using a within-animal control. One advantage of the rat for such work is that the bulk of fibers from each eye cross to the opposite side of the brain, such that the use of a split-brain procedure, combined with occlusion of one eye, can restrict visual input from training largely to one hemisphere. Chang and Greenough (1982) performed such an experiment, again using the changing maze patterns. A control group indicated that there were no interhemispheric differences as a result of insertion of the eye occluder (an opaque ratsized contact lens) for a few hours each day. The group trained with the same eye covered each day, in contrast, had more apical dendritic branches on visual cortex neurons in the hemisphere opposite the trained eye, a result incompatible with generally acting hormonal or metabolic effects. Thus the changes brought about by maze training were specifically a consequence of visual input from the training experience.

One further experiment increases our confidence in both the generality of the morphological effects of training in adult rats and in the unlikelihood that these effects result from general hormonal or metabolic causes (Greenough et al., 1985b). In it, rats were trained to reach, bilaterally or unilaterally, either with the forepaw they preferred to use or the nonpreferred forepaw, into a tube for food. A strong preference for reaching with one paw was accomplished by placing a partition next to the tube that made reaching with the opposite forepaw difficult. Extensive training on the nonpreferred paw permanently reversed reaching preference, as had been demonstrated previously (Peterson, 1951). It is not clear that something like "handedness" in humans is being reversed in these rats, as opposed to the animals' merely using the paw with which they had developed more skill or even thinking that the contingency required them to continue reaching with the trained paw. We examined the neurons in the forelimb region of the cortex whose axons project to the spinal region that governs reaching. Animals trained with both paws had dendrites that were more highly branched than those of nontrained animals, and hemispheres opposite trained forelimbs in unilaterally trained animals had more branches than the other hemisphere. Analysis of the hindlimb region of motor cortex in unilaterally trained rats indicated no similar pattern of assymetry, so the structural change was specific to both the hemisphere and the cortical area most directly involved in the learned task. We must realize, however, that this reaching task involves many other areas of the brain, as became evident when we examined metabolism of various brain areas in rats performing the task (see Greenough, 1984). The complex tasks used in developmental psychology research are similarly likely to involve multiple brain areas, and explanations of the role of the brain in such tasks that focus on a single region (e.g. Diamond, 1985), while interesting, are likely to be incomplete.

Experience-dependent information storage: possible mechanisms

Given that complex environment experience and experience in learning tasks alter these estimates of synapse number, the process whereby the new synapses arise is of significant interest. There appear to be two obvious possibilities. (1) The process of synapse overproduction that we described with regard to early sensory-system development might continue. That is, excess synapses, the existence of which would be transient unless they were confirmed by some aspect of neural activity, might be continually produced on a nonsystematic basis. Since the nature and timing of these sorts of experiences could not be anticipated, synapse formation would have to occur chronically throughout the brain (or in regions that remain plastic). The effects of environmental complexity or training would arise because a proportion of these synapses became permanent as a result of experience-associated neural activity (Changeux and Danchin, 1977; Cotman and Nieto-Sampedro, 1984; Greenough, 1978). (2) The production of new synapses in later development and adulthood might be dependent upon experience-associated neural activity. That is, synapses would be formed as a result of the activity of neurons in information-processing and/ or neuromodulatory systems. The synapses might be generated nonsystematically at the outset, with some aspect of patterned neuronal activity determining the survival of a subset of them (Greenough, 1984). The synapses formed in this case would be localized to regions involved in the information-processing activity that caused their formation.

The first hypothesis is attractive, given the tendency of evolution to conserve mechanisms. It also provides a very simple way for a proper set of connections to come to encode a memory. The second hypothesis has its own attractions, such as the relatively lower amount of metabolic resources required for local, experience-dependent synapse formation and the reduction in potential "noise" in the nervous system that might be associated with chronic generation and degeneration of synapses. Most of the same genes would probably be involved in the construction or stabilization of synapses, regardless of the initiating event. Moreover, the initiating event for intrinsic and extrinsic triggering of synapse formation could involve a final common pathway or common mechanism, such as the activation of neuromodulatory systems. Finally, the second hypothesis has been made far more attractive by the recent appearance of data that are more consonant with it than with the first.

Rapid, active synapse formation in the adult brain

Two lines of evidence have emerged that can be interpreted as suggesting a dynamic synapse-formation process in response to experience-associated neural activity in the adult brain. The first arises from a phenomenon induced by electrical stimulation of neurons that has been proposed as a model for adult long-term memory, long-term potentiation (LTP). In the hippocampus and a number of other brain regions, stimulation of axons at high frequencies can give rise to an increased postsynaptic response to test stimuli (Bliss and Lømo, 1973; see Teyler and Fountain, 1987). With proper stimulus sequences, this elevated responsiveness can persist for up to several weeks. There are several hypotheses as to its neural basis. One, that additional synapses are formed, is based on the work of Lee et al. (1980, 1981), who reported that synapses form in the hippocampus *in vivo* and in an *in vitro* tissue slice preparation following LTP-inducing stimulation. The synapses form surprisingly rapidly. Chang and Greenough (1984) noted that synapses formed within 10–15 minutes *in vitro*. This rate of formation is simply too rapid to arise from the chronic synapse turnover proposed in the first hypothesis. Regardless of whether LTP is related to memory, or synapse formation to LTP, the fact remains that the adult brain, or at least the hippocampus, is capable of generating new synapses rapidly in response to neural activity.

The second finding involves what we believe to be a marker of newly forming synapses, polyribosomal aggregates (PRA), the protein-synthesizing "factories" of cells. Steward

(1983) reported that PRA were found frequently within postsynaptic spines (otherwise rare) during the process of re-formation of synapses that occurs following damage to a part of the hippocampus. Hwang and Greenough (1984) similarly found, in a developmental study, a large increase in the number of PRA in spines in rat visual cortex during periods of peak synapse formation, compared to adult values. Thus, in both situations, PRA in spines appear to indicate the formation of new synapses. We do not know, of course, that synapse formation in late development or adulthood resembles early development or the response to damage. However, if it does, a recent finding suggests that behavioral experience can promote synapse formation, as the second hypothesis above suggests. If animals in environments of different complexity formed equivalent numbers of synapses, but more synapses were confirmed or stabilized in ECs, we might expect the frequency of PRA in spines to be equivalent across the groups. Greenough et al. (1985b) studied synapses in upper visual cortex of rats reared for 30 days after weaning in EC, SC, or IC environments. PRA were considerably more frequent in spines in the EC animals, suggesting that more new synapses were forming.

Given our knowledge that there are more synapses per neuron in EC rats, and other data indicating that PRA in spines marks newly formed synapses, this result suggests that experience-dependent synapse formation occurs in the developmental environmental complexity paradigm. Of course we must keep in mind that PRA may aggregate in spines to perform functions associated with increased activity of synapses or modification of their strength. We now need to find other ways to identify newly forming synapses and must determine whether similar increases in spine-located PRA occur in adult animals during learning. The data to this point, however, suggest that synapses form *in response to experience from which information is to be stored* in the postweaning environmental complexity paradigm.

Summary of later development and adult learning

The data reviewed here suggest that there is a fundamental difference between the processes governing the formation of synapses in early, age-locked sensory system development and those governing synapse formation during later development and adulthood. Experience-expectant processes found in early development appear to produce a surplus of synapses, which are then pruned back by experience to a functional subset. In later development and adulthood, synapses appear to be generated in response to events that provide information to be encoded in the nervous system. This later experience-dependent synapse formation may differ from that of early development in that it is localized to regions involved in processing information arising from the event, but may be similar in that synapses are initially formed on a relatively unpatterned basis, with aspects of neural activity resulting from the event determining the selective preservation of a subset of them. The cumulative effect of many such individual experiences may appear to be a smoothly increasing supply of synapses, as shown in figure 11.4.

Some Cautionary Notes

Presumably we need not point out to most readers that neuroscience involves significant amounts of disagreement and controversy, as do other disciplines, and some of what is said

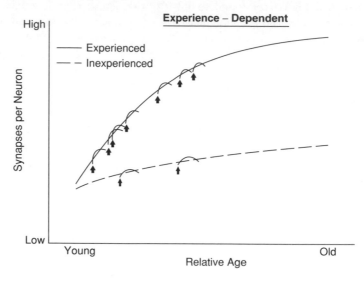

Figure 11.4 Schematic diagram of synapse formation and selective retention during an experience-dependent process. The arrowheads mark salient experiences that generate local synaptic overproduction and deletion (small curves). The cumulative effect of such synaptic blooms and prunes is a smooth increase in synapses per neuron, which is greater for the animals with more experience. (From Black and Greenough, 1986, vol. 4, p. 38; copyright 1986 by Lawrence Erlbaum Associates; reprinted by permission.)

here would be considered controversial by certain of our colleagues. For simplicity, we have painted a much more straightforward picture here than probably exists. For example, there is significant evidence for an active synapse-formation component in early sensory development. Winfield (1981), for example, noted that the peak number of synapses per neuron was lower in visually deprived than in normal kittens, suggesting that visual stimulation promotes extra synapse formation (although it remains possible that this reflects reduced preservation of synapses in a population that is intrinsically generated over time). There is also evidence for a burst of synapse formation and axonal and/or dendritic growth at eye opening or first exposure to light in rodents. Several studies have indicated a burst of synapse formation at about the time of eye opening (Blue and Parnavelas, 1983; Hwang and Greenough, 1984; Miller, 1981; Miller and Peters, 1981), although there is some evidence that the burst may begin prior to eye opening (e.g. Valverde, 1971), leaving open the possibility of an intrinsic trigger. Exposure of rats to light for the first time at later than the normal age of eye opening may also trigger some synapse formation (Cragg, 1967), as well as the synthesis of protein (Rose, 1967), including tubulin, a major molecular component of axons and dendrites (Cronly-Dillon and Perry, 1979). In an artificial imprinting situation, in which chicks were exposed to light for the first time in the form of a flashing amber stimulus, RNA and protein synthesis in the forebrain increased dramatically (Bateson et al., 1973; Horn et al., 1973). And, during the recovery that can be made to occur in monocularly deprived monkeys by reversing which eye is sutured shut, there is evidence for active extension of the axons associated with the previously deprived eye (LeVay et al., 1980). Thus, while synapse overproduction appears to be a dominant aspect of the early organization of the visual system, it is likely to be accompanied by some experience-dependent growth. Nonetheless, on the basis of the evidence to date, the relative emphasis on intrinsic generation and experiential selection on a sensory system-wide basis seems quite clear in early development, and the generation of synapses in later development and adulthood appears to be much more dependent upon extrinsically originating events. It thus seems reasonable to view sensitive period versus continuing developmental information-storage phenomena from this perspective.

Finally, our dichotomy of information-storage mechanisms is based upon studies of a limited number of brain regions. Although many developing systems within the brain other than the visual system go through phases of synapse overproduction, and experience effects on various aspects of the development of these systems have been reported, it remains quite possible that other systems may operate in different ways. Similarly, experience-dependent synapse formation is quite probably not characteristic of all regions of the later-developing and adult nervous system, and there may be other mechanisms with quite different properties whereby nervous systems store information. Recently, for example, we found that an electrophysiologically detectable phenomenon in the hippocampal dentate gyrus (perhaps similar to LTP), which was apparent immediately after postweaning rearing in a complex environment, had entirely disappeared within 30 days (Green and Greenough, 1986). In contrast, dendritic branching differences induced in visual cortex in this paradigm are relatively stable for at least that long (Camel et al., 1986).

Thus, while the separation of experience effects upon brain development into categories based upon the existence of neural anticipation of the experience is compatible with current data, these categories may well not be comprehensive. Nonetheless, recognition (1) that a common aspect of early development of sensory systems may be overproduction of synapses in expectation of experiences that will determine their selective survival, and (2) that later developmental and adult information storage may involve synapse formation triggered by experience, may offer a new level of understanding of phenomena previously described as merely related or unrelated to sensitive periods in development.

Some guidelines for studying effects of experience on development

Monolithic approaches, in which the development of the brain (or the organism) is treated as a unitary phenomenon, are unlikely to be very useful and, in fact, may be misleading. For example, Epstein (1974a, b) has proposed that "phrenoblysis," or spurts of growth of the whole brain during selected periods of development (purportedly corresponding to stages of cognitive development), characterizes species as diverse as humans and mice. While findings of others have failed to replicate Epstein's observations in either species (e.g. Hahn et al., 1983; McCall et al., 1983) and Epstein's analytical procedures have been discredited (Marsh, 1985), the general concept, that the brain as a whole develops in bursts or stages, continues to attract attention to phenomena that probably do not exist (e.g. Spreen et al., 1984). Certainly any recommendations that educational practices be modified to accommodate such bursts (e.g. Epstein and Toepfer, 1978) are not appropriate at this stage. Several lines of evidence indicate that, while discrete brain regions definitely progress through something like "spurts," in terms of such processes as the generation of nerve cells and of connections between them, different brain regions do so out of synchrony and in a reliable developmental sequence. First, some older but generally ignored data on human cerebral cortex development (Conel, 1939–67), which we have plotted in figure 11.5, show rather striking differences in the pattern of growth across brain regions. While many regions of the

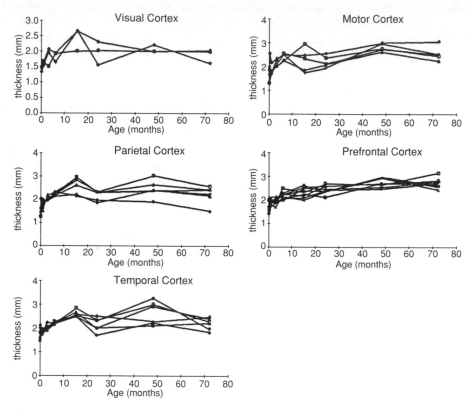

Figure 11.5 Cortical thickness in humans is plotted as a function of age and region of the cerebral cortex. Symbols within regions identify particular sites that were measured (data from Conel, 1939–1967). Postnatal changes in cortical thickness indirectly reflect the addition or deletion of brain components, for example, synapses, neurons and supporting cells, blood vessels. A tendency for a peak in cortical thickness between 10 and 20 months of age is evident at many sites in visual, parietal, temporal, and motor cortex, and a second peak may also occur near 50 months of age at some sites. A clear pattern of peaks and troughs is much less evident in prefrontal cortex, which seems to increase gradually in thickness over the first four years of life.

cortex show some synchrony in the pattern of thickness fluctuations with age, other regions are not in synchrony with them. Rather than showing clear peaks, for example, the prefrontal cortex appears to continue to grow thicker throughout the first six years of life. A similar relative delay in the development of frontal brain regions is evident in the protracted (10–14 years) process of achieving stable synaptic density values in human frontal cortex (Huttenlocher, 1979), compared with the rapid stabilization (1–2 years) seen in human visual cortex (Huttenlocher et al., 1982). A metabolic parallel, perhaps, to these reports is the Chugani and Phelps (1986) report that glucose utilization in human infants was initially highest in sensorimotor cortex and only later rose in the frontal cortex.

In the light of these findings, the report by Rakic et al. (1986) that there is a striking temporal synchrony across cortical areas in developmental changes in density of synapses is rather surprising. Interpreting synaptic density measures can be difficult, since they do not clearly reflect either the number of synapses within a functional area or the number of synapses per nerve cell. Turner and Greenough (1985) found that while the number of synapses per neuron was about 20 percent higher in rats reared in complex environments, the density of synapses (in neuropil, as in Rakic et al., 1986) did not differ in these groups, apparently because the tissue volume of the dendrites, axons, glial cells, blood vessels, etc. necessary for additional synapses pushed the new synapses as far apart as they were in IC rats. As Bennett et al. (1964) had shown years earlier, the volume of the cortex as a whole simply increases to accommodate these needs.

Thus, while counterexamples exist, it seems clear that asynchrony in brain development merits theoretical attention. Theorists have argued that by staggering the developmental schedule for maturation of different brain regions, the human species (and other mammals, for which such patterns are also evident) may have gained substantial advantages, most importantly by allowing one developmental system to provide a suitable framework for a subsequent, experience-sensitive system (Black and Greenough, 1986; Turkewitz and Kenny, 1982). This "stage setting" possibility is most interesting for human development, for example, where early social and communicative skills can establish the foundations for adult language, and where early visual and motor skills can help the infant master spatial and causal relations. The active participation of the infant in acquiring and organizing experience becomes paramount if one process is setting the stage for a subsequent experience-dependent process. In summary, sensitive periods must be characterized in terms of their time course, the brain regions and mechanisms employed, and the organism's involvement in shaping experience.

This perspective may be helpful to both developmental psychologists and neuroscientists in explaining the meaning of infancy. For example, a conjecture that a particular developmental process has a sensitive period(s) (e.g. language acquisition) can now generate testable hypotheses about neural changes that must accompany it. For example, a fixed time course for language acquisition would suggest a peak in cortical thickness or synaptic numbers shortly before the start of a hypothetical experience-expectant period. Such predictions could be quite specific about what brain regions are involved and when the changes occur. After examination of appropriate brain tissue, findings of different time courses or the involvement of other brain regions can reflect back on the original theory, suggesting different influences and constraints. Given the complex and long period of language acquisition, a theory invoking a single, protracted "sensitive period" may eventually be expanded to reflect the multiple involvement of many brain regions, each with its own time course and experiential sensitivities, as has recently been proposed for visual development (Harwerth et al., 1986).

ACKNOWLEDGMENTS

Preparation of this paper and research not otherwise reported was supported by NIMH 40631, NIMH 35321, NIII RR 07030, PHS 5 T-32EY07005, PHS 5 T-32GM7143, ONR N00014-85-K-0587, the Retirement Research Foundation, the System Development Foundation, and the University of Illinois Research Board.

REFERENCES

Bateson, P. P. G. (1979). How do sensitive periods arise and what are they for? *Animal Behavior* 27, 470–86.

Bateson, P. P. G., Rose, S. P. R., and Horn, G. (1973). Imprinting: Lasting effects on uracil incorporation into chick brain. *Science* 181, 576–8.

Bear, M. F. and Singer, W. (1986). Modulation of visual cortical plasticity by acetylcholine and noradrenaline. *Nature* 320, 172–6.

Bennett, E. L., Diamond, M. C., Krech, D., and Rosenzweig, M. R. (1964). Chemical and anatomical plasticity of brain. *Science* 146, 610–19.

Bennett, E. L., Rosenzweig, M. R. Morimoto, H., and Hebert, M. (1979). Maze training alters brain weights and cortical RNA/DNA ratios. *Behavioral and Neural Biology* 26, 1–22.

Black, J. E. and Greenough, W. T. (1986). Induction of pattern in neural structure by experience: Implications for cognitive development. In M. E. Lamb, A. L. Brown, and B. Rogoff (eds.), *Advances in Developmental Psychology* (Vol. 4, pp. 1–50). Hillsdale, NJ: Erlbaum.

Blakemore, C. and Van Sluyters, R. C. (1975). Innate and environmental factors in the development of the kitten's visual cortex. *Journal of Physiology* 248, 663–716.

Blasdel, G. G., Mitchell, D. E., Muir, D. W., and Pettigrew, J. D. (1977). A physiological and behavioural study in cats of the effect of early visual experience with contours of a single orientation. *Journal of Physiology* 265, 615–36.

Bliss, T. V. P. and Lomo, T. (1973). Long-lasting potentiation of synaptic transmission in the dentate area of the anaesthetized rabbit following stimulation of the perforant path. *Journal of Physiology* 232, 331–56.

Blue, M. E. and Parnavelas, J. G. (1983). The formation and maturation of synapses in the visual cortex of the rat: I. Quantitative analysis. *Journal of Neurocytology* 12, 697–712.

Boothe, R. G., Greenough, W. T., Lund, J. S., and Wrege, K. (1979). A quantitative investigation of spine and dendritic development of neurons in visual cortex (area 17) of *Macaca nemestrina* monkeys. *Journal of Comparative Neurology* 186, 473–90.

Brown, M. C., Jansen, J. K. S., and Van Essen, D. (1976). Polyneuronal innervation of skeletal muscle in new-born rats and its elimination during maturation. *Journal of Physiology* 261, 387–422.

Brown, R. T. (1968). Early experience and problem solving ability. *Journal of Comparative and Physiological Psychology* 65, 433–40.

Brunjes, P. C., Schwark, H. D., and Greenough, W. T. (1982). Olfactory granule cell development in normal and hyperthyroid rats. *Developmental Brain Research* 5, 149–59.

Buisseret, P. and Imbert, M. (1976). Visual cortical cells: Their developmental properties in normal and dark-reared kittens. *Journal of Physiology* 255, 511–25.

Camel, J. E., Withers, G. S., and Greenough, W. T. (1986). Persistence of visual cortex dendritic alterations induced by postweaning exposure to a "superenriched" environment in rats. *Behavioral Neuroscience* 100, 810–13.

Chang, F.-L. F. and Greenough, W. T. (1982). Lateralized effects of monocular training on dendritic branching in adult split-brain rats. *Brain Research* 232, 283–92.

Chang, F.-L. F. and Greenough, W. T. (1984). Transient and enduring morphological correlates of synaptic activity and efficacy change in the rat hippocampal slice. *Brain Research* 309, 35–46.

Changeux, J.-P. and Danchin, A. (1977). Biochemical models for the selective stabilization of developing synapses. In G. A. Cottrell and P. M. Usherwood (eds.), *Synapses* (pp. 705–12). New York: Academic Press.

Chomsky, N. (1980). On cognitive structures and their development: A reply to Piaget. In M. Piatelli-Palmarini (ed.), *Language and Learning* (pp. 35–52). Cambridge, MA: Harvard University Press.

Chugani, H. T. and Phelps, M. E. (1986). Maturational changes in cerebral function in infants determined by [18] FDG positron emission to mography. *Science* 231, 840–43.

Clopton, B. M. and Winfield, J. A. (1976). Effect of early exposure to patterned sound on unit activity in rat inferior colliculus. *Journal of Neurophysiology* 39, 1081–9.

Coleman, P. D., Flood, D. G., Whitehead, M. C., and Emerson, R. C. (1981). Spatial sampling by dendritic trees in visual cortex. *Brain Research* 214, 1–21.

Coleman, P. D. and Riesen, A. H. (1968). Environmental effects on cortical dendritic fields: I. Rearing in the dark. *Journal of Anatomy* 102, 363–74.

Conel, J. L. (1939–1967). *The Postnatal Development of the Human Cerebral Cortex* (Vols. 1–8). Cambridge, MA: Harvard University Press.

Corrigan, J. G. and Carpenter, D. L. (1979). Early selective visual experience and pattern discrimination in hooded rats. *Developmental Psychobiology* 12, 67–72.

Cotman, C. W. and Nieto-Sampedro, M. (1984). Cell biology of synaptic plasticity. *Science* 225, 1287–94.

Crabtree, J. W. and Riesen, A. H. (1979). Effects of the duration of dark rearing on visually guided behavior in the kitten. *Developmental Psychobiology* 12, 291–303.

Cragg, B. G. (1967). Changes in visual cortex on first exposure of rats to light: Effect on synaptic dimensions. *Nature* 215, 251–3.

Cragg, B. G. (1975a). The development of synapses in kitten visual cortex during visual deprivation. *Experimental Neurology* 46, 445–51.

Cragg, B. G. (1975b). The development of synapses in the visual system of the cat. *Journal of Comparative Neurology* 160, 147–66.

Cronly-Dillon, J. and Perry, G. W. (1979). The effect of visual experience on tubulin synthesis during a critical period of visual cortex development in the hooded rat. *Journal of Physiology* 293, 469–84.

Cynader, M., Berman, N., and Hein, A. (1976). Recovery of function in cat visual cortex following prolonged deprivation. *Experimental Brain Research* 25, 139–56.

Cynader, M. and Chernenko, G. (1976). Abolition of direction selectivity in the visual cortex of the cat. *Science* 193, 504–5.

Cynader, M. and Mitchell, D. E. (1980). Prolonged sensitivity to monocular deprivation in dark-reared cats. *Journal of Neurophysiology* 43, 1026–40.

Diamond, A. (1985). Development of the ability to use recall to guide action, as indicated by infants' performance on AB. *Child Development* 56, 868–83.

Diamond, M. C. (1967). Extensive cortical depth measurements and neuron size increases in the cortex of environmentally enriched rats. *Journal of Comparative Neurology* 131, 357–64.

Diamond, M. C., Rosenzweig, M. R., Bennett, E. L., Lindner, B., and Lyon, L. (1972). Effects of environmental enrichment and impoverishment on rat cerebral cortex. *Journal of Neuro-biology* 3, 47–64.

Dunn, A. J. (1980). Neurochemistry of learning and memory: An evaluation of recent data. *Annual Review of Psychology* 31, 343–90.

Eayrs, J. T. and Ireland, K. F. (1950). The effect of total darkness on the growth of the newborn albino rat. *Journal of Endocrinology* 6, 386–97.

Eimas, P. D. (1975). Speech perception in early infancy. In L. B. Cohen and P. Salapatek (eds.), *Infant Perception* (pp. 193–231). New York: Academic Press.

Epstein, H. T. (1974a). Phrenoblysis: Special brain and mind growth periods: I. Human brain and skull development. *Developmental Psychobiology* 7, 207–16.

Epstein, H. T. (1974b). Phrenoblysis: Special brain and mind growth periods: II. Human mental development. *Developmental Psychobiology* 7, 217–24.

Epstein, H. T. and Toepfer, C. F., Jr. (1978). A neuroscience basis for reorganizing middle grades education. *Educational Leadership* 35, 656–60.

Feng, A. S. and Rogowski, B. A. (1980). Effects of monaural and binaural occlusion on the morphology of neurons in the medial superior olivary nucleus of the rat. *Brain Research* 189, 530–4.

Ferchmin, P. A., Bennett, E. L., and Rosenzweig, M. R. (1975). Direct contact with enriched environments is required to alter cerebral weights in rats. *Journal of Comparative and Physiological Psychology* 88, 360–7.

Fernald, A. (1984). The perceptual and affective salience of mother's speech to infants. In L. Feagans, C. Garvey, and R. Golinkoff (eds.), *The origins and growth of communication* (pp. 5–29). Norwood, NJ: Ablex.

Fifkova, E. (1968). Changes in the visual cortex of rats after unilateral deprivation. *Nature* 220, 379–81.

Fifkova, E. (1970). The effect of unilateral deprivation on visual centers in rats. *Journal of Comparative Neurology* 140, 431–8.

Fiske, J. (1909). *The Meaning of Infancy*. Boston: Houghton Mifflin. (Original work published 1883).

Floeter, M. K. and Greenough, W. T. (1979). Cerebellar plasticity: Modification of purkinje cell structure by differential rearing in monkeys. *Science* 206, 227–9.

Forgays, D. G. and Forgays, J. W. (1952). The nature of the effect of free-environmental experience in the rat. *Journal of Comparative and Physiological Psychology* 45, 322–8.

Fox, M. W. (1966). Neuro-behavioral ontogeny: A synthesis of ethological and neurophysiological concepts. *Brain Research* 2, 3–20.

Globus, A. (1975). Brain morphology as a function of presynaptic morphology and activity. In A. H. Riesen (ed.), *The developmental neuropsychology of sensory deprivation* (pp. 9–91). New York: Academic Press.

Globus, A., Rosenzweig, M. R., Bennett, E. L., and Diamond, M. C. (1973). Effects of differential experience on dendritic spine counts in rat cerebral cortex. *Journal of Comparative and Physiological Psychology* 82, 175–81.

Gold, P. E. (1984). Memory modulation: Neurobiological contexts. In G. Lynch, J. L. McGaugh, and N. M. Weinberger (eds.), *Neurobiology of Learning and Memory* (pp. 374–82). New York: Guilford.

Goldman-Rakic, P. S. (1987). Development of cortical circuitry and cognitive function. *Child Development* 58, 601–22.

Gordon, B., Presson, J., Packwood, J., and Scheer, R. (1979). Alteration of cortical orientation selectivity: Importance of asymmetric input. *Science* 204, 1109–11.

Gouze, J.-L., Lasry, J.-M., and Changeux, J.-P. (1983). Selective stabilization of muscle innervation during development: A mathematical model. *Biological Cybernetics* 46, 207–15.

Green, E. J. and Greenough, W. T. (1986). Altered synaptic transmission in dentate gyrus of rats reared in complex environments: Evidence from hippocampal slices maintained in vivo. *Journal of Neurophysiology* 55, 739–50.

Green, E. J., Greenough, W. T., and Schlumpf, B. E. (1983). Effects of complex or isolated environments on cortical dendrites of middle-aged rats. *Brain Research* 264, 233–40.

Greenough, W. T. (1976). Enduring brain effects of differential experience and training. In M. T. Rosenzweig and E. L. Bennett (eds.), *Neural Mechanisms of Learning and Memory* (pp. 255–78). Cambridge, MA: MIT Press.

Greenough, W. T. (1978). Development and memory: The synaptic connection. In T. Teyler (ed.), *Brain and Learning* (pp. 127–45). Stamford, CT: Greylock.

Greenough, W. T. (1984). Structural correlates of information storage in the mammalian brain: A review and hypothesis. *Trends in Neurosciences* 7, 229–33.

Greenough, W. T. and Chang, F.-L. C. (1985). Synaptic structural correlates of information storage in mammalian nervous systems. In C. W. Cotman (ed.), *Synaptic Plasticity and Remodeling* (pp. 335–72). New York: Guilford.

Greenough, W. T., Hwang, H. M., and Gorman, C. (1985a). Evidence for active synapse formation, or altered postsynaptic metabolism, in visual cortex of rats reared in complex environments. *Proceedings of the National Academy of Sciences* (USA) 82, 4549–52.

Greenough, W. T., Juraska, J. M., and Volkmar, F. R. (1979). Maze training effects on dendritic branching in occipital cortex of adult rats. *Behavioral and Neural Biology* 26, 287–97.

Greenough, W. T., Larson, J. R., and Withers, G. S. (1985b). Effects of unilateral and bilateral training in a reaching task on dendritic branching of neurons in the rat motor-sensory forelimb cortex. *Behavioral and Neural Biology* 44, 301–14.

Greenough, W. T., Madden, T. C., and Fleishmann, T. B. (1972). Effects of isolation, daily handling, and enriched rearing on maze learning. *Psychonomic Science* 27, 279–80.

Greenough, W. T. and Maier, S. F. (1972). Molecular changes during learning: Behavioral strategy: A comment on Gaito and Bonnet. *Psychological Bulletin* 78, 480–2.

Greenough, W. T., McDonald, J., Parnisari, R., and Camel, J. E. (1986). Environmental conditions modulate degeneration and new dendrite growth in cerebellum of senescent rats. *Brain Research* 380, 136–43.

Greenough, W. T. and Schwark, H. D. (1984). Age-related aspects of experience effects upon brain structure. In R. N. Emde and R. J. Harmon (eds.), *Continuities and Discontinuities in Development* (pp. 69–91). Hillsdale, NJ: Plenum.

Greenough, W. T. and Volkmar, F. R. (1973). Pattern of dendritic branching in occipital cortex of rats reared in complex environments. *Experimental Neurology* 40, 491–504.

Greenough, W. T., Volkmar, F. R., and Juraska, J. M. (1973). Effects of rearing complexity on dendritic branching in frontolateral and temporal cortex of the rat. *Experimental Neurology* 41, 371–8.

Guillery, R. W. (1972). Binocular competition in the control of geniculate cell growth. *Journal of Comparative Neurology* 144, 117–30.

Gyllensten, L., Malmfors, T., and Norrlin, M. L. (1966). Growth alteration in the auditory cortex of visually deprived mice. *Journal of Comparative Neurology* 126, 463–70.

Hahn, M. E., Walters, J. K., Lavooy, J., and DeLuca, J. (1983). Brain growth in young mice: Evidence on the theory of phrenoblysis. *Developmental Psychobiology* 16, 377–83.

Harwerth, R. S., Smith III, E. L., Duncan, G. C., Crawford, M. L. J., and von Noorden, G. K. (1986). Multiple sensitive periods in the development of the primate visual system. *Science* 232, 235–8.

Hebb, D. O. (1949). *The Organization of Behavior*. New York: Wiley.

Hirsch, H. V. B. and Spinelli, D. N. (1970). Visual experience modifies distribution of horizontally and vertically oriented receptive fields in cats. *Science* 168, 869–71.

Holloway, R. L. (1966). Dendritic branching: Some preliminary results of training and complexity in rat visual cortex. *Brain Research* 2, 393–6.

Horn, G., Rose, S. P. R., and Bateson, P. P. G. (1973). Monocular imprinting and regional incorporation of tritiated uracil into the brains of intact and "split-brain" chicks. *Brain Research* 56, 227–37.

Hubel, D. H. and Wiesel, T. N. (1970). The period of susceptibility to the physiological effects of unilateral eye closure in kittens. *Journal of Physiology* 206, 419–36.

Huttenlocher, P. R. (1979). Synaptic density in human frontal cortex – developmental changes and effects of aging. *Brain Research* 163, 195–205.

Huttenlocher, P. R., de Courten, C., Garey, L. J., and Van Der Loos, H. (1982). Synaptogenesis in human visual cortex – evidence for synapse elimination during normal development. *Neuroscience Letters* 33, 247–52.

Hwang, H. M. and Greenough, W. T. (1984). Spine formation and synaptogenesis in rat visual cortex: A serial section developmental study. *Society for Neuroscience Abstracts* 14, 579.

Hymovitch, B. (1952). The effects of experimental variations on problem solving in the rat. *Journal of Comparative and Physiological Psychology* 45, 313–21.

Juraska, J. M. (1984). Sex differences in dendritic response to differential experience in the rat visual cortex. *Brain Research* 295, 27–34.

Juraska, J. M., Fitch, J., Henderson, C., and Rivers, N. (1985). Sex differences in the dendritic branching of dentate granule cells following differential experience. *Brain Research* 333, 73–80.

Juraska, J. M., Greenough, W. T., Elliott, C., Mack, K. J., and Berkowitz, R. (1980). Plasticity in adult rat visual cortex: An examination of several cell populations after differential rearing. *Behavioral and Neural Biology* 29, 157–67.

Kasamatsu, T. and Pettigrew, J. D. (1976). Depletion of brain catecholamines: Failure of ocular dominance shift after monocular occlusion in kittens. *Science* 194, 206–9.

Krech, D., Rosenzweig, M. R., and Bennett, E. L. (1962). Relations between brain chemistry and problem-solving among rats raised in enriched and impoverished environments. *Journal of Comparative and Physiological Psychology* 55, 801–7.

Lee, K. S., Oliver, M., Schottler, F., and Lynch, G. (1981). Electron microscopic studies of brain slices: The effects of high-frequency stimulation on dendritic ultrastructure. In G. A. Kerkut and H. V. Wheal (eds.), *Electrophysiology of Isolated Mammalian CNS Preparations* (pp. 189–212). New York: Academic Press.

Lee, K. S., Schottler, F., Oliver, M., and Lynch, G. (1980). Brief bursts of high-frequency stimulation produce two types of structural change in rat hippocampus. *Journal of Neurophysiology* 44, 247–58.

LeVay, S., Wiesel, T. N., and Hubel, D. H. (1980). The development of ocular dominance columns in normal and visually deprived monkeys. *Journal of Comparative Neurology* 191, 1–51.

Leventhal, A. G. and Hirsch, H. V. B. (1975). Cortical effect of early selective exposure to diagonal lines. *Science* 190, 902–4.

Marsh, R. W. (1985). Phrenoblysis: Real or chimera? *Child Development* 56, 1059–61.

McCall, R. B., Meyers, E. C., Jr., Hartman, J., and Roche, A. F. (1983). Developmental changes in head-circumference and mental-performance growth rates: A test of Epstein's phrenoblysis hypothesis. *Developmental Psychobiology* 16, 457–68.

Meisami, E. (1975). Early sensory influences on regional activity of brain ATPases in developing rats. In M. A. B. Brazier (ed.), *Growth and Development of the Brain* (pp. 51–74). New York: Raven.

Miller, M. (1981). Maturation of rat visual cortex: I. A quantitative study of Golgi-impregnated pyramidal neurons. *Journal of Neurocytology* 10, 859–78.

Miller, M. and Peters, A. (1981). Maturation of rat visual cortex: II. A combined Golgi–electron microscope study of pyramidal neurons. *Journal of Comparative Neurology* 203, 555–73.

Mirmiran, M. and Uylings, H. B. M. (1983). The environmental enrichment effect upon cortical growth is neutralized by concomitant pharmacological suppression of active sleep in female rats. *Brain Research* 261, 331–4.

Mitchell, D. E., Freeman, R. D., Millodot, M., and Haegerstrom, G. (1973). Meridional amblyopia: Evidence for modification of the human visual system by early visual experience. *Vision Research* 13, 535–58.

Mitchell, D. E. and Timney, B. (1984). Postnatal development of function in the mammalian nervous system. In J. M. Brookhart and V. R. Mountcastle (eds.), *Handbook of physiology, Section I: The nervous system* (Vol. 3, pp. 507–55). Bethesda, MD: American Physiological Society.

Mos, L. P. (1976). Light rearing effects on factors of mouse emotionality and endocrine organ weight. *Physiological Psychology* 4, 503–10.

Movshon, J. A. and Van Sluyters, R. C. (1981). Visual neuronal development. *Annual Review of Psychology* 32, 477–522.

Mower, G. D., Christen, W. G., and Caplan, C. J. (1983). Very brief visual experience eliminates plasticity in the cat visual cortex. *Science* 221, 178–80.

Myers, R. D. and Fox, J. (1963). Differences in maze performance of group- vs. isolation-reared rats. *Psychological Reports* 12, 199–202.

O'Brien, R. A. D., Ostberg, A. J., and Vrbova, G. (1978). Observations on the elimination of polyneural innervation in developing mammalian skeletal muscle. *Journal of Physiology* 282, 571–82.

Olson, C. R. and Freeman, R. D. (1978). Monocular deprivation and recovery during sensitive period in kittens. *Journal of Neurophysiology* 41, 65–74.

O'Shea, L., Saari, M., Pappas, B., Ings, R., and Stange, K. (1983). Neonatal 6-hydroxydopamine attenuates the neural and behavioral effects of enriched rearing in the rat. *European Journal of Pharmacology* 92, 43–7.

Parnavelas, J. G. and Globus, A. (1976). The effect of continuous illumination on the development of cortical neurons in the rat: A Golgi study. *Experimental Neurology* 51, 637–47.

Parnavelas, J. G., Globus, A., and Kaups, P. (1973). Continuous illumination from birth affects spine density of neurons in the visual cortex of the rat. *Experimental Neurology* 40, 742–7.

Pearlman, C. (1983). Impairment of environmental effects on brain weight by adrenergic drugs in rats. *Physiology and Behavior* 30, 161–3.

Peterson, G. M. (1951). Transfers of handedness in the rat from forced practice. *Journal of Comparative and Physiological Psychology* 44, 184–90.

Pettigrew, J. D. and Kasamatsu, T. (1978). Local perfusion of noradrenaline maintains visual cortical plasticity. *Nature* 271, 761–3.

Purves, D. and Lichtman, J. W. (1980). Elimination of synapses in the developing nervous system. *Science* 210, 153–7.

Pysh, J. J. and Weiss, M. (1979). Exercise during development induces an increase in Purkinje cell dendritic tree size. *Science* 206, 230–2.

Rakic, P., Bourgeois, J.-P., Eckenhoff, M. F., Zecevic, N., and Goldman-Rakic, P. S. (1986). Concurrent overproduction of synapses in diverse regions of the primate cerebral cortex. *Science* 232, 232–5.

Ramon y Cajal, S. (1893). New findings about the histological structure of the central nervous system. *Archiv fur Anatomic und Physiologie (Anatomie)*, pp. 319–428.

Rasch, E., Swift, H., Riesen, A. H., and Chow, K. L. (1961). Altered structure and composition of retinal cells in dark-reared mammals. *Experimental Cell Research* 25, 348–63.

Ravizza, R. J. and Herschberger, A. C. (1966). The effect of prolonged motor restriction upon later behavior of the rat. *Psychological Record* 16, 73–80.

Rose, S. P. R. (1967). Changes in visual cortex on first exposure to light. *Nature* 215, 253–55.

Rose, S. P. R. (1981). What should a biochemistry of learning and memory be about? *Neuroscience* 6, 811–21.

Rosenzweig, M. R., Bennett, E. L., and Diamond, M. C. (1972). Chemical and anatomical plasticity of brain: Replications and extensions. In J. Gaito (ed.), *Macromolecules and behavior* (2nd ed., pp. 205–77). New York: Appleton-Century-Crofts.

Rothblat, L. A. and Schwartz, M. (1979). The effect of monocular deprivation on dendritic spines in visual cortex of young and adult albino rats: Evidence for a sensitive period. *Brain Research* 161, 156–61.

Ruiz-Marcos, A. and Valverde, F. (1969). The temporal evolution of the distribution of dendritic spines in the visual cortex of normal and dark raised mice. *Experimental Brain Research* 8, 284–94.

Ryugo, D. K., Ryugo, R., Globus, A., and Killackey, H. P. (1975). Increased spine density in auditory cortex following visual or somatic deafferentation. *Brain Research* 90, 143–6.

Schneider, G. E. (1981). Early lesions and abnormal neural connections. *Trends in Neurosciences* 4, 187–92.

Schüz, A. (1978). Some facts and hypotheses concerning dendritic spines and learning. In M. A. B. Brazier and H. Petsche (eds), *Architectonics of the Cerebral Cortex* (pp. 129–35). New York: Raven.

Senden, M. von (1960). *Space and Sight: The Perception of Space and Shape in the Congenitally Blind Before and After Operation.* Glencoe, IL: Free Press.

Sherman, S. M. (1973). Visual field defects in monocularly and binocularly deprived cats. *Brain Research* 49, 25–45.

Sherman, S. M. (1977). The effect of cortical and tectal lesions on the visual fields of binocularly deprived cats. *Journal of Comparative Neurology* 172, 231–46.

Singer, W. (1986). Neuronal activity as a shaping factor in postnatal development of visual cortex. In W. T. Greenough and J. M. Juraska (eds), *Developmental Neuropsychobiology*. New York: Academic Press.

Spreen, O., Tupper, D., Risser, A., Tuokko, H., and Edgell, D. (1984). *Human Developmental Neuropsychology*. New York: Oxford University Press.

Steward, O. (1983). Polyribosomes at the base of dendritic spines of CNS neurons: Their possible role in synapse construction and modification. *Cold Spring Harbor Symposia on Quantitative Biology* 48, 745–59.

Tanzi, E. (1893). Facts and inductions in current histology of the nervous system. *Rivista sperimentale di freniatria e medicina legale delle mentali alienazioni* 19, 419–72.

Tees, R. C. (1979). The effect of visual deprivation on pattern recognition in the rat. *Developmental Psychobiology* 12, 485–97.

Tees, R. C. and Cartwright, J. (1972). Sensory preconditioning in rats following early visual deprivation. *Journal of Comparative and Physiological Psychology* 81, 12–20.

Teyler, T. J. and Fountain, S. B. (1987). Neuronal plasticity in the mammalian brain: Relevance to behavioral learning and memory. *Child Development* 58, 698–712.

Thelen, E. (1980). Rhythmical behavior in infancy: An ethological perspective. *Developmental Psychology* 17, 237–57.

Thinus-Blanc, C. (1981). Volume discrimination learning in golden hamsters: Effects of the structure of complex rearing cages. *Developmental Psychobiology* 14, 397–403.

Thompson, W., Kuffler, D. P., and Jansen, J. K. S. (1979). The effect of prolonged reversible block of nerve impulses on the elimination of polyneural innervation of newborn rat skeletal muscle fibres. *Neuroscience* 4, 271–81.

Tieman, S. B. and Hirsch, H. (1982). Exposure to lines of only one orientation modifies dendritic morphology of cells in the visual cortex of the cat. *Journal of Comparative Neurology* 211, 353–62.

Timney, B., Mitchell, D. E., and Cynader, M. (1980). Behavioral evidence for prolonged sensitivity to effects of monocular deprivation in dark-reared cats. *Journal of Neurophysiology* 43, 1041–54.

Turkewitz, G. and Kenny, P. A. (1982). Limitations on input as a basis for neural organization and perceptual development: A preliminary theoretical statement. *Developmental Psychobiology* 15, 357–68.

Turner, A. M. and Greenough, W. T. (1985). Differential rearing effects on rat visual cortex synapses: I. Synaptic and neuronal density and synapses per neuron. *Brain Research* 329, 195–203.

Uylings, H. B. M., Kuypers, K., Diamond, M. C., and Veltman, W. A. M. (1978). Effects of differential environments on plasticity of dendrites of cortical pyramidal neurons in adult rats. *Experimental Neurology* 62, 658–77.

Uylings, H. B. M., Kuypers, K., and Veltman, W. A. M. (1978). Environmental influences on neocortex in later life. *Progress in Brain Research* 48, 261–74.

Valverde, F. (1970). The Golgi method: A tool for comparative structural analyses. In W. J. H. Nauta and S. O. E. Ebbesson (eds.), *Contemporary Research Methods in Neuroanatomy* (pp. 12–31). New York: Springer-Verlag.

Valverde, F. (1971). Rate and extent of recovery from dark-rearing in the mouse. *Brain Research* 33, 1–11.

Werker, J. F. and Tees, R. C. (1984). Cross-language speech perception: Evidence for perceptual reorganization during the first year of life. *Infant Behavior and Development* 7, 49–63.

Wiesel, T. N. and Hubel, D. H. (1963). Single-cell responses in striate cortex of kittens deprived of vision in one eye. *Journal of Neurophysiology* 26, 1003–17.

Wiesel, T. N. and Hubel, D. H. (1965). Comparison of the effects of unilateral and bilateral eye closure on cortical unit responses in kittens. *Journal of Neurophysiology* 28, 1029–40.

Wiesel, T. N. and Raviola, E. (1977). Myopia and eye enlargement after neonatal lid fusion in monkeys. *Nature* 266, 66–8.

Winfield, D. A. (1981). The postnatal development of synapses in the visual cortex of the cat and the effects of eyelid closure. *Brain Research* 206, 166–71.

Brain Adaptation to Experience: an Update

William T. Greenough

Since the Greenough, Black and Wallace paper was published in 1987, a number of findings have increased our understanding of the function of brain differences arising from experience. In particular, we have found that the synaptic changes are accompanied by an orchestrated set of changes in other elements of the brain tissue. In addition, a recent experiment makes us more confident that the synaptic and dendritic changes, which alter the "wiring diagram" of the brain, are specifically associated with learning. The results of this experiment have also provided a new perspective on mechanisms of brain adaptation to behavioral demands.

Changes in Nonsynaptic Brain Components

A major advance in our understanding of the brain's response to experience, still unfolding to some degree, was the finding that the experience-dependent formation of synapses is accompanied by changes in the brain's *blood supply* and in *astrocytes*, cells that metabolically support the activities of nerve cells and their synapses. When we wrote "apparently because the tissue volume of the dendrites, axons, glial cells, blood vessels, etc. necessary for additional synapses pushed the new synapses as far apart as they were in IC rats," in late 1986, we had very little to back it up. In fact, the only study published on EC (environmental complexity), SC (social condition) and IC (individual cage) rat blood vessels had reported that the density of vessels was *lower* in EC rats (Diamond et al., 1964). Our more recent work has indicated that work to be in error; in fact, blood vessel density is dramatically higher in young EC rats, while the capacity to generate new vessels declines with age. In young animals placed in the EC housing condition, the number of *capillaries*, the blood vessels that mediate transfer of nutrients from blood to brain, increases dramatically (Black et al., 1987). Similarly, the amount of astrocyte tissue is increased in young EC rats relative to SC and IC rats (Sirevaag and Greenough, 1991). Astrocytes are glial cells that maintain the metabolic environment of neurons and their synapses in a manner that optimizes synaptic and neuronal function. Synapses use a very large amount of metabolic energy and the developing brain apparently adapts itself to their numbers, and perhaps also to their level of activity, which is likely to be considerably higher in the exciting and stimulating world of the EC rat.

For capillaries, at least, the dramatic adaptation of the young rat, in which the amount of capillary per nerve cell is nearly double that of the IC rat, is not an ability that the animal retains if its exposure to EC is delayed to young adulthood. Adult EC rats can increase capillary numbers somewhat, but only enough to keep the same density within the expanding cortical tissue volume, in contrast to the greatly increased capillary density in the young EC rat (Black et al., 1991). Middle-age rats first exposed to EC show an even smaller capillary response to EC exposure in the visual cortex, although other areas or conditions may exhibit greater responsiveness (Black et al., 1989). We have not studied age effects on astrocytes.

In short, the brain retains in this case the ability to generate new synapses but it loses to a significant degree the ability to support them metabolically with advancing age. Whether this may lead to what Smith (1984) called a "power failure" for synapses – a situation in which they cannot keep up with the demands of behavior – remains an open question.

Do the Brain Differences Arise from Learning or from Neural Activity?

While it makes sense that changing the wiring diagram of the brain would alter its functional organization such that new information could be incorporated, there is no direct evidence that this is the case. One could conceive that neurons, like muscles, simply grow larger with increased levels of use and that brain blood vessels, like muscle vessels, proliferate to support the neurons. An experiment that addressed this issue compared animals learning a long series of complicated motor skills with animals that exercised by running on a treadmill or in an activity wheel such that little new learning was possible. A control group had neither exercise nor learning but were handled by the experimenters each day in a manner comparable to that of the other groups. (The rats were ten months old, about half the way to the "middle-age" groups described earlier.) The experiment used the cerebellum, a sensorimotor part of the brain (we had previously found that the complexity of housing conditions affects the cerebellum in a manner similar to its effects on the visual cortex: Floeter and Greenough, 1979; Greenough et al., 1986). The results of this experiment (Black et al., 1990) showed that both learning and exercise had effects, but that they were quite different. In the animals that learned, the number of synapses per cerebellar output cell increased, as we would have expected based upon our visual cortical results with the complex environment animals. The blood vessels in the learning animals just "kept up" with the changes in the tissue volume necessary to accommodate the new synapses. In contrast, both exercise groups exhibited no change in the number of synapses, but substantially increased the density of capillaries. Clearly, in cases where sufficient demand exists, the mature adult brain becomes capable of a response that we previously thought was limited to the juvenile.

The results of this experiment really revised the way we think about *learning*, or experience-expectant information storage in general, as an independent process as opposed to brain adaptation to the demands placed upon it by the animal's behavior. As psychologists oriented towards higher mental processes, we had tended to think of learning as something special and different from the sort of thing that the blood supply does in a muscle when it is repeatedly exercised. There are still ways in which this is true – other evidence from our laboratory also indicates that mere activation of neurons is insufficient to bring about synaptic change (Chang and Greenough, 1984). But the fundamental change that has occurred in our thinking has come from looking at how the cerebellum "views" the problems in this experiment. The appropriate role for any part of the body is to adapt in an optimal way to the conditions that the organism's needs are placing upon it. In the cases of the conditions used in this experiment, one adaptation apparently required establishing more capillaries such that the cerebellum could comfortably support sustained involvement in mediating routine but taxing motor output over long periods. The other adaptation involved changing the wiring diagram to incorporate the ability to perform novel skills. One might easily argue that from the point of view of the role of the cerebellum in optimizing its owner's chances of surviving in the natural environment, the two adaptations are equivalent. Both capillary increases and synapse increases are appropriate to the rats' behavioral needs. In short, from a survival viewpoint, what we call learning is not unique. It is just one of a range of adaptations that nervous systems may adopt to optimize behavioral performance.

REFERENCES

Black, J. E., Isaacs, K. R., Anderson, B. J., Alcantara, A. A., and Greenough, W. T. (1990). Learning causes synaptogenesis, whereas motor activity causes angiogenesis, in cerebellar cortex of adult rats. *Proceedings of the National Academy of Sciences (USA)* 87, 5568–72.

Black, J. E., Polinsky, M., and Greenough, W. T. (1989). Progressive failure of cerebral angiogenesis supporting neural plasticity in aging rats. *Neurobiology of Aging* 10, 353–8.

Black, J. E., Sirevaag, A. M., and Greenough, W. T. (1987). Complex experience promotes capillary formation in young rat visual cortex. *Neuroscience Letters* 83, 351–5.

Black, J. E., Zelazny, A. M., and Greenough, W. T. (1991). Capillary and mitochondrial support of neural plasticity in adult rat visual cortex. *Experimental Neurology* 111, 204–9.

Chang, F.-L. F. and Greenough, W. T. (1984). Transient and enduring morphological correlates of synaptic activity and efficacy change in the rat hippocampal slice. *Brain Research* 309, 35–46.

Diamond, M. C., Krech, D., and Rosenzweig, M. R. (1964). The effects of an enriched environment on the histology of the rat cerebral cortex. *Journal of Comparative Neurology* 123, 111–20.

Floeter, M. K. and Greenough, W. T. (1979). Cerebellar plasticity: modification of Purkinje cell structure by differential rearing in monkeys. *Science* 206, 227–9.

Greenough, W. T., McDonald, J. W., Parnisari, R. M., and Camel, J. E. (1986). Environmental conditions modulate degeneration and new dendrite growth in cerebellum of senescent rats. *Brain Research* 380, 136–43.

Sirevaag, A. M. and Greenough, W. T. (1991). Plasticity of GFAP-immunoreactive astrocyte size and number in visual cortex of rats reared in complex environments. *Brain Research* 540, 273–8.

Smith, C. B. (1984). Aging and changes in cerebral energy metabolism. *Trends in Neuroscience* 7, 203–8.

12

Do Cortical Areas Emerge from a Protocortex?

Dennis D. M. O'Leary

The neocortex is unique to mammals. Although it differs greatly in complexity between mammalian species, in all mammals it can be divided on both morphological and functional grounds into a sizable number of "areas."[1,2] There are phylogenetic differences in neocortical parcellation which reflect the addition of higher order "associational" areas and an increase in the specialization of regions of neocortex to perform specific functions.[3] Much attention has been directed toward understanding the organization and operation of the neocortex. Recently, though, an increased amount of effort has been focused on determining how areas of the neocortex acquire their unique characteristics.[4] Although this question relates to an understanding of the mechanisms underlying the phylogenetic expansion of the neocortex in terms of the size and the number of definable areas, studies of neocortical development provide the best opportunity for answers. One can imagine two extreme positions of how distinct areas are developed: the neuroepithelium which gives rise to the neocortex may be regionally specified to generate area unique lineages of neurons that reflect the area-specific features of the adult neocortex, or alternatively, the neocortical neuroepithelium may generate uniform lineages across its extent and rely on subsequent interactions to bring about the differentiation of areas. I will consider here an increasing body of evidence which suggests that many prominent features distinctive of the differentiation of areas of the neocortex are not determined at the time of neurogenesis, but rather are established through subsequent epigenetic interactions involving a variety of mechanisms.

Some Distinctions and Similarities between Cortical Areas in the Adult

Areas of the adult neocortex are clearly dissimilar. Neocortical areas can be distinguished from one another by differences in connections, both outputs and inputs, as well as by distinctions in architecture, from different distributions of receptors for neurotransmitters

"Do Cortical Areas Emerge from a Protocortex?" first appeared in *Trends in the Neurosciences* 12 (Elsevier Trends Journals 1989), pp. 400–6, and is reprinted by kind permission.

to variations in cell sizes and densities. These area-specific characteristics contribute to the unique functional properties of the various neocortical areas. But, in spite of the many striking differences between areas, certain features are shared. The most obvious common feature is that by convention all neocortical areas have six primary layers. Although the appearance of individual layers changes at the borders between areas, the chief characteristics of each layer are retained. For example, the same basic scheme of laminar organization of sources of cortical outputs applies to all: neurons in layer 6 project to the thalamus and claustrum, neurons in layer 5 send their axons to all other subcortical targets, and layers 2 and 3 are the principal source of projections to other neocortical areas, ipsilaterally and contralaterally.[5,6]

Even the basic cellular constituents seem to be consistent from one area to another. Although cortical thickness varies considerably, the number of neurons found in a "radial traverse" through the six layers is surprisingly constant between diverse cortical areas within a species, as well as across species.[7,8] A notable exception is that the number of neurons found in a radial traverse in primary visual cortex (area 17) is higher than in other areas.[7-9] The proportion of cells classified by shape as pyramidal or non-pyramidal is also constant between two very different areas, the primary motor and visual areas.[10] Similarly, the predominant cortical inhibitory cell, the GABAergic neuron, is present in roughly equivalent proportions in all areas examined.[8] Cortical neurons that might use other neurotransmitters or modulators, for example those immunoreactive for choline acetyltransferase (the synthesizing enzyme for the neurotransmitter acetylcholine),[11] as well as interneurons of various peptide phenotypes,[12-15] are also found in all neocortical areas. In short, all of the basic morphological and chemically defined types of cortical neurons identified to date are widely distributed within the adult neocortex.

Based on these and other structural and functional consistencies between areas of the adult neocortex, it has been proposed by both neuroanatomists and neurophysiologists, especially Lorente de No,[16] Creutzfeld,[17] Mountcastle,[18] Powell[19] and Eccles,[20] that different primary cortical areas share a common organizational scheme. This suggestion has been addressed experimentally in two independent sets of experiments in which somatosensory or auditory cortex was induced to process visual information by misrouting, during development, retinal axons to somatosensory thalamus[21] or to auditory thalamus[22] (figure 12.1). In these animals, the receptive field and response properties of cells in somatosensory or auditory cortex to visual stimuli resemble those normally seen in visual cortex. The most straightforward explanation for these findings is that the primary sensory areas of the neocortex normally process sensory information relayed through the thalamus in a fundamentally similar way, implying that the basic organization of cells and connections that underlie functional properties is also similar. This interpretation is supported by the finding that some cells in the somatosensory cortex to which visual input is directed can respond both to visual and somatosensory stimuli in modality-appropriate ways.[21] An alternative explanation is that the intrinsic organizations of neocortical sensory areas are not normally similar at mature stages, but that their development can be altered by visual input. However, even this suggests that primary sensory areas arise from regions of developing neocortex that are initially similar or to some extent pluripotent.

In summary, it appears that areas of the adult neocortex are constructed with the same basic set of cells organized in a fundamentally similar way, yet, by definition, each area has distinctive features.

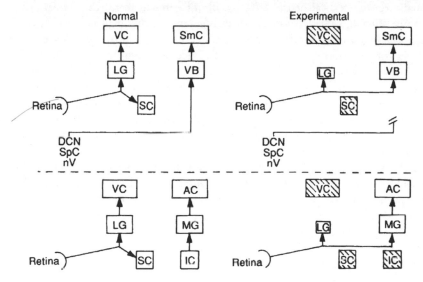

Figure 12.1 Aberrant routing of visual input into somatosensory and auditory cortex. Top left: in normal hamsters, the retina projects to the primary visual thalamic nucleus, the lateral geniculate nucleus (LG), and the superior colliculus (SC). The LG relays visual information to the visual cortex (VC). Somatosensory information is sent from the dorsal column nuclei (DCN), spinal cord (SpC) and the trigeminal nuclei (nV) to the primary somatosensory thalamic nuclei, termed the ventrobasal complex (VB), which in turn relays it to the somatosensory cortex (SmC). Top right: the retina can be induced to project to VB, by reducing its normal targets (by removing at birth the SC and the VC, which results in atrophy of the LG) and making terminal space available in the VB (by removing at birth its normal input). Under these conditions, SmC receives visual input from VB (see ref. 21). Bottom left: in normal ferrets, the retina projects to the LG and the SC. The LG projects to several visual cortical areas. The primary auditory thalamic nucleus, the medial geniculate (MG), receives auditory information from the inferior colliculus (IC), and relays it to the auditory cortex (AC). Bottom right: the retina can be induced to project to MG by a similar strategy to that described above; retinal targets are reduced (by removing the SC and visual cortical areas 17 and 18, which results in atrophy of the LG) and terminal space is made available in MG (by removing IC). Under these conditions, AC receives visual input from MG (see ref. 22). (Figure modified from figures appearing in refs 22 and 23.)

Early Events in Cortical Development

A discussion of differentiation of the areas of the neocortex should include the early stages of cortical development. Cortical neurons are generated in the neuroepithelium of the lateral ventricle. They migrate away from this site along the processes of radial glial cells and form the cortical layers in a deep-to-superficial sequence.[4,24] Previous studies have suggested that the young neurons are deposited in a radial fashion within the developing cortical plate. The first direct demonstration of this has come recently from studies in which a progenitor cell is infected with a recombinant retrovirus carrying a marker gene which allows for later identification of its progeny. Using this approach, it has been shown that clonally related cortical neurons are usually distributed in roughly radial arrays.[25,26] Occasionally, though, clonally related cells can be tangentially displaced within the cortex over distances that are substantial relative to the size of individual cortical areas.[26] These findings bear on the issue of area differentiation, since in its simplest form the concept of a specification of the neuroepithelium to give rise to specific cortical areas requires that neurons generated by a specific proliferative region remain segregated within the overlying cortical plate from neurons produced by neighboring proliferative regions.[4] A re-examination of this issue using two distinguishable viral markers that are now available[27] should allow for a firm determination of the frequency and magnitude of tangential displacements of clonally related neurons.

The findings from mouse chimera studies suggest that if the neocortical neuroepithelium does become regionally specified, specification must be a relatively late event. Neurons derived from blastula fusions of two strains of mice seem to be randomly dispersed within the mature neocortex,[28] implying that proliferative cells mix within the neocortical neuroepithelium close to the time that the first neurons become postmitotic. At these and later stages, morphological distinctions that could suggest the subdivision of the neocortical neuroepithelium into regions are not apparent,[29] while discontinuities indicative of the mosaic organization of certain other proliferative zones, for example the thalamic neuroepithelium, can be clearly discerned.[30] But any regional specification of the neocortical neuroepithelium should be revealed by a parallel expression of unique molecules in distinct patterns. Interestingly, antibodies to the peptides encoded by four proto-oncogenes (*sis-*, *src-*, *ras-*, and *myc-*), and against the intermediate filament protein vimentin, co-stain patches of radial glial cells spanning the neocortical neuroepithelium of rats,[31] whereas other antibodies to components of the neuroepithelium, D1.1[31,32] and Rat-401,[33] stain it homogeneously. Presently, this is the best evidence for a structural or molecular regionalization within the neocortical neuroepithelium. However, since the patchy pattern of peptide staining emerges from a uniformly stained neuroepithelium only at very *late* stages of neurogenesis,[31] it is not clear how such regionalization would play a role in an early specialization of the neuroepithelium.

Generation of a "Protocortex"

The developing neocortex is distinct from the adult form in notable ways. First, it contains transient structures. The earliest recognized cortical structure is a cellular layer,[34] termed the preplate, that does not persist into adulthood. The neurons that populate this layer are the first to be generated by the neocortical neuroepithelium, but die over the course of development.[35] Later generated neurons that form the cortical plate aggregate within the preplate and split it into two layers. The upper layer develops into layer 1, while the lower layer, termed the subplate, becomes part of the axon tracts underlying layer 6. Presently, it is not clear if the preplate is simply a phylogenetic remnant, or if it plays a critical role in cortical development before its demise.[36]

Additionally, the neocortex is more uniform across its extent during development than at maturity, as it lacks many of the area-specific features characteristic of the adult. For instance, the primary somatosensory cortex of adult rodents contains a one-to-one representation of the mystacial vibrissae found on the muzzle, and sinus hairs present on the head and limbs, in the form of aggregations of layer 4 neurons and thalamic afferents referred to as barrels[37] (see figure 12.2). However, barrels are not apparent as the cortex is

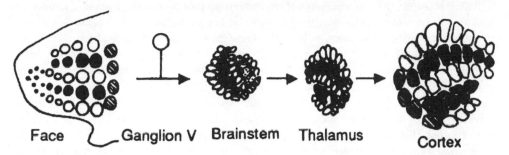

Face   Ganglion V   Brainstem   Thalamus   Cortex

Figure 12.2 Patterning of cytoarchitectural units in somatosensory cortex. The pattern of 'barrels' in the posteromedial barrel subfield of somatosensory cortex of rodents is an isomorphic representation of the geometric arrangement of mystacial vibrissae found on the animal's face. Similar patterns are present in the brainstem and thalamic nuclei that relay inputs from the face to the barrel cortex. Alterations of the pattern of mystacial vibrissae, either genetically or by removal of vibrissae follicles during a critical period of development, result in a corresponding alteration of the cortical barrel pattern. Cutting the axons of trigeminal ganglion (ganglion V) neurons (thus blocking the flow of sensory information from the periphery to the brainstem) early on prevents barrel formation (see refs 38, 69–71).

assembled, but emerge later from an initially uniform cortical plate.[38] Another example of uniformity in the developing neocortex can be taken from the development of area-specific outputs. In the adult neocortex, the unique outputs of specific areas are reflected in part by the limited distributions of types of cortical projection neurons, including those that send axons to subcortical targets such as the superior colliculus (corticotectal neurons), certain medullary nuclei and the spinal cord (pyramidal tract neurons), or through the corpus callosum to the contralateral cortex (callosal neurons). However, during development all of these classes of projection neurons are widely distributed across the neocortex (table 12.1). The restricted distributions of projection neurons in the adult, then, do not reflect regional differences in the ability of the neocortical neuroepithelium to generate general classes of cortical projection neurons.

Table 12.1 Selected reports of developmentally widespread distributions of cortical projection neurons

Type of projection neuron	Mammalian order	References
Pyramidal tract/	Rodents	39, 40, 41
Corticospinal	Marsupials	42
	Lagomorphs	43
Corticotectal	Rodents	44
Callosal (commissural)	Rodents	45, 46
	Marsupials	47
	Lagomorphs	48
	Carnivores	49, 50, 51
	Primates	52, 53

Taken together, these comparisons of the organization of developing and adult neocortex lead to a reasonable conclusion that the entire extent of the neocortical neuroepithelium is competent to generate most, if not all, of the basic classes of cortical neurons, both permanent and transient. Further, early in its development, the neocortex not only contains large, transient populations of neurons, but also lacks the architectonic divisions characteristic of area diversity in the adult neocortex. The relative uniformity of the early neocortex compared with its adult form suggests that many of the area-specific features characteristic of the adult are not predetermined within the neuroepithelium. The neocortical neuroepithelium may generate a "protocortex" from which well-defined areas gradually emerge in a manner dependent upon influences that operate after neurogenesis. If different regions of the protocortex are indeed similar and their differentiation is not rigidly predetermined, one would expect that they would be capable of considerable plasticity in their expression of area-specific features. In the following sections, this issue will be examined.

Development of Area-Specific Outputs

The set of output projections of a given neocortical area in the adult is a subset of the projections that it originally elaborates. Although just a subset is retained by a given area, these early, widespread projections are made only to specific sets of targets appropriate for the general class of projection neuron from which they arise;[54,55,57] the subset retained in the adult varies between areas. The output of a neocortical area is remodeled chiefly through the selective elimination of particular axon collaterals or long distal segments of the primary axons without a concomitant death of the projection neurons. For example, in adult rats, pyramidal tract neurons (which extend a long axon through the pyramidal tract and innervate medullary nuclei and the spinal cord) are restricted to cortical layer 5, but of sensorimotor areas only. In neonates, though, while already limited to layer 5, these neurons are distributed throughout the entire neocortex.[39,40] Pyramidal tract neurons located in regions of developing neocortex completely devoid of them in adults, such as the primary visual and auditory areas, subsequently lose their pyramidal tract axons,[39,56] but retain collateral branches to other subcortical targets appropriate for their cortical location.[57] The fate of this axon is not a fixed property of pyramidal tract neurons, but is dependent on the area location of the neuron in the developing cortex.[58,59] Thus, although the appropriate laminar position of cortical projection neurons is probably specified at or near the time they become postmitotic,[60] their adult areal distribution is achieved through a process of selective axon elimination that occurs well after the cortex is assembled.

Selective axon elimination also brings about the developmental restriction of initially widely distributed populations of callosally projecting neurons.[61–64] The stabilization or elimination of callosal axons seems to be influenced by sensory input. This is suggested by the presence of an abnormally widespread distribution of callosal neurons in visual cortical areas of adult rodents, cats and primates in which visual input to the developing cortex was altered naturally by genetics (Siamese cats)[65] or experimentally by removing or changing, in a number of ways, retinal inputs to visual thalamus.[66,67] Such findings imply that thalamocortical input, or inputs relayed through thalamus, may regulate the process of selective axon elimination, and thus the output of a given region of neocortex.

Differentiation of Area-Specific Architecture

The cytoarchitectural differentiation of a region of neocortex is not a fixed property, and is capable of considerable plasticity. To illustrate this point, we return to the barrel-field of rodents. Cortical barrels develop through an interaction with thalamic afferents that relay sensory information from the periphery. The existence of cortical barrels is the manifest-ation of a series of afferent-induced barrel-like parcellations beginning in the brainstem and passing through the thalamus to the cortex[38] (figure 12.2). A number of markers, including certain lectins, can reveal early stages of this process.[68] Manipulations of the sensory periphery, all of which modify or block sensory input through the trigeminal system, alter or even prevent barrel formation.[38,69] Somatosensory cortex is able also to reorganize and form a normal pattern of barrels following small lesions made in the barrel-field during an early postnatal critical period.[70] Perhaps the best evidence that the barrel pattern is not predetermined comes from observations made on strains of mice inbred for abnormal sets of mystacial vibrissae. In these mice, supernumerary vibrissae are represented in the cortex through the induced formation of additional barrels, but only if the anomalous vibrissa follicle is innervated by a suprathreshold number of sensory axons.[71] These observations indicate that the differentiation of barrel morphology and the unique patterning of groups of barrels are not fixed properties of somatosensory cortex, but are induced by inputs relayed to the cortex from the sensory periphery, suggesting that at least this feature of cortical cytoarchitecture is not predetermined within the neuroepithelium.

Are the Borders between Cortical Areas Fixed?

How is an extra barrel accommodated in somatosensory cortex? Does the area undergo some local or overall reorganization to allow for the space occupied by the barrel, or does the area expand its size at the expense of neighboring neocortical areas? Unfortunately, the size of an individual barrel is too small to make any firm statements. But recent findings in primates suggest that the border between primary visual cortex (area 17) and a secondary visual area (area 18) appears to be capable of a large shift with dramatic consequences on the subsequent differentiation of the affected piece of cortex.[4,67] Such a border shift seems to occur in macaque monkeys bilaterally enucleated at mid-fetal stages (see figure 12.3 legend, and reference 4 for arguments). This manipulation results in a 50 percent loss in the number of lateral geniculate neurons, the primary source of thalamic input to area 17. The total number of neurons in area 17, and its overall size, are correspondingly reduced, but the thickness and appearance of the layers are normal.[72] Features characteristic of area 17, including the unique laminar distributions of receptors for neurotransmitters and the presence of functional subunits specific to area 17, are retained within the reduced area identified as area 17 based on cytoarchitectural appearance.[4] But more importantly, a region of cortex normally contained within area 17 takes on the architectural appearance of area 18, and apparently lacks other characteristics which define area 17. Even the output of this region is altered and resembles that of area 18. A large number of callosally projecting neurons are present within area 18 up to its new border with area 17, with few or none found in the region cytoarchitecturally identified as area 17;[67] callosal neurons are rarely, if at all, encountered in area 17 of normal macaque monkeys.[53] These findings indicate that the biochemical, cytoarchitectural, and connectional differentiation of a part of neocortex

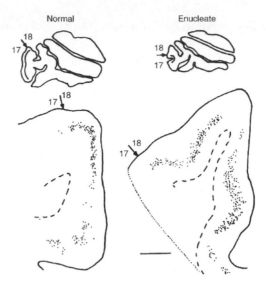

Figure 12.3 Borders between cortical areas are not fixed. A border shift between visual cortical areas 17 and 18 seems to occur in macaques bilaterally enucleated during the third month of gestation. The drawings are of sagittal sections of brains from normal (left) and bilaterally enucleated (right) newborn macaques. The top illustrations are low-power drawings to show the extent of area 17 (bold line) and the location of its border with area 18. The bottom drawings are higher power plots of callosally projecting neurons (which are normally present in area 18 but not area 17) taken from the same sections displayed above. (Figure modified from ref. 67.) In similarly enucleated macaques analysed as adults, the total number of neurons is reduced by about 50 percent within the region defined by cytoarchitecture as area 17, but the thickness and appearance of the layers, the number of neurons in a traverse across the six layers, and cell density in this region are comparable to that in area 17 of normal adults.[4,70] The reduced number of neurons cannot be attributed to fewer cells generated since the enucleations are done after neurogenesis. Further, it is unlikely that the result is a consequence of increased cell death since a selective loss of entire columns of cortical neurons has never been observed (and is highly improbable), and neuronal death distributed across all of area 17 would result in a substantial reduction of the number of neurons per column and a thinning of the cortex rather than the observed reduction in surface area. Thus, a reasonable conclusion is that a part of cortex that normally would mature into area 17 has instead developed properties characteristic of the adjacent area 18. (See ref. 4 for detailed arguments in support of a border shift.)

can be developmentally controlled by epigenetic factors. Again, a critical, regulatory role for thalamic input in this phenomenon has been suggested.[4]

Are Cortical Areas Interchangeable?

Similar conclusions can be drawn from a set of studies that indicate that the regional location of a piece of developing neocortex has a decisive influence on the subsequent acquisition of many area-specific properties. This has been demonstrated by transplanting pieces of late fetal neocortex to be heterotopic positions within the neocortex of newborn rodents. The layer 5 projections to subcortical targets permanently established by such transplants are dependent upon the transplant's position within the neocortex (figure 12.4). Visual cortical neurons transplanted to the sensorimotor region extend and permanently retain axons to the spinal cord, a subcortical target of sensorimotor cortex.[58,59] Conversely, sensorimotor cortical neurons transplanted to the visual region extend and then lose spinal

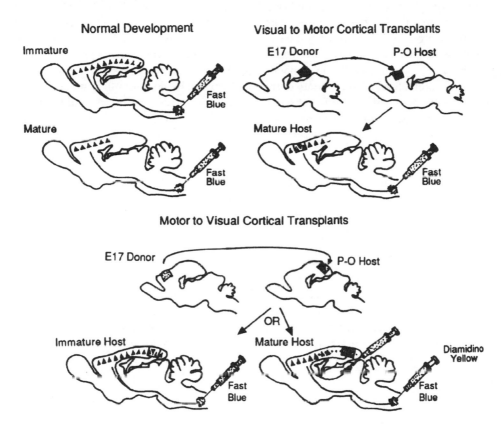

Figure 12.4 Development of area-specific outputs is not a fixed property of cortical areas. Top left: during normal development in rats, layer 5 neurons in all regions of the immature neocortex develop a pyramidal tract axon and can be labeled retrogradely with the dye Fast Blue injected into the pyramidal decussation. A similar injection made in mature rats labels layer 5 neurons confined to sensorimotor areas of cortex. The restriction from the widespread, immature distribution to the limited, mature one is achieved through a selective elimination of pyramidal tract axons without neuron loss (see ref. 39). Heterotopic transplantation of fetal cortex shows that this elimination of pyramidal tract axons is dependent upon the cortical location of developing neurons (see refs 58, 59). Top right: embryonic day 17 (E17) visual cortical neurons transplanted to the motor region of a newborn (P-O) host develop and permanently retain pyramidal tract axons as demonstrated by Fast Blue labeling from the pyramidal decussation after maturation. Bottom: motor cortical neurons transplanted to the visual region can be labeled with Fast Blue injected into the pyramidal decussation (PD) at immature stages, but not at maturity. However, in the same mature hosts, the transplanted neurons can be labeled with a second dye, Diamidino Yellow, injected into the superior colliculus, a permanent target of visual cortex but only a transient target of motor cortex. Thus, the transplants form permanent projections characteristic of their new cortical location. (Figure modified from ref. 59.)

axons, but retain a projection to a subcortical target of visual cortex, the superior colliculus.[59] The heterotopic transplants also establish callosal and thalamic connections, both input and output, appropriate for their *new* location.[59,73,74] In sum, the inputs and outputs of heterotopically transplanted neurons resemble those of the neurons normally present in that cortical location. Heterotopic transplants of neocortex can also take on the cytoarchitectural appearance of the host cortical region. For example, pieces of occipital (visual) cortex placed in the presumptive barrel-field of primary somatosensory cortex develop morphological features that resemble barrels when innervated by thalamic afferents.[75] From this observation it can be inferred that thalamic afferents are able to organize in a foreign piece of cortex, and that the transplanted cells can respond to the afferents in ways necessary to express the cytoarchitectural features appropriate to their new cortical locale. It can be concluded from this class of experiments that different regions of the protocortex are sufficiently alike that, if heterotopically placed in the developing neocortex, they will come to acquire many of the area-specific properties normally associated with their new location.

Mechanisms Involved in the Differentiation of the Protocortex

All, or most, of the epigenetically influenced developmental processes that operate throughout the developing nervous system[76] are likely to play a role in the differentiation of the protocortex. Some of these processes elaborate upon existing components. For instance, the shapes and sizes of the dendritic arbors of specific classes of neurons, which contribute to differences in cytoarchitecture, can be greatly influenced by afferent input[38] and target-derived factors.[77] Other processes, such as selective axon elimination, synapse elimination and neuronal death, which can be thought of as regressive in nature, serve to remove, in a regionally specific manner, excess of functionally inappropriate components. We have already seen that selective axon elimination contributes to the development of area-specific outputs. Synapse elimination has been reported to occur in several diverse cortical areas,[70] and is probably involved in the shaping of many cortical features. It is best documented as underlying the developmental remodeling of geniculocortical inputs to visual cortex,[79] a process driven by a relative asynchrony in activity patterns among competing sets of inputs.[80] Neuronal death is a likely contributor to the sculpting of inter-area differences in the number of neurons found in specific layers. In rodents, about 30 percent of cortical neurons die.[81] Most of this loss occurs in the superficial layers, primarily in layers 2 and 3, and to a lesser extent in layer 4.[9,81] There is evidence that the number of cells in layer 4 is governed by the density of thalamic input, and that the number of cells present in the superficial layers is determined by a combination of differential cell loss and changes in neuronal differentiation,[9,82] factors which are believed to contribute to the greater number of neurons found in a radial traverse in area 17 compared with other areas.[9] Although I have only briefly considered a few, clearly a wide range of developmental processes can act on the protocortex to establish area-specific features characteristic of the adult neocortex.

Regional Differences in the Protocortex

The processes just described contribute to the differentiation of the protocortex, but can they account for all of the differences seen between neocortical areas in the adult? Let us consider two features reported for area 17 of monkeys of the genus *Macaca*. First, in adult macaques area 17 has more than twice as many neurons in a radial traverse compared with other primary sensory areas, with the extra neurons contained in layers 4 and above.[7,8] The increased number of neurons in area 17 might reflect not only a reduced amount of cell loss, but also a regionally specific increase in neuronal production. Here it is worth recalling the patchy distribution of radial glial cells that stain in rats with antibodies to proto–oncogene peptides.[31] Within a patch, an increased proportion of neuroepithelial cells can be labeled with [^{3}H]thymidine (a marker of DNA synthesis), and the patches appear over the period that neurons which will populate the most superficial cortical layers are being generated. Although this observation can be interpreted in several ways, one intriguing possibility is that it reflects localized increases in the generation of superficial neurons.[31] Second, area 17 of macaques reportedly does not have a callosal projection even during development,[53] and in this sense is unlike area 17 in all non–primate mammals examined to date, where, as mentioned earlier, neurons throughout area 17 transiently extend callosal axons. Macaques may have evolved a higher degree of specification of the output of area 17. If true, this feature may prove to be unique for area 17, since other cortical areas in macaques, namely the secondary visual area 18[53] and primary somatosensory cortex,[52] do develop transiently widespread callosal connections. However, an argument against this possibility is the finding in macaques that parts of cortex that normally are contained within area 17 do have callosal connections following eye removal at mid–fetal stages.[67]

Nevertheless, there are likely to be differences across the protocortex, whether present as subtle gradients or as sharp discontinuities. One likely possibility would be molecular distinctions between regions, and even within regions, of the protocortex, which promote the formation of appropriate connectional relationships, for example between thalamic nuclei and cortical areas, as well as underlie the topographic ordering of the input and output connections of the neocortex. These molecules would probably be present on the surface of select subsets of cells. To date, though, cells immunoreactive for antibodies that recognize distinct neuronal surface antigens are present in all neocortical areas, whether the number stained is substantial, as for Cat-301-positive neurons,[83] or exceedingly small, as for Tor-23-positive neurons.[84] However, specific areas of limbic cortex (often termed allocortex and distinct from neocortex), do stain selectively for an antibody that recognizes a surface molecule (named limbic-associated membrane protein), both in the mature[85] and developing brain.[86] The same molecule is associated with subcortical components of the limbic system.[85] Similar markers will probably be found for neocortex.

Concluding Remarks

The neocortical neuroepithelium generates a fairly uniform structure, here termed the protocortex, that does not have the architectonic divisions present in the adult neocortex. Many of the area-specific features characteristic of well-defined cortical areas emerge from the protocortex long after the conclusion of neurogenesis through a process that can be regulated by influences, for example afferent inputs, that vary across the developing neocortex. However, differences are likely to exist from one region of the protocortex to another – differences laid down at the time of neurogenesis that contribute to the development of area-specific properties. The extent to which area-specific properties are determined at the time of neurogenesis, that is, the degree to which the neocortical neuroepithelium is regionally specified to generate the definable characteristics of specific neocortical areas,[4] is presently not resolved and may well vary from species to species. However, most studies relevant to this issue provide evidence for epigenetic regulation of area differentiation; the mere existence of cytoarchitectonically defined areas in the adult neocortex is presently the most compelling evidence for their predetermination within the neocortical neuroepithelium. The neocortex shows considerable plasticity in the development of area-specific features, but many of these findings are based on perturbation studies, and therefore such plasticity does not unequivocally demonstrate that area-specific features are not predetermined, but rather that they are not irreversibly predetermined. Nonetheless, different regions of the developing neocortex have the capability to acquire many of the area-specific characteristics normally associated with other cortical areas, indicating that there are significant similarities among these regions. These similarities may reflect a phylogenetic conservation of the ability of all parts of the neocortical neuroepithelium to generate the ensemble of basic structural components of the neocortex, thereby establishing a protocortex from which defined areas emerge.

ACKNOWLEDGMENTS

I thank B. Stanfield for valuable discussions, A. Burkhalter, J. Lichtman, B. Schlaggar, C. Shatz and T. Woolsey for their thoughtful comments on the manuscript, T. Woolsey for help with making figures 12.1 and 12.2 and the NEI, NINCDS, the McKnight Endowment Fund for Neuroscience and the Sloan Foundation for support.

REFERENCES

1   Brodmann, K. (1909). *Lokalisationslehre der Groshirnrinde in ihren Pricipen dargestellt aus Grund des Zellenbaue*, Barth.
2   Krieg, W. J. S. (1946). *F. Comp. Neurol.* 84, 221–75.
3   Van Essen, D. C. (1985). in *Cerebral Cortex, Vol. 3: Visual Cortex* (Peters, A. and Jones, E. G., eds.), pp. 259–330, Plenum.
4   Rakic, P. (1988). *Science* 241, 170–6.
5   Gilbert, C. D. (1983). *Annu. Rev. Neurosci.* 6, 217–48.
6   Jones, E. G. (1984). in *Cerebral Cortex, Vol. 1: Cellular Components of the Cerebral Cortex* (Peters, A. and Jones, E. G. eds.), pp. 521–53, Plenum.
7   Rockel, A. J., Hiorns, R. W., and Powell, T. P. S. (1980). *Brain* 103, 221–44.
8   Hendry, S. H. C., Schwark, H. D., Jones, E. G., and Yan, J. (1987). *F. Neurosci.* 4, 2497–517.
9   Finlay, B. L. and Slattery, M. (1983). *Science* 219, 1349–51.
10 Winfield, D. A., Gatter, K. C., and Powell, T. P. S. (1980). *Brain* 103, 245–58.
11 Sofroniew, M. V., Campbell, P. E., Cuello, A. C., and Eckenstein, F. (1985). in *The Rat Nervous System, Vol. 1: Forebrain and Midbrain* (Paxinos, G., ed.), pp. 471–86, Academic Press.
12 Fuxe, K., Hokfelt, T., Said, S. I., and Mutt, V. (1979). *Neurosci. Lett.* 5, 241–6.
13 Hendry, S. H. C., Jones, E. G., and Emson, P. C. (1984). *F. Neurosci.* 4, 2497–517.
14 Peters, A., Miller, M., and Kimerer, L. M. (1983). *Neuroscience* 8, 431–48.
15 Morrison, J. H., Benoit, P. J., Magistretti, P. J., and Bloom, F. E. (1983). *Brain Res.* 262, 344–51.
16 Lorente de No, R. (1949). in *Physiology of the Nervous System* (Fulton, J. F., ed.), pp. 288–315, Oxford University Press.
17 Creutzfeld, O. D. (1977). *Naturwissenschaft* 64, 507–17.

18 Mountcastle, V. B. (1978). in *The Mindful Brain* (Mountcastle, V. B. and Edelman, G. M., eds.), pp. 7–50, MIT.

19 Powell, T. P. S. (1981). in *Brain Mechanisms and Perceptual Awareness* (Pompeiano, O. and Ajmone Marsan, C., eds.), pp. 1–19, Raven.

20 Eccles, J. C. (1984). in *Cerebral Cortex, Vol. 2: Functional Properties of Cortical Cells* (Jones, E. G. and Peters, A., eds.), pp. 1–36, Plenum.

21 Metin, C. and Frost, D. O. (1989). *Proc. Natl Acad. Sci. USA* 86, 357–61.

22 Sur, M., Garraghty, P. E., and Roe, A. W. (1988). *Science* 242, 1437–41.

23 Frost, D. O. (1981). *J. Comp. Neurol.* 203, 227–56.

24 Rakic, P. (1974). *Science* 183, 425–7.

25 Luskin, M. B., Pearlman, A. L., and Sanes, J. R. (1988). *Neuron* 1, 635–47.

26 Walsh, C. and Cepko, C. L. (1988). *Science* 241, 1342–5.

27 Galileo, D. S., Gray, G. E., Owens, G. C., Majors, J., and Sanes, J. R. *Soc. Neurosci. Abstr.* (in press).

28 Goldwitz, D. (1987). *Dev. Brain Res.* 35, 1–9.

29 Smart, I. H. M. and Sturrock, R. R. (1979). in *The Neostriatum* (Divac, I. and Oberg, R. G. E., eds.), pp. 127–46, Pergamon.

30 Altman, J. and Bayer, S. A. (1988). *J. Comp. Neurol.* 275, 346–77.

31 Johnson, J. G. and Van Der Kooy, D. (1989). *Proc. Natl Acad. Sci. USA* 86, 1066–70.

32 Levine, J. M., Beasley, L., and Stallcup, W. B. (1984). *J. Neurosci.* 4, 820–31.

33 Frederikson, K. and McKay, R. D. G. (1988). *J. Neurosci.* 8, 1144–51.

34 Marin-Padilla, M. (1978). *Anat. Embryol.* 152, 109–26.

35 Luskin, M. B. and Shatz, C. J. (1985). *J. Neurosci.* 5, 1062–75.

36 Shatz, C. J., Chun, J. J. M., and Luskin, M. B. in *Cerebral Cortex, Vol. 7* (Jones, E. G. and Peters, A., eds.), Plenum (in press).

37 Woolsey, T. A. and Van Der Loos, H. (1970). *Brain Res.* 17, 205–42.

38 Woolsey, T. A. in *Development of Sensory Systems in Mammals* (Coleman, J. R., ed.), Wiley (in press).

39 Stanfield, B. B., O'Leary, D. D. M., and Fricks, C. (1982). *Nature* 298, 371–3.

40 Bates, C. A. and Killackey, H. P. (1984). *Dev. Brain Res.* 13, 265–73.

41 O'Leary, D. D. M. and Stanfield, B. B. (1986). *Dev. Brain Res.* 27, 87–99.

42 Cabana, T. and Martin, G. F. (1984). *Dev. Brain Res.* 15, 247–63.

43 Distel, H. and Hollander, H. (1980). *J. Comp. Neurol.* 192, 505–18.

44 Thong, I. G. and Dreher, B. (1986). *Dev. Brain Res.* 25, 227–38.

45 Ivy, G. O. and Killackey, H. P. (1981). *J. Comp. Neurol.* 195, 367–89.

46 Olavarria, J. and Van Sluyters, R. C. (1985). *J. Comp. Neurol.* 239, 1–26.

47 Cabana, T. and Martin, G. F. (1985). *Anat. Embryol.* 17, 121–8.

48 Chow, K. K., Baumbach, H. D., and Lawson, R. (1981). *Exp. Brain Res.* 42, 122–6.

49 Innocenti, G. M., Fiore, L., and Caminiti, R. (1977). *Neurosci. Lett.* 4, 237–42.

50 Innocenti, G. M. and Caminiti, R. (1980). *Exp. Brain Res.* 38, 824–7.

51 Feng, J. Z. and Brugge, J. F. (1983). *J. Comp. Neurol.* 214, 416–26.

52 Killackey, H. P. and Chalupa, L. M. (1986). *J. Comp. Neurol.* 244, 331–48.

53 Dehay, C., Kennedy, H., Bullier, J., and Berland, M. (1988). *Nature* 331, 348–59.

54 O'Leary, D. D. M. and Terashima, T. *Soc. Neurosci. Abstr.* (in press).

55 Koester, S. E. and O'Leary, D. D. M. *Soc. Neurosci. Abstr.* (in press).

56 O'Leary, D. D. M. and Terashima, T. (1988). *Neuron* 1, 901–10.

57 O'Leary, D. D. M. and Stanfield, B. B. (1985). *Brain Res.* 336, 326–33.

58 Standfield, B. B. and O'Leary, D. D. M. (1985). *Nature* 313, 135–7.

59 O'Leary, D. D. M. and Stanfield, B. B. (1989). *J. Neurosci.* 9, 2230–46.

60 McConnell, S. K. (1988). *J. Neurosci.* 8, 945–74.

61 Innocenti, G. M. (1981). *Science* 212, 824–7.

62 O'Leary, D. D. M., Stanfield, B. B., and Cowan, M. W. (1981). *Dev. Brain Res.* 1, 607–17.

63 Ivy, G. O. and Killackey, H. P. (1982). *J. Neurosci.* 6, 735–43.

64 Chalupa, L. M. and Killackey, H. P. (1989). *Proc. Natl Acad. Sci. USA* 86, 1076–9.

65 Shatz, C. J. (1977). *J. Comp. Neurol.* 173, 497–518.

66 Innocenti, G. M. (1985). in *Cerebral Cortex, Vol. 5: Sensory-motor Areas and Aspects of Cortical Connectivity* (Jones, E. G. and Peters, A., eds.), pp. 291–353, Plenum.

67 Dehay, C., Horsburgh, G., Berland, M., Killackey, H., and Kennedy, H. (1989). *Nature* 337, 265–7.

68 Cooper, N. G. F. and Steindler, D. A. (1986). *J. Comp. Neurol.* 249, 157–86.

69 Van der Loos, H. and Welker, E. (1985). in *Development, Organization, and Processing in Somatosensory Pathways*, pp. 53–67, Alan R. Liss.

70 Seo, M. L. and Ito, M. (1987). *Exp. Brain Res.* 65, 251–60.

71 Welker, E. and van der Loos, H. (1986). *J. Neurosci.* 6, 3355–73.

72 Rakic, P. and Williams, R. W. (1986). *Soc. Neurosci. Abstr.* 12, 1499.

73 Chang, F. L. F., Steedman, J. G., and Lund, R. D. (1986). *J. Comp. Neurol.* 244, 401–11.

74 O'Leary, D. D. M. (1988). *Soc. Neurosci. Abstr.* 14, 1113.

75 Schlaggar, B. L. and O'Leary, D. D. M. (1988). *Soc. Neurosci. Abstr.* 14, 475.

76 Purves, D. and Lichtman, J. W. (1985). *Principles of Neural Development Sinauer.*

77 Voyvodic, J. T. (1989). *J. Neurosci* 9, 1997–2010.

78 Rakic, P., Bourgeois, J. P., Eckenhoff, M. F., Zecevic, N., and Goldman-Rakic, P. S. (1986). *Science* 232, 232–5.

79 LeVay, S., Wiesel, T. N., and Hubel, D. H. (1981). in *The Organization of the Cerebral Cortex*, pp. 29–45, MIT.

80 Stryker, M. P. and Harris, W. A. (1986). *J. Neurosci.* 6, 2117–33.

81 Huemann, D., Lueba, G., and Rabinowicz, G. (1978). *J. Hirnforsch.* 19, 385–93.

82 Windrem, M. S., Jan de Beur, S. M., and Finlay, B. L. (1986). *Soc. Neurosci. Abstr.* 12, 867.

83 Hendry, S. H. C., Jones, E. G., Hockfield, S., and McKay, R. D. G. (1988). *J. Neurosci.* 8, 518–42.

84 Stephenson, D. T. and Kushner, P. D. (1988). *J. Neurosci.* 8, 3035–56.

85 Levitt, P. (1984). *Science* 223, 299–301.

86 Horton, H. L. and Levitt, P. (1988). *J. Neurosci.* 8, 4653–61.

13

Emergence of Order in Visual System Development

Carla J. Shatz

The formation of precise connectivity is generally thought to involve two distinct sets of mechanisms: those that require neuronal activity and those that are activity independent (reviewed in ref. 1). Many studies in both vertebrates and invertebrates suggest that the early events of axon outgrowth, pathfinding, and target selection are relatively accurate and do not require action potentials and synaptic transmission. These studies have shown that axon growth cones can select correct pathways and targets by responding to a variety of specific molecular cues laid out on cell surfaces, in the extracellular matrix, or even diffusing from distant sources. Once axons invade their targets, however, the initial connections they make with individual target neurons frequently are not accurate. Rather, the process of forming the adult precision of connectivity involves the correction of many initial errors; this process of error correction almost always requires neural activity.

Here, I wish to consider how neural activity contributes to the emergence of the adult pattern of precise connectivity in the mammalian visual system. In the adult visual system, information about the world is sent from the eye to more central visual structures via the output neurons of the retina, the ganglion cells (2). Axons of the retinal ganglion cells project to several visual relay structures within the brain, such as the lateral geniculate nucleus (LGN). The connections between ganglion cells and LGN neurons are precise and stereotyped. One important example of this precision is that the connections are topographically organized; neighboring retinal ganglion cells send their axons to contact the same or nearby target neurons within the LGN, setting up a retinotopic map. In addition, within the LGN, retinal ganglion cell axons from one eye are strictly segregated from those arising from the other eye to form a series of alternating eye-specific layers. There are several pairs of LGN layers because each pair receives inputs from a subset of functionally distinct retinal ganglion cells (reviewed in ref. 3).

LGN Layers Are Not Present Initially in Development

How is the segregated pattern of eye input from ganglion cells to the LGN wired up during development? Many lines of experiments now indicate that when connections between retinal ganglion cells and LGN neurons first form they are not as precise as in the adult. Intraocular injections of anterograde tracers (4–6) or filling of individual ganglion cell axons with horseradish peroxidase (HRP) (7) reveal that the eye-specific layers are not present initially; ganglion cell axons from the two eyes are intermixed with each other throughout a large portion of the LGN (figure 13.1). With ensuing development, the layers emerge as axons gradually remodel their branches by retracting sidebranches from inappropriate LGN regions and growing extensive terminal arbors within the region appropriate to their eye of origin.

The presence of extensive intermixing of retinogeniculate axons, followed by segregation into layers, suggests that the process by which segregation is achieved may involve competitive interactions between ganglion cell axons from the two eyes. Such interactions might permit right and left-eye axons to compete for LGN neurons that themselves are not intrinsically different from each other with respect to eye of origin. Some of the first evidence in favor of the idea that competitive interactions between retinal ganglion cell axons give rise to the eye-specific layers has come from studies in many species in which one eye is removed during development and the pattern of the retinogeniculate projection from the remaining eye is examined at later developmental times or in adulthood. The results are generally consistent in showing that axons from the remaining eye are capable of occupying the entire LGN, including territory that normally would have been innervated by the enucleated eye (refs. 8 and 9; see ref. 10 for review and ref. 11 for a possible exception). These observations indicate that inputs from both eyes are necessary for segregation to occur, and they suggest that LGN neurons themselves are not rigidly specified with respect to the ocular identity of their retinal innervation.

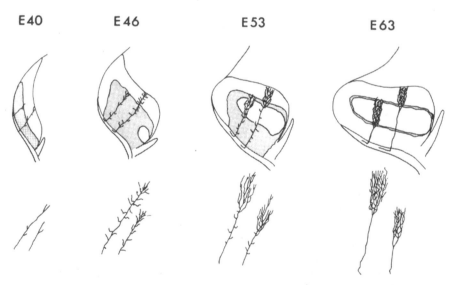

E 40   E 46   E 53   E 63

Figure 13.1 The relationship between the changes in the global pattern of the retinogeniculate projection and the development of individual retinogeniculate axons is summarized. Shaded areas indicate regions within the LGN simultaneously occupied by ganglion cell axons from the two eyes. Stick figures show the appearance of representative axons from the ipsilateral (shorter axon) and contralateral eyes at each age, based on their appearance by using the *in vitro* HRP-filling technique. By embryonic day 63 (E63), just before birth, the eye-specific layers are almost completely formed: axons from the contralateral eye have terminal arbors largely restricted to LGN layer A (top layer), while those from the ipsilateral eye are largely restricted to layer A1 (middle layer). (Modified from ref. 7.)

Studies, both of the mammalian visual system and elsewhere in the central and peripheral nervous systems, suggest that the transformation from a mixed to a segregated state occurs during a period in which the axonal inputs destined to segregate from each other are first capable of forming functioning synaptic connections with common postsynaptic target cells (for reviews see refs. 12–16). This evidence has generated the current hypothesis, considered below, that segregation is achieved via an activity-mediated competitive process requiring the formation and elimination of synaptic connections.

In the developing retinogeniculate pathway, the cellular machinery necessary to sustain activity-driven synaptic competition is present. Ultrastructural examination of identified retinogeniculate axons has demonstrated directly that ganglion cell axons from each eye form many synapses, both in territory ultimately destined to become innervated by that eye and also in the territory that will come to belong to the other eye (17). Not only are synapses present during the fetal period, but they are also capable of functional transmission (ref. 18; see also below). By electrically stimulating the optic nerves and recording from LGN neurons with extracellular microelectrodes *in vitro*, we found that even before the onset of segregation there is functional synaptic transmission. Moreover, during the period of extensive anatomical intermixing (E40–E59 in cat), about 90 percent of the LGN neurons studied physiologically received convergent excitatory inputs from stimulation of both optic nerves. In contrast, in the adult, the vast majority of LGN neurons receive excitatory input from only one nerve. The most reasonable interpretation of these observations, particularly in the context of the anatomical experiments considered above, is that prior to the completion of segregation many LGN neurons indeed receive monosynaptic excitation from both nerves. The emergence of the eye-specific layers is then accompanied by a functional change in the synaptic physiology of the retinogeniculate pathway: from binocular to monocular excitation.

Action-Potential Activity Is Required for the Formation of the Eye-Specific Layers

It is important to note that in every mammalian species studied so far the eye-specific layers form during a period in which vision is not possible: the photoreceptor outer segments are not yet present or functional (19, 20). Therefore, unlike other developing systems, such as the neuromuscular junction or the primary visual cortex, in which action potentials are evoked via use-dependent activity, here, it is necessary to postulate that activity is present as spontaneously generated action potentials. Elegant experiments by Galli and Maffei (21) indicate that this is indeed the case. They made extracellular microelectrode recordings from fetal rat retinal ganglion cells *in vivo* and demonstrated that ganglion cells indeed can fire spontaneously. The nature of this spontaneous activity and whether it is relayed to the LGN neurons will be considered more fully below.

There are now several excellent examples in which activity-dependent competition is known to be required for the final patterning of axonal connections in the vertebrate visual system. These include the postnatal development of the system of ocular dominance columns in layer 4 of the visual cortex (14, 22–24) and the experimentally induced formation of eye-specific stripes in the optic tecta of frogs (25, 26) and goldfish (27, 28). In each instance, blocking retinal ganglion cell activity [by means of injections of tetrodotoxin (TTX), a blocker of voltage dependent sodium channels] or blocking synaptic transmission (by the use of glutamate receptor blockers such as 2-amino-5-phosphonovaleric acid) prevents segregation of eye input (reviewed in refs. 15 and 16). By analogy with these examples, it should be possible to prevent or at least delay retinogeniculate segregation by blocking retinogeniculate transmission. Blockade was achieved by implanting osmotic minipumps *in utero* in cat fetuses and infusing TTX intracranially for the 2-week period during which the eye-specific layers largely form (between E42 and E56; figure 13.1). Infusions of TTX (but not vehicle) prevented the segregation of ganglion cell axons into layers (29). Moreover, as shown in figure 13.2, the axons were not simply stunted or arrested in their growth, but, rather, they grew extensively and, in fact, were about 35 percent larger in total linear extent than were untreated axons (30).

These observations indicate that TTX can affect the development of two basic features of ganglion cell arbor morphology: the shape of the axon (normally restricted to a cylindrical terminal arbor) and its location (normally within a single eye-specific layer). One possible explanation for how TTX has exerted its effect is that it has acted in a nonspecific manner to deregulate the growth state of retinal ganglion cells, a possibility

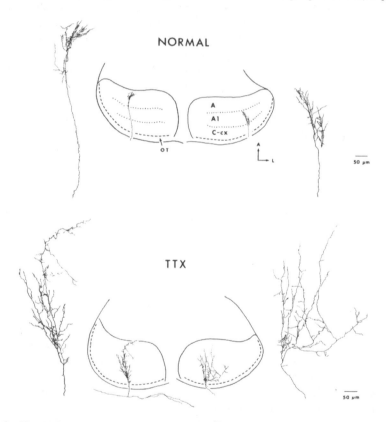

Figure 13.2   Examples of the terminal arborizations of retinogeniculate axons at E58 in normal animals *(upper)* and in animals that received minipump infusion of TTX between E42 and E58 *(lower)*. In both cases, axons were labeled by using the *in vitro* HRP-filling technique. In the normal case, axons from the contralateral *(left)* and ipsilateral *(right)* eyes are shown, and their restricted arborization within the appropriate LGN layer (either layer A or layer A1) is indicated *(center)*. With TTX treatment, axons branch extensively and indiscriminately within the LGN without regard for (implied) laminar borders. [Reproduced with permission from ref. 30 (copyright 1988 Macmillan Magazines Limited).]

suggested by studies showing that action potentials can have an inhibitory effect on axonal growth *in vitro* (31, 32). However, the effect cannot be entirely nonspecific since ganglion cell axons come to an abrupt halt at the LGN border, indicating that they can still respond to many cues even in the presence of TTX. In the context of all the evidence presented above, the most reasonable explanation for the alteration in axon arbor morphology following TTX treatment is that it has acted to block spontaneously generated action potentials and synaptic transmission, which in turn are required for the formation of the normal specific patterns of axonal arborization. It is as if, in the absence of activity, the normal elimination of side branches fails to occur, and, instead, each side branch continues to elongate to form a significant portion of the terminal arbor. If so, then the conservative remodeling of axon arbors seen during normal retinogeniculate development is unlikely to reflect a highly prespecified intrinsic program of axonal growth. Rather, such economical growth is more likely due to the presence of intense competitive interactions that are activity dependent.

The Spontaneous Firing of Neighboring Retinal Ganglion Cells Is Correlated

How can the firing of retinal ganglion cells give rise to a segregated pattern of eye input within the LGN? Action potentials by themselves are not sufficient. It is the precise temporal and spatial patterning of neural activity, in conjunction with the presence of special kinds of synapses, that are necessary (14, 33, 34). For example, Stryker and Strickland (35) have shown that if all of the axons in the optic nerves from both eyes are electrically stimulated synchronously during the postnatal period in which the ocular dominance columns normally form in layer 4 of primary visual cortex, segregation of the LGN axons representing the two eyes is prevented, just as occurred with TTX. In contrast, if the two nerves are stimulated asynchronously, such that ganglion cell axons in one nerve never fire at the same time as those in the other nerve, then segregation to form the columns in layer 4 proceeds. This important experiment illustrates the fact that "cells that fire together wire together," in the sense that the timing of action potential activity is critical in determining which synaptic connections between LGN neurons and layer 4 cortical neurons are retained and strengthened and which are weakened and eliminated. (Note that at the postnatal age that these experiments were performed, retinal ganglion cell axons have already segregated to form the eye-specific layers in the LGN and the stimulation does not affect the LGN layers.) Similarly, Eisele and Schmidt (36) demonstrated that strobe rearing (in which the activity of all ganglion cells becomes correlated due to the visual stimulus), like TTX, blocks the sharpening of the regenerating retinotectal projection in goldfish. Although in these particular experiments all of the ganglion cells in one eye are experimentally made to fire simultaneously, under normal circumstances, vision itself acts naturally to correlate the activity of neighboring ganglion cells since they receive inputs from the same or immediately adjacent parts of the visual world. Thus, these required correlations are normally generated as a consequence of visual experience.

What about earlier in development, when ganglion cell axons segregate into the layers within the LGN but the photoreceptors are not present? Even without vision, somehow neighboring ganglion cells within each eye ought to fire in near synchrony with each other, while the firing of cells in the two eyes should be asynchronous. To search for spatiotemporal patterns of spontaneous firing within the retina, it is necessary to monitor simultaneously the action potential activity of many ganglion cells in the developing retina during the early times when the eye-specific layers are forming. Two recent technical advances have made it possible to record simultaneously from many ganglion cells in the developing retina: multielectrode recording and optical recording. In these experiments, we studied ferret retinas because, as in other mammalian retinas, ferret ganglion cell axons sort to form the eye-specific layers prior to vision (5, 37, 38). The ferret, however, has the advantage of being born in a very immature state, almost a month before the cat, thereby obviating the need for fetal surgery.

By placing neonatal ferret retinas onto a special 61-electrode array (39) *in vitro*, we were able to record extracellularly the spontaneously generated action potentials from up to 100 cells simultaneously (40, 41). In confirmation of the *in vivo* recordings of Galli and Maffei (21), each cell on the multielectrode array fired in a very stereotyped and rhythmic pattern: high-frequency bursts of action potentials lasting several seconds, followed by long silent pauses lasting 0.5–2 min in duration. The biggest surprise came when the spatiotemporal firing patterns on the array were analyzed. First, we discovered that almost all of the cells on the array fired action potentials within about 5 s of each other and then paused together for up to 2 min before firing again. This observation showed that the activity of ganglion cells is indeed correlated. Further analysis demonstrated that the activity of neighboring cells on the array is more highly correlated than that of distant cells. Even more remarkable, as shown in figure 13.3, the spatial pattern of firing resembled a wave of activity that sweeps across the retina at about 200 μm/s. Each "wave" is followed by a silent period lasting up to 2 min, after which another wave is generated but in a completely different and apparently random direction. Finally, we found that these spontaneously generated retinal waves are present throughout the period when eye-specific layers form in the ferret between P1 and P21, but they then disappear by P30, just before eye-opening and the onset of visual function.

From an engineering standpoint, these waves seem beautifully designed to provide the postulated local correlations in the firing of nearby ganglion cells while also ensuring a

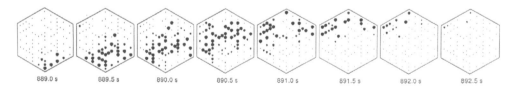

889.0 s	889.5 s	890.0 s	890.5 s	891.0 s	891.5 s	892.0 s	892.5 s

Figure 13.3   The pattern of spike activity over the multielectrode recording array is plotted for eight successive intervals during one burst of ganglion cell firings covering the time interval from 889 s to 893 s during the recording session. Each frame shows the averaged firing rate during an 0.5-s interval. Each of 82 neurons is represented with a small dot at its approximate spatial location on the electrode array. The dot area for each cell is proportional to its average firing rate during the relevant 0.5-s interval: the larger the diameter, the higher the average firing rate. During this recording, ganglion cells located in the lower right hand corner of the array commenced firing together at the beginning of a burst (889.0 s), and then activity progressed in a wave-like fashion across the array so that at the end of the burst period (892.5 s), ganglion cells at the upper left hand edge of the array were active. Recordings are from a postnatal day 5 (P5) ferret retina. [Reproduced with permission from ref. 40 (copyright 1991 American Association for the Advancement of Science).]

sufficient time delay so that the firing of more distant cells, also correlated with each other, is not synchronized across the entire retina. Such a pattern of firing could help to refine the topographic map conveyed by ganglion cell axons to each eye-specific layer in the LGN. Moreover, the fact that wave direction appears to be entirely random during each successive burst implies that ganglion cells in corresponding locations in the two retinas are highly unlikely ever to fire synchronously – a requirement for eye-specific layers to form. Thus, even before the onset of vision, the retina spontaneously generates stereotyped patterns of correlated firing that are entirely appropriate to subserve the process of activity-dependent sorting of connections. Experiments aimed at disrupting the waves are now needed to demonstrate that they are required for the formation of the layers in the LGN.

These observations naturally raise the question of what neural substrate is responsible for generating the observed correlations in the firing of retinal ganglion cells? During the period when the waves are present, the outer retina, including photoreceptors and bipolar cells, is very immature (37). The principal synaptic inputs to retinal ganglion cells at these ages appear to be from the amacrine cells (42, 43), suggesting that they too might participate in a circuit that generates correlations in firing. Another possibility is that nonsynaptic mechanisms, such as the release of a diffusible, excitatory substance – e.g., potassium, an excitatory amino acid, etc. – might contribute. And finally, the coupling of neuronal firing via gap junctions, known to be present between subsets of ganglion cells and amacrine cells in the adult mammalian retina (44), could also occur.

We have begun to investigate some of these possibilities by pursuing two separate lines of experiments. First, using optical recording techniques that permit dynamic changes in intracellular calcium to be monitored, we have found that not only ganglion cells but also retinal interneurons – most likely amacrine cells based on their size and location – undergo spontaneous calcium bursting that is correlated among many near neighbors (figure 13.4; ref. 45). Recent whole-cell recordings from ganglion cells in the neonate combined with calcium imaging also indicate that the ganglion cells receive a barrage of excitatory postsynaptic currents (EPSCs) during each wave (46). Second, intracellular injections of neurobiotin, an agent known to cross gap junctions, reveals tracer coupling between retinal ganglion cells and amacrine cells from P1 onwards in ferret retinas (47). Neurobiotin coupling at the earliest ages is rare, but it becomes quite extensive by the third postnatal week. Taken together, these results imply that an early tangential network of amacrine cells and ganglion cells may act together to generate the synchronized patterns of spontaneous activity in the developing retina.

Retinogeniculate Synapses Can Undergo Activity-Dependent Strengthening

A major issue raised from the experiments described above is whether the correlations in the firing of neighboring ganglion cells can be detected and used within the LGN to cause strengthening of appropriate synapses and weakening of inappropriate ones. Two lines of preliminary experiments suggest that this is likely to be the case. To address the question of whether the bursts of action potentials generated by retinal ganglion cells are relayed to LGN neurons, an obvious experiment would be to record from the LGN neurons *in vivo* at the appropriate ages and see if they are driven to spike by the retinal inputs; however, the spontaneously generated retinal activity is sensitive to anesthetics (R. O. L. Wong, D. A. Baylor, M. Meister, and C. J. S., unpublished results). To circumvent this problem, my

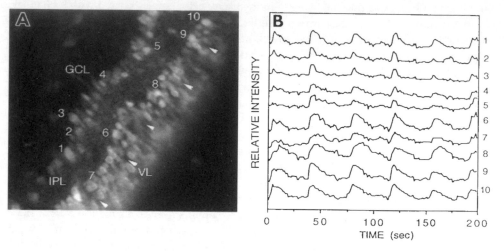

Figure 13.4   Both ganglion cells and amacrine cells show correlated calcium oscillations. *(A)* Cross-sectional view of a P10 retina showing spontaneous activity both in the ganglion cell layer (GCL, cells 1–5) and in the forming amacrine cell layer (cells 6–10). Spontaneously active cells are shown in red, whereas inactive ones are coded in blue. IPL, inner plexiform layer; VL, ventricular layer. *(B)* Recordings of the spontaneous fluctuations in intracellular calcium of the 10 cells marked in *A*. (Bar = 10 *μm*.) [Reproduced with permission from ref. 45 (copyright 1995 Macmillan Magazines Limited).]

colleagues R. Mooney, A. A. Penn, and R. Gallego and I developed a preparation in which the entire visual pathway from retina to LGN is dissected intact and placed *in vitra*. Extracellular microelectrode recordings from the optic nerves or LGN (figure 13.5) indicate that the retinal ganglion cells not only are active and generate bursts of action potentials with a period similar to that observed *in viva*, but also that LGN neurons are driven to fire spikes (48). Thus, it is highly likely that the retinal waves are relayed across the synapse to LGN neurons during the period in which the eye-specific layers form. As mentioned above, for an activity-dependent mechanism to operate in the formation of the eye-specific layers, there must be special synaptic mechanisms at the retinogeniculate synapse to strengthen connections when action potentials from different presynaptic inputs arrive within near synchrony of each other and also to weaken them if cells fire asynchronously. Many years ago, Hebb (49) proposed the existence of synapses that could undergo strengthening whenever activity in a pre-synaptic cell occurred simultaneously with that in the postsynaptic cell. Such "Hebb synapses" have the property that if many inputs coincide in activating a cell, then they all undergo strengthening. Clear evidence showing that synapses with this special property actually exist in the central nervous system comes from studies of the hippocampus and the phenomenon of long-term potentiation, in which the pairing of pre- and postsynaptic activity can cause increases in the strength of synaptic transmission specifically between the paired cells that can last from hours to days (reviewed in refs. 50 and 51). Hebb synapses are almost certainly also present in the visual cortex during the postnatal period in which ocular dominance columns form, although their properties are less well understood than those in the hippocampus (52–55).

    Can the synapses established between retinal ganglion cells and LGN neurons undergo activity-dependent changes at the relevant developmental ages? To examine this question,

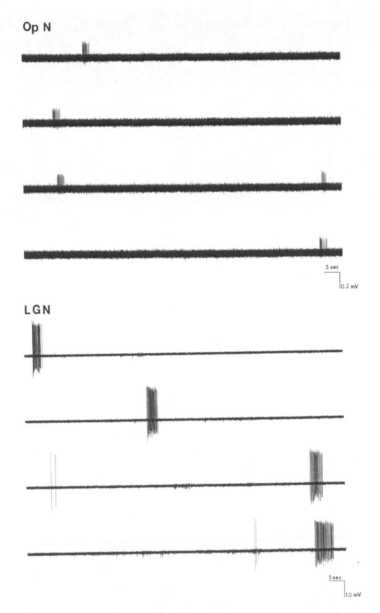

Figure 13.5 Examples of extracellular microelectrode recordings from a single axon in the optic nerve (Op N) *(Upper)* or from a single postsynaptic neuron in the LGN *(Lower)* of a neonatal mouse brain preparation consisting of the retinas, Op Ns, and LGNs dissected and maintained *in vitro*. Spontaneously generated bursts of action potentials in both Op N and LGN neuron occur about once per minute. Note different voltage scales in the two examples. (Data are from A. A. Penn, R. Gallego, R. Mooney, and C.J.S.)

we prepared slices of the LGN from ferrets between P1 and P21 and made whole-cell voltage clamp recordings *in vitro* to monitor the efficacy of synaptic transmission (56). Ganglion cell axons were stimulated by inserting electrodes into the optic tract, just

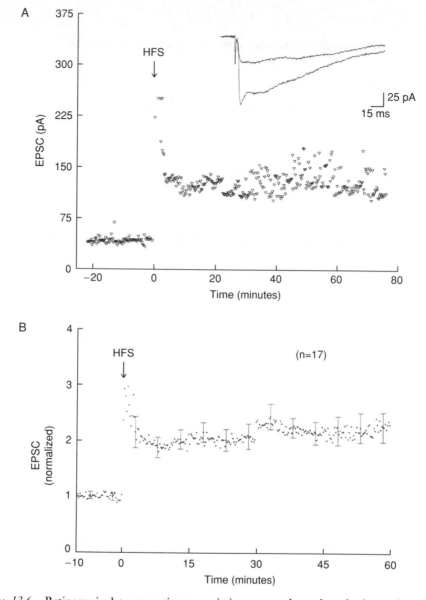

Figure 13.6 Retinogeniculate synaptic transmission can undergo long-lasting enhancement. *(A)* Example from an LGN slice from a P21 ferret. At the beginning of the recording, single shocks delivered to the optic nerve evoked monosynaptic EPSCs in the LGN neuron. Following several bursts of high-frequency stimulation (HFS) of the optic tract, a long-term increase in the amplitude of the evoked EPSC that lasted for up to 80 min resulted. Recordings were made in the presence of picrotoxin. EPSCs were recorded with perforated-patch, whole-cell techniques. Superimposed EPSCs shown at the top of the figure were evoked before and 60 min after HFS. *(B)* Ensemble average of 17 positive cases of synaptic enhancement observed in LGN slices from P6–P21 ferrets. For each case the amplitude of the EPSC at each point was normalized to the average of 40 traces immediately preceding the test stimulus. [Reproduced with permission from ref. 56 (copyright 1993 Cell Press).]

adjacent to the LGN in the slice. Three to six bursts of high frequency stimulation of the optic tract caused a significant enhancement of retinogeniculate synaptic transmission that lasted for several tens of minutes to an hour in about 40 percent of all the cells recorded. Examples of such enhancement of transmission, recorded from ferret LGN slices, are shown in figure 13.6. In some instances, we could also prevent this increase by using 2-amino-5-phosphonovaleric acid to block N-methyl-D-aspartate (NMDA) receptors, known to be present in LGN neurons at this age (56–58). Blockade of NMDA receptors *in vivo* between P14 and P21 is also known to prevent the final refinement of retinal ganglion cell axons into sub-layers receiving input from on-center or off-center ganglion cells (38). Thus, these observations suggest that the activity-dependent synaptic enhancement observed *in vitra* could indeed represent a cellular mechanism underlying the process of segregation of ganglion cell axons within the LGN.

In some ways these experiments have raised more questions than they have answered. Is the stereotyped bursting pattern of firing of retinal ganglion cells the most effective pattern for evoking synaptic enhancement? What are the long-term consequences of enhancement of synaptic transmission – e.g., does it result in morphological change? To what extent is the cellular mechanism underlying synaptic strengthening during development similar to that known to occur in the hippocampus during long-term potentiation (59)? And finally, is there a process of activity-dependent weakening of synaptic transmission since, as discussed above, some of the synaptic contacts between retinal ganglion cells and LGN neurons that are present early on are ultimately eliminated.

Concluding Remarks

The development of retinogeniculate connections in mammals is one of many examples in which the adult pattern of connections is not established initially but rather is sculpted from an immature pattern. Here, I have put forward the argument that the formation of the adult pattern of the eye-specific layers in the mammalian LGN requires activity-driven competitive interactions between ganglion cell axons from the two eyes for common postsynaptic neurons. Of course, this cannot be the whole story since the layers always form in the same pattern and since there is also a segregation of subtypes of functionally distinct retinal ganglion cell axons within different layers and from each other even within the same layer. Just how many of these other important details of LGN organization may be accounted for by timing differences in the generation of different classes of retinal ganglion cells (60), by competitive interactions between ganglion cells within the same eye (61), or by specific molecular differences between cells remain to be determined. Nevertheless, the implication that activity-driven competition plays an essential role in wiring of the visual system even before vision raises the possibility that spontaneous neural activity may shape connections elsewhere in the nervous system during fetal development.

The requirement for neuronal activity in producing the adult precision of connections is a genetically conservative means of achieving a high degree of precision in wiring. To specify precisely each neural connection between retina and LGN by using specific molecular markers would require an extraordinary number of genes, given the thousands of connections that are formed. The alternative, to specify precise pathways and targets with molecular cues and then using the rules of activity-dependent sorting to achieve ultimate precision in connectivity, is far more economical. Indeed, once axons recognize and grow into their appropriate targets, the same general rules of activity-dependent competition can apply throughout the nervous system. A major challenge for the future will be to elucidate the cellular and molecular bases for these rules.

ACKNOWLEDGMENTS

I wish to thank the many colleagues and collaborators whose essential contributions made this review article possible, including Do Baylor, G. Campbell, M. Feller, R. Gallego, Po A. Kirkwood, Do Vo Madison, Mo Meister, R. Mooney, A. Penn, M. Siegel, D. W. Sretavan, M. P. Stryker, R. O. L. Wong, and R. M. Yamawaki. The original research work presented in this article was supported in part by grants from the National Institutes of Health (EYO2858 and MH48108), the National Science Foundation (IBN92-12640), and the March of Dimes. C. J. S. is an investigator of the Howard Hughes Medical Institute.

REFERENCES

1   Goodman, C. S. and Shatz, C. J. (1993). *Cell72/Neuron* 10, 1–20.
2   Rodieck, R. W. (1979). *Annu. Rev. Neurosci.* 2, 193–255.
3   Sherman, S. M. (1985). *Prog. Psychobiol. Physiol. Psychol.* 11, 233–313.
4   Rakic, P. (1977). *Philos. Trans. R. Soc. London B* 278, 245–60.
5   Linden, D. C., Guillery, R. W., and Cucchiaro, J. (1981). *J. Comp. Neurol.* 203, 189–211.
6   Shatz, C. J. (1983). *J. Neurosci.* 3, 482–99.
7   Sretavan, D. W. and Shatz, C. J. (1986). *J. Neurosci.* 6, 234–51.
8   Rakic, P. (1981). *Science* 214, 928.
9   Chalupa. L. M. and Williams, R. W. (1984). *Hum. Neurobiol.* 3, 103–7.
10 Shatz, C. J. and Sretavan, D. W. (1986). *Annu. Rev. Neurosci.* 9, 171–207.
11 Guillery, R. W., Lamantia, A. S., Robson, J. A., and Huang, K. (1985). *J. Neurosci.* 5, 1370–9.
12 Purves, D. and Lichtman, J. W. (1980). *Science* 210, 153–7.
13 Fawcett, J. W. and O'Leary, D. D. M. (1985). *Trends Neurosci.* 8, 201–6.
14 Miller, K. D., Keller, J. B., and Stryker, M. P. (1989). *Science* 245, 605–15.
15 Constantine-Paton, M., Cline, H. T., and Debski, E. (1990). *Annu. Rev. Neurosci.* 13, 129–54.
16 Shatz, C. J. (1990). *Neuron* 5, 1–10.
17 Campbell, G. and Shatz, C. J. (1992). *J. Neurosci.* 12, 1847–58.
18 Shatz, C. J. and Kirkwood, P. A. (1984). *J. Neurosci.* 4, 1378–97.
19 Donovan, A. (1966). *Exp. Eye Res.* 5, 249–54.
20 Robinson, S. R. (1991). in *Vision and Visual Dysfunction*, ed. Cronly-Dillon, J. (Macmillan, New York), vol. 3, pp. 69–128.
21 Galli, L. and Maffei, L. (1988). *Science* 242, 90–1.
22 LeVay, S., Stryker, M. P., and Shatz, C. J. (1978). *J. Comp. Neurol.* 179, 223–44.
23 LeVay, S., Wiesel, T. N., and Hubel, D. H. (1980). *J. Comp. Neurol.* 191, 1–51.
24 Stryker, M. P. and Harris, W. (1986). *J. Neurosci.* 6, 2117–33.
25 Reh, T. A. and Constantine-Paton, M. (1985). *J. Neurosci.* 5, 1132–43.
26 Cline, H. T., Debski, E. A., and Constantine-Paton, M. (1987). *Proc. Natl. Acad. Sci. USA* 84, 4342–5.
27 Meyer, R. L. (1982). *Science* 218, 589–91.
28 Boss, V. C. and Schmidt, J. T. (1984). *J. Neurosci.* 4, 2891–905.
29 Shatz, C. J. and Stryker, M. P. (1988). *Science* 242, 87–9.
30 Sretavan, D. W., Shatz, C. J., and Stryker, M. P. (1988). *Nature (London)* 336, 468–71.

31 Cohan, C. S. and Kater, S. B. (1986). *Science* 232, 1638–40.

32 Frank, E. (1987). *Trends Neurosci.* 10, 188–90.

33 Willshaw, D. J. and von der Malsburg, C. (1976). *Proc. R. Soc. London B* 194, 431–45.

34 Mastronarde, D. N. (1989). *Trends Neurosci.* 12, 75–80.

35 Stryker, M. P. and Strickland, S. L. (1984). *Invest. Ophthalmol. Visual Sci.* 25, Suppl., 278.

36 Eisele, L. L. and Schmidt, J. T. (1988). *J. Neurobiol.* 19, 395–411.

37 Grenier, J. V. and Weidman, T. A. (1981). *Exp. Eye Res.* 33, 315–32.

38 Hahm, J. O., Langdon, R. B., and Sur, M. (1991). *Nature (London)* 351, 568–70.

39 Regher, W. G., Pine, J., Cohan, C. S., Mischke, M. D., and Tank, D. W. (1989). *J. Neurosci. Methods* 30, 91–4.

40 Meister, M., Wong, R. O. L., Baylor, D. A., and Shatz, C. J. (1991). *Science* 252, 939–43.

41 Wong, R. O. L., Meister, M., and Shatz, C. J. (1993). *Neuron* 11, 923–38.

42 Maslim, J. and Stone, J. (1986). *Brain Res.* 373, 35–48.

43 Wong, R. O. L., Yamawaki, R. M., and Shatz, C. J. (1992). *Eur. J. Neurosci.* 4, 1387–97.

44 Vaney, D. I. (1991). *Neurosci. Lett.* 125, 187–90.

45 Wong, R. O. L., Chernjavsky, A., Smith, S. J., and Shatz, C. J. (1995). *Nature (London)* 374, 716–18.

46 Feller, M. B., Wellis, D. P., Werblin, F. S., and Shatz, C. J. (1995). *Soc. Neurosci. Abstr.* 21, 1504.

47 Penn, A. A., Wong, R. O. L., and Shatz, C. J. (1994). *J. Neurosci.* 14, 3862–80.

48 Penn, A. A., Gallego, R., Mooney, R., and Shatz, C. J. (1995). *Soc. Neurosci. Abstr.* 21, 1504.

49 Hebb, D. O. (1949). *The Organization of Behavior* (Wiley, New York).

50 Madison, D. V., Malenka, R. C., and Nicoll, R. A. (1991). *Annu. Rev. Neurosci.* 14, 379–97.

51 Malenka, R. C. (1994). *Cell* 78, 535–8.

52 Artola, A. and Singer, W. (1987). *Nature (London)* 330, 649–52.

53 Komatsu, Y., Fujii, K., Maeda, J., Sakaguchi, H., and Toyama, K. (1988). *J. Neurophysiol.* 59, 124–41.

54 Shultz, D. and Fregnac, Y. (1992). *J. Neurosci.* 12, 1301–18.

55 Kirkwood, A., Dudek, S. M., Gold, J. T., Aizenman, C. D., and Bear, M. F. (1993). *Science* 260, 1518–21.

56 Mooney, R., Madison, D. V., and Shatz, C. J. (1993). *Neuron* 10, 815–25.

57 Esguerra, M., Kwon, Y. H., and Sur, M. (1992). *Neuroscience* 8, 545–55.

58 White, C. A. and Sur, M. (1992). *Proc. Natl. Acad. Sci. USA* 89, 9850–4.

59 Kandel, E. R. and O'Dell, T. J. (1992). *Science* 258, 243–5.

60 Walsh, C., Polley, E. H., Hickey, T. L., and Guillery, R. W. (1983). *Nature (London)* 302, 611–14.

61 Dubin, M. W., Stark, L. A., and Archer, S. M. (1986). *J. Neurosci.* 6, 1021–36.

PART V

Brain Plasticity and Cognition

Editors' Introduction to Part V

The realization that many aspects of brain development are open to influence by sensory experience raises the issue of what impact it has on cognition and how this latent plasticity is constrained. On the one hand, we have the observations reported in the earlier parts about the apparent equipotentiality of cerebral cortex: within certain broad constraints, parts of cortex can replace other parts, and different regions of cortex may subserve the same function at different times in development. On the other hand, we have the commonly observed correspondence between particular regions of cortex and particular functions in adults. Indeed, most of classical neuropsychology and behavioral neuroscience is based upon this assumption. One way to begin to resolve this apparent paradox is to consider the various constraints that might operate on the plasticity latent in the brain. The readings in this part illustrate a range of factors which may provide such constraints.

One source of constraint may be the extent to which different sensory systems respond to changes in normal patterns of input. Neville and Bavelier describe a series of studies that examine whether normally hearing and congenitally deaf individuals differ in their responses to visual stimuli. The motivation for these studies is the hypothesis that auditory deprivation might induce plasticity in other intact sensory systems. In accord with this view, deaf adults showed enhanced event-related potential (ERP) responses to patterns thought to engage the magnocellular (M) stream but not to parvocellular (P) stream stimuli. Moreover, deaf individuals showed larger signal changes in a brain imaging study that focused on motion processing circuits in the temporal lobe. This suggests that certain visual systems, those associated with the dorsal stream, may be more susceptible than others to alterations in sensory input. At the same time, individuals who became deaf in later childhood did not show the enhanced ERP, suggesting that the time period of visual plasticity may be limited. Evidence from studies on the auditory and tactile sensitivity of congenitally blind individuals provide additional support for the idea that different neural and cognitive systems respond to altered experience in distinct ways.

Neville and Bavelier next focus on the domain of language, in part because of the consistent association that has been found between areas in the left hemisphere and the perceptual and productive aspects of language. Given that the left hemisphere has a predisposition to support language, what constraints account for this regularity? At the same time, if the left hemisphere is specially predisposed toward language processing, how do we account for the ability of the right hemisphere to take over after damage early in life to the left (see Stiles this section)? Neville and Bavelier examine these questions by comparing the similarities and differences between individuals who learn language with different primary modes of expression, sign language and English, and who learn language at different points in development.

The main results Neville and Bavelier discuss can be summarized as follows. Within languages, there may be different patterns of functional specialization according to the type of information processed, lexical/semantic information versus grammatical form. At the same time, the learning of gesture-based languages such as American Sign Language (ASL) may induce specific functional specializations in individuals who learn the language early, but not those who learn it later. These specializations include the activation of right hemisphere circuits rarely invoked in the brains of hearing adults by the processing of written or spoken English. Finally, it appears that some of the differential brain activation patterns that are observed in adults stem from initially overlapping and undifferentiated functional signatures early in childhood. Together, these results support the argument that the specific form and timing of language experience an individual undergoes shapes the development and functional organization of the brain. That is, the development of mature brain structures for language is constrained by different types of functions that are characteristic of languages generally and by the specific aspects of individual languages, such as their primary modes of expression and perception.

Stiles et al. provide related evidence about brain mechanisms of language processing but do so from a different perspective. These authors explore constraints on plasticity by studying children with focal brain lesions. They stress a prospective approach, whereby recovery from and compensation for brain damage are investigated as they occur. The prospective approach allows researchers to determine early patterns of impairment and abilities, the relation between these patterns and those observed in adults with similar damage, and how these patterns change over time. The patterns observed by Stiles et al. demonstrate both plasticity and constraints on plasticity following early brain lesions. In some cases, children show better performance than adults with damage to the same brain regions, suggesting the plasticity of other brain regions to take on the functions typically subserved by the damaged tissue. However, subtle deficits are often observed in such cases, sometimes emerging well after the brain lesions occur, suggesting constraints on the plasticity of the brain to compensate for damage. Stiles et al. suggest that these are soft constraints, or innate predispositions that influence which brain regions get recruited for different functions.

Similar to Neville and Bavelier, Stiles et al. point out that different domains may vary in how much plasticity they allow. For instance, Stiles et al. demonstrate that language processing appears to be more plastic than spatial processing. In spatial processing, children with focal brain lesions show similar deficits to adults with similar lesions; left hemisphere damage leads to difficulty in defining parts, whereas right hemisphere damage leads to difficulty in configural relations. These results suggest that the intact hemisphere is not plastic enough to take over the spatial processing functions of the damaged hemisphere, so children and adults show similar profiles. In contrast, in the case of language, children with focal brain lesions show very different patterns of deficit than adults with similar lesions. For example, in children, right hemisphere damage rather than left impairs comprehension, posterior rather than anterior damage impairs certain aspects of production, and the effects of lateralized frontal damage are symmetric rather than greater for the left hemisphere. Stiles et al. suggest that language may be more plastic than spatial cognition because language expresses meaning, which is encoded across widely distributed brain regions, and because of the different task demands involved in comprehending and producing language for the first time versus using it fluently.

The reading by Merzenich and colleagues provides data that supports and extends these points. In one example, the authors describe how owl monkeys trained to perform a difficult object retrieval task showed widespread changes in the size of areas in the cerebral cortex devoted to sensory and motor aspects of the task. Merzenich and colleagues go on to discuss how one form of language learning deficit, specific language impairment or SLI, may be understood and possibly even partially remediated based on specific hypotheses about the process of developmental brain plasticity. Based on the work of their collaborator, Paula Tallal, the authors hypothesize that SLI is caused in part by the effects of abnormal abilities to process rapidly changing sound patterns. Since some of the most critical distinctions between words occur over rapid timecourses, a deficit in processing rapid transitions in sound could profoundly impair speech perception. In collaboration with Tallal, the authors designed an intervention program for children with SLI that both slowed down the rate of speech and gave extended practice on rapid sound discriminations. Within several months of retraining, the authors report that all of the children with SLI showed normal or above normal discrimination of rapidly presented speech sounds and significant improvement in normal speech perception. Unlike the monkey studies, the source of the plasticity in the children responding to treatment is not known; however, the authors speculate that the training regime may have had its largest effect in modifying perceptual systems so that rapid speech transitions that were once missed are now discriminated. Finally, Merzenich and colleagues describe how a movement disorder associated with rapid and repetitive hand movements might be remediated by a scheme in which hand and finger movements are distinctly separated both in time and space. Clearly the sources of constraint on brain plasticity and behavior processes are as varied as the contexts in which perceptual, cognitive, and motor behavior occur. Merzenich et al. share the view that a greater understanding of brain plasticity will lead to other effective treatments for congenital or acquired neurological disorders. However, it should be stressed that these treatments remain controversial, and their effectiveness has yet to be demonstrated in a way that convinces all scientists.

The final reading of this section, by Marler, examines how internal and external constraints jointly contribute to adaptive developmental outcomes. Marler discusses some examples of how specific species of birds acquire the characteristic song of their species. In several of these cases, Marler argues, rather than instinct and learning being opposing, they may be viewed as complementary. Marler develops some of the concepts first put forward by the founders of ethology, Tinbergen and Lorenz (see Part I), such as the notions of sensitive period and innate releasing mechanisms, to argue that such forms of innate responsiveness may also facilitate and guide learning. Studies have revealed that certain species of young sparrows are able to learn about their species-specific song even if they are exposed to several songs during development. For example, young swamp sparrows "tune in" to the song syllables of their own species, even when the experimenter attempts to fool the young birds by exposing them to synthetic songs structured like that of a closely related species. Swamp sparrows reared without hearing other birds' songs produce abnormal songs, demonstrating the importance of experience. Thus, the young of many songbird species start with some form of "innate" song template which helps them to select their species song from the many other sounds to which they are exposed.

Another point made by Marler concerns the differences in mechanisms that result in the acquisition of the species-specific song in the wild, even between quite closely related species, such as song sparrows and swamp sparrows. For example, while the swamp sparrow responds to its species syllables within a song, song sparrows base their learning preferences more on a number of "syntactic" features, such as number of segments, phrase structure, and tempo. This, and several other examples, help to make the point that selection pressures operate on behavioral phenotypes, not directly on genotypes. When studying the mechanisms underlying the ontogeny of a behavior, we should expect to find a variety of degrees of genotypic contribution as long as they produce the same result. To a certain extent then, evolution doesn't care about the exact mechanisms that give rise to an outcome, it only cares about the outcome itself.

FURTHER READING

Bolhuis, J. J. (1991). Mechanisms of avian imprinting: A review. *Biological Review 66*. (A review of most of what is known from experimental studies of imprinting in social birds).

Johnson, M. H. and Morton, J. (1991). *Biology and Cognitive Development: The Case of Face Recognition*. Oxford, UK: Blackwell. (Argues that there are two processes that guide imprinting in the domestic chick which may have analogues in the perception of faces by human infants).

Karni, A., Tanne, D., Rubenstein, B. S., Askenasy, J. J. M., and Sagi, D. (1994). Dependence on REM sleep of overnight improvement in perceptual skill. *Science* 265, 679–82. (Describes how the plasticity may depend on processes of consolidation that occur during sleep).

Merzenich, M. M., Jenkins, W. M., Johnston, P., Schreiner, C., Miller, S. L., and Tallal, P. (1996). Temporal processing deficits of language-learning impaired children ameliorated by training. *Science* 271(5), 77–81. (A more detailed report on the effects of training SLI children with modified acoustic stimuli).

Neville, H. J., Bavelier, D., Rauschecker, J., Karni, A., Lalwani, A., Braun, A., Clark, V., Jezzard, P., and Turner, R. (1998). Cerebral organization for language in deaf and hearing subjects: biological constraints and effects of experience. *Proceedings of the National Academy of Sciences* 95, 922–9. (Additional information about brain imaging experiments studying cortical systems for language processing in deaf and hearing adults).

Payne, B. R. and Cornwell, P. (1994). System-wide repercussions of damage to the immature visual cortex. *Trends in Neuroscience* 17(3). (Describes how plasticity in response to brain injury varies depending on when in development the insult occurs).

Rieser, J. J., Pick, H. L., Ashmead, D. H., and Garing, A. E. (1995). Calibration of human locomotion and models of perceptual-motor organization. *Journal of Experimental Psychology: Human Perception and Performance* 21(3), 480–97. (Provides evidence for the view that functional aspects of behavior, not specific sensory-motor subsystems, may be shaped by learning and plasticity).

Sathian, K. and Zangaladze, A. (1997). Tactile learning is task specific but transfers between fingers. *Perception and Psychophysics* 59(1), 119–28. (Plasticity can be both specific and general).

Tallal, P., Miller, S. L., Bedi, G., Byma, G., Wang, X., Nagaranjan, S. S., Schreiner, C., Jenkins, W. M., and Merzenich, M. M. (1996). Acoustically modified speech improves language comprehension in language-learning impaired children. *Science* 271(5), 81–3. (Companion article to Merzenich et al. 1996).

14

Specificity and Plasticity in Neurocognitive Development in Humans

Helen J. Neville *and* Daphne Bavelier

Cognitive neuroscience has rapidly expanded during the decade of the brain. Progress in cognitive science and in the development of techniques that permit noninvasive monitoring of the human brain have permitted extensive, ongoing mapping and differentiation of sensory and cognitive systems in the mature human mind/brain. The burgeoning literature on the normal adult brain serves as the point of departure for a major opportunity and challenge for the coming decade and century – the characterization of the processes that lead to the development and differentiation of the mature brain (developmental cognitive neuroscience).

Discussions of neurocognitive development have long been dominated (and stifled) by the "nature–nurture" debate. Most current investigators acknowledge both the role of biological constraints imposed by the genotype and the role of environmental inputs in gene expression and other chemical and physiological developmental events. It is clear that neurocognitive development relies on a dynamic and complex interplay between predetermined genetic events and environmental events. In this chapter we argue that the degree of interplay is highly variable across different neurocognitive systems, leading to different degrees and timing of sensitivities to environmental inputs for different brain functions. These differences in developmental specificity and plasticity prevent simple generalization and call for a careful characterization of the developmental events within each system and subsystem.

This chapter offers (1) evidence on the development of the anatomy of the developing cerebral cortex in humans; (2) a review of developmental plasticity of higher visual functions, considering separately functions of the ventral and dorsal visual pathways; (3) a brief discussion of reports on plasticity within the development of other sensory systems; and (4) a consideration of developmental plasticity and specificity of language functions with an emphasis on the comparison of lexical and grammatical functions.

Anatomy and Physiology of the Developing Human Brain

Although a thorough review of the structural, chemical, and physiological development of the human brain is beyond the scope of this chapter, this section aims at summarizing the state of knowledge on postnatal human development from infancy to adulthood.

In most species, including humans, the developing brain displays progressive and regressive events during which axons, dendrites, synapses, and neurons show exuberant growth and major loss leading to a remodeling of the neural circuitry. This period of remodeling is hypothesized to be a time during which environmental factors can have a major impact on cortical organization. Several studies of primary sensory areas have shown that sensory inputs are of central importance in selecting the axons, dendrites, synapses, and neurons that form functional neural circuits (Rakic, 1976; Hubel and Wiesel, 1977; Sur, Pallas, and Roe, 1990). For example, during a specific time period (the sensitive period), visual deprivation induced by monocular eyelid suture results in shrinkage of ocular dominance columns serving the closed eye. Outside the critical period, visual deprivation has little effect on the pattern of ocular dominance (Blakemore et al., 1978; Hubel and Wiesel, 1977; Horton and Hocking, 1997). Little is known about the factors that control the duration and timing of sensitive periods, however the onset of the sensitive period is affected by input. For example, in cats, binocular deprivation results in delayed onset of the sensitive period for ocular dominance formation (Cynader and Mitchell, 1980; Mitchell, 1981). Similar observations have been made in the auditory system of songbirds (Marler, 1970) and humans. The maturation of an early auditory evoked response displays an extended time course of development after cochlear implantation in congenitally deaf children (Ponton et al., 1996). The number of years of auditory experience, rather than chronological age per se, was predictive of the maturational time course.

Different neural systems and associated behavioral capabilities are affected by environmental input at highly variable time periods, supporting the idea that they develop along distinct time courses (Mitchell, 1981, Harwerth et al., 1986; Curtiss, 1989; Neville, Mills, and Lawson, 1992; Maurer and Lewis, 1998). For example, visual processes thought to arise within the retina (cf. the sensitivity of the scotopic visual system) display relatively short sensitive periods. By contrast, binocular functions that rely on later developing cortical neurons display considerably longer sensitive periods (Harwerth et al., 1986). This variability in the timing of experience-dependent modification may depend upon the rate of maturation of the neural systems that mediate different functions, with later developing cortical areas having more opportunity to be affected by incoming input.

The proposal that different brain systems in the human display distinct developmental time courses is supported by anatomical and physiological measurements. Recently developed neuroanatomical techniques can be used to provide estimates of the density of neurons, axons, dendrites, or synapses in tissue. Huttenlocher and collaborators (Huttenlocher, 1994; Huttenlocher and Dabholkar, 1997) have used electron microscopy to map out the synaptic remodeling that occurs during human development. These authors have compared synaptogenesis and synapse elimination within several different brain areas (Huttenlocher, 1994). In primary visual cortex a burst in synaptogenesis occurs at about 3 to 4 months of age, with the maximum density reached at 4 months. In contrast, synaptogenesis in the middle prefrontal cortex takes longer, reaching a maximum synaptic density at about 3.5 years of age. Furthermore, the time course for synapse elimination occurs significantly later in the middle frontal gyrus (until age 20) than in the primary visual cortex (converged on adult levels by age 4; see figure 14.1; Huttenlocher and Dabholkar, 1997). Recently, Huttenlocher and colleagues have described developmental changes in synaptic density for different cortical areas important in language processing–primary auditory cortex, the angular gyrus (Broadman's area 40), and Broca's area (Huttenlocher, 1994; Huttenlocher and Dabholkar, 1997). At birth synaptic development (as measured by the time course of synaptic density) in the auditory cortex is more advanced than in the two

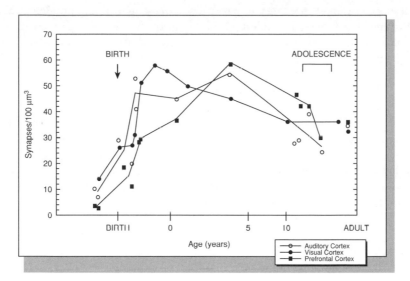

Figure 14.1 Mean synaptic density in synapses/100 μm³ in auditory (open circles), calcarine (filled circles), and prefrontal (squares) cortex at various ages. From Huttenlocher, P. R. and Dabholkar, A. S. (1997). Regional differences in synaptogenesis in human cerebral cortex. *Journal of Comparative Neurology* 387, 85. Reprinted with permission from John Wiley & Sons Inc.

language areas; but by 4 years of age, synaptic density is similar in these areas and is significantly greater than in the adult (by about a factor of 2). These findings suggest different time courses of synaptogenesis for different brain systems. A recent report suggests there may also be considerable postnatal variability in neuron loss and neurogenesis in the human brain (Shankle et al., 1998a). However, other neuroanatomic features of the human brain appear to show concurrent developmental patterns from region to region (Shankle et al., 1998b). In macaque monkeys, Rakic and colleagues (1986) have reported concurrent time courses of synaptogenesis across several different brain areas. However, there is variability between areas in the duration of the maximum densities of synapses, in the elimination phases, and in the timing of synaptogenesis on dendritic shafts and spines (Bourgeous, et al., 2000).

Anatomical measures of synapse proliferation in the human brain (Huttenlocher and Dabholkar, 1997) describe developmental time courses similar to those observed in physiological studies using PET with FDG, a technique that traces glucose metabolism. Chugani and collaborators (1996) have described the patterns of brain glucose utilization during human development. These studies show a rapid rise in cerebral metabolism during infancy, perhaps reflecting the burst of synaptogenesis described in the structural studies. This is followed by a decrease in brain glucose metabolism later in childhood, in much the same time frame as is observed for the loss of synapses. In the metabolic studies, primary sensory and motor cortex, the hippocampal region, and the cingulate cortex have an earlier increase in glucose metabolism than other cortical regions; and the prefrontal cortex is one of the latest structures to show increased glucose metabolism. These structural and physiological findings support the view of different maturational timetables for distinct brain structures with primary cortices developing before higher association cortices.

Much more research is necessary to characterize the structural and physiological development of the human brain and to link variability in the development of these parameters to variability in the time course of sensory, motor, and cognitive development in the child.

Developmental Specificity of Visual Functions in Humans

We now have powerful brain imaging methods to study aspects of the physiology of sensory and language processing in humans. Event-related brain potentials (ERPs) and functional magnetic resonance imaging (fMRI) are two such techniques. ERPs are voltage fluctuations in the EEG in response to a controlled stimulus. The latencies of different positive and negative components in an ERP reveal the time course of activation (within microseconds) of the neuronal populations that are recruited during the processing of that stimulus. The fMRI technique measures changes in blood flow and oxygenation, permitting mapping of brain regions metabolically active following the presentation of a controlled stimulus. In contrast to the ERP, this technique has a good spatial resolution (about 1 mm) but a restricted temporal resolution.

Dorsal and Ventral Visual Subsystems

In several experiments employing ERPs, we have observed that sensory and attentional processing of visual information presented to the central and peripheral visual fields elicit activity in different neural pathways in normal hearing subjects. Congenital auditory deprivation is associated with specific enhancements of behavioral performance and ERPs in response to visual information presented in the peripheral (but not the foveal) visual fields (Neville, Schmidt, and Kutas, 1983; Neville and Lawson, 1987a, b, c). These data suggest that the systems mediating the representation of peripheral visual space may be more modifiable than those representing central visual space. There is anatomical evidence that the visual periphery is represented most strongly along the dorsal visual pathway that projects from V1 toward the posterior parietal cortex and includes areas important for the processing of spatial location and motion information. By contrast, central space is largely represented along the ventral pathway that projects from V1 to anterior regions of the inferior temporal lobe and includes areas important for processing form and color information (Ungerleider and Mishkin, 1982; Baizer, Ungerleider, and Desimone, 1991). These results prompted the hypothesis that there may be a greater sensitivity to altered experience for other dorsal visual pathway functions.

In order to investigate this hypothesis, we employed stimuli designed to selectively activate either the magnocellular system (M stimuli) which projects strongly to the dorsal pathway, or the parvocellular system, which projects strongly (but not solely: see Stoner and Albright, 1993; Sawatari and Callaway, 1996) to the ventral pathway (P stimuli). The parvo system is highly responsive to color information and to stimuli of high spatial frequency, while the magno system is highly responsive to motion and to stimuli of low spatial frequency and low contrast (Livingstone and Hubel, 1988; Merigan and Maunsell, 1993).

Stimuli were presented at five different locations including the fovea and 8 degrees from the foveal stimulus in the upper and lower left and right visual fields. The parvo (P) stimuli were isoluminant blue and green high spatial frequency gratings (adjusted for the cortical magnification factor) continuously visible at all locations. ERPs were evoked by a brief change in color; randomly at one location the blue bars changed to red for 100 ms. The magno (M) stimuli consisted of low spatial frequency gratings of light and dark gray bars with a low luminance contrast. The evoking stimulus consisted of the bars at one location (random) moving transversely to the right. Subjects fixated centrally and monitored all locations for the rare occurrence of a black square at one of the locations. We first asked whether ERPs to these different stimuli would provide evidence for the activation of distinct neural systems in normal hearing subjects and then asked whether congenital auditory deprivation would have selective effects on these different aspects of processing (Armstrong Neville and Bavelier, 1995, 1998).

In normal hearing subjects the distribution of the ERPs elicited by the parvo and magno stimuli displayed many similarities, and this may be attributable to the spatial proximity (within 1 cm) of the ventral and dorsal stream areas in humans, as indicated in recent fMRI studies (Sereno et al., 1995; Tootell et al., 1995). On the other hand, there were reliable differences in the activity patterns elicited by the stimuli. Magno stimuli elicited responses that were larger dorsally than were responses to parvo stimuli, consistent with our initial hypotheses. Additionally, both the current source density maps and the grand averaged waveforms demonstrate that, whereas the peripheral M stimuli elicited ERPs largest over cortex contralateral to the field of presentation, the P stimuli evoked a bilateral response. This pattern of results may be attributable in part to the deep ventromedial location of V4 which could generate a bilateral pattern of activation. Area MT, on the other hand, is located more laterally and would therefore generate a stronger contralateral response. Thus, these differences are consistent with anatomical differences of ventral and dorsal stream areas.

In addition, magno stimuli elicited ERP responses with considerably earlier latencies than those elicited by parvo stimuli, consistent with evidence from animal studies that show faster conduction within the magnocellular pathway. In addition, for several early components (beginning at 110 ms), P stimuli presented in the upper and lower visual fields (VF) evoked different response amplitudes while magno stimuli did not. These results may be accounted for by the retinotopic organization of V4 and MT/MST. fMRI data from humans (Sereno et al., 1995) have shown that upper and lower VF representations in several ventral stream areas including V4 are centimeters apart; however, in areas MT and MST, the representations are adjacent. Thus, a difference in response to parvo stimuli in the upper and lower VF is consistent with ventral stream activation, and the similarity of responses to magno stimuli in the upper and lower VF is consistent with dorsal stream activation. In summary, these stimuli were successful in evoking distinct ERP responses that may index the activation of separate streams or modes of visual processing in normal hearing subjects.

Effects of Auditory Deprivation

Our prior research, coupled with evidence that different systems within vision display different developmental time courses and modification by visual experience (Sherman, 1985), led us to hypothesize that processing of the magno stimuli would be selectively enhanced in congenitally deaf subjects.

Subjects were 11 congenitally, profoundly and bilaterally deaf subjects born to deaf parents. Whereas hearing subjects' reaction times were faster to targets occurring in the central than in the peripheral visual field, deaf subjects responded equally quickly to targets in the central and peripheral fields. Several specific group differences occurred in the amplitude and distribution of early sensory responses recorded over anterior and temporal regions. Deaf subjects displayed significantly greater amplitudes than hearing subjects – but this effect occurred only for magno stimuli, not for parvo stimuli (see figure 14.2). Further, whereas in hearing subjects, P stimuli elicited larger responses than did M stimuli, in deaf subjects responses to M stimuli were as large as those to P stimuli. In addition, at 150 ms ERPs to the M stimuli displayed a source-sink generator in temporal cortex that was clearly present in the deaf subjects but not in the hearing subjects. Currently, we are acquiring results from a group of hearing subjects born to deaf parents who acquired ASL as a first language. This research should allow us to determine whether certain group effects observed in this experiment are attributable to auditory deprivation and others to acquisition of a visuospatial language (ASL) since, in previous research, we have observed separate effects of these two factors (Neville and Lawson, 1987c).

These data suggest that there is considerable specificity in the aspects of visual processing that are altered following auditory deprivation; specifically, the dorsal visual processing stream may be more modifiable in response to alterations in afferent input than is the ventral processing pathway. This hypothesis is in broad agreement with the proposal put forward by Chalupa and Dreher (1991) that components of the visual pathway that are

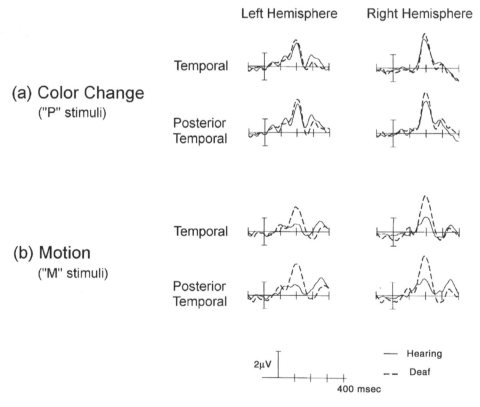

Figure 14.2 ERPs elicited by (a) color change and (b) motion in normally hearing and congenitally deaf adults. Recordings from temporal and posterior temporal regions of the left and right hemispheres. Reprinted with permission from Neville and Bavelier, 1998.

specialized for high acuity vision exhibit fewer developmental redundancies ("errors"), decreased modifiability, and more specificity than do those displaying less acuity and precision. It may also be that the dorsal visual pathway has a more prolonged maturational time course than the ventral pathway, permitting extrinsic influences to exert an effect over a longer time. While little evidence bears directly on this hypothesis, anatomical data suggest that, in humans, neurons in the parvocellular layers of the LGN mature earlier than those in the magnocellular laminae (Hickey, 1977) and, in nonhuman primates, the peripheral retina is slower to mature (Lachica and Casagrande, 1988; Packer, Hendrickson, and Curcio, 1990; Van Driel, Provis, and Billson, 1990). Additionally, data suggest that the development of the Y-cell pathway (which is strongest in the periphery of the retina) is more affected by visual deprivation than is development of the W- and X-cell pathways (Sherman and Spear, 1982). Investigators have also reported that the effects of congenital visual deprivation (due to cataracts) are more pronounced on peripheral than foveal vision (and by implication on the dorsal pathway) (Mioche and Perenin, 1986; Bowering et al., 1997). Moreover, in developmental disabilities including dyslexia, specific language impairment, and Williams syndrome, visual deficits are more pronounced for dorsal than ventral visual pathway functions (Lovegrove, Garzia, and Nicholson, 1990; Eden et al., 1996; Atkinson et al., 1997). An additional hypothesis that may account for the greater effects on peripheral vision is that in development the effects of deprivation and enhancement are equivalent within all cortical regions. Those areas with less extent to begin with (e.g., MT, peripheral visual representations) would display the largest proportional effects of both enhancement and vulnerability. A similar hypothesis has been proposed to account for the larger effects of visual deprivation on ocular dominance formation within the periphery in monkeys (Horton and Hocking, 1997).

Sensitive Period Effects and Mechanisms

We have observed that individuals who became deaf after the age of 4 years (due to delayed expression of the gene that leads to cochlear degeneration) typically do not display the increased visual ERPs that we attributed to auditory deprivation (Neville, Schmidt, and Kutas, 1983; Neville and Lawson, 1987c). We considered several mechanisms that might mediate the effects themselves and the developmental time limits on them. One possibility is that they are mediated by an early, normally transient, redundancy of connections between the auditory and visual systems (as has been observed in cats and hamsters: see Dehay, Bullier, and Kennedy, 1984; Frost, 1984; Innocenti and Clarke, 1984). In the absence of competition from auditory input, visual afferents may be maintained on what would normally be auditory neurons. Our results from studies of later deafened individuals suggest that in humans this redundancy may diminish by the fourth year of life. One way we tested this hypothesis was to study the differentiation of visual and auditory sensory responses in normal development (see figure 14.3). In normal adults, auditory stimuli elicit ERP responses that are large over temporal brain regions but small or absent over occipital regions. By contrast, in 6-month-old children we observed that auditory ERPs are equally large over temporal and visual brain regions, consistent with the idea that there is less specificity and more redundancy of connections between auditory and visual cortex at this time. Between 6 and 36 months, however, we observed a gradual decrease in the amplitude of the auditory ERP over visual areas, while the amplitude over the temporal areas was unchanged. These results suggest that early in human development there exists a redundancy of connections between auditory and visual areas and that this overlap gradually decreases between birth and 3 years of age. This loss of redundancy may be the boundary condition that determines when auditory deprivation can result in alterations in the organization of the visual system. Ongoing studies of hearing and deaf infants and children employing the parvo and magno stimuli described above will test for the specificity of these effects.

RESPONSES TO SPEECH

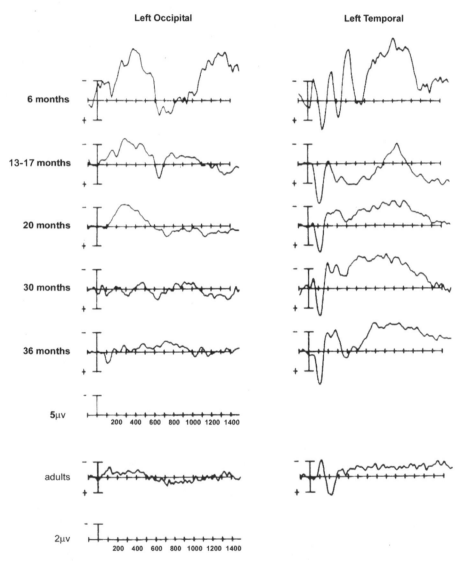

Figure 14.3 ERPs to auditory (speech) stimuli recorded over temporal and occipital regions in normal adults (bottom) and in children aged 6–36 months. (From Neville, H. J. (1995). Developmental specificity in neurocognitive development in humans. In M. Gazzaniga (ed.), *The Cognitive Neurosciences*, p. 88. Cambridge, MA: MIT Press. Reprinted with permission of MIT Press.)

fMRI Study of Motion Perception

We have further pursued the hypothesis that deafness alters the functional organization of the dorsal visual stream, by employing fMRI (Tomann et al., 1998). Specifically, we assessed whether early auditory deprivation alters cerebral activation during motion processing. In addition, we hypothesized that these changes would be most marked when visual attention was required in view of the central role of dorsal parietal regions in spatial attention. Motion processing was compared between congenitally deaf (native signers/born to deaf parents) and hearing individuals as visual attention was manipulated. Subjects fixated centrally and viewed an alternation of radial flow fields (converging and diverging) and static dots. While the first run required only passive viewing, visual attention was manipulated in all other runs by asking subjects to detect velocity and/or luminance changes.

Under conditions of active attention, deaf individuals showed a greater number of voxels activated and a larger percent signal change than did hearing subjects in temporal cortex including areas MT-MST (figure 14.4). Thus, congenital deafness alters the cortical organization of motion processing, especially when attention is required. Interestingly, the recruitment of the intraparietal sulcus was also significantly larger in deaf than in hearing subjects. This result, like our earlier ERP study of spatial attention (Neville and Lawson, 1987b; Neville, 1995), suggests that early auditory deprivation may also alter the cortical organization of visual attention. Ongoing studies will determine the precise location and the specificity of these effects.

Visual Motion

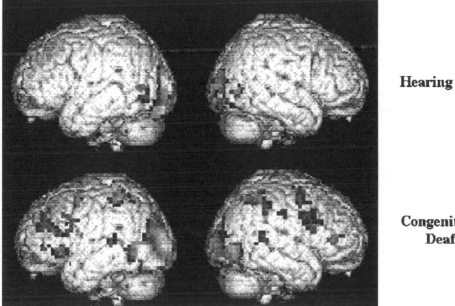

Hearing

Congenitally Deaf

Figure 14.4 Activation (fMRI, 1.5T) in normally hearing and congenitally deaf adults in responses to visual motion.

Developmental Specificity in Other Neurocognitive Domains

Developmental plasticity has also been documented in humans within other sensory modalities. There are several reports that early peripheral blindness leads to changes in the visually deprived cortex. Measures of glucose utilization have shown an increased metabolism in the visual cortex of early blind humans as compared to subjects who became blind after the completion of visual development. These studies report that metabolic activity within the occipital cortex of early blind individuals is higher than that found in blindfolded sighted subjects and equivalent to that of sighted subjects with their eyes open (Wanet-Defalque et al., 1988; Veraart et al., 1990; Uhl et al., 1994). Additionally, ERP studies indicate a larger slow negative DC potential shift over the occipital lobe in early blind than in sighted persons during tactile and auditory tasks (Uhl et al., 1991, 1994; Röder et al., 1996, 1997). Recently, a number of studies have confirmed the functional participation of visual areas during somatosensory tasks in early blind individuals. Using PET, Sadato and colleagues (Sadato et al., 1996) compared tactile discrimination in early blind braille readers and control subjects. Blind subjects revealed activation of visual cortical areas whereas these regions were deactivated in controls. The functional relevance of visual areas in tactile discrimination was further established in a transcranial magnetic stimulation experiment (Cohen et al., 1997). Transient stimulation of the occipital cortex induced errors on a tactile task in early blind subjects but had no effect on the sighted controls. It is worth noting that not all aspects of somatosensory processing recruit visual areas in blind subjects. For example, simple tactile stimuli that did not require discrimination produced little activation in visual areas of blind subjects (Sadato et al., 1996). This finding is in agreement with the hypothesis that different neurocognitive systems and subsystems exhibit different sensitivities to altered experience.

This point is further supported by the research of Röder and colleagues (1997) who have studied auditory localization abilities in blind humans. ERPs were recorded as congenitally blind adults and sighted controls attended either to central or peripheral sound sources in order to detect a rare noise burst either at the 0- or the 90-degree loudspeaker (on different blocks). Behavioral data revealed a higher spatial resolution in the blind, particularly when they were attending to the periphery. Gradients of ERP amplitudes suggested a sharper auditory spatial attention focus in the blind compared to the sighted for peripheral sounds. The results suggest that, on across auditory and visual modalities the representation of peripheral space is more altered by early sensory experience than is the representation of central space. It is interesting that, on close examination of the behavioral data presented in Rice (1965) on blind humans and Rauschecker and Kneipert (1993) on blind cats, a similar effect is observed – i.e., an advantage in sound localization for the blind that is largest at peripheral locations.

Development Specificity of Language Functions in Humans

It is reasonable to assume that the rules and principles that govern the development of the sensory systems also guide the development of language-relevant brain systems. Thus, differences in the rate of differentiation and degree of specification may be apparent within language and help to identify different functional subsystems. In a series of experiments we have studied the development of the neural systems important in lexical/semantic and

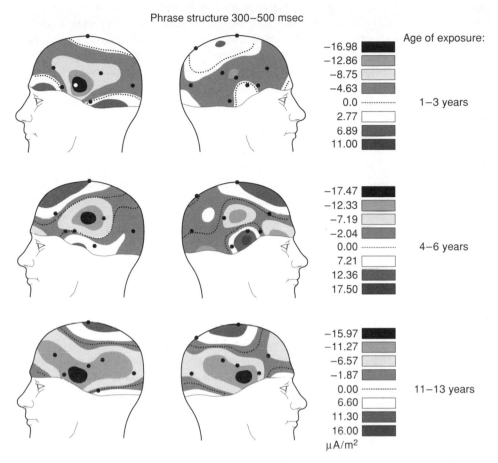

Figure 14.5 Current source density (CSD) analyses of responses to grammatical anomalies (violations of phrase structure) in English. Early Learners of English (1–3 years) display a left lateralized activation but delays in age of exposure (4–13 years) are associated with bilateral activation.

grammatical processing. In normal, right-handed, monolingual adults nouns and verbs ("open-class" words) that provide lexical/semantic information elicit a different pattern of brain activity (as measured by ERPs) than do function words including prepositions and conjunctions ("closed-class" words) that provide grammatical information in English (Neville, Mills, and Lawson, 1992; Nobre and McCarthy, 1994). In addition, sentences that are semantically nonsensical (but grammatically intact) elicit a different pattern of ERPs than do sentences that contain a violation of syntactic structure (but leave the meaning intact) (Neville et al., 1991; Osterhout, McLaughlin, and Bersick, 1997). These results are consistent with several other types of evidence suggesting that different neural systems mediate the processing of lexical/semantic and grammatical information in adults. Specifically, they imply a greater role for more posterior temporal-parietal systems in lexical/semantic processing and for frontal-temporal systems within the left hemisphere in grammatical processing. This overall pattern appears ubiquitous in adults, and many investigators have suggested that the central role of the left hemisphere in language processing is strongly genetically determined. Certainly, the fact that most individuals, regardless of the language they learn, display left hemisphere dominance for that language indicates that this aspect of neural development is strongly biased. Nonetheless, it is likely that language-relevant aspects of cerebral organization are dependent on and modified by language experience. Many investigators have studied this question by comparing cerebral organization in individuals who learned a second language at different times in development (Perani, et al., 1996; Dehaene, et al., 1997; Kim, et al., 1997). In general, age of exposure to language appears to affect cerebral organization for that language. Moreover, there appears to be specificity in these effects: In Chinese–English bilinguals delays of as long as 16 years in exposure to English had very little effect on the organization of the brain systems active in lexical/semantic processing. In contrast, delays of only 4 years had significant effects on those aspects of brain organization linked to grammatical processing (figure 14.5; Weber-Fox and Neville, 1996). These results and parallel behavioral results from the same study suggest that aspects of semantic and grammatical processing differ markedly in the degree to which they depend upon language input. Specifically, grammatical processing appears more vulnerable to delays in language experience.

Studies of Deaf Adults

Further evidence on this point was provided by ERP studies of English sentence processing by congenitally deaf individuals who learned English late and as a second language (American Sign Language or ASL was the first language of these subjects; Neville, Mills, and Lawson, 1992). Deaf subjects displayed ERP responses to nouns and to semantically anomalous sentences in written English that were indistinguishable from those of normal hearing subjects who learned English as a first language. These data are consistent with the hypothesis that some aspects of lexical/semantic processing are largely unaffected by the many aspects of language experience that differ between normally hearing and congenitally deaf individuals. By contrast, deaf subjects displayed aberrant ERP responses to grammatical information like that presented in function words in English. Specifically, they did not display the specialization of the anterior regions of the left hemisphere characteristic of native hearing/speaking learners. These data suggest that the systems mediating the processing of grammatical information are more modifiable and vulnerable in response to altered language experience than are those associated with lexical/semantic processing.

Studies of ASL

Recently, we have employed the ERP and fMRI techniques to pursue this hypothesis further and also to obtain evidence on the question of whether the strongly biased role of the left hemisphere in language occurs independently of the structure and modality of the language first acquired (Neville et al., 1997, 1998). ERPs recorded to response to open- and closed-class signs in ASL sentences displayed similar timing and anterior/posterior distributions to those observed in previous studies of English. But, whereas in native speakers of English responses to closed-class English words were largest over anterior regions of the left hemisphere, in native signers closed-class ASL signs elicited bilateral activity that extended posteriorly to include parietal regions of both the left and right hemispheres. These results imply that the acquisition of a language that relies on spatial contrasts and the perception of motion may result in the inclusion of right hemisphere regions into the language system. As seen in figure 14.6, both hearing and deaf native signers displayed this effect. However, hearing people who acquired ASL in the late teens did not show this effect, suggesting there may be a limited time (sensitive) period when this type of organization for grammatical processing can develop. By contrast, the response to semantic information was not affected by age of acquisition of ASL, in keeping with the results from studies of English suggesting that these different subsystems within language display different degrees of developmental plasticity.

In fMRI studies comparing sentence processing in English and ASL we also observed evidence for biological constraints and effects of experience on the mature organization of the language systems of the brain. As seen at the top of figure 14.7, when hearing adults read English (their first language), there is robust activation within the left (but not the right) hemisphere and in particular within the inferior frontal (Broca's) regions. When deaf people read English (their second language, learned late and imperfectly), we did not observe activation of these regions within the left hemisphere (figure 14.7, middle). Is the absence of left-hemisphere activation in the deaf linked to lack of auditory experience with language or to incomplete acquisition of the grammar of the language? ASL is not sound-based, but displays each of the characteristics of all formal languages including a complex grammar (that makes extensive use of spatial location and hand motion) (Klima and Bellugi, 1979). Studies of the same deaf subjects when viewing sentences in their native ASL clearly show activation within the same inferior frontal regions of the left hemisphere that are active when native speakers of English process English (figure 14.7, bottom). These data suggest a strong biological bias for these neural systems to mediate grammatical language regardless of the structure and modality of the language acquired. However, if the language is not acquired within the appropriate time window, this strong bias is not expressed. Biological constraints and language experience interact epigenetically, as has been described for many other systems described in developmental biology.

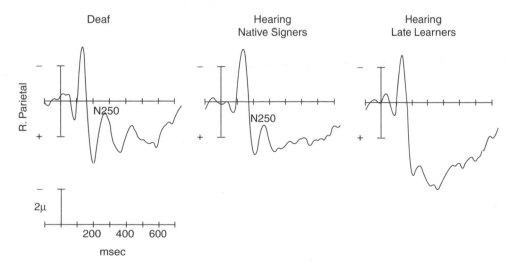

Figure 14.6 ERPs to closed class signs in ASL sentences from 10 deaf and 10 hearing native signers and 10 late learners of ASL. Recordings from parietal areas of the right hemisphere.

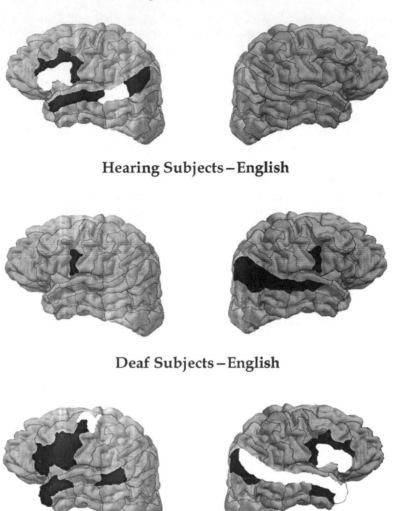

Hearing Subjects – English

Deaf Subjects – English

Deaf Subjects – ASL

Figure 14.7 Cortical areas showing increases in blood oxygenation on fMRI when normal hearing adults read English sentences (top), when congenitally deaf native signers read English sentences (middle) and when congenitally deaf native signers view sentences in their native sign language (American Sign Language).

The fMRI data also indicate a robust role for the right hemisphere in processing ASL. These results suggest that the nature of the language input, in this case the co-occurrence of location and motion information with language, shapes the organization of the language systems of the brain. Further research is necessary to specify the different times in human development when particular types of input are required for optimal development of the many systems and subsystems important in language processing.

Effects of Primary Language Acquisition on Cerebral Organization

The research summarized above implies that language experience determines the development and organization of language-relevant systems of the brain. A strong test of this hypothesis would be to chart the changes in brain organization as children acquire primary language, and to separate these from more general maturational changes (Mills, Coffey-Corina, and Neville, 1993, 1997; Neville and Mills, 1997). We compared patterns of neural activity relevant to language processing in 13- and 20-month-old infants to determine whether or not changes in cerebral organization occur as a function of specific changes in language development when chronological age is held constant. ERPs were recorded as children listened to a series of words whose meaning was understood by the child, words whose meaning the child did not understand, and backward words. Specific and different ERP components discriminated comprehended words from unknown and from backward words. Distinct lateral and anterior–posterior specializations were apparent in ERP responses to the different types of words. At 13 months of age the effects of word comprehension were apparent over anterior and posterior regions of both the left and right hemispheres. However, at 20 months of age the effects occurred only over temporal and parietal regions of the left hemisphere. This increasing specialization of language-relevant systems is not however solely dependent on chronological age. In comparisons of children of the same age who differ in size of vocabulary it is clear that language experience/knowledge is strongly predictive of the maturity of cerebral organization: 13-month-old infants with large vocabularies also display more focal left temporal/parietal effects of word meaning than do those with small vocabularies.

A similar effect is found in the development of the differential processing of open- and closed-class words. We compared ERPs to open- and closed-class words in infants and young children from 20 to 42 months of age. All children understood and produced both the open- and closed-class words presented. At 20 months, ERPs in response to open- and closed-class words did not differ. However, both types of words elicited ERPs that differed from those elicited by unknown and backward words. These data suggest that in the earliest stages of language development, when children are typically speaking in single-word utterances or beginning to put two words together, open- and closed-class words elicit similar patterns of brain activity. At 28 to 30 months of age, when children typically begin to speak in short phrases, ERPs to open- and closed-class words elicited different patterns of brain activity However, the more mature left hemisphere asymmetry to closed-class words was not observed. By 3 years of age most children speak in sentences and use closed-class words appropriately to specify grammatical relations and, like adults, ERPs from 3-year-olds displayed a left-hemisphere asymmetry to closed-class words. Figure 14.8 illustrates the development of the left-hemisphere asymmetry to closed-class words in current source density maps across the three age groups. The results across the three groups are consistent with the hypothesis that, initially, open- and closed-class words are processed by similar brain systems, and that these systems become progressively specialized with increasing language experience. Further evidence on this hypothesis comes from an examination of ERPs from children who were the same age but differed in language abilities. The 20-month-old children who scored below the 50th percentile for vocabulary

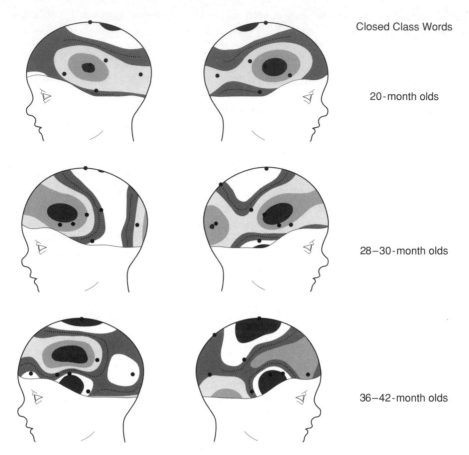

Closed Class Words

20-month olds

28–30-month olds

36–42-month olds

Figure 14.8 Current source density (CSD) analyses of neural activity to closed-class words at 200 msec. The CSDs illustrate sinks, i.e., activity flowing into the head, and sources, i.e., activity flowing out of the head, at three age groups. Top: at 20 months the CSD shows sinks over both the left and the right hemispheres. Middle: at 28–30 months the CSD shows sinks that are bilateral but slightly more prominent over the right than the left hemisphere. Bottom: at 36–42 months the CSD shows a sink over left anterior regions.

size did not show ERP differences to open- and closed-class words. In contrast, those above the 50th percentile displayed ERP differences to open- and closed-class words that were similar to the patterns shown in 28–30 months old. These data strongly suggest that the organization of brain activity is linked to language abilities rather than to chronological age per se.

Summary and Conclusions

The results from the language studies, taken as a whole, point to different developmental time courses and developmental vulnerabilities of aspects of grammatical and semantic/lexical processing. They thus provide support for conceptions of language that distinguish these subprocesses within language. Similarly, following auditory deprivation, processes associated with the dorsal visual pathway were more altered than were functions associated with the ventral pathway, providing support for conceptions of visual system organization that distinguish functions along these lines. A general hypothesis that may account for the different patterns of plasticity within both vision and language is that systems employing fundamentally different learning mechanisms display different patterns of developmental plasticity. It may be that systems displaying experience-dependent change throughout life including the topography of sensory maps (Merzenich et al., 1988; Gilbert, 1995; Kaas, 1995); lexical acquisition (i.e., object–word associations); and the establishment of form, face and object representations (i.e., ventral pathway functions) rely upon very general, associative learning mechanisms that permit learning and adaptation throughout life. By contrast, systems important for computing dynamically shifting relations between locations, objects, and events (including the dorsal visual pathway and the systems of the brain that mediate grammar) appear dependent on and modifiable by experience primarily during more limited periods in development. This could account both for the greater developmental deficits and enhancements of dorsal pathway function following various developmental anomalies and for the greater effects of altered language experience on grammatical functions. Further research is necessary to characterize systems that become constrained in this way and those that can be modified throughout life. This type of developmental evidence can contribute to fundamental descriptions of the architecture of different cognitive systems. Additionally, in the long run, they may contribute to the design of educational and habilitative programs for both normally and abnormally developing children.

ACKNOWLEDGMENTS

This research has been supported by grants from National Institutes of Health, DC00128, and DC00481. We are grateful to our many collaborators on the several studies summarized here, and to Linda Heidenreich for manuscript preparation. We thank Jeff Goodhill for his careful reading of this manuscript.

REFERENCES

Armstrong, B. (1995). Effects of auditory deprivation on color and motion processing: an ERP study. Unpublished doctoral thesis, UCSD.

Atkinson, J., King, J., Braddick, O., Nokes, L., Anker, S., and Braddick, F. (1997). A specific deficit of dorsal stream function in Williams' syndrome. *NeuroReport* 8, 1919–22.

Baizer, J. S., Ungerleider, L. G., and Desimone, R. (1991). Organization of visual inputs to the inferior temporal and posterior parietal cortex in macaques. *J. Neurosci.* 11, 168–90.

Blakemore, C., Garey, L. J., and Vital-Durand, F. (1978). The physiological effects of monocular deprivation and their reversal in the monkey's visual cortex. *Physiol.* (Lond.) 283, 223–62.

Bourgeois, J. P., Goldman-Rakic, P. S., and Rakic, P. (2000). Formation, Elimination, and Stabilization of synapses in the primate cerebral cortex. In *The New Cognitive Neuro Sciences*. M. S. Gazzaniga, ed. Cambridge, MA: MIT Press, pp. 45–53.

Bowering, E. R., Maurer, D. Lewis, T. L., and Brent, H. P. (1997). Constriction of the visual field of children after early visual deprivation. *J. Pediatr. Ophthalmol. Strabismus* 34, 347–56.

Chalupa, L. and Dreher, B. (1991). High precision systems require high precision "blueprints": A new view regarding the formation of connections in the mammalian visual system. *J. Cogn. Science* 3, 209–19.

Chugani, H. T., Müller, R.-A., and Chugani, D. C. (1996). Functional brain reorganization in children. *Brain Dev.* 18, 347–56.

Cohen, L. G., Celnik, P., Pascual-Leone, A., Corwell, B., Faiz, L., Dambrosia, J., Honda, M., Sadato, N., Gerloff, C., Catalá, M. D., and Hallett, M. (1997). Functional relevance of cross-modal plasticity in blind humans. *Nature* 389, 180–3.

Curtiss, S. (1989). The independence and task-specificity of language. In *Interaction in Human Development*. M. Bornstein and J. Bruner, eds. Hillsdale, NJ: Lawrence Erlbaum, pp. 105–37.

Cynader, M., and Mitchell, D. (1980). Prolonged sensitivity to monocular deprivation in dark reared cats. *J. Neurophysiol.* 43, 1026–40.

Dehaene, S., Dupoux, E., Mehler, J., Cohen, L., Perani, D., van de Moortele, P.-F., Lehérici, S., and Le Bihan, D. (1997). Anatomical variability in the cortical representation of first and second languages. *NeuroReport* 17, 3809–15.

Dehay, C., Bullier, J., and Kennedy, H. (1984). Transient projections from the fronto-parietal and temporal cortex to areas 17, 18, and 19 in the kitten. *Exp. Brain Res.* 57, 208–12.

Eden, G. F., Van Meter, J. W., Rumsey, J. M., Maisog, J. M., Woods, R. P., and Zeffiro, T. A. (1996). Abnormal processing of visual motion in dyslexia revealed by functional brain imaging. *Nature* 382, 66–9.

Frost, D. O. (1984). Axonal growth and target selection during development: Retinal projections to the ventrobasal complex and other "nonvisual" structures in neonatal Syrian hamsters. *J. Comp. Neurol.* 230, 576–92.

Gilbert, C. D. (1995). Dynamic properties of adult visual cortex. In *The Cognitive Neurosciences*. M. S. Gazzaniga, ed. Cambridge, MA: MIT Press, pp. 73–89.

Harwerth, R., Smith, E., Duncan, G., Crawford, M., and von Noorden, G. (1986). Multiple sensitive periods in the development of the primate visual system. *Science* 232, 235–8.

Hickey, T. L. (1977). Postnatal development of the human lateral geniculate nucleus: Relationship to a critical period for the visual system. *Science* 198, 836–8.

Horton, J. C. and Hocking, D. R. (1997). Timing of the critical period for plasticity of ocular dominance columns in macaque striate cortex. *J. Neurosci.* 17, 3684–709.

Hubel, D. H. and Wiesel, T. N. (1977). Functional architecture of macaque monkey visual cortex. *Proc. R. Soc. Lond.* 198, 1–59.

Huttenlocher, P. R. (1994). Synaptogenesis, synapse elimination, and neural plasticity in human cerebral cortex. In *Threats to Optimal Development: Integrating Biological, Psychological, and Social Risk Factors*, Volume 27. C. A. Nelson, ed. Hillsdale, NJ: Lawrence Erlbaum Associates, Inc., pp. 35–54.

Huttenlocher, P. R. and Dabholkar, A. S. (1997). Regional differences in synaptogenesis in human cerebral cortex. *J. Comp. Neurol.* 387, 167–78.

Innocenti, G. and Clarke, S. (1984). Bilateral transitory projection to visual areas from auditory cortex in kittens. *Dev. Brain Res.* 14, 143–8.

Kaas, J. H. (1995). The reorganization of sensory and motor maps in adult mammals. In *The Cognitive Neurosciences*. M. S. Gazzaniga, ed. Cambridge, MA: MIT Press, pp. 51–71.

Kim, K. H. S., Relkin, N. R., Lee, K.-M., and Hirsch, J. (1997). Distinct cortical areas associated with native and second languages. *Nature* 388, 171–4.

Klima, E. S. and Bellugi, U. (1979). *The Signs of Language*. Cambridge, MA: Harvard University Press.

Lachica, E. A. and Casagrande, V. A. (1988). Development of primate retinogeniculate axon arbors. *Visual Neuroscience* 1, 103–23.

Livingstone, M. and Hubel, D. (1988). Segregation of form, color, movement and depth: Anatomy, physiology, and perception. *Science* 240, 740–9.

Lovegrove, W., Garzia, R., and Nicholson, S. (1990). Experimental evidence for a transient system deficit in specific reading disability. *J. Am. Optom. Assoc.* 61, 137–46.

Marler, P. (1970). A comparative approach to vocal learning: Song development in white-crowned sparrows. *Journal of Comparative and Physiological Psychology Monograph* 71, 1–25.

Maurer, D. and Lewis, T. L. (1998). Overt orienting toward peripheral stimuli: Normal development and underlying mechanisms. In *Cognitive Neuroscience of Attention: A developmental perspective.* J. E. Richards, ed., Hillsdale, NJ: Lawrence Erlbaum, pp. 51–102.

Merigan, W. and Maunsell, J. (1993). How parallel are the primate visual pathways? *Ann. Rev. Neurosci.* 16, 369–402.

Merzenich, M., Recanzone, G., Jenkins, W., Allard, T., and Nudo, R. (1988). Cortical representational plasticity. In *Neurobiology of Neocortex.* P. Rakic and W. Singer, eds. John Wiley and Sons, pp. 41–67.

Mills, D. L., Coffey-Corina, S. A., and Neville, H. J. (1993). Language acquisition and cerebral specialization in 20-month-old infants. *J. Cogn. Neurosci.* 5, 317–34.

Mills, D. L., Coffey-Corina, S. A., and Neville, H. J. (1997). Language comprehension and cerebral specialization from 13 to 20 months. *Developmental Neuropsychology* 13, 397–445.

Mioche, L. and Perenin, M. (1986). Central and peripheral residual vision in humans with bilateral deprivation amblyopia. *Exp. Brain Res.* 62, 259–72.

Mitchell, D. E. (1981). Sensitive periods in visual development. In *Development of Perception.* R. Aslin, J. Alberts, and M. Petersen, eds. New York: Academic Press, pp. 3–43.

Neville, H. J. (1995). Developmental specificity in neurocognitive development in humans. In *The Cognitive Neurosciences.* M. Gazzaniga, eds. Cambridge, MA: MIT Press, pp. 219–31.

Neville, H. J. and Bavelier, D. (1998). Variability of developmental plasticity within sensory and language systems: Behavioral, ERP and fMRI studies. *Proceedings of the Conference on Advancing Research on Developmental Plasticity: Integrating the Behavioral Science and the Neuroscience of Mental Health.* Wash. DC, US Govt. Printing Office, pp. 174–84.

Neville, H. J., Bavelier, D., Corina, D., Rauschecker, J., Karni, A., Lalwani, A., Braun, A., Clark, V., Jezzard, P., and Turner, R. (1998). Cerebral organization for language in deaf and hearing subjects: Biological constraints and effects of experience. *Proc. Natl. Acad. Sci. USA* 95, 922–9.

Neville, H. J., Coffey, S. A., Lawson, D. S., Fischer, A., Emmorey, K., and Bellugi, U. (1997). Neural systems mediating American Sign Language: Effects of sensory experience and age of acquisition. *Brain Lang.* 57, 285–308.

Neville, H. J. and Lawson, D. (1987a). Attention to central and peripheral visual space in a movement detection task: An event-related potential and behavioral study. I. Normal hearing adults. *Brain Res.* 405, 253–67.

Neville, H. J. and Lawson, D. (1987b). Attention to central and peripheral visual space in a movement detection task: An event-related and behavioral study. II. Congenitally deaf adults. *Brain Res.* 405, 268–83.

Neville, H. J. and Lawson, D. (1987c). Attention to central and peripheral visual space in a movement detection task. III. Separate effects of auditory deprivation and acquisition of a visual language. *Brain Res.* 405, 284–94.

Neville, H. J. and Mills, D. L. (1997). Epigenesis of language. *Mental Retardation and Developmental Disabilities Research Reviews* 3, 282–92.

Neville, H. J., Mills, D. L., and Lawson, D. (1992). Fractionating language: Different neural subsystems with different sensitive periods. *Cerebral Cortex* 2, 244–58.

Neville, H. J., Nicol, J., Barss, A., Forster, K., and Garrett, M. (1991). Syntactically based sentence processing classes: Evidence from event-related brain potentials. *J. Cogn. Neurosci.* 3, 155–70.

Neville, H. J., Schmidt, A., and Kutas, M. (1983). Altered visual evoked potentials in congenitally deaf adults. *Brain Res.* 266, 127–32.

Nobre, A. and McCarthy, G. (1994). Language-related ERPs: Scalp distributions and modulation by word type and semantic priming. *J. Cogn. Neurosci.* 6, 233–55.

Osterhout, L., McLaughlin, J., and Bersick, M. (1997). Event-related brain potentials and human language. *Trends in Cognitive Sciences* 1, 203–9.

Packer, O., Hendrickson, A., and Curcio, A. (1990). Developmental redistribution of photo-receptors across the *Macaca nemestrina* (Pigtail Macaque) retina. *J. Comp. Neurol.* 298, 472–93.

Perani, D., Dehaene, S., Grassi, F., Cohen, L., Cappa, S. F., Dupoux, E., Fazio, F., and Mehler, J. (1996). Brain processing of native and foreign languages. *NeuroReport* 7, 2439–44.

Ponton, C. W., Don, M., Eggermont, J. J., Waring, M. D., Kwong, B., and Masuda, A. (1996). Auditory system plasticity in children after long periods of complete deafness. *NeuroReport* 8, 61–5.

Rakic, P. (1976). Prenatal genesis of connections subserving ocular dominance in the rhesus monkey. *Nature* 261, 467–71.

Rakic, P., Bourgeois, J., Eckenhoff, M., Zecevic, N., and Goldman-Rakic, P. (1986). Concurrent overproduction of synapses in diverse regions of the primate cerebral cortex. *Science* 232, 232–5.

Rauschecker, J. and Kniepert, U. (1993). Auditory localization behaviour in visually deprived cats. *Eur. J. Neurosci.* 6, 149–60.

Rice, C., Feinstein, S., and Schusterman, R. (1965). Echo-detection ability of the blind: Size and distance factors. *J. Exp. Psychol.* 70, 246–51.

Röder, B., Rösler, F., and Hennighausen, E. (1997). Different cortical activation patterns in blind and sighted humans during encoding and transformation of haptic images. *Psychophysiology* 34, 292–307.

Röder, B., Rösler, F., Hennighausen, E., and Näcker, F. (1996). Event-related potentials during auditory and somatosensory discrimination in sighted and blind human subjects. *Cognitive Brain Research* 4, 77–93.

Röder, B., Teder-Salejarvi, W., Sterr, A., Rösler, F., Hillyard, S. A., and Neville, H. J. (1997). Auditory-spatial tuning in sighted and blind adults: Behavioral and electrophysiological evidence. *Society for Neuroscience* 23, 1590.

Sadato, N., Pascual-Leone, A., Grafman, J., Ibanez, V., Deiber, M.-P., Dold, G., and Hallet, M. (1996). Activation of the primary visual cortex by Braille reading in blind subjects. *Nature* 380, 526–8.

Sawatari, A. and Callaway, E. M. (1996). Convergence of magno- and parvocellular pathways in layer 4B of macaque primary visual cortex. *Nature* 380, 442–6.

Sereno, M. I., Dale, A. M., Reppas, J. B., Kwong, K. K., Belliveau, J. W., Brady, T. J., Rosen, B. R., and Tootell, R. G. (1995). Borders of multiple visual areas in humans revealed by functional magnetic resonance imaging. *Science* 268, 889–93.

Shankle, W. R., Kimball, R. A., Landing, B. H., and Hara, J. (1998b). Developmental patterns in the cytoarchitecture of the human cerebral cortex from birth to 6 years examined by correspondence analysis. *Proc. Natl. Acad. Sci. USA* 95, 4023–8.

Shankle, W. R., Landing, B. H., Rafii, M. S., Schiano, A., Chen, J. M., and Hara, J. (1998a). Evidence for a postnatal doubling of neuron number in the developing human cerebral cortex between 15 months and 6 years. *Journal of Theoretical Biology* 191, 115–40.

Sherman, S. M. (1985). Development of retinal projections to the cat's lateral geniculate nucleus. *TINS* 8, 350–5.

Sherman, S. M. and Spear, P. (1982). Organization of visual pathways in normal and visually deprived cats. *Psychol. Rev.* 62, 738–855.

Stoner, G. B. and Albright, T. D. (1993). Image segmentation cues in motion processing: Implications for modularity in vision. *J. Cogn. Neurosci.* 5, 129–49.

Sur, M., Pallas, S., and Roe, A. (1990). Cross-modal plasticity in cortical development: Differentiation and specification of sensory neocortex. *TINS* 13, 227–33.

Tomann, A., Mitchell, T., Neville, H. J., Corina, D., Liu, G., and Bavelier, D. (1998). Cortical reorganization for motion processing in congenitally deaf subjects. *Cognitive Neuroscience Society* 5, 14.

Tootell, R. B., Reppas, J. B., Kwong, K. K., Malach, R., Born, R. T., Brady, T. J., Rosen, B. R., and Belliveau, J. W. (1995). Functional analysis of human MT and related visual cortical areas using magnetic resonance imaging. *J. Neurosci.* 15, 3215–30.

Uhl, F., Franzen, P., Lindinger, G., Lang, W., and Deecke, L. (1991). On the functionality of the visually deprived occipital cortex in early blind persons. *Neurosci. Lett.* 124, 256–9.

Uhl, F., Kretschmer, T., Lindinger, G., Goldenberg, G., Lang, W., Oder, W., and Deecke, L. (1994). Tactile mental imagery in sighted persons and in patients suffering from peripheral blindness early in life. *Electroencephalogr. Clin. Neurophysiol.* 91, 249–55.

Ungerleider, L. G. and Mishkin, M. (1982). Two cortical visual systems. In *Analysis of Visual Behavior*. D. J. Ingle, M. A. Goodale, and R. J. Mansfield, eds. Cambridge: The MIT Press, pp. 549–86.

Van Driel, D., Provis, J. M., and Billson, F. A. (1990). Early differentiation of ganglion, amacrine, bipolar, and Muller cells in the developing fovea of human retina. *J. Comp. Neurol.* 291, 203–19.

Veraart, C., DeVolder, A., Wanet-Defalque, M., Bol, A., Michel, C., and Goffinet, A. (1990). Glucose utilization in human visual cortex is abnormally elevated in blindness of early onset but decreased in blindness of late onset. *Brain Res.* 510, 115–21.

Wanet-Defalque, M., Veraart, C., DeVolder, A., Metz, R., Michel, C., Dooms, G., and Goffinet, A. (1988). High metabolic activity in the visual cortex of early blind human subjects. *Brain Res.* 446, 369–73.

Weber-Fox, C. and Neville, H. J. (1996). Maturational constraints on functional specializations for language processing: ERP and behavioral evidence in bilingual speakers. *J. Cogn. Neurosci.* 8, 231–56.

15

Linguistic and Spatial Cognitive Development in Children with Pre- and Perinatal Focal Brain Injury: A Ten-Year Overview from the San Diego Longitudinal Project

Joan Stiles, Elizabeth A. Bates, Donna Thal, Doris A. Trauner, *and* Judy Reilly

For the past ten years a group of investigators based in San Diego has been studying the effects of pre- and perinatal focal brain injury on the development of linguistic and spatial cognitive functions. When this project began, even the most basic question concerning whether or not it is possible to identify specific deficits associated with early injury was still a subject of debate. Early studies on the effects of focal brain injury emphasized the "resilience" of young children to the effects of early injury and argued that early available mechanisms subserving a transient capacity for plastic change allow children with early injury to develop normal or near-normal cognitive functioning following injuries to the brain that would leave an adult permanently impaired (Alajouanine and Lhermitte, 1965; Brown and Jaffe, 1975; Carlson, Netley, Hendrick, and Pritchard, 1968; Gott, 1973; Hammill and Irwin, 1966; Krashen, 1973; Lenneberg, 1967; McFie, 1961; Reed and Reitan, 1971). These arguments did not, however, go unchallenged. Other investigators argued that a more fine-grained analysis of behavior showed evidence of persistent cognitive deficit (Day and Ulatowska, 1979; Dennis, 1980; Dennis and Kohn, 1975; Dennis and Whitaker, 1976; Kohn, 1980; Kohn and Dennis, 1974; Rudel and Teuber, 1971; Vargha-Khadem et al., 1983, 1985; Woods, 1980; Woods and Carey, 1979). These apparently contradictory sets of claims suggested a complex interplay between plasticity and specialization of function in the developing brain, but the nature and course of that interaction remained unclear. One limitation of that early work on both sides of the debate was its reliance on retrospective accounts of development in which the outcome of development following early injury is used to infer developmental process.

In order to understand the long-term effects of early neurological insult, it is necessary to investigate processes of recovery and/or compensation as they occur. A prospective approach to the study of development following early injury makes it possible to determine:

(1) whether there is *early* evidence of impairment; (2) whether the profile of impairment in early childhood is the same as or different from that observed in adults with similar injury; and (3) whether there is change in the profile over time.

A small number of investigators have adopted this approach to the study of children with focal brain injury. For example, Aram and her colleagues (Aram and Ekelman, 1986; Aram et al., 1983; 1985; Rankin et al., 1981) have reported data from cross-sectional studies of children under 5 years of age, providing evidence for global linguistic and cognitive deficits in children with early acquired focal brain injury. Longitudinal follow-ups of these children in the school-age period suggest that these early deficits persist with development (Aram, 1988; Aram and Ekelman, 1988; Aram et al., 1985). These studies are important because they provide strong evidence that early focal brain injury does result in significant functional deficits. However, studies by Aram and other investigators also show that the deficits associated with early brain injury are often quite subtle and may require finer-grained measures to be detected. For example, Riva, Cazzaniga, Pantaleoni, Milani, and Fedrizzi (1987) have uncovered grammatical deficits on the Token Test in children with left hemisphere damage (LHD) that are only evident when that test is reanalyzed to extract specific syntactic patterns (see also Dennis and Whitaker, 1976). Similar profiles of early, subtle deficit have been reported for children with frontal lobe injury. Eslinger and his colleagues (Eslinger and Grattan, 1991) report that among younger children the effects of injury to frontal lobe regions may be quite mild. However, they note that with development, patterns of deficit become more pronounced. They suggest that this late emerging pattern may reflect the fact that demands for behaviors mediated by the frontal lobes may become more pronounced as children reach adolescence, thus suggesting a kind of latent deficit profile. This pattern of late emerging deficit has been reported by Levine and her colleagues (Levine, 1993) on measures of IQ. They report a systematic decline in IQ scores beginning in early adolescence. This profile is not confined to children with frontal lobe injury, rather it appears to hold for the focal lesion population as a whole.

One of the most intriguing findings from this longitudinal investigation of the effects of early brain injury on development is that studies of language and visuospatial processing provide different answers to the questions of initial deficit, of mapping to adult profiles of deficit, and of change over time. The differences in these two domain-specific profiles are striking enough that they might have led an individual investigator working in isolation to posit very different theoretical accounts of developmental change following early brain injury. Yet within the context of this project, we are confronted with the fact that the data have been obtained from the same children. One challenge of this work will be the need to reconcile these differences, and provide a single account of development following early focal brain injury that encompasses what is becoming a diverse and challenging set of findings.

The Population of Children with Early Focal Brain Injury

The studies reported here focus on a group of children with early occurring focal brain injury. The children included in these studies were selected on the basis of the presence of a single, unilateral brain lesion that was acquired prior to, or at birth. Location and size of the lesions were ascertained by obtaining neuro-imaging procedures (MRI or CT scans) on every subject. Individuals were excluded if there was evidence of multi-focal or diffuse brain damage, or if there was evidence of intrauterine drug exposure. Most of the children were born full-term. Finally, on gross assessment, the children in the population do well behaviorally, both individually and as a group. They do not manifest gross cognitive deficits. In fact, they typically score within the normal range on standardized IQ measures, and attend public schools.

Language

We based our first round of hypotheses on a handful of relatively uncontroversial claims about adult aphasia that appear in virtually every neurology textbook. For example, there is general agreement that the left hemisphere (LH) is specialized for language in most normal adults (Bryden, 1982; Damasio and Damasio, 1992; Galaburda et al., 1994; Gazzaniga, 1994; Hellige, 1993). It is also generally believed that the perisylvian regions of the LH are especially important for phonological, lexical and grammatical functions (Damasio, 1989; Damasio and Damasio, 1992; Geschwind, 1972; Rasmussen and Milner, 1977). Furthermore, anterior versus posterior damage along the left Sylvian fissure is reliably correlated with the syndromes described by Broca and Wernicke, respectively (Damasio and Damasio, 1992; Goodglass, 1993; Naeser, Helm-Estabrooks, Haas, Aurbach, and Levine, 1984).

More recent research suggests that the right hemisphere (RH) also plays a role in language processing, complementing the functions mediated by the left. Studies have shown that RH injuries have specific effects on the comprehension and production of humor (Brownell, Michel, Powelson, and Gardner, 1983), metaphors (Brownell, Simpson, Birhle, Potter, and Gardner, 1990), and idioms (VanLancker and Kempler, 1986). They also may create problems with cohesion and coherence in narratives (Garner, 1983; Hough, 1990; Joanette, Goulet, and Hannequin, 1990; Kaplan, Brownell, Jacobs, and Gardner, 1990).

Extrapolating from these studies, there was ample reason to hypothesize that the LH, particularly the perisylvian area, may be innately specialized for acquisition of core aspects of language, whereas the RH might come into play as children begin to use language for a variety of discourse functions. We predicted that: (1) children with LHD would develop more severe language impairments than those with right hemisphere damage (RHD) (left-specialization hypothesis); (2) children with damage to anterior regions of the LH, especially the perisylvian area, would develop more severe language production deficits (Broca hypothesis); (3) children with damage to posterior regions of the LH, particularly the posterior portion of the left temporal lobe, would develop more severe language comprehension deficits (Wernicke hypothesis); and (4) children with RHD would demonstrate problems in telling a story or using language to make inferences.

In the sections that follow, we will describe four studies that span the range from 10 months to 12 years of age. The first three studies describe a group of children that was identified prior to the onset of measurable language skills. They were tested longitudinally (in cross-sectional studies) from prespeech through the period when typically developing children begin to regularly use grammatical sentences. The fourth study describes the acquisition of more complex syntax and narrative skills in children from 3 to 12 years.

Babbling and first words. The first study was a multiple case study of five infants with focal brain injury who were compared to ten typically developing children matched for level of language development at three data points (Marchman, Miller, and Bates, 1991). Language was measured with the MacArthur Communicative Development Inventory (CDI) (Fenson, Dale, Reznick, Thal, Bates, Hartung, Pethick, and Reilly, 1993) and a

30-minute spontaneous communication sample. Four of the children had LH lesions and one had a RH lesion. Two of the LH lesions were posterior. All of the other lesions were anterior.

All children with focal brain injury were delayed in gesture and word production at all three data points on the CDI. For the children with anterior lesions, however, word production began to move into the normal range at the third data point. The two children with left posterior (LP) lesions, on the other hand, remained below the 5th percentile. The anterior–posterior differences also appeared in the spontaneous communication samples. As a group, the children with focal brain injury did not differ from their typically developing peers on the number or length of vocalizations produced. However, their phonological development paralleled their lexical development: children with focal brain injury produced fewer "true" consonants and a smaller proportion of labial consonants than the age matched normal control children. By the third data point, however, children with anterior lesions had begun to use "true" consonants as frequently as the controls.

These results provided evidence that children with focal brain injury are indeed impaired in the early stages of language acquisition. The profiles of impairment also were different from those of adults with similar lesions, since children with anterior lesions (left and right) began to move into the normal range for word production by 21–22 months of age while those with LP lesions remained significantly delayed.

Early lexical development

Thal et al. (1991) used the CDI to extend these findings to 27 children with focal brain injury who were between 12 and 35 months of age. Results reinforced those of Marchman et al. (1991), indicating delays for the group as a whole in vocabulary comprehension (for the period over which it was measured) and production (throughout the full 12 to 35 month range).

Results also provided evidence that relationships between behavioral profiles and lesion site during development are not the same as those seen in adults. First, significant delays in vocabulary comprehension were found only in children with RHD. Second, particularly severe *expressive* delays were seen in children with LP lesions. Children without LP, on the other hand, moved into normal range. Thus, LP lesions appear to be associated with significant delays in *expressive* language, a pattern that only partially maps onto the profile of adults with focal brain injury.

From first words to grammar

Bates, Thal, Trauner, Fenson, Aram, Eisele, and Nass (1997), further extended these findings in 3 additional studies. In Study 1, children with LHD and RHD were compared using percentile scores on the CDI. Binomial tests indicated that more children than expected by chance were delayed in comprehension and word production and that more children with RHD (but *not* LHD) than expected by chance fell into the delayed range (below the 10th percentile). Even more surprising, *none* of the children with lesions involving the left temporal cortex (+LT), the presumed site of Wernicke's area, were in the risk range for word comprehension. Thus, in the age range from 10–17 months, there is weak evidence for RH specialization for language comprehension and clear disconfirmation of the Wernicke hypothesis. This is compatible with comprehension results for older children (Eisele and Aram, 1994; Trauner et al., 1996) as well as the earlier study reported by the San Diego group (Thal et al., 1991). Similar analyses of gesture production indicated no significant delays associated with LH or +LT, but support for RH disadvantage in gesture production, comparable to the findings for comprehension.

There was neither a significant left–right difference nor evidence for different effects for +LT on word production percentile scores. Note, however, that this null result is confounded by the surprising finding that comprehension deficits were greater in the RH. Hence it was important to control for the number of words that a child *understands* in order to assess whether there are site-specific effects on *the ability to produce those words*. To control for the confound, Bates et al. examined the proportion of receptive vocabulary that was produced. This analysis did yield a significant disadvantage for +LT. In other words, a LH disadvantage for expressive language was present in 10- to 17-month-old children with focal brain injury when differences in word comprehension were controlled. The fact that this LH disadvantage comes primarily from children with damage involving the left temporal lobe provides yet another challenge to the Wernicke hypothesis.

In Study 2, 19- to 31-month-old children with focal brain injury were compared on percentile scores for word production and two measures of early grammar: mean length in morphemes of the three longest utterances reported by parents (M3L), and the proportion of total vocabulary comprising grammatical function words. These comparisons produced a number of surprises. First, a significant number of children continued to be at risk for delays in expressive language. There were no significant differences overall between LH and RH for word production or grammar, but children with +LT were at a greater disadvantage for both vocabulary and M3L. The left temporal disadvantage appeared to be even stronger when there was also damage to the left frontal lobe, a finding that is compatible with hypotheses based on the adult literature. However, delays were equally serious for children with *right* frontal lobe damage, suggesting that frontal effects are symmetrical during this period of development. There were significant differences between LH and RH on the proportion of grammatical function words in their vocabulary, with LH lower than right, but this reflected a *right hemisphere advantage* rather than a left hemisphere disadvantage.

Finally, in Study 3, free speech samples of 20- to 44-month-old children with focal brain injury were compared on a general measure of grammatical complexity (mean length of utterance [MLU] in morphemes). As a group, subjects were about 4 months behind normal controls on MLU: about 52 percent fell in the lowest 10 percent for their age and LH/RH comparisons did not reach significance. However +LT were significantly lower than children without left temporal damage (–LT). Only 31 percent of the –LT sample fell into the lowest 10 percent for their age while 85 percent of the +LT sample did so (significant by a likelihood ratio, $p < .002$). These results contradict the Wernicke hypothesis, and extend the left temporal findings reported above. However, in contrast with Study 2, frontal involvement did not increase the risk for expressive language delays in this analysis, providing little evidence for the Broca hypothesis.

The series of studies by Bates et al. (1997) does not follow the pattern expected based on lesion site–symptom correlations in adults with focal brain injury. This contradiction may reflect the very different task demands that confront infants and adults in the language domain. Infants and toddlers are learning language *for the first time*, whereas the task for adults is to use that knowledge for fluent and efficient communication. It appears that in the acquisition and development of the linguistic system, children draw on a broader array of brain structures. However, the Bates et al. (1997) results do provide evidence that the left temporal lobe is of major importance to the emergence of LH specialization for language under normal conditions.

Discourse and grammar from 3–12 years

Our study of older children is based on narratives elicited from 31 children with focal brain injury (13 with RHD and 18 with LHD) between 3 years, 6 months (3,6) and 9 years, 6 months (9,6) and age and gender matched controls (Reilly, Bates, and Marchman, 1998). In our narrative task, the children were asked to look through a wordless picture book, *Frog, where are you?* (Mayer, 1969), and then, while looking at the book, to tell the story to an adult. Our analyses focused on microstructures (lexical types and tokens, morphology and syntax) and macrostructures (narrative components and theme).

Children with focal brain injury produced shorter stories overall than the controls, and they included fewer story components. Their stories contained a smaller number of prepositions, fewer word types and fewer word tokens. There were developmental changes in lexical output that included an increase in both the use and range of evaluative terms, and an increased use of pronouns that are co-referential with a noun in the same sentence, but no clear effects of lesion group. By age 5, the children with focal brain injury were comparable to the controls in vocabulary production during a story-telling task.

Morphological development continued to lag behind in the children with focal brain injury. By age 5, the controls made very few morphological errors; the children with focal brain injury did not reach the same level of proficiency until seven. Similar to our findings for the emergent stages of language development above, this selective disadvantage in the acquisition of morphology before 7 was primarily in +LT.

Syntax was analyzed from two perspectives: frequency of complex sentences and diversity of complex structures. All children used more complex syntax as they got older, but the children with focal brain injury lagged behind the controls across the full age range from 3.5 to 12 years. Among the youngest children (3,6 5,0), children with RHD clustered with controls, whereas children with LHD rarely used complex syntax. Among older children (5,0–9,6), all children with focal brain injury, regardless of lesion site, performed below the controls. If we plot the developmental trajectories across all ages, children with LHD show the same slope as controls but at a significantly lower level, whereas the slope for children with RHD is essentially flat. Since complex syntax is a mechanism for integrating and relating events in a story, this profile may be evidence of a broader RH integrative deficit. Note, however, that there was no evidence of a RH disadvantage in overall level of performance.

Syntactic diversity was measured by applying a scale of 0 to 5 to the number of complex sentence types in each child's story. Among the younger children, +LT produced significantly fewer complex types compared to −LT; however, this profile did not hold after age 5, when both scored significantly lower than controls.

Children with focal brain injury included significantly fewer story episodes in narratives, and the stories tended to focus on local story events rather than tying events together with a theme. This suggests a delay in integrating the macrostructure with individual events as well as in making inferences about the motivations of the characters. The transition from a sequential description of local events to coherent narrative with an integrating theme occurred between age 5 and 6 in controls; it did not appear consistently until 7 to 8 in the stories from children with focal brain injury. Again, we see no clear patterns relating to lesion side or site.

Overall, we found delays in children with focal brain injury on both linguistic and narrative measures. In addition, +LT appeared to be the most vulnerable for acquisition of new linguistic structures before 5–7 years of age. This profile of delay is reminiscent of the initial delays in language described above in infants and toddlers with focal brain injury. The production delays observed for core linguistic structures do *not* map onto the lesion profiles observed in adults with analogous injuries. However, these findings are compatible with the idea that the left temporal lobe plays an important role in the emergence of the LH specialization for language typically observed in normal adults. Finally, these data suggest that delays in linguistic abilities are not completely resolved by 5 years of age. They may, instead, reassert themselves as children with focal brain injury face new linguistic challenges. What we appear to be witnessing is a dynamic and repetitive process, very much like normal language acquisition, but with a somewhat delayed developmental trajectory.

As we have seen, results from examination of the acquisition of language by children with focal brain injury contradict predictions based on adults with comparable injuries. As we are about to see, the data for spatial cognition in the same population tell another story.

Spatial Analytic Processing

Spatial analysis is defined as the ability to specify both the parts and the overall configuration of a pattern. Studies with adults have shown that different patterns of spatial deficit are associated with LHD and RHD (e.g., Arena and Gainotti, 1978; Delis et al., 1986; 1998; Gainotti and Tiacci, 1970; McFie and Zangwill, 1960; Piercy et al., 1960; Ratcliff, 1982; Swindell et al., 1988; Warrington et al., 1966). Injury to LP brain regions results in disorders in defining the parts of a spatial array, while patients with RHD have difficulty with the configural aspects of spatial pattern analysis. We have found similar patterns of disorder in our studies of young children with early focal brain injury

Spatial classification

Our study of spatial classification (Stiles-Davis et al., 1985) was the first to explicitly establish a specific disorder of spatial integrative ability in 2- to 3-year-olds with RHD. In this task children were presented with stimulus sets containing two classes of objects (e.g., blocks and small plates, small dolls and wooden rings, cups and spoons) and simply encouraged to play. This procedure elicits systematic class grouping activity in both normal children and children with focal brain injury. The results showed that children with RHD were selectively impaired in their ability to form spatial groupings. Specifically, while RHD children would stack objects or place one object in another, they did not place objects next to one another to extend their constructions out in space. Normal and LHD children regularly placed objects next to each other as early as 24-months.

Block construction

In order to elaborate the spatial classification findings, we conducted a large study using a more structured spatial grouping task. In this study 3- to 5-year-old children were asked to copy a series of model block constructions (Stiles, Stern, Trauner, and Nass, 1996). This study was designed to allow us to examine both the products of children's construction efforts, and the procedures they used in grouping the blocks. Children in both LHD and RHD groups showed evidence of impairment on these tasks. Children with LHD initially showed delay on the task, producing simplified constructions. By the time they were 4 years of age, they showed an interesting dissociation in performance. Most of the children were able to produce accurate copies of the target constructions, however the procedures they used in copying the forms were greatly simplified. This dissociation between product and process persisted at least through age 6. RHD children were initially delayed. By age 4, they produced disordered, poorly configured constructions. However, at this age the procedures they used to generate their ill-formed constructions were comparable to age-matched controls. However, by the time these children were 6 years of age their profile of performance changed. By that time they were able to accurately copy the target construction, but like their LHD peers, they used simple procedures to generate these constructions. This study suggests that there is indeed impairment in spatial processing following early injury, and there is compensation with development. However, close examination of how spatial constructions are generated suggests persistent deficit. These findings have been replicated in a second study of American and Italian children with localized brain injury (Vicari et al., 1998). This also demonstrated that children with isolated subcortical injury show the same profiles of deficit as children with cortical involvement.

Drawing

Our study of drawing in the focal lesion population has shown that children with RHD initially have considerable difficulty drawing organized pictures (Stiles–Davis et al., 1988). In a simple free drawing task, children were asked to draw a house. By age 3.5 to 4, normal children produce well organized houses, with an outer form representing the building and appropriately positioned inner features representing doors and windows. By age 5, the house drawings of children with LHD are indistinguishable from those of normal controls. However, during the late preschool period drawings by children with RHD are disordered and lack integration. The lack of organization suggests deficits in the ability to integrate parts to form a coherent whole. This is consistent with Swindell and colleagues' (1988) characterization of drawings by adult patients with RHD as, "scattered, fragmented, and disorganized . . . subjects often overscored lines and added extraneous scribblings" (p. 19).

This notable impairment in drawing among the children with RHD does not persist. Our longitudinal studies have shown considerable improvement with age. Improvement in the organization of their drawings is striking, but the drawings also exhibit striking similarity over time. This similarity may reflect the development of graphic formulas. Graphic formulas are common in the normal development course of drawing. Children begin to use graphic formulas from their earliest drawings (Stiles, 1995) and their use persists through adulthood. Thus the development of graphic formulas would not be an abnormal feature of drawing among children with RHD. The development of formulas may, however, offer a useful compensatory strategy by allowing children to represent common objects, while minimizing the spatial processing demands. If the children's improvement on the drawing task is achieved through the compensatory strategy of graphic formula production, then they should be more dependent on formulaic representation than normally developing children. Reliance on graphic formulas was tested using a task developed by Karmiloff-Smith (1990) in which children are asked to first draw a house, and then an impossible house (Stiles et al., 1997). The most common solution to this task among normal children is to distort the spatial configuration of the house. The drawings of children with LHD are indistinguishable from those of normal controls (see figure 15.1a). However, in our longitudinal sample of 5 RHD children tested every 6 to 12 months for a period from 3 to 6 years, configural distortion was not used (see figure 15.1b). Instead the children derived a number of non-configurational solutions for solving the problem, including verbal descriptions, formula substitution (drawing another formulaic object and asserting it was a house), reduction (putting a dot on the page and saying the house is very

A. Children with Left Hemisphere Damage

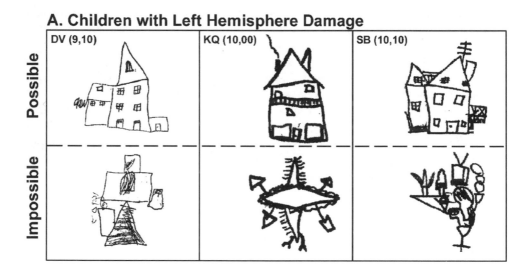

B. Children with Right Hemisphere Damage

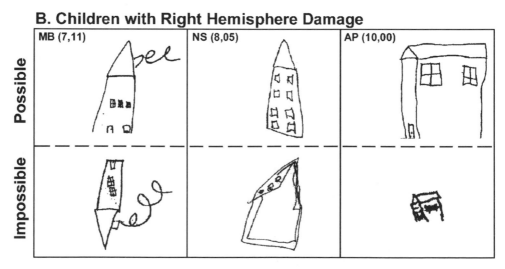

Figure 15.1   Drawings of possible and impossible houses from children with left (A) or right (B) hemisphere brain injury.

small), and invisibility. Once again, these data indicate that while these children are developing and their performance on specific spatial tasks improves, the processes by which they master these tasks may differ from those of normally developing children. This suggests a pattern of specific, subtle, and persistent deficit in spatial processing.

Processing hierarchical forms

Any visually presented pattern can be conceived of as a structured hierarchy consisting of local level elements and more global level assemblies. One example of a simple pattern hierarchy is the hierarchical form stimulus. It consists of a large letter composed of appropriately arranged smaller letters, such as a large H made up of small Ss. Hierarchical stimuli have been used in studies of normal adults (e.g., Kinchla and Wolfe, 1979; Martin, 1979; Navon, 1977; Palmer, 1980; Palmer and Bucher, 1981) and children (Dukette and Stiles, 1996; 2001; Stiles-Davis et al., 1988). They have also been used successfully to identify differential patterns of spatial deficit in adults with focal left and right posterior brain injury (Delis et al., 1986; 1988; Lamb et al., 1989, 1990; Robertson and Delis, 1986). Specifically, adult patients with RHD have difficulty processing the global level of the form, while patients with LHD have difficulty with the local level.

Data from one study of hierarchical form processing among children with LHD or RHD are consistent with data from adult patients. In this task children were asked to study and remember a hierarchical pattern. After a brief distracter task they were asked to reproduce the form from memory (see figure 15.2 for examples from younger children). Two age groups were tested, 5- to 7-year-olds, and 9- to 11-year-olds. The younger children with LHD had difficulty producing both the global and the local level of pattern structure, while young children with RHD were able to accurately produce the local level elements but had difficulty with the global level. Older children with LHD were impaired only with production of local level stimuli, and older children with RHD continued to show impairment with the global level. For each group the level of impairment was more pronounced

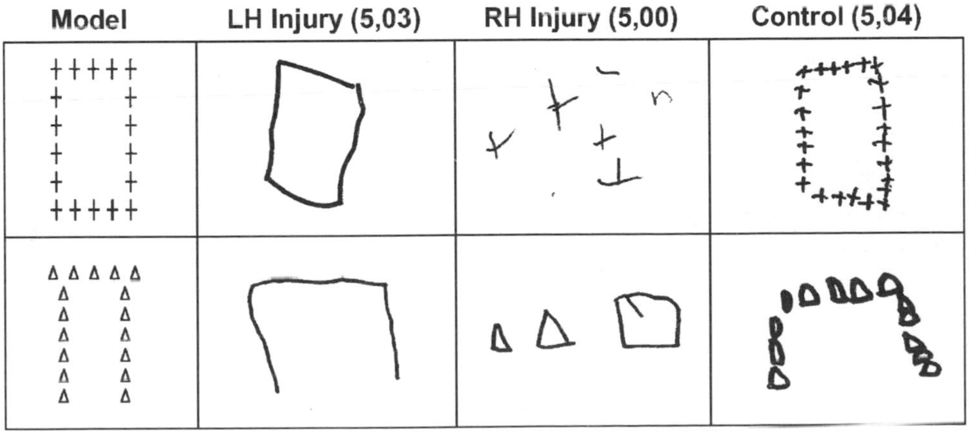

Figure 15.2 Memory reproductions of two model hierarchical forms by three 5-year-old children, one with prenatal LH brain injury, one with prenatal RH brain injury, and a normal control child.

for the younger than the older children. For the young children with LHD, the severe impairment in ability to produce local elements, also affects their ability to generate a well configured larger form. The reverse profile was not observed for the children with RHD. It was possible for them to accurately generate local level elements, even though they were unable to configure them appropriately.

Summary and Conclusion

We have provided a brief overview of results from the first large-scale prospective study of behavioral development in children with early focal brain injury. It has taken more than ten years to accumulate a large enough database to justify the (tentative) conclusions presented here. It also goes without saying that all of these findings will need to be replicated in other laboratories. Furthermore, because our findings are still primarily cross-sectional in nature, they must be tested and extended in longitudinal work. With those caveats in mind, we want to underscore that research with this population has yielded a number of surprises, including results that are not always compatible with the view of brain organization that one typically finds in surveys of lesion studies in human adults. We end this chapter with three lessons from research with this population, followed by three questions that are left unanswered by this work.

Lesson #1: Against predeterminism

The idea that the mind–brain is organized into distinct faculties or "modules" goes back to the eighteenth century, to the phrenological proposals of Gall and Spurzheim. This phrenological perspective is often accompanied by a developmental corollary: familiar patterns of brain organization for higher cognitive functions can be found in the mature adult because those patterns were there from the beginning, as innate properties of the human brain. The fact that children in this population outperform adults with homologous injuries can be used to argue against any strong form of predeterminism, predestination, or preformationism. All of the findings that we have reviewed in this chapter point in the same direction: children with early focal brain damage ultimately reach levels of performance well ahead of those observed in adults with homologous injuries. To be sure, brain damage is not a good thing, and children who have suffered some form of focal brain injury typically perform (as a group) reliably below normal controls, sometimes in relatively predictable patterns depending on their site and side of injury. However, our developmental findings suggest that these initial biases are imperfect, indirect, "soft constraints" that can be overcome.

Lesson #2: Against equipotentiality

When studies of children with early brain injury first appeared in the neuroscience literature, they were sometimes used to argue in favor of a *tabula rasa* view of the mind–brain, a view in which cortical tissue is, initially, capable of taking on an infinite number of functions, with no bias toward any particular cognitive domain. In its strongest form, the equipotentiality hypothesis is flatly impossible: if it were true, there would be no way to explain why familiar forms of brain organization are observed so often in the neurologically intact adult brain. For example, current estimates are that the LH plays a special role in the mediation of language in 95–98 percent of normal individuals. There must be some kind of bias present from the beginning of life in order to explain the well-documented hemispheric specialization for language and spatial cognitive functioning. By carrying out prospective studies of linguistic and cognitive development, we have uncovered subtle but specific patterns of deficit and delay that work against any strong and simple form of the equipotentiality hypothesis. Some form of cortical specialization (or "cortical preference") is clearly there from the beginning of life, although it can give way to an alternative "division of labor" when things go awry. Our challenge for the future is to specify the nature of those early biases, and the developmental processes by which alternative forms of brain organization emerge over time.

Lesson #3: Children are not adults

The patterns of lesion–symptom mapping that we have uncovered in our work differ markedly from the patterns revealed in adult neuropsychology literature. In all the domains that we have studied to date, there are quantitative differences in the effects of homologous injuries on children and adults: the effects on children are generally more subtle (i.e., not as severe, compared with performance by normals in the same age range), and performance improves markedly over time – sometimes to the point where (at least on casual inspection) the deficit seems to have disappeared altogether. These quantitative differences provide further evidence for a conclusion that has emerged in the last 20–30 years of research in developmental neurobiology: the developing brain is highly plastic, and alternative forms of brain organization are possible for the "same" behavioral task (although there is emerging evidence that the processes associated with these alternative forms may differ from those observed with typical organizational profiles).

Within the language domain, the differences are also qualitative. We outlined four simple hypotheses derived from more than 100 years of research on adults with unilateral brain injury: (1) LH specialization for most linguistic tasks, (2) left frontal specialization for expressive language (i.e., the Broca hypothesis), (3) left temporal specialization for receptive language (i.e., the Wernicke hypothesis), and (4) RH specialization for some discourse functions. We did not find unequivocal support for any of these hypotheses, and some of them were flatly contradicted by our results.

For example, none of our infants with left temporal lesions were in the bottom 10th percentile for word comprehension; in fact, although results are probabilistic in nature, there is some reason to believe that RHD is a greater risk factor for comprehension. These findings run against the Wernicke hypothesis, and against LH specialization for basic language functions. In line with the adult literature, we do find evidence that children with LHD are more delayed in expressive language. However, this finding is only evident from 10 months of age (the dawn of language) up to but not beyond 5–7 years. Furthermore, the effect is coming primarily from children with left temporal involvement (against the Wernicke hypothesis). Frontal involvement is an additional risk factor between 19 and 31 months of age, but in this time window it doesn't seem to matter whether frontal damage occurs in the left or the RH (against the Broca hypothesis). Some time after 5–7 years of age, we no longer have any evidence for differences due to side of lesion (left vs. right) or intra-hemisphere site of lesion (frontal or temporal). The RH cases display a flatter developmental profile in the use of complex syntax for narrative purposes, in line with the idea that the RH may be specialized for discourse. However, there are no significant differences between the left and right hemisphere groups in absolute level of performance after 5–7 years of age. The only firm conclusion that holds in our data for older children with congenital lesions is that brain damage does exact a cost, lowering the group profile below normal controls – though still well within the normal range.

Although we have no ready explanation for these quantitative and qualitative differences in patterning, these findings do remind us of an important point: the children in our prospective studies are encountering language and other higher cognitive functions for the first time. What we are looking at is, in essence, the effect of early focal brain injury on the learning process. Our results suggest that the brain mechanisms responsible for language learning are not the same mechanisms that govern the maintenance and fluent use of language in normal adults. In other words, we do not believe that language literally moves (bags packed) from one brain region to another across the course of development. Rather, the learning process may recruit brain areas that are no longer needed once the learning itself is complete, and the task in question has become a routine part of daily life. This conclusion is, in fact, compatible with recent studies of learning and processing in normal adults using positron emission tomography (PET) and functional magnetic resonance imaging (fMRI) – studies that show differential patterns of brain activity for the same task in novices compared with experts (Raichle, 1994), and differential patterns of activity in the same individuals as a new task is mastered and/or as the same task is administered with increasingly difficult and complex stimuli (Just et al., 1996).

These conclusions are easy to defend, in light of our own work and many other studies in the literature. However, as we have noted, they raise more questions than they answer. Let us end by posing three of the most puzzling questions that we now face.

Question #1: Why is language more plastic than spatial cognition?

Our results for spatial cognition are, as noted, qualitatively similar to the lesion–symptom patterns that have been reported for brain-injured adults. In the spatial domain, RHD seems to be associated with a deficit in the integration of information; by contrast, LHD results in a deficit in the extraction of pattern detail. By contrast, our findings for language development are not at all compatible with the classic aphasia types observed in adults. Deficits in word comprehension and gesture appear to be associated with RHD rather than LHD. Deficits on the production of words and grammar are greater in our LHD sample, as we might expect from adult aphasiology. However, the intrahemispheric patterns observed in children are quite different from those observed in adults, including an asymmetrical LP effect on both vocabulary and grammar, and an additional frontal effect on expressive language that is observed to an equal degree with right frontal and left frontal involvement. More puzzling still, none of these side or site specific effects are observed in our cross-sectional findings after 5–7 years of age, even though our older children have exactly the same congenital etiology as the younger cases. This is not true for our extensive school-age studies of spatial cognition. Why are the findings for language so different from our findings for spatial cognition?

It is possible that language is more plastic than other behavioral functions simply because it is a phylogenetically recent phenomenon. Perhaps there has not been sufficient time for language to evolve into a fixed and irreversible neural system. Although we acknowledge this possibility, we suspect that this is not the answer. Language is different from the other systems that we have studied to date in a number of crucial respects, with implications for the nature and plasticity of the neural systems that subserve it. First, language is the system that we use to express meaning; indeed, the boundaries of language include semantics as well as grammar and phonology. Because meaning encompasses all of our experience, the system that we have evolved to encode those meanings must by definition include information derived from widely distributed neural systems.

But what about linguistic form, independent of meaning? Could there be a tightly bounded, predetermined region that handles phonology and/or grammar? In principle, this is certainly possible, and to a limited extent it has to be true – at least for speech sounds. The basic input–output architecture used by speech appears to be a universal property of the human brain. As Sigmund Freud pointed out long ago in his seminal book on aphasia (Freud, 1953), it is quite likely that, under default circumstances, the continuous sheets of cortex that subserve the rest of language will organize around these basic input–output "hot spots," leading to the familiar pattern of broad perisylvian specialization for language. At the same time, we now know that this pattern can appear in either hemisphere after early brain injury, and we also know from recent neural imaging studies of normal adults that homologous areas of activation are observed on both sides of the brain in many language tasks, although the activation is typically greater on the left (Just et al., 1996).

This brings us to a central issue in the definition of "language areas": are these regions specialized for speech and language *only* (i.e., as special purpose mechanisms – Fodor, 1983), or is it the case that language "borrows" perceptual and motor systems that also do other kinds of work? At the moment, most of the evidence points to the latter option. For example, a recent fMRI study demonstrated that, in addition to carrying out linguistic functions, the various subcomponents of Broca's participate in the planning and execution of one or more non-speech tasks (Erhard et al., 1996). Similar results have been reported for the left temporal regions that are the putative site of Wernicke's area. In short, although it is possible that some aspects of language processing are carried out in highly localized brain regions, those regions may subserve a wider range of function. This may be one reason why these areas show so much plasticity: language is a problem that the brain solves with a range of different general-purpose tools, and for that reason, a number of different solutions are possible.

This brings us to a related point: if language is a parasitic system, running on hardware that evolved for other purposes, it is fair to ask whether the lesion–symptom patterns that we have observed in language, spatial cognition and affect are related in some way? For example, we have noted that RHD children show a relatively flat profile in the development of complex syntax. Is this language profile related to the information-integration deficits observed in spatial cognition? Do the same integration problems observed in RHD contribute in some fashion to the delays in word comprehension displayed by RHD children in the early phases of development? In fact, learning what a word means for the first time is, by definition, a multimodal integration problem. In the same vein, we may ask whether the deficits in perceptual analysis associated with left temporal lesions are implicated in some way in the expressive language delays that children with such lesions display between 10 and 60 months of age. The evidence suggests that left temporal cortex is especially well-suited to the extraction of pattern detail, temporal as well as spatial. This fact may give left temporal cortex a "competitive edge" in the language learning process. But why should this "edge" appear most clearly in expressive language, rather than comprehension? We have suggested elsewhere (e.g., Bates et al., 1997; Elman et al., 1996; Stiles and Thal, 1993) that learning-to-produce actually requires a much more fine-grained form of perceptual analysis than learning-to-comprehend, because the child must pull enough detail out of the acoustic signal to permit the construction of an intelligible motor template. In other words, understanding what "giraffe" means in context requires far less analysis of the signal than saying the word "giraffe" for the very first time. Of course these suggestions are still quite speculative, but it is a place to start – which brings us to the next question.

Question #2: What is a "bias"?

We have suggested a compromise between the warring claims of equipotentiality and predeterminism, in which different regions of cortex start out not with innate knowledge, but with "soft constraints," innate predispositions to process information a certain way. This is what Elman et al. (1996), refer to as "architectural innateness," as opposed to "representational innateness." Because of its initial predispositions, a particular region of the brain may be *recruited* to carry out specific aspects of (for example) a linguistic or visual–spatial task, in the same way that a tall child is recruited into the game of basketball. On this view, the division of labor that we see in the adult brain is the product of development rather than its cause. This approach is compatible with findings in developmental neurobiology over the last two decades, suggesting that cortical specialization is driven by activity and experience, in the default situation and in the alternative situations that arise after early brain injury (for reviews, see Elman et al., 1996, ch. 5; Nelson, 1999; Stiles, 1998; 2000). However, we still know very little about the features of different cortical regions that are responsible for these initial predispositions. What do we mean, in concrete neurocomputational terms, when we say that a region is specialized for information integration, or for the extraction of fine-grained pattern detail? Unfortunately, very little is currently known about the neural microcircuitry of the developing human brain. For example, are there concrete, measurable differences from region to region or hemisphere to hemisphere in cell density and cell types within and across cortical layers, the distribution of neurochemicals, and so forth? What are the computational consequences of such differences, if they exist? We know what questions to ask, but there are very few answers available right now, and our conjectures about innate predispositions for learning cannot be turned into testable hypotheses until such information becomes available.

Question #3: Why does plasticity sometimes fail?

We end by pointing out that there are populations of children with deficits in language, cognition and communication that do not display the extraordinary plasticity evidenced by children with early focal brain injury. Examples include children with Specific Language Impairment (SLI), autism, and several different forms of mental retardation including Williams Syndrome and Down Syndrome. All of these populations are currently under study in our San Diego research center, using many of the same behavioral and electrophysiological measures that we administer in our focal lesion studies. On almost every measure, our children with focal brain injury eventually surpass the other clinical groups, even though recent neural imaging studies of SLI, autism, Williams Syndrome and Down Syndrome provide no evidence for frank lesions of any kind. It seems evident from these comparisons that some forms of early brain injury lead to severe and persistent long-term deficits, without the profiles of recovery and/or compensation that we observe in the group with focal brain injury.

Why does plasticity fail in these cases? There are several possibilities: (1) diffuse, "microlesions" that are invisible in neural imaging studies but are nevertheless so pervasive that they preclude normal development, (2) abnormalities in the cytoarchitecture arising during neurogenesis and/or migration, (3) abnormalities in control of synaptogenesis, apoptosis or other regulatory mechanisms in brain development, and/or (4) neurochemical abnormalities affecting either basic metabolic processes or neurotransmitter production. Although these possibilities are no more than sheer speculation today, they may lend themselves to a rigorous test through the combined application of structural and functional brain imaging techniques.

To summarize, we have raised more questions than we have resolved in this chapter, but some lessons have been learned, and there are good reasons to hope that our new questions will be answered. Interdisciplinary research is difficult, requiring time and patience. But our experience to date suggests that this collaborative approach is well worth the effort.

REFERENCES

Alajouanine, T. and Lhermitte, F. (1965). Acquired aphasia in children. *Brain* 88, 553–62.

Aram, D. M. (1988) Language sequelae of unilateral brain lesions in children. In F. Plum (ed.), *Language, Communication, and the Brain* (pp. 171–97). New York: Raven Press.

Aram, D. M. and Ekelman, B. L. (1986). Cognitive profiles of children with early onset of unilateral lesions. *Developmental Neuropsychology* 2(3), 155–72.

Aram, D. M. and Ekelman, B. L. (1988). Scholastic aptitude and achievement among children with unilateral brain lesions. *Neuropsychologia* 26(6), 903–16.

Aram, D. M., Ekelman, B. L., Rose, D. F., and Whitaker, H. A. (1985). Verbal and cognitive sequel following unilateral lesions acquired in early childhood. *Journal of Clinical and Experimental Neuropsychology* 7(1), 55–78.

Aram, D. M., Rose, D. F., Rekate, H. L., and Whitaker, H. A. (1983). Acquired capsular/striatal aphasia in childhood. *American Medical Association* 40, 614–17.

Arena, R. and Gainotti, G. (1978). Constructional apraxia and visuoperceptive disabilities in relation to laterality of cerebral lesions. *Cortex* 11, 463–73.

Bates, E. A., Thal, D., Trauner, D., Fenson, J., Aram, D., Eisele, J. A., and Nass, R. (1997). From first words to grammar in children with focal brain injury. *Developmental Neuropsychology* 13(3), 275–343.

Brown, J. W. and Jaffe, J. (1975). Hypothesis on cerebral dominance. *Neuropsychologia* 13(1), 107–10.

Brownell, H., Michel, D., Powelson, J., and Gardner, H. (1983). Surprise but not coherence: Sensitivity to verbal humor in right-hemisphere patients. *Brain and Language* 18, 20–7.

Brownell, H., Simpson, T., Bihrle, A., Potter, H., and Gardner, H. (1990). Appreciation of metaphoric alternative word meanings by left and right brain-damaged patients. *Neuropsychologia* 28, 375–84.

Bryden, M. (1982). *Laterality: Functional asymmetry in the intact brain*. New York: Academic Press.

Carlson, J., Netley, C., Hendrick, E., and Pritchard, J. (1968). A reexamination of intellectual abilities in hemidecorticated patients. *Transactions of the American Neurological Association* 93, 198–201.

Damasio, A. (1989). Time-locked multiregional retroactivation: A systems-level proposal for the neural substrates of recall and recognition. *Cognition* 33, 25–62.

Damasio, A. and Damasio, H. (1992). Brain and language. *Scientific American* 267, 88–95.

Day, P. S. and Ulatowska, H. K. (1979). Perceptual, cognitive, and linguistic development after early hemispherectomy: Two case studies. *Brain and Language* 7, 17–33.

Delis, D. C., Kiefner, M. G., and Fridlund, A. J. (1988). Visuospatial dysfunction following unilateral brain damage: dissociations in hierarchical hemispatial analysis. *Journal of Clinical and Experimental Neuropsychology* 10(4), 421–31.

Delis, D. C., Robertson, L. C., and Efron, R. (1986). Hemispheric specialization of memory for visual hierarchical stimuli. *Neuropsychologia* 24(2), 205–14.

Dennis, M. (1980). Capacity and strategy for syntactic comprehension after left or right hemidecortication. *Brain and Language* 10, 287–317.

Dennis, M. and Kohn, B. (1975). Comprehension of syntax in infantile hemiplegics after cerebral hemidecortication. *Brain and Language* 2, 472–82.

Dennis, M. and Whitaker, H. A. (1976). Language acquisition following hemidecortication: Linguistic superiority of the left over the right hemisphere. *Brain and Language* 3, 404–33.

Dukette, D. and Stiles, J. (1996). Children's analysis of hierarchical patterns: Evidence from a similarity judgement task. *Journal of Experimental Child Psychology* 63(1), 103–40.

Dukette, D. and Stiles, J. (2001). The effects of stimulus density on children's analysis of heirarchical patterns. *Developmental Science* 4(2), 233–51.

Eisele, J. A. and Aram, D. M. (1994). Comprehension and imitation of syntax following early hemisphere damage. *Brain and Language* 46, 212–31.

Elman, E., Bates, E. A., Johnson, M., Karmiloff-Smith, A., Parisi, D., and Plunkett, K. (1996). *Rethinking innateness: A connectionist perspective on development.* Cambridge, MA: MIT Press/Bradford Books.

Erhard, P., Kato, T., Strick, P. L., and Ugurbil, K. (1996). Functional MRI activation pattern of motor and language tasks in Broca's area (Abstract). *Society for Neuroscience* 22, 260.2, 656.

Eslinger, P. J. and Grattan, L. M. (1991). Frontal lobe damage in children and adults: A comparative review. *Developmental Neuropsychology* 7(3), 283–326.

Fenson, L., Dale, P., Reznick, J. S., Thal, D., Bates, E. A., Hartung, J., Pethick, S., and Reilly, J. (1993). *The MacArthur Communicative Development Inventories: User's guide and technical manual.* San Diego: Singular Publishing Group.

Fodor, J. A. (1983). *The Modularity of Mind: An essay on faculty psychology.* Cambridge, MA: MIT Press.

Freud, S. (1953). *On Aphasia: A critical study.* New York: International Universities Press. (Original work published in 1891).

Gainotti, G. and Tiacci, C. (1970). Patterns of drawing disability in right and left hemispheric patients. *Neuropsychologia* 8, 379–84.

Galaburda, A. M., Wang, P. P., Bellugi, U., and Rossen, M. (1994). Cytoarchitectonic anomalies in a genetically based disorder: Williams syndrome. *NeuroReport* 5, 753–7.

Garner, W. R. (1983). Asymmetric interactions of stimulus dimensions in perceptual information processing. In T. J. Tighe and B. E. Shepp (eds.), *Perception, Cognition, and Development: Interactional analyses* (pp. 1–37). Hillsdale, NJ: Lawrence Erlbaum Associates.

Gazzaniga, M. (1994). Language and the cerebral hemispheres. *Discussions in Neuroscience* 10, 106–9.

Geschwind, N. (1972). Language and the brain. *Scientific American* 226(4), 76–83.

Goodglass, H. (1993). *Understanding aphasia.* San Diego: Academic Press.

Gott, P. S. (1973). Cognitive abilities following right and left hemispherectomy. *Cortex* 9, 266–74.

Hammill, D. and Irwin, O. C. (1966). I.Q. differences of right and left spastic hemiplegic children. *Perceptual and Motor Skills* 22, 193–4.

Hellige, J. B. (1993). *Hemispheric Asymmetry: What's right and what's left.* Cambridge, MA/ London: Harvard University Press.

Hough, M. (1990). Narrative comprehension in adults with right and left hemisphere brain damage: Theme organization. *Brain and Language* 38, 253–77.

Joanette, Y., Goulet, P., and Hannequin, D. (1990). *Right Hemisphere and Verbal Communication.* New York: Springer-Verlag.

Just, M. A., Carpenter, P. A., Keller, T. A., Eddy, W. F., and Thulborn, K. R. (1996). Brain activation modulated by sentence comprehension. *Science* 274 (5284), 114–16.

Kaplan, J., Brownell, H., Jacobs, J., and Gardner, H. (1990). The effects of right hemisphere damage on the pragmatic interpretation of conversational remarks. *Brain and Language* 38, 315–33.

Karmiloff-Smith, A. (1990). Constraints on representational change: Evidence from children's drawing. *Cognition* 34, 57–83.

Kinchla, R. A. and Wolfe, J. M. (1979). The order of visual processing: "Top-down," "bottom-up," or "middle-out". *Perception and Psychophysics* 25(3), 225–31.

Kohn, B. (1980). "Right hemisphere speech representation and comprehension of syntax after left cerebral injury." *Brain and Language* 9, 350–61.

Kohn, B. and Dennis, M. (1974). Selective impairments of visuospatial abilities in infantile hemiplegics after right cerebral hemidecortication. *Neuropsychologia* 12, 505–12.

Krashen, S. D. (1973). Lateralization, language learning, and the critical period: Some new evidence. *Language Learning* 23(1), 63–74.

Lamb, M. R., Robertson, L. C., and Knight, R. T. (1989). Attention and interference in the processing of global and local information: Effects of unilateral temporal–parietal junction lesions. *Neuropsychologia* 27(4), 471–83.

Lamb, M. R., Robertson, L. C., and Knight, R. T. (1990). Component mechanisms underlying the processing of hierarchically organized patterns: Inferences from patients with unilateral cortical lesions. *Journal of Experimental Psychology: Learning, Memory and Cognition* 16, 471–83.

Lenneberg, E. H. (1967). *Biological Foundations of Language.* New York: John Wiley and Sons, Inc.

Levine, S. C. (1993). *Effects of Early Unilateral Lesions: Changes over the course of development.* Hillsdale, NJ: Lawrence Erlbaum Associates, Inc.

Marchman, V. A., Miller, R., and Bates, E. A. (1991). Babble and first words in children with focal brain injury. *Applied Psycholinguistics* 12(1), 1–22.

Martin, M. (1979). Local and Global Processing: The Role of Sparsity. *Memory and Cognition* 7(6), 476–84.

Mayer, M. (1969). *Frog, where are you?* New York: Dial Press.

McFie, J. (1961). The effects of hemispherectomy on intellectual functioning in cases of infantile hemiplegia. *Journal of Neurology, Neurosurgery, and Psychiatry* 24, 240–9.

McFie, J. and Zangwill, O. L. (1960). Visual–constructive disabilities associated with lesions of the left cerebral hemisphere. *Brain* 83, 243–60.

Naeser, M., Helm-Estabrooks, N., Haas, G., Auerbach, S., and Levine, H. (1984). Relationship between lesion extent in "Wernicke's area" on computed tomographic scan and predicting recovery of comprehension in Wernicke's aphasia. *Archives of Neurology* 44(1), 73–82.

Navon, D. (1977). Forest before trees: The precedence of global features in visual perception. *Cognitive Psychology* 9, 353–83.

Nelson, C. A. (1999). Neural plasticity and human development. *Current Directions in Psychological Science* 8(2), 42–5.

Palmer, S. E. (1980). What makes triangles point: Local and global effects in configurations of ambiguous triangles. *Cognitive Psychology* 12, 285–305.

Palmer, S. E. and Bucher, N. M. (1981). Configural effects in perceived pointing of ambiguous triangles. *Journal of Experimental Psychology: Human Perception and Performance* 7(1), 88–114.

Piercy, M., Hecaen, H., and de Ajuriaguerra, J. (1960). Constructional apraxia associated with unilateral cerebral lesions: Left and right sided cases compared. *Brain* 83, 225–42.

Raichle, M. E. (1994). Positron emission tomographic studies of verbal response selection. In D. C. Gajdusek, G. M. McKhann, and C. L. Bolis (eds.), *Evolution and Neurology of Language. Discussions in Neuroscience* 10, 130–6.

Rankin, J. M., Aram, D. M., and Horwitz, S. J. (1981). Language ability in right and left hemiplegic children. *Brain and Language* 14, 292–306.

Rasmussen, T. and Milner, B. (1977). The role of early left-brain injury in determining lateralization of cerebral speech functions. *Annals of the New York Academy of Sciences* 229, 355–69.

Ratcliff, G. (1982). Disturbances of spatial orientation associated with cerebral lesions. Chapter 13 in M. Potegal (ed.), *Spatial Abilities: Development and physiological foundations* (pp. 301–31). New York: Academic Press.

Reed, J. C. and Reitan, R. M. (1969). Verbal and performance differences among brain-injured children with lateralized motor deficits. *Perceptual and motor shills* 29(3), 747–52.

Reilly, J. S., Bates, E. A., and Marchman, V. A. (1998). Narrative discourse in children with early focal brain injury. *Brain and Language* 61(3), 335–75.

Riva, D., Cazzaniga, L., Pantaleoni, C., Milani, N., and Fedrizzi, E. (1987). Acute hemisplegia in childhood: The neuropsychological prognosis. *Journal of Pediatric Neurosciences* 2, 239–50.

Robertson, L. C. and Delis, D. C. (1986). "Part–whole" processing in unilateral brain damaged patients: Dysfunction of hierarchical organization. *Neuropsychologia* 24(3), 363–70.

Rudel, R. G. and Teuber, H. L. (1971). Spatial orientation in normal children and in children with early brain damage. *Neuropsychologia* 9, 401–7.

Stenberg, C., Campos, J., and Emde, R. (1983). The facial expression of anger in seven-month-old infants. *Child Development* 54, 178–84.

Stiles, J. (1995). Plasticity and development: Evidence from children with early occurring focal brain injury. In B. Julesz and I. Kovacs (eds.), *Maturational windows and cortical plasticity in human development: Is there reason for an optimistic view?* Addison-Wesley Publishing.

Stiles, J. (1998). The effects of early focal brain injury on lateralization of cognitive function. *Current Directions in Psychological Science* 7(1), 21–6.

Stiles, J. (2000). Neural plasticity and cognitive development. *Developmental Neuropsychology* 18(2), 237–72.

Stiles, J., Stern, C., Trauner, D., and Nass, R. (1996). Developmental change in spatial grouping activity among children with early focal brain injury: Evidence from a modeling task. *Brain and Cognition* 31, 46–62.

Stiles, J. and Thal, D. (1993). Linguistic and spatial cognitive development following early focal brain injury: Patterns of deficit and recovery. In M. Johnson (ed.), *Brain Development and Cognition: A reader* (pp. 643–64). Oxford: Blackwell Publishers.

Stiles, J., Trauner, D., Engel, M., and Nass, R. (1997). The development of drawing in children with congenital focal brain injury: Evidence for limited functional recovery. *Neuropsychologia* 35(3), 299–312.

Stiles-Davis, J., Janowsky, J., Engel, M., and Nass, R. D. (1988). Drawing ability in four young children with congenital unilateral brain lesions. *Neuropsychologia* 26(3), 359–71.

Stiles-Davis, J., Sugarman, S., and Nass, R. (1985). The development of spatial and class relations in four young children with right cerebral hemisphere damage: Evidence for early and spatial-constructive deficit. *Brain and Cognition* 4, 388–412.

Swindell, C. S., Holland, A. L., Fromm, D., and Greenhouse, J. B. (1988). Characteristics of recovery of drawing ability in left and right brain-damaged patients. *Brain and Cognition* 7(1), 16–30.

Thal, D. J., Marchman, V. A., Stiles, J., and Aram, D. (1991). Early lexical development in children with focal brain injury. *Brain and Language* 40(4), 491–527.

Trauner, D., Ballantyne, A., Friedland, S., and Chase, C. (1996). Disorders of affective and linguistic prosody in children after early unilateral brain damage. *Annals of Neurology* 39, 361–7.

VanLancker, D. and Kempler, D. (1986). Comprehension of familiar phrases by left- but not by right-hemisphere-damaged patients. *Brain and Language* 32, 265–77.

Vargha-Khadem, F., O'Gorman, A. M., and Watters, G. V. (1983). Aphasia in children with "prenatal" versus postnatal left hemisphere lesions: A clinical and CT scan study. *11th meeting of the International Neuropsychological Society*, Mexico City.

Vargha-Khadem, F., O'Gorman, A. M., and Watters, G. V. (1985). Aphasia and handedness in relation to hemispheric side, age at injury and severity of cerebral lesion during childhood. *Brain*, Sept., 677–96.

Vicari, S., Stiles, J., Stern, C., and Resca, A. (1998). Spatial grouping activity in children with early cortical and subcortical lesions. *Developmental Medicine and Child Neurology* 40, 90–4.

Warrington, E. K., James, M., and Kinsbourne, M. (1966). Drawing disability in relation to laterality of cerebral lesion. *Brain* 89, 53–82.

Woods, B. T. (1980). The restricted effects of right-hemisphere lesions after age one: Wechsler test data. *Neuropsychologia* 18(1), 65–70.

Woods, B. T. and Carey, S. (1979). Language deficits after apparent clinical recovery from childhood aphasia. *Annals of Neurology* 6, 405–9.

16

Cortical Plasticity Underlying Perceptual, Motor, and Cognitive Skill Development: Implications for Neurorehabilitation

Michael M. Merzenich, Beverly A. Wright, William Jenkins, Christian Xerri, Nancy Byl, Steve Miller, *and* Paula Tallal

During the past decade, there has emerged a new understanding of how changes in the brain account for perceptual, cognitive, and motor skill learning. Studies have shown that the brain reorganizes its effective inputs and local circuits through the course of learning. With skill mastery, brain representations are demonstrably specialized in the various specific tasks that underlie skill performance. This capacity for brain "remodeling" is lifelong.

To cite a very simple example, we trained New World owl monkeys and squirrel monkeys to pick up small round objects (food pellets) from shallow wells on a flat surface (Nudo et al., 1996a). The objects were about 1/3 the diameter of the slender fingers of these monkeys. This task required that a monkey fully extend its arm, differentially control and drop one or two or three fingers into a shallow well, palpate the pellet at the bottom of the well and manipulate it to remove it, grasp the small round object as it was ejected from the well, and carry it up to the mouth.

Performance was invariably initially ragged; the round pellet was usually fumbled and dropped during early attempts. However, performance improved dramatically with practice. In a few days, after a few hundred or thousand "practice trials," small-object retrieval was nearly flawless. Few pellets were dropped. The daily allotment of 100 pellets was picked up in a short working time period. The hand and arm movements were fluid, the grasp of the small objects decisive and secure, and the movement sequence beautifully stereotyped for success.

After skill mastery, examination of several cortical areas revealed a "new" brain that was highly specialized for this simple task (Nudo et al., 1996a). Areas of the brain representing somatosensation (SI cortical areas 3b and 1) were elaborated, specifically for that area of skin that the individual monkey used to palpate, manipulate, and control the grasp of these small round objects (Xerri et al., 1999). The much more refined information from this exercised skin derived from this elaborated, far more topographically detailed representation, presumably supported the more reliable perception of the surfaces, shapes, and movements of these small round objects as they were palpated and manipulated as a critical part of grasping and retrieving them.

When the region of the brain that represents sensory information from muscles was examined, it was also clearly specialized. The brain representation of sensory information fed back from muscles and joints (SI cortical area 3a) was now more refined, specifically supporting the more precise and differentiated movements that the monkey had to develop to perfect this small-object manipulation and grasping.

When the area representing movement output control patterns (cortical area 4) was examined, it was found to be specialized to elaborate and refine the representations of just those special movements and movement combinations that must occur for a reliable, almost-always-successful motor act (Nudo et al., 1996a).

In fact, if you could look all across the brain in a subject trained at a simple sensorimotor skill like this one, studies documenting behavioral specific response properties of neurons in trained monkeys indicate that you would presumably record major changes in neural activity within 15 or 20 cortical areas (Aizawa et al., 1991; Mitz et al., 1991; Germain and Lamarre, 1993; Merzenich and Samashima, 1993; Aosaki et al., 1994; Merzenich and Jenkins, 1994). Each area would have undergone progressive change as it plays its special role in the progressive learning of the simple skill. Tens of millions or hundreds of millions of neurons would have changed the way they respond through the course of learning this skill. Billions of synaptic connections providing extrinsic inputs or linking brain cells to one another will have been changed. Collectively, this dramatic brain remodeling almost certainly *is* the cortical part of the skill acquisition.

Consequences of "Ministrokes" Induced in these Cortical Zones

Cortical lesions have been introduced into two of these remodeled cortical zones in monkeys trained at this small-object retrieval task (Nudo et al., 1996b; Xerri et al., 1998). A lesion that completely destroyed the behaviorally elaborated representations in cortical area 3b of just those fingertip surfaces that a monkey used to palpate and grasp the small objects resulted in a marked degradation of the earlier-mastered retrieval behavior (Xerri et al., 1999). A New World monkey suffering such a microlesion that destroyed its true primary skin representation behaved as if this fingertip was anesthetic, adopting a strategy of opening the hand to determine whether or not a pellet had been retrieved (it often had not) as a part of every grasp/retrieval trial. Retrieval success was initially substantially maintained, because prior to the lesion the behavior had come to be performed "automatically." However, task performance rapidly degraded, and the monkey began to use a variety of alternative grasping strategies to eject and grasp these small objects. After several days of such practice, the monkey appeared to recover the sensibility on the fingers that had earlier been primarily involved in the behavior. The monkey soon began using those fingers again, in successful pellet retrievals. Over a period of days, it again progressively improved at this task, ultimately usually achieving pre-lesion training performance levels.

When the cortical representations of the skin surfaces of the hand were again reconstructed in these stroke-recovered monkeys, they were found to be dramatically altered once again (Xerri et al., 1998). The representations of the surfaces of the hand were especially strikingly modified in cortical areas 3a and 1, two other SI zones in the anterior parietal cortex that can represent hand surfaces. In both regions, there was now a major elaboration of just those skin surfaces that provided inputs that guided palpation, ejection, and grasping of the small round objects in the retrieval behavior. Before the lesion, the most striking elaboration of the skin representation that was recorded had been in cortical area

3b. After the lesion restricted to just those zones of area 3b and subsequent training and behavioral recovery, there were equally prominent representational elaborations in *alternative* cutaneous response zones in areas 3a and 1 (Xerri et al., 1999).

When the ministroke in cortical area 4 destroyed the representation of movements critical for performing the behavior, as has been studied elegantly by Nudo and colleagues (1996b), the monkey's movement control was again strikingly degraded. Some monkeys neglected their hands; the consequence was a dramatic further degradation of the movement representation of the hand. If the monkey again heavily practiced the behavior and recovered proficiency at this small-object-retrieval task, the representation of movements critical to this task reemerged in cortical area 4 in zones formerly representing other hand or forelimb movements (Nudo et al., 1996b).

These simple ministroke recovery experiments strengthen the argument that these massive, collective cortical representational changes *are* the cortical part of skill acquisition. They clearly manifest a representational plasticity/learning contribution to stroke recovery, consistent with the conclusions of earlier stroke recovery studies (Cole and Glees, 1954; Schaefer and Meyer, 1974; Lacour and Xerri, 1981; Jenkins and Merzenich, 1987; Goldberger, 1988). They demonstrate that functional recovery can be accounted for by the reemergence of the representation of functions critical for the behavior, in cortical zones that were concerned primarily with other primary activities prior to the lesion.

A Different View of the Origins of Human Disability

An emerging understanding of this lifelong "brain plasticity" has led to an important rethinking about the origins, and the treatments, of human ability and disability. In general, most neurological science during the past two decades has focused on molecular or genetic or physical brain defect explanations for human disabilities or neurological illnesses. We now understand that there is a potentially powerful role played by the "functional-self-creation plasticity processes" of the brain. Consider two simple examples: (1) the origins of and a plasticity-based treatment of a developmental disability, specific language impairment; and (2) the origins of and a plasticity-based treatment of an acquired adult disability, occupationally based movement disorders of the hand.

Origins and Therapeutic Remediation of Specific Language Impairments

Seven to eight percent of children entering school are identified as specifically language impaired (SLI); i.e., (1) they are delayed in their language learning when they are benchmarked against their chronological age or their nonverbal intelligence and (2) they have no other known neurological deficits (Beitchman et al., 1986; Tomblin, 1996). Most of these children will fail to successfully initiate reading in a timely way. There are genetic contributions to the language disabilities of many of these children (Arnold, 1961; Tallal et al., 1991; Lewis et al., 1993; Pennington, 1995). There are physical differences between the brains of at least some SLI individuals as compared with normals that are arguably related to their language impairment (Flynn et al., 1992; Hagman et al., 1992; Galaburda and Livingstone, 1993; Neville et al., 1993; Galaburda et al., 1994; Hari and Kiesila, 1996). In general, these genetic factors and these physical differences have been presumed to be "causes" of the specific language impairment and the consequent dyslexia (reading failure) that usually emerges in these children.

At the same time, we also know that functional self-creation processes in the brain are necessarily contributing massively to the processes of language creation in every child. Could they be a contributing cause of this disability? Consider the changes that occur in the brain of a child learning normal or abnormal language skills in terms of our earlier example of a subject learning to pick up small round objects. In an adult brain, picking up small objects a few hundred or thousand times over a period of a few days resulted in a "new" brain in which responses were altered on a wide scale as the brain progressively specialized, parallel with progressive improvements at this simple skill. In achieving that specialization, the basic activities of tens of millions or hundreds of millions of brain cells and the functions of hundreds of millions or billions of synapses are remodeled.

By the time a SLI child enters primary school, he/she has undergone several *million* "practice trials" in the development of language skills. The brain of the child is unquestionably highly specialized at the representation of their defective language. The creation of a functional language is the product of massive brain remodeling inducing enduring changes in hundreds of millions of neurons. Whether these processes are the cause of the disability or not, they must be contributing powerfully to the emergent language phenomenology in these children.

A Language-Impaired Child is a Specialist at a Particular Form of Language Processing

Every language-impaired child is heavily "practicing" his/her disabling language skills. Why has the child's progressive learning about language resulted in a debilitating form of language? Why does a child continue to use a marginally successful brain-processing strategy for language? If the brain is so plastic, why doesn't the child simply correct the problem on his/her own? Why is the child apparently ensnared by brain processes that appear to be highly resistant to change?

Studies indicate that more than 10 percent of children, including most children that fit the clinical definition of "specifically language-impaired," have actually created their early language constructs in an alternative way. Unlike normal children, they integrate sound information over relatively long chunks of time, of the order of one-fifth to one-third of a second (Tallal and Piercy, 1974; Merzenich et al., 1993; Tallal et al., 1993; Farmer and Klein, 1995; Merzenich and Jenkins, 1995; Kraus et al., 1996; McAnally and Stein, 1996). If the interferences in their sound input stream are measured in masking experiments, it is seen that most of these children have very consistent *and highly abnormal* temporal integration/segmentation abilities marked by especially strong and prolonged backward masking effects (Wright et al., 1997). What are these children practicing to produce such consistent, abnormal, successive sound event interferences?

Psychophysical studies have led us to the hypothesis that they are simply taking in integrated sound chunks that extend over the period length of syllables without reliably developing the further crucial step of making rapid intrasyllabic distinctions. Furthermore, we hypothesize that they are storing information about speech using this long-time-chunk (approximately syllable-length) representational mode − as contrasted with the normal, intrasyllabic feature-distinguishing (phoneme-based) mode. The brains of these children have not developed the skill of separately segmenting and distinguishing the brief, successive sound features from which syllables are constructed. Consistent with that view, these children have impoverished phonetic reception abilities (Vellutino and Scanlon, 1987; Hodgson, 1992; Watson and Miller, 1993; Bird et al., 1995; Stothard and Hulme, 1995; Vellutino et al., 1995).

The cortical plasticity/learning processes in these children *are* working powerfully throughout the period of their language development; they are not "learning disabled" in any general sense. These children have a normal capacity to learn, as is reflected by their normal nonverbal intelligence. In their language learning, they are trained specialists at receiving and interpreting speech using an alternative long-time-chunking aural representational processing mode. Once their special skills have been developed through many hundreds of thousands or millions of "practice events," they hypothetically then get the most information about sound using this – i.e., their special – speech representation mode. Therein lies their trap. These children have evolved an expertise at a language representational system that lacks the symbolic representational power of normal, phonologically based language. Their substantially nonphonologically based language representation does not provide a basis for reliable sound-to-phonologically based orthographic script translation.

Other Aspects of the Deficits of SLI Children

Three other aspects of the specialization in speech perception in these children contribute importantly to their impairment. First, they are also significantly impaired in the way their brain distinguishes different spectral (tonal) parts of sound (Wright et al., 1997). As noted above, these individuals have massive interferences between fast, successive sounds; e.g., between the successive sound pieces of speech. They also have abnormal interferences between the tonal parts of speech. Like the temporal processing deficit, this "spectral processing deficit" arises, we believe, because of the brain's heavy practice at integrating and chunking sounds over syllable-length time periods. At the same time, the temporal interferences between successive sounds are most powerful when those sounds have more similar spectral (tonal) contents. These spectrally specific interactions have been a source of confusion for speech scientists who have tried to define the "rules" governing errors in speech reception and comprehension in these special children.

Second, the interferences that apply for a given phonetic element in running speech are a very complicated function of the specific context in which it occurs. Perceptual generalization is a critical aspect of our normal phonological representational schema. For these children, the rules of perceptual generalization that apply for normal children cannot work. Because they are destined to be asked to use generalized, aurally based perceptual constructs as a basis for translating sounds in alphabetic terms, difficulty in initiating reading is a not-surprising outcome.

Third, other coping behaviors and learning consequences can be expected to arise as a consequence of this alternative language representation mode. The perceptual and cognitive skills of different affected children might be expected to progressively elaborate, possibly in manifold ways, in this population.

Why is the Trap Sprung on these Children?

What underlies the creation of this second form of language representation in so many children? What goes wrong? Hypothetically, anything that degrades the very early treatment of sound by the brain in very early childhood could give rise to this alternative language mode (Merzenich et al., 1993; Merzenich and Jenkins, 1995). For example, if sound is consistently perceived as muffled during the first 6 or 8 or 10 months of life, the brain would be expected to adopt this alternative, syllable-based processing mode. In such circumstances, the child cannot make reliable and therefore consistently behaviorally rewardable distinctions between fast, successive phonemic events, but it can learn to make distinctions about the far more powerful signal modulations that distinguish successive syllables. You could think of the child as adopting that alternative language-processing mode as a "fall-back" position for a brain that is having significant difficulty making fine distinctions about intrasyllabic sound inputs.

There are almost certainly multiple causes that could initiate this alternative language learning progression (Merzenich et al., 1993; Merzenich and Jenkins, 1995), some of which undoubtedly can be inherited. For example, such a problem could arise from defective or delayed or middle ear infection-impaired hearing. It could arise from a variety of developmental delays in the brain. It could arise in a perfectly normal brain opting to derive information about speech using an alternative strategy. Recent studies have recorded the origins of this problem within the first year of life (Benasich and Tallal, 1996). Language learning-impaired children simply do not progress in their development of hearing of fast, successive sounds as do normal children. They are heavily practicing sound processing with syllable length sound chunking by their first birthday.

Functional Self-Creation Processes can at Least Partially "Correct" this Developmental Learning Progression in SLI Children

Brain plasticity studies have shown that a monkey can be trained to make many-fold improvements in its ability to identify rapidly successive sounds with a particular form of practice (Recanzone et al., 1993). A monkey can also be trained to specialize at distinguishing slow events received in long time chunks by an intense regime of practice, again paralleled by major neuronal response remodeling (Beitel et al., 1996). Related scientific experiments conducted by visual and auditory psychophysicists have shown that major improvements in the ability to detect or recognize rapidly successive stimuli can be achieved with practice (Karni and Sagi, 1991, 1993; Ahissar and Hochstein, 1993). Could this kind of progressive, adaptive training be used to help a SLI child change his/her processing mode from a slow-time-chunk, syllable-based mode to a fast-time-chunk, phonologically based mode? To address that question, a series of training tools for 5- to 9-year-old SLI children were created and were applied in a special 20-day-long, 3-hour per day "summer school" organized by Professor Paula Tallal in her Rutgers University laboratories (Merzenich et al., 1996; Tallal et al., 1996). These training exercises, modeled after exercises applied in earlier monkey and human psychophysical studies, were implemented in the form of CD ROM-mounted audiovisual "games."

The first set of games was designed to train the child to make progressively faster (in speech, progressively more high-speed, natural) accurate distinctions about successive acoustic stimuli. All SLI children improved at these skills. Their abilities to recognize fast consonant sounds invariably improved markedly with training, and at a non-speech, fast-successive-element recognition task, gains in two summer school studies of 7 and 11 children averaged 5-fold and 15-fold, respectively. At the end of training, many children were approaching normal performance abilities at some variations of this task. In parallel with this training, the phonetic reception abilities of these children also improved, and they continued to improve, differentially re control children, after training was completed. These children were initially severely receptively impaired. *By several months after training, all 18 children tested at or above normal in their phonetic reception abilities.*

A second set of exercises was designed to rapidly improve the language skills of these language-delayed children by conducting training exercises that employed synthetically disambiguated speech. This speech was extended in time, and its fast, weak phonetic elements were differentially amplified to make it more intelligible to SLI children. On the average, SLI children improved about two years in their language age by working at these language training tasks over a 20-day period. Moreover, with their parallel fast-element-recognition training, their language training gains generalized to natural speech. Language-processing gains were strongly correlated ($r = 0.86$ and 0.85) with the number of practice trials that children were able to complete over these 20 days in fast-element-recognition exercises, in two studies of 7 and 11 SLI children.

It seems unlikely that these results can be accounted for by the development of two or more years of cognitive skill training accomplished through this relatively limited period of language training. We hypothesize that the main gains in measured achievement levels actually derive from the fact that the trained child now has a much improved ability to perform on the language measurement tests because of his/her clarified speech signal reception capabilities. By this view, pre-test versus post-test language battery comparisons would be akin to pre-test versus post-test visual test battery comparisons with the "after" battery administered 1 month after corrective lenses were given to a visually impaired child. By this view, widescale performance changes are recorded because the child is receiving a temporally-spectrally clarified acoustic signal, which is now being segmented and analyzed by the brain on a time scale on which critical phonetic distinctions can be accurately processed.

Whatever the ultimate complete explanations for these very large and rapid changes in language processing, these studies show that we *can* train most SLI children to make more accurate distinctions about progressively faster (more natural, higher-speed) speech element sequences. As a consequence, these impaired children developed more competent speech reception. With only 20 days of training, they were apparently able to effectively shift their processing mode from a substantially nonphonological mode to a phonologically more competent mode. With limited parallel practice, other trained language skills were rapidly brought up nearer to age-appropriate levels, although the true origins of these very rapid, large-scale changes in receptive and expressive language measures are not yet completely understood (Merzenich et al., 1996; Tallal et al., 1996).

These results demonstrate that the problem in at least most of these children is not an irreversible one. In functional terms, these individuals do not appear to have substantially defective learning machinery, per se. Differences in brain imaging or brain morphology recorded in these children must at least often reflect *effects* of their peculiar learning histories, rather than their causes. In any event, the powerful functional self-creation powers of the brain can apparently be marshalled quickly and effectively to convert a child's brain from operating as a syllable-based speech processor that is relatively poor at making intrasyllabic distinctions to a more normal and more cognitively powerful phoneme-based speech processor that is making reliable intrasyllabic distinctions.

What do Integrative Neuroscience Studies Reveal about the Learning Required to Remediate this kind of Problem?

A scientific understanding of the probable contribution of the brain plasticity-based development of a defective language representation to the language disabilities of these children carries with it a very important precaution: There can be no quick fix for this kind of problem. This developmental disability has been very hard won through years of practice and the functional brain development that it has driven. SLI children are dedicated experts at using their special processing strategies, not just in speech reception, but in the cognitive skills, including special coping skills, that flow directly from it. Only very intensive exercises applied over an extended time period can be expected to generate any real cortical plasticity-based correction.

Cognitive neuroscience studies also reveal the most effective strategies for driving brain change. The subject must be attentive and motivated. The training must be progressive and adapted to each training subject. The training schedule must be repetitious and the training schedule intense. A computer-based adaptive training approach like the one applied in these experimental studies in SLI children is an appropriate way of achieving these requisite conditions for driving rapid neurological change.

The Origins of Occupationally Based Movement Disorders of the Hand

A second example of a cortical plasticity/learning-induced disability has been studied intensively by us in monkey and human models: the origins of focal dystonias of the hand (FDh) accompanying a "repetitive strain injury." This second model of a common human disability reveals another interesting aspect of cortical functional-self-creation plasticity processes. Although plasticity in learning usually operates to generate elaborating, differentiating, representational changes that drive progressively more refined behavioral performance, under special circumstances *the same change mechanisms can drive de-differentiating brain remodeling that grossly degrades behavioral performance*.

FDh is a common part of a repetitive strain injury (Sheehy and Marsden, 1982; Newmark and Hochberg, 1987; Cohen and Hallett, 1988; Bureau of National Affairs, 1991; Millender et al., 1992). It is usually manifested by the loss of control of digital movements when the hand is brought down into what had been a heavy-use posture, then replicating heavily practiced sensory stimulus events. For example, a pianist or typist can lose the ability to produce rapidly successive movements with two fingers. In the dystonic hand, when either one of the two digits is brought down onto the keyboard, the other moves uncontrollably. Movement from any other digit onto the two offending digits occurs with normal facility, but movement between the two involved digits is frozen.

This condition commonly arises out of a period of heavy hand use that specifically involves the fingers that express the dystonia. It was earlier hypothesized that this common problem is an *expected* negative aspect of input coincidence-based (Hebbian) plasticity mechanisms (Merzenich et al., 1990; Merzenich and Jenkins, 1993). That is because an integrative time constant that is at least several tens of milliseconds long governs synaptic effectiveness-change mechanisms. If inputs are driven into the cortex from normally differentiated input sources within these time limits in a learning context, they will be integrated by the plasticity machinery of the brain. The consequent *de*-differentiation of sensory feedback information from the hand would be expected to result in an inability to control previously independent finger movements, because after such training induced integration, the brain would interpret input coming back from either of the two fingers as coming from a single (now integrated, two-finger) input source.

To test this simple hypothesis, adult owl monkeys were trained at a task at which weak but temporally sharp vibratory stimuli were delivered to the hand while it was engaged in a digital grasp. In this simulation of the genesis of a "writer's cramp," the vibratory shocks were meant to simulate stimulus events delivered back to the grasping fingers via the writing instrument. In our model, these weak vibratory events nearly simultaneously engaged wide digital surfaces. The four conditions critical for driving de-differentiating changes in hand representations in the cortex were met by this task: Inputs were generated (1) nearly simultaneously from multiple-digit skin surfaces and muscle and joint afferents, (2) in a highly stereotypic manner, (3) in a repetitive task, and (4) with stimuli delivered under behaviorally attentive conditions.

This training resulted in a profound de-differentiation of the representations of sensory feedback information from the digits of these monkeys, by which the independent representations of sensory feedback information from the fingers were largely destroyed in parallel with the emergence of a dystonic hand (Byl et al., 1995a, 1997; Wang et al., 1995). In such a FDh monkey, the normal topographic representation of feedback sensory information that guides hand movement was grossly degraded. Now, (1) many or most neurons representing finger surfaces had receptive fields that were 10 to 20 or more times larger than normal; (2) in sharp contradistinction to the normal condition, receptive fields commonly extended across large surfaces of single or multiple digits; and (3) unlike the normal case, receptive fields commonly extended across large parts of both the dorsal and volar hand. In comparison to normals, input from any given digital location was represented very widely across the most topographic (area 3b) cortical representation of the hand, and now, there could be an equally dramatic de-differentiation of the representation of muscle afferent inputs in cortical area 3a.

This de-differentiation leading to a dystonic hand is of an increasingly wide occurrence because of contemporary workplace demands on human hand use. Why has it not occurred to most medical specialists who treat these individuals that *attended, heavy hand use is learning*, and that learning-induced plasticity could partly underlie the problems that can emerge from hand use? In our view, it is because the common models of the origins or treatments of human disability and disease do not yet acknowledge the powerful, in place, lifelong functional self-creation mechanisms of the brain.

Consider how that understanding could affect the way a complex problem like a "repetitive strain injury" marked by a FDh is treated. What do plasticity studies indicate about the possible treatment of this common condition? First, it has now been demonstrated that these individuals have degraded haptic and small-figure recognition abilities that would be a part of any fine tactually guided movement task (Byl et al., 1995b). There is an increasingly clear concept of what the brain requires to generate progressively more elaborated, differentiated representations of sensory feedback information and movements. The true correction of this problem hypothetically requires a *re*-differentiation, through training, of these cortical representations. Such training has been applied in a qualitative way in human studies by using haptic and stimulus discrimination and recognition tasks, with encouraging initial success. The development of computer-guided training should greatly facilitate the delivery of the heavy requisite schedules of stimuli and should provide a basis for monitoring the progressive refinement of sensory feedback information and movement control.

Second, as these studies are elaborated, they should clarify exactly what use conditions in the workplace account for the genesis of the problem. For a worker at risk, workplace monitoring of potentially destructive behaviors and prophylactic exercises could be constructed into a workday routine.

Third, once it is understood that massive, learning-induced changes in brain representations are occurring in repetitive strain injury patients, it is logical to ask whether or not these brain changes have anything to do with the genesis of the inflammation or pain that are other common aspects of the repetitive strain injury syndrome.

Closing Comment

Neuroscience is creating an increasingly detailed understanding of the neuroplasticity processes underlying the learning/plasticity-based elaboration of functional abilities. That science is also revealing how normal brain plasticity processes contribute to the expressions of neurological dysfunction and impairment recorded in developmental disabilities, and throughout life, in large human populations. It has also led to new rehabilitation models in which cortical plasticity processes have been marshalled to ameliorate or reverse underlying causes or consequences of severe human disability. Important successes in ameliorating language-learning impairments and occupationally based movement disorders represent the beginnings of an important new era in integrative neuroscience-based neurological rehabilitation, in which brain plasticity-based training methods will be used to attack the fundamental behavioral deficits marking *many* chronic neurological disabilities and "diseases."

REFERENCES

Ahissar, M. and Hochstein, S. (1993). Attentional control of early perceptual learning. *Proc. Natl. Acad. Sci.* 90, 5718.

Aizawa, H., Inase, M., Mushiake, H., Shima, K., and Tanji, J. (1991). Reorganization of activity in the supplementary motor area associated with motor learning and functional recovery. *Exp. Brain Res.* 84, 778.

Aosaki, T., Tsubokawa, H., Ishida, A., Watanabe, K., Graybiel, A. M., and Kimura. M. (1994). Responses of tonically active neurons in the primate's striatum undergo systematic changes during behavioral sensorimotor conditioning. *J. Neurosci.* 14, 3969.

Arnold, G. E. (1961). The genetic background of developmental language disorders. *Folia Phoniatr.* 13, 246.

Beitchman, J. H., Nair, R., and Patel, P. G. (1986). Prevalence of speech and language disorders in 5-year-old kindergarten children in the Ottawa-Carlton region. *J. Speech Hear. Disord.* 51, 98.

Beitel, R. E., Schreiner, C. E., Wang, X., Cheung, S. W., and Merzenich, M. M. (1996). Amplitude modulated tones: Effects of carrier frequencies on psychophysical discrimination and responses of primary auditory cortical neurons in the owl monkey. *J. Neurosci. Abstr.* 22, 1623.

Benasich, A. A. and Tallal, P. (1996). Auditory temporal processing thresholds, habituation, and recognition memory over the first year. *Infant Behav. Dev.* 19, 339.

Bird, J., Bishop, D. V., and Freeman, N. H. (1995). Phonological awareness and literacy development in children with expressive phonological impairments. *J. Speech Hear. Res.* 38, 446.

Bureau of National Affairs. (1991). *Cumulative Trauma Disorders in the Workplace: Costs, prevention and progress.* Bureau of National Affairs, Washington, D.C.

Byl, N. N., Merzenich, M. M., and Jenkins, W. M. (1995a). A primate genesis model of focal dystonia and repetitive strain injury: I. Learning-induced de-differentiation of the representation of the hand in the primary somatosensory cortex in adult monkeys. *Neurology* 47, 508.

Byl, N., Merzenich, M. M., Cheung, S., Bedenbaugh, P., Nagarajan, S. S., and Jenkins, W. M. (1997). Primate model for studying focal dystonia and repetitive strain injury: Effects on the primary somatosensory cortex. *Phys. Ther.* 77(3), 269–84.

Byl, N., McKenzie, A., Wilson, F., Melnick, M., Scott, P., Oakes, A., Jenkins, W., and Merzenich, M. (1995b). Discriminative tactile processing in patients with repetitive injury syndromes: Tendinitis or focal dystonia. *J. Orthop. Sports Phys. Ther.* 3, 234.

Cohen, L. and Hallett, M. (1988). Hand cramps: Clinical features and electromyographic patterns in focal dystonia. *Neurology* 38, 1005.

Cole, J. and Glees, P. (1954). Effects of small lesions in sensory cortex in trained monkeys. *J. Neurophysiol.* 17, 1.

Farmer, M. E. and Klein, R. M. (1995). The evidence for a temporal processing deficit linked to dyslexia: A review. *Psychon. Bull. Rev.* 2, 460.

Flynn, J. M., Deering, W., Goldstein, M., and Rahbar, M. H. (1992). Electrophysiological correlates of dyslexic subtypes. *J. Learn Disabil.* 25, 133.

Galaburda, A. and Livingstone, M. (1993). Evidence for a magnocillular effect in developmental dyslexia. *Ann. N.Y. Acad. Sci.* 682, 70.

Galaburda, A. M., Menard, M. T., and Rosen, G. D. (1994). Evidence for aberrant auditory anatomy in developmental dyslexia. *Proc. Natl. Acad. Sci.* 91, 8010.

Germain, L. and Lamarre, Y. (1993). Neuronal activity in the motor and premotor cortices before and after learning the associations between auditory stimuli and motor responses. *Brain Res.* 611, 175.

Goldberger, M. E. (1988). Partial and complete deafferentation of cat hindlimb: The contribution of behavioral substitution to recovery of motor function. *Exp. Brain Res.* 73, 343–53.

Hagman, J. O., Wood, F., Buchsbaum, M. S., Tallal, P., Flowers, L., and Katz, W. (1992). Cerebral brain metabolism in adult dyslexic subjects assessed with positron emission tomography during performance of an auditory task. *Arch. Neurol.* 49, 734.

Hari, R. and Kiesila, P. (1996). Deficit of temporal auditory processing in dyslexic adults. *Neurosci. Lett.* 205, 138.

Hodgson, J. (1992). The status of metalinguistic skills in reading development. *J. Learn. Disabil.* 5, 96.

Jenkins, W. M. and Merzenich, M. M. (1987). Reorganization of neocortical representations after brain injury. A neurophysiological model of the bases of recovery from stroke. *Prog. Brain Res.* 71, 249.

Karni, A. and Sagi, D. (1991). Where practice makes perfect in texture discrimination. Evidence for primary visual cortex plasticity. *Proc. Natl. Acad. Sci.* 88, 4966.

——. (1993). The time course of learning a visual skill. *Nature* 365, 250.

Kraus, N., McGee, T. J., Carrell, T. D., Zecker, S. G., Nico, T. G., and Koch, D. B. (1996). Neurophysiologic responses and behavioral discrimination deficits in children with learning problems (comments). *Science* 273, 867.

Lacour, M. and Xerri, C. (1981). Vestibular compensation: New perspective. In *Lesion-induced Neuronal Plasticity in Sensorimotor Systems* (ed. H. Flohr and W. Precht), p. 240. Springer-Verlag, Berlin.

Lewis, B. A., Cox, N. J., and Bayard, P. J. (1993). Segregation analysis of speech and language disorders. *Behav. Genet.* 23, 191.

McAnally, K. I. and Stein, J. F. (1996). Auditory temporal coding in dyslexia. *Proc. R. Soc. Lond. B. Biol. Sci.* 263, 961.

Merzenich, M. M. and Jenkins, W. M. (1993). Reorganization of cortical representations of the hand following alterations of skin inputs induced by nerve injury, skin island transfers, and experience. *J. Hand Ther.* 6, 89.

———. (1994). Cortical representation of learned behaviors. In *Memory concepts* (ed. P. Anderson et al.), p. 247. Elsevier, Amsterdam.

———. (1995). Cortical plasticity, learning and learning dysfunction. In *Maturational Windows and Adult Cortical Plasticity* (ed. B. Julesz and I. Kovacs), p. 247. Addison-Wesley, Reading, Massachusetts.

Merzenich, M. M. and Samashima, K. (1993). Cortical plasticity and memory. *Curr. Opin. Neurobiol.* 3, 187.

Merzenich, M. M., Recanzone, G. M., Jenkins, W. M., and Grajski, K. A. (1990). Adaptive mechanisms in cortical networks underlying cortical contributions to learning and non-declarative memory. *Cold Spring Harbor Symp. Quant. Biol.* 55, 873.

Merzenich, M. M., Schreiner, C., Jenkins, W., and Wang, X. (1993). Neural mechanisms underlying temporal integration, segmentation, and input sequence representation: Some implications for the origin of learning disabilities. *Ann. N.Y. Acad. Sci.* 682, 1.

Merzenich, M. M., Jenkins, W. M., Johnston, P., Schreiner, C., Miller, S. L., and Tallal, P. (1996). Temporal processing deficits of language-learning impaired children ameliorated by training. *Science* 271, 77.

Millender, L. H., Louis, D. S., and Simmons, B. P. (1992). *Occupational Disorders of the Upper Extremity*. Churchill Livingstone, New York.

Mitz, A. R., Godschalk, M., and Wise, S. P. (1991). Learning-dependent neuronal activity in the premotor cortex: Activity during the acquisition of conditional motor associations. *J. Neurosci.* 11, 1855.

Neville, H. J., Coffey, S. A., Holcomb, P. J., and Tallal, P. (1993). The neurobiology of sensory and language processing in language-impaired children. *J. Cogn. Neurosci.* 5, 235.

Newmark, J. and Hochberg, F. (1987). Isolated painless manual incoordination in musicians. *J. Neurol. Neurosurg. Psychiatry* 50, 291.

Nudo, R. J., Milliken, G. W., Jenkins, W. M., and Merzenich, M. M. (1996a). Use-dependent alterations of movement representations in primary motor cortex of adult squirrel monkeys. *J. Neurosci.* 16, 785.

Nudo, R. J., Wise, B. M., Sifuentes, F., and Milliken, G. W. (1996b). Neural substrates for the effects of rehabilitative training on motor recovery after ischemic infarct. *Science* 272, 1791–4.

Pennington, B. F. (1995). Genetics of learning disabilities. *J. Child Neurol.* (suppl. 1) 10, 69.

Recanzone, G. H., Schreiner, C. E., and Merzenich, M. M. (1993). Plasticity in the frequency representation of primary auditory cortex following discrimination training in adult owl monkeys. *J. Neurosci.* 13, 87.

Schaefer, K. P. and Meyer, D. L. (1974). Compensation of vestibular lesions. In *Handbook of Sensory Physiology* (ed. H. H. Kornhuber), p. 463. Springer-Verlag, Berlin.

Sheehy, M. P. and Marsden, C. D. (1982). Writer's cramp – A focal dystonia. *Brain* 105, 461.

Stothard, S. E. and Hulme, C. (1995). A comparison of phonological skills in children with reading comprehension difficulties and children with decoding difficulties. *J. Child Psychol. Psychiatry Allied Discip.* 36, 399.

Tallal, P. and Piercy, M. (1974). Developmental aphasia: Rate of auditory processing and selective impairment of consonant perception. *Neuropsychologia* 12, 83.

Tallal, P., Miller, S., and Fitch, R. H. (1993). Neurobiological basis of speech: A case for the preeminence of temporal processing. *Ann. N.Y. Acad. Sci.* 682, 27.

Tallal, P., Townsend, J., Curtiss, S., and Wulfech, B. (1991). Phenotypic profiles of language-impaired children based on genetic/family history. *Brain Lang.* 41, 81.

Tallal, P., Miller, S. L., Bedi, G., Byma, G., Wang, X., Nagarajan, S. S., Schreiner, C., Jenkins, W. M., and Merzenich, M. M. (1996). Acoustically modified speech improves language comprehension in language-learning impaired children. *Science* 271, 81.

Tomblin, H. B. (1996). The big picture of SLI: Results of an epidemiological study of SLI among kindergarten children. Paper presented at the 17th Annual Symposium on Research in Child Language Disorders, Madison, Wisconsin.

Vellutino, F. R. and Scanlon, D. M. (1987). Phonological coding, phonological awareness, and reading ability: Evidence from a longitudinal and experimental study. *Merrill-Palmer Q.* 33, 321.

Vellutino, F. R., Scanlon, D. M., and Spearing, D. (1995). Semantic and phonological coding in poor and normal readers. *J. Exp. Child Psychol.* 59, 76.

Wang, X., Merzenich, M. M., Sameshima, K., and Jenkins, W. M. (1995). Remodelling of hand representation in adult cortex determined by timing of tactile stimulation. *Nature* 378, 71.

Watson, B. U. and Miller, T. K. (1993). Auditory perception, phonological processing, and reading ability/disability. *J. Speech Hear. Res.* 36, 850.

Wright, B. A., Lombardino, L. J., King, W. M., Puranik, C. S., Leonard, C. M., and Merzenich, M. M. (1997). Deficits in auditory temporal and spectral processing in language-impaired children. *Nature* 387 (6629), 176–8.

Xerri, C., Merzenich, M., Peterson, B. E., and Jenkins, W. (1998). Plasticity of primary somatosensory cortex paralleling sensorimotor skill recovery from stroke in adult monkeys. *J. Neurophysiol.* 79(4), 2119–48.

Xerri, C. and Merzenich, M. et al. (1999). Representational plasticity in cortical area 3b paralleling tactual-motor skill acquisition in adult monkeys. *Cereb. Cortex* 9(3), 264–76.

17

The Instinct to Learn

Peter Marler

I sense from the classical debate between Piaget and Chomsky (Piattelli-Palmarini, 1980) that at least some of us are all too prone to think of learning and instinct as being virtually antithetical. According to this common view, behavior is one or the other, but it is rarely, if ever, both. Lower animals display instincts, but our own species, apart from a few very basic drives, displays instincts rarely. Instead, we are supposed to be the manifestation of what can be achieved by the emancipation from instinctive control (Gould and Marler, 1987).

It is self-evident that this antithesis is false. Just as instincts are products of interactions between genome and environment, even the most extreme case of purely arbitrary, culturally transmitted behavior must, in some sense, be the result of an instinct at work. Functions of instincts may be generalized or highly specialized, but without them learning could not occur. Thus, the question I pose is not "Do instincts to learn exist?" but rather "What is their nature, and by what behavioral and physiological mechanism do they operate?" How do they impinge on the pervasive plasticity that behavior displays at so many points in the course of its development? I suggest that concepts from the classical ethology of Konrad Lorenz (1950) and Niko Tinbergen (1951) are instructive in a search for answers to these questions.

Of the several concepts with which Lorenz and Tinbergen sought to capture the essence of instinctive behavior in animals (listed in table 17.1), I concentrate especially on three. First is the notion of *sensitive periods* as phases of development with unusual potential for lability. Second and third are the complementary ideas of *releasers (or sign stimuli)* and *innate release mechanisms*, invoked by ethologists to explain the remarkable fact that many organisms, especially in infancy, are responsive to certain key stimuli during interactions with their social companions and with their physical environments, when they first encounter them. This responsiveness implies the possession of brain mechanisms that attune them innately to certain kinds of stimulation.

In recent years, I have come to believe that many such mechanisms have richer and more interesting functions than simply to serve as design features for animals as automata. They also provide the physiological machinery to facilitate and guide learning processes, as one set of components in what I think can be appropriately viewed as instincts to learn.

"The Instinct to Learn" first appeared in *The Epigenesis of Mind: Essays on Biology and Cognition*, edited by S. Carey and R. Gelman (Lawrence Erlbaum Associates, 1991, pp. 37–66), and is reprinted by kind permission.

Table 17.1   Concepts from classical ethology relevant to the instinct to learn

Sensitive periods
Imprinting
Fixed action patterns
Releasers
Innate release mechanisms
(Instincts to learn)

I use birdsong to make the case for instincts to learn as an approach that is productive and logical, even with behavior that is clearly and obviously learned. As a research strategy, it prepares us directly for posing the right kinds of questions in neurophysiological investigations of the underlying mechanisms. It is a position that follows naturally, once the crucial point is appreciated that instincts are not immutable and completely lacking in ontogenetic plasticity, as has so often been assumed in the past, but are themselves, by definition, susceptible to the influence of experience. I present evidence that even the most creative aspects of song development are imbued with instinctive influences, by which I refer to the aspects of the phenotype of the learning organism that are attributable to its genetic constitution (Johnston, 1988). These influences pervade all aspects of ontogeny. We cannot begin to understand how a young bird learning to sing interacts with its social and physical environments, and assimilates information from these interactions, without taking full account of innate contributions to the assimilation process. Each species accommodates most readily to those aspects of experience that are compatible with its nature.

One of the best illustrations of local dialects in birdsong is the white-crowned sparrow (figure 17.1). This is a very simple case. With rare exceptions, each male has a single song type, which has about a 2-second duration. Some song features conform very closely to the local dialect, and others are unique to each individual male. The dialects are so marked that someone with a cultivated ear would be able to tell where he or she was in California, blindfolded, simply by listening to their songs (Baker and Cunningham, 1985; Baptista, 1975, 1977). The fact that the dialects are learned becomes obvious when a male bird is reared without hearing the song of its own kind. A much simpler song develops, lacking all traces of the local accent (Marler, 1970; Petrinovich, 1985). What is the nature of this learning process, and what, if any, are the contributions of instinctive processes? We can detect such contributions in many aspects of the process of learning to sing.

Innate Learning Preferences

If we present a young bird with an array of different songs or tutors to learn from, are they equipotential as stimuli, or are some preferred over others? If there are preferences, do species differ in the songs they favor, or is a song that is a strong learning stimulus for one species, strong for others as well?

As a key feature of the research on which this report is based, a comparative approach has been taken. The underlying principle is simple. Young males of two species, the swamp and the song sparrow, were brought into the laboratory and reared under identical conditions. This gave us the opportunity to observe whether they interacted similarly or

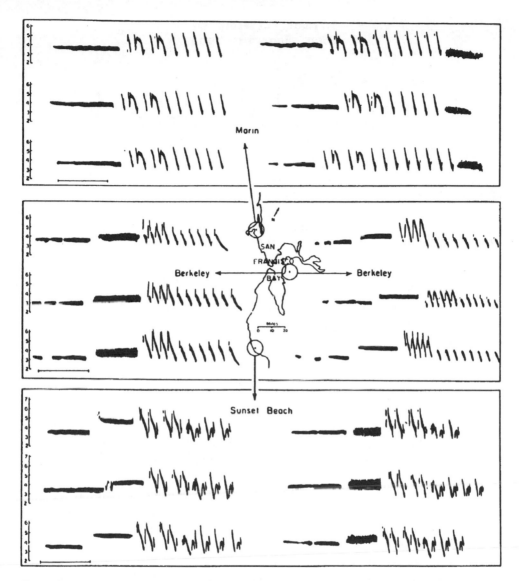

Figure 17.1   An illustration of song dialects in the white-crowned sparrow in the San Francisco Bay area. Songs of 18 males are illustrated, 6 from Marin County, 6 in the Berkeley area, and 6 from Sunset Beach, to the south. Each male has a single song type, for the most part. Local dialects are most evident in the second, trilled portion of the song (from Marler, 1970). These dialects have been studied in much greater detail by Baptista (1975).

differently with the experimental situations in which they were reared. Despite their close genetic relatedness, their songs are very different (figure 17.2). One is simple; the other is complex. They differ in the overall "syntax" of their songs and in the "phonology" of the individual notes. They differ in repertoire size, a male song sparrow having about three times as many song types as a male swamp sparrow (three in one case, 10 to 12 in the other).

Normal, Crystallized
Song Sparrow Song

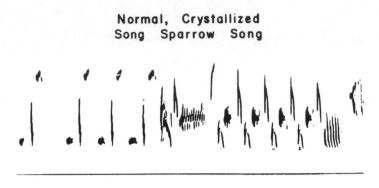

Normal, Crystallized
Swamp Sparrow Song

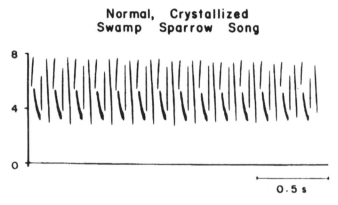

0.5 s

Figure 17.2 Sound spectrograms of normal song and swamp sparrow songs. They differ in both syntax and phonology, and also in the size of individual song repertoires, which average about three song types in swamp sparrows and 10–12 in song sparrows.

How do males of these two species react if we bring them into the laboratory as nestlings, raise them by hand so that their opportunity to hear song in nature is limited, and expose them to tape recordings with equal numbers of swamp sparrow songs and song sparrow songs? When we analyze the songs that they produce, it becomes clear that each displays a preference for songs of its own species (figure 17.3).

In most of the experiments I report on, birds were raised by hand, after being taken as nestlings from the field at an age of 3–5 days. We do this because it is more difficult to raise them from the egg. Might they have learned something in the egg, or the first few days of life before being brought into the laboratory, that has an influence on development of singing behavior, perhaps leading them to favor songs of the species heard during that period?

To check on the possibility of pre- or perinatal experience of species-specific song on learning preferences, eggs from wild nests of the same two species were taken early in incubation, hatched in the laboratory, and raised with absolutely no opportunity to hear adult song of their species. They displayed similar learning preferences (figure 17.3). The preference for conspecific song is thus innate (Marler and Peters, 1989). Interestingly, the song sparrow preference is less extreme in birds raised under both conditions. Dooling and Searcy (1980) uncovered a similar trend by looking at heart-rate changes in three-week-old

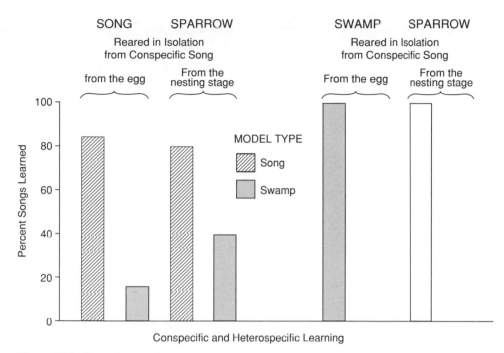

Figure 17.3 Learning preferences of male song and swamp sparrows either raised in the laboratory from the egg or exposed to song in nature during the nestling phase and only then brought into the laboratory. Birds were given a choice of tape recordings to learn, some of their own species' song and some of the other species. The results show that both have an innate preference for learning songs of their own species, but the preference is stronger in swamp sparrows than in song sparrows. Song experience during the nestling phase evidently has no effect on learning preferences.

song and swamp sparrows in response to song (figure 17.4). It may be that, as found in some other birds (Baptista and Petrinovich, 1984, 1986; Clayton, 1988; Pepperberg, 1988), social interaction with live tutors is more important in song sparrows than in swamp sparrows, because song sparrows are not known to imitate swamp sparrows in nature, even though they live in close proximity. In swamp sparrows, learning from tape recordings and live tutors has been shown to take place in a very similar fashion (Marler and Peters, 1988b). Social influences notwithstanding, in both species the preference *can* be sustained solely on the basis of acoustic features of song. What are the acoustic features on which these preferences are based? The answer is different in the two species.

By using computer-synthesized songs in which different acoustic features were independently varied, we found that the learning preference of male swamp sparrows is based not on syntactical features of the song but on the phonology of the syllables. As illustrated in figure 17.5, male swamp sparrows presented with simplified songs consisting either of swamp sparrow syllables or song sparrow syllables unerringly favor those with conspecific syllables, irrespective of the temporal pattern in which they are presented. They then recast them in the normal syntactical pattern, whether or not this pattern has been available to them in the songs they have heard. In choosing models for learning, the song syllable is clearly the primary focus of interest for a swamp sparrow.

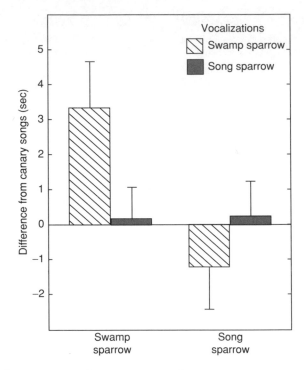

Figure 17.4   Cardiac responses of young swamp and song sparrows to recorded songs of their own and of the other species. The responses are calibrated in relation to the neutral stimulus of a canary song. Each responds most strongly to songs of its own species. The swamp sparrows discriminated more strongly than the song sparrows, in which the preference was not statistically significant. The trend matches that in song learning preferences (figure 17.3). These data were gathered at an age of 3–4 weeks, prior to any song production. (After Dooling and Searcy, 1980.)

In contrast, song sparrows, with their more complex songs, base their learning preference not only on syllabic structure but also on a number of syntactical features, including the number of segments, their internal phrase structure – whether syllables are trilled or unrepeated, and such attributes as the tempo in which they are delivered. There is no evidence that young male swamp sparrows refer to any of these syntactical features when they choose models for song learning (Marler and Peters, 1980, 1988a, 1989).

The evidence of differences in innate responsiveness to song features from species to species is thus clear and unequivocal, implying the existence of something like Lorenzian "innate-release mechanisms." This innate responsiveness is employed not to develop fixed behaviors, as we might once have thought, but as the basis for a learning process. Having focused attention on the particular set of exemplars that satisfy the innate criteria, sparrows then learn them, in specific detail, including the local dialect (if this is a species that possesses dialects). In the swamp sparrow, the dialects are defined by the patterning of notes within a syllable (Marler and Pickert, 1984) as displayed in figure 17.6. Balaban (1988) has shown that both males and females acquire responsiveness to these dialect variations. Thus, the birds go far beyond the dictates of the initial ethological lock-and-key mechanism.

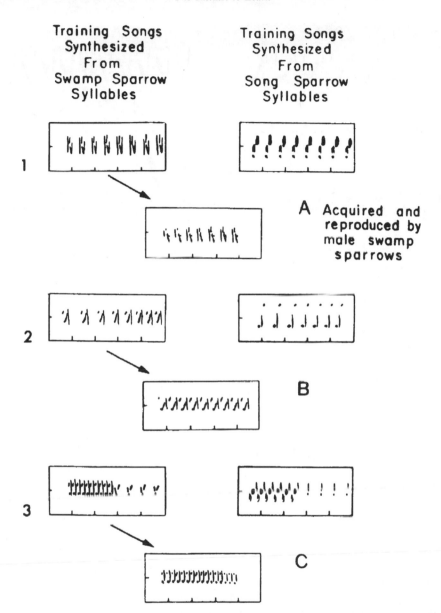

Figure 17.5 A diagram of song learning preference in male swamp sparrows. Three pairs of computer-synthesized songs are illustrated with the same syntax but composed of syllables either from song sparrow or from swamp sparrow songs. In each case, male swamp sparrows preferred syllables of their own species, irrespective of the syntactical arrangement in which they were presented. In each case, the syllable chosen was produced with typical swamp sparrow syntax, regardless of the syntactical structure of the learned model.

A further point, the importance of which cannot be overstressed, is that birds are not completely bound by these innate preferences. If conspecific songs are withheld, sparrows can be persuaded to learn nonpreferred songs (figure 17.7), especially if these are accompanied

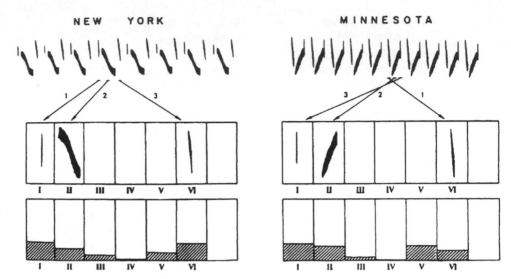

Figure 17.6 Swamp sparrow songs are constructed from six basic note types (I–VI), present in similar proportions in different populations (histograms at the bottom). Two typical songs from New York and Minnesota are illustrated, with different rules for ordering note types within syllables. In New York three-note syllables, type I notes are typically in first position and type VI notes in final position, with one of the other note types between. In Minnesota three-note songs an opposite rule tends to prevail, as illustrated (Marler and Pickert, 1984). Wild males and females are both responsive to these differences in syllable construction (Balaban, 1988).

by further, strong stimulation, as with a live interactive tutor of another species (Baptista and Petrinovich, 1984, 1986). Thus, the process of choosing models for song learning is probabilistically controlled, not absolutely determined. Given the normal ecology of the species, however, conspecific song tutoring will usually be available for innate preferences to be exercised, thus establishing a certain predictable trajectory to the learning process.

How might one model the mechanisms underlying such learning preferences? There is ample experimental evidence that birds can hear the songs of other species perfectly well and can discriminate between them with precision, even at the level of individual differences (Dooling, 1989). Yet they either fail to learn them in retrievable form in the normal course of song acquisition, or, if they do learn them, they forget them again. One caveat here is that we still lack a direct test of what has been memorized, and we have to rely instead on what is produced as a memorization index. Even in the earliest productions of imitations, in plastic song, copies of songs of other species are not usually in evidence. By this criterion, these sparrows behave as though any song presented as a stimulus is subjected to normal sensory processing but is then quickly lost from memory in the usual course of events, unless the exposure is massive, continuing day after day, and associated with strong arousal. There is an urgent need to develop memorization assays that are independent of song production.

When conspecific stimuli are presented, it is as though the bird suddenly becomes attentive, and a brief time window is opened during which the stimulus cluster in view becomes more salient, more likely to be memorized, and probably destined to be used later for guiding song development. One tends to think in terms of parallel processing, with certain circuits responsible for general auditory processing and others committed to the

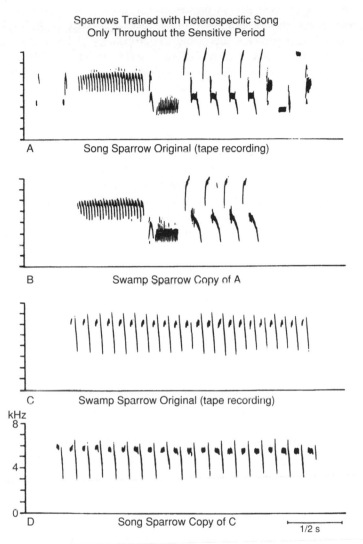

Sparrows Trained with Heterospecific Song Only Throughout the Sensitive Period

A   Song Sparrow Original (tape recording)

B   Swamp Sparrow Copy of A

C   Swamp Sparrow Original (tape recording)

kHz

D   Song Sparrow Copy of C

1/2 s

Figure 17.7   If song and swamp sparrows are raised in the laboratory and presented only with tape-recorded songs of the other species, on rare occasions they will imitate them. Examples are illustrated of a swamp sparrow copy (B) of part of a song sparrow model (A) and a song sparrow copy (D) of a swamp sparrow model (C). Male swamp sparrows rarely imitate song sparrow song. Song sparrows imitate swamp sparrow song more often (cf. figure 17.3), but when they do so they usually recast the swamp sparrow syllables into song sparrow-like syntax (cf figure 17.20).

identification of stimuli as worthy of the special attention of the general processing machinery, if and when they are encountered. This interaction might be thought of as a teaching process, with special mechanisms serving – especially in infancy – to instruct general mechanisms about what to pay special attention to during learning and about how the learning process can most efficiently be structured. In adulthood, once their function of establishing certain developmental trajectories has been accomplished, special mechanisms may cease to function or even cease to exist.

One may think of the sign stimuli present in conspecific songs operating not only as behavioral triggers but also as cues for learning, serving as what might be thought of as "enabling signals," their presence increasing the probability of learning other associated stimuli that might otherwise be neglected (Rauschecker and Marler, 1987). I believe that this function is served by many ethological "releasers," and it may even be the *primary* function for many of them.

Vocal Learning Templates

Sparrows are able to generate some aspects of normal, species-specific song syntax irrespective of the syntax of the models to which they have been exposed in the past. This potential is most clearly displayed in the songs of birds raised in isolation, completely deprived of access to adult song of their own or any other species. Figure 17.8 shows examples of natural song and examples of the simpler form of song that develops in males reared in isolation. There are many abnormalities in the songs of males raised in isolation, and quantitative study reveals that the variation is great. Neverthless, by using a comparative approach, it can be clearly shown that each species is capable of generating some basic features of normal song syntax irrespective of whether these have been experienced in the form of song stimulation by others. The syntax of a swamp sparrow is rather resistant to change by experience, in comparison with the song sparrow, although stimulation by multipartite songs does result in the production of a certain proportion of bipartite song patterns (Marler and Peters, 1980). Male swamp sparrows copy syllables more readily than whole songs. This is less true of song sparrows. When they are allowed to hear conspecific song, they will sometimes imitate the entire syntax of the particular model experienced (figure 17.8), even though they are innately responsive to conspecific syntax. Once more, the invocation of innate influences in no way implies a commitment to immutability.

Again, we may pose the question, "What kind of physiological mechanism underlies this ability?" Some insight is gained by studying the singing behavior of birds that are deaf. We know that the sense of hearing is important not only to permit a bird to hear the songs of others but also to enable it to hear its own voice (Konishi, 1965; Nottebohm, 1968). Male sparrows deafened early in life, prior to any singing, develop songs that are highly abnormal, exceedingly variable, almost amorphous in structure (figure 17.8), although certain basic species differences are sometimes still detectable (Marler and Sherman, 1983).

This highly degraded form of song results both if a male is deafened before song stimulation and also after song stimulation but before the development of singing (Konishi, 1965). Thus, there seems to be no internal brain circuitry that makes memorized songs directly available to guide motor development. To transform a memorized song into a produced song, the bird must be able to hear its own voice.

This contrast between the songs of hearing and deaf birds inspired the concept of vocal learning templates, existing in two forms: one innate and the other acquired. Acquired templates, resulting from enrichment, modification, substitution, or interaction with other mechanisms as a consequence of experience, were originally conceived of as transforms of the same basic mechanisms as innate templates (Konishi, 1965; Marler, 1976; Marler and Sherman, 1983). It now seems possible that they are functionally and neuroanatomically separate, although interconnected and interreactive, as indicated earlier. Innate auditory song templates have a potential direct influence on early learning preferences, in some circumstances, and on the later production of songs. They also serve as a vehicle for

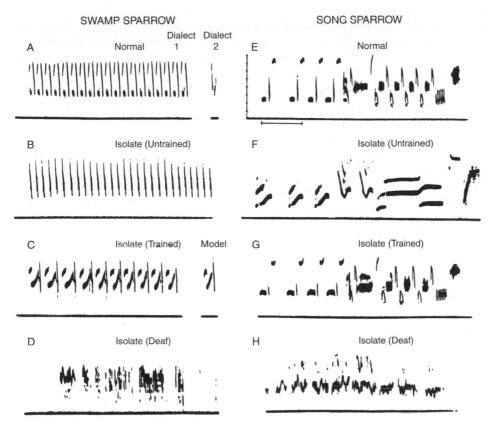

Figure 17.8 Sound spectrograms illustrating typical songs of swamp and song sparrows produced under four conditions. First row: normal learning in the wild (A and E, with one syllable of a second dialect also shown in A). Row 2: acoustic isolation, but with intact hearing (B and F). Row 3: isolated, but trained with tape recordings of normal songs of their species (C and G). Row 4: isolated and deafened (D and H). Frequency markers indicate 1 kHz intervals and the time marker 0.5 secs.

bringing innate influences to bear on the effects of intervening experience. Auditory templates for vocal learning provide one model of the kind of brain mechanisms underlying this particular instinct to learn. Many of the attributes of this model are applicable to other systems of behavioral development. Ontogeny is guided by sensory feedback from motor activity, with referral of this feedback to templates with specifications that can be supplemented, modified, or overridden by experience. The specifications incorporate innate contributions that may be unique to one species, as is the case with those stressed in this paper, or they may be more generally distributed across species, such as specifications for the tonality that characterizes many birdsongs (Nowicki and Marler, 1988).

Plans for Motor Development

Songs of many birds, such as sub-oscine flycatchers, develop completely normally in isolation. When such a song begins to be performed, the first efforts are clearly identifiable as immature versions of what will ultimately be the normal crystalized song. These early attempts may be noisy and fragmented, but the maturational progression is clear and predictable (Kroodsma, 1984). In birds that learn their songs, the developmental progression is quite different. There is a more complex ontogenetic sequence, from subsong, through plastic song, to crystallized song (figure 17.9). The general pattern of song development in 16 male swamp sparrows in the laboratory is diagrammed in figure 17.10. There is considerable individual variation, but a modal pattern can neverthless be discerned that comprises three stages: subsong, plastic song, and crystallized song. This program unfolds similarly in males raised in isolation, suggesting that it is hormonally controlled (but see Marler et al., 1988).

We still know less about subsong than any other aspect of birdsong development. Figure 17.11 shows examples of early subsong from male swamp and song sparrows. It illustrates the fact that the structure of subsong is quite different from that of mature song. It is typical of bird species with learned songs that a kind of metamorphosis intervenes between subsong and later stages of song development. The amorphous structure and noisy spectral organization of sparrow subsong is typical.

Despite its lack of structure, careful analysis reveals subtle species differences. Auditory templates appear to be operating even at this early stage. A difference in note duration present in normal song and in those of isolates (Marler and Sherman, 1985) also occurs in the subsong of hearing song and swamp sparrows (figure 17.11) but is lacking in the early subsong of deaf birds (figure 17.12). Subsong is believed to be critical for several aspects of the development of the general motor skills of singing and also for honing the ability to guide the voice by the ear, which is a prerequisite for vocal imitation (Nottebohm, 1972; Marler and Peters, 1982b); however, direct evidence has been hard to obtain.

Only in the second stage, plastic song, do the more obvious signs of mature song structure appear. Figure 17.13 presents samples of developing song in a single male swamp sparrow, starting with subsong and proceeding through plastic song to the stable form of crystallized song. As plastic song progresses, rehearsal of previously memorized song patterns begins. These continue to stabilize gradually until crystallization occurs. Note that normal species-specific syntax – a single trill – emerges late in swamp sparrows,

---

THE SPECIAL SIGNIFICANCE OF SUBSONG

SPECIES WITH LEARNED SONGS

SUBSONG → PLASTIC SONG → CRYSTALLIZED SONG

SPECIES WITH UNLEARNED SONGS

IMMATURE SONG → CRYSTALLIZED SONG

Figure 17.9 The developmental sequence is different in bird species with learned and unlearned songs. Subsong is radically different from mature song in structure, and undergoes a metamorphosis in the progression through plastic song.

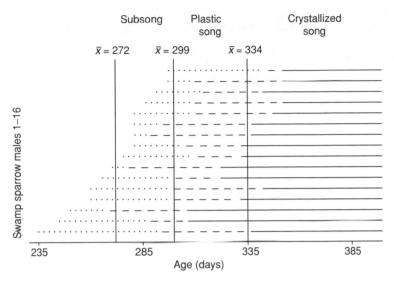

Figure 17.10 Patterns of song development in 16 male swamp sparrows, each raised in individual isolation. They are displayed with the latest developers at the top and the earliest developers at the bottom. Despite considerable individual variation, a species-typical pattern can be discerned.

irrespective of whether such patterns have been heard from others or not, suggesting that an innately specified central motor program is accessed at this stage.

Larger repertoires of songs occur during plastic song than in crystallized song (Marler and Peters, 1982a). Male swamp sparrows greatly overproduce song material at intermediate stages of development, as can be seen more clearly by summing data on numbers of songs present, in an individual repertoire during the transition from plastic to crystallized song (figure 17.14). A typical crystallized repertoire consists of two or three song types, but in early plastic song the repertoire may be four or five times greater. Thus, more is memorized than is manifest in the final products of motor development.

The process of discarding songs during crystallization is not a random one. For one thing, birds that have been persuaded to learn songs of other species by "hybridizing" them with conspecific song elements are more likely to reject these "hybrid" songs during the attrition process (Marler and Peters, 1982a). In addition, there are also opportunities for experience to interact with development to influence the final outcome. There is often a premium in songbirds on countersinging against rivals with similar themes if they are available. The transition from plastic song to full song takes place at a stage of life when a young male is striving to establish his first territory, and, by a "pseudolearning" process, stimulation by the songs of rivals at this time may favor the retention of song themes that most closely match those of rivals in the attrition process. There is also a fascinating suggestion from the work of King and West (1988) on the brown-headed cowbird that females can influence the choice of crystallized song by giving courtship responses to song types that they favor during the plastic song phase.

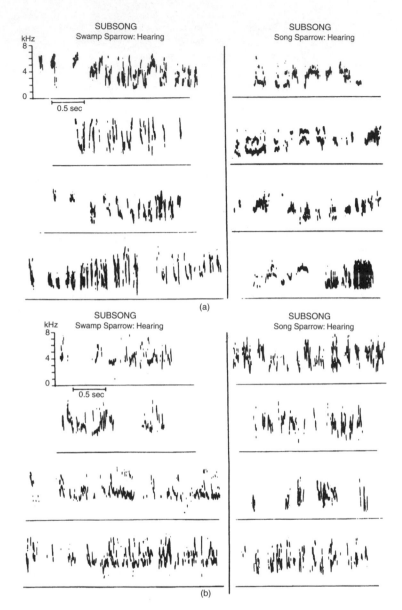

Figure 17.11 Sound spectrograms of early subsong from swamp and song sparrows with hearing intact, as compared with subsong produced after early deafening. In the birds with hearing intact, note duration averages longer in the song sparrows. This difference is absent in subsong of deaf birds produced at the same age.

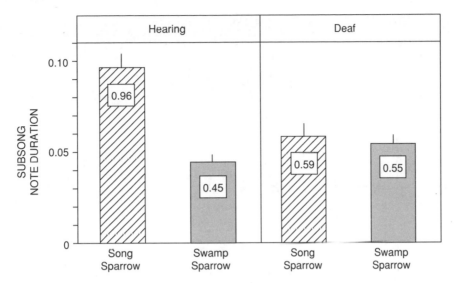

Figure 17.12 Histograms of mean note durations in subsong of song and swamp sparrows with hearing intact and after deafening. It is evident that auditory song templates are already operating even at this early age, to generate species differences in subsong structure.

Steps in Learning to Sing

The diverse strategies that different birds use in learning to sing are accompanied by certain underlying consistencies. For example, there are always several phases in the process of learning to sing. Sensory and perceptual processing tends to precede production (figure 17.15). Songs pass into storage during the acquisition phase, when a bird subjects songs to auditory processing, and commits some of them to memory. It seems logical that the knowledge necessary to develop patterns of action should be acquired before development of these actions commences. After acquisition, internalized representations of songs, or parts of them, may be stored for an appreciable time before the male embarks on the process of retrieving them and generating imitations. In figure 17.16, time intervals are plotted between the last exposure to tape-recorded songs of 16 male swamp sparrows, each separately housed, ending at about 60 days of age, and production of the very first hints of identifiable imitations. This storage interval was surprisingly long, on the order of 8 months, an impressive achievement.

The period of storage before retrieval of stored representations from memory begins varies greatly from species to species. It is not known whether this is a phase of passive storage or whether consolidation or active reorganization of memorized material is taking place. Subsong may occur during storage, and even during acquisition, but the onset of rehearsal is the sign that plastic song has begun. Themes are rehearsed and stabilized, and eventually song crystallization occurs.

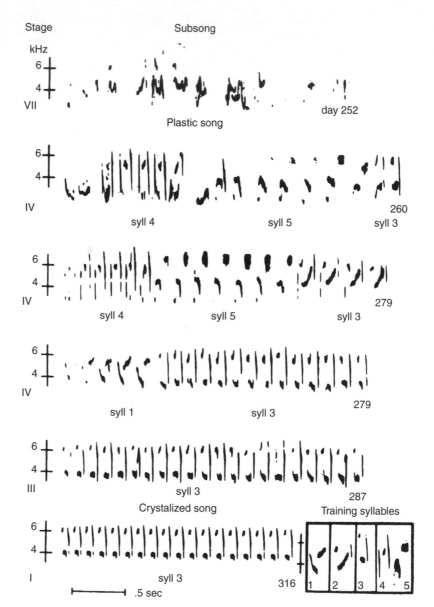

Figure 17.13 Samples from the process of song development in a single male swamp sparrow, ranging from subsong to crystallized song. The age of the bird is indicated on the right ranging from 252 to 316 days of age. This bird was trained with tape-recorded songs, syllables of some of which are indicated in the boxed insert (1–5). As indicated by the labels, early efforts to reproduce imitations of these months later are imperfect in early plastic song, but they improve as progress towards crystallized song is made. The overproduction of song types during plastic song can also be seen. The two song types in the crystallized repertoire of this male consisted of syllable types 2 and 3.

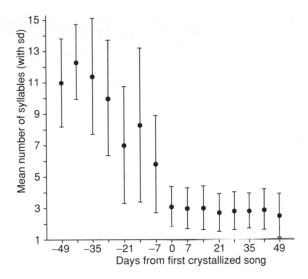

Figure 17.14 A plot of mean syllable repertoires of 16 male swamp sparrows at different stages of song development, arranged around day 0 as the time of crystallization. There is extensive overproduction of song types during plastic song, and the repertoire is drastically reduced as development proceeds towards crystallization of the mature repertoire, averaging three song types per bird. (From Marler and Peters, 1982.)

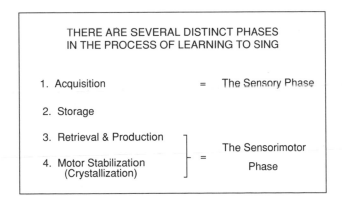

Figure 17.15 Steps in the process of learning and reproducing a song.

Sensitive Periods for Acquisition

Another aspect of instincts to learn is the timing of the acquisition phase. Is it brief, or extended? Does it occur only once, or repeatedly during life? There are striking differences between species in the timing of song acquisition (figure 17.17). In some birds, acquisition is age-dependent and is restricted to a short period early in life. In other species, song remains changeable from year to year, apparently with a continuing ability to acquire new songs

P. Marler

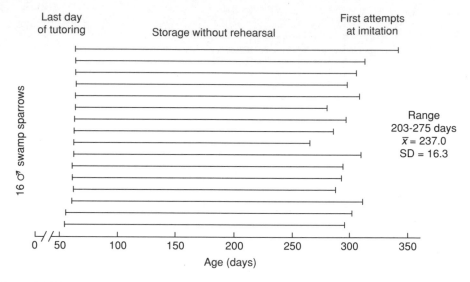

Figure 17.16 The period of storage of learned songs without rehearsal in 16 male swamp sparrows trained with tape-recorded song prior to 60 days of age. Songs were recorded and analyzed every two weeks, and the age was noted at which the first identifiable imitations were reproduced, some eight months after last exposure to the models.

SENSITIVE PERIODS	
Age-Dependent Learning	Age-Independent Learning
Zebra Finch	Canary
Chaffinch	Mockingbird
Sparrows	Starling

Figure 17.17 Examples of bird species with age-dependent and age-independent song learning.

throughout life. Even close relatives, such as sparrows and canaries, may differ strikingly in the timing of sensitive periods, providing ideal opportunities for comparative investigation of variations in the neural and hormonal physiology that correlate with song acquisition. Such species differences can have a direct and profound impact on the potential for behavioral plasticity.

Much of the behavioral information on sensitive periods is inadequate to serve well as a springboard for comparative physiological investigation. In an effort to develop a more systematic, experimental approach to this problem, we played tape-recorded songs to male sparrows in the laboratory throughout their first year of life, changing song types every week or two (Marler and Peters, 1987, 1988b; Marler, 1987). By recording and analyzing the songs produced, we were able to extrapolate back to the time when acquisition occurred. Figure 17.18 shows the results for a group of male swamp sparrows, with a clear sensitive period for song acquisition beginning at about 20 days of age and then closing out about 3–4 months later, before the onset of plastic song. A similar picture of song acquisition was obtained with a changing roster of live tutors, brought into song by

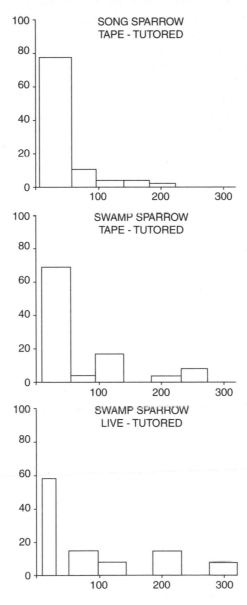

Figure 17.18   The sensitive period for song acquisition peaks in male song sparrows between 20 and 50 days of age (top). The peak is attenuated somewhat in male swamp sparrows and extends to a later age, both when they are tutored with tape recordings (middle) and when they are given live tutors (bottom). These results were obtained by training birds with a constantly changing program of either tape recordings or live tutors and then inferring the age at which acquisition occurred from analyses of songs produced later. (From Marler and Peters, 1987, 1988b.)

testosterone therapy (figure 17.18). Differences between species in the timing of sensitive periods are sometimes gross but may also be subtle, as can be seen by comparing the timing of song acquisition from tape recordings in male song sparrows (figure 17.18). Here, the sensitive period is even more compressed into early adolescence. These birds provide ideal opportunities for pursuing questions about the neural and hormonal changes that are correlated with these sensitive periods and perhaps bear a causal relationship with them (Marler et al., 1987, 1988; Nordeen et al., 1988).

Although sensitive periods for song acquisition are clearly significant components of instincts to learn, it is important to be aware once again that these are not fixed traits (Marler, 1987). There are degrees of lability, depending on such factors as the strength of stimulation – whether a tape recording or a live tutor is used (Baptista and Petrinovich, 1984, 1986). Physiological factors that correlate with the season are also relevant. In some species, young may be hatched so late that singing, which is a seasonal activity in most species, has ceased for the year. In such cases, it has been shown that closure of the sensitive period may be delayed until the following spring, apparently in response to the changing photoperiod (Kroodsma and Pickert, 1984). Deprivation of access to conspecific models can also delay closure of the sensitive period (Clayton, 1988). Once more, the invocation of innate influences does not mean sacrifice of the potential for behavioral flexibility; rather, instincts to learn set a species-specific context within which experience operates.

Innate Inventiveness

Thus far in this account of song learning, the emphasis has been placed on the production of more-or-less precise imitations of songs heard from other birds. In fact, an element of inventiveness often intrudes. This may take several forms. One revelation from the sensitive period experiments described in the previous section is that sparrows are able to recombine components both of the same song and of songs acquired at different times. Recasting or re-editing of components of learned models into new sequences is commonly exploited as one means for generating novelty and also for producing the very large individual repertoires that some birds possess (Krebs and Kroodsma, 1980). Often, models are broken down into phrases or syllables and then reordered into several different sequences that become stable themes (Marler, 1984). Song sparrows are especially prone to indulge in such recombinations with songs acquired in later phases of the sensitive period (Marler and Peters, 1988b). This correlates with a decline in the completeness with which entire learned songs are accurately reproduced (figure 17.19). This tendency to recombine segments of learned models has the effect of creating new songs from old, by reuse of the same basic raw materials.

Species differ greatly in the faithfulness with which they adhere to learned models, although imitations are rarely identical with their models, even in the best mimics. Some species imitate learned models closely, and local dialects are common in birds, but a degree of personal individuality is also virtually universal. In every case examined, this individuality has proved to provide a basis in nature for personal identification of companions and for distinguishing neighbors from strangers (reviewed in Falls, 1982).

Some degree of inventiveness is, in fact, universal, but species differ greatly in the extent to which they indulge in creative activity in song development. Figure 17.20 illustrates just one example of a song sparrow exposed in the laboratory to a variety of simple synthetic songs. This bird generated an approximation of typical song sparrow syntax in highly

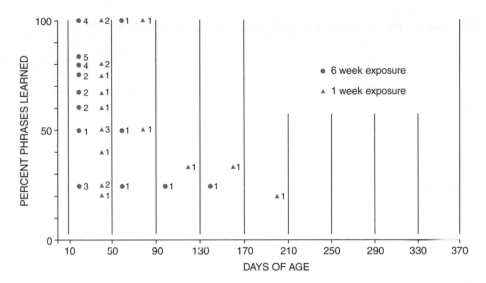

Figure 17.19　When song sparrows reproduce songs acquired early in the sensitive period, they are more likely to reproduce them with the original syntax of the model than with songs acquired later in the sensitive period. For each age block, two sets of data are illustrated, from tape recorded songs heard for a six-week period (left) and for a one-week period (right). Songs acquired later are more likely to be broken up into separate phrases that are then recombined in different ways to produce new songs. (From Marler and Peters, 1987.)

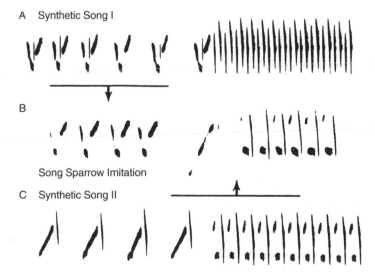

Figure 17.20　Song sparrows often create new themes by breaking learned songs down into their component syllables and recombining them in various ways. Illustrated here is the song of a laboratory-reared song sparrow exposed to an array of synthetic songs. It learned two of these (A and C) and recombined parts of them, as illustrated, to create a crude approximation of normal song sparrow song syntax.

creative fashion by drawing two components from one model and one from another model. Some species provide abundant illustrations of this kind of innovative process, both in the laboratory and in the field.

The rules for parsing acquired songs down into components and recombining them are species-specific, however. There is also species variation in the faithfulness with which a bird adheres to the structure of a given imitation. Some, like sparrows, are conservative. They recast syllables often, but they adhere to the basic syllabic structure, which makes them good subjects for studies of learning. Other species, such as the red-winged blackbird, are compulsive improvisers (Marler et al., 1972), subjecting themes to continuous experimentation and embroidery during development, until the originals are barely recognizable.

Even more intriguing is the suggestion that improvisation and invention may be most consistently applied to certain segments of songs, with other segments left as pure, unadulterated imitations. A species like the white-crowned sparrow, in which birds in a given locality adhere closely to a given dialect, nevertheless has song segments or features that are more free for individual improvisation. Thus cues for personal identification may be encoded in one segment or feature, cues for the local dialect in another, and cues for species recognition in yet another set, the arrangement varying from species to species (Marler, 1960).

Conclusions

It is less illogical than it first appears to speak of instincts for inventiveness. Song development is a creative process, but the inventiveness that birds often display is governed by sets of rules. Each species has its own distinctive set of physiological mechanisms for constraining or facilitating improvisation, guiding learning preferences, directing motor development, and establishing the timing of sensitive periods. Songs are learned, and yet instinctive influences on the learning process intrude at every turn.

Instincts to learn offer priceless opportunities to pinpoint the ways in which physiological or neuroanatomical changes can affect the process of learning a new behavior. Given the striking contrasts in song development in birds that are very close genetic relatives and are otherwise very similar in structure and physiology, presumably quite limited changes in neural organization or the timing of a hormonal event can have profound effects on the course of learning. Already the proverbial bird brain has yielded many secrets about the neural biology of vocal plasticity (Konishi, 1985; Nottebohm, 1987). Yet there is a sense in which we have hardly begun to exploit the potential of comparative studies as a source of new insights into the role of innate species differences in structure and physiology in the operation of instincts to learn.

There is a need in studies of behavioral development to overcome behavioristic prejudice against the invocation of innate contributions. It is as a consequence of such prejudice against the term "innate" that most students of animal behavior have eschewed its use altogether. The result is that ethological investigations of processes of behavioral epigenetics have, for the most part, been rendered impotent. The initiative has been left to geneticists and developmental biologists, who take it for granted that the genome plays a major role in all aspects of behavioral development (Marler and Sherman, 1985).

There is nothing illogical in applying the term "innate" to *differences* between organisms. As Hinde (1970) asserted, "Evidence that a difference in behavior is to be ascribed to genetic differences must come ultimately from the rearing of animals, known to differ genetically, in similar environments" (p. 431). It is both valid and productive for students of development to address Dobzhansky's (1962) question, "To what extent are the *differences* observed between persons due to genotypic or to environmental causes?" (p. 44).

ACKNOWLEDGMENTS

Research was conducted in collaboration with Susan Peters and supported in part by grant No. BRSG SO7 RR07065, awarded by the Biomedical Research Support Grant Program, Division of Research Resources, National Institutes of Health, and by grant number MH 14651. Esther Arruza prepared the figures and typed the manuscript. I thank Judith and Cathy Marler and Eileen McCue for rearing the birds. I am indebted to Susan Peters, Stephen Nowicki, Susan Carey, and Rochel Gelman for discussion and valuable criticism of the manuscript and to the New York Botanical Garden Institute of Ecosystem Studies at the Mary Flagler Cary Arboretum for access to study areas.

REFERENCES

Baker, M. C. and Cunningham, M. A. (1985). The biology of birdsong dialects. *Behavioral and Brain Sciences* 8, 85–133.

Balaban, E. (1988). Cultural and genetic variation in swamp sparrows (*Melospiza georgiana*). II. Behavioral salience of geographic song variants. *Behaviour* 105, 292–322.

Baptista, L. F. (1975). Song dialects and demes in sedentary populations of the white-crowned sparrow (*Zonotrichia leucophrys nuttalli*). *University of California Publications in Zoology* 105, 1–52.

Baptista, L. F. (1977). Geographic variation in song and dialects of the Puget Sound white-crowned sparrow. *Condor* 79, 356–70.

Baptista, L. F. and Petrinovich, L. (1984). Social interaction, sensitive phases and the song template hypothesis in the white-crowned sparrow. *Animal Behaviour* 32, 172–81.

Baptista, L. F. and Petrinovich, L. (1986). Song development in the white-crowned sparrow: social factors and sex differences. *Animal Behaviour* 34, 1359–71.

Clayton, N. S. (1988). Song tutor choice in zebra finches and Bengalese finches: The relative importance of visual and vocal cues. *Behaviour* 104, 281–99.

Dobzhansky, T. (1962). *Mankind Evolving*. New Haven, CT: Yale University Press.

Dooling, R. J. (1989). Perception of complex, species-specific vocalizations by birds and humans. In R. J. Dooling and S. Hulse (eds.), *The Comparative Psychology of Audition* (pp. 423–44). Hillsdale, NJ: Lawrence Erlbaum Associates.

Dooling, R. J. and Searcy, M. H. (1980). Early perceptual selectivity in the swamp sparrow. *Developmental Psychobiology* 13, 499–506.

Falls, J. B. (1982). Individual recognition by sounds in birds. In D. E. Kroodsma and E. H. Miller (eds.), *Acoustic Communication in Birds*, Vol. 2 (pp. 237–78). New York: Academic Press.

Gould, J. L. and Marler, P. (1987). Learning by instinct. *Scientific American* 256, 74–85.

Hinde, R. A. (1970). *Animal Behaviour: A Synthesis of Ethology and Comparative Psychology*, 2nd edn. New York: McGraw-Hill.

Johnston, T. D. (1988). Developmental explanation and the ontogeny of birdsong: Nature/nurture redux. *Behavioural and Brain Sciences* 11, 631–75.

King, A. P. and West, J. J. (1988). Searching for the functional origins of song in eastern brown-headed cowbirds, *Molothrus ater ater*. *Animal Behaviour* 36, 1575–88.

Konishi, M. (1965). The role of auditory feedback in the control of vocalization in the white-crowned sparrow. *Zeitschrift für Tierpsychologie* 22, 770–83.

Konishi, M. (1985). Birdsong: From behavior to neuron. *Annual Review of Neuroscience* 8, 125–70.

Krebs, J. R. and Kroodsma, D. E. (1980). Repertoires and geographical variation in bird song. In J. S. Rosenblatt, R. A. Hinde, C. Beer, and M. C. Busnel (eds.), *Advances in the Study of Behaviour* (pp. 143–77). New York: Academic Press.

Kroodsma, D. E. (1984). Songs of the alder flycatcher (*Empidonax alnorum*) and willow flycatcher (*Empidonax traillii*) are innate. *Auk* 101, 13–24.

Kroodsma, D. E. and Pickert, R. (1984). Sensitive phases for song learning: Effects of social interaction and individual variation. *Animal Behaviour* 32, 389–94.

Lorenz, K. Z. (1950). The comparative method in studying innate behavior patterns. *Symposium Society Experimental Biology* 4, 221–68.

Marler, P. (1960). Bird songs and mate selection. In W. N. Tavolga (ed.), *Animal Sounds and Communication* (pp. 348–67). American Institute of Biological Sciences Symposium Proceedings.

Marler, P. (1970). A comparative approach to vocal learning: Song development in white-crowned sparrows. *Journal of Comparative and Physiological Psychology* 71, 1–25.

Marler, P. (1976). Sensory templates in species-specific behavior. In J. Fentress (ed.), *Simpler Networks and Behavior* (pp. 314–29). Sunderland, MA: Sinauer Associates.

Marler, P. (1984). Song learning: Innate species differences in the learning process. In P. Marler and H. S. Terrace (eds.), *The Biology of Learning* (pp. 289–309). Berlin: Springe-Verlag.

Marler, P. (1987). Sensitive periods and the role of specific and general sensory stimulation in birdsong learning. In J. P. Rauschecker and P. Marler (eds.), *Imprinting and Cortical Plasticity* (pp. 99–135). New York: John Wiley and Sons.

Marler, P., Mundinger, P., Waser, M. S., and Lutjen, A. (1972). Effects of acoustical stimulation and deprivation on song development in red-winged blackbirds (*Agelaius phoeniceus*). *Animal Behaviour* 20, 586–606.

Marler, P. and Peters, S. (1980). Birdsong and speech: Evidence for special processing. In P. Eimas and J. Miller (eds.), *Perspectives on the Study of Speech* (pp. 75–112). Hillsdale, NJ: Lawrence Erlbaum Associates.

Marler, P. and Peters, S. (1982a). Developmental overproduction and selective attrition: New processes in the epigenesis of birdsong. *Developmental Psychobiology* 15, 369–78.

Marler, P. and Peters, S. (1982b). Subsong and plastic song: Their role in the vocal learning process. In D. E. Kroodsma and E. H. Miller (eds.), *Acoustic Communication in Birds:* Vol. 2 (pp. 25–50). New York: Academic Press.

Marler, P. and Peters, S. (1987). A sensitive period for song acquisition in the song sparrow, *Melospiza melodia*: A case of age-limited learning. *Ethology* 76, 89–100.

Marler, P. and Peters, S. (1988a). The role of song phonology and syntax in vocal learning preferences in the song sparrow, *Melospiza melodia*. *Ethology* 77, 125–49.

Marler, P. and Peters, S. (1988b). Sensitive periods for song acquisition from tape recordings and live tutors in the swamp sparrow, *Melospiza georgiana*. *Ethology* 77, 76–84.

Marler, P. and Peters, S. (1989). Species differences in auditory responsiveness in early vocal learning. In S. Hulse and R. Dooling (eds.), *The Comparative Psychology of Audition* (pp. 243–73). Hillsdale, NJ: Lawrence Erlbaum Associates.

Marler, P., Peters, S., Ball, G. F., Dufty, A. M., Jr., and Wingfield, J. C. (1988). The role of sex steriods in the acquisition of birdsong. *Nature* 336, 770–72.

Marler, P., Peters, S., and Wingfield, J. (1987). Correlations between song acquisition, song production, and plasma levels of testosterone and estradiol in sparrows. *Journal of Neurobiology* 18, 531–48.

Marler, P. and Pickert, R. (1984). Species-universal microstructure in the learned song of the swamp sparrow (*Melospiza georgiana*). *Animal Behaviour* 32, 673–89.

Marler, P. and Sherman, V. (1983). Song structure without auditory feedback: Emendations of the auditory template hypothesis. *Journal of Neuroscience* 3, 517–31.

Marler, P. and Sherman, V. (1985). Innate differences in singing behaviour of sparrows reared in isolation from adult conspecific song. *Animal Behaviour* 33, 57–71.

Nordeen, K. W., Marler, P., and Nordeen, E. J. (1988). Changes in neuron number during sensory learning in swamp sparrows. *Society of Neuroscience Abstracts* 14, 89.

Nottebohm, F. (1968). Auditory experience and song development in the chaffinch (*Fringilla coelebs*). *Ibis* 110, 549–68.

Nottebohm, F. (1972). Neural lateralization of vocal control in a passerine bird. II. Subsong, calls and a theory of vocal learning. *Journal of Experimental Zoology* 1979, 35–49.

Nottebohm, F. (1987). Plasticity in adult avian central nervous system: Possible relation between hormones, learning, and brain repair. In F. Plum (ed.), *Higher Functions of the Nervous System* (pp. 85–108). Washington: American Physiological Society.

Nowicki, S. and Marler, P. (1988). How do birds sing? *Music Perception* 5, 391–426.

Pepperberg, I. M. (1988). The importance of social interaction and observation in the acquisition of communicative competence: Possible parallels between avian and human learning. In T. R. Zentall and B. G. Galef, Jr. (eds.), *Social Learning: A Comparative Approach* (pp. 279–99). Hillsdale, NJ: Lawrence Erlbaum Associates.

Petrinovich, L. (1985). Factors influencing song development in the white-crowned sparrow (*Zonotrichia leucophrys*). *Journal of Comparative Psychology* 99, 15–29.

Piattelli-Palmarini, M. (ed.). (1980). *Language and Learning*. Cambridge, MA: Harvard University Press.

Rauschecker, J. P. and Marler, P. (1987). Cortical plasticity and imprinting: Behavioral and physiological contrasts and parallels. In J. P. Rauschecker and P. Marler (eds.), *Imprinting and Cortical Plasticity* (pp. 349–66). New York: John Wiley and Sons.

Tinbergen, N. (1951) *The Study of Instinct*. Oxford: Clarendon Press.

PART VI

Self-organization and Development

Editors' Introduction to Part VI

In Part I we saw that an alternative to analyzing development into nature and nurture components was to view development as a constructive process in which structure emerges from an interaction of lower level components (Oyama, Piaget). This part contains specific examples of attempts to provide constructive accounts of developmental change at the cognitive, behavioral, neural, and computational levels. In all of these approaches, development is viewed as occurring through the self-organization of many interacting components, rather than arising from any instruction or plan.

In the first reading in this section, Thelen discusses a dynamic systems framework for the study of development. This framework provides qualitative and quantitative descriptions of how complex systems change state, and has been especially successfully applied to the development of rhythmical activities such as walking and sleep/wake cycles. Within dynamic systems theory, as in Piagetian theory (Part I), apparently stable states are, in fact, the result of the interaction between several dynamic processes. When factors contributing to the dynamic stability change to a sufficient extent, this can push the system out of one "attractor" state and into another.

In the update to her original article, Thelen reviews enduring principles in dynamic systems and discusses how the framework has been extended to cognitive and social domains. One dynamic systems principle is the equal importance of all of the components that interact to produce behavior. This principle proved useful for understanding infant behavior in the Piagetian A-not-B task (also discussed by Nelson in Part III and by Diamond in Part VII). A second principle is the continuity of behaviors in time, highlighting the need for microgenetic studies that focus on transitions. Such studies have demonstrated that variability in behavior (another major principle) can be critical for change. Another dynamic systems principle is nonlinearity in development; small changes can produce large effects. Such nonlinearities are also critical in the neural network framework (as discussed by Bates and Elman in Part VII, and in the second reading in this part, by Karmiloff-Smith).

Karmiloff-Smith describes a constructivist approach to developmental disorders. The constructivist approach differs significantly from nativist approaches, which attribute disorders to genetic impairments in domain-specific cognitive modules, and from empiricist approaches, which focus on environmental causes rather than genetic abnormalities. From the constructivist perspective, developmental disorders result from an interaction between genes that lead to low-level abnormalities (e.g., in neuronal migration and density) and the environment. To understand a disorder, one must understand the process of development that results from this interaction. This complex process is unlikely to result in one-to-one mappings between genes and behaviors, or simple patterns of damage and preservation in specific modules.

Karmiloff-Smith describes several examples that illustrate the importance and complexity of the developmental process underlying developmental disorders. In the case of Williams syndrome, planning and problem-solving are typically impaired whereas face processing and language are relatively spared. One might be tempted to attribute this pattern to genes that impair and preserve specific associated modules. Instead, consistent with the constructivist approach, there is no clear one-to-one mapping between genes and outcomes; patients may have some of the genetic abnormalities without the associated phenotypes. Further, spared abilities in Williams syndrome appear to be achieved using atypical strategies and brain regions, suggesting that these skills do not simply reflect the preservation of cognitive modules. Karmiloff-Smith also describes the case of Specific Language Impairment, which may result from an interaction between the environment and a basic auditory processing deficit, rather than a deficit in a "grammar gene" (see also Merzenich et al.'s discussion of this example in Part V). The Diamond reading (Part VII) provides another compelling example in the case of phenylketonuria (PKU), a genetic condition that can lead to mental retardation. Again, the genetic abnormality does not specify the outcome of mental retardation; rather, mental retardation in PKU results from a complex interaction between the environment and a gene that codes for an enzyme ultimately affecting the levels of dopamine in the brain. An understanding of this developmental process led to successful treatments based on altering the protein content of children's diets.

The final reading in this section, by O'Reilly and Johnson, describes a neural network model of object recognition. The model implemented specific mechanisms that might underlie some of the constructivist, self-organizing processes described in the preceding readings. Based on an interaction between the model's experience (a simplified environment of moving objects) and basic initial properties of the model (its connectivity and learning algorithm), the model learned to recognize objects in different locations despite the associated differences in visual input.

The architecture of the model was based upon the anatomy of a brain region that contributes to object recognition in the chick (and that may be analogous to mammalian association cortex). Recurrent excitatory connections and lateral inhibitory connections allowed active units in the model to remain active, because active units continued to send activation to themselves via the recurrent excitatory connections, and they prevented other competing units from becoming active via the lateral inhibitory connections. Thus, when an object was presented to the network, certain units became active, and they tended to stay active even as the object moved around. A Hebbian learning rule led the model to associate this pattern of activity with the object in different locations. So, whenever the object appeared in any of these locations, the network came to activate the same units, or the same object representation. In this way, the model learned to recognize objects in its environment. The model thus provided an explicit, mechanistic account of how one aspect of object recognition might arise through the interaction of basic neural properties and visual input from the environment. The model illustrates the kinds of neural and computational mechanisms that might subserve self-organizing development more generally.

FURTHER READING

Horn, G. (1991). Cerebral function and behavior investigated through a study of filial imprinting. In P. Bateson (ed.), *The Development and Integration of Behavior. Essays in Honor of Robert Hinde*. Cambridge: Cambridge University Press. (Experimental studies of imprinting in the chick that served as the foundation of the O'Reilly and Johnson model.)

Johnson, M. H. and Morton, J. (1991). *Biology and Cognitive Development: The Case of Face Recognition*. Oxford: Blackwell. (Extension of the neurocognitive model of imprinting in the chick to the problem of face recognition in human infants.)

Elman, J. L., Bates, E. A., Johnson, M. H., Karmiloff-Smith, A., Parisi, D., and Plunkett, K. (1996). *Rethinking Innateness: A Connectionist Perspective on Development*. Cambridge, MA: MIT Press. (Wide ranging discussion of the strengths of connectionist models in explorations of cognitive development.)

Oliver, A., Johnson, M. H., Karmiloff-Smith, A., and Pennington, B. (2000). Deviations in the emergence of representations: A neuroconstructivist framework for analysing developmental disorders. *Developmental Science* 3, 1–23.

O'Reilly, R. C. and Munakata, Y. (2000). *Computational Cognitive Neuroscience: Understanding the Mind by Simulating the Brain*. Cambridge, MA: MIT Press. (Introduction to neural network simulations of perceptual and cognitive phenomena.)

Thelen, E. and Smith, L. B. (1994). *A Dynamic Systems Approach to the Development of Cognition and Action*. Cambridge, MA: MIT Press. (Comprehensive survey of the application of dynamic systems ideas to problems in psychological development.)

18

Self-organization in Developmental Processes: Can Systems Approaches Work?

Esther Thelen

> The induction of novel behavioral forms may be the single most important unresolved problem for all the developmental and cognitive sciences.
>
> (Wolff, 1987, p. 240)

What does behavior come from? As modest observers of humans and other animals in their early times of life, we must ask this question every day. It is the most profound of questions. Nearly every field of human inquiry – philosophy, theology, cosmology, physics, geology, history, biology, anthropology – asks in some way about the origins of new forms. How can we start with a state that is somehow less and get more? What is the ultimate source of the "more"?

Traditionally, developmentalists have sought the source of the "more" either in the organism or in the environment. In one case, new structures and functions arise as a result of instructions stored beforehand, encoded in the genes or in the nervous system (and ultimately in the genes) and read out during ontogeny like the program on a computer tape. Alternatively, the organism gains in form by absorbing the structure and patterning of its physical or social environment through its interactions with that environment.

Of course, no contemporary developmentalist would advocate either pole in the nature–nurture dichotomy. Everyone now is an interactionist or a transactionalist or a systems theorist. We have example after example in both human and other animal research of the reciprocal effects of organism and environment in effecting developmental change. We would likely find no cases that would show anything else. Why then, can Wolff claim that the induction of new forms remains a great unsolved problem?

At one level, it seems clear that no current developmental models – whether they invoke interactional, transactional, or systems concepts, have been especially successful in accounting for a wide range of empirical data. That is, we lack general principles of development that apply across species or across domains in one species, and that can account for both the exquisite regularities and the often frustrating nonlinearities, regressions, and variabilities that characterize the emergence of new forms.

"Self-organization in Developmental Processes: Can Systems Approaches Work?" first appeared in *Systems and Development. The Minnesota Symposium in Child Psychology, volume 22*, edited by M. Gunnar and E. Thelen (Lawrence Erlbaum Associates, 1989, pp. 77–117), and is reprinted by kind permission.

Recently, several authors have criticized current developmental theorizing on perhaps an even deeper level. Oyama (1985), for example, cogently argued that by assigning the sources of ontogenetic change to either instructions from within the organism or information in the environment we have never come to grips with the ultimate origins of new forms. We seek to find the plans pre-existing somewhere that impose structure on the organism. Nativism and empiricism thus both share the assumption that "information can pre-exist the processes that give rise to it" (p. 13). This assumption of prior design located inside or "out there," leads to an inevitable logical trap – who or what "turns on" the genes, who or what decides what information out there is "good." However elaborate our story of regulator genes, feedback loops, comparators, and schema, Oyama claimed that we finally require a cause – and the old homunculus rears its head, although in more sophisticated guise. *Postulating an interaction of genes and environment in no way removes this logical impasse*. It merely assigns the pre-existing plans to two sources instead of one.

In a similar vein, Haroutunian (1983) criticized Piaget – surely our most thorough going interactionist – for failing to acknowledge the logical consequences of equilibration through accommodation and assimilation. Piaget's logical nemesis is also infinite regress. How can equilibration produce new forms through accommodation and assimilation that are not properties of these functions themselves? How does the organism know to differentiate schema in the right direction? If the organism is testing hypotheses about the world, against what standards are those hypotheses tested? Piaget's solution, Haroutunian claimed, was an implicit genetic nativism.

Are there, then, any candidates for general developmental principles that will avoid the logical pitfalls of dualistic theories and yet provide more than just rhetoric, principles that will provide structure to guide empirical research, formulate testable hypotheses, and integrate data within and across species and domains?

For many years, developmentalists have recognized that systems principles of biological organization offer a conceptually elegant solution to the problem of new forms. Systems principles are well-known: wholeness and order, adaptive self-stabilization, adaptive self-organization, hierarchical structuring (Laszlo, 1972). In addition to the classic statements of Von Bertalanffy (1968), Laszlo (1972), Waddington (1972), and Weiss (1969), a number of recent excellent essays and reviews detail the application of systems theory to development (e.g. Brent, 1978, 1984; Kitchener, 1982; Lerner, 1978; Overton, 1975; Sameroff, 1983; Wolff, 1987).

It is specifically the principle of *self-organization* that rescues developmentalists from the logical hole of infinite regress. That is, in biological systems, *pattern and order can emerge from the process of the interactions of the components of a complex system* without the need for explicit instructions. In Oyama's (1985) terminology:

> Form emerges in successive interactions. Far from being imposed on matter by some agent, it is a function of the reactivity of matter at many hierarchical levels, and of the responsiveness of those interactions to each other.... Organismic form ... is constructed in developmental processes.

Systems formulations are intuitively attractive for many developmental issues, in addition to the question of the origins of novel forms. Despite this, systems remain more of an abstraction for most working developmentalists than a coherent guide to investigation or synthesis. I believe there are a number of reasons why systems have not "worked."

Oyama suggested that the resistance to concepts like emergent order stems both from the prevailing reductionist and mechanistic approaches in biology and from a long tradition of belief in causation by design. Invoking emergent order seems like a retreat into vitalism. Equally important, I believe, is that we have had no accessible translation of systems principles to empirical design, methodology, and interpretation. By their very nature, systems are complex, multicausal, nonlinear, nonstationary, and contingent. The inherent nonlinearity and nonstationarity poses a real challenge to our needs for prescription and predictability. As a result, workers will often resort to a systems explanation only after their more direct main-effect or interactional models fail to explain a body of data. Systems views are often relegated to the discussion sections of papers: If everything affects everything else in a complicated way, then it must be a system (Woodson, 1988). Such *post hoc* incantation can dilute systems concepts to the point of vacuousness. Thus, although we need complexity and multicausality in our models because we have complexity and multicausality in our organisms, systems views seemingly lead to insurmountable obstacles for empirical analysis.

Certain contemporary work in physics, chemistry, biology, and psychology may now weaken the traditional resistance to the idea that organisms can produce pattern without prescription. The active fields of synergetics and nonlinear dynamics in physics, chemistry, and mathematics, for example, show in mathematically precise ways, how complex systems may produce emergent order, that is, without a prescription for the pattern existing beforehand (see, for example, Haken, 1983, 1985; Madore and Freedman, 1987; Prigogine, 1980; Prigogine and Stengers, 1984). Where is the "design" that allows aggregations of molecules to form laser lights, flow patterns in fluids, crystals, cloud formations, and other nonrandom collectives of simple subunits? In biology, field theories of morphogenesis in plants and animals allow for the highly complex differentiation of structural and functional elements from more simple, nongenetic factors such as gradients, nearest neighbor calculations, cell-packing patterns, and so on (e.g. French et al., 1976; Gierer, 1981; Meakin, 1986; Mittenthal, 1981). Developmental neurophysiologists are using terms such as *self-assembly* to describe the establishment and refinement of neural networks as a dynamic and contingent process (e.g. Barnes, 1986; Dammasch et al., 1986; Singer, 1986).

There is a growing trend toward viewing adult nervous system function also as a dynamic and self-organizing process; that is, modeling function as the emergent property of the assembly of elemental units, none of which contains the prescription or command center (Skarda and Freeman, 1987; Szentagothai, 1984). This work ranges from mathematical formulations of simple behaviors in relatively primitive organisms – locomotion in the lamprey eel, for example (Cohen et al., 1982), to computational models of the highest human brain functions such as memory and language (e.g. Hopfield and Tank, 1986; Rumelhart and McClelland, 1986; Shrager et al., 1987). I rely especially on the theoretical and empirical studies of human motor behavior of Kelso and his colleagues (Kelso et al., 1980; Kelso and Tuller, 1984; Kugler et al., 1980) based on dynamic principles, and in which the details of coordinated movement are seen to arise from the synergetic assembly of muscle collectives.

What these diverse formulations share – and what offers the empirical challenge to students of behavioral development – is the assumption that a higher order complexity can result from the cooperativity of simpler components. Vitalistic forces need not be invoked; it is the unique utilization of energy that can create "order out of chaos." Thus, the order and regularity observed in living organisms is a fundamental consequence of their thermodynamics; that they are open systems that use energy flow to organize and maintain stability. This means that unlike machines, biological systems can actively evolve toward a state of higher organization (Von Bertalanffy, 1968).

But will systems work for developmentalists? In the remainder of this chapter, I outline a number of principles derived from the field of synergetics (the physics of complex systems) that have special relevance for the study of developing systems. I then suggest that these principles may be useful in two ways. First, on a metaphoric or heuristic level, I offer a characterization of developing systems that may serve as a guide for examining and understanding multicausal and nonlinear phenomena in ontogeny. I apply the systems metaphor to several domains of early sensorimotor development in humans and other animals, and I suggest how synergetic principles may lead to testable systems hypotheses about the origins of new forms. Finally, I present examples from an ongoing study of infant motor coordination designed to use synergetic principles. Please note that I invoke these concepts with great caution and in the spirit of exploration. When the principles of complex systems have been applied to biological systems (e.g. Kelso and Schöner, 1987), the phenomena modeled have been relatively simple and many variables could be rigorously controlled. We normally do not have that level of control over naturally developing organisms, nor can we be confident of the stationarity of our behavior over the measurement interval.

My introduction to synergetic principles came through my interest in early motor development. A fundamental question for understanding motor behavior is how a system composed of many, many "degrees of freedom" – muscle groups, joints, neuronal elements, and so on – "compressed" these degrees of freedom into coordinated movement with precise spatial and temporal patterning. The traditional theories invoking either "motor programs" or feedback-based machine models were beset with the same logical problem that faces developmental theories: the origins of new forms. Kelso and his colleagues have used synergetic principles to show how the neuromuscular system can be "self-organizing"; that is, how trajectories and coordinative modes can emerge without the need for prescriptive solutions (see Kelso and Tuller, 1984). A basic assumption is that synergetic principles of organization are so general that they may be applied across systems and time spans; that new forms arise in development by the same processes by which they arise in "real-time" action (see Fogel and Thelen, 1987; Kugler et al., 1982; Thelen, 1986b; Thelen and Fogel, 1989; Thelen et al., 1987).

Pattern Formation in Complex and Developing Systems

Compression of the degrees of freedom and self-organization

Complex systems are systems with many elements or subsystems. These elements can combine with each other in a potentially very large number of ways; the system has an enormous number of "degrees of freedom" (figure 18.1). Under certain thermodynamic conditions – thermodynamic non-equilibrium (a directed flow of energy) – these elements can self-organize to generate patterned behavior that has much fewer dimensions than the original elements. That is, when the participating elements or subsystems interact, the original degrees of freedom are compressed to produce spatial and temporal order. The multiple variables can then be expressed as one or a few *collective variables*.

At any point in time, the behavior of the complex system is dynamically assembled as a product of the interactions of the elements in a particular context. At the same time that

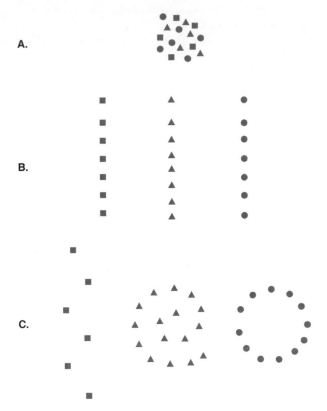

Figure 18.1 Schematic depiction of self-organization in a complex system. **A**, A complex system consists of a very large number of noisy elements or subsystems with very many degrees of freedom. **B**, Under certain thermodynamic conditions, such systems can self-organize to produce lower dimensional dynamics; the degrees of freedom are reduced. **C**, The dynamical system, in turn, exhibits behavioral complexity; it can have multiple patterns, multiple stable states, and adaptable configurations.

information is compressed, the resulting lower dimensional behavior can be highly complex and patterned. Behavioral complexity may be manifest in patterns evolving in space and time, in multiple patterns and stable states, and in remarkable adaptability to perturbations. Note that there is no prescription for this order existing prior to the dynamic assembly, either in the individual elements or in the context; the order grows out of the relations.

These phenomena are best illustrated by a dramatic, nonbiological example: the now-famous Belousov–Zhabotinskii autocatalytic chemical reaction. When simple chemicals – bromate ions in highly acidic medium – are placed in a shallow glass dish, a remarkable series of events begins (see figure 18.2):

> A dish, thinly spread with a lightly colored liquid, sits quietly for a moment after its preparation. The liquid is then suddenly swept by a spontaneous burst of colored centers of chemical activity. Each newly formed region creates expanding patterns of concentric, circular rings. These collide with neighboring waves but never penetrate. In some rare cases, rotating one-, two- or three-armed spirals may emerge. Each pattern grows, impinging on its

neighboring patterns, winning on some fronts and losing on others, organizing the entire surface into a unique pattern. Finally, the patterns decay and the system dies, as secondary reactions drain the flow of the primary reaction. (Madore and Freedman, 1987, p. 253)

It would, of course, be impossible to describe the Belousov–Zhabotinskii reaction in terms of the behavior of the individual ions. There are too many of them and a nearly infinite number of degrees of freedom. The dramatic patterns, however, represent a much more compressed description. Whereas the behavior of the individual atoms is random and chaotic, the patterns show order in both space and time. Although they compress the original degrees of freedom, these patterns are themselves complex.

Where do these beautiful patterns and elaborate designs come from? No pattern generator or schema can be found. The order is truly emergent from the initial conditions: the mix of the chemicals and the constraints of the container, the room temperature, and so on. Scientists can simulate these self-organizing properties by a computer program that sets up very simple initial conditions. When the program runs, the sequence of pattern emerges, but a program for the pattern itself was never written.

Figure 18.2 Evolving forms in the Belousov-Zhabotinskii reaction. The spontaneous development of structure can be seen in a sequence of photographs (left panels in each pair) that shows waves of chemical activity propagating through a receptive liquid medium. These complex forms can be remarkably well modeled by a simple computer simulation (right panels). (From Madore, B. F. and Freedman, W. L. (1987) Self-organizing structures. *American Scientist* 75, 561. Reprinted with permission of Sigma Xi, The Scientific Research Society.)

The parallel between the Belousov–Zhabotinskii reaction and the events of early biological morphogenesis is striking. From the fertilized egg, a seeming homogeneous bag of
chemicals, the embryo divides, cleaves, invaginates, becomes polarized and lateralized,
develops layers, and so on. Models of early morphogenesis have much in common with
those used to simulate the Belousov–Zhabotinskii reaction as they call on gradient fields,
states of excitation, nearest neighbor effects, and simple rules of interaction.

But unlike the chemical reaction, which decays as the elements reach thermodynamic
equilibrium, the embryo is supplied with a continual supply of energy through metabolic
processes. It remains in this thermodynamic nonequilibrium, and as it utilizes energy, its
emergent forms not only remain, but become more elaborated, each pattern generating its
own subpatterns and so on until a great number of functional structures have been
generated. Of course the process is not random as species quite precisely reproduce
themselves. In this case however, the genome may be thought to greatly underspecify the
resultant product. Much evidence exists that genetic information sets the initial conditions,
so to speak, but does not encode the topology that enfolds.

On a different level, behavior in developing organisms is likewise a result of the unique
cooperativity of the subsystems in a context. Because of the thermodynamic status of living
organisms, complexity in behavior may be an emergent property. No iconic representations
of the behavior, either in the form of genetic codes, maturational timetables, reflexes, or
cognitive schemes need exist *a priori*. As such, behavior is never hard-wired, but flexibly
assembled within certain organismic constraints and the demands of the context or task.
Order, therefore, is a product of *process*, not instruction. It is noteworthy that contemporary
parallel models of neuronal and higher brain function are predicated on the processing of
many individual subunits, none of which contains the icon or command of the resultant
memory unit, perceptual trace, or word representation.

This formulation allows us to make another important claim. Because biological systems
are openly exchanging energy with their surrounds, the state of the organism and the
context for action (the task demands) are formally equivalent in the assembly of the
cooperative interaction. Therefore, there is no dichotomy between organism and environment. Neither has privileged status in effecting change. It is as meaningless to talk of a
decontextualized organism as of an environment without biological meaning to the animal.
However, we may identify parameters either within or without the organism which act as
agents of change, without being prescriptives for change.

Dynamic stability

Self-assembled behavior of complex systems is dynamically stable in any given context.
Given a particular biological organization, and a particular context, we can say that the
system prefers a certain range of behavioral outputs (characterized in dynamic terminology
as an abstract *attractor* state; Abraham and Shaw, 1982). The system will "settle into" this
dynamic stability from a number of initial states and will tend to return to its attractor
regimes when perturbed. In figure 18.3, I have illustrated a hypothetical state space, the
"fitness space" of an individual. The two axes of this state space are defined as the possible
states of two measured variables of fitness, body temperature, and heart rate. Normal adult
humans occupy a certain preferred part of this space. Illness or exercise may shift you
temporarily to one portion of the space, but your system "wants" to return to the dark
central spot and will do so after the perturbation of illness or exercise. This is a dynamic

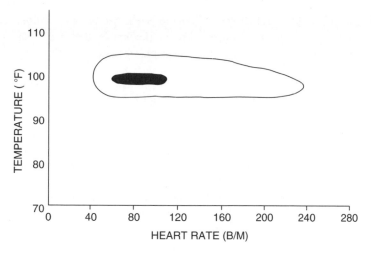

Figure 18.3 Hypothetical "fitness space" of a normal human individual showing dynamic range of heart rate and temperature. Individual "prefers" to spend time in the dark center portion, but is not limited to it. When perturbed, the system normally returns to the center oval.

stability because the system is not rigidly fixed to a confined region of the state space, but tends to stay in and return to a constrained region.

Dynamic systems theory identifies a number of such attractor regimes (figure 18.4). Behaviors that tends to converge around a single or several output states are called *point attractor* systems, whereas repetitive or cyclical behavior is characterized as a *limit cycle attractor*. A special attractor regime currently of great biological interest is the *chaotic* or strange attractor. Chaotic systems are globally deterministic, but locally nondeterministic. They look noisy by conventional statistical tests, but they are not. Their behavior can be captured by certain sets of equations, thus, they have fewer degrees of freedom than truly random noise (Skarda and Freeman 1987).

The attractor concept helps to understand how behavior can be both stable and variable. Developing organisms are neither stereotyped and "hard-wired" nor are they random. Behavior fluctuates, but within limits. That is, organisms tend to show a delimited number of behavioral patterns, which within certain boundary conditions, will act like dynamic

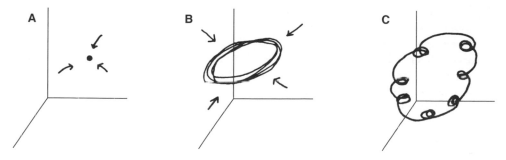

Figure 18.4 Three hypothetical attractors plotted in three-dimensional state space. **A**, Point attractor. **B**, Limit cycle attractor. **C**, Chaotic attractor. Arrows indicate that dynamic trajectories tend to converge on these behavior patterns of the collective variable.

attractors. These states will be the preferred configuration from a number of initial conditions, and they will be relatively resistant to perturbation. As a consequence of this dynamic assembly, developing organisms remain flexible in the face of tasks, but only within the constraints of their energetically stable possible states.

Attractors stabilize and destabilize during ontogeny

Because the components of developing systems are always in flux, the attractor states themselves have dynamic trajectories. Some behavior becomes more stable, more tightly constrained, more skilled, and less subject to perturbations. New walkers, like new drivers, must focus all their attention to the task and are easily distracted and dislodged. With experience, the skill becomes so stable that conversation, even chewing gum, is possible, and the walker can compensate for all manner of obstacles. Increasing skill can be conceptualized as an increasingly stable attractor.

Likewise, many ontogenetic phenemona require attractors to destabilize; behavior becomes less reliable, more disruptable, and more variable. For example, in infant mammals, sucking is a highly stable attractor state. All intact infant mammals must suckle in a skilled and reliable manner at birth. However, with weaning, suckling becomes more context dependent, less obligatory, more variable, and more likely to be interrupted. Eventually, the motor pattern itself disappears, as adults cannot reproduce the behavior.

I have characterized the continual and gradual changes during development as the stabilization and destabilization of preferred attractor states. What about the notorious discontinuities in development? As I discuss in the following sections, discontinuous changes also require the disruption of stable states.

Discontinuous phase shifts

Complex systems may exhibit multiple behavioral patterns. An important characteristic of such complex systems is that they switch between patterns *in a discontinuous manner*, by exhibiting discrete phase transitions. That is, the shift from one stable behavioral mode (attractor regime) to another behavioral regime occurs without stable intermediate states (Haken, 1983). *Bifurcations* are phase shifts where the collective variable jumps into two or more discrete, stable modes. Complex systems may undergo multiple bifurcations (figure 18.5), resulting in increasing behavioral complexity. Phase shifts and bifurcations give rise, therefore, to new forms and multiple states.

Developing organisms are well known to display qualitatively discrete phases during ontogeny. Sometimes, the animal seems even to lose behavioral forms or regress to less mature performance. The premier developmental question is, of course, the nature of the transition from one developmental stage to another – the emergence of new forms. How does a system retain continuity and yet produce discontinuous manifestations?

Control parameters

Developmental theorists may well look to synergetic principles for help with the perennial puzzle of continuity-within-discontinuity. In complex systems, behavior that is ordered

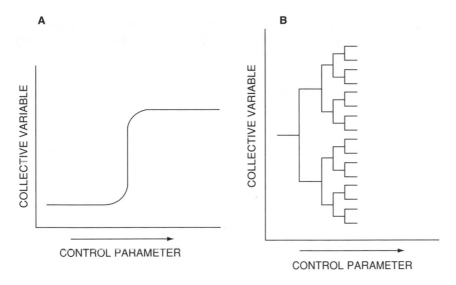

Figure 18.5 The appearance of new forms through discontinuous phase shift. A, Scaling on a control parameter shifts the system into a new state without a stable intermediate. B, Scaling on a control parameter induces multiple stable behavioral states.

results from the cooperativity of the subsystems. But at points of change – phase shifts – not all of the elements drive the system into a new phase. An important synergetic principle is that at a phase transition, scaling on only one or a few *control parameters* shifts the entire system. Because of the holistic nature of cooperative systems, this change in a crucial variable beyond a critical point reverberates to a system-wide reorganization (Kelso and Schöner, 1987). Again, because organismic and contextual variables are equally important in the dynamic assembly of behavior, there is no formal difference between exogenous and endogenous sources of change. The control parameter must in no way be envisioned as a prescription for change. Control parameters do not themselves encode or represent change. They may be rather unspecific, like physical parameters of pressure, temperature, or energy to the system, but they act to reorganize the system in specific ways. Continuity is maintained because most of the components of the system have not materially changed; discontinuity is manifest because the components relate to one another in a different fashion, and their low-dimensional, collective behavior has undergone a qualitative shift.

Here I would like to illustrate such a nonequilibrium phase shift and the role of the control parameter with a compelling real-time example from the human motor system, which has been elegantly modeled by Kelso and his colleagues using synergetic principles (Haken et al., 1985; Kelso et al., 1986; Schöner et al., 1986). Kelso asked human subjects to flex and extend their index fingers in time to a metronome, beginning at a slow pace and with the fingers moving out-of-phase, that is, with one finger flexing while the other was extending. As the experimenter increased the metronome pacing, subjects spontaneously and instantaneously shifted their coordination pattern from out-of-phase to in-phase at repeatable critical points in the speed scalar. (No such shift occurs if subjects begin with in-phase movements.) The degrees of freedom contributing to finger-flexing movements were compressed by the motor system such that the behavior could be described by much fewer variables – in this case the relative phasing between fingers. Although out-of-phase movements were stable at lower speeds, at a critical point the system assumed a new, and presumably more stable regime. No prescription for this phase shift is assumed; the new coordinative pattern arose from the task demands and the thermodynamics of the combined elements that produced it. In this case, a single control parameter – the energy delivered to the system to increase the speed, appeared to drive the phase shift. The anatomical and physiological elements participating in the ensemble were reorganized to produce a different output while themselves remaining stable.

Control parameters in developing systems

We have proposed that at developmental transitions, one or several components of the complex system may act as control parameters, including variables in the context or in the environment (Fogel and Thelen, 1987; Thelen, 1988). Although all of the elements or subsystems are essential for the systems output, only one or a few of the subsystems will trigger transitions, which, in turn, will lead to system-wide reorganization.

This principle helps explain the heterochronic, asynchronous, and often nonlinear character of behavioral ontogeny. We commonly observe "pieces" of a functional behavior long before the performance of the mature behavior. These pieces seem to be used out of sequence, in inappropriate or different functional contexts, only under certain experimental conditions, or otherwise not properly "connected" with the other elements needed for goal-directed activity.

Theories that assume that developmental change is driven by a unified timetable in the form of maturational plans, neurological reorganizations, or cognitive structures have had difficulty accounting for both the anticipations of function and regressions. In this systems approach, we strongly emphasize that contributing components may mature at different rates. The component processes are thus developing in parallel, but not synchronously or symmetrically. Figure 18.6 depicts a developing system composed of many component profiles in a heterarchical, rather than a hierarchical assembly. At any point in time, behavior is a compression of these components within a specific task context. This means that some elements of functional actions may be in place long before the performance but may not be manifest until the slowest component allows the system to dynamically assemble in a new form (the *rate-limiting* component).

Because it is the task, not instructions that exist prior to the task, which assembles the components, these subsystems may be opportunistically appropriated for different actions for different ontogenetic goals. The component is continuously available, but as it is only manifest in a task, its expression is task specific. For example, leg kicks may be used by young infants as expressive or exploratory behaviors, although these coordinated activities may be later recruited for locomotor systems. Fogel and Thelen (1987) and Thelen (1981) give other examples of coordinative patterns transiently recruited for tasks quite unrelated to their mature forms.

How control parameters drive developmental change

Scalar changes in a single control parameter.   In particular, we have proposed that control parameters can act to trigger developmental transitions in two ways. First, there may be scalar changes in one or more existing components that reach the critical values that initiate

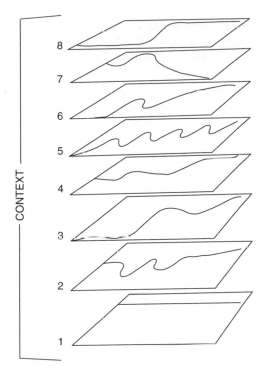

Figure 18.6 Developing systems pictured as a layered ensemble of subsystems, each with its own developmental trajectory. The low-dimensional behavior (collective variable) is assembled only within a contextual frame. No subsystem has hierarchical priority.

a phase shift. These may be identified at many levels of analysis: incremental growth in anatomical systems, increase (or decrease) of neural elements or concentrations of neuro-transmitters, changing perceptual, cognitive or motor abilities or memory capacity, or change of attentional mechanisms.

Contextual factors may, however, be equally potent in effecting the appearance of new forms. We have especially stressed the role of the social partners of young animals in promoting developmental change (Fogel and Thelen, 1987). Social conspecifics often create contexts that support or facilitate the organization of systems by substituting for organismic elements that are later developing. Human parents, for example, continually provide access to objects, appropriate "frames" for social dialogue, correctly scaled language opportunities, and so on, which provide a task context within which the child's organismic capabilities may coalesce. Without these supportive contexts, the infant performs at a less mature level.

I offer the phenomenon of the newborn stepping response as an illustration of how, in a systems approach, a scalar change in a crucial control parameter can lead to the emergence (or in this case, the disappearance!) of ontogenetic forms. The regression of the coordinated stepping seen in normal newborns has conventionally been interpreted as the result of maturing cortical inhibitory centers. Donna Fisher and I (Thelen and Fisher, 1982) found, however, that a simple contextual manipulation – placing the infant supine – "restored" the patterned behavior even in infants who performed no steps when held upright. We proposed that the developmental transition from stepping to no-stepping was triggered

by a simple, nonneural scaling of a body composition parameter, the increase of nonmus-
cular or fat tissue, which made the legs comparatively heavy and weak and prevented the
infant from lifting the leg upright, but only when the infant was in the biomechanically
demanding upright posture (Thelen and Fisher, 1982). My colleagues and I have shown
that stepping in young infants can be elicited or supressed by a number of contextual
manipulations that systematically change the biomechanical demands on the legs, including
postural changes, submerging in water, adding weights, and placing infants on motorized
treadmills (Thelen, 1986a; Thelen et al., 1984; Thelen et al., 1982).

In dynamic systems terminology, then, the low-dimensional behavior of stepping, characterized by a definable relation between the excursions of the joints of each limb and
between the two legs, is not a product of some abstract "program" for stepping that exists
before the performance. Rather, it is the interaction of the contributing components,
including the biomechanical elements in relation to a specific task context, which determines
whether the infant steps or does not step. The body composition control parameter effects a
developmental shift in one context, but perhaps not in other contexts. In other words, under
certain conditions, the stepping topography represents a preferred and stable output of the
system. Changing the internal or external conditions causes the system to reassemble in
another attractor state. We therefore cannot define the system removed from the context.

The control parameters themselves change during ontogeny.   Conventional single-causal
models of developmental change assume that the control parameter in any one domain
remains stationary over long periods of developmental time (i.e. that cognitive reorganizations
or cortical growth organize diverse aspects of behavior over a long time span). Our systems
view, however, proposes that the control parameters themselves shift as the contributing
components grow and differentiate and as the physical and social contexts of the organism
change as a result of its development. This is the second source of transitions. The process of
development itself is nonlinear, and as the systems regroup and coalesce, these nonlinearities
serve as a continuing wellspring for new forms. In figure 18.7, I represent these changing
control parameters as the migration of a surface in three-dimensional state space.

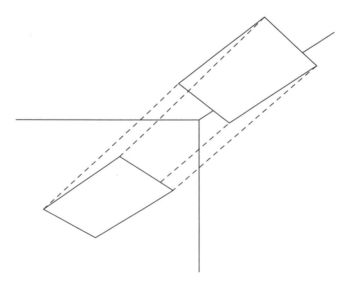

Figure 18.7   Developing system depicted as a surface in three-dimensional state space. With
time, the surface itself migrates in the space, resulting in changing control parameters.

Control parameters for developmental shifts at different ages and in different domains cannot be identified *a priori*. Identifying the sources of change remains an empirical exercise at every level of analysis. This is important because sometimes it is the nonobvious contributions to the system that drive the shift, as I illustrated with the newborn stepping system. Although, for example, the onset of verbal language appears to reflect a major cognitive reorganization, it is at least an open possibility that what in fact delimits the appearance of words is articulatory control over the vocal apparatus. Thus, although brain development may be a necessary condition for the appearance of new behavioral modes, it may not be sufficient, because we can never assume a one-to-one mapping of the structural basis of behavior and its performance in any individual or at any time. We can find many other instances of developing systems where only careful experimental analysis can dissect the interacting systems to reveal the driving subsystems.

For example, coordinated stepping behavior while upright reappears in the repertoire of normal infants at about ten months. I have proposed elsewhere that the control parameter driving this developmental shift (from no-stepping to stepping) is different from the one responsible for the earlier transition (Thelen, 1984). In particular, voluntary walking emerges when elements of both balance and extensor muscle strength reach values critical for allowing infants to support their weight on one leg in a stable manner while the other is lifted for the step. When we support newly stepping infants by holding their hands, or by providing then with walkers, we augment these control parameters and allow the system to display its more mature patterns (i.e. infants can successfully step).

Adaptive behavior emerges from successive bifurcations

Ontogenetic systems thus increase in complexity by a cascade of successive bifurcations or phase shifts. As the system reorganizes through the scalar change in a component, the newly emergent forms themselves act as control parameters. Changes in any one domain therefore may become amplified and have system-wide reverberations. What may appear to be a small change or acquisition may trigger a succession of major developmental landmarks – I provide examples here. I emphasize, however, that the track of successive bifurcations is a stochastic rather than a deterministic process. Ontogenetic outcomes are similar in the members of a species because certain attractor regimes are dynamically stable and certain configurations are more likely than others. Individual differences are possible because the fluctuations of the internal and external millieu provide elements of uncertainty and because the collective variable is exquisitely sensitive to the task. That is, the system may find alternative configurations to meet task constraints. For example, the task of moving toward a goal may be accomplished by young infants by a variety of locomotor modes – rolling, crawling, creeping, scooting, propelling in a wheeled device, and so on. The precise configuration is a function of the maturational and motivational state of the infant and the constraints of the support surface, provision of the wheeled device and so on.

Phase transitions result from the amplification of fluctuations

By what processes do control parameters induce changes of form? In complex systems, change results from the amplification of naturally occurring fluctuations or instabilities as the control parameter is scaled past a critical value (Kelso et al., 1986).

As a result of their complexity and multiple degrees of freedom, biological systems are *dynamically* stable. This means that they exist within a range of possible states and fluctuate among those states. As one component is gradually changed, there exists a point where the coalition of elements is no longer stable. Normal fluctuations become amplified until this noise disrupts the dynamic stability and the system autonomously reorganizes into a new stable state. Note again that fluctuations may become amplified from such control parameters acting outside as well as within the organism (figure 18.8).

Stability can be measured in complex systems in two ways. First, if the system is driven by a small perturbation away from its stationary state, it will tend to return to that stationary state. The time it takes to return to stationarity is a function of the stability of the system, and surprisingly, independent of the size of the perturbation, if it is small. Second, the inherent noise in any system acts as perturbations on the behavior. If the system is stable, the noise produces few variations from the stable state. At points of instability, however, the noise drives the collective behavior into more variable manifestations (figure 18.8).

From these considerations, we can make two powerful predictions about nonequilibrium systems at the point of phase transitions. First, that we should be able to detect the essential enhanced fluctuations at phase transitions in the form of increased variability in our behavioral measure. (This assumes we have chosen the correct collective variable to describe the behavior of interest, a nontrivial problem and one I discuss further later.) Second, because the system is inherently less stable at these transitions, it should be more sensitive to perturbations and thus restore itself to its stable attractor more slowly when perturbed.

These predictions were rigorously confirmed in the bilateral rhythmical finger movement experiments by Kelso and colleagues previously mentioned. These investigators found clear evidence of enhanced fluctuations in the relative phase measure just before and during the spontaneous phase shift from out-of-phase to in-phase coordination (Kelso et al., 1986). In addition, when they mechanically perturbed the movements, they observed a slower return to an equilibrium state at or near the phase transition (Scholz et al., 1987).

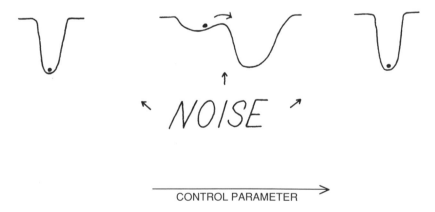

Figure 18.8 Phase shifts result from the amplification of normally occurring fluctuations or noise. The stability of a complex system is depicted in the steepness of a potential well; stable systems have steep wells. It is difficult to dislodge the ball from the steep well. At certain values of a control parameter, the internal fluctuations overwhelm the system stability and the system seeks new stable modes.

What does this mean for developing organisms? That ontogenic change results from a dialectic process of equilibrium arising from disequilibrium has long been a feature of developmental theories, including those of Piaget, Vygotsky, Lerner, Langer, Riegel, Overton, and Werner. However, the empirical instantiation of equilibration has been of little concern. Certainly, contemporary Piagetian research has centered more on the validity of a structural approach and the validation of invariant sequences than on Piaget's actual process of change.

If phase shifts through amplification of fluctuations are characteristic of systems in general, we should, by using the appropriate empirical strategy, be able to detect these phenomona. Indeed, such a demonstration would offer strong support to the autonomous or self-organizing abilities of developing systems.

Using Dynamical Systems Principles to Understand Development: Some Examples

Thelen et al. (1987) and Fogel and Thelen (1987) show how dynamic principles can help explain persistent puzzling aspects of early motor and expressive-communicative development. Here I present some additional examples.

Behavioral states in the newborn period: Self-organization and phase shifts

Thelen et al. (1987) suggested that the clustering of discrete variables seen in newborn state behavior was an important illustration of phase shifts or discontinuities in behavioral organization. Wolff (1987) has recently written an eloquent analysis of state behavior from a dynamic systems perspective.

In this treatment, Wolff emphasized the nonlinearity of state as a behavioral organizer in the newborn period. This nonlinearity means that there is no one-to-one correspondence between the input to the system and its response. Newborns are indeed very nonlinear: Their motor patterns form discrete clusters, and a stimulus presented in one cluster (such as sleep) may lead to a very different response than when the identical stimulus is presented during another cluster (such as alert wakefulness). Transitions from one behavioral state to another usually occur relatively abruptly, with unstable intermediate conditions.

Wolff explicitly rejected the traditional conceptualization of infant state as points along a continuum of behavioral arousal or activation. The traditional view assumes that one central agency such as the brainstem drives the discrete motor patterns, but is extrinsic to them. Rather, the cluster of behaviors we identify as state, Wolff argued, represent self-organizing aggregates of movement patterns, which are stable and resist perturbation. No outside executive assembles these clusters; states "fall out" because the system can exist only in one of several stable attractor regimes. These attractor regimes may themselves be different as development progresses; that is, the ensemble of interactive motor patterns may change with age.

Presumably, a number of control parameters can disrupt the dynamic stability of one state and lead to a qualitative shift to a new state. If a sleeping infant is tickled very gently, he or she may remain asleep, however, if we increase the tactile stimulation, there will likely be a point where the stability of the sleep state is disrupted, and the infant awakens. If he or she immediately falls asleep again, we would judge the infant's sleep state to be very deep;

that is, the attractor regime is very stable. If the infant stays awake, we could assume that she was close to the transition point to wakefulness and the tickling acted as a control parameter driving the phase shift. Likewise, nonnutritive sucking may be the control parameter to shift the fussy infant into a more quiet state (see also Fogel and Thelen, 1987).

Evidence from the early development of sleep states supports this self-assembly view. In premature infants, differentiation of active and quiet sleep states occurs progressively with age from a more indeterminate sleep type. Curzi-Dascalova et al. (1988) showed that this differentiation could be characterized by the association of increasing numbers of state criteria behaviors from 31 to 41 weeks of gestational age. They recorded EEG, eye movements, tonic chin EMG, gross limb movements, and respiration. In the youngest premature infants, only the EEG and eye movement patterns "hung together" to distinguish active and quiet states from indeterminate sleep. By 41 weeks, states were reliably characterized by larger constellations of variables. As sleep states entrap more components, they also become more stable, in terms of well-defined and regular cycles. State development looks not so much like the maturation of a single controlling structure as the progressive strengthening of stable attractor states that serve, in turn, as major organizers of behavior.

Variability and instability at phase shifts: Three examples

The three examples I offer – two recent human studies and the well-studied weaning period in rat pups – fulfill dynamic predictions: that increased variability and more sensitivity to perturbation will accompany ontogenetic transitions.

Postural Stability.   Shumway-Cook and Woollacott (1985) studied the development of postural stability in three groups of children aged 15–31 months, 4–6 years, and 7–10 years. The children stood on a moveable platform that provided a rapid forward or backward displacement of a few centimeters to which subjects respond by an appropriate postural compensation. The experimenters measured the onset latency of the contraction of the stabilizing muscle groups in the lower leg and the delay between the onset of the activation of the lower leg and thigh muscles over a number of trials. The oldest group of children and adults showed consistent responses that rapidly adapted over succeeding trials; that is, the subjects damped their responses to minimize overcompensation to the perturbation. The youngest children also showed consistent, rather longer latency responses, but they did not habituate to the destabilizing trials – a less mature strategy. In the transition group of four- to six-year-olds, the response latencies were not only significantly longer than in the younger and older groups, but also the variability was greatly increased, both within and between subjects (figure 18.9). Postural compensation, like stepping, is a dynamic product of the neurological mechanisms detecting the perturbation and producing the corrective response and biomechanical considerations, in this case, the natural sway frequency of the body. (Children have a faster sway rate than adults, Forssberg and Nashner, 1982.) These authors speculated that the rapid change of body proportion seen in the 4–6 age range may have disrupted the stable, but less adaptable, earlier stage. In dynamic terminology, the body proportion may have acted as one (although likely not the only) control parameter. In addition, the four to six-year-old group performed more poorly when they were given discrepant information about their postural stability from two sensory modalities, vision and ankle and foot proprioception. Younger infants apparently rely largely on visual input, whereas older subjects are able to rapidly integrate the two sources. In the transition group, however, the perturbation proved to be much more disruptive.

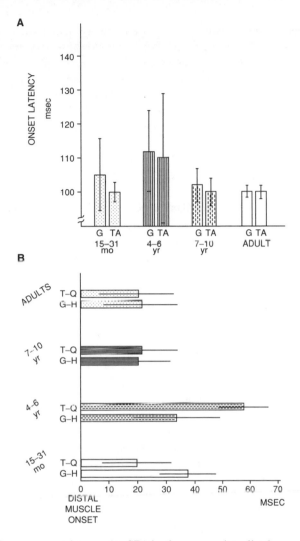

Figure 18.9   **A,** Average onset latency (+ SD) in the appropriate distal muscle in response to a forward sway translation (G) or backward sway translation (TA) as a function of age. Response latencies are slower and more variable in children 4–6. **B,** Temporal delay between distal and proximal muscle activation as a function of age. Children ages 4–6 demonstrate greatest temporal delay in activation of proximal muscles suggesting diminished synergic coupling between distal and proximal muscles. (From Shumway-Cook, A. and Woolacott, M. H. (1985) The growth of stability: Postural control from a developmental perspective. *Journal of Motor Behavior* 17, 137. Reprinted with permission of the Helen Dwight Reid Educational Foundation. Published by Heldref Publications, 1319 Eighteenth St., NW, Washington, DC, 20036–1802. Copyright © 1985.)

Piagetian conservation.   Church and Goldin-Meadow (1986) presented a compelling measure of instability in transitions in a classic Piagetian conservation task. When these authors asked five- to eight-year-old children to explain their conservation judgments nearly all children gestured spontaneously as they spoke. Some children, however, conveyed information in their gestures about the task that did not match the information of their spoken explanation. These "discordant" children were far less consistent in the nature of their explanations of the various conservation tasks and in matching the actual judgment of conservation with their explanation. These authors suggested that the discordant children "appeared to have pieces of information that they had not yet consolidated into a coherent explanatory system" (p. 59). In dynamic terms, the tasks did not elicit a stable attractor state – either conservation or nonconservation. If we consider verbal production as one compression of the degrees of freedom and gestural production as yet another way that the system can reduce the dimensionality for a lower dimensional output, we have a dramatic example of the fluid assembly of the components, especially at a time when system has not settled in to a more stable regime.

Indeed, the children in the discordant group proved to be much more sensitive to environmental perturbations. When the experimenters explicitly trained these children on conservation principles or even just allowed them practice with the materials, the children improved both on their judgments and on their explanations. Concordant children did not benefit from training. This intervention, therefore, acted as the crucial control parameter that pushed the unstable system into new forms. The stable systems of the concordant children could not be disrupted. It is consistent with a Piagetian interpretation to conclude that naturally occurring experience with conservation-like tasks would eventually shift the system into the conserving mode.

Weaning in rat pups.   In the rat pup, the shift from suckling to independent ingestion of food is a well-defined behavioral transition. In the first two weeks of life, rats meet their nutritional needs exclusively by suckling and after 28 days they only eat and drink independently. The shift in feeding modes is most pronounced between days 21 and 24 (Hall and Williams, 1983).

Although under natural conditions the transition is relatively discrete, experimental manipulations have revealed that the process is a complex one, reflecting the synergetic and symbiotic relationship between the behavior and physiology of both the mother and the pup. Noteworthy from the present systems view is the mobility of the component subsystems and their ability to coalesce in particular task-specific configurations that can be relatively independent of age.

For example, although the rat pups do not normally eat and drink independently for several weeks after birth, Hall and Bryan (1980) have shown that even newborn rat pups will ingest liquid or semisolid food from the floor of a test chamber. In young pups, this oral activity was activated only when the ambient temperature was high. The presence of food and external warmth served as control parameters to shift the rat pups into an ontogenetically more mature performance, independent ingestion.

Equally intriguing is the demonstration by Pfister et al. (1986) of a context-determined prolongation of suckling. These experimenters provided weaning-aged rat pups with a succession of nursing dams and their 16- to 21-day-old litters. Under these conditions, rats continued to nurse until as much as 70 days of age, long beyond the time they were eating independently, but they attached to the nipple and withdrew milk only when the younger littermates had attached. A combination of the social facilitation of nursing littermates, a dam who allowed continued nursing, and the continuation of the suckling experience here coalesced to maintain the animal in a stable state characteristic of an earlier ontogenetic stage.

It is noteworthy that during the natural weaning transition, ingestive behavior in a choice situation was highly variable and subject to disruption. The youngest rat pups in Stoloff and Blass's (1983) forced choice experiment consistently chose to suckle and the over 28-day group never chose suckling over eating. However, the 21–24 day transition group exhibited highly unstable and variable responses, and their choice behavior was described as "markedly affected by each manipulation undertaken in this experiment" (p. 451).

These results make it unlikely that there is a "weaning clock" somewhere in the rat pup, ticking off time or metering out some "weaning substance." Rather, weaning may be a phenomenon emergent from this confluence of ongoing systems, each with constraints and demands. In recently completed work, Thiels (1987) has shown that at the weaning transition, rat pups show increases not only in independent eating and drinking, *but also in many other actions as well* (see figure 18.10). The increased locomotor ability of the pup, its increased size and energy demands, its abilities to move away from the mother to seek food, and so on, are all contributions to the weaning transition and potential control parameters. No specific weaning instructions need be invoked. Weaning falls out, so to speak, from an ensemble of dynamic processes.

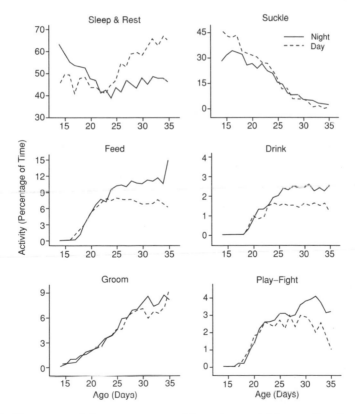

Figure 18.10 Percentage of time rat pups spend in various activities as a function of age. Note increase of many independent functions between ages 20–25 days. (From Thiels, 1987, reprinted with permission.)

The development of early lateral preferences: phase shifts and attractors

By the age of two, human children show lateral preferences for hand use almost as consistently as adults. Developmentalists have long been intrigued with the developmental origins of laterality, especially because hemispheric specialization for manual behavior may be related to specialization for speech. Nonetheless, it is not easy to determine when and how this preference is manifested in infancy. Lateral preferences often appear to wax and wane, making prediction from infant hand use to adult handedness very difficult.

The strong, predominantly rightward, asymmetrical head posture seen in the newborn period makes it likely that the central nervous system is laterally biased from birth. Indeed, neonatal head preference is a good predictor of hand-use preference in the second year (Michel and Harkins, 1986). There is considerable debate over whether the asymmetries of head posture are manifestations of the same lateralities that are later expressed in handedness, or whether these head postures induce handedness through biasing hand–eye contact and arm movements (see Young et al. (1983) for further elaboration of this debate and several models of laterality development).

In a recent review, Michel (1987) offered a plausible scenario by which the initial head biasing has cascading effects leading to eventual laterality in handedness. Head orientation leads to an asymmetry of visual regard of the hand and arm movement, which in turn, may induce asymmetrical reaching, and later manipulation. Thus, the infant's own experiences generate laterality in progressively developing skills.

If, however, the system is inherently biased, why is infant handedness so shifting and unstable? Michel suggested that the actual manifestation of the preferred hand is a function of both the infant's level of manual skill and the particular task. For example, Michel et al. (1986) tested 6- to 13-month-old infants for lateral preference in three manual skills: reaching for objects, manipulating objects, and coordinating complementary bimanual actions. Infants generally showed consistent hand-use preferences among the tasks (and about 75 percent were right handed). However, there were some surprising shifts. Although all of the 12-month-old infants preferred the same hand for reaching and bimanual manipulation, 56 percent of the 13-month-olds chose the opposite hand for bimanual manipulations from the hand they used for reaching. It is important to note that bimanual manipulation becomes a common skill for infants only in about the twelfth month. Michel speculated that many of the reaches of the 13-month-old infants were with the nonpreferred hand so that the preferred hand could be left free to begin bimanual manipulation. When bimanual manipulation becomes practiced, presumably infants could both reach and manipulate with the preferred hand. Lateral preference is a useful metric only when combined with a task analysis.

This account of lateral preference is consistent with a dynamic systems view. Let us depict strong, adult-like lateral preferences for hand use as two point attractors whose stability is represented by the steepness of the well seen at the bottom left of figure 18.11. The attractor for the right hand is very strong; the ball "prefers" to roll to the bottom of the well and will return there very quickly when perturbed. Right-handed people may be able to use the left hand for some tasks, but they prefer not to under ordinary circumstances. However, if their right arms were in a cast and sling, they would recruit the left hand to do tasks not ordinarily undertaken. That is, given a strong perturbation (broken arm), the ball can be shaken out of the deep well into another attractor state (left hand use), as a qualitative phase shift.

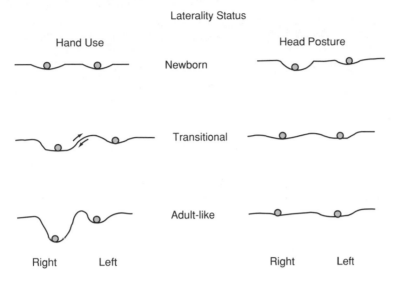

Figure 18.11 Lateral preference depicted as a series of point attractor states. Hand use attractors are the left-hand panel, head posture attractors on the right-hand panel. Transitional states are bistable and are especially sensitive to task context.

We can characterize newborn head posture as a relatively strong attractor, which entrains the arm and hand system to become progressively more laterally differentiated. However, in the transitional period, the attractor basins are shallow. Even rather small perturbations will drive the ball out of the well, up over the wall, and into the opposite hand attractor. The system is especially sensitive to the task and skill-level interaction because each new demand acts as a perturbation. Thus, the onset of bimanual manipulation acts as a control parameter and disrupts the stability of the reaching laterality, leading to a phase shift.

How does this account differ from a model of development as simply increasing hemispheric laterality? Here I emphasize the systems nature of lateral preference, which is always assembled "softly" in relation to the task and action patterns available to the infant. The system prefers certain places in the state space, but it is not restricted to them. Accomplishing the task is always a higher priority than the particular means by which the infant executes the action, so that the attractors are shallow enough to allow for flexibility in the face of obstacles. Likewise, the system becomes lateralized only as it supports adaptive actions. At the same time as the hand use attractors are becoming lateralized and stable, the head posture attractors are becoming progressively weaker. It is not adaptive for action to have an obligatory, or even strongly preferred head posture. Similarly, spontaneous leg movements develop from an initial strong asymmetry to symmetrical activity, reflecting the demands of locomotion and postural support for bilateral symmetry (Thelen et al., 1983).

Although hand use preference may indeed reflect an increasing hemispheric specialization, this explanation alone misses the richness and complexity of the process of change over time. We sometimes view the nonlinearity and nonstationarity of behavior over time as noise in the smooth trajectory toward maturity. The lesson from nonlinear dynamical systems is that these aberrations are the very stuff of ontogenetic change. It is at these transitions that the system reveals what holds it together and what drives it to new forms. A synergetic strategy of development will exploit these nonlinearities for a deeper understanding of process.

An Empirical Strategy Based on Systems Principles

We know that self-organizing phenomena in physics, chemistry, and some biological systems may be modeled with precision and elegance. This goal may not be attainable with behaving and developing organisms. Can principles of complex systems help developmentalists in our everyday unraveling of real life behavior? Do we have just another set of agreeable postulates which are neither objectionable nor useful?

I believe the lessons from complex systems analysis can serve developmentalists well, not only as a conceptual framework, but as an empirical strategy that is independent of level and content domain. Nothing I propose here for operationalizing systems is, in itself, new. Developmentalists have been using these methods – observational, longitudinal, experimental – since the adoption of scientific methods for studying ontogeny. What may be new, however, is the systematic linking of these strategies to synergetic principles:

1   The focus is on process not just outcome measures.
2   No component or subsystem has ontological priority.
3   Task and context, not instructions, assemble behavior.
4   Control parameters are not stationary. (The state space itself evolves through time.)

The first requirement for a systems approach is to identify the essential collective variables and their behavior. What is the best way to describe, for any particular organism and set of developmental questions, how the system compresses the degrees of freedom? Note that this description of the collective states can be done in many domains and at many levels of analysis. For infant animals, this may be a measure of perceptual performance or motor output, a psycho–physiological measure, or variables indexing social interaction. The dynamical description is level-independent. However, the choice of an appropriate collective variable is neither a trivial nor a simple matter because ontogeny is so often nonlinear. Because we are interested in the processes of developmental change, it is likely that our first approach would be longitudinal. For animals like humans, where significant individual variability often renders group means meaningless, the analysis may require a case-study design.

Because we assume in this perspective that the task or context, not pre-existing instructions, assembles the system into a measurable collective variable, it is essential that our developmental descriptions also contain a task analysis. This also may be difficult, especially in long-term longitudinal studies, because the meaning of the task or context itself changes with the development of the infant. For example, grasping a 1-inch cube is not the same task for a three-month-old as for a 12-month-old simply because of the body scale changes in the dimensions of the hand relative to the object (Newell, 1986). Nonetheless, it is a mistake to assume that sources of developmental shifts are organismic when they may indeed be in the match between the organism and the task.

The second step in this analysis is to identify the developmental transitions or where the organism shifts from one stable mode of performance to a new mode. Again, if there is variability in the age–dependent onset of new behaviors, or if complex contextual eliciting factors are involved, such shifts may be best discovered in the course of individual developmental profiles. Synergetic theory predicts that at such transitions, the system will show enhanced fluctuations and loss of stability. In developmental data we would expect an increase in the variability of our collective variable – that is, an increase in the deviations from the mean performance when compared to either the earlier stable performance or the new behavioral mode.

Experimentally induced perturbations or facilitations at the point of transitions can test the stability of the system. Developmentalists may probe a transition by experimentally perturbing the infant with an appropriate contextual manipulation (or, in nonhuman species, a surgical or pharmacological intervention). Systems near phase transitions are predicted to recover more slowly than those in more stable states.

The third, and crucial, step is to try to identify the control parameters: the one or few variables in the complex system that drives the shift. How can this be done? First, we would expect that a component or subsystem acting as a control parameter would itself show scalar changes in the time period of the phase transition. One clue to identifying control parameters is to look for variables that themselves change rapidly prior to or during the phase shift. This is not foolproof, however! In dynamic systems even small changes in crucial scalars can amplify fluctuations and lead to new equilibrium states.

If we understand our developing organism fairly well, we can make reasonable guesses about which components may drive developmental systems. Nonetheless, it may be a mistake to assume a control parameter *a priori*. A more fruitful strategy would be to map several likely control parameters so that they may be tested individually.

Once candidates for control parameters are identified, we can perform experimental manipulations or exploit the natural variability among individuals to confirm whether changes in the single parameter drive the system reorganization. The former tactic is more easily employed if we can discover a contextual manipulation that will serve as a substitute for a natural control parameter. In humans, neural or organismic variables may need correlational methods or observation of nonnormal populations.

The final step in a synergetic strategy would be the integration of the different levels of description. In the abstract, the dynamics at the neural level should be coupled to the dynamics at the behavioral level, and so on, regardless of the level used. For example, Kelso and Scholz (1985) have related amplifications in fluctuations at phase transitions seen in the kinematics of finger movements to similar phenomena measured at the level of muscle contractions. Such elegant mappings may be quite difficult over developmental time.

A Synergetic Approach to Locomotor Development

The onset of independent, upright locomotion – learning to walk – can be viewed as a dramatic phase shift in motor development. One day, the infant cannot walk alone, and the next day he or she toddles by herself. Traditional explanations attribute this milestone to maturational changes in an executive function such as increasing cortical or cognitive control of movement. My colleagues and I have suggested that walking alone is not so much commanded as emergent. No "walking" schema *per se* need exist; the behavior is rather the stable compression of many variables in an organism with a particular neural, anatomical, and biomechanical configuration, with certain motivations and goals, and supported on a permissive substrate. The benefit of viewing walking as a multicomponent emergent phenomenon is to open a window on how the skill is actually constructed during development.

For a synergetic strategy we must first ask: By what collective variable can we capture the compression of the degrees of freedom involved when people walk? A number of kinematic and kinetic variables might suffice. We focus on one essential characteristic of human bipedal walking: the regular, 180 degrees out-of-phase alternation of the legs needed to maintain both upright stability and forward progress. (Humans could use other symmetrical gait patterns such as hopping or galloping, but presumably they are less efficient.) When infants begin to locomote in the upright position, they use an alternating gait, although they are more variable in their phasing than in older toddlers and children (Clark et al., 1988). How do they acquire this ability? Is this a pattern that emerges with independent locomotion? What component skills do infants need to step? How does the environment support this skill?

Infants are capable of regularly alternating movements of their legs long before the onset of upright locomotion. Even in the newborn period, supine leg kicks may alternate, but the limbs appear loosely coupled. Throughout the first year, leg kicks seem to be like a weak, cyclic attractor. Alternation is a preferred, but not very stable state (Thelen, 1985).

This stability greatly increased, however, with a simple contextual manipulation. When I supported seven-month-old infants, who normally do not step, over a motorized treadmill, I saw dramatic increases not only in their step rate, but in the strictly alternating excursions of their limbs (Thelen, 1986). These treadmill steps were not simple reflexes, but dynamic and adaptive motor coordinations. Infants not only adjusted their step rate in accord with the speed of the treadmill in a manner identical to independent walkers, but also were able to compensate for extreme perturbations – one leg driven at twice the speed of the opposite leg – to maintain the right–left alternation (Thelen et al., 1987). It is unlikely that, at seven months, either the onset of stepping or the continual compensations were mediated by conscious or voluntary processes.

Figure 18.12 illustrates such leg alternation in a single eight-month-old infant girl (CH). CH's leg excursions were tracked by means of an optico–electronic motion detection system through a series of trials beginning with the treadmill belts turned off and continuing through seven more trials where the speed of the belts was gradually scaled up. The speed adjustment was made after 5 seconds in each trial except the first moving belt trial. It is easy to see where the 5-second perturbation occurred and CH's subsequent adjustment to maintain alternation. After the eighth trial, the belt was again turned off. In this second no-movement trial, CH performed some leg movements, but they were poorly coordinated. Finally, we perturbed coordination by moving one belt twice as fast as the other, but the infant still kept on walking!

Thus, the collective variable of interest is a measure of interlimb phasing – the relative coordination of one limb to another. These patterned movements represent the low-dimensional output of a system composed of many components – neurological networks, bones, joints, muscles with characteristic strength and tone, and motivational and attentional elements, including the infant's state, physiological parameters, and so on.

We may ask about the developmental course of this coordinative ability, and especially about two transitions. First, at what point in ontogeny does this neuromotor ability develop? Second, what allows coordinated upright stepping to become manifest during the last few months of the first year? Our ultimate question is, which of the essential elements in the system will serve as control parameters in effecting the development shifts?

Beverly Ulrich, my collaborator in this work, and I began our synergetic strategy with an effort to understand the dynamics of our collective variable over developmental time. We used a multiple case-study, longitudinal design by observing nine infants each month from

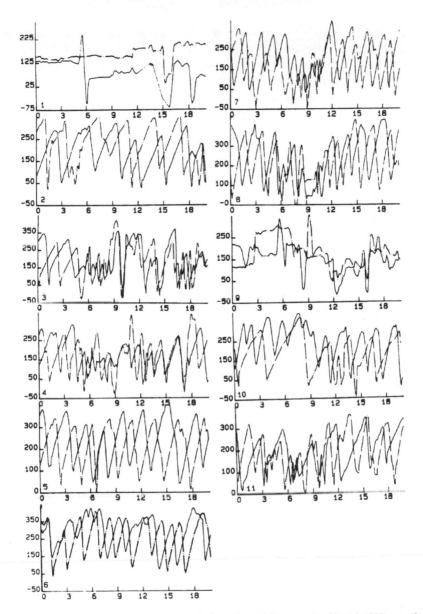

Figure 18.12 Excursions of the right and left foot of an eight-month-old girl (CH) as a function of treadmill speed condition. Trials 1 and 9 are with the belt turned off. In trials 2–8 the speed is gradually increased; the increase occurs after 5 seconds of the trial. Note CH's adjustment. Trials 10 and 11 are "split-belt" trials, where one belt is moving at twice the speed of the opposite belt. Note the continuation of alternation.

age one month until they walked independently or refused the treadmill (usually between seven and nine months). Each infant participated in two identical experimental sessions each month to assess within-age variability and to elicit optimal performance. The treadmill task is identical to the series of trials just described for infant CH, one of the subjects in the

study. In addition, we obtained Bayley scales of motor development, behavioral state
assessments, and anthropometric measurements because previous research suggested that
these variables affected stepping performance.

I present here some preliminary results in the single infant, CH, to illustrate the
paradigm. In figure 18.13, we plot the cycle durations of alternating steps taken by infant
CH as a function of age and treadmill speed trial. (Remember that trials 1 and 9 are on

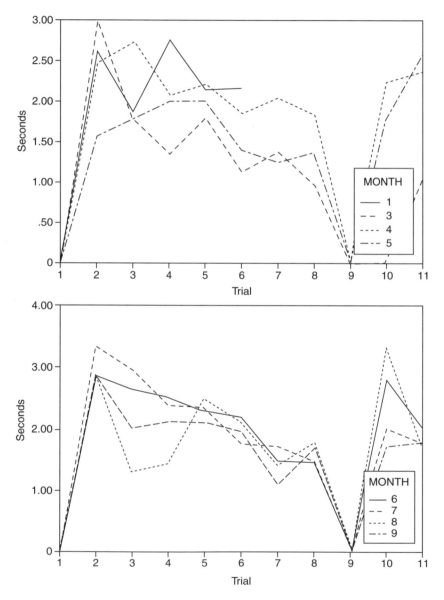

Figure 18.13 Cycle durations of alternating steps performed by CH as a function of treadmill
speed. Each trace represents the "better" day of each month's testing. Trials as in figure 18.12.
Note decrease in cycle durations as belt speed increases and increased sensitivity to treadmill
speed, especially in months 5–8. CH did not step at all in month 2.

stationary belts and that the belt speed was gradually increased in trials 2–8). In general, cycle duration was inversely related to belt speed, but in months 1–3, CH's performance was erratic. By month 4, however, she adjusted her steps to the belt speed, and she continued to do so, although the very fastest belt speeds sometimes appeared to inhibit performance. (We do not know whether this reflected an inability of the legs to cycle at such a high frequency or a fatigue effect, but other infants also showed this decrement at the highest speeds.)

We can also look at a more precise index of bilateral coordination, the relative phasing between the movements of each leg. In mature stepping, the step cycle of one leg is initiated at 50 percent of the cycle duration of the opposite leg (the limbs are precisely 180 degrees out-of-phase). In figure 18.14, we can see that in the early months, CH's interlimb phasing is very variable, but that it approaches the adult-like 50 percent value more consistently in the second half of the year. The coupling between the limbs becomes tighter. The other infants in our sample showed remarkably similar developmental trends.

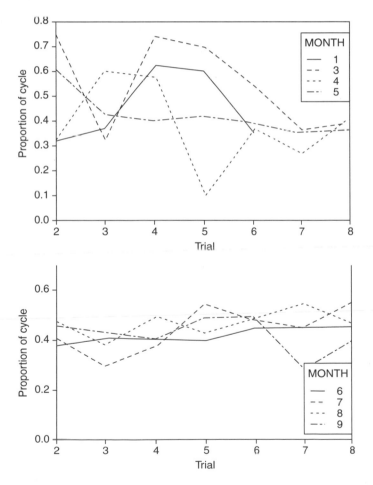

Figure 18.14 Relative phase lags between left and right foot steps in infant CH as a function of age and treadmill speed. Lags are expressed as the proportion of the step cycle of one leg when step in the opposite leg was initiated.

These descriptive data give us a picture of the dynamics of change of the ability to coordinate the two legs. Some ability, albeit rather primitive, is manifest at the first month. In CH, we saw no abrupt transitions from no stepping to fully articulated stepping on the treadmill, but rather a gradual increase in steps with age. This suggested that the basic mechanism whereby limbs respond to a backward stretch by alternating swings is in place at a very early age, but that the system is not very stable. The attractor becomes progressively stronger with age.

These results are only the first step in a synergetic strategy; an understanding of the dynamics of our collective variable over developmental time. It is an essential (but often laborious) step to identify the points of transition when the system is unstable and when the control parameter dynamics can be explored. In the case of treadmill-elicited stepping, this analysis points to the first three to four months as the period of most rapid change, reflected in instability and variability. We have some indication of a relative decrement in treadmill performance at months 1 and 2 and then a more rapid improvement. What, then, are the control parameters shifting the system at these transition times?

One source of clues is to look at the other elements of the system indexed by the anthropometric, state, and motor maturity measures. In figure 18.15, for example, we show CH's stepping performance plotted with several other anthropometric indices. The first few months are a time of especially rapid changes in the rate of weight gain, and in

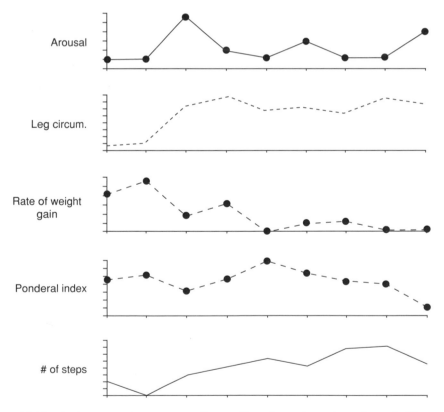

Figure 18.15 Anthropometric measures, "arousal" scale, and number of treadmill steps of infant CH from months 1 through 10. Anthropometric indices include rate of weight gain, summed circumferences of the thigh and calf, and Ponderal Index, weight/length^3. Note that there are rapid changes in the first four months on all variables.

measures of chubbiness and leg volume. Do these other system variables act as control parameters for treadmill stepping? Clearly, we cannot answer this question on the basis of correlational and case-study data. Many other things change very rapidly in the first few months of life that may affect this behavior. Nonetheless, this method does allow us to dissect our system to see what components are in place and what components are rapidly changing and may be candidates for control parameters. This then suggests possible experimental manipulations to test causal hypotheses.

Conclusion

In this view, ontogenetic change is the reorganization of components to meet adaptive tasks. It assigns the sources of new forms to the self-organizing properties of systems that use energy in a particular configuration. Pattern and complexity can emerge from the cooperativity of more simple elements. It says that developing systems are stable and predictable where their adaptive demands have constrained, through phylogenetic mechanisms, their range of solutions. (All mammals must suckle; at birth, the architecture of the suckling system leads to a very stable periodic attractor.) But this view also accounts for the variability and flexibility of these same systems when the task demands are not strict, or when experimental manipulations challenge the developing organisms with unique circumstances. (Suckling can also be curtailed, or prolonged, or the action patterns used for other goals, such as exploration.) Because prescriptions for action do not exist outside of the context that elicits action, components are free to assemble and reassemble within the constraints of the organism and the task. The physical and social context of the developing animal is more than just a supportive frame; it is an essential component of the assembled system. In such systems, new forms arise when the stability of the system is disrupted when random fluctuations are amplified by the scaling of a critical component. The process of developmental change is thus normally accompanied by a period of instability, where the system is exploring, so to speak, another level of stability.

A dynamic systems perspective may require new empirical strategies in which variability is the substance rather than the noise. By identifying developmental transitions, where the system may be "fooled" into progressions and regressions, we can then test the limits of the organism and the context in eliciting new forms. In reality, many developmentalists have implicitly adopted such an empirical strategy; this perspective provides a rationale consistent with pattern-formation processes in other physical and biological systems.

ACKNOWLEDGMENTS

I thank Scott Kelso and Alan Fogel for their important contributions to the ideas presented here and Beverly Ulrich and David Niles for their invaluable collaboration on the research. This chapter was supported by National Science Foundation Grant BNS 85 09793, National Institutes of Health Grant ROI HD 22830, and a Research Career Development Award from the National Institutes of Health.

REFERENCES

Abraham, R. H. and Shaw, C. D. (1982). *Dynamics – The geomentry of behavior*. Santa Cruz, CA: Aerial Press.

Barnes, D. M. (1986). Brain architecture: Beyond genes. *Science* 233, 155–6.

Brent, S. B. (1978). Prigogine's model for self-organization in monequilibrium systems: Its relevance for developmental psychology. *Human Development* 21, 374–87.

Brent, S. B. (1984). *Psychological and Social Structures*. Hillsdale, NJ: Lawrence Erlbaum Associates.

Church, R. B. and Goldin-Meadow, S. (1986). The mismatch betwen gesture and speech as an index of transitional knowledge. *Cognition* 23, 43–71.

Clark, J. E., Whitall, J., and Phillips, S. J. (1988). Human interlimb coordination: The first 6 months of independent walking. *Developmental Psychobiology* 21, 445–56.

Cohen, A. H., Holmes, P. J., and Rand, R. H. (1982). The nature of coupling between segmental oscillators of the lamprey spinal generator for locomotion: A mathematical model. *Journal of Mathematical Biology* 13, 345–69.

Curzi-Dascalova, L., Peirano, P., and Morel-Kahn, F. (1988). Development of sleep states in normal premature and full-term newborns. *Developmental Psychobiology* 21, 431–44.

Dammasch, I. E., Wagner, G. P., and Wolff, J. R. (1986). Self-stabilization of neural networks, 1: The compensation algorithm for synaptogenesis. *Biological Cybernetics* 54, 211–22.

Fogel, A. and Thelen, E. (1987). The development of expressive and communicative action in the first year: Reinterpreting the evidence from a dynamic systems perspective. *Developmental Psychology* 23, 747–61.

Forssberg, H. and Nashner, L. M. (1982). Ontogenetic development of postural control in man: Adaptation to altered support and visual conditions during stance. *Journal of Neuroscience* 2, 545–52.

French, V., Bryant, P. J., and Bryant, S. V. (1976). Pattern regulation in epimorphic fields. *Science* 193, 969–81.

Gierer, A. (1981). Generation of biological patterns and form: Some physical, mathematical, and logical aspects. *Progress in Biophysics and Molecular Biology* 37, 1–47.

Haken, H. (1983). *Synergetics: An introduction*, 3rd edn. Heidelberg, Berlin: Springer-Verlag.

Haken, H. (ed.). (1985). *Complex Systems: Operational approaches in neurobiology, physics, and computers*. Heidelberg, Berlin: Springer.

Haken, H., Kelso, J. A. S., and Bunz, H. (1985). A theoretical model of phase transitions in human hand movements. *Biological Cybernetics* 51, 347–56.

Hall, W. G. and Bryan, T. E. (1980). The ontogeny of feeding in rats: II. Independent ingestive behavior. *Journal of Comparative and Physiological Psychology* 93, 746–56.

Hall, W. G. and Williams, C. L. (1983). Suckling isn't feeding, or is it? A search for developmental continuities. *Advances in the Study of Behavior* 13, 219–54.

Haroutunian, S. (1983). *Equilibrium in the Balance: A study of psychological explanation*. New York: Springer-Verlag.

Hopfield, J. J. and Tank, D. W. (1986). Computing with neural circuits: A model. *Science* 233, 625–33.

Kelso, J. A. S., Holt, K. G., Kugler, P. N., and Turvey, M. T. (1980). On the concept of coordinative structures as dissipative structures: II. Empirical lines of convergence. In G. E. Stelmach and J. Requin (eds.), *Tutorials in Motor Behavior* (pp. 49–70). New York: North-Holland.

Kelso, J. A. S. and Scholz, J. P. (1985). Cooperative phenomena in biological motion. In H. Haken (ed.), *Complex Systems: Operational approaches in neurobiology, physical systems, and computers* (pp. 124–49). Berlin: Springer.

Kelso, J. A. S., Scholz, J. P., and Schöner, G. (1986). Non-equilibrium phase transitions in coordinated biological motion: Critical fluctuations. *Physics Letters A*, 118, 279–84.

Kelso, J. A. S. and Schöner, G. (1987). Toward a physical (synergetic) theory of biological coordination. In R. Graham (ed.), *Lasers and Synergetics*. Heidelberg, Berlin: Springer.

Kelso, J. A. S. and Tuller, B. (1984). A dynamical basis for action systems. In M. S. Gazzaniga (ed.), *Handbook of Cognitive Neuroscience* (pp. 321–56). New York: Plenum Press.

Kitchener, R. F. (1982). Holism and the organismic model in developmental psychology. *Human Development* 25, 233–49.

Kugler, P. N., Kelso, J. A. S., and Turvey, M. T. (1980). On the concept of coordinative structures as dissipative structures: I. Theoretical lines of convergence. In G. E. Stelmach and J. Requin (eds.), *Tutorials in Motor Behavior* (pp. 3–47). New York: North-Holland.

Kugler, P. N., Kelso, J. A. S., and Turvey, M. T. (1982). On the control and co-ordination of naturally developing systems. In J. A. S. Kelso and J. E. Clark (eds.), *The Development of Movement Control and Co-ordination* (pp. 5–78). New York: Wiley.

Laszlo, E. (1972). *Introduction to Systems Philosophy*. New York: Harper and Row.

Lerner, R. M. (1978). Nature, nurture, and dynamic interaction. *Human Development* 21, 1–20.

Madore, B. F. and Freedman, W. L. (1987). Self-organizing structures. *American Scientist* 75, 252–9.

Meakin, P. (1986). A new model for biological pattern formation. *Journal of Theoretical Biology* 118, 101–13.

Michel, G. F. (1987). Self-generated experience and the development of lateralized neurobehavioral organization in infants. In J. S. Rosenblatt (ed.), *Advances in the Study of Behavior* (Vol. 17). New York: Academic Press.

Michel, G. F. and Harkins, D. A. (1986). Postural and lateral asymmetries in the ontogeny of handedness during infancy. *Developmental Psychobiology* 19, 247–58.

Michel, G. F., Ovrut, M. R., and Harkins, D. A. (1986). Hand-use preference for reaching and object manipulation in 6- through 13-month-old infants. *Genetic, Social, and General Psychology Monographs* 111, 409–27.

Mittenthal, J. E. (1981). The rule of normal neighbors: a hypothesis for morphogenetic pattern regulation. *Developmental Biology* 88, 15–26.

Newell, K. M. (1986). Constraints on the development of coordination. In M. G. Wade and H. T. A. Whiting (eds.), *Motor Development in Children: Aspects of coordination and control* (pp. 341–60). Dordrecht, Netherlands: Martinus Nijhoff Publishers.

Overton, W. F. (1975). General systems, structure, and development. In K. F. Riegel and G. C. Rosenwald (eds.), *Structure and Transformation: Developmental and historical aspects* (pp. 61–81). New York: Wiley.

Oyama, S. (1985). *The Ontogeny of Information: Developmental systems and evolution*. Cambridge: Cambridge University Press.

Pfister, J. F., Cramer, C. P., and Blass, E. M. (1986). Suckling in rats extended by continuous living with dams and their preweanling litters. *Animal Behaviour* 34, 415–20.

Prigogine, I. (1980). *From Being to Becoming*. San Francisco: W. H. Freeman.

Prigogine, I. and Stengers, I. (1984). *Order Out of Chaos: Man's new dialogue with nature*. New York: Bantam.

Rumelhart, D. E. and McClelland, J. L. (eds.). (1986). *Parallel Distributed Processing: Explorations in the microstructure of cognition. Vol. I: Foundations*. Cambridge, MA: Bradford Books/ MIT Press.

Sameroff, A. J. (1983). Developmental systems: Contexts and evolution. In P. H. Mussen (ed.), *Handbook of Child Psychology. Vol. I: History, theory, and methods*, 4th edn. (pp. 237–94). New York: Wiley.

Scholz, J. P., Kelso, J. A. S., and Schöner, G. (1987). *Nonequilibrium Phase Transitions in Coordinated Biological Motion: Critical slowing down and switching time*. Manuscript.

Schöner, G., Haken, H., and Kelso, J. A. S. (1986). A stochastic theory of phase transitions in human hand movement. *Biological Cybernetics* 53, 1–11.

Shrager, J., Hogg, T., and Huberman, B. A. (1987). Observation of phase transitions in spreading activation networks. *Science* 236, 1092–4.

Shumway-Cook, A. and Woollacott, M. H. (1985). The growth of stability: Postural control from a developmental perspective. *Journal of Motor Behavior* 17, 131–47.

Singer, W. (1986). The brain as a self-organizing system. *European Archives of Psychiatry and Neurological Sciences* 236, 4–9.

Skarda, C. A. and Freeman, W. J. (1987). How brains make chaos in order to make sense of the world. *Behavioral and Brain Sciences* 10, 161–95.

Stoloff, M. L. and Blass, E. M. (1983). Changes in appetitive behavior in weanling-age rats: Transitions from suckling to feeding behavior. *Developmental Psychobiology* 16, 439–53.

Szentagothai, J. (1984). Downward causation? *Annual Review of Neuroscience* 7, 1–11.

Thelen, E. (1981). Kicking, rocking, and waving: Contextual analysis of rhythmical stereotypes in normal human infants. *Animal Behavior* 29, 3–11.

Thelen, E. (1984). Learning to walk: Ecological demands and phylogenetic constraints. In L. P. Lipsitt (ed.), *Advances in Infancy Research, Vol. 3* (pp. 213–50). Norwood, NJ: Ablex.

Thelen, E. (1985). Developmental origins of motor coordination: Leg movements in human infants. *Developmental Psychobiology* 18, 1–22.

Thelen, E. (1986a). Treadmill-elicited stepping in seven-month-old infants. *Child Development* 57, 1498–506.

Thelen, E. (1986b). Development of coordinated movement: Implications for early development. In H. T. A. Whiting and M. G. Wade (eds.), *Motor Skill Acquisition in Children* (pp. 107–24). Dordrecht, Netherlands: Martinus Nijhoff.

Thelen, E. (1988). Dynamical approaches to the development of behavior. In J. A. S. Kelso, A. J. Mandell, and M. R. Shlesinger (eds.), *Dynamic Patterns in Complex Systems* (pp. 348–69). Singapore: World Scientific Publishers.

Thelen, E. and Fisher, D. M. (1982). Newborn stepping: An explanation for a "disappearing reflex." *Developmental Psychology* 18, 760–75.

Thelen, E., Fisher, D. M., and Ridley-Johnson, R. (1983). Shifting patterns of bilateral coordination and lateral dominance in the leg movements of young infants. *Developmental Psychobiology* 16, 29–46.

Thelen, E., Fisher, D. M., and Ridley-Johnson, R. (1984). The relationship between physical growth and a newborn reflex. *Infant Behavior and Development* 7, 479–93.

Thelen, E., Fisher, D. M., Ridley-Johnson, R., and Griffin, N. (1982). The effects of body build and arousal on newborn infant stepping. *Developmental Psychobiology* 15, 447–53.

Thelen, E. and Fogel, A. (1989). Toward an action-based theory of infant development. In J. Lockman and N. Hazen (eds.), *Action in Social Context*. New York: Plenum.

Thelen, E., Kelso, J. A. S., and Fogel, A. (1987). Self-organizing systems and infant motor development. *Developmental Review* 7, 39–65.

Thelen, E., Ulrich, B., and Niles, D. (1987). Bilateral coordination in human infants: Stepping on a split-belt treadmill. *Journal of Experimental Psychology: Human Perception and Performance* 13, 405–10.

Thiels, E. (1987). *Behavioral and energetic factors in weaning in Norway rats.* Unpublished doctoral dissertation, Indiana University.

Von Bertalanffy, L. (1968). *General System Theory.* New York: George Braziller.

Waddington, C. H. (1972). Form and information. In C. H. Waddington (ed.), *Towards a Theoretical Biology, Vol. 4* (pp. 109–45). Edinburgh: Edinburgh University Press.

Weiss, P. A. (1969). The living system: Determinism stratified. In A. Koestler and J. R. Smithies (eds.), *Beyond Reductionism: New perspectives in the life sciences* (pp. 3–55). Boston: Beacon Press.

Wolff, P. H. (1987). *The Development of Behavioral States and the Expression of Emotions in Early Infancy: New proposals for investigation.* Chicago: University of Chicago Press.

Woodson, R. H. (1988). Individual, development, and ontogeny. Manuscript. Dept of Psychology. University of Texas at Austin.

Young, G., Segalowitz, S. J., Corter, C. M., and Trehub, S. E. (eds.). (1983). *Manual Specialization and the Developing Brain*. New York: Academic Press.

Chapter Update

Systems Approaches Can *Work!*

This 1989 paper was the result of nearly a decade of my grappling with issues of development in light of the new theories of human movement that emerged in the early 1980s. The key moment for me was reading two chapters that appeared in a 1980 volume of otherwise conventional papers in motor behavior (Stelmach and Requin, 1980). The main authors of the papers, Peter Kugler, Scott Kelso, and Michael Turvey, were colleagues at Haskins Institute in New Haven. In these chapters, they presented an amalgam of ideas – from physiologists Bernstein and von Holst, physicists Haken, Iberall, and Prigogine, systems theorists von Bertanlanffy, Pattee, and Yates, and were inspired by Turvey's work on perception from a Gibsonian perspective (Kugler, Kelso, and Turvey, 1980; Kelso, Holt, Kugler and Turvey, 1980). Despite the dense writing and the eyestrain print, I saw that these ideas of self-organization were not only a brilliant solution to the issues of motor control, but that they could also be applied to any systems that change.

Systems ideas have been around in biology and psychology for many years. What distinguished the new formulation, however, was its solid grounding in both formal theory and experimental results. Could the tenets of system theory be useful for understanding development as well, especially for bringing together theoretical ideas and rigorous empirical work? Thus, the goal of my chapter was to pose this question and to suggest some strategies to make that happen.

In the decade since the 1989 chapter, I, and others, have conducted programs of research grounded in the belief that developing organisms can be best understood as dynamic systems. The intervening time has seen a number of major books on these new ideas (Elman, Bates, Johnson, Karmiloff-Smith, Parisi, and Plunkett, 1996; Fogel, Lyra and Valsiner, 1997; Newell and Molenaar, 1998; Smith and Thelen, 1993; Thelen and Smith, 1994; Van Geert, 1994) and dynamic systems has been accepted as a major theoretical approach (e.g. Lewis, 2000, Goldhaber, 2000; Thelen and Smith, 1998). In some ways, the promise of the new theory has been fulfilled, but in other ways, more work still needs to be done.

For the purposes of this update, it is useful first to review the major principles of dynamic systems that have continued to be important in thinking about development. Then we can discuss how these principles have been implemented in empirical research and modeling.

1. *Multiple causation and self-organization.* The idea that complex living systems, with many, heterogeneous parts, produce coherent behavior in a self-organized manner, has inspired many studies and simulations. The critical point here is that in such systems, all components are important. No agents are privileged and causality is circular. What allows self-organization to happen is that such systems are "open" to the environment and thus the physical and social worlds are as important in producing behavior as the organism. In such systems, new forms can arise as a function of the relationship of the parts.

For example, in my own studies of infant motor development, I was inspired by dynamic systems ideas to measure multiple, interacting components to begin to understand system change. For instance, in a longitudinal study of the development of infant reaching, my colleagues and I recorded multiple measures from the same small sample of infants at very dense intervals. Thus, we could relate the onset of reaching and improvements in that skill to control of muscle forces (Thelen, Corbetta, Kamm, Spencer, Schneider and Zernicke, 1993; Zaal, Daigle, Gottlieb, and Thelen, 1999), the underlying patterns of muscle activation (Spencer and Thelen, 2000), and to system-wide postural reorganizations (Spencer, Vereijken, Diedrich, and Thelen, in press). Likewise, in our re-interpretation of Piaget's "A-not-B" error from a dynamic perspective, we showed that there were multiple influences on the task, including the task design, visual cue, movement and posture, and memory of previous actions (Diedrich, Thelen, Corbetta and Smith, 2000; Smith, Thelen, Titzer and McLin, 1999; Thelen, Schöner, Scheier and Smith, 2001). We have recently simulated this dynamic interplay of causality in a formal field model, generated novel predictions from the model, and then tested them empirically (Thelen, et al., 2001). To me, this work is an especially gratifying demonstration that systems approaches can work, and in particular, are able to produce a mutually informative collaboration between theory, model, and experiment.

The notions of self-organization are also predominant in another important breakthrough of the last decade, the use of connectionist models. Ellman et al. (1996) give the most comprehensive overview and rationale for these modeling techniques. In brief, connectionist models demonstrate that patterns can emerge from initially non-patterned networks through simple rules and their own repeated activity. Rumelhart and McClelland's (1986) simulation of the ontogeny of the past tense in language learning is the classic example, but recent efforts to use these networks to simulate the development of object representation are also noteworthy (Mareschal, Plunkett and Harris, 1999; Munakata, 1998; Munakata, McClelland, Johnson, and Siegler, 1997).

Finally, mention must be made of the use of dynamic principles to understand the emergent principles of social interactions. In these cases, it is not the organism and the physical environment that constitute the system, but two or more individuals communicating with one another, either adults, or adults and children. In his important work, Fogel (1993; Fogel, Lyra and Valsiner, 1997) shows by minute analysis of dyadic interactions, that such interchanges are mutually co-regulated so that the meaning of the interaction is literally constructed through the relationship.

2. *Continuity in time.* The second useful insight from the dynamic perspective is that behavior always occurs continuously in time, such that current actions are a function of events and experiences in the past, and, in turn, set the stage for actions in the future. Although this is, of course, the hallmark of development, process approaches have not always been the standard of the field. In the last decade, there has been renewed interest in time, and especially in the relationship between short (or real-time) processes (action and learning) and changes over a developmental time scale.

One consequence is more attention to longitudinal studies, often using small sample sizes, but with a dense sampling schedule that enables the researcher to determine the pathways of change. I feel no small satisfaction, for example, to have two of our longitudinal studies of infant reaching, based on only four participants, published in one of the premier journals of experimental psychology, *Journal of Experimental Psychology: Human Perception and Performance*! What such designs relinquish in generalizability, they gain in detailed insight of process.

A second new focus on process consistent with a dynamic approach is termed *microgenesis* (Granott and Parziale, in press; Siegler and Jenkins, 1989). Microgenetic studies focus on transitions, and especially in identifying and manipulating experimentally variables that may be critical for developmental change. Many microgenetic studies involve training children in particular tasks to accelerate skills in a certain domain. For instance, Siegler and Jenkins (1989) showed that practice in particular, more efficient strategies for learning arithmetic helped children whose strategies were less mature.

3. *Nonlinearity.* There has been a remarkable attention in the last decade to the presence of nonlinearity in development. In dynamic systems, small changes in one or more components can have large, and cascading effects. This means that processes that are continuous can show what appear to be startling discontinuities. Indeed the differences in the initial differences may be so small, that the direction of these changes may not be knowable, resulting in a natural indeterminacy in developing systems (Fogel, Lyra, and Valsiner, 1997).

The most important theoretical work in this area has been by Paul van Geert (1994), who uses a particular kind of mathematical dynamic system (logistic equations) to model non-linear growth. Again, using only simple growth rules as initial conditions, van Geert's models produce complex, stage-like developmental profiles, fluctuations, and periods of exuberant growth and plateaus, much like real developmental data. Van Geert's efforts have been mainly directed to simulating patterns of language development (largely because of the rich corpus of dense longitudinal data in this domain), but others have used similar dynamic equations to model brain growth (Fischer and Rose, 1994; Thatcher, 1998), and interpersonal dynamics (Newtson, 1998).

4. *Transitions and variability.* Related to both the issues of nonlinearity and microgenesis, dynamic systems approaches have also highlighted the importance of transitions and variability as a window for understanding change. For example, in longitudinal studies of treadmill stepping (Thelen and Ulrich, 1991) and reaching (Thelen, Corbetta, and Spencer, 1996) we have identified times when behavior undergoes transitions and when it is stable by looking at the variability. Dynamic systems predicts that behavior that is relatively less variable will be less likely to be perturbed or changed by an intervention, indicating that the system has found a relatively stable attractor state. Thus, Vereijken and Thelen (1997) found that infants were more likely to benefit from training in treadmill stepping when their movement patterns were highly variable than when the patterns were stable.

In dynamic systems thinking, variability is the key to change because when system components are too tightly coupled, the intrinsic noise inherent in any biological system is damped down. Conversely, when the components are more loosely coupled, the system is more flexibly able to adapt to changes in the organism or in the environment. Lampl and Johnson (1998) provide a beautiful demonstration of the dynamics of developing complex biological systems in their models of human growth. By extremely careful measurements, they show that growth of fetuses, infants, and children is not linear, but occurs in spurts and plateaus. In infants, for instance, growth occurs in pulses of between 0.5 and 1.6 cm in 24 hours and then 2 to 63 days with no detectable growth. They claim that these growth dynamics are the natural result of "the output of complex, interrelated underlying processes that combine both endogenous signals and the physiological effects of the organism's interaction with environmental input" (p. 30). Indeed they see this dynamic pattern as a measure of a "robust and flexible" system "in which network and external forces substantially influence component behavior." "Variability in the amplitude and frequency of discrete events a mechanism providing pathway divergence for the attainment of reproductive adulthood amidst highly variable environmental circumstances" (p. 31).

Have they worked? I think the answer to the question I posed in 1989 is a loud "Yes." We have seen the ideas of dynamic systems more widely accepted over the last decade and making an entry to nearly all domains of developmental study. But there is still much work to be done before we have shown conclusively that a dynamic approach is the most powerful way to conceptualize development. First, I believe that the qualitative appeal of the theory and the abstract models from it have themselves progressed faster than the empirical applications. In other words, many developmentalists like the ideas of dynamic systems but do not know what to do with them in their research. This has not changed much since 1989. Collecting appropriate time-based and intensive sets of data is very difficult, especially when compared to cross-sectional experiments. We are still developing appropriate statistical tools to deal with time-series data and to look at intensive single-subject design. On the modeling side, theorists are creating increasingly sophisticated mathematical models (e.g. Newell and Molenaar, 1998), but there are fewer examples where the models do more than fit curves of existing data. Dynamic models are very powerful. What is needed is more work where models make unique predictions that can be tested against new experiments.

One strength of a dynamic approach is to unite dynamics across time scales and across levels. This also should be on our future agenda. How do brain and behavior dynamics intersect in real or developmental time (c.f. Fischer and Rose, 1994; Thatcher, 1998)? What about the coupled interactions of perception, action, and cognition (cf. Thelen et al., 2001)? I believe studies asking such questions will prove the key to future progress using a dynamic approach.

REFERENCES

Corbetta, D. and Thelen, E. (1996). The developmental origins of bimanual coordination. *Journal of Experimental Psychology: Human Perception and Performance* 22, 502–22.

Diedrich, F. J., Thelen, E., Corbetta, D., and Smith, L. B. (2000). Motor memory is a factor in infant perseverative errors. *Developmental Science* 3(4), 479–94.

Elman, J. L., Bates, E. A., Johnson, M. H., Karmiloff-Smith, A., Parisi, D., and Plunkett, K. (1996). *Rethinking Innateness: A connectionist perspective on development*. Cambridge, MA: MIT Press.

Fischer, K. W. and Rose, S. P. (1994). Dynamic development of coordination of components in brain and behavior. In G. Dawson and K. W. Fischer (eds.), *Human Behavior and the Developing Brain* (pp. 3–66). New York: Guilford Press.

Fogel, A. (1993). *Developing through Relationships*. London: Harvester Wheatsheaf.

Fogel, A., Lyra, M. C. D. P., and Valsiner, J. (1997). *Dynamics and Indeterminism in Developmental and Social Processes*. Mawah, NJ: Erlbaum.

Goldhaber, D. E. (2000). *Theories of Human Development: Integrative perspectives*. Mountain View, CA: Mayfield.

Granott, N. and Parziale, J. (eds.). (in press). *Microdevelopment: Transition processes in development and learning*. Cambridge: Cambridge University Press.

Kelso, J. A. S., Holt, K. G., Kugler, P. N., and Turvey, M. T. (1980). On the concept of coordinative structures as dissipative structures: II. Empirical lines of convergence. In G. E. Stelmach and J. Requin (cds.), *Tutorials in Motor Behavior* (pp. 49–70). Amsterdam: North-Holland.

Kugler, P. N., Kelso, J. A. S., and Turvey, M. T. (1980). On the concept of coordinative structures as dissipative structures: I. Theoretical lines of convergence. In G. E. Stelmach and J. Requin (eds.), *Tutorials in Motor Behavior* (pp. 3–47). Amsterdam: North-Holland.

Lampl, M. and Johnson, M. L. (1998). Normal human growth as saltatory: Adaptation through irregularity. In In K. M. Newell and P. C. M. Molenaar, *Applications of Nonlinear Dynamics to Developmental Process Modeling*. Mahwah, NJ: Erlbaum.

Lewis, M. D. (2000). The promise of self-organizing dynamic systems for a general model of human development. *Child Development* 71(1), 36–43.

Mareschal, D., Plunkett, K., and Harris, P. (1999). A computational and neuropsychological account of object-oriented behaviours in infancy. *Developmental Science* 2, 306–17.

Munakata, Y. (1998). Infant perseveration and implications for object permanence theories: A PDP model of the AB task. *Developmental Science* 1: 161–84.

Munakata, Y., McClelland, J. L., Johnson, M. H., and Siegler, R. S. (1997). Rethinking infant knowledge: Towards an adaptive process account of successes and failures in object permanence tasks. *Psychological Review* 104, 686–713.

Newell, K. M. and Molenaar, P. C. M. (1998). *Applications of Nonlinear Dynamics to Developmental Process Modeling*. Mahwah, NJ: Erlbaum.

Newtson, D. (1998). Dynamical systems and the structure of behavior. In K. M. Newell and P. C. M. Molenaar, *Applications of Nonlinear Dynamics to Developmental Process Modeling*. Mahwah, NJ: Erlbaum.

Rumelhart, D. E. and McClelland, J. L. (1986). On learning the past tenses of English verbs. In D. E. Rumelhart and J. L. McClelland (eds.), *Parallel Distributed Processing: Explorations in the microstructure of cognition: Vol. 1. Foundations* (pp. 318–62). Cambridge, MA: MIT Press.

Siegler, R. S. and Jenkins, E. (1989). *How Children Discover New Strategies*. Hillsdale, NJ: Erlbaum.

Smith, L. B. and Thelen, E. (1993). *Dynamic Systems in Development: Applications*. Cambridge, MA: Bradford Books/MIT Press.

Smith, L. B., Thelen, E., Titzer, R., and McLin, D. (1999). Knowing in the context of acting: The task dynamics of the A-not-B error. *Psychological Review* 106, 235–60.

Spencer, J. P., Vereijken, B., Diedrich, F. J., and Thelen, E. (2000). Posture and the emergence of manual skills. *Developmental Science* 3(2), 216–33.

Spencer, J. P. and Thelen, E. (2000). Spatially-specific changes in infants' muscle coactivity as they learn to reach. *Infancy* 1, 275–302.

Stelmach, G. E. and Requin, J. (1980). *Tutorials in Motor Behavior*. Amsterdam: North-Holland.

Thatcher, R. W. (1998). A predator-prey model of human cerebral development. In K. M. Newell and P. C. M. Molenaar (eds.) *Applications of Nonlinear Dynamics to Developmental Process Modeling* (pp. 87–128). Mahwah, NJ: Lawrence Erlbaum Associates.

Thelen, E., Corbetta, D., Kamm, K., Spencer, J. P., Schneider, K., and Zernicke, R. F. (1993). The transition to reaching: Mapping intention and intrinsic dynamics. *Child Development* 64, 1058–98.

Thelen, E., Corbetta, D., and Spencer, J. P. (1996). The development of reaching during the first year: The role of movement speed. *Journal of Experimental Psychology: Human Perception and Performance* 22, 1059–76.

Thelen, E., Schöner, G., Scheier, C., and Smith, L. B. (2001). The dynamics of embodiment: A field theory of infant perseverative reaching. *Behavioral and Brain Sciences* 24(1), 1–33.

Thelen, E. and Smith, L. B. (1994). *A Dynamic Systems Approach to the Development of Cognition and Action*. Cambridge, MA: Bradford Books/MIT Press.

Thelen, E. and Smith, L. B. (1997). Dynamic systems theories. In R. M. Lerner (ed.), *Theoretical Models of Human Development*. Volume 1 of the *Handbook of Child Psychology* (5th edition; pp. 563–634). Editor-in-chief: William Damon. New York: Wiley.

Thelen, E. and Ulrich, B. D. (1991). *Hidden Skills: A dynamical systems analysis of treadmill stepping during the first year. Monographs of the Society for Research in Child Development.* Vol. 56, No. 223.

Van Geert, P. (1994). *Dynamic Systems of Development: Change between complexity and chaos.* New York: Prentice-Hall/Harvester.

Vereijken, B. and Thelen, E. (1997). Training infant treadmill stepping: The role of individual pattern stability. *Developmental Psychobiology* 30, 89–102.

Zaal, F. T. J. M., Daigle, K., Gottlieb, G., and Thelen, E. (1999). An unlearned principle for controlling natural movements. *Journal of Neurophysiology* 82, 255–9.

19

Development Itself is the Key to Understanding Developmental Disorders

Annette Karmiloff-Smith

All scientists studying normal and atypical development – from the staunchest Chomskyan nativist to the most domain-general empiricist – agree that development involves contributions from both genes and environment. The gulf between the theories lies in how genes and environment are claimed to contribute to developmental outcomes. At some level, of course, we all concur in the existence of some degree of innate specification. The difference in positions concerns how rich and how domain-specific the innately specified component is, whether development is the result of predetermined epigenesis[1] (mere triggering) or probabilistic epigenesis,[1] and what happens when things go wrong. These differences in position influence the focus of the questions asked (nature or nurture, on the one hand, versus the mechanisms of progressive developmental change, on the other) and the way in which developmental disorders are studied.

Let's briefly take the example of language. For the staunch nativist, a set of genes specifically targets domain-specific modules as the end product of their epigenesis (e.g. a syntactic module,[2] a morphological module,[3] or a more narrowly pre-specified module for, say, canonical linkage rules in grammar[4]). Under this non-developmental view, the environment simply acts as a trigger for identifying and setting (environmentally-derived) native-tongue realizations of (pre-specified) parameters of universal grammar. The child is born innately expecting nouns, verbs, canonical linking rules, agreement between asymmetrical sentence elements, and so forth, but not yet knowing how they are realized in her/his native tongue.[5] The deletion, reduplication or mispositioning of genes is assumed to result in very specific impairments in the endstate.[3–6] For the empiricist, by contrast, much of the structure necessary for building language and the rest of the human mind is discovered directly in the structure of the physical and social environment.

These two extremes are not the only options, however. The neuroconstructivist approach to normal and atypical development fully recognizes innate biological constraints but, unlike the staunch nativist, considers them to be initially less detailed and less domain-specific as far as higher-level cognitive functions are concerned. Rather, development itself is seen as playing a crucial role in shaping phenotypical outcomes, with the protracted period of postnatal growth as essential in influencing the resulting domain specificity of the developing neocortex.[7,8] A clearer way to capture this idea is to specify that the interaction is not in fact between genes and environment. Rather, on the gene side, the interaction lies in the outcome of the indirect, cascading effects of interacting genes and their environments and, on the environment side, the interaction comes from the infant's *progressive* selection and processing of different kinds of input. For both the strict nativist and the empiricist, the notion of "environment" is a static one, whereas development (both normal and atypical) is of course dynamic. The child's way of processing environmental stimuli is likely to change repeatedly as a function of development, leading to the progressive formation of domain-specific representations.

Most nativists interested in language argue that what is innately specified are *representations* of universal grammar. Other theorists recognize that knowledge representations *per se* are unlikely to be pre-specified in neocortex (although see Ref. 9 for an alternative, selectionist view of pre-specified representations). Rather than representational innateness, they opt for dedicated domain-specific mechanisms within innately specified modules, the presumed absence of which in a developmental disorder will inform about their specific function in normal development.[10,11] Such arguments seem to be heavily influenced by so-called evolutionary psychology.[12] According to this view, phylogenesis has led to increasing pre-specification for ontogenesis, such that there are genetically-coded responses to evolutionary pressures, leading, through relatively predetermined epigenesis, to hardwired circuitry for language, theory of mind, and other specific forms of higher-level cognitive processing. In this "Swiss army knife" view of the brain, domain specificity is the starting point of ontogenesis, with development relegated to a relatively secondary role. A different view is that although evolution has pre-specified many constraints on development, it has made the human neocortex increasingly flexible and open to learning during postnatal development. In other words, evolution is argued to have selected for adaptive outcomes and a strong capacity to learn, rather than prior knowledge.[7] Within such a perspective, it is more plausible to think in terms of a variety of what one might call domain-relevant mechanisms that might gradually *become* domain-specific as a result of processing different kinds of input.

What does such a distinction entail? First we need to draw a distinction between domain-specific and domain-general mechanisms. Take, for example, inhibition. For the domain-general theorist, when the inhibitory mechanism is impaired, it will affect all systems across the board. By contrast, for the domain-specific theorist, the infant brain will contain, say, an inhibitory process *A* for theory-of-mind computations, an inhibitory process *B* for language-relevant computations, and yet another for sensorimotor development, and so forth. For this position, when the theory-of-mind inhibitory process is impaired, it will affect solely theory-of-mind computations, but leave intact linguistic, sensorimotor, and other domains. It is a subtly different distinction that I wish to draw between domain-relevant and domain-specific mechanisms. Unlike the domain-general theorist, this position does not argue for domain-general mechanisms simply applied across all domains. Rather, it suggests that biological constraints on the developing brain might have produced a number of mechanisms that do not start out as strictly domain-specific, that is, dedicated to the exclusive processing of one and only one kind of input. Instead, a mechanism starts out as somewhat more relevant to one kind of input over others, but it is usable – albeit in a less efficient way – for other types of processing too. This allows for compensatory processing and makes development channelled but far less predetermined than the nativist view. Once a domain-relevant mechanism is repeatedly used to process a certain type of input, it becomes domain-specific as a result of its

developmental history.[7,13] Then, in adulthood, it can be differentially impaired. For example, a learning mechanism that has a feedback loop will be more relevant to processing sequential input than to processing static, holistic input. With time such a mechanism would become progressively dedicated to processing, say, sequentially presented linguistic input. In other words, rather than evolution providing pre-specified representations, this change in perspective places the mechanisms of progressive ontogenetic change on centre stage.

The Implications for Developmental Disorders

The neuroconstructivist modification in perspective crucially influences the way in which atypical development is considered. In this approach, the deletion, reduplication or mispositioning of genes will be expected to subtly change the course of developmental pathways, with stronger effects on some outcomes and weaker effects on others. A totally specific disorder will, *ex hypothesis*, be extremely unlikely, thereby changing the focus of research in pathology. Rather than solely aiming to identify a damaged module at the cognitive level, researchers are encouraged to seek more subtle effects beyond the seemingly unique one, as well as to question whether successful behaviour (the presumed "intact" part of the brain) is reached by the same processes as in normal development. This change in perspective means that atypical development should not be considered in terms of a catalogue of impaired and intact functions, in which non-affected modules are considered to develop normally, independently of the others. Such claims are based on the static, adult neuropsychological model which is inappropriate for understanding the dynamics of developmental disorders[14,15] (see Box 19.1).

The neuroconstructivist approach highlights how tiny variations in the initial state could give rise to domain-specific differences in endstates[7, 13, 15] (see Box 19.2). With a shift in focus from dissociations to cross-syndrome associations, disorders might turn out to lie on more of a continuum than commonly thought. Thus, two very distinct phenotypical outcomes could start with only slightly differing parameters but, with development, the effects of this small difference might be far reaching. This contrasts with the notion that a whole cognitive module is initially impaired. Rather, phenotypical outcomes could stem from small differences in one or more of the following parameters: developmental timing, gene dosage, neuronal formation, neuronal migration, neuronal density, biochemical efficiency affecting firing thresholds, variations in transmitter types, dendritic arborization, synaptogenesis, and pruning. The effects of alterations in these initial parameters might also vary in strength at different developmental periods.[14] Furthermore, some problems might stem from lack of connections between brain regions or between the two hemispheres.[16,17] In some cases, like Down syndrome, cognitive problems could stem from a failure to progressively specialize or modularize as a function of development, whereas in others specialization might occur too rapidly leaving less opportunity for environmental constraints to play a role in shaping the developmental outcome. These are all indirect and at a much lower level than the notion of direct damage to innately-specified cognitive modules invoked by strict nativists to explain developmental disorders. It is these subtle differences that are likely to explain the range of phenotypical outcomes that atypical development can display. Such differences might affect the resulting organism at multiple levels.

Box 19.1   The postulates of the static adult neuropsychological model and its application to developmental disorders

- The method of double dissociation is used to identify specialized functions: Patient 1 has function A intact and function B impaired, whereas for Patient 2 the opposite obtains.
- This leads to the conclusion that the brain is organized into specialized circuits or modules which can be differentially damaged.

Thus far, the argument might be valid with respect to the fully-formed adult brain (although for arguments against the reduction of double dissociation to autonomy of modules, see Refs a, b; and for those against modularity of adult processing, see Ref. c). The subsequent conclusions are, in my view, open to serious challenge:

- Similar dissociations are found in certain developmental disorders.
- This leads to the conclusion that modules are innately specified in the human brain, with impaired genes mapped to impaired modules, alongside otherwise normal brain development.
- Developmental disorders are then explained in terms of the juxtaposition of damaged and intact sets of modules.

This ignores both the probabilistic dynamics of gene expression during embryogenesis and of progressive brain development during postnatal growth. When one considers the dynamics of development, the notion of the juxtaposition of spared and impaired higher-level cognitive processes is challenged, suggesting that in some developmental disorders, ostensibly "intact" performance might turn out to be achieved through different cognitive processes (see Box 19.5).

References

a   Plaut, D. (1995). Double dissociations without modularity: evidence from connectionist neuropsychology. *J. Clin. Exp. Neuropsychol.* 17, 291–331
b   Van Orden, G. C., Jansen op de Haar, M., and Bosman, A. M. T. (1997). Complex dynamic systems also predict dissociations, but they do not reduce to autonomous components. *Cognit. Neuropsychol.* 14, 131–65
c   Marslen-Wilson, W. D. and Tyler, L. K. (1987). Against modularity, in *Modularity in Knowledge Representations and Natural Language Understanding* (Garfield, J. L., ed.), pp. 37–62, MIT Press

---

These multiple levels – brain volume, regional anatomy, brain chemistry, hemispheric asymmetry, the temporal patterns of brain activity, physical characteristics and cognitive behavioural outcome – have recently been studied in some detail with respect to one neurodevelopmental disorder, Williams syndrome (see Boxes 19.3, 19.4 and 19.5). Consideration of the multiple two-way mappings from the biological to the cognitive levels leads to different hypotheses about so-called "intact" abilities; that is, even where normal *behavioural* levels are found in a developmental disorder in a given domain, they might be achieved by different *cognitive* processes. This turns out to be the case for Williams syndrome, in which face processing and language are particularly proficient alongside other serious impairments, but the proficiency seems to be achieved through different cognitive processes (see Box 19.5).

Are Some Developmental Disorders Truly Specific?

Despite the arguments in the previous section, some developmental disorders (e.g. autism,[18,19] Asperger syndrome,[20] dyslexia,[21] Turner's syndrome,[22] Specific Language Impairment[14]) appear at first sight to involve very specific deficits at the cognitive level. Autism, for example, is argued to be the result of impairment of the domain-specific mechanism of metarepresentation, dedicated solely to the processing of social stimuli[10,19] – a deficit in the so-called "theory-of-mind" module. When other, non-social impairments are noted, they are explained either in terms of secondary effects[10] or of an additional, unrelated cognitive impairment,[23] with other parts of the brain assumed to be intact. A similar approach has been taken with respect to Specific Language Impairment (SLI). This phenotype suggests, by its very name, a specific linguistic deficit alongside otherwise intact intelligence, as if grammar developed in total isolation of the rest of the growing brain. Researchers differ as to what they claim the specific deficit to be: the inability to make canonical links from grammar to semantics,[4] feature blindness with respect to morphology,[3,24] and so forth (for comprehensive reviews, see Refs 14, 25). The common suggestion, however, is that there is a specific genetic underpinning to the derivation of certain grammatical rules, which is impaired in these forms of SLI but leaving the rest of development intact.

It is clear that disorders like autism and SLI have a genetic origin and that evolutionary pressures have contributed to whatever is innately specified. This is a truism. The question is whether, on the one hand, the deficit results from damage to a domain-specific starting point at the cognitive level, as a result of evolution specifying dedicated processing systems for grammar, theory of mind and so forth, or whether, on the other hand, evolution has specified more general constraints for higher-level cognition and there is a more indirect way for genetic defects to result in domain-specific outcomes as a function of development.

The case of SLI (Ref. 14) shows how this second alternative might hold. Developmental timing plays a crucial role. If, early on, the infant's processing of fast auditory transitions is even slightly delayed in maturation, then certain aspects of grammar might, with development, emerge as more impaired than others. Grammatical disorders would then be the indirect, developmental effect of a subtle, initial acoustic deficit. Such a position is supported by the fact that training solely at the acoustic level has been shown to have positive repercussions at the grammatical level.[26] However, some adolescents and adults with SLI do not display a processing deficit.[3,4,25] It is none the less possible that by later childhood or adulthood, an initial deficit in acoustic processing which had a huge effect at one point in development might no longer be detectable (owing, for example, to subsequent long-term compensation or to ceiling effects and the lack of sufficiently subtle measures; S. Rosen, pers. commun.), but its early effects could continue to have a significant impact. This stresses the importance of developmental timing in understanding developmental disorders. Although atypical processing of fast auditory transitions might not turn out to be the final cause of SLI, this view aptly illustrates how a less pre-specified approach to language can result in a language-specific representational impairment through the process of development itself. This is why a truly developmental approach is so crucial.

The neuroconstructivist account modifies the way a developmental disorder like SLI will be studied. It suggests that focus must be placed on at risk populations in early infancy, before

Box 19.2   Single and multiple gene disorders, but no Swiss army knives

A report in the press recently heralded the discovery of a specific gene for hearing. The *Science* article[a] on which it was based, however, illustrates how indirect the effects of the gene are. Geneticists studying eight generations of a Costa Rican family found a 50 percent incidence of acquired deafness, with onset around age 10 and complete deafness by age 30. A single gene mutation was identified, with the last 52 amino acids in the gene's protein product misformed, and the first 1,213 amino acids formed correctly. This gene produces a protein that controls the assembly of actin. Actin organizes the tiny fibres found in cell plasma which determine a cell's structural properties, such as rigidity. Because the genetic impairment is tiny and the protein functions sufficiently well to control the assembly of actin in most parts of the body, no other deficits are observable. However, it turns out that hair cells are especially sensitive to loss of rigidity, such that even this tiny impairment has a huge effect on them, resulting in deafness. In other words, what might look like a specialized gene for a complex trait like hearing is, on closer examination, very indirect – hearing is dependent on the interaction of huge numbers of genes, one of which affects the rigidity of hair cells and has cascading effects on the others. A "gene for hearing" might be a convenient shorthand, but it could be a very misleading one, impeding the researcher from seeking to understand the probabilistic dynamics of development.

A second illustration comes from a computational model of the development of the ventral and dorsal pathways of visual cortex. There are several things we know about these pathways. First, they operate on somewhat different time schedules in early infancy: infants track novel objects (dorsal pathway) before they can categorize them (ventral pathway). Second, double dissociations exist in adult brain damage, such that patients can locate objects without being able to identify them, or vice versa.[b] This has led some neuropsychologists to argue that the two pathways must be innately specified. But is this conclusion necessary? Their specialization in adulthood could have emerged from development itself. A computational model illustrates how this might occur.[c] A simple three-layer feedforward network was used. At the hidden layer, two channels were fed with identical input (see fig.). The only difference was the speed with which activation levels changed (channel A rapidly, channel B slowly). Despite processing identical inputs, channel A progressively came to represent where objects were (mimicking the dorsal pathway in the brain), whereas channel B came to represent what each object was (ventral pathway). These functions were not pre-specified in the network but emerged from its developmental history, caused by a

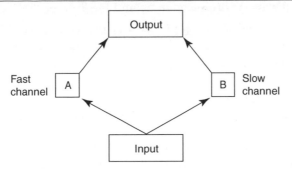

Fig. A simple three-layer feedforward network model of specialization in neural pathways. (See text for details.)

small difference in a starting state parameter. Thus, when neuropsychologists find dissociations in brain-damaged adults in visual form agnosia, this does not mean that the "where" and "what" pathways are necessarily pre-specified in the infant neocortex for spatio/temporal information versus form/colour/shape information. A small difference simply in firing thresholds (which might be innate) could give rise to such specialized functions indirectly, via the gradual processing during early infancy of differences between moving versus static stimuli. And a lack of such a difference in firing thresholds could result in domain-specific abnormality in one of these pathways. Again, the shorthand of talking about innate "where" and "what" pathways could be seriously misleading. They might only *become* what they are after processing the input. This leads to an important speculation: domain-specific outcomes might not even be possible without the process of development itself.

These two examples highlight the importance of giving serious consideration to very indirect causes of albeit very specific outcomes.

References

a   Lynch, E. D. et al. (1997). Nonsyndromic deafness DFNA1 associated with mutation of a human homolog of the *Drosophila* gene *diaphanous*. *Science* 278, 1315–18

b   Goodale, M. A. and Milner, A. D. (1992). Separate visual pathways for perception and action. *Trends Neurosci.* 15, 20–25

c   O'Reilly, R. C. and McClelland, J. L. (1992). The self-organization of spatially invariant representations. *Technical Report PDP.CNS.92.5*, Carnegie Mellon University

Box 19.3   Williams syndrome: genetic and brain levels

Williams syndrome (WS) is caused by a microdeletion on the long arm of chromosome 7 at q. 11,23 (Refs a, b). The genes on the deleted area have not all been identified, but they include:

- the elastin gene (*ELN*), not expressed in the brain, and thought to cause the vascular abnormalities;
- the *Limkinasel* gene (*LIMK1*) expressed in the brain, and claimed to cause the spatial deficits;
- the gene for DNA replication factor C2 (*RFC2*), and syntaxin 1A (*STX1A*) which affects the way chemicals are released in the brain;
- the *frizzled* gene (*FZD3*), affecting the way in which cells signal to one another during development.

All patients with classic WS are hemizygous for *ELN*, *LIMK1*, *STX1A* and *RFC2*. While these discoveries seem to offer a neat mapping between genes and particular phenotypical outcomes, our recent study challenges these conclusions.[c] Three patients were identified with hemizygotic *ELN* and *LIMK1* deletions, two of whom also had *RFC2* deletions and one the *STX1A* deletion. However, none had the facial dysmorphology, the mental retardation or the specific spatio-constructive problems typical of people with Williams syndrome. The explanation of the WS phenotype clearly cannot be sought in simple gene/outcome mappings, but lies at the level of developmental timing and downstream effects of the complex interaction between all the deleted genes and the rest of the developing organism.

At the brain level, WS has been mainly described in terms of adult brains.[d] No work has yet been done on the developing infant brain. Some important discoveries about the fully-formed adult brain include:

- the WS brain is 80 percent of normal volume
- the total cerebral grey matter is significantly reduced
- there is abnormal layering, orientation, clustering and size of neurones
- the anterior regions are smaller than in normal controls but larger than in Down syndrome brains
- the dorsal hemispheres show cortical malformation
- the cerebrum is particularly small
- the limbic structures of the temporal lobe are small but proportionally similar to normal controls
- the frontal cortex displays a near normal proportional relation with posterior cortex, although both are reduced in size.

Although limbic structures and frontal cortex are both proportionally similar in WS compared with normal brains, their functions show very different levels of impairment, with socio–affective behaviour being relatively good[e] and executive functions being particularly impaired.[f] Thus, the existence of normal anatomical proportions cannot be used to infer normal functions in the domains that they subserve in normal adults.

Our study using magnetic resonance spectroscopy has shown that brain biochemistry is also atypical in people with WS (Ref. g). Significant correlations were found between abnormal brain chemistry in the cerebellum and various neuropsychological tests, including Verbal and Performance IQ, British Picture Vocabulary Scale, and Ravens Progressive Matrices. The strongest correlation was with very poor results on a task measuring speed of processing, suggesting decreased neuronal efficiency in WS.

Finally, several studies have investigated brain activation in WS, particularly with respect to their domains of relative proficiency (language and face processing; see Box 5).[h] Event-related potentials of individuals with WS show abnormal patterns for both face processing and language. More importantly, such patterns are found at no age across normal development, suggesting aberrant rather than delayed development in WS (Ref. h). Neither do people with WS show the progressive hemispheric asymmetries typical of normal development.[h] Furthermore, infants with WS spend far more time than controls focused on faces and language,[i] suggesting that more of the developing brain might be devoted to processing such inputs.

In sum, brain volume, brain anatomy, brain chemistry, hemispheric asymmetry, and the temporal patterns of brain activity are all atypical in people with WS. How could the resulting cognitive system be described in terms of a normal brain with parts intact and parts impaired, as the popular view holds?[j,k] Rather, the brains of infants with WS develop differently from the outset, which has subtle, widespread repercussions at the cognitive level (see Box 19.5).

References

a Frangiskakis, J. M. et al. (1996). *LIM-kinase1* hemizygosity implicated in impaired visuospatial constructive cognition. *Cell* 86, 59–69

b Tassabehji, M. K. et al. (1996). LIM-kinase detected in Williams syndrome. *Nat. Genet.* 13, 272–3

c Tassabehji, M. K. et al. (1997). Genotype–phenotype correlations in Williams Syndrome. *Am. J. Hum. Genet.* 61, 11

d Galaburda, A. M. et al. (1994). Cytoarchitectonic anomalies in a genetically based disorder: Williams syndrome. *NeuroReport* 5, 753–7

e Karmiloff-Smith, A. et al. (1995). Is there a social module? Language, face processing and theory-of-mind in subjects with Williams syndrome. *J. Cogn. Neurosci.* 7, 196–208

f Wang, P. P. et al. (1992). The specific neurobehavioral profile of WS is associated with neocerebellar hemispheric preservation. *Neurology* 42, 1999–2002

g Rae, L., Karmiloff-Smith, A., Lee, M. A., Dixon, R. M., Grant, J., Blamire, A. M., Thompson, C. H., Styles, P., and Radda, G. K. (1998). Brain biochemistry in Williams syndrome: evidence for a role of the cerebellum in cognition? *Neurology* 51, 33–40

h Neville, H. J., Mills, D. L., and Bellugi, U. (1993). Effects of altered auditory sensitivity and age of language acquisition on the development of language-relevant neural systems: preliminary studies of Williams syndrome, in *Cognitive Deficits in Developmental Disorders: Implications for Brain Function* (Broman, S. and Grafman, J., eds.), pp. 67–83, Erlbaum

i Mervis, C. B., Morris, C. A., Bertrand, J., and Robinson, B. F. Williams syndrome: Findings from an integrated program of research. In *Neurodevelopmental Disorders: Contributions to a New Framework from the Cognitive Neurosciences* (Tager-Flusberg, H. ed.), MIT Press (in press)

j Pinker, S. (1994). *The Language Instinct*, Harmondsworth, Penguin

k Bickerton, D. (1997). Constructivism, nativism and explanatory adequacy. *Behav. Brain Sci.* 20, 557–8

Box 19.4   Clinical characteristics of the Williams syndrome phenotype

Williams syndrome (WS) is a rare genetic disorder that occurs in 1 in 20,000 live births. Its clinical features[a] include dysmorphic faces (see A–C), congenital heart and renal disorders due to a narrowing of the large arteries, musculo-skeletal abnormalities, growth retardation, hyperacusis, and infantile hypercalcaemia. The physical abnormalities are accompanied by moderate to severe mental retardation, a specific personality profile, very poor visuospatial constructive skills and relatively good language and face processing abilities (see Box 19.5).

Reference

a   Udwin, O. and Dennis, J. (1995). Williams syndrome, in *Clinics in Developmental Medicine No. 138: Behavioural Phenotypes* (O'Brien, G. and Yule, W., eds.), pp. 201–4, MacKeith Press, London

WS Behavioural Features

- Low IQ: 50-65 range

- Uneven cognitive profile: language>spatial cognition

- Seemingly very sociable

- Able to talk to large audience

- Sensitive to others' emotions

- Use of erudite-sounding words

The typical facial dysmorphology in WS, illustrated in three patients (photographs reproduced with permission of parents), aged 2 years, 10 years and 18 years, respectively. To be noted are the full cheeks, flared nostrils, wide mouth, full lips, pointed ears, and dental irregularities.

the onset of language, and longitudinally thereafter, to ascertain whether the timing of subtle developmental processes is out of synchrony and grows in importance as the child starts to process more complex linguistic input. Furthermore, the neuroconstructivist approach predicts that because of the way genes interact in their developmental expression, we should seek co-occurring, more subtle impairments which might have nothing to do with language. In fact, it has been shown that people with language-related deficits, such as SLI or dyslexia, often display an impairment (albeit lesser) in various forms of motor control such as balance.[27] This indicates that we might not be dealing with an initially language-specific impairment, but a deficit that turns out to be more detrimental to spoken and/or written language over developmental time (i.e. caused by an earlier language-relevant deficit), but that also gives rise to (weaker) problems in other areas. There is unlikely to be such a thing as impaired "genes for reading" or "genes for grammar." Rather, genetic impairments lead to a disruption in probabilistic epigenesis pushing individuals onto different developmental pathways which eventually result in reading or grammatical deficits.[26–28]

The neuroconstructivist approach would seek the initial disruption in innate mechanisms such as level of firing thresholds, differences in inhibition, and so forth. These are clearly at a lower-level, less richly domain-specific form than is commonly invoked by strict nativists who argue for innately specified representations of universal grammar. Neuroconstructivists would seek domain-relevant computational biases and the effects of differential developmental timing.[7] This is because we hypothesize that, rather than bringing greater pre-specialization to neocortex, evolution has provided the human neocortex with a greater and more varied capacity to learn via the process of development itself.[29] This clearly requires innate constraints but, because of the unusually slow period of human postnatal brain development, the child's gradual processing of different types of input is likely to have a strong influence on the way in which neocortex structures itself.

Conclusions

One of the major problems with very specific accounts of developmental disorders of higher-level cognition is that so far no gene (or set of genes) has been identified that is expressed solely in a specific region of neocortex (see Ref. 30 for discussion). Yet, such theories claim that neocortex is pre-specified for functions such as theory of mind or language and that this is why they can dissociate in adulthood. This is the basis for most brain imaging studies. Some authors go as far as claiming that epigenetic selection acts on preformed synaptic substrates and that to learn is to stabilize pre-existing synaptic combinations and to eliminate the surplus.[31] By contrast, current knowledge suggests that genes that are expressed in neocortex tend to do so throughout most regions, resulting in a similar six-layer structure and a similar overall pattern of intrinsic connectivity.[30] Combinations of neuroanatomical features, cortical layers and brain cytoarchitectural regions are found to be remarkably similar in all regions of the brain from birth to 72 months. In other words, for quite some time the developmental patterns of different cytoarchitectural regions are indistinguishable from one another.[32] A single set of instructions might structure the different areas of neocortex, leaving the interaction with different environmental inputs to influence specific forms of synaptogenesis and dendritic arborization. In fact, neocortical specialization has already been shown to be very progressive across developmental time.[33] So if there is early genetic impairment, then it could be relatively widespread in the developing neocortex, even though its effects might be

Box 19.5   Williams syndrome: the resulting cognitive–behavioural pheno-type

Classic Williams syndrome (WS) has been characterized along the following lines (for more details, see Refs a–c):

- IQs mainly in the 50s (range: 45–87)
- serious deficits in spatio-constructive skills, but spatio-perceptual skills as would be predicted by Mental Age
- serious deficits in numerical cognition
- serious deficits in problem solving and planning
- intact syntactic capacities alongside aberrant semantics
- intact face processing capacities
- relatively spared social cognition skills.

The above conclusions stemmed mainly from standardized tests used to assess intact and impaired functions, an approach inspired theoretically by the adult neuropsychological model of deficit. However, even in cases where behavioural scores are equivalent to chronologically matched controls, it is essential to go beyond behavioural success and study the underlying cognitive processes in detail.[d,e] For example, our study of face-processing capacities of people with WS (Ref. e) showed that, although their scores were equivalent to normal controls, the way in which they solved the task was different. Whereas normal controls used predominantly configural (holistic) processing, the subjects with WS reached their good scores by using predominantly componential (feature-by-feature) processing. In other words, different *cognitive* processes led to similar *behavioural* outcomes. The notion that WS displays a normal, intact face-processing module is thereby challenged. None the less, the neuroconstructivist view could accept that people with WS might have developed a face-processing module. However, it would be argued that, rather than simply being triggered, such a module – like the normal face-processing module – is the result of a developmental process of modularization, but emerging in this case from an atypical ontogenetic pathway.

A similar story obtains for WS language acquisition. Several studies now suggest that neither syntax nor semantics is entirely normal in WS, despite earlier claims to the contrary. First, there is a discrepancy between vocabulary Mental Age (MA) and syntactic MA, the former being considerably higher.[f] Second, high vocabulary scores in WS patients camouflage the fact that they learn the lexicon in a somewhat different way from normally developing children.[g] Third, they show dissociations within syntax itself, with problems in forming agreement between elements in phrase structure, difficulties in processing embedded relative clauses and subcategorization frames (the distinction between transitive and intransitive verbs), and so forth.[f,h,i] Furthermore, even when language is fluent, Williams syndrome cannot be used to claim, as some have,[j] that syntax develops independently of cognition. The use of IQ scores is very misleading in this respect. To state that a person has fluent language but an IQ of 51 indeed appears theoretically surprising and could lead to the conclusion that syntax develops in isolation from the rest of the brain. But to state that the same person has fluent language and an MA of 7 yrs changes the conclusion. In other words, those people with WS who have relatively fluent language might indeed have low IQs, but their MAs in non-verbal cognition, although seriously behind their chronological age, are usually well over 5, the age at which most language has been acquired in normally developing children.

In sum, not only are brain anatomy, brain chemistry, and temporal brain processes atypical, but Williams syndrome also displays an abnormal cognitive phenotype in which, even where behavioural scores are equivalent to those of normal controls, the cognitive processes by which such proficiency is achieved are different.

Our ongoing longitudinal behavioural and brain-imaging studies of atypical infants (with Janice Brown, Sarah J. Paterson, Marisa Gsödl, Michelle de Haan, Mark Johnson and others) already point to important differences in the initial state of WS patients compared with controls. The atypical groups' patterns are not one of juxtaposition of intact and impaired functions, as different end states might suggest. Interestingly, too, although WS linguistic performance ends up resembling normal language far more than Down syndrome performance, our preliminary results with infants show how important it is to distinguish the cognitive level from the behavioural level (see Box 19.6). Fluent linguistic behaviour might stem from different processes at the cognitive level of description. Our initial results suggest that Down syndrome language comprehension has a delayed but relatively normal developmental pathway in infancy, whereas WS language development seems to be deviant from the outset. It is only by focusing studies of developmental disorders at their roots in early infancy that we will ultimately be able to chart longitudinally the varying developmental pathways that progressively lead to different phenotypical outcomes.

References

a   Udwin, O. and Yule, W. (1991). A cognitive and behavioural phenotype in Williams syndrome. *J. Clin. Exp. Neuropsychol.* 13, 232–44

b   Bellugi, U., Wang, P., and Jernigan, T. L. (1994). Williams syndrome: an unusual neuropsychological profile, in *Atypical Cognitive Deficits in Developmental Disorders: Implications for Brain Function* (Broman, S. and Grafman, J., eds.), pp. 23–56, Erlbaum

c   Mervis, C. B. et al. Williams syndrome: findings from an integrated program of research, in *Neurodevelopmental Disorders: Contributions to a New Framework from the Cognitive Neurosciences* (Tager-Flusberg, H., ed.), MIT Press (in press)

d   Pennington, B. (1997). Using genetics to dissect cognition. *Am. J. Hum. Genet.* 60, 13–16

e   Karmiloff-Smith, A. (1997). Crucial differences between developmental cognitive neuroscience and adult neuropsychology. *Dev. Neuropsychol.* 13, 513–24

f   Karmiloff-Smith, A. et al. (1997). Language and Williams syndrome: how intact is "intact"? *Child Dev.* 68, 246 62

g   Stevens, T. and Karmiloff-Smith, A. (1997). Word learning in a special population: do individuals with Williams syndrome obey lexical constraints? *J. Child Lang.* 24, 737–65

h   Karmiloff-Smith, A. et al. (1998). Linguistic dissociations in Williams syndrome: evaluating receptive syntax in on-line and off-line tasks. *Neuropsychologia* 6, 342–51

i   Volterra, V. et al. (1996). Linguistic abilities in Italian children with Williams syndrome. *Cortex* 32, 67–83

j   Bickerton, D, (1997). Constructivism, nativism and explanatory adequacy. *Behav. Brain Sci.* 20, 557–8 surprisingly differential in outcome. To be biologically and developmentally plausible, we must go beyond the more obvious deficit to seek far subtler effects on other aspects of the developing system. Even if future research were to uncover a specific regional pattern of neocortical gene expression – which is not ruled out by the position developed in this paper – the neuroconstructivist approach would force a reinterpretation of the meaning of localized gene expression, encouraging researchers to take serious account of the developmental time course. The systemic properties of ontogenesis and the developmental effects of the interconnectedness of brain regions, together with a structuring rather than merely triggering role for environmental input, would still be likely to result in a cascade of subtle deficits rather than a single, higher-level one.

Because both normal and abnormal development is progressive, a change of focus is essential in future research into pathology. Rather than concentrate on the study of disorders solely at their end state in school-aged children and adults, which is most commonly the case, it becomes essential to study disorders in early infancy, and longitudinally, to understand how alternative developmental pathways might lead to different phenotypical outcomes. Furthermore, if we accept that behavioural outcomes could stem from different cognitive processes, then matching control groups on the basis of behavioural scores, rather than underlying processes, might also be open to challenge.

One essential step towards a deeper understanding of developmental disorders is to model their various manifestations. In an important contribution to the field, Morton and Frith devised a structural framework for causal modelling within which to explore a variety of theories concerning different abnormal phenotypes.[34] Work of this nature is crucial in developing more constrained theories of developmental disorders. The authors present their discussion in terms of a framework rather than the embodiment of a particular theory. However, the 55 different models that they explore are all unidirectional in their causal chains, and so do not capture the basic assumptions of the neuroconstructivist approach. The figure in Box 19.6 illustrates how the neuroconstructivist approach differs from both the nativist and empiricist approaches to developmental psychopathology. It pinpoints the various theoretical assumptions discussed in this paper and the different research strategies to which they lead.

The complex dynamics of both normal and atypical development indicate, in my view, that the neuroconstructivist approach is the most viable theoretical framework within which to explore developmental disorders. These must be approached from early infancy onwards, and simultaneously at multiple levels: the genetic, the brain in its spatial and temporal dynamics, the cognitive, the environmental and the behavioural, as well as stressing the multiple two-way rather than unidirectional chains that interact all the way from genetic causes through to ultimate behavioural outcomes. This is because the dynamics of development itself are the key to understanding developmental disorders.

Outstanding Questions

- Some argue that evolution has provided the human cortex with increasingly detailed pre-specification prior to ontogenetic development. To what extent can the ontogenetic data be accounted for in terms of evolution selecting for less specific factors, such as increased neocortical plasticity and a greater range of learning mechanisms, to ensure adaptive outcomes rather than prior knowledge? Is it more useful to entertain the possibility that the highest level of evolution is to pre-specify simply a number of domain-relevant mechanisms which, after processing specific aspects of the

Box 19.6 Models of developmental disorders of known genetic aetiology

The figure illustrates how the neuroconstructivist approach differs in its theoretical assumptions and resulting research strategies from both the nativist and empiricist accounts. Boxes and arrows are clearly not the most appropriate notation for a dynamic system, but the current representation hopefully captures some of the essential differences between neuroconstructivism and the other two theories. At the cognitive level, the neuroconstructivist approach stresses the difference between innate representations (invoked by most nativist linguists) and much lower-level innate computational and timing constraints from which representations progressively emerge as a function of development and of interaction with different types of environmental input. The multiple interactions between all levels, invoked by the neuroconstructivist approach, highlight why it is essential to start studies of developmental disorders in early infancy and then to trace the subsequent processes of development itself.

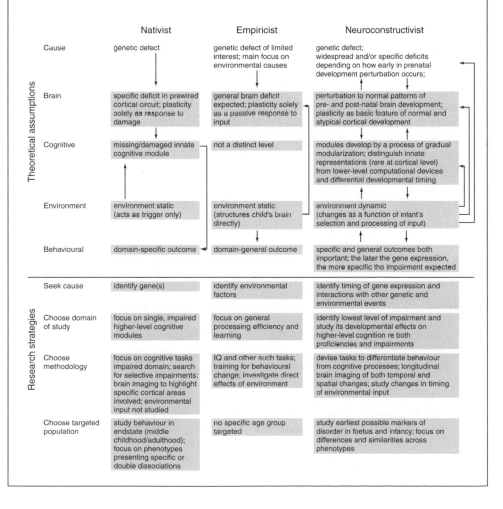

		Nativist	Empiricist	Neuroconstructivist
Theoretical assumptions	Cause	genetic defect	genetic defect of limited interest; main focus on environmental causes	genetic defect; widespread and/or specific deficits depending on how early in prenatal development perturbation occurs;
	Brain	specific deficit in prewired cortical circuit; plasticity solely as response to damage	general brain deficit expected; plasticity solely as a passive response to input	perturbation to normal patterns of pre- and post-natal brain development; plasticity as basic feature of normal and atypical cortical development
	Cognitive	missing/damaged innate cognitive module	not a distinct level	modules develop by a process of gradual modularization; distinguish innate representations (rare at cortical level) from lower-level computational devices and differential developmental timing
	Environment	environment static (acts as trigger only)	environment static (structures child's brain directly)	environment dynamic (changes as a function of infant's selection and processing of input)
	Behavioural	domain-specific outcome	domain-general outcome	specific and general outcomes both important; the later the gene expression, the more specific the impairment expected
Research strategies	Seek cause	identify gene(s)	identify environmental factors	identify timing of gene expression and interactions with other genetic and environmental events
	Choose domain of study	focus on single, impaired higher-level cognitive modules	focus on general processing efficiency and learning	identify lowest level of impairment and study its developmental effects on higher-level cognition re both proficiencies and impairments
	Choose methodology	focus on cognitive tasks impaired domain; search for selective impairments; brain imaging to highlight specific cortical areas involved; environmental input not studied	IQ and other such tasks; training for behavioural change; investigate direct effects of environment	devise tasks to differentiate behaviour from cognitive processes; longitudinal brain imaging of both temporal and spatial changes; study changes in timing of environmental input
	Choose targeted population	study behaviour in endstate (middle childhood/adulthood); focus on phenotypes presenting specific or double dissociations	no specific age group targeted	study earliest possible markers of disorder in foetus and infancy; focus on differences and similarities across phenotypes

environment, *become* increasingly domain-specific, that is, specialized, during ontogenesis? How might this change our perspective on developmental disorders?

- What can we learn about subtle differences in the environmental input to atypically developing infants and children? In this respect, is it useful to replace the static notion of "environment" by that of the "child's progressive processing of environmental input"? To what extent does the infant/child contribute to its own subsequent brain specialization by selecting aspects of its environment to attend to at different times in development?

- How influential is subcortical specialization in the structuring of neocortex?

- Are developmental disorders really specific, or do they lie on a continuum, with seeming dissociations due to relatively small differences in developmental timing, gene dosage, neuronal formation, neuronal migration, neuronal density, biochemical efficiency affecting firing thresholds, variations in transmitter types, dendritic arborization, synaptogenesis, and pruning?

- Just as modularity theorists can show that specific disorders also predict more general impairments, so non-modularity theorists can show that dynamic systems predict dissociations that do not reduce to autonomous modules. Is the double-dissociation method necessarily the right tool for furthering our knowledge of developmental disorders?

- If we do discover a truly specific disorder of higher-level cognition with no other subtle impairments, how could this be explained without violating what is known about the probabilistic epigenetics of biological development? Can one region of neocortex develop abnormally with no effects on any other region?

- How do acquired developmental disorders differ from genetically-based disorders?

- If we take development seriously, is atypical ontogenesis necessarily a window on the structure/functioning of the normal mind/brain, as seems to be taken for granted by many of those studying developmental disorders?

ACKNOWLEDGEMENTS

I should like to thank Mike Anderson, Susan Carey, Mark Johnson and Steven Rose, as well as the anonymous reviewers, for comments on an earlier version of this paper.

REFERENCES

1   Gottlieb, G. (1992). *Individual Development and Evolution: The Genesis of Novel Behavior*, Oxford University Press.

2   Lightfoot, D. W. (1989). The child's trigger experience: degree–0 learnability. *Behav. Brain Sci.* 12, 321–75.

3   Gopnik, M. (1997). Language deficits and genetic factors. *Trends Cognit. Sci.* 1, 5–9.

4   Van der Lely, H. (1994). Canonical linking rules: forward versus reverse linking in normally developing and specifically language-impaired children. *Cognition* 51, 29–72.

5   Pinker, S. (1994). *The Language Instinct*, Harmondsworth, Penguin.

6   Clahsen, H. (1989). The grammatical characterisation of developmental dysphasia. *Linguistics* 27, 897–920.

7   Elman, J. L. et al. (1996). *Rethinking Innateness: A Connectionist Perspective on Development*, MIT Press.

8   Quartz, S. R. and Sejnowsky, T. J. (1997). A neural basis of cognitive development: a constructivist manifesto. *Behav. Brain Sci.* 20, 537–56.

9   Changeux, J.-P. and Dehaene, S. (1989). Neuronal models of cognitive functions. *Cognition* 33, 63–109.

10 Frith, U. and Happé, F. (1998). Why specific developmental disorders are not specific: On-line and developmental effects in autism and dyslexia. *Developmental Science* 1, 267–72.

11 Baron-Cohen, S. (1994). How to build a baby that can read minds: cognitive mechanisms in mindreading. *Cahiers de Psychol. Cognit.* 13, 513–52.

12 Tooby, J. and Cosmides, L. (1990). On the universality of human nature and the unique-ness of the individual: the role of genetics and adaptation. *J. Personal.* 58, 17–67.

13 Karmiloff-Smith, A. (1995). Annotation: the extraordinary cognitive journey from foetus through infancy. *J. Child Psychol. Child Psychiatry* 36, 1293–313.

14 Bishop, D. V. M. (1997). *Uncommon Understanding: Development and Disorders of Language Comprehension in Children*, Psychology Press.

15 Karmiloff-Smith, A. (1997). Crucial differences between developmental cognitive neuro-science and adult neuropsychology. *Dev. Neuropsychol.* 13, 513–24.

16 Liegeois, F. and de Schonen, S. (1997). Simultaneous attention in the two visual hemifields and interhemispheric integration: a developmental finding on 20–26-month-old infants. *Neuropsychologia* 35, 381–5.

17 Mancini, J. et al. (1994). Face recognition in children with early right or left brain damage. *Dev. Med. Child Neurol.* 36, 156–66.

18 Frith, U. (1989). *Autism: Explaining the Enigma*, Blackwell Science.

19 Leslie, A. M. (1992). Pretence, autism and the theory-of-mind module. *Curr. Dir. Psychol. Sci.* 1, 18–21.

20 Frith, U., ed. (1991). *Autism and Asperger Syndrome*, Cambridge University Press.

21 Frith, C. and Frith, U. (1996). A biological marker for dyslexia. *Nature* 382, 19–20.

22 Skuse, D. H. et al. (1997). Evidence from Turner's syndrome of an imprinted X-linked locus affecting cognitive function. *Nature* 387, 705–8.

23 Happé, F. G. E. (1996). Studying weak central coherence at low levels: children with autism do not succumb to visual illusions (a research note). *J. Child Psychol. Psychiatry.* 37, 873–7.

24 Gopnik, M. (1990). Feature-blind grammar and dysphasia. *Nature* 344, 715.

25 Temple, C. M. (1997). Cognitive neuropsychology and its application to children. *J. Child Psychol. Psychiatry* 38, 27–52.

26 Tallal, P. et al. (1996). Language comprehension in language-learning impaired children improved with acoustically modified speech. *Science* 271, 81–4.

27 Fawcett, A. J., Nicolson, R. I., and Dean, P. (1996). Impaired performance of children with dyslexia on a range of cerebellar tasks. *Ann. Dyslexia* 46, 259–83.

28 Pennington, B. (1997). Using genetics to dissect cognition. *Am. J. Hum. Genet.* 60, 13–16.

29 Gerhart, J. and Kirschner, M. (1997). *Cells, Embryos and Evolution*, Blackwell Science.

30 Johnson, M. H. (1997). *Developmental Cognitive Neuroscience*, Blackwell Science.

31 Dehaene-Lambertz, G. and Dehaene S. (1997). In defence of learning by selection: neurobiology and behavioral evidence revisited. *Behav. Brain Sci.* 20, 560–1.

32 Shankle, W. R. et al. (1998). Developmental patterns in the cytoarchitecture of the human cerebral cortex from birth to six years examined by correspondence analysis. *Proc. Natl. Acad. Sci. U.S.A.* 95, 4023–38.

33 Neville, H. J. (1991). Neurobiology of cognitive and language processing: effects of early experience, in *Brain Maturation and Cognitive Development: Comparative and Cross-Cultural Perspectives* (Gibson, K. R. and Peterson, A. C., eds.), pp. 355–80, Aldine de Gruyter Press, New York.

34 Morton, J. and Frith, U. (1995). Causal modelling: a structural approach to developmental psychopathology, in *Manual of Developmental Psychopathology* (Vol. 1) (Cicchetti, D. and Cohen, D. J., eds.), pp. 357–90, John Wiley & Sons.

20

Object Recognition and Sensitive Periods: A Computational Analysis of Visual Imprinting

Randall C. O'Reilly *and* Mark H. Johnson

1 Introduction

General approaches to the computational problem of spatially invariant object recognition have come and gone over the years, but the problem remains. In both the symbolic and neural network paradigms the research emphasis has shifted from underlying principles to special case performance on real world tasks such as handwritten digit recognition or assembly-line part recognition. We have adopted a different approach, which is to link the computational principles and behavior of a model to those of a biological object recognition system, wherein the research emphasis is on the ability to use empirical data to constrain and shape the model. If the model makes unique and testable behavioral predictions based on its identified neural properties, then experimental research can be used to test the computational theory of object recognition embodied in the model.

We have developed a model of invariant visual object recognition based on the environmental regularity of object existence: objects, though they might exhibit motion relative to the observer, have a tendency to persist in the environment. This regularity can be capitalized upon by introducing a corresponding persistence of the activation states (referred to as *hysteresis*) of neurons responsible for object recognition. When combined with a Hebbian learning rule that strengthens the connections between coactive neurons, these neurons become associated with the many different images of a given object, resulting in an invariant representation (Földiák, 1991; O'Reilly and McClelland, 1992). In the O'Reilly and McClelland (1992) version of the algorithm, specific neural properties, detailed below, lead to hysteresis. Instead of attempting to test for evidence of the algorithm in the complex mammalian nervous system, we have taken the approach of studying the relatively well known and simpler vertebrate object recognition system of the domestic chick.

Visual object recognition in the chick has been studied behaviorally for nearly 50 years under the guise of filial imprinting, which is the process whereby young precocial[1] birds learn to recognize the first conspicuous object that they see after hatching. Visual imprinting is studied using dark-reared chicks which are exposed to a conspicuous object for a training period which usually lasts for several hours. Hours or days later, the chick is given a preference test in which it is released in the presence of two objects – the training object and a novel object. The extent to which the chick attempts to approach the familiar object as opposed to the novel one results in a *preference score* which correlates with the strength of imprinting. The original work of Lorenz (1935, 1937) on imprinting has given rise to half a century of active research on this process by ethologists and psychologists, and more recently by neuroscientists interested in the neural basis of imprinting. Recently, the area of the chick brain that subserves this imprinting process has been identified, and some of its neurobiological properties studied. Therefore, it is now possible to assess a model of imprinting in the chick both with regard to its fidelity to these properties and the behavioral effects they produce.

With a variety of neuroanatomical, neurophysiological and biochemical techniques, Horn, Bateson and their collaborators established that a particular region of the chick forebrain, referred to as the Intermediate and Medial part of the Hyperstriatum Ventrale (IMHV), is essential for imprinting (see Horn, 1985; Horn and Johnson, 1989; Johnson, 1991, for reviews). This region receives input from the main visual projection areas of the chick, and may be analogous to mammalian association cortex on both embryological and functional grounds (Horn, 1985). A Golgi study of the histology and connectivity of the IMHV (Tömböl, Csillag and Stewart, 1988) revealed the presence of the principal anatomical features necessary for hysteresis of the principal excitatory cells of this region as proposed by O'Reilly and McClelland (1992). These features, recurrent excitatory connections and lateral inhibition, constitute an essential component of our object recognition model. In addition, evidence consistent with a Hebbian learning rule operating in this region has been found in morphometric studies of synaptic modification and changes in the density of postsynaptic NMDA receptors (e.g. Horn, Bradley and McCabe, 1985; McCabe and Horn, 1988). Thus, both the hysteresis and the Hebbian learning properties of our model are likely to be present in the region of the chick brain thought to be responsible for object recognition.

Our model captures several findings from the imprinting literature that might initially appear to require more specialized mechanisms. Perhaps the best known of these is the critical or sensitive period for imprinting. A sensitive period means that a strong preference for a given object can only be established during a specific period of life, and that the animal is relatively unaffected by subsequent exposure to different objects. This kind of behavior is not typical of neural network models, which typically exhibit strong (even "catastrophic") interference effects from subsequent learning. Further, Lorenz's original theory has been revised to reflect the fact that the termination of the sensitive period is experience-driven (Sluckin and Salzen, 1961; Bateson, 1966), so that one cannot simply posit a hard-wired maturational process responsible for terminating the sensitivity of the network. Our model shows how a self-terminating sensitive period is a consequence of a system incorporating hysteresis and a covariance Hebbian learning rule.

Another behavioral finding is temporal blending, where chicks blend two objects if they appear in close temporal proximity to each other (Chantrey, 1974; Stewart, Capretta, Cooper and Littlefield, 1977). This temporal dependency alone is consistent with the idea that the object recognition system uses hysteresis to develop invariant representations of objects. However, our model demonstrates a paradoxical interaction between stimulus similarity and temporal blending, such that more similar stimuli experience relatively *less* blending. This phenomenon can be directly related to the same hysteresis and covariance Hebbian learning rule properties as the sensitive period phenomenon.

To claim that our model of object recognition is applicable to brains other than that of the domestic chick, we would need evidence of hysteresis and Hebbian associative learning in structures such as the mammalian visual cortex. Several lines of such evidence are present. First, and most relevant for our model, the intra-cortical connectivity of the visual system contains recurrent excitatory connections and lateral inhibition (see Douglas and Martin, 1990, for a review, and Douglas, Martin and Whitteridge, 1989; Bush and Douglas, 1991, for models). There are also embryological similarities between the Hyperstriatum Ventrale in chicks and neocortex in mammals (Horn, 1985), and Johnson and Morton, (1991) argue for a correspondence between IMHV and mammalian visual object recognition centers in their relationship to "subcortical" processing. Finally, it is possible that the temporally extended parvocellular inputs to the form pathway of the mammalian visual system (e.g. Livingstone and Hubel, 1988; Maunsell, Nealey, and DePriest, 1990) are an additional source of hysteresis in mammals. With regard to the Hebbian associative learning, several studies have found evidence for associative long-term potentiation (LTP) in visual cortex (e.g. Fregnac, Shulz, Thorpe, and Bienenstock, 1988).

We adopt a multi-level approach to modeling the behavioral phenomena and neural substrate. The basic mechanism of translation-invariant object recognition can be specified and implemented with a relatively abstract neural network model, as it is based on rather general properties of neural circuitry, and not on the detailed properties of individual neurons. Using an abstract neural network model offers the further advantage of simplicity and explanatory clarity – since the model only has a few properties, the phenomena that result can be related more directly to these properties. However, caution is required in relating such a simple model to both detailed behavioral and neural data; in general this model makes qualitative rather than quantitative predictions. Thus, a more realistic neural model, based on anatomical and physiological measurements of actual IMHV neurons, is an important next step in this research.

2   The Neural Basis of Object Recognition in Imprinting: IMHV

2.1   *The role of IMHV in object recognition*

Several studies have shown that the IMHV region of the chick brain is critical for visual imprinting, which is clearly required for object recognition. Specifically, lesions of IMHV prior to imprinting prevent the acquisition of preferences, and its destruction after imprinting renders a chick amnesic for existing preferences, and these effects are specific to imprinting and do not affect other tasks that do not depend on object recognition (McCabe, Cipolla-Neto, Horn, and Bateson, 1982; Horn, 1985; Horn and Johnson, 1989; Johnson, 1991). Other evidence shows that IMHV is involved in other tasks that do require object recognition. For example, IMHV lesions impair the ability of chicks to recognize a particular individual member of their own species (Johnson and Horn, 1987), and the ability to recognize individual members of the species in a mate choice situation (Bolhuis, Johnson, Horn, and Bateson, 1989). Davies, Taylor, and Johnson (1988) demonstrated object recognition deficits in chicks with IMHV lesions in the context of a *one-trial passive avoidance learning* (PAL) task. Perhaps the best description of the functional effect of IMHV lesions would be that it induces object agnosia (Horn, 1985; Johnson, 1991). Also, changes in synaptic morphology and cell activity in IMHV have been recorded following imprinting, and these changes have been directly linked to visual learning as opposed to other task factors (Horn et al., 1985; McCabe and Horn, 1988; Payne and Horn, 1984; Brown and Horn, 1992).

2.2. Neural properties of IMHV

IMHV is a small "sausage-shaped" region immediately around the midpoint between the anterior and posterior poles of the cerebral hemispheres. It receives input from the main visual projection areas of the chick, including a prominent input from the avian forebrain primary visual projection area (the Hyperstriatum Accessorium, HA), and is embryologically and functionally related to mammalian association cortex (Horn, 1985). See figure 20.1 for a diagram of this visual input to IMHV. In addition, IMHV is extensively connected to other regions of the avian brain (Bradley, Davies, and Horn, 1985), including those thought to be involved in motor control, such as the archistriatum.

Our model incorporates the following two characteristics of the cytoarchitectonics of IMHV as identified by Tömböl et al. (1988) (figure 20.1): (a) the existence of positive feedback loops between the two types of spiny excitatory principal neurons (PNs), type 1 and 2; and (b) the extensive inhibitory circuitry mediated by the local circuit neurons (LCNs), which receive excitatory input from the PNs and project inhibition back to them. These properties are also characteristic of mammalian cortex (Douglas and Martin, 1990), and are not commonly observed in neighboring regions of the chick brain that have been studied (Tömböl et al., 1988). We propose that these properties lead to a hysteresis of the activation state of PN's in IMHV, which contributes to the development of translation invariant object-based representations. In our model, we assume that type 2 PNs are the main *target* of projections to IMHV from area HA, while type 1 PNs are probably the main *source* of projections to IMHV from area HA, because they have long bifurcating axons that project outside the region.

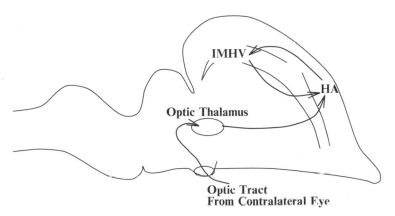

Figure 20.1 Visual inputs to IMHV from the thalamic pathway. Shown is a saggital view (strictly diagrammatic, as some areas are out of the plane with others) of the chick brain, with visual information coming in through the optic tract, which then synapses in the optic nucleus of the thalamus. This then projects to area HA (Hyperstriatum Accessorium), which connects reciprocally with IMHV. This pathway may correspond to the retina $\Rightarrow$ LGN $\Leftrightarrow$ V1, V4 $\Leftrightarrow$ IT pathway in mammals. There are other routes of visual input to IMHV, which are not shown in this figure (see Horn, 1985). The brain of a 2 day old chick is approximately 2 cm long.

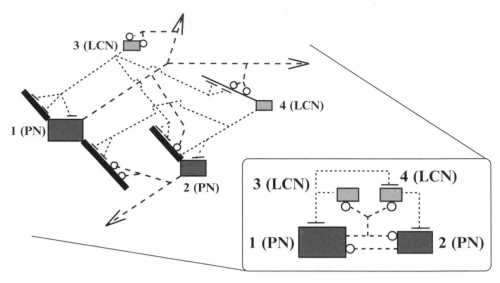

Figure 20.2 Schematic drawing summarizing the circuitry of IMHV at two levels of detail (simplified version in the box). Excitatory contacts are represented by open circles, and inhibitory ones by flat bars. Shown are the local circuit inhibitory neurons (LCN) and their reciprocal connectivity with the excitatory principal neurons (PN), and the recurrent excitatory connectivity between the principal neurons. In the detailed version, the thick solid lines are dendrites, while the axons are dashed or dotted lines. Both the inhibition and recurrent excitatory connectivity are used in the simplified model to produce hysteresis in the activation state of the IMHV. (After Tömböl et al., 1988.)

3   The Self-Organization of Invariant Representations

Despite the relative ease of its everyday execution, visual object recognition is a difficult computational problem. One of the principal reasons for this difficulty is also a clue to a potential solution: there are a practically infinite number of different images that a given object can project onto the retina. Deciphering which of the many thousands of familiar objects a given image represents is difficult because of this many-to-many correspondence. However, the ways in which a given object can produce different images on the retina are limited to a few dimensions of variability, corresponding to translation, dilation, rotation, etc.

The algorithm proposed by Földiák (1991) and O'Reilly and McClelland (1992) collapses across irrelevant dimensions by capitalizing on the idea that the visual environment naturally presents a sequence of images of the same object undergoing a transformation along one or more of these dimensions. The sequence of translating images all correspond to the same object in the world – one could refer to this information as "identity from persistence." In computational terms, the world imposes a temporal smoothness constraint on the existence of objects which can be used to regularize the ill-posed problem of visual object recognition (c.f. Poggio, Torre, and Koch, 1985; Yuille, 1990). Interestingly, several studies have shown that the stimulus motion is important for the acquisition of imprinting (Sluckin, 1972; Hoffman and Ratner, 1973) – this is not likely to be a simple attentional phenomenon because motion – this is not likely to be a simple attentional phenomenon because motion is not needed for the expression of a previously acquired preference.

The temporal smoothness of the environment can be capitalized upon by a smoothness constraint (i.e., hysteresis, or persistence) in the activation state of units in an artificial neural network, combined with an associative learning rule that causes temporally contiguous patterns of input activity to become represented by the same subset of higher-level units. These higher-level units develop representations that are invariant over the differences between the temporally contiguous patterns. Biologically, the necessary hysteresis comes from the combined forces of lateral inhibition, which prevents other units from becoming active, and recurrent, excitatory activation loops, which cause active units to remain so through mutual excitation (O'Reilly and McClelland, 1992).

3.1 Network architecture

The detailed architecture of the model (shown in figure 20.3) is designed around the anatomical connectivity of IMHV and its primary input area, HA, as described previously. The input layer of the network, layer 0, represents area HA, which contains cells with properties similar to the simple and complex retinotopic feature detectors described by Hubel and Wiesel in the cat visual cortex (Hubel and Wiesel, 1962; Horn, 1985). Layers 1 and 2 in the model correspond to IMHV type 2 and type 2 principal neurons, respectively

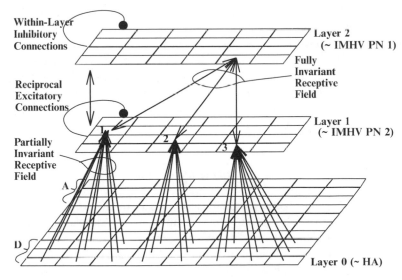

Figure 20.3 Network architecture used for the simplified model of IMHV, showing the three layers (Layer 0 represents HA, Layer 1 represents IMHV PN type 2, Layer 2 represents IMHV PN type 1), and their interconnectivity. The network is shown being trained on stimulus *D*, and the 3 different units numbered 1–3 in layer 1 have partially invariant fields which capture local invariance over portions of the different positions of stimulus *D*. These different units project reciprocally to the layer 2 unit which has a fully invariant representation of stimulus *D* by combining the partially invariant fields from layer 1.

(note that IMHV does not actually have a laminar structure). Layer 2 sends outputs to layer 1 of the model, which in turn sends outputs to layer 2, creating the recurrent feedback loop important for hysteresis. There are 10 × 8 or 80 units in layer 0, and 24 units each in layers 1 and 2.

Strong lateral inhibition is present within each layer of the model, in the form of relatively large negative weights (fixed to values of −3.0) between all units in the layer. These weights reflect the influence of a large number of GABAergic inhibitory LCNs in IMHV and its relatively low levels of spontaneous activity. The inhibition enabled only one unit in each layer to become active at any time – this Winner-Take-All (WTA) extreme in the model is easier to implement and analyze than the more distributed activity that likely occurs in the real system.

3.2   Activation function and learning rule

The need for recurrent excitatory activation loops and lateral inhibition in our network requires a recurrent network in the tradition of the interactive activation and competition (IAC) model (McClelland and Rumelhart, 1981) and the Hopfield network (Hopfield, 1984). For simplicity, the IAC activation function of McClelland and Rumelhart (1981) was used, with stepsize .05, decay 1, and a range of −1 to 1 with a provision that only positive activations are propagated to other units (see Appendix A for the exact equation used). Layer 2 had a lower decay (.5) because it does not receive any excitatory input from higher layers that are known to exist in the chick but are not present in the model.

Associative learning is implemented with a simple Hebbian covariance learning rule. The specific learning rule used in the present simulations is a modification of the Competitive Learning scheme (Rumelhart and Zipser, 1986) (see Appendix B for the formulation), although other similar rules have been used with equal success (c.f. Földiák, 1991; O'Reilly and McClelland, 1992). It is important that the learning rule be a covariance formulation (Sejnowski, 1977), having both increase and decrease components which work together to shape the receptive fields of units both towards those inputs which excite them, and away from those that do not. This is consistent with a combined LTP/D (*long-term potentiation/depression*) mechanism (e.g., Artola, Brocher, and Singer, 1990; Bear and Malenka, 1994).

3.3   Training and testing

Training in the model consisted of presenting a set of feature bits (assumed to correspond to a given object) in sequential positions across the input layer 0 (simulated HA) with either right or left motion (randomly chosen). At each position of a stimulus, the weights between all units in the system were adjusted according to the Hebbian learning rule once the activation state of the network had reached equilibrium for each position (defined here as the point at which the maximum change in activation went below a threshold of .0005). The activation state was initialized to zero between different objects, but not between positions of a single object, enabling a state resulting from an object in one position to exert the desired hysteresis effect on the state with the object in the next position.

Four "objects" were used in the simulations, which consisted of three active features in any of the 8 possible retinotopic locations represented in the input layer (see figure 20.4). The arrangement of the feature bits into columns simply represents 8 different views of an

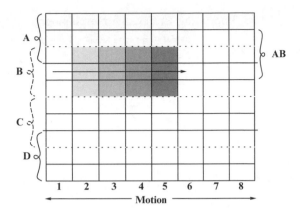

Figure 20.4   Stimuli used in training the network, consisting of 3 feature bits active in any of 8 different positions. For visual clarity, the positions were arranged along the horizontal axis, and the object features along the vertical, with 1 bit of overlap between two pairs of the 4 primary stimuli. Object *AB* was a hybrid stimulus used in some simulations that had 2 bits in common (overlap) with both *A* and *B*, while the others had 1 bit in common with their neighbor.

object, which could in theory correspond to any transformation sequence, not just horizontal translation. There was 1 bit out of the three features in common between neighboring stimuli, so that object A overlapped with B by 1 bit, as did C with D. B and C did not overlap.

Because it is not possible to record preferential approach behavior from the network, some proxy for this kind of preference measure must be used. We recorded the activation level over the putative output neurons of IMHV in the model, layer 2, when different stimuli were presented to determine the preference. Because of the extreme inhibitory competition between units, the activation level of the single active unit is not indicative of the level of excitation this unit is receiving.[2] To circumvent this potential measurement artifact, we instead used the total excitatory input to layer 2 (i.e., for all units in the layer) as an indication of preference. The actual preference scores were computed by averaging the total excitatory input over all the different positions for each stimulus, resulting in a raw preference score for each stimulus. These raw preference scores were converted into percentage preference measures between two stimuli (e.g., A over D) by dividing each raw score by the total for both stimuli. This is analogous to the *preference score* measure used in many behavioral studies (Horn, 1985).

4   Basic Imprinting and Learning Capacity

Before addressing the more challenging behavioral phenomena with our model, we first establish its basic imprinting properties and capacity for learning about multiple objects. The latter is especially important because one does not want a putative sensitive period phenomenon to reduce to a simple capacity limitation of the model. The basic simulation of the imprinting effect involved presenting a single stimulus over many epochs while recording the development of the preference for this stimulus. The imprinting results are shown in figure 20.5, which indicates that a preference for the training stimulus over a novel, dissimilar, object does develop over time. This effect is simply due to the selective

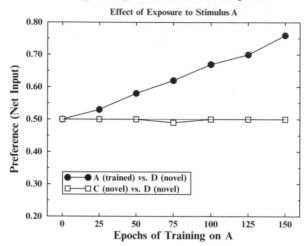

Figure 20.5   The basic imprinting effect, showing the preference for the imprinted stimulus *A* as compared to a novel stimulus, *D*. The preference for a control stimulus *C* as compared to *D* is also shown. This preference does not deviate from chance (0.5).

enhancement of weights to units which respond to the imprinted stimulus, and is not a surprising or novel result.

The capacity simulation was run by training on all four stimuli (objects A–D), and showing that the model developed individuated representations for each object that were invariant across the entire range of positions of the object. Each epoch of training consisted of sweeping each stimulus in turn across the input layer, covering all 8 positions of each object. The order in which the stimuli were presented was randomized, with a "delay" (implemented by zeroing the activation states) between each sweep of the stimuli. Training continued for 100 epochs.

The receptive fields for the two simulated IMHV layers developed invariant representations in a graded fashion. That is, the first layer developed representations specific to one stimulus in any of several (but not all) different positions of that stimulus, making it partially invariant with respect to position. Layer 2, however, did have fully invariant representations, so that a single pattern of activation coded for a single stimulus in any position.

As a result of being further from the moving input, there is a greater degree of hysteresis in layer 2 than in layer 1 of the model, which is reflected in the kinds of receptive fields that form in the two layers. See O'Reilly and McClelland (1992) for more discussion of the graded invariance transformation over increasingly deeper layers.

5   Reversibility and the Sensitive Period

5.1   Behavior

Lorenz (1937) originally claimed that an imprinted preference was irreversible. Jaynes (1956) pointed that there are two senses in which imprinting could be irreversible. First, that after imprinting a bird will never again direct its filial responses to a novel object. Alternatively, that while a bird can direct its filial responses to a second object, it always retains information about the first object. There is a considerable amount of evidence that imprinting is not irreversible in the first sense (e.g., Klopfer and Hailman, 1964b, 1964a; Klopfer, 1967; Salzen and Meyer, 1968; Kertzman and Demarest, 1982). Much evidence supports the second, and weaker, form of the irreversibility claim (for review see Bolhuis and Bateson, 1990; Bolhuis, 1991). Thus, while imprinted preferences can be reversed by prolonged exposure to a second object, a representation of the original object remains.

A number of factors affect whether imprinted preferences can be reversed, and if so, the extent of reversal. These factors include the length of exposure to the first object experienced by the chick, and length of subsequent exposure to a second object. For example, a prolonged exposure to the first object will prevent reversal of preference for a second object (Shapiro and Thurston, 1978). With shorter exposure to the first object, a very brief period of exposure to a second object will not result in a reversal of preference, while a longer period of exposure to a second object will (Salzen and Meyer, 1968). Data from Bolhuis and Bateson (1990), shown in figure 20.6, illustrates this effect. The chicks were trained for either 3 or 6 days, and preference tests revealed a strong preference for the training object. Then, the chicks were exposed to a second object for 3 or 6 days, and preferences were reversed. The extent to which a reversal occurs depends on the length of exposure to the first stimulus (longer exposure reduces the subsequent extent of reversibility). While Bolhuis and Bateson (1990) did not systematically manipulate the length of exposure to the second stimulus, other studies have shown that this variable influences the degree of reversal (Salzen and Meyer, 1968; Einsiedel, 1975).

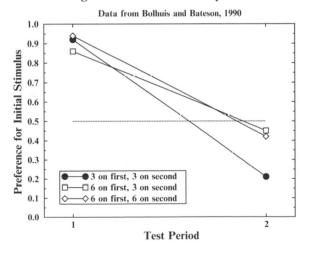

Figure 20.6 Data showing an initial preference for the first object after either 3 or 6 days recorded on test 1, and a reversal of this preference after a period of exposure of 3 or 6 days to the other stimulus, as recorded in test 2. A decreased level of reversal is observed with greater exposure to the first object.

5.2   Simulation

The implementation of reversibility in the model was straightforward: train on one stimulus for a variable amount of time, then train on a different one for a variable amount of time. For the basic effect, we trained on stimulus A for 100 epochs (100 sweeps across the input layer), and then trained again with stimulus D from various points of training on A. The results are shown in figure 20.7a for a network that was exposed to A for 100 Epochs, and then exposed to D for up to 300 epochs. Thus, reversibility occurs despite a relatively strong initial preference for A, with D being preferred to A after more than 150 epochs of exposure to D. This finding is consistent with those cited above. Further, the strength of preference for D increases with longer training on that object. Also shown in this figure is the continued preference for A, the initial training object, over a novel stimulus, B. This finding shows that a representation of the first object still exists, and is consistent with the second, weaker form of irreversibility observed in the chick (Cook, 1993).

That the network displayed reversibility is not terribly surprising, as many neural networks will continue to adapt their weights as the environment changes. However, unlike many networks which display a "catastrophic" level of interference from subsequent learning (cf. McCloskey and Cohen, 1989), this model retained a relatively intact preference for the initial stimulus over a completely novel one. The explanation for this preserved learning effect will be presented below.

While reversibility seems to occur in the network and in chicks, there is also support for the idea of a *self-terminating* sensitive period where sufficiently long exposure to an imprinting stimulus will prevent the preference from being reversed (e.g., Shapiro and Thurston, 1978). Indeed, in the model, a sensitive period is observed with just 25 more epochs of exposure to A before exposing the network to stimulus D. This additional

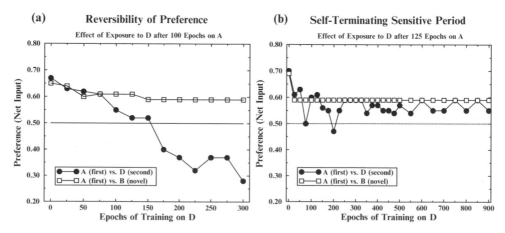

Figure 20.7   (a) The basic reversibility effect from training on *D* after initial imprinting on *A*. The comparison of the preference for *A* vs. *D* shows a reversal (from above 50% preference to below 50% preference). The preference for *A* over a second object *B*, remains stable despite the training on *D*. (b) A sensitive period effect from 125 epochs of imprinting on *A* before exposing to *D*. The *A* vs. *D* preference does not reverse, indicating a preserved preference for *A* despite up to 900 epochs of exposure to *D*.

exposure prevents any amount of further training on D from reversing the initial prefer-ence for A (figure 20.7b). This kind of sensitive period is self-terminating because it is determined solely by exposure to the object, and not by some other maturational change in the system.

5.3 *Discussion*

Both the sensitive period effect and the preserved preference effect described above can be explained by an interaction between the subtractive component of the covariance Hebbian learning rule and hysteresis effects. The subtractive component of the learning rule causes a receiving unit's weights to decrease for all inactive sending units, whenever the receiving unit is active. Hysteresis causes a unit to remain active, and thus to decrease its weights from inactive senders, over a contiguous period of time. If a unit is active for multiple locations of a given object, the weights from each location will be increased once (when that location is active in the input), but decreased multiple times (when other locations are active). Weights from locations of other objects, which are never active when the unit is active, are uniformly decreased.

Thus, the initial training in the network is dominated more by this weight decrease than the increase, and it results in two specific effects. One effect is that a unit that was active for a given object on one epoch will be *less* likely to be active the next epoch. As a result, a different unit will become active the next time, and adjust its weights for the same object. In this way, the repeated presentation of a given object will result in a *recruitment* process where multiple units will become tuned to the same object. This recruitment process happens gradually, with all of the recruited units taking turns becoming active. The other effect is that the uniform weight decrease from other object locations causes units to become *tuned* to one object over others. Over enough time, this causes the weights to the other object features to go to zero, making it effectively impossible to retune such a unit to respond to a different object.

In the present simulation, as training continues on the imprinting stimulus, both the tuning and recruitment effects get stronger, so that by a certain point (125 epochs in the present simulations), a majority of the units become selective to the imprinting stimulus, and are unavailable for recruitment to any new training stimulus because their weights to the other object features are near zero. Once this majority has been established, no amount of exposure to a different stimulus will cause these units to be recruited to the new stimulus, and the balance of preference will not shift. Instead, the retraining will cause the minority of initially unrecruited or less strongly recruited units to become selective to the new stimulus.

The tuning and recruitment processes also explain the retention of preference for a trained stimulus over a novel one even after re-training. The recruited units, being tuned to a particular object, do not become recruited by the other object, and the original preference for the object is preserved.

Thus, the two computationally important and biologically supported features of our model, hysteresis and a covariance Hebbian learning rule, are critical for its self-terminating sensitive period behavior. However, the specific properties of both of these components will affect the quantitative nature of the reversibility phenomenon in the chick. For example, changing the number of hidden units in the network extends the amount of training necessary to get the sensitive period effect.

5.4   Predictions

The model's behavior is consistent with the empirical studies described, and it makes some clear, if not particularly counter-intuitive, predictions regarding the properties of neurons in IMHV. The falsification of any of these would pose a challenge to the model.

- A neuron in IMHV that shows a preference for a given stimulus will tend to retain this preference even after re-training. Further, this propensity for retention of initial preference will be correlated with the selectivity and/or strength of the initial preference.
- More neurons in IMHV will show a strong preference for the first training stimulus after the sensitive period for reversibility than before it.
- Early on in training, neurons in IMHV should exhibit phasic or noisy correlations (i.e. correlated for a period then not, then correlated again) with the stimulus presentation as the balance between weight increase and decrease forces is struck.

6   Generalization

At a behavioral level, a number of studies have shown that generalization from the imprinting stimulus occurs to objects having the same shape or color (Jaynes, 1956, 1958; Cofoid and Honig, 1961). More recently, Bolhuis and Horn (1992) found evidence that generalization varies systematically with stimulus similarity.

The model generalizes because overlapping input patterns tend to activate the same units in higher layers. This is a basic property of most neural network models. The central finding from the simulations is that generalization appears to vary in a non-linear fashion with respect to stimulus similarity. Thus, for the basic imprinting simulation, after initial training on A, the network generalized to stimulus AB (a hybrid of A and B, having $\frac{2}{3}$ overlap with each), but not to stimulus B, which had only $\frac{1}{3}$ overlap with A (figure 20.8). This non-linearity is due to the lateral inhibition, which causes weakly activated units to become inhibited by more active units.

Similar results were found when generalization was tested in the reversibility simulation. In this case, the initial exposure to A generalized to AB, and not B, and subsequent exposure to D caused the preference for A and AB to reverse. This reversed preference was less than the preference for D over B, indicating that the non-linear generalization from the initial exposure is preserved following reversal (see figure 20.9a). The reversibility simulations were also run with AB as the retraining stimulus, which is highly similar ($\frac{2}{3}$ overlap) to the original stimulus A. As shown in figure 20.9b, the preference for A relative to a novel stimulus (D) increases slightly, rather than decreases after exposure to AB. This follows from the fact that the same units are active in both cases, causing learning to benefit both stimuli.

Another interesting effect shown in the figure is that the retraining on AB generalizes to stimulus B, because of B's $\frac{2}{3}$ overlap with AB. Thus, initially quite distinct objects, A and B, can be made to elicit the same preference from the network, and activate the same units, by providing a "bridge" between them. Control simulations using different orderings of initial and subsequent stimuli (e.g., exposing to A and B, then AB) indicate that order is not important for this effect. Ryan and Lea (1989) describe findings in the chick consistent with

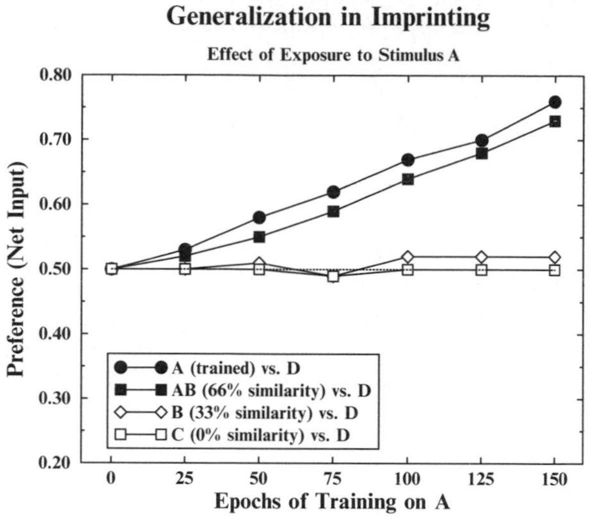

Generalization in Imprinting

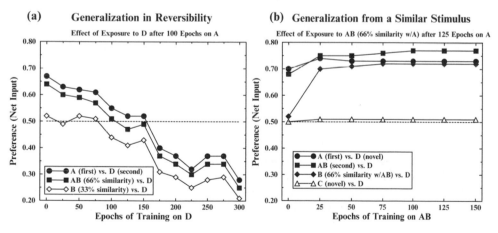

Figure 20.8　Generalization of imprinting on stimulus A to stimulus AB ($\frac{2}{3}$ overlap with A), as revealed by a comparison with the measured preference for D. Note that stimulus B, which has a $\frac{1}{3}$ overlap with A, does not experience significant imprinting from exposure to A, revealing a non-linearity in generalization.

Figure 20.9　(a) Generalization of the reversibility effect from exposure to D after 100 epochs on A. Stimulus AB ($\frac{2}{3}$ overlap with A) shows both the initial preference, and the reversal of this preference from exposure to D. Note that stimulus B remains less preferred than A or AB, due to non–linear generalization effects. (b) Training on a highly similar stimulus (AB) to the original imprinting stimulus A increases the preference of A relative to a novel stimulus (D). While there is a reversal of preference for A relative to AB, this effect is minor relative to the increase in preference compared to the novel stimulus. Also, the AB stimulus, being equally similar to A and B, causes the system to generalize to B as well, which shows a similar level of preference relative to the novel stimulus as A.

our model's behaviour. They exposed chicks to a stimulus composed of four balls, all one of two colors. One group saw the stimulus gradually change by flipping the color of one ball every four days, while the other group's stimulus was changed all at once. The chicks with the gradually changing stimulus developed an equally strong preference for both colors of the stimulus, while the others did not. The authors argue that these chicks had undergone *category enlargement.*

Finally, using stimulus AB for retraining prevented the termination of the critical period for imprinting, since, after retraining on AB, it will be preferred to A even after any number of epochs of initial exposure to A. However, the preference for A did not diminish relative to a novel stimulus (it actually increased slightly), and the level of preference of AB over A was not strong. This is a direct consequence of the fact that many of the same units in the model that were active for A are active for AB. Some evidence from imprinting on highly similar objects, such as two live hens, suggests that preferences remain fluid for a longer period (Kent, 1987).

6.1   Predictions

Again, the model's behavior is consistent with the empirical studies described, but we consolidate here the clear predictions that the model makes.

- The shape of the generalization window in chicks will be non-linear with respect to stimulus similarity, with a rather sharp boundary to the range of stimuli that generalize and those that do not.
- The generalization of preference should be preserved under reversal due to subsequent training on a novel, dissimilar stimulus.
- The objects within the generalization window will activate many of the same principal neurons in IMHV, while those not in the window will not. This finding would establish the neural basis of generalization as predicted from our model.
- Secondary training on a stimulus that is very similar to the original imprinting stimulus, but also similar to another stimulus, will result in a "widening" of the imprinting preference, so that all three stimuli will now show a similar level of preference to a novel stimulus.
- Retraining with a stimulus that is sufficiently similar to the original will not result in a decrease in preference relative to a completely novel stimulus, and only a weak reversal of preference over the initial stimulus.
- The termination of the sensitive period will occur at a variable time depending on the degree of similarity between the retraining stimulus and the original imprinting stimulus.

7   Temporal Contiguity and Blending

7.1   Behavior

A number of authors have reported that *blending*, a phenomenon related to generalization, can occur when two objects are presented in close temporal or spatial contiguity. For example, Chantrey (1974) varied the inter-stimulus-interval (ISI) between the presentation of two objects from 15 seconds to 30 minutes. By subsequently attempting to train chicks on a visual discrimination task involving the two objects he was able to demonstrate that when the objects had been presented in close temporal proximity (under 30 seconds gap between them) they became *blended* together to some extent. This result was replicated by Stewart et al. (1977) who also controlled for the total amount of exposure to the stimuli.

7.2 Simulations

According to our assumptions about the specific nature of the learning taking place in IMHV, temporal contiguity should be a very important variable in determining what the network considers to be the same object. In the "identity from persistence" algorithm, an object is *defined* as that which coheres over time. If this kind of learning is indeed taking place in IMHV, then one would expect to find the kinds of blending effects found by Chantrey (1974) due to close temporal contiguity. To stimulate the effects of delay in the model, we used the re-initialization of the activation state as a proxy for a delay long enough to allow the neural activation states to decay to values near resting, or at least retain little information about previous states. The exact length of time that this corresponds to in the chick is not known, so we manipulated "delay" as a binary variable. The delay condition networks were re-initialized between each sweep of a stimulus across the input layer, while the no-delay networks were not.[3]

In the model, we measure blending by looking directly at the unit's weights to determine what they have encoded. If a unit has weights that have been enhanced from features belonging to two or more different stimuli, then this unit has a representation that blends the distinction between these objects. If the unit only has strong weights from features for one stimulus, then the unit has a representation that differentiates between stimuli. Thus, to measure blending, we simply count the number of units that have non-differentiating representations. To allow for noise in the weights, we take an arbitrary threshold at .36788 (1/e) times the strength of the strongest weight into a unit as a cutoff for considering that weight to be enhanced.

Figure 20.10 shows the level of blending for training on stimuli A and D in the delay and no-delay conditions. Clearly, the absence of a delay causes almost total blending in the representations that form, so that the network would be unable, based on the active units, to distinguish whether stimulus A or stimulus D was present in the environment. The explanation for this effect is simple – a different position of a given object and an entirely different object are no different to a naive network. Thus, the intermingling without a delay of two different stimuli causes the network to treat them as different "positions" of the same stimulus. Note that without hysteresis, this effect would not arise, making the blending phenomenon a crucial source of empirical support for our hysteresis-based algorithm.

Intuitively, one might expect that the effect of similarity of stimuli on blending would be to increase it, so that more similar objects will be subject to greater blending effects. This was tested in the model by training with stimulus A in conjunction with AB or B, in the delay and no-delay conditions, and comparing the results to those found with stimulus D. Figure 20.11 shows that the effect of similarity on blending is not the same for both delay and no-delay conditions. In the delay condition, the more similar the stimuli were, the more blending occurred. This is the predicted direction of the effect. However, in the no-delay condition, the more similar the two stimuli, the *less* blending occurred: the level of blending in the no-delay condition was inversely proportional to the similarity of the stimuli.

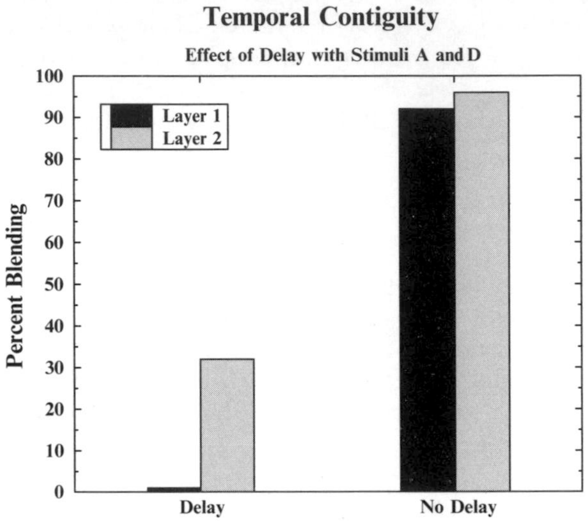

Temporal Contiguity

Effect of Delay with Stimuli A and D

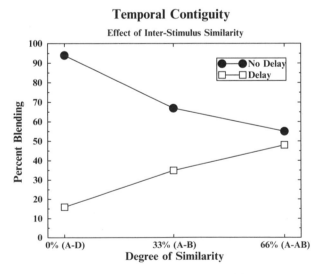

Figure 20.10   Temporal contiguity manipulation (delay vs. no–delay) affects number of blended representations, so that the no–delay condition causes considerably increased blending of the two stimuli. Blending is measured by examining the receptive fields of the units in each of the two layers of the model.

Temporal Contiguity

Effect of Inter-Stimulus Similarity

Figure 20.11   Temporal contiguity manipulation (delay vs. no–delay) interacts with similarity of the stimuli, so that in the delay condition, more similar stimuli (AB, *B*) show greater blending than dissimilar stimuli (D). The no–delay condition causes increased blending in inverse proportion to the amount of blending in the delay case. This data is the average of both layers 1 and 2, but each layer individually shows the same pattern.

The somewhat paradoxical inverse relationship between blending in the delay and no-delay conditions depends critically on hysteresis and the covariance formulation of the learning rule, in the form of the tuning property discussed previously. Specifically, the more active a receiving unit is, the more it will tune its weights, and thus cause itself to become more selective (less blended) in the future. We can understand the combined effects of similarity and no-delay as causing the units to initially become active very often, both because of input overlap (similarity) and hysteresis continued through the absence of delays. This results in a greater amount of tuning, which in turn causes the units to have more selective representations by the end of training.

7.3 Predictions

- When dissimilar stimuli are used in a temporal blending experiment, significant blending will be observed in short delay conditions. However, when stimuli which share many visual features are used, evidence for blending will be more difficult to detect. We propose that the difficulties in extending the Chantrey (1974) findings to other stimuli and experimental conditions (Stewart et al., 1977) is due to the relative similarity of the stimuli used.
- The temporal blending effect should be apparent in neural recording studies. With two dissimilar training stimuli, a short temporal gap training condition should result in more cells responding to both stimuli. In contrast, a long temporal gap condition with the same two stimuli should reveal more neurons responsive to one or the other stimulus.
- Some IMHV neurons initially activated by both of two similar stimuli should become gradually more sensitive to one or the other as training proceeds, while others should remain active for both. The gradient of overall similarity in IMHV firing patterns should be towards more distinct patterns for the two stimuli as exposure increases, reflecting the tuning process at work.

8 Discussion

Through a series of simulations and analysis of the mechanisms behind them, we have been able to evaluate a simple neural network model of invariant object recognition by relating its behavior and neural properties to those of the domestic chick during imprinting. The model exhibits a range of behaviors in different analogs of experimental manipulations from reversibility and sensitive periods to generalization and temporal blending that qualitatively agree with empirical results. The model also produces some counter-intuitive predictions regarding temporal blending as it interacts with similarity, in addition to a number of more straightforward predictions. Further, the relative simplicity of the model has enabled its behaviors to be related to certain properties that the model incorporates from the neuronal structure of IMHV. This lends support to the idea that these neural circuit properties have a functional role in object recognition within IMHV corresponding to their role in our model.

Further, the sensitive period issues explored in our model may have utility outside the sphere of visual imprinting in birds. For example, several authors have pointed out similarities between some of the phenomena associated with imprinting, and observations about the development and plasticity of the primate cortex (e.g. Rauschecker and Marler, 1987). In particular, there may be strong parallels between the reversibility effects examined in this paper, and the extent of recovery of visual acuity following monocular occlusion in the kitten (e.g., Mitchell, 1991).

Aside from the specific predictions made regarding each of the different behavioral effects found in imprinting, we feel the model leads to several broader conclusions. To the extent that our account of IMHV fits the behavioral and neural data, it provides support for the computational model of object recognition upon which our account is based. Given the challenging nature of the object recognition problem from a computational standpoint, the existence of a simplified animal model of object recognition would provide a valuable tool for further exploration and understanding of how neural systems recognize objects.

Appendix A – IAC Activation Function

The IAC activation function (in a slightly modified form) contains an input and a decay term (with the relative contribution of these two factors controlled by modifying the level of the decay term, α) controlled by a rate parameter λ:

$$\Delta a_i = \lambda(f(net_i) - \alpha(a_i - rest))$$

where $f(net_i)$ is the following input function:

$$f(net_i) = \begin{cases} net_i(max - a_i) & net_i > 0 \\ net_i(a_i - min) & net_i < 0 \end{cases}$$

and net_i is the net input to the unit:

$$net_i = \sum_j o_j w_{ji} + \sum_{l, l \neq i} o_l w_{li}$$

with l indexing over the other units in the same layer with inhibitory connections, and o_j representing the positive-only activation value of unit j (0 otherwise).

Appendix B – Hebbian Weight Update Rule

The weight update rule used throughout was as follows:

$$\frac{1}{\lambda}\Delta w_{ij} = \begin{cases} (1.0 - w_{ij}) & a_j > 0, a_i > 0 \\ -w_{ij} & a_j > 0, a_i < 0 \\ 0 & \text{otherwise} \end{cases}$$

where λ is the learning rate.

The rule depends on the signs of the pre- and postsynaptic terms (a_i and a_j, respectively), as the inhibition within a layer will drive all but a single unit into the negative activation range. Without hysteresis, this unit would always be the one with the largest net input from the current input pattern, making this formulation in combination with the lateral inhibition roughly equivalent to the Competitive Learning scheme (Rumelhart and Zipser, 1986). The hysteresis can cause an already-active unit that might not have the largest amount of input from the current pattern to remain active, which is the basis of the translation invariance learning, and in this way the system differs from Rumelhart and Zipser (1986). Note that it differs also from the Földiák (1991) scheme in that the hysteresis or trace component of the activation is implemented in the activation function through the influence of lateral inhibition and mutual excitation, and not directly in the weight update function.

NOTES

1 That is, young which are capable of fending for themselves from birth.
2 This is an artifact of the Winner-Take-All nature of our model, and is probably not the case in the real system.
3 Note that all simulations to this point involving multiple stimuli per epoch have been run with a "delay."

REFERENCES

Artola, A., Brocher, S., and Singer, W. (1990). Different voltage-dependent thresholds for inducing long-term depression and long-term potentiation in slices of rat visual cortex. *Nature* 347, 69–72.

Bateson, P. P. G. (1966). The characteristics and context of imprinting. *Biological Reviews* 91, 177–220.

Bear, M. F. and Malenka, R. C. (1994). Synaptic plasticity: LTP and LTD. *Current Opinion in Neurobiology* 4, 389–99.

Bolhuis, J. J. (1991). Mechanisms of avian imprinting: A review. *Biological Reviews* 66, 303–45.

Bolhuis, J. J. and Bateson, P. P. G. (1990). The importance of being first: A primacy effect in filial imprinting. *Animal Behavior* 40, 472–83.

Bolhuis, J. J. and Horn, G. (1992). Generalization of learned preferences in filial imprinting. *Animal Behavior* 44, 185–7.

Bolhuis, J. J., Johnson, M. H., Horn, G., and Bateson, P. P. G. (1989). Long-lasting effects of IMHV lesions on social preferences in domestic fowl. *Behavioral Neuroscience* 103, 438–41.

Bradley, P., Davies, D. C., and Horn, G. (1985). Connections of the hyperstriatum ventrale in the domestic chick *gallus domesticus*. *Journal of Anatomy* 140, 577–89.

Brown, M. W. and Horn, G. (1992). Neurones in the intermediate and medial part of the hyperstriatum ventrale (IMHV) of freely moving chicks respond to visual and/or auditory stimuli. *Journal of Physiology* 452, 102P.

Bush, P. C. and Douglas, R. J. (1991). Synchronization of bursting action potential discharge in a model network of neocortical neurons. *Neural Computation* 3, 19–30.

Chantrey, D. F. (1974). Stimulus pre-exposure and discrimination learning by domestic chicks: Effect of varying interstimulus time. *Journal of Comparative and Physiological Psychology* 87, 517–25.

Cofoid, D. A. and Honig, W. K. (1961). Stimulus generalization of imprinting. *Science* 134, 1692–4.

Cook, S. E. (1993). Retention of primary preferences after secondary filial imprinting. *Animal Behavior* 46, 405–7.

Davies, D. C., Taylor, D. A., and Johnson, M. H. (1988). Restricted hyperstriatal lesions and passive avoidance learning in the chick. *Journal of Neuroscience* 8, 4662–8.

Douglas, R. J. and Martin, K. A. C. (1990). Neocortex. In G. M. Shepherd (ed.), *The Synaptic Organization of the Brain* (ch. 12, pp. 389–438). Oxford: Oxford University Press.

Douglas, R. J., Martin, K. A. C., and Whitteridge, D. (1989). A cannonical microcircuit for neocortex. *Neural Computation* 1, 480–8.

Einsiedel, A. A. (1975). The development and modification of object preferences in domestic white leghorn chicks. *Developmental Psychobiology* 8(6), 533–40.

Földiák, P. (1991). Learning invariance from transformation sequences. *Neural Computation* 3(2), 194–200.

Frégnac, Y., Shulz, D., Thorpe, S., and Bienenstock, E. L. (1988). A cellular analogue of visual cortical plasticity. *Nature* 333, 367–70.

Hoffman, H. S. and Ratner, A. M. (1973). A reinforcement model of imprinting. *Psychological Review* 80, 527–44.

Hopfield, J. J. (1984). Neurons with graded response have collective computational properties like those of two-state neurons. *Proceedings of the National Academy of Sciences* 81, 3088–92.

Horn, G. (1985). *Memory, Imprinting, and the Brain: An inquiry into mechanisms*. Oxford: Clarendon Press.

Horn, G., Bradley, P., and McCabe, B. J. (1985). Changes in the structure of synapses associated with learning. *Journal of Neuroscience* 5, 3161–8.

Horn, G. and Johnson, M. H. (1989). Memory systems in the chick: Dissociations and neuronal analysis. *Neuropsychologia* 27, 1–22.

Hubel, D. H. and Wiesel, T. N. (1962). Receptive fields, binocular interaction, and functional architecture in the cat's visual cortex. *Journal of Physiology* 160, 106–54.

Jaynes, J. (1956). Imprinting: The interaction of learned and innate behavior. I. Development and generalization. *Journal of Comparative and Physiological Psychology* 49, 200–6.

Jaynes, J. (1958). Imprinting: The interaction of learned and innate behavior. IV. Generalization and emergent discrimination. *Journal of Comparative and Physiological Psychology* 51, 238–42.

Johnson, M. H. (1991). Information processing and storage during filial imprinting. In P. G. Hepper (ed.), *Kin Recognition* (pp. 335–57). Cambridge: Cambridge University Press.

Johnson, M. H. and Horn, G. (1987). The role of a restricted region of the chick forebrain in the recognition of conspecifics. *Behavioural Brain Research* 23, 269–75.

Johnson, M. H. and Morton, J. (1991). *Biology and Cognitive Development: The case of face recognition*. Oxford: Blackwell.

Kent, J. P. (1987). Experiments on the relationship between the hen and chick: The role of the auditory mode in recognition and the effects of maternal separation. *Behaviour* 102, 1–14.

Kertzman, C. and Demarest, J. (1982). Irreversibility of imprinting after active vs. passive exposure to the object. *Journal of Comparative and Physiological Psychology* 96, 130–42.

Klopfer, P. H. (1967). Stimulus preferences and imprinting. *Science* 156, 1394–6.

Klopfer, P. H. and Hailman, J. P. (1964a). Basic parameters of following and imprinting in precocial birds. *Z. Tierpsychol.* 21, 755–62.

Klopfer, P. H. and Hailman, J. P. (1964b). Perceptual preferences and imprinting in chicks. *Science* 145, 1333–4.

Livingstone, M. and Hubel, D. (1988). Segregation of form, color, movement, and depth: Anatomy, physiology, and perception. *Science* 240, 740–9.

Lorenz, K. (1935). Der kumpan in der umwelt des vogels. *Journal of Ornithology* 83, 137–213, 289–413.

Lorenz, K. (1937). The companion in the bird's world. *Auk* 54, 245–73.

Maunsell, J. H. R., Nealey, T. A., and DePriest, D. D. (1990). Magnocellular and parvocellular contributions to responses in the middle temporal visual area (MT) of the macaque monkey. *Journal of Neuroscience* 10(10), 3323–34.

McCabe, B. J., Cipolla-Neto, J., Horn, G., and Bateson, P. P. G. (1982). Amnesic effects of bilateral lesions placed in the hyperstriatum ventrale of the chick after imprinting. *Experimental Brain Research* 48, 13–21.

McCabe, B. J. and Horn, G. (1988). Learning and memory: Regional changes in N-methyl-D-aspartate receptors in the chick brain. *Proceedings of the National Academy of Sciences* 85, 2849–53.

McClelland, J. L. and Rumelhart, D. E. (1981). An interactive activation model of context effects in letter perception: Part 1. An account of basic findings. *Psychological Review* 88(5), 375–407.

McCloskey, M. and Cohen, N. J. (1989). Catastrophic interference in connectionist networks: The sequential learning problem. In G. H. Bower (ed.), *The Psychology of Learning and Motivation*, vol. 24 (pp. 109–64). San Diego, CA: Academic Press, Inc.

Mitchell, D. E. (1991). The long-term effectiveness of different regimens of occlusion on recovery from early monocular deprivation in kittens. *Philosophical Transactions of the Royal Society (London)* B 333, 51–79.

O'Reilly, R. C. and McClelland, J. L. (1992). *The Self-organization of Spatially Invariant Representations* (Parallel Distributed Processing and Cognitive Neuroscience PDP. CNS.92.5). Carnegie Mellon University, Department of Psychology.

Payne, J. K. and Horn, G. (1984). Differential effects of exposure to an imprinting stimulus on "spontaneous" neuronal activity in two regions of the chick brain. *Brain Research* 232, 191–3.

Poggio, T., Torre, V., and Koch, C. (1985). Computational vision and regularization theory. *Nature* 317, 314–19.

Rauschecker, J. P. and Marler, P. (1987). *Imprinting and Cortical Plasticity: Comparative aspects of sensitive periods*. New York: Wiley.

Rumelhart, D. E. and Zipser, D. (1986). Feature discovery by competitive learning. In D. E. Rumelhart, J. L. McClelland and PDP Research Group (eds.), *Parallel Distributed Processing. Volume 1: Foundations* (ch. 5, pp. 151–93). Cambridge, MA: MIT Press.

Ryan, C. M. E. and Lea, S. E. G. (1989). Pattern recognition, updating, and filial imprinting in the domestic chicken (*gallus gallus*). In M. L. Commons, R. J. Herrnstein, S. Kosslyn, and D. Mumford (eds.), *Models of Behaviour: Behavioural approaches to pattern recognition and concept formation: quantitative analyses of behavior*, vol. 8 (pp. 89–110). Hillsdale, NJ: Lawrence Erlbaum Associates, Inc.

Salzen, E. A. and Meyer, C. C. (1968). Reversibility of imprinting. *Journal of Comparative Physiology* 66, 269–75.

Sejnowski, T. J. (1977). Storing covariance with nonlinearly interacting neurons. *Journal of Mathematical Biology* 4, 303–21.

Shapiro, L. J. and Thurston, K. G. (1978). The effect of enforced exposure to live models on the reversibility of attachments in white peking ducklings. *The Psychological Record* 28 (479–85).

Sluckin, W. (1972). *Imprinting and Early Learning*, 2nd edn. London: Methuen.

Sluckin, W. and Salzen, E. A. (1961). Imprinting and perceptual learning. *Quarterly Journal of Experimental Psychology* 13, 65–77.

Stewart, D. J., Capretta, P. J., Cooper, A. J., and Littlefield, V. M. (1977). Learning in domestic chicks after exposure to both discriminanda. *Journal of Comparative and Physiological Psychology* 91, 1095–109.

Tömböl, T., Csillag, A., and Stewart, M. G. (1988). Cell types of the hyperstriatum ventrale of the domestic chicken *gallus domesticus*: A golgi study. *Journal für Hinforschung* 29(3), 319–34.

Yuille, A. L. (1990). Generalized deformable models, statsitical physics, and matching problems. *Neural Computation* 2(1), 1–24.

PART VII

New Directions

Editors' Introduction to Part VII

The next several decades promise to bring an exponential increase in our knowledge about the relation between brain development and cognition. Recent developments in molecular biology, in brain imaging, and in the development of specific, quantitative theories of information processing will allow us to test hypotheses about the relationship between brain growth and cognitive development which have been thus far impossible. This final section discusses some of the novel theoretical and methodological tools that will make these advances possible. While some of the approaches may, in the long run, prove more useful than others, they illustrate the breadth of currently active approaches, and in our view, some particularly promising directions for future research.

Bates and Elman argue strongly for the utility of computational models in efforts to understand the mechanisms of changes that may underlie both brain and cognitive development. Specifically, they endorse models based on a computational framework called parallel distributed processing (PDP), or alternatively, connectionism or neural networks. This approach invokes systems of processing elements which are thought to mimic some aspects of processing characteristic of populations of neurons (see O'Reilly and Johnson, Part VI). Bates and Elman argue that neural networks may be better able to describe processes of change than other computer-based approaches to cognition, which in their view, have largely failed. Indeed, these authors suggest that computational models based on the PDP framework may offer specific instantiations of some of the developmental ideas first articulated by Piaget (see Part I). The use of computational models in research on brain and behavior relations in adults has become quite common, but with few exceptions (e.g., Munakata et al., 1997; Elman et al., 1996), remains relatively rare in studies of development. Bates and Elman argue that this situation is ripe for change.

The essay by Diamond illustrates an interdisciplinary, multi-level approach to the study of brain and cognition early in life. The focal point for this work is the effect of a congenital metabolic disorder, phenylketonuria (PKU), on the emergence of perceptual and cognitive function in human infants. In most cases, PKU is diagnosed around the time of birth and is usually treated by dietary restriction. Diamond shows, however, that children who have been diagnosed and systematically treated for PKU still show residual perceptual and cognitive deficits. These deficits are linked to abnormal functioning of prefrontal cortex by observations that children with early treated PKU may have reduced levels of the neurotransmitter dopamine, a chemical messenger that is vital to the normal operation of many brain systems, including the prefrontal cortex. Diamond also shows how an animal model of PKU may permit specific predictions about the disorder's behavioral and cognitive outcomes in humans. The essay provides a working model for how brain and cognitive development might be studied at multiple, interacting levels of analysis, from molecules to behavior.

In a related vein, Pennington describes how molecular approaches, specifically, those which link behavior to genetics, can provide additional essential sources of constraint on developmental theories of brain function (see also the readings by Oyama and Gottlieb in Part I). Specifically, because a large fraction of the human genome is expressed exclusively or mainly in the nervous system, questions about where and when genes are expressed in the brain and what impact their expression has on development are of fundamental importance. Not only have genetic methods begun to shed light on a variety of congenital disorders, but recent advances in molecular biology have permitted theories about the effects of genetic mechanisms on brain function to be tested directly by studying animals with specific gene deletions or mutations. The recent publication of a draft of the human genome has only highlighted our fundamental ignorance about what most of our genes do and how they influence brain development and function. Pennington's chapter illustrates some of the tools that may become increasingly important to developmental cognitive neuroscience.

It is clear from recent developments in neuroscience research that many old dogmas, such as the "fact" that neurogenesis in adult mammals is isolated to a limited range of species or to specific brain regions, may be forced to give way as new methods are developed and new evidence accumulates (e.g., Kemperman and Gage, 1999). This is likely to be especially true for the study of human brain and cognitive development because our base of knowledge remains relatively small. The three essays in this section offer a hopeful view of the challenges and opportunities ahead.

FURTHER READING

Bornstein, M. H., ed. (1987). *Sensitive Periods in Development: Interdisciplinary perspectives.* Hillsdale, NJ: Erlbaum. (A useful reference collection on sensitive periods in a variety of species.)

Carey, S. and Gelman, R., eds. (1991). *The Epigenesis of Mind: Essays on biology and cognition.* The Jean Piaget Symposium Series. Hillsdale, NJ: Lawrence Erlbaum Associates. (A uniformly excellent collection of chapters at the interface between biology and cognitive development.)

Diamond, A., ed. (1990). *The Development and Neural Basis of Higher Cognitive Functions.* New York: New York Academy of Sciences. (A comprehensive collection of chapters related to the topic.)

Elman, J. L., Bates, E. A., Johnson, M. H., Karmiloff-Smith, A., Parisi, D., and Plunkett, K. (1996). *Rethinking Innateness: A connectionist perspective on development.* Cambridge, MA: MIT Press. (Wide ranging discussion of the strengths of connectionist models in explorations of cognitive development.)

Gibson, K. R. and Peterson, A. C., eds. (1991). *Brain Maturation and Cognitive Development: Comparative and cross-cultural perspectives.* Hawthorne, NY: Aldine de Gruyter Press. (Contains several useful reference chapters.)

Gould, E., Reeves, A. J., Graziano, M. S., and Gross, C. G. (1999). Neurogenesis in the neocortex of adult primates. *Science* 286(5439), 458–552. (Describes evidence overturning long-standing assumption that neurogenesis in primate cerebral cortex ends before birth.)

Gunnar, M. R. and Nelson, C. A. (1992). *Developmental Behavioral Neuroscience. The Minnesota Symposium on Child Psychology, Volume 24*. Hillsdale, NJ: Erlbaum. (Contains several useful and stimulating papers.)

Hahn, M. E., Hewitt, J. K. et al., eds. (1990). *Developmental Behavior Genetics: Neural, biometrical, and evolutionary approaches*. Oxford: Oxford University Press. (A useful reference source for developmental behavior genetics.)

Kemperman, G. and Gage, F. H. (1999). New nerve cells for the adult brain. *Scientific American*, May 1999, 48–53. (A readable summary of recent evidence concerning the genesis of new neurons in the adult brain.)

Munakata, Y., McClelland, J. L., Johnson, M. H., and Siegler, R. S. (1997). Rethinking infant knowledge: Toward an adaptive process account of successes and failures in object permanence tasks. *Psychological Review* 104(4), 686–713. (Discussion of how computational models and integrated behavioral experiments can yield novel views about an important psychological milestone.)

21

Connectionism and the Study of Change

Elizabeth A. Bates *and* Jeffrey L. Elman

Developmental psychology and developmental neuropsychology have traditionally focused on the study of children. But these two fields are also supposed to be about the study of change, i.e. changes in behavior, changes in the neural structures that underlie behavior, and changes in the relationship between mind and brain across the course of development. Ironically, there has been relatively little interest in the mechanisms responsible for change in the last 15–20 years of developmental research. The reasons for this de-emphasis on change have a great deal to do with a metaphor for mind and brain that has influenced most of experimental psychology, cognitive science and neuropsychology for the last few decades, i.e., the metaphor of the serial digital computer. We will refer to this particular framework for the study of mind as the *First Computer Metaphor*, to be contrasted with a new computer metaphor, variously known as connectionism, parallel distributing processing, and/or neural networks. In this brief chapter, we will argue that the First Computer Metaphor has had some particularly unhappy consequences for the study of mental and neural development. By contrast, the *Second Computer Metaphor* (despite its current and no doubt future limitations) offers some compelling advantages for the study of change, at both the mental and the neural level.

The chapter is organized as follows: (1) a brief discussion of the way that change has (or has not) been treated in the last decade of research in developmental psychology, (2) a discussion of the First Computer Metaphor, and its implications for developmental research, (3) an introduction to the Second Computer Metaphor, and the promise it offers for research on the development of mind and brain, ending with (4) a response to some common misconceptions about connectionism.

1   What Happened to the Study of Change?

Traditionally, there are three terms that have been used to describe changes in child behavior over time: maturation, learning, and development. For our purposes here, these terms can be defined as follows.

(a) *Maturation*. As the term is typically used in the psychological literature (although this use may not be entirely accurate from a biological perspective – Bates et al., in press; Elman et al., 1996; Johnson, 1997), "maturation" refers to the timely appearance or unfolding of behaviors that are predetermined, in their structure and their sequence, by a well-defined genetic program. The role of experience in a strong maturational theory is limited to a "triggering" function (providing the general or specific conditions that allow some predetermined structures to emerge) or a "blocking" function (providing conditions that inhibit the expression of some predetermined event). The environment does not, in and of itself, provide or cause behavioral structure.

(b) *Learning*. "Learning" is typically defined as a systematic change in behavior as a result of experience. Under some interpretations, learning refers to a copying or transfer of structure from the environment to the organism (as in "acquisition" or "internalization"). Under a somewhat weaker interpretation, learning may refer to a shaping or alteration of behavior that is caused by experience, although the resulting behavior does not resemble structures in the environment in any direct or interesting way.

(c) *Development*. As defined by Werner (1948) in his elaboration of the "orthogenetic principle," "development" refers to any positive change in the internal structure of a system, where "positive" is further defined as an increase in the number of internal parts (i.e., differentiation), accompanied by an increase in the amount of organization that holds among those parts. Under this definition, the term "development" is neutral to the genetic or experiential sources of change, and may include emergent forms that are not directly predictable from genes or experience considered separately (i.e., the sum is greater than and qualitatively different from the parts).

Although all three terms have been used to describe behavioral change in the psychological literature, the most difficult and (in our view) most interesting proposals are the ones that have involved emergent form, i.e., changes that are only indirectly related to structure in the genes or the environment (Bates et al., 1998; Elman et al., 1996; MacWhinney, 1999). We are referring here not to the banal interactionism in which black and white yield grey, but to a much more challenging interactionism in which black and white converge and interact to yield an unexpected red. Because this interactionist view appears to be the only way to explain how new structures arise, it may be our only way out of a fruitless nature/nurture debate that has hampered progress in developmental psychology for most of its history.

Within our field, the most complete interactionist theory of behavioral change to date is the theory offered by Jean Piaget, across a career that spanned more than fifty years (Piaget, 1952, 1970a, 1970b, 1971). Piaget's genetic epistemology concentrated on the way that new mental structures emerge at the interface between an active child and a structured world. The key mechanism for change in Piaget's theory is the consummate biological notion of adaptation. Starting with a restricted set of sensorimotor schemes (i.e., structured "packages" of perception and action that permit activities like sucking, reaching, tracking, and/ or grasping), the child begins to act upon the world (assimilation). Actions are modified in response to feedback from that world (accommodation), and in response to the degree of internal coherence or stability that action schemes bear to one another (reciprocal assimilation). The proximal cause that brings about adaptation is a rather poorly defined notion of equilibration, i.e., the re-establishment of a stable and coherent state after a perturbation that created instability or disequilibrium. In the infant years, adaptation of simple sensorimotor schemes to a structured world leads to an increasingly complex and integrated set of schemes or "plans," structures that eventually permit the child to "re-present" the world (i.e., to call potential perceptuo-motor schemes associated with a given object or event into an organized state-of-readiness, in the absence of direct perceptual input from the represented object or event). This developmental notion of representation comprised Piaget's explanation for the appearance of mental imagery, language and other symbolic or representational forms somewhere in the second year of life. After this point, the process of adaptation continues at both the physical and representational level (i.e., operations on the real world, and operations on the new "mental world"), passing through a series of semistable "stages" or moments of system-wide equilibrium, ultimately leading to our human capacity for higher forms of logic and reasoning.

This "bootstrapping" approach to cognitive development does involve a weak form of learning (as defined above), but the mental structures that characterize each stage of development are not predictable in any direct way from either the structure of the world or the set of innate sensorimotor schemes with which the child began. Furthermore, Piaget insisted that these progressive increases in complexity were a result of activity ("construction"), and not a gradual unfolding of predetermined forms (maturation). In this fashion, Piaget strove to save us from the nature/nurture dilemma. Behavioral outcomes were determined not only by genes, or by environment, but by the mathematical, physical and biological laws that determine the kinds of solutions that are possible for any given problem. As Piaget once stated in a criticism of his American colleague Noam Chomsky, "That which is inevitable does not have to be innate" (Piaget, 1970a).

There was a period in the history of developmental psychology in which Piagetian theory assumed a degree of orthodoxy that many found stifling. Decades later, it now appears that much of Piaget's theory was wrong in detail. For one thing, it is now clear that the infant's initial stock of innate sensorimotor schemes is far richer than Piaget believed. It is also clear that Piaget overestimated the degree of cross-domain stability that children are likely to display at any given point in development (i.e., the notion of a coherent "stage"). Once the details of his stage theory were proven inadequate, all that really remained were the principles of change that formed the bedrock of Piaget's genetic epistemology – notions of adaptation and equilibration that struck many of his critics as hopelessly vague, and a notion of emergent form that many found downright mystical. Piaget was aware of these problems, and spent the latter part of his career seeking a set of formalisms to concretize his deep insights about change. Most critics agree that these efforts failed. This failure, coupled with new empirical information showing that many other aspects of the theory were incorrect, has led to a widespread repudiation of Piaget. Indeed, we are in a period of "anti-Piagetianism" of patricidal dimensions.

But what have we put in Piaget's place? We have never replaced his theory with a better account of the epistemology of change. In fact, the most influential developmental movements of the last two decades have essentially disavowed change. Alas, we fear that we are back on the horns of the Nature–Nurture dilemma from which Piaget tried in vain to save us.

On the one hand, we have seen a series of strong nativist proposals in the last few years, including proposals by some neo-Gibsonian theorists within the so-called "competent infant movement" (Baillargeon, 1999; Baillargeon and de Vos, 1991; Spelke, 1990, 1991; Spelke and Newport, 1998), and proposals within language acquisition inspired by Chomsky's approach to the nature and origins of grammar (Hyams, 1986; Lightfoot, 1991; Roeper and Williams, 1987). In both these movements, it is assumed that the essence of what it means to be human is genetically predetermined. Change – insofar as we see change at all – is attributed to the maturation of predetermined mental content, to the release of preformed material by an environmental "trigger," and/or to the gradual removal of banal sensory and motor limitations that hid all this complex innate knowledge from view. Indeed, the term "learning" has taken on such negative connotations in some quarters that efforts are underway to eliminate it altogether. The following quotes from Piatelli-Palmarini (1989) illustrate how far things have gone:

> "I, for one, see no advantage in the preservation of the term learning. We agree with those who maintain that we would gain in clarity if the scientific use of the term were simply discontinued." (p. 2)

> "Problem-solving . . . adaptation, simplicity, compensation, equilibration, minimal disturbance and all those universal, parsimony-driven forces of which the natural sciences are so fond, recede into the background. They are either scaled down, at the physico-chemical level, where they still make a lot of sense, or dismissed altogether." (pp. 13–14)

On the other hand, the neo-Vygotskian movement and associated approaches to the social bases of cognition have provided us with another form of preformationalism, insisting that the essence of what it means to be human is laid out for the child in the structure of social interactions (Bruner and Sherwood, 1976; Rogoff, 1990). In these theories, change is viewed primarily as a process of internalization, as the child takes in preformed solutions to problems that lie in the "zone of proximal development," i.e., in joint activities that are just outside his current ability to act alone. Related ideas are often found in research on "motherese," i.e., on the special, simplified and caricatured form of language that adults direct to small children (for a review, see Ferguson and Snow, 1978). In citing these examples, we do not want to deny that society has an influence on development, because we are quite sure that it does. Our point is, simply, that the pendulum has swung too far from the study of child-initiated change. The most influential movements in developmental psychology for the last two decades are those that have de-emphasized change in favor of an emphasis on some kind of preformation: either a preformation by Nature and the hand of God, or a preformation by the competent adult.

Why have we accepted these limits? Why haven't we moved on to study the process by which new structures really do emerge? We believe that developmental psychology has been influenced for many years by a metaphor for mind in which it is difficult to think about change in any interesting form – which brings us to the First Computer Metaphor.

2 The First Computer Metaphor and its Implications for Development

At its core, the serial digital computer is a machine that manipulates symbols. It takes individual symbols (or strings of symbols) as its input, applies a set of stored algorithms (a program) to that input, and produces more symbols (or strings of symbols) as its output. These steps are performed one at a time (albeit very quickly) by a central processor. Because of this serial constraint, problems to be solved by the First Computer must be broken down into a hierarchical structure that permits the machine to reach solutions with maximum efficiency (e.g., moving down a decision tree until a particular subproblem is solved, and then back up again to the next step in the program).

Without question, exploitation of this machine has led to huge advances in virtually every area of science, industry, and education. After all, computers can do things that human beings simply cannot do, permitting quantitative advances in information processing and numerical analysis that were unthinkable a century ago. The problem with this device for our purposes here lies not in its utility as a scientific tool, but in its utility as a scientific metaphor, in particular as a metaphor for the human mind/brain. Four properties of the serial digital computer have had particularly unfortunate consequences for the way that we have come to think about mental and neural development.

(1) *Discrete representations*. The symbols that are manipulated by a serial digital computer are discrete entities. That is, they either are or are not present in the input. There is no such thing as 50 percent of the letter A or 99 percent of the number 7. For example, if a would-be user types in a password that is off by only one key-stroke, the computer does not respond with "What the heck, that's close enough." Instead, the user is damned just as thoroughly as he would be if he did not know the password at all.

People (particularly children) rarely behave like this. We can respond to partial information (degraded input) in a systematic way; and we often transform our inputs (systematic or not) into partial decisions and imperfect acts (degraded output). We are error-prone, but we are also forgiving, flexible, willing, and able to make the best of what we have. This mismatch between human behavior and the representations manipulated by serial digital computers has of course been known for some time. To resolve this well-known discrepancy, the usual device adopted by proponents of the First Computer Metaphor for Mind is the competence/performance distinction. That is, it is argued that our knowledge (competence) takes a discrete and idealized form that is compatible with the computer metaphor, but our behavior (performance) is degraded by processing factors and other sources of noise that are irrelevant to a characterization of knowledge and (by extension) acquisition of knowledge. This is a perfectly reasonable intellectual move, but as we will see in more detail below, it has led to certain difficulties in characterizing the nature of learning that often result in the statement that learning is impossible.

(2) *Absolute rules*. Like the symbolic representations described above, the algorithms contained in a computer program also take a discrete form. If the discrete symbols that trigger a given rule are present in the input, then that rule must apply, and give an equally discrete symbol or string of symbols as its output. Conversely, if the relevant symbols are not present in the input, then the rule in question will not apply. There is no room for anything in between, no coherent way of talking about 50 percent of a rule, or (for that matter) weak vs. strong rules. Indeed, this is exactly the reason why computers are so much more reliable than human beings for many computational purposes.

Presented with the well-known mismatch between human behavior and the absolute status of rules in a serial digital computer, proponents of the First Computer Metaphor for Mind usually resort to the same competence/performance described above. Alternatively, there have been attempts to model the probabilistic nature of human behavior by adding weights to rules, a device that permits the model to decide which rule to apply (or in what order of preference) when a choice has to be made. The problem is that these weights are in no way a natural product or property of the architecture in which they are embedded, nor are they produced automatically by the learning process. Instead, these weights are arbitrary, ad hoc devices that must be placed in the system by hand – which brings us to the next point.

(3) *Learning as programming*. The serial digital computer is not a self-organizing system. It does not learn easily. Indeed, the easiest metaphor for learning in a system of this kind is programming; that is, the rules that must be applied to inputs of some kind are placed directly into the system – by man, by Nature or by the hand of God. To be sure, there is a literature on computer learning in the field of artificial intelligence. However, most of these efforts are based on a process of hypothesis testing. In such learning models, two essential factors are provided a priori: a set of hypotheses that will be tested against the data, and an algorithm for deciding which hypothesis provides the best fit to those data. This is by its

very nature a strong nativist approach to learning. It is not surprising that learning theories of this kind are regularly invoked by linguists and psycholinguists with a strong nativist orientation. There is no graceful way for the system to derive new hypotheses (as opposed to modifications of a pre-existing option). Everything that really counts is already there at the beginning.

Once again, however, we have an unfortunate mismatch between theory and data in cognitive science. Because the hypotheses tested by a traditional computer-learning model are discrete in nature (based on the rule and representations described above), learning (a.k.a. "selection") necessarily involves a series of discrete decisions about the truth or falsity of each hypothesis. Hence we would expect change to take place in a crisp, step-wise fashion, as decisions are made, hypotheses are discarded, and new ones are put in their place. But human learning rarely proceeds in this fashion, being characterized more often by error, vacillation and backsliding. In fact, the limited value of the serial digital computer as a metaphor for learning is well known. Perhaps for this reason, learning and development have receded into the background in modern cognitive psychology, while the field has concentrated instead on issues like the nature of representation, processes of recognition and retrieval, and the various stages through which discrete bits of information are processed (e.g., various buffers and checkpoints in a serial process of symbol manipulation). Developmental psychologists working within this framework (or indirectly influenced by it) have moved away from the study of change and self-organization toward a catalogue of those representations that are there at the beginning (e.g. the "competent infant" move-ment in cognition and perception; the parameter-setting movement in developmental psycholinguistics), and/or a characterization of how the processes that elaborate infor-mation mature or expand across the childhood years (i.e., changes in performance that "release" the expression of pre-existing knowledge).

(4) *The hardware/software distinction.* One of the most unfortunate consequences of the First Computer Metaphor for cognitive science in general and developmental psychology in particular has been the acceptance of a strong separation between software (the know-ledge – symbols, rules, hypotheses, etc. – that is contained in a program) and hardware (the machine that is used to implement that program). From this perspective, the machine itself places very few constraints on our theory of knowledge and (by extension) behavior, except perhaps for some relatively banal concerns about capacity (e.g., there are some programs that one simply cannot run on a small personal computer with limited memory).

The distinction between hardware and software has provided much of the ammunition for an approach to philosophy of mind and cognitive science called Functionalism (Fodor, 1981).[1] Within the functionalist school, the essential properties of mind are derived entirely from the domains on which the mind must operate: language, logic, mathematics, three-dimensional space, etc. To be sure, these properties have to be implemented in a machine of some kind, but the machine itself does not place interesting constraints on mental representations (i.e., the objects manipulated by the mind) or functional architecture (i.e., the abstract system that manipulates those objects). This belief has justified an approach to cognition that is entirely independent of neuroscience, thereby reducing the number and range of constraints to which our cognitive theories must respond. As a by-product (since divorces usually affect both parties), this approach has also reduced the impact of cognitive theories and cognitive phenomena on the field of neuroscience.

The separation between biology and cognition has had particularly serious consequences for developmental psychology, a field in which biology has traditionally played a major role (i.e., a tradition that includes Freud, Gesell, Baldwin, and Piaget, to name a few). Not only have we turned away from our traditional emphasis on change, but we have also turned away from the healthy and regular use of biological constraints on the study of developing minds. Ironically, some of the strongest claims about innateness in the current literature have been put forth in complete disregard of biological facts (Bates, Thal, Finlay and Clancy, in press; Elman, Bates, Johnson, Karmiloff-Smith, Parisi and Plunkett, 1996). For example, claims about the innateness of detailed cortical representations (e.g., an innate theory of physics, or innate theory of mind) are difficult to square with what we now know about (a) the plastic and activity-dependent nature of the processes that set up cortical microcircuitry, and (b) the mathematical bottleneck involved in setting up a brain with 10^{14} connections using fewer than 10^6 genes, 98 percent of which humans share with chimpanzees (Gerhart and Kirschner, 1998). The underlying assumption appears to be that our cognitive findings have priority, and if there is a mismatch between cognitive and biological conclusions, we probably got the biology wrong (which may be the case some of the time – but surely not all the time!).

It seems to us that we need all the constraints that can be found to make sense of a growing mass of information about cognitive development, language development, perceptual development, social development. Furthermore, we suspect that developmental neuroscience would also profit from a healthy dose of knowledge about the behavioral functions of the neural systems under study. Finally, we would all be better off if we could find a computational model (or class of models) in which it would be easier to organize and study the mutual constraints that hold between mental and neural development – which brings us to the next computer metaphor.

3   The Second Computer Metaphor and Its Implications for Development

During the 1950s and '60s, when the First Computer Metaphor for mind began to influence psychological research, some information scientists were exploring the properties of a different and competing computational device called the Perceptron (Rosenblatt, 1958, 1962). The roots of this approach can be traced to earlier work in cybernetics (Minsky, 1956; von Neumann, 1951, 1958) and in neurophysiology (Eccles, 1953; Hebb, 1949; McCulloch and Pitts, 1943). In a perceptron network, unlike the serial digital computer, there was not a clear distinction between processor and memory, nor did it operate on symbols in the usual sense of the term. Instead, the perceptron network was composed of a large number of relatively simple "local" units that worked in parallel to perceive, recognize and/or categorize an input. These local units or "nodes" were organized into two layers, an "input set" and an "output set." In the typical perceptron architecture, every unit on the input layer was connected by a single link to each and every unit on the output layer (see figure 21.1). These connections varied in degree or strength, from 0 to 1 (in a purely excitatory system) or from -1 to $+1$ (in a system with both activation and inhibition). A given output unit would "fire" as a function of the amount of input that it received from the various input units, with activation collected until a critical firing threshold was reached (see also McCulloch and Pitts, 1943). Individual acts of recognition or categorization in a perceptron reflect the collective activity of all these units. Knowledge is a property of the connection strengths that hold between the respective input and output layers; the machine can be said to "know" a pattern when it gives the correct output for a given class of inputs (including novel members of the input class that it has never seen before, i.e., generalization).

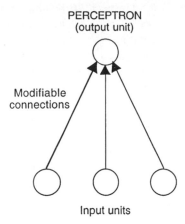

Figure 21.1   A simple perceptron network.

There are some obvious analogies between this system and the form of computation carried out in real neural systems, e.g., excitatory and inhibitory links, summation of activation, firing thresholds, and above all the distribution of patterns across a large number of interconnected units. But this was not the only advantage that perceptrons offered, compared with their competitors. The most important property of perceptrons was (and is) their ability to learn by example.

During the teaching and learning phase, a stimulus is registered on the input layer in a distributed fashion, by turning units on or off to varying degrees. The system produces the output that it currently prefers (based, in the most extreme *tabula rasa* case, on a random set of connections). Each unit in this distributed but "ignorant" output is then compared with the corresponding unit in the "correct" output. If a given output unit within a distributed pattern has "the right answer," its connection strengths are left unchanged. If a given output has "the wrong answer," the size of the error is calculated by a simple difference score (i.e., "delta"). All of the connections to that erroneous output are then increased or decreased in proportion to the amount of error that they were responsible for on that trial. This procedure then continues in a similar fashion for other trials. Because the network is required to find a single set of connection weights which allow it to respond correctly to all of the patterns it has seen, it typically succeeds only by discovering the underlying generalizations which relate inputs to outputs. The important and interesting result is that the network is then able to respond appropriately not only to stimuli it has seen before, but to novel stimuli as well. The learning procedure is thus an example of learning inductively.

Compared with the cumbersome hypothesis-testing procedures that constitute learning in serial digital computers, learning really appears to be a natural property of the Perceptron. Indeed, perceptrons are able to master a broad range of patterns, with realistic generalization to new inputs as a function of their similarity to the initial learning set. The initial success of these artificial systems had some impact on theories of pattern recognition in humans. The most noteworthy example is Selfridge's "Pandemonium Model" (Selfridge, 1958), in which simple local feature detectors or "demons" work in parallel to recognize a complex pattern. Each demon scans the input for evidence of its preferred feature; depending on its degree of certainty that the relevant feature has appeared, each demon "shouts" or "whispers" its results. In the Pandemonium Model (as in the Perceptron), there is no final arbiter, no *homunculus* or central executive who puts all these daemonical inputs together. Rather, the "solution" is an emergent property of the system as a whole, a global pattern produced by independent, local computations. This also means that results or solutions can vary in their degree of resemblance to the "right" answer, capturing the rather fuzzy properties of human categorization that are so elusive in psychological models inspired by the serial digital computer.

So far so good. And yet this promising line of research came to a virtual end in 1969, when Minsky and Papert published their famous book *Perceptrons*. Minsky and Papert (who were initial enthusiasts and pioneers in perceptron research) were able to prove that perceptrons are only capable of learning a limited class of first-order, linearly separable patterns. These systems are incapable of learning second-order relations like "A or B but not both" (i.e., logical exclusive OR), and by extension, any pattern of equivalent or greater complexity and interdependence. This fatal flaw is a direct product of the fact that perceptrons are two-layered systems, with a single direct link between each input and output unit. If A and B are both "on" in the input layer, then they each automatically "turn on" their collaborators on the output layer. There is simply no place in the system to record the fact that A and B are both on simultaneously, and hence no way to "warn" their various collaborators that they should shut up on this particular trial. It was clear even in 1969 that this problem could be addressed by adding another layer somewhere in the middle, a set of units capable of recording the fact that A and B are both on simultaneously, and therefore capable of inhibiting output nodes that would normally turn on in the presence of either A or B. So why not add a set of "in between" units, creating three- or four- or N-layered perceptrons? Unfortunately, the learning rules available at that time (e.g., the simple delta rule) did not work with multilayered systems. Furthermore, Minsky and Papert offered the conjecture that such a learning rule would prove impossible in principle, due to the combinatorial complexity of delta calculations and "distribution of blame" in an N-layered system. As it turns out, this conjecture was wrong (after all, a conjecture is not a proof). Nevertheless, it was very influential. Interest in the Perceptron as a model of complex mental processes dwindled in many quarters. From 1970 on, most of artificial intelligence research abandoned this architecture in favor of the fast, flexible and highly programmable serial digital computer. And most of cognitive psychology followed suit. (For a somewhat different account of this history, see Papert, 1988; a good collection of historically important documents can be found in Anderson and Rosenfeld, 1989. A good tutorial on how to do connectionist simulations is Plunkett and Elman, 1997, and Golden, 1996, provides an excellent technical overview of neural networks.)

Parallel distributed processing was revived in the late 1970s and early 1980s, for a variety of reasons. In fact, the computational advantages of such systems were never entirely forgotten (Anderson, 1972; Feldman and Ballard, 1980; Hinton and Anderson, 1981; Kohonen, 1977; Willshaw et al., 1969), and their resemblance to real neural systems continued to exert some appeal (Grossberg, 1968, 1972, 1987). But the current "boom" in parallel distributed processing or "connectionism" was inspired in large measure by the discovery of a learning rule that worked for multilayered systems (Le Cun, 1985; Rumelhart et al., 1986a). The Minsky–Papert conjecture was overturned, and there are now many impressive demonstrations of learning in multilayered neural nets, including learning of n-order dependencies like "A or B but not both" (Rumelhart et al., 1986b).[2] Multilayer networks have been shown to be universal function approximators, which means they can approximate any function to any arbitrary degree of precision (Hornik, Stinchcombe, and White, 1989). Such a network is shown in figure 21.2.

Another reason for the current popularity of connectionism derives from technical advances in the design of parallel computing systems. It has become increasingly clear to computer scientists that we are close to the absolute physical limits on speed and efficiency in serial systems – and yet the largest and fastest serial computers still cannot come close to the speed with which our small, slow, energy-efficient brains recognize patterns and decide where and how to move. As Carver Mead has pointed out (Mead, 1989), it is time to "reverse-engineer Nature," to figure out the principles by which real brains compute information. It is still the case that most connectionist simulations are actually carried out on serial digital computers (which mimic parallelism by carrying out a set of would-be parallel computations in a series, and waiting for the result until the next wave of would-be parallel computations is ready to go). But new, truly parallel architectures are coming on line (e.g., the now-famous Connection Machine) to implement those discoveries that have been made with pseudo-parallel simulations. Parallel distributed processing appears to be the solution elected by Evolution, and (if Mead is right) computer science will have to move in this direction to capture the kinds of processing that human beings do so well.

For developmental psychologists, the Second Computer Metaphor holds some clear advantages for the study of change in human beings. The first set involves the same four areas in which the First Computer Metaphor has let us down: the nature of representations, rules or "mappings," learning, and the hardware/software issue. The last two are advantages peculiar to connectionist networks: nonlinear dynamics, and emergent form.

(1) *Distributed representations.* The representations employed in connectionist nets differ radically from the symbols manipulated by serial digital computers. First, these representations are "coarse-coded," distributed across many different units. Because of this property, it is reasonable to talk about the degree to which a representation is active or the amount of a representation that is currently available in this system (i.e., 50 percent of an "A" or 99

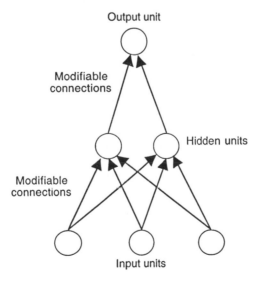

Figure 21.2 A multilayer network. The "hidden units" allow such networks to form internal representations. Multilayer networks of this sort have been shown to be able to approximate any function to any arbitrary degree of accuracy.

percent of the number "7"). This also means that patterns can be built up or torn down in bits and pieces, accounting for the graded nature of learning in most instances, and for the gradual or graded patterns of breakdown that are typically displayed by brain-damaged individuals (Hinton and Shallice, 1991; Marchman, 1993; Seidenberg and McClelland, 1989; Schwartz et al., 1990). Second, the same units can participate in many different patterns, and many different patterns coexist in a superimposed fashion across the same set of units. This fact can be used to account for degrees of similarity between patterns, and for the ways in which patterns penetrate, facilitate and/or interfere with one another at various points in learning and development (for an expanded discussion of this point, see Bates et al., 1991; Elman et al., 1996).

(2) *Graded Rules.* Contrary to rumor, it is not the case that connectionist systems have no rules. However, the rules or "mappings" employed by connectionist nets take a very different form from the crisp algorithms contained within the programs employed by a serial digital computer. These include the learning rule itself (i.e. the principle by which the system reduces error and "decides" when it has reached a good fit between input and output), and the functions that determine when and how a unit will fire. But above all, the "rules" in a connectionist net include the connections that hold among units, i.e. the links or "weights" that embody all the potential mappings from input to output across the system as a whole. This means that rules (like representations) can exist by degree, and vary in strength.

It should also be clear from this description that it is difficult to distinguish between rules and representations in a connectionist net. The knowledge or "mapping potential" of a network comprises the units that participate in distributed patterns, and the connections among those units. Because all these potential mappings coexist across the same "territory," they must compete with one another to resolve a given input. In the course of this competition, the system does not "decide" between alternatives in the usual sense; rather, it "relaxes" or "resolves" into a (temporary) state of equilibrium. In a stochastic system of this kind, it is possible for several different networks to reach the same solution to a problem, each with a totally different set of weights. This fact runs directly counter to the tendency in traditional cognitive and linguistic research to seek "the rule" or "the grammar" that underlies a set of behavioral regularities. In other words, rules are not absolute in any sense – they can vary by degree within a given individual, and they can also vary in their internal structure from one individual to another. We believe that these properties are far more compatible with the combination of universal tendencies and individual variation that we see in the course of human development, and they are compatible with the remarkable neural and behavioral plasticity that is evident in children who have suffered early brain injury (Bates et al., 1997; Elman et al., 1996; Marchman, 1993).

(3) *Learning as structural change.* As we pointed out earlier, much of the current excitement about connectionist systems revolves around their capacity for learning and self-organization. Indeed, the current boom in connectionism has brought learning and development back onto center stage in cognitive science. These systems really do change as a function of learning, displaying forms of organization that were not placed there by the programmer (or by nature, or by the Hand of God). To be sure, the final product is co-determined by the initial structure of the system and the data to which it is exposed. These systems are not anarchists, nor solipsists. But in no sense is the final product "copied" or programmed in. Furthermore, once the system has learned it is difficult for it to "unlearn," if by "unlearning" we mean a return to its pristine prelearning state. This is true for the reasons described in (1) and (2): the knowledge contained in connectionist nets is contained in and defined by its very architecture, in the connection weights that

currently hold among all units as a function of prior learning. Knowledge is not "retrieved" from some passive store, nor is it "placed in" or "passed between" spatially localized buffers. Learning is structural change, and experience involves the activation of potential states in that system as it is currently structured.

From this point of view, the term "acquisition" is an infelicitous way of talking about learning or change. Certain states become possible in the system, but they are not acquired in the usual sense, i.e., found or purchased or stored away like nuts in preparation for the winter. This property of connectionist systems permits us to do away with problems that have been rampant in certain areas of developmental psychology, e.g., the problem of determining "when" a given piece of knowledge is acquired, or "when" a rule finally becomes productive. Instead, development (like the representations and mappings on which it is based) can be viewed as a gradual process; there is no single moment at which learning can be said to occur (but see nonlinearity, below).

(4) *Software as Hardware*. We have stated that knowledge in connectionist nets is defined by the very structure of the system. For this reason, the hardware/software distinction is impossible to maintain under the Second Computer Metaphor. This is true whether or not the structure of connectionist nets as currently conceived is "neurally real", i.e., like the structure that holds in real neural systems. We may still have the details wrong (indeed, we probably do), but the important point for present purposes is that there is no further excuse for ignoring potential neural constraints on proposed cognitive architectures. The distinction that has separated cognitive science and neuroscience for so long has fallen, like the Berlin Wall. Some cognitive psychologists and philosophers of science believe that is not a good thing (and indeed, the same might be said someday for the Berlin Wall). But we are convinced that this historic change is a good one, especially for those of us who are interested in the co-development of mind and brain. We are going in the right direction, even though we have a long way to go.

(5) *Nonlinear dynamics*. Connectionist networks are nonlinear dynamical systems, a fact that follows from several properties of connectionist architecture including the existence of intervening layers between inputs and outputs (permitting the system to go beyond linear mappings), the nonlinear threshold functions that determine how and when a single unit will fire, and the learning rules that bring about a change in the weighted connections between units. Because these networks are nonlinear systems, they can behave in unexpected ways, mimicking the U-shaped learning functions and sudden moments of "insight" that challenged old Stimulus–Response theories of learning, and helped to bring about the cognitive revolution in the 1960s (MacWhinney and Leinbach, 1991; Plunkett and Marchman, 1991a, b).

(6) *Emergent form*. Because connectionist networks are nonlinear systems, capable of unexpected forms of change, they are also capable of producing truly novel outputs (see also Elman et al., 1996; MacWhinney, 1999). In trying to achieve stability across a large number of superimposed, distributed patterns, the network may hit on a solution that was "hidden" in bits and pieces of the data; that solution may be transformed and generalized across the system as a whole, resulting in what must be viewed as a qualitative shift. This is the first precise, formal embodiment of the notion of emergent form – an idea that stood at the heart of Piaget's theory of change in cognitive systems. As such, connectionist systems may have the very property that we need to free ourselves from the nature–nurture controversy. New structures can emerge at the interface between "nature" (the initial architecture of the system) and "nurture" (the input to which that system is exposed). These new structures are not the result of black magic, or vital forces. They are the result of laws that govern the integration of information in nonlinear systems – which brings us to our final section.

4   Some Common Misconceptions about Connectionism

It is no doubt quite clear to the reader that we are enthusiastic about the Second Computer Metaphor, because we believe that it will help us to pick up a cold trail that Piaget first pioneered, moving toward a truly interactive theory of change. But we are aware of how much there is to do, and how many pitfalls lie before us. We are also aware of some of the doubts and worries about this movement that are currently in circulation. Perhaps it would be useful to end this essay with some answers to some common misconceptions about connectionism, with special reference to the application of connectionist principles within developmental psychology.

Worry # 1. "Connectionism is nothing but associationism, and we already know the limits of associationism" (e.g., Fodor and Pylyshyn, 1988). As we pointed out above, multilayer connectionist nets are nonlinear dynamical systems, whereas the familiar associationist models of the past rested on assumptions of linearity. This is both the good news, and the bad news. The good news is that nonlinear systems can learn relationships of considerable complexity, and they can produce surprising and (of course) nonlinear forms of change. The bad news is that no one really understands the limits and capabilities of nonlinear dynamical systems. Maybe this is also good news: we have finally met our goal, after years of physics envy, because we have finally reached the same frontiers of ignorance as the physicists! Presumably, the limits of these systems will someday be known (although probably not within our lifetimes). But right now, it would be grossly premature to claim that connectionist networks can "never" perform certain functions. Anyone who claims that we already know the limits of this kind of associationism has been misinformed.

Worry #2. "There are no interesting internal representations in connectionist nets" (e.g., Pinker and Prince, 1988). There are indeed complex and rich representations in connectionist networks, and transformations that do the same work as rules in classical systems. However, these rules and representations take a radically different form from the familiar symbols and algorithms of serial digital computers and/or generative linguistics. The representations and rules embodied in connectionist nets are implicit and highly distributed. Part of the challenge of modern research on neural networks is to understand exactly what a net has learned after it has reached some criterion of performance. So far, the answer appears to be that the solutions that networks find very often look quite different than their symbolic counterparts (for examples, see Elman, 1989, 1990, 1991).

Worry #3. "Connectionist nets only yield interesting performance on cognitive problems when the experiment 'sneaks in' the solution by (a) fixing the internal weights until they work, or (b) laying out the solution in the input" (e.g., Lachter and Bever, 1988). Part of the fascination of connectionist modeling lies in the fact that it offers the experimenter so many surprises. These are self-organizing systems that learn how to solve a problem. As the art is currently practiced, NO ONE fiddles with the internal weights but the system itself, in the course of learning. Indeed, in a simulation of any interesting level of complexity, it would be virtually impossible to reach a solution by "hand-tweaking" of the weights. As for the issue of "sneaking the solution into the input," we have seen several simulations in which the Experimenter did indeed try to make the input as explicit as possible – and yet the system stubbornly found a different way to solve the problem. Good connectionist modelers approach their simulations with the same spirit of discovery and breathless anticipation that is very familiar to those who carry out real experiments with real children.

Aside from being close to impossible, cheating would not be any fun at all – and the hand-crafting of solutions is usually considered a form of cheating.

Worry #4. "The supposed commitment to neural plausibility is a scam; no one really takes it seriously." Connectionists work at many different levels between brain and behavior. In current simulations of higher cognitive processes, it is true that the architecture is "brain-like" only in a very indirect sense. In fact, the typical 100-neuron connectionist toy is "brain-like" only in comparison with the serial digital computer (which is wildly unlike nervous systems of any known kind). The many qualities that separate real brains from connectionist simulations have been described in detail elsewhere (Churchland and Sejnowski, 1992; Crick, 1989; Hertz, Krogh, and Palmer, 1991). The real questions are: (a) is there anything of interest that can be learned from simulations in simplified systems, and (b) can connectionists "add in" constraints from real neural systems in a series of systematic steps, approaching something like a realistic theory of mind and brain? Of course we still do not know the answer to either of these questions, but there are many researchers in the connectionist movement who are trying to bring these systems closer to neural reality. For example, efforts are underway to study the computational properties of different neuronal types. Some researchers are exploring analogues to synaptogenesis and synaptic pruning in neural nets. Others are looking into the computational analogues of neural transmitters within a fixed network structure. The current hope is that work at all these different levels will prove to be compatible, and that a unified theory of the mind and brain will someday emerge. Of course we are a long way off, but the commitment by most of the researchers that we know in this field is a very serious one. It has launched a new spirit of interdisciplinary research in cognitive neuroscience, one with important implications for developmental psychology.

Worry #5. "Connectionism is anti-nativist, and efforts are underway to reinstate a *tabula rasa* approach to mind and development" (e.g., Kirsh, 1992; Pinker, 1999). It is true that many current simulations assume something like a *tabula rasa* in the first stages of learning (e.g. a random "seeding" of weights among fully connected units before learning begins). This has proven to be a useful simplifying assumption, in order to learn something about the amount and type of structure that has to be assumed for a given type of learning to go through. But there is no logical incompatibility between connectionism and nativism. Indeed, just as many historians have argued that Franklin Delano Roosevelt saved capitalism, connectionism may prove to be the salvation of nativist approaches to mind. The problem with current nativist theories is that they offer no serious account of what it might mean in biological terms for a given structure or idea to be innate. In neural networks, it is possible to explore various avenues for building in innate structure, including minor biases that have major structural consequences across a range of environmental conditions (Elman, 1994; Elman et al., 1996; Jacobs et al., 1991; Jacobs and Jordan, 1992; Jacobs, 1999). In fact, within connectionist models there are coherent ways to talk about 90 percent or 10 percent of any innate idea! This is an approach that has not been explored in any detail to date, but the possibilities are intriguing, and might (ironically enough) end up being connectionism's greatest contribution to developmental cognitive neuroscience.

5   Epilogue: New Directions in Developmental Connectionism

The story is far from over – so this is not a true epilogue – but since we first wrote this chapter it has become even clearer how connectionist models are offering new insights into developmental phenomena. Consider the following (by no means exhaustive) examples:

- *U-shaped curves.* In the course of learning a number of tasks, children frequently exhibit various "U-shaped" patterns of behavior in which good initial performance is followed by poorer performance, which eventually again improves. One of the best known cases of this is the acquisition of the past tense of English. Networks that are trained on similar tasks exhibit the same patterns of behavior (MacWhinney et al., 1989; Plunkett and Juola, 1999; Plunkett and Marchman, 1991a, 1991b, 1993; Rumelhart and McClelland, 1986). Furthermore, the sorts of differences in learning of regular forms (e.g., those which add "-ed") compared with irregulars ("sing"–"sang") have now been explored in network models of many other languages (e.g., German, Arabic; Hare, Elman, and Daugherty, 1995; Nakisa, Plunkett, and Hahn, in press; Plunkett and Nakissa, 1997).
- *Critical periods in brain plasticity.* Developmental changes in brain plasticity – the ability to recover from early lesions – suggest that there are "critical periods" during which the brain is more plastic and able to learn. Marchman (1993) has shown that such changes in plasticity can also arise merely as a by-product of learning itself, and do not necessarily require some kind of exogenous (learning-independent) change in the structure or function of the brain. The same changes in brain structure that occur as a result of learning may also make recovery from stroke more difficult, and make later learning harder.
- *Lesioning networks.* Networks that are trained on tasks such as reading or verb morphology demonstrate, when "lesioned," symptoms and patterns of recovery which closely resemble the patterns of human aphasics (Farah and McClelland, 1991; Hinton and Shallice, 1991; Marchman, 1993; Martin et al., 1994; Plaut and Shallice, 1993; Seidenberg and McClelland, 1989). Finally, the kinds of dissociations in behavior that may be found as a result of brain damage, in which regular forms are better preserved than irregulars (or vice versa), have been simulated by lesioning networks in which the regular/irregular distinction is not directly encoded (Juola and Plunkett, 1998; Joanisse and Seidenberg, 1999).
- *Learning rediscovered.* There have been a number of recent demonstrations of apparently precocious knowledge in young infants (e.g., very early learning of language-like patterns; object permanence). Some researchers have taken this as evidence for innate knowledge, and the existence of abstract rules and symbols. But similar results have been easily replicated in networks that are sensitive to statistical properties in their environment, suggesting that the environment is a richer source of information than might be thought, and that young infants are using a relatively simple learning algorithm to extract this information (Mareschal, Plunkett, and Harris, 1995; Munakata, McClelland, Johnson, and Siegler, 1999; Seidenberg and Elman, 1999).
- *Readiness phenomena.* Children are known to go through phases in which behavior changes slowly and is resistant to new learning. At other points in time children show heightened sensitivity to examples and rapid changes in behavior. Networks exhibit similar readiness phenomena (Elman et al., 1996, chapter 6; McClelland, 1989).
- *The importance of starting small.* Some aspects of grammatical structure are particularly hard to learn, and it has been claimed that these structures must therefore be innate. Paradoxically, these structures can be learned in networks as long as learning begins when the network has a limited working memory (similar to that of an infant or young child). This limitation turns out to be crucial for learning the more complex aspects of language.

- *Activity-dependent origins of brain structure.* Visual cortex in mammals is well known to include neurons that are selectively sensitive to highly specific visual inputs. These neurons include edge detectors, center-surround cells, and motion detectors. Biologically plausible network models have been constructed which demonstrate that such specialized response properties do not have to be prespecified. They emerge naturally and inevitably from cells which are initially uncommitted, simply as a function of a simple learning rule and exposure to stimulation (Linsker, 1986, 1990; Miller, Keller, and Stryker, 1989; Sereno and Sereno, 1991). These artificial networks even develop the characteristic zebra-like striped patterns seen in ocular dominance columns in real cortex (Miller, Keller, and Stryker, 1989).
- *Learning the categories of language.* Must children have innate knowledge of linguistic categories such as "noun" or "verb"? Or can these notions be learned? Network simulations as well as corpus analyses have shown that such categories can be learned merely from the distributional properties in the language that young children hear (Elman, 1990; Mintz, Newport, and Bever, 1995).

These examples (as well as many others described in Elman et al., 1996) lead us to believe we will soon see a revival of Piagetian theory within a connectionist framework – not a mindless reinterpretation of the old theory in modern jargon, but a return to Piaget's program of genetic epistemology, instantiating his principles of equilibration and adaptation in concrete systems that really work – and really change. As we said before, Piaget spent the later decades of his life seeking a way of formalizing the theory, to answer critics (including Piaget himself) who charged that his principles of change were much too vague. We think that Piaget would have loved these new possibilities if he had lived to see them. We now have an opportunity to pick up the threads of his old program and move it forward into an exciting new decade, incorporating all the new insights and new empirical information that has been gained in the interim, without abandoning the fundamental commitment of developmental psychology to the study of change.

NOTES

1 This particular school of Functionalism has little to do with, and is indeed diametrically opposed to, an approach within linguistics and psycholinguistics alternatively called Functional Grammar or Cognitive Linguistics. (For discussions, see Bates and MacWhinney, 1989; Givón, 1984; Lakoff, 1987; Langacker, 1987.)
2 A number of readable introductions to connectionism are now available. (See Bechtel and Abrahamsen, 1991; Churchland and Sejnowski, 1992; Dayhoff, 1990. An excellent but more technical introduction can be found in Hertz et al., 1991.)

REFERENCES

Anderson, J. A. (1972). A simple neural network generating an interactive memory. *Mathematical Bio-Sciences* 8, 137–60.

Anderson, J. A. and Rosenfeld, E. (1989). *Neurocomputing: Foundations of research.* MIT Press/ Bradford Books.

Baillargeon, R. (1999). Young infants' expectation about hidden objects: A reply to three challenges. *Developmental Science* 2, 115–32.

Baillargeon, R. and de Vos, J. (1991). Object permanence in young infants: Further evidence. *Child Development* 62, 1227–46.

Bates, E. A., Elman, J. L., Johnson, M., Karmiloff-Smith, A., Parisi, D., and Plunkett, K. (1998). Innateness and emergentism. In W. Bechtel and G. Graham (eds.), *A Companion to Cognitive Science* (pp. 590–601). Malden, MA and Oxford: Blackwell Publishers.

Bates, E. A., Thal, D., Finlay, B. L., and Clancy, B. (in press). Early language development and its neural correlates. To appear in F. Boller and J. Grafman (series eds.) and I. Rapin and S. Segalowitz (Vol. eds.), *Handbook of Neuropsychology, Vol. 7: Child Neurology* (2nd edn.). Amsterdam: Elsevier.

Bates, E. A., Thal, D., and Marchman, V. (1991). Symbols and syntax: A Darwinian approach to language development. In N. Krasnegor, D. Rumbaugh, E. Schiefelbusch, and M. Studdert-Kennedy (eds.), *The Biological and Behavioral Determinants of Language Development*. Hillsdale, NJ: Erlbaum.

Bates, E. A., Thal, D., Trauner, D., Fenson, J., Aram, D., Eisele, J., and Nass, R. (1997). From first words to grammar in children with focal brain injury. In D. Thal and J. Reilly (eds.), Special issue on Origins of Communication Disorders. *Developmental Neuropsychology* 13, 275–343.

Bechtel, W. and Abrahamsen, A. (1991). *Connectionism and the Mind*. Oxford: Basil Blackwell.

Bruner, J. S. and Sherwood, V. (1976). Peekaboo and the learning of rule structures. In J. S. Bruner, A. Jolly, and K. Sylva (eds.), *Play: Its role in development and evolution*. New York: Basic Books, Inc.

Churchland, P. and Sejnowsky, T. (1992). *The Net Effect*. Cambridge, MA: MIT Press/ Bradford Books.

Clancy, B., Darlington, R. B., and Finlay, B. L. (2000). The course of human events: Predicting the timing of primate neural development. *Developmental Science* 3, 57–66.

Crick, F. (1989). The recent excitement about neural networks. *Nature* 337, 129–32.

Dayhoff, J. (1990). *Neural Network Architectures*. New York: Van Nostrand Reinhold.

Eccles, J. L. (1953). *The Neurophysiological Basis of Mind*. Oxford: Clarendon.

Elman, J. L. (1989). Structured representations and connectionist models. In *The Eleventh Annual Conference of the Cognitive Science Society*. Hillsdale, NJ: Erlbaum.

Elman, J. L. (1990). Finding structure in time. *Cognitive Science* 14, 179–211.

Elman, J. L. (1991). Distributed representations, simple recurrent networks, and grammatical structure. *Machine Learning* 7, 195–225.

Elman, J. L. (1993). Learning and development in neural networks: The importance of starting small. *Cognition* 48, 71–99.

Elman, J. L., Bates, E. A., Johnson, M. H., Karmiloff-Smith, A., Parisi, D., and Plunkett, K. (1996). *Rethinking Innateness: A connectionist perspective on development*. Cambridge, MA: MIT Press/Bradford Books.

Farah, M. J. and McClelland, J. (1991). A computational model of semantic memory impairment: Modality specificity and emergent category specificity. *Journal of Experimental Psychology: General* 120, 339–57.

Feldman, J. A. and Ballard, D. H. (1980). *Computing with Connections*. TR 72. University of Rochester: Computer Science Department.

Ferguson, C. and Snow, C. (1978). *Talking to Children*. Cambridge: Cambridge University Press.

Fodor, J. A. (1981) *Representations*. Brighton: Harvester Press.

Fodor, J. A. and Pylyshyn, Z. W. (1988). Connectionism and cognitive architecture: A critical analysis. In S. Pinker and J. Mehler (eds.), *Connections and Symbols* (pp. 3–71). Cambridge, MA: MIT Press/Bradford Books.

Givón, T. (1984). *Syntax: A functional-typological introduction. Volume I*. Amsterdam: John Benjamins.

Golden, R. (1996). *Mathematical Models for Neural Network Analysis and Design*. Cambridge, MA: MIT Press.

Grossberg, S. (1968). Some physiological and biochemical consequences of psychological postulates. *Proceedings of the National Academy of Science, USA* 60, 758–65.

Grossberg, S. (1972). Neural expectation: Cerebellar and retinal analogs of cells fired by learnable or unlearned pattern classes. *Kybernetik* 10, 49–57.

Grossberg, S. (1987). *The Adaptive Brain*, 2 vols. Amsterdam: Elsevier.

Hare, M., Elman, J. L., and Daugherty, K. G. (1995). Default generalization in connectionist networks. *Language and Cognitive Processes* 10, 601–30.

Hebb, D. (1949). *The Organization of Behavior*. New York: Wiley.

Hertz, J., Krogh, A., and Palmer, R. (1991). *Introduction to the Theory of Neural Computation*. Redwood City, California: Addison Wesley.

Hinton, G. E. and Shallice, T. (1991). Lesioning a connectionist network: Investigations of acquired dyslexia. *Psychological Review* 98, 74–95.

Hinton, G. E. and Anderson, J. A. (1981). *Parallel Models of Associative Memory*. Hillsdale, NJ: Erlbaum.

Hornik, K., Stinchcombe, M., and White, H. (1989). Multilayer feedforward networks are universal approximators. *Neural Networks* 2, 359–66.

Hyams, N. (1986). *Language Acquisition and the Theory of Parameters*. Dordrecht and Boston: Reidel.

Jacobs, R., Jordan, M., and Barto, A. (1991). Task decomposition through competition in a modular connectionist architecture: The what and where visual tasks. *Cognitive Science* 15, 219–50.

Jacobs, R. and Jordan, M., (1992). Computational consequences of a bias toward short connections. *Journal of Cognitive Neuroscience* 4, 323–36.

Joanisse, M. F. and Seidenberg, M. S. (1999). Impairments in verb morphology after brain injury: A connectionist model. *Proceedings of the National Academy of Sciences of the United States of America* 96, 7592–7.

Johnson, M. H. (1997). *Developmental Cognitive Neuroscience: An introduction*. Cambridge, MA: Blackwell Publishers.

Juola, P. and Plunkett, K. (1998). Why double dissociations don't mean much. In Morton Ann Gernsbacher and Sharon J. Derry (eds.), *Proceedings of the Twentieth Annual Conference of the Cognitive Science Society* (pp. 561 6). Mahwah, NJ: Erlbaum.

Kellman, P. J., Spelke, E. S., and Short, K. R. (1986). Infant perception of object unity from translatory motion in depth and vertical translation. *Child Development* 57, 72–86.

Kirsh, D. (1992). PDP Learnability and innate knowledge of language. *Center for Research in Language Newsletter*, Vol. 6, no. 3. University of California, San Diego.

Kohonen, T. (1977). *Associative Memory: A system-theoretical approach*. Berlin: Springer.

Lachter, J. and Bever, T. G. (1988). The relation between linguistic structure and associative theories of language learning: A constructive critique of some connectionist learning models. In S. Pinker and J. Mehler (eds.), *Connections and Symbols* (pp. 3–71). Cambridge, MA: MIT Press/Bradford Books.

Lakoff, G. (1987). *Fire, Women, and Dangerous Things: What categories reveal about the mind*. Chicago: University of Chicago Press.

Langacker, R. (1987). *Foundations of Cognitive Grammar: Theoretical perspectives. Volume I*. Stanford: Stanford University Press.

Le Cun, Y. (1985). Une procédure d'apprentissage pour réseau à seuil assymétrique. In *Cognitiva 85: à la Frontière de l'Intelligence Artificielle des Sciences de la Connaissance des Neurosciences* (Paris 1985), 599–604.

Lightfoot, D. (1991). The child's trigger experience – Degree-0 learnability. *Behavioral Brain Sciences*, 14(2).

Linsker, R. (1986). From basic network principles to neural architecture (series). *Proceedings of the National Academy of Sciences, USA 83*, 7508–12, 8390–4, 8779–83.

Linsker, R. (1990). Perceptual neural organization: Some approaches based on network models and information theory. *Annual Review of Neuroscience* 13, 257–81.

MacWhinney, B., Leinbach, J., Taraban, R., and McDonald, J. (1989). Language learning: Cues or rules? *Journal of Memory and Language* 28, 255–77.

MacWhinney, B. (1991). Implementations are not conceptualizations: Revising the verb-learning model. *Cognition* 40, 121–57.

MacWhinney, B. (ed.) (1999). *The Emergence of Language*. Mahwah, NJ: Lawrence Erlbaum.

Mareschal, D., Plunkett, K., and Harris, P. (1995). Developing object permanence: A connectionist model. In J. D. Moore and J. F. Lehman (eds.), *Proceedings of the Seventeenth Annual Conference of the Cognitive Science Society* (170–5). Mahwah, NJ: Erlbaum.

Marchman, V. A. (1993). Constraints on plasticity in a connectionist model of the English past tense. *Journal of Cognitive Neuroscience* 5, 215–34.

Martin, N., Dell, G. S., Saffran, E. M., and Schwartz, M. F. (1994). Origins of paraphasias in deep dysphasia: Testing the consequences of a decay impairment to an interactive spreading activation model of lexical retrieval. *Brain and Language* 47(1), 52–88.

McClelland, J. L. (1989). Parallel distributed processing: Implications for cognition and development. In R. G. M. Morris (ed.), *Parallel Distributed Processing: Implications for Psychology and Neurobiology* (pp. 9–45). Oxford: Clarendon Press.

McClelland, J. and Rumelhart, D. (1986). *Parallel Distributed Processing: Explorations in the microstructure of cognition, Vol. 2*. Cambridge, MA: MIT Press/Bradford Books.

McCulloch, W. and Pitts, W. (1943). A logical calculus of ideas immanent in nervous activity. *Bulletin of Mathematical Biophysics* 5, 115–33. Reprinted in J. Anderson and E. Rosenfeld (eds.), *Neurocomputing: Foundations of research*. Cambridge, MA: MIT Press.

Mead, C. (1989). Analog VLSI and neural systems. Inaugural address presented to the Institute for Neural Computation, October 1989. University of California, San Diego.

Miller, K. D., Keller, J. B., and Stryker, M. P. (1989). Ocular dominance column development: Analysis and simulation. *Science* 245, 605–15.

Minsky, M. (1956). Some universal elements for finite automata. In C. E. Shannon and J. McCarthy (eds.), *Automata Studies* (pp. 117–28.). Princeton: Princeton University Press.

Minsky, M. and Papert, S. (1969). *Perceptrons*. Cambridge, MA: MIT Press.

Mintz, T. H., Newport, E. L., and Bever, T. G. (1995). Distributional regularities of form class in speech to young children. In Jill Beckman (ed.), Proceedings of the 25th annual meeting of the North Eastern Linguistics Society. Amherst, MA: GLSA.

Munakata, Y., McClelland, J. L., Johnson, M. H., and Siegler, R. S. (1999). Rethinking infant knowledge: Toward an adaptive process account of successes and failures in object permanence tasks. *Psychological Review* 4, 686–713s.

Nakisa, R., Plunkett, K., and Hahn, U. (in press). A cross-linguistic comparison of single and dual-route models of inflectional morphology. In P. Broeder and J. Murre (eds.), *Cognitive Models of Language Acquisition*. Cambridge, MA: MIT Press.

Papert, S. (1988). One AI or Many? *Daedalus: Artificial Intelligence*. Winter 1988.

Piaget, J. (1952). *The Origins of Intelligence in Children*. New York: International Universities Press.

Piaget, J. (1970a). *Structuralism*. New York: Basic Books.

Piaget, J. (1970b). *Genetic Epistemology*. New York: Columbia University Press.

Piaget, J. (1971). *Biology and Knowledge: An essay on the relations between organic regulations and cognitive processes*. Chicago: University of Chicago Press.

Piatelli-Palmarini, M. (1989). Evolution, selection, and cognition: From "learning" to parameter setting in biology and the study of language. *Cognition* 31, 1–44.

Pinker, S. (1999). *Words and Rules: The ingredients of language*. New York: Basic Books.

Pinker, S. and Prince, A. (1988). On language and connectionism: Analysis of a parallel distributed processing model of language acquisition. In S. Pinker and J. Mehler (eds.), *Connections and Symbols* (pp. 3–71). Cambridge, MA: MIT Press/Bradford Books.

Plaut, D. C. and Shallice, T. (1993). Deep dyslexia: A case study of connectionist neuropsychology. *Cognitive Neuropsychology* 10(5), 377–500.

Plunkett, K. and Elman J. L. (1997). *Exercises in Rethinking Innateness: A handbook for connectionist simulations*. Cambridge, MA: MIT Press.

Plunkett, K. and Juola, P. (1999). A connectionist model of English past tense and plural morphology. *Cognitive Science* 23, 463–90.

Plunkett, K. and Marchman, V. (1991a). U-shaped learning and frequency effects in a multi-layered perceptron: implications for child language acquisition. *Cognition* 38, 43–102.

Plunkett, K. and Marchman, V. (1991b). From rote learning to system building. (Technical Report 9020). Center for Research in Language, University of California, San Diego.

Plunkett, K. and Nakisa, R. C. (1997). A connectionist model of the Arabic plural system. *Language and Cognitive Processes* 12, 807–36.

Roeper, T. and Williams, E., eds. (1987). *Parameter Setting*. Dordrecht and Boston: Reidel.

Rogoff, B. (1990). *Apprenticeship in Thinking: Cognitive development in social context*. New York: Oxford University Press.

Rosenblatt, F. (1958). The Perceptron: a probabilistic model for information storage and organization in the brain. *Psychological Review* 65, 386–408.

Rosenblatt, F. (1962). *Principles of Neurodynamics*. New York: Spartan.

Rumelhart, D., Hinton, G., and Williams, R. (1986a). Learning representations by back-propagating errors. *Nature* 323, 533–6.

Rumelhart, D., McClelland, J., and the PDP Research Group (1986b). *Parallel Distributed Processing: Explorations in the microstructure of cognition, Vol. 1*. Cambridge, MA: MIT/Bradford Books.

Schwartz, M. F., Saffran, E. M., and Dell, G. S. (1990). Comparing speech error patterns in normals and jargon aphasics: Methodological issues and theoretical implications. Presented to the Academy of Aphasia, Baltimore, MD.

Seidenberg, M. S. and Elman, J. L. (1999). Do infants learn grammar with algebra or statistics? *Science* 284, 434–5.

Seidenberg, M. S. and McClelland, J. L. (1989). A distributed developmental model of visual word recognition and naming. *Psychological Review* 96, 523–68.

Selfridge, O. G. (1958). Pandemonium: A paradigm for learning. In *Mechanisation of Thought Processes: Proceedings of a Symposium Held at the National Physical Laboratory, November 1958*. London: HMSO, pp. 513–26.

Sereno, M. I. and Sereno, M. E. (1991). Learning to see rotation and dilation with a Hebb rule. In R. P. Lippman, J. Moody, and D. S. Touretzky (eds.), *Advances in Neural Information-Processing Systems 3* (pp. 320–6). San Mateo, CA: Morgan Kaufman.

Spelke, E. (1990). Principles of object perception. *Cognitive Science* 14, 29–56.

Spelke, E. (1991). Physical knowledge in infancy: Reflections on Piaget's theory. In S. Carey and R. Gelman (eds.), *The Epigenesis of Mind: Essays on biology and cognition* (pp. 133–69). Hillsdale, NJ: Erlbaum.

Spelke, E. S. and Newport, E. L. (1998). Nativism, empiricism, and the development of knowledge. In W. Damon (series ed.) and D. Kuhn and R. Siegler (Vol. eds.), *Handbook of Child Psychology: Vol. 1. Theoretical models of human development* (5th edn., pp. 275–340). New York: Wiley.

Thal, D., Marchman, V., Stiles, J., Aram, D., Trauner, D., Nass, R., and Bates, E. E. (1991). Early lexical development in children with focal brain injury. *Brain and Language* 40, 491–527.

Von Neumann, J. (1951). The general and logical theory of automata. In L. A. Jeffress (ed.), *Cerebral Mechanisms in Behavior*. New York: Wiley.

Von Neumann, J. (1958). *The Computer and the Brain*. New Haven: Yale University Press.

Werner, H. (1948). *Comparative Psychology of Mental Development*. New York: International Universities Press.

Willshaw, D. J., Buneman, O. P., and Longuet-Higgins, H. C. (1969). Nonholographic associative memory. *Nature* 222, 960–2.

Zipser, D. and Andersen, R. A. (1988). A back-propagation programmed network that simulates response properties of a subset of posterior parietal neurons. *Nature* 331, 679–84.

22

A Model System for Studying the Role of Dopamine in Prefrontal Cortex During Early Development in Humans

Adele Diamond

Dorsolateral prefrontal cortex (DL-PFC) undergoes an extremely protracted period of maturation and is not fully mature until adulthood (Yakovlev and Lecours, 1967; Huttenlocher, 1979, 1984, 1990; Orzhekhovskaya, 1981; Huttenlocher et al., 1982; Thatcher et al., 1987; Rosenberg and Lewis, 1994; Sowell et al., 1999). Growing evidence indicates, however, that some of the cognitive advances seen as early as the first year of life (6–12 months) are made possible, in part, by early changes in DL-PFC (e.g., Fox and Bell, 1990; Diamond, 1991a, b; Bell and Fox, 1992, 1997). One maturational change in DL-PFC that might help make possible these early cognitive advances is increasing levels of the neurotransmitter, dopamine, in DL-PFC.

Prefrontal cortex is richer in dopamine than any other region of the cerebral cortex (e.g., Bjorklund et al., 1978; Brown et al., 1979; Levitt et al., 1984; Lewis et al., 1988; Gaspar et al., 1989; Williams and Goldman-Rakic, 1993, 1995; Lewis et al., 1998). Not surprisingly, given its high concentration in prefrontal cortex, dopamine plays an important role in DL-PFC function in adult human and non-human primates (e.g., Brozoski et al., 1979; Sawaguchi et al., 1988; Sawaguchi and Goldman-Rakic, 1991; Luciana et al., 1992; Watanabe et al., 1997; Akil et al., 1999).

We know that during the period that infant rhesus macaques are improving on tasks dependent on DL-PFC (the A-not-B, delayed response, and object retrieval tasks) the level of dopamine is increasing in their brain (Brown et al., 1976; Brown and Goldman, 1977), the density of dopamine receptors in their prefrontal cortex is increasing (Lidow and Rakic, 1992), and the distribution within their DL-PFC (Brodmann's area 9) of axons containing the rate-limiting enzyme for the production of dopamine (tyrosine hydroxylase) is markedly changing (Lewis and Harris, 1991; Rosenberg and Lewis, 1995). Moreover, in adult rhesus macaques, the cognitive abilities that depend on DL-PFC (as indexed by tasks such as delayed response) rely critically on the dopaminergic projection to prefrontal cortex (e.g., Brozoski et al., 1979; Sawaguchi et al., 1990; Taylor et al., 1990; Taylor et al., 1990; Sawaguchi and Goldman-Rakic, 1991).

Evidence such as that summarized here makes it plausible that one change in the prefrontal neural circuit helping to make possible some of the cognitive advances that occur in infants between 6–12 months of age might be changes in the dopaminergic innervation of prefrontal cortex. Maturational changes in the prefrontal dopamine system are protracted, and therefore it is conceivable that later maturational changes in that system might help make possible subsequent improvements in the cognitive abilities dependent on prefrontal cortex as well. (To propose that changes in the dopamine innervation of prefrontal cortex play a role in making possible some of the cognitive advances during development is not to negate the role of experience nor the role of other maturational changes in the prefrontal neural system, such as in the communication between prefrontal cortex and other neural regions.)

To begin to look at the role of the dopamine projection to DL-PFC in helping to subserve cognitive functions early in life in humans, we have been studying children who, the evidence suggests, have reduced levels of dopamine in prefrontal cortex but otherwise remarkably normal brains. These are children treated early and continuously for a genetic disorder called "phenylketonuria" (PKU), who have levels of an amino acid (phenylalanine [Phe]) in their bloodstream that are 3–5 times normal (6–10 mg/dl).

Where is DL-PFC?

The cerebral cortex is distinguished from subcortex by generally having six different layers of cells (subcortical regions have fewer layers) and by being the outer mantle of the brain (closer to the surface), whereas subcortical structures are buried deep inside the brain below the cortex. In general, cortical regions are phylogenetically newer regions of the brain than subcortical regions, mature later during development, and receive more highly processed information that has already passed through subcortical structures. During primate evolution, the cerebral cortex changed from being smooth to having marked "hills" (called "gyri") and "valleys" (called "sulci"). This infolding made possible the extraordinary expansion in size of the cerebral cortex within a cranium that expanded much less markedly in size. This was a very adaptive solution to getting much more surface area into a limited space.

The central sulcus divides the front of the brain from the back. All of the cerebral cortex in front of the central sulcus is frontal cortex (see figure 22.1). The most posterior region of frontal cortex, directly in front of the central sulcus, is primary motor cortex (Brodmann's area 4). The anterior boundary of motor cortex is the precentral sulcus. In front of that is premotor cortex and the supplementary motor area (SMA), two distinct subregions of Broadmann's area 6. All of the cortex in front of that is prefrontal cortex (areas 8, 9, 10, 12, 44, 45, 46, 47, and 9/46). Prefrontal cortex is not only the most anterior region of frontal cortex, but the only region of frontal cortex with a granule cell layer.

While the brain as a whole has increased in size during evolution, the proportion of the brain devoted to prefrontal cortex has increased much more dramatically, especially in humans (Brodmann, 1912). For example, prefrontal cortex makes up 25 percent of the cortex in the human brain, but only 15 percent in chimpanzees, 7 percent in dogs, and 4 percent in cats. Prefrontal cortex is an association area; its functions are primarily integrative, neither exclusively sensory nor motor. In accord with its late maturational timetable and massive expansion during primate evolution, prefrontal cortex is credited with underlying the most sophisticated cognitive abilities, often called "executive processes," such as reasoning, planning, problem-solving, and coordinating the performance of multiple tasks (e.g., Warren and Akert, 1964; Goldman-Rakic, 1987; Shallice, 1988; Pennington and Ozonoff, 1996; Postle et al., 1999).

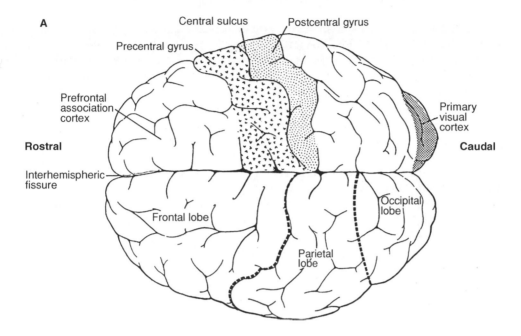

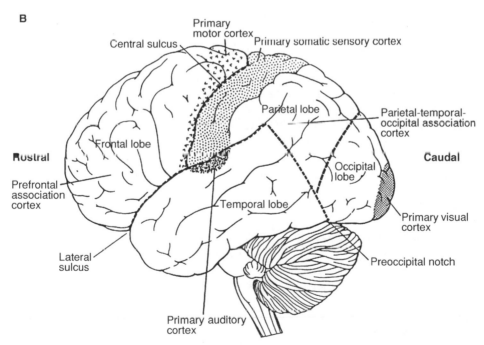

Figure 22.1 Diagram of the human brain, indicating the location of dorsolateral prefrontal cortex.

Within prefrontal cortex, the mid-dorsolateral subregion (areas 9, 46, and 9/46) has increased disproportionately in size during evolution even compared to the other regions of prefrontal cortex. Mid-DL-PFC consists of the middle section of the superior and middle frontal gyri, extending from behind the frontal pole (area 10) to area 8 (see figure 22.1; Petrides and Pandya, 1999). DL-PFC has historically been defined by its reciprocal connections with the parvocellular subdivision of the mediodorsal nucleus of the thalamus (Walker, 1940; Rose and Woolsey, 1948; McLardy, 1950; Akert, 1964; Kievit and Kuypers, 1977; Tobias, 1975; Jacobson et al., 1978; Goldman-Rakic and Porrino, 1985; Siwek and Pandya, 1991). The size of the parvocellular portion of the mediodorsal nucleus has increased phylogenetically in proportion to the increase in size of DL-PFC and disproportionately compared even to other regions of the mediodorsal nucleus (Pines, 1927; Clark, 1930; Khokhryakova, 1979).

No area of the brain acts in isolation. A neural region functions as part of a system of functionally and anatomically interrelated structures. Through its reciprocal connections with the *superior temporal cortex* (Petrides and Pandya, 1988; Seltzer and Pandya, 1989), *posterior parietal cortex* (area 7a; Goldman-Rakic and Schwartz, 1982; Schwartz and Goldman-Rakic, 1984; Petrides and Pandya, 1984; Selemon and Goldman-Rakic, 1988; Cavada and Goldman-Rakic, 1989; Johnson et al., 1989), *anterior and posterior cingulate* (Vogt et al., 1987), premotor cortex (Künzle, 1978; Barbas and Mesulam, 1985, 1987), SMA (Wiesendanger, 1981; McGuire et al., 1991), *retrosplenial cortex* (Morris et al., 1999; Morris et al., 1999; see also Petrides and Pandya, 1999, concerning all of these interconnections), and the *neocerebellum* (Sasaki et al., 1979; Leiner et al., 1989; Yamamoto et al., 1992; Middleton and Strick, 1994; Middleton and Strick, 1997; Schmahmann and Pandya, 1995; Diamond, 2000), mid-DL-PFC can modulate the activity of those regions, as well as receive information from, and be modulated by, these regions. In addition, mid-DL-PFC sends a strong projection to the caudate nucleus (Kemp and Powell, 1970; Goldman and Nauta, 1977; Selemon and Goldman-Rakic, 1985; Arikuni and Kubota, 1986). The projections from DL-PFC, posterior parietal cortex, and the superior temporal cortex are intricately interdigitated throughout the brain, including in the caudate nucleus, providing multiple opportunities for these neural regions to communicate with, and influence, one another (Goldman-Rakic and Schwartz, 1982; Schwartz and Goldman-Rakic, 1984; Selemon and Goldman-Rakic, 1985, 1988; Johnson et al., 1989).

Evidence that DL-PFC subserves Cognitive Abilities even during Infancy

The "A-not-B" task has been used in scores of laboratories throughout the world to study cognitive development in infants since it was first introduced by Piaget (1954 [1936]). Under the name "delayed response," an almost-identical task has been the classic paradigm for studying the functions of DL-PFC in macaques since it was first introduced for that purpose by Jacobsen (1935, 1936). In the A-not-B/delayed response task, the participant watches as a desired object is hidden in one of two hiding places that differ only in their left–right location, and then a few seconds later is allowed to reach to find that object. The participant must hold in mind over those few seconds where the object was hidden. Over trials, the participant must update his or her mental record to reflect where the reward was hidden last. When the participant reaches correctly, he or she is rewarded by being allowed to retrieve the desired object. In this manner, the behavior of reaching to that hiding location is reinforced and hence the tendency to emit that response is strengthened. When the reward is then hidden at the other location, the participant must inhibit the natural tendency to repeat the rewarded response and instead respond according to the representation held in mind of where the reward was just hidden. Thus, the A–not-B task requires holding information in mind (where the reward was last hidden) and inhibition of a prepotent response tendency. By roughly $7\frac{1}{2}$–8 months of age, infants reach correctly to the first hiding location with delays as long as 3 sec. When the reward is then hidden at the other hiding place, however, infants err by going back to the first location (called the "A–not-B error"). As infants get older, they are able to succeed at longer and longer delays. Thus, for example, one sees the A–not-B error (correct at the first location, but incorrectly repeating that response on the reversal trials) at delays of 5 sec in infants of 9 months and at delays of 7–8 sec in infants of 10 months (Diamond, 1985; Diamond and Doar, 1989).

In the object retrieval task (Diamond, 1981, 1988, 1990a), nothing is hidden and there is no delay. A toy is placed within easy reach in a small, clear box, open on one side. Difficulties arise when the infant sees the toy through one of the closed sides of the box. Here, the infant must integrate seeing the toy through one side of the box with reaching through a different side. There is a strong pull to try to reach straight for the toy; that prepotent response must be inhibited when a detour reach is required. The following variables are manipulated: (a) which side of the box is open (top, front, left, or right), (b) distance of the toy from the box opening, (c) position of the box on the testing surface (e.g., near the front edge of table or far), (d) box size, and (e) box transparency. The experimental variables jointly determine through which side of the box the toy is seen. Initially, infants reach only at the side through which they are looking. They must look through the opening, and continue to do so to reach in and retrieve the toy. As they get older, the memory of having looked through the opening is enough; infants can look through the opening, sit up, and reach in while looking through a closed side. Still older infants do not need to look along the line of reach at all. Infants progress through a well-demarcated series of 5 stages of performance on this task between 6 and 12 months of age (e.g., Diamond, 1981, 1988, 1990a).

Although the A–not-B/delayed response task and the object retrieval task appear to share few surface similarities, human infants improve on these tasks during the same age period (6–12 months; Diamond, 1988, 1991a, b) and so do infant rhesus macaque ($1\frac{1}{2}$–4 months; Diamond and Goldman-Rakic, 1986; Diamond, 1988, 1991a, b). Indeed, although there is considerable individual variation in the rate at which different infants improve on any of these tasks, the age at which a given infant reaches "Phase 1B" on the object retrieval task is remarkably close to the age at which that same infant can first uncover a hidden object in the A–not-B/delayed response paradigm (Diamond, 1991a, b). Developmental improvements on both in human infants are related to the same changes in the EEG pattern over frontal leads and in frontal-parietal EEG coherence (*re: A–not-B*: Fox and Bell, 1990; Bell and Fox, 1992, 1997; *re: object retrieval*: Fox, personal communication) Both the A–not-B/delayed response task and the object retrieval task depend on DL-PFC and are sensitive to the level of dopamine there.

There is no behavioral task more firmly linked to DL-PFC than the A–not-B/delayed response task. Lesions that destroy DL-PFC disrupt performance of A–not-B and delayed response in adult macaques (e.g., Butters et al., 1969; Goldman and Rosvold, 1970; Diamond and Goldman-Rakic, 1989) and infant macaques (Goldman et al., 1970; Diamond

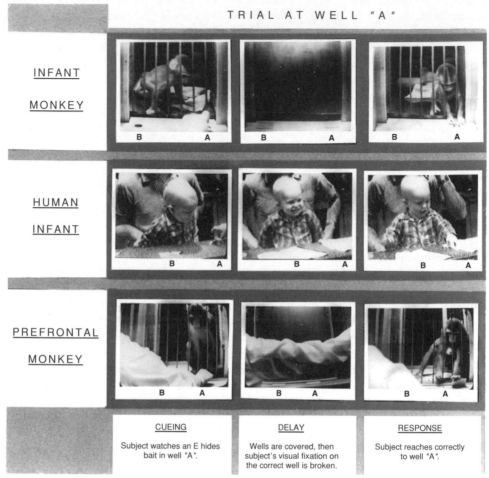

Figure 22.2 Illustration of a 1½-month-old infant rhesus macaque, 8-month-old human infant, and an adult rhesus macaque in whom dorsolateral prefrontal cortex had been removed bilaterally performing the A-not-B/delayed response task. All are correct at the first hiding place (A). After 2 trials, there is a switch and the reward is hidden at the second hiding place (B). Although they all watch the hiding at B, and although the delay at B is no longer than at A, they all err by reaching back to A. This error is called the "A-not-B error" because they are correct on the A trials, but not on the B trials; they reach to A, not B.

(B)

TRIAL AT WELL "B"

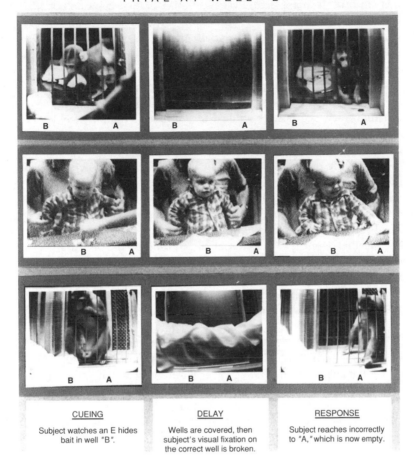

CUEING	DELAY	RESPONSE
Subject watches an E hides bait in well "B".	Wells are covered, then subject's visual fixation on the correct well is broken.	Subject reaches incorrectly to "A," which is now empty.

and Goldman-Rakic, 1986; Diamond, 1990b), while performance of other tasks such as delayed nonmatching to sample (Bachevalier and Mishkin, 1986) and visual discrimination (Goldman et al., 1970) is unimpaired. Lesions of other brain regions do not affect A-not-B or delayed response performance at the same brief delays (e.g., medial temporal lobe [Diamond et al., 1989]; posterior parietal cortex [Harlow et al., 1952; Diamond and Goldman-Rakic, 1989; Bauer and Fuster, 1976]). Successful delayed response performance has been linked to dorsolateral PFC by techniques as varied as *reversible cooling* (where function is only temporarily disrupted, and an animal can serve as his own control; e.g., Fuster and Alexander, 1970; Bauer and Fuster, 1976), *single unit recording* (where the functions of individual neurons are studied in the intact brain; e.g., Niki, 1974; Fuster and Alexander, 1971; Fuster, 1973), and *2-deoxyglucose metabolic labeling* (where the functions of diverse neural regions are studied in the intact brain; Bugbee and Goldman-Rakic, 1981). Blocking dopamine receptors in DL-PFC produces deficits on the delayed response task as severe as when DL-PFC is removed altogether (Brozoski et al., 1979). Indeed, there is a precise dose-dependent relation between how large a dose of the dopamine antagonist is injected and performance on the delayed response task (Sawaguchi and Goldman-Rakic, 1991). Disruption of the prefrontal dopamine system by injections of MPTP (1-methyl-4-phenyl-1,2,3,6-tetrahydropy-ridine) also impairs performance on the task (Schneider and Kovelowski, 1990). Destruction of the dopamine neurons in the ventral tegmental area (VTA) that project to prefrontal cortex impairs performance on the task as well (Simon et al., 1980). Pharmacological activation of D2 dopamine receptors in normal human adults has been found to facilitate performance on the task (Luciana et al., 1992).

DL-PFC lesions in the macaque also disrupt performance on the object retrieval task (Diamond and Goldman-Rakic, 1985; Diamond, 1990b), while lesions of the medial temporal lobe (Diamond et al., 1989) or of posterior parietal cortex (Diamond and Goldman-Rakic, 1989) do not. MPTP injections, which reduce the level of dopamine in prefrontal cortex, also produce deficits on the task (e.g., Saint-Cyr et al., 1988; Taylor et al., 1990a, b; Schneider and Roeltgen, 1993). (MPTP also affects the level of dopamine in the striatum, but lesions of the striatum do not impair performance on the object retrieval task [Crofts et al., 1999].) Cumulative doses of 15–75 mg of MPTP do not produce Parkinso-nian-type motor deficits in rhesus macaques, although larger doses do. At the lower doses of MPTP [15–75 mg], monkeys are impaired on the object retrieval and A-not-B/delayed response tasks [e.g., Schneider and Kovelowski, 1990; Taylor et al., 1990], although they perform normally on other tasks such as visual discrimination.)

Importantly, human infants, infant rhesus macaques, and infant and adult rhesus macaques with lesions of DL-PFC fail the A-not-B/delayed response task under the same conditions and in the same ways. The same is true for the object retrieval task. Thus, for example, on A-not-B: macaques with lesions of DL-PFC and human infants of $7\frac{1}{2} - 9$ months succeed when there is no delay (*macaques*: Harlow et al., 1952; Bättig et al., 1960; Goldman et al., 1970; *infants*: Harris, 1973; Gratch et al., 1974), succeed when allowed to circumvent the memory requirements by continuing to stare at or strain toward the correct well during the delay (*macaques*: Bättig et al., 1960; Miles and Blomquist, 1960; Pinsker and French, 1967; *infants*: Cornell, 1979; Fox et al., 1979), succeed if a landmark reliably indicates where the reward is located (*macaques*: Pohl, 1973; *infants*: Butterworth et al., 1982), fail even at brief delays of only 2–5 sec (*macaques*: Goldman and Rosvold, 1970; Diamond and Goldman-Rakic, 1989; *infants*: Gratch and Landers, 1971; Fox et al., 1979; Diamond, 1985; Diamond and Doar, 1989) and fail if the hiding places differ either in left–

right or up–down location (*macaques*: Goldman et al., 1970; Fuster, 1980; *infants*: Gratch and Landers, 1971; Butterworth, 1976). See figure 22.2.

Similar close parallels in the parameters determining success or failure, and in the characteristics of performance, hold for the object retrieval task (*infants*: Diamond, 1981; 1990b, 1991a; *macaques with lesions of DL-PFC*: Diamond and Goldman-Rakic, 1985; Diamond, 1990b; 1991a; *MPTP-treated macaques*: Saint-Cyr et al., 1988; Taylor et al., 1990a, b; Schneider and Roeltgen, 1993). Human infants of $7\frac{1}{2}$–9 months, rhesus macaques with lesions of DL-PFC, and macaques treated with MPTP all succeed on the object retrieval task when they are looking through the open side of the box. They fail when they are looking through a closed side, and they fail by trying to reach straight through the transparent barrier instead of detouring around it. Human infants of $7\frac{1}{2}$–9 months, rhesus macaques with lesions of DL-PFC, and macaques treated with MPTP perform better when the box is opaque than when the box is transparent. They lean over to look in the box opening when the left or right side of the box is open and recruit the contralateral hand to reach in the opening (see figure 22.3), and show that "awkward reach" on both the left and right sides of the box.

The Cognitive Abilities Subserved by DL-PFC and Required for Success on the A–not–B and Object Retrieval Tasks

Note that many of the manipulations discussed above for the A–not–B task indicate that the presence of the delay is critical, since even very young infants and prefrontally-lesioned macaques perform well when there is no delay or when the requirements of the delay can be circumvented. This suggests that the ability to hold in mind the information on where the reward was last hidden (this might be termed "sustained attention" or the information-maintenance component of "working memory" [Baddeley, 1992]) is critical to success on this task. The information that must be held in mind is relational (Was the reward hidden on the right or the left most recently? "Left" is only left in relation to right and, similarly, "recent" implies a before and after relation.) There is also a characteristic pattern to the errors made by infants and by prefrontally-lesioned macaques on the A–not–B task: Their errors tend to be confined to the reversal trials and to the trials immediately following a reversal error when the reward continues to be hidden at the new location (Diamond, 1985, 1990a, 1991a, b). If the only source of error on the task were failure to keep the critical information in mind, then one would expect errors to be random, but they are not (Diamond et al., 1994a). The non-random pattern of errors, and the fact that participants occasionally look at the correct location (as if they remember that the reward is there) while at the same time reaching back to the previously correct location (Diamond, 1990a, 1991a; see also Hofstadter and Reznick, 1996) suggests that success on the task also requires resisting, or inhibiting, the tendency to repeat the previous response. (I have suggested that there is a predisposition to repeat the previous response because it had been rewarded. Smith et al. (1999) suggest that there is a predisposition to repeat the previous response simply because the response was made before [not because of reinforcement], just as it is easier for neurons in visual cortex to process a visual stimulus if they have previously processed that visual stimulus. Either account of the source of the predisposition works equally well for my theoretical position. The important point is that there is a tendency to repeat the previous response; the source of that predisposition is unimportant for my argument.)

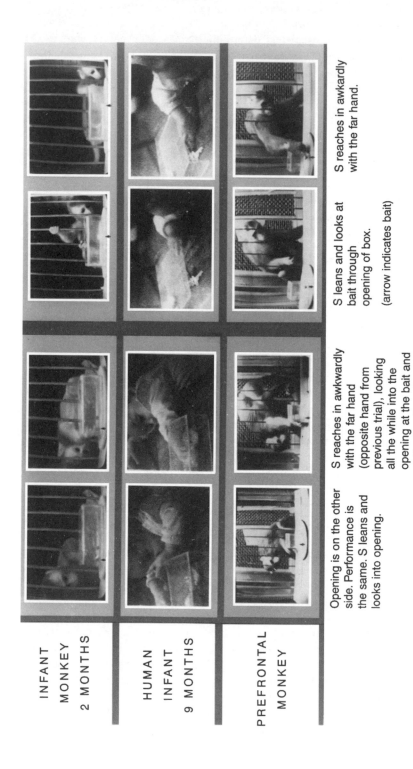

Figure 22.3 Illustration of a 2-month-old infant rhesus macaque, 9-month-old human infant, and an adult rhesus macaque in whom dorsolateral prefrontal cortex had been removed bilaterally performing the object retrieval task. They lean and look in the side opening of the transparent box, and then while continuing to look through the opening, recruit the contralateral hand to reach in and retrieve the reward. This is seen on both sides of the box and does not reflect a hand preference. Because of its appearance, the recruitment of the contralateral arm is dubbed the "awkward reach."

A few errors can be elicited simply by taxing how long information must be held in mind even when no inhibition is required, such as by using a long delay at the first hiding location (e.g., Sophian and Wellman, 1983). Similarly, a few errors can be elicited simply by taxing inhibitory control even when the participant does not have to remember where the reward was hidden; for example, a few infants err on the reversal trial even when the covers are transparent (e.g., Butterworth, 1977; Willatts, 1985). However, the overwhelming majority of errors occur when participants must both hold information in mind and also exercise inhibitory control (i.e., on reversal trials when the covers are opaque and a delay is imposed).

A fragile memory of where the reward was hidden would be sufficient on the initial trials at A because there is no competition. However, when the side of hiding is reversed, the fragile memory of where the reward was hidden now has to compete with the conditioned tendency to repeat the rewarded response of reaching to A, and so sometimes that fragile memory is not sufficient to win the battle. At the core of my hypothesis about the cause of the A-not-B error has always been the notion of a competition or battle between the information held in mind (i.e., where the toy was last hidden) and the prepotent tendency (a type of procedural or implicit memory) formed by the experience of previous trials. The key element is conflict: What is required is not simply holding in mind the newest information, but that stored information has to win against a competitor (a conditioned tendency), which is probably subcortical in origin, since even extremely simple organisms can show conditioned tendencies.

The pattern of performance discussed above for the object retrieval task highlights the importance, for success at that task, of being able to inhibit the strong tendency to reach straight in the side of the box through which one is looking. Behaviors such as the "awkward reach" also highlight the importance of holding the location of the box opening in mind when looking at the reward and holding the location of the reward in mind when looking at the box opening, and of integrating the two pieces of information. Focusing exclusively on the reward or the box will not work for this task; both must be taken into account. Reaching through the opening when looking through a closed side requires integrating in one's mind looking at the reward along one route with reaching for the reward along a completely different route. Infants of $8\frac{1}{2}-9$ months and prefrontally-lesioned macaques are only able to succeed when the left or right side of the transparent box is open by simplifying the task. They lean over to look in the opening, hence lining up the opening and the reward so that they can see both at once and so that their line of sight is the same as the line along which they will reach.

I have emphasized that DL-PFC is recruited when one must both hold information in mind and inhibit a prepotent response. Other investigators have characterized the functions of DL-PFC more broadly, proposing that when one must both hold information in mind and manipulate or process that information, then DL-PFC becomes critical (Petrides, 1994; 1995b; Owen et al., 1996; Smith et al., 1998; D'Esposito et al., 1999; Owen et al., 1999; Postle et al., 1999; Smith and Jonides, 1999). Under such conceptualizations, holding information in mind plus inhibiting a dominant response becomes part of a subset of "holding information in mind + another cognitive operation." I am in full accord with such formulations. In general, tasks that require DL-PFC are more difficult than tasks that do not. Tasks that require simply holding one piece of information in mind (such as delayed nonmatching to sample) are too easy to require DL-PFC (e.g., Bachevalier and Mishkin, 1986). However, if one increases how much information must be held in mind so that the task is as difficult as one that requires both holding information in mind plus inhibition

(Diamond et al., 1998) or as difficult as one that requires alphabetizing the information held in mind (Postle et al., 1999) then that task, too, will activate DL-PFC.

In sum, human infants of $7\frac{1}{2}-9$ months, infant macaques of $1\frac{1}{2}-2\frac{1}{2}$ months, adult macaques with bilateral removals of DL-PFC, infant macaques of 5 months in whom DL-PFC was removed at 4 months, and adult macaques who have received MPTP injections to disrupt the prefrontal dopamine system fail the A-not-B/delayed response and object retrieval tasks under the same conditions and in the same ways (see table 22.1). This does not prove that maturational changes in DL-PFC during infancy contribute to the emergence of success on these tasks during infancy, but this body of work makes that hypothesis plausible.

Evidence of Improvement in the Cognitive Abilities that depend on DL-PFC during Early Childhood

DL-PFC continues to mature until early adulthood. Marked improvements on tasks that require working memory + inhibition (tasks thought to require the functions of DL-PFC) are seen in children between 3 and 6 years of age. At 3 years of age, one can see errors reminiscent of the A-not-B error seen in infants and in prefrontally-lesioned macaques, but with a slightly more difficult task. On this task, children who are 3 years old can sort cards correctly by the first criterion they are given (*either color or shape*: Zelazo et al., 1996; Zelazo et al., 1995; Kirkham et al., submitted), just as infants of $7\frac{1}{2}-9$ months and prefrontally-lesioned macaques are correct at the first hiding place, and just as adults with prefrontal cortex damage are correct at sorting cards according to the first criterion (*Wisconsin Card Sort test*: Milner, 1963, 1964; Drewe, 1974). Three-year-old children err when correct performance demands switching to a new criterion, i.e., when cards previously sorted by color (or shape) must now be sorted according to the other criterion (shape or color), just as infants of $7\frac{1}{2}-9$ months and prefrontally-lesioned macaques err when required to switch and search for the reward at the other location, and just as adults with prefrontal cortex damage err when required to switch to a new sorting criterion.

Although 3-year-old children fail to sort by the new sorting criterion (sticking steadfastly to the previously correct criterion), they can correctly state the new sorting criterion (Zelazo et al., 1996; Kirkham et al., submitted). Similarly, infants of $7\frac{1}{2}-9$ months can sometimes tell you with their eyes that they know the reward is in the new hiding place even as they persist in reaching back to the previously correct location (Diamond, 1990a, 1991a, b; Hofstadter and Reznick, 1996), and patients with prefrontal cortex damage can sometimes tell you correctly the new sorting criterion even as they persist in sorting by the previously correct criterion (Milner, 1963, 1964; Luria and Homskaya, 1964). When there are only two sorting criteria (color and shape) and only two values for each criterion (e.g., red/blue, truck/star) children are able to succeed at the card sorting task by $4\text{--}4\frac{1}{2}$ years of age. If the task is made more complicated, by, for example, adding a third sorting dimension, then children cannot succeed until they are $5\text{--}5\frac{1}{2}$ years old. The problem for the children appears to be in relating two or more dimensions to a single stimulus (thinking of a stimulus as either red or blue and also thinking about that same stimulus as either a truck or a star) and in inhibiting the tendency to repeat their previously correct way of categorizing the stimulus.

Similarly, children 3 years old have great difficulty with "appearance–reality" tasks (e.g., Flavell, 1986, 1993) where, for example, they are presented with a sponge that looks like a

Table 22.1 Performance of human infants, infant rhesus monkeys, and adult rhesus monkeys with selective ablations on the same three tasks

	A-not-B	*Delayed Response*	*Object Retrieval*
Human infants show a clear developmental progression from 7½ to 12 months.	Diamond, 1985	Diamond & Doar, 1989	Diamond, 1988
Adult monkeys with lesions of prefrontal cortex fail.	Diamond & Goldman-Rakic, 1989	Diamond & Goldman-Rakic, 1989	Diamond & Goldman-Rakic, 1985
Adult monkeys with lesions of parietal cortex succeed.	Diamond & Goldman-Rakic, 1989	Diamond & Goldman-Rakic, 1989	Diamond & Goldman-Rakic, 1985
Adult monkeys with lesions of the hippocampal formation succeed.	Diamond, Zola-Morgan, & Squire, 1989	Squire & Zola-Morgan, 1983	Diamond, Zola Morgan, & Squire, 1989
Infant monkeys show a clear developmental progression from 1 to 4 months.	Diamond & Goldman-Rakic, 1986	Diamond & Goldman-Rakic, 1986	Diamond & Goldman-Rakic, 1986
5-month-old infant monkeys, who received lesions of prefrontal cortex at 4 months, fail.	Diamond & Goldman-Rakic, 1986	Diamond & Goldman-Rakic, 1986	
Disruption of the prefrontal dopamine system impairs performance in monkeys.		Taylor et al., 1990a, b; Schneider & Roeltgen, 1993	Schneider & Kovelowski, 1990; Sawaguchi & Goldman-Rakic, 1991

rock. Three-year-olds typically report, for example, that it looks like a rock and really is a rock, whereas a child of 4–5 years correctly answers that it looks like a rock but really is a sponge. The problem for the younger children is in relating two conflicting identities to the same object (e.g., Rice et al., 1997) and in inhibiting the response that matches their perception (thus manipulations that reduce the perceptual salience, by removing the object during questioning, find significantly better performance by children of 3–4 years [e.g., Heberle et al., 1999]). "Theory of mind" and "false belief" tasks are other tasks that require holding two things in mind about the same situation (the true state of affairs and the false belief of another person) and inhibiting a prepotent impulse (in this case, to give the veridical answer). For example, the child must keep in mind where the hidden object is now and where another person saw it placed before, and the child must inhibit the inclination to say where the object really is and instead say where the other person would think it is, even though the child knows that answer to be "wrong" because the object is not there now. Here, as well, manipulations that reduce the perceptual salience of the true state of affairs aid children of 3–4 years (Fritz, 1991; Zaitchik, 1991). Carlson et al. (1998) reasoned that pointing veridically to true locations and identities is likely to be a well-practiced and reinforced response in young children, and that children of 3–4 years have trouble inhibiting that tendency when they should point to the false location, as is required on false belief tasks. Carlson et al. (1998) found that when they gave children a novel response by which to indicate the false location, children of 3–4 years performed much better on the false belief task.

Many of the advances of Piaget's "preoperational" child of 5–7 years over a child of 3–4 years, who is in the stage of "concrete operations," similarly reflects the development of the ability to hold more than one thing in mind and to inhibit the strongest response tendency of the moment. Evidence that children 3 or 4 years old have difficulty keeping two things in mind at the same time, or that they tend to focus on only one aspect of a problem, can be seen in (a) their failure on tests of liquid conservation (they fail to attend to both height and width, attending only to height), (b) their difficulty on tests of perspective-taking where they must mentally manipulate a scene to say what it would look like from another perspective and must inhibit the strong tendency to give the most salient response (i.e., their current perspective), (c) their difficulty in comparing an old idea with a new one and hence seeing the contradiction, and (d) their difficulty in working through a two-step problem without losing track of what they are doing. By 5 or 6 years of age, children are capable of doing all of these things. Certainly, part of the difficulty posed by Piaget's liquid conservation task (Piaget and Inhelder, 1941) is the salience of the visual perception that the tall, thin container appears to have more liquid in it. Thus, if an opaque screen is placed between the child and the containers before the child answers, younger children are much more likely to answer correctly (Bruner, 1964).

Many investigators have similarly found evidence of improved ability to exercise inhibitory control over one's behavior between 3 and 6 years of age, especially when children must hold two things in mind and relate them to one another. For example, in the delay of gratification paradigm, when faced with the choice of a smaller, immediate reward or a later, larger reward, children of 3–4 years are unable to inhibit going for the immediate reward although they would prefer the larger one. By 5–6 years of age, children are much better at waiting for the bigger reward (Mischel and Mischel, 1983). Similarly, on the windows task, where children are rewarded for pointing to a box that is visibly empty, and are not rewarded for pointing to a box in which they can see candy, 3-year-olds fail to inhibit the tendency to point to the baited box (Russell et al., 1991). Children 3–4 years of age also tend to fail go/no-go tasks because they cannot inhibit responding. They appear to understand and remember the task instructions (e.g., they can verbalize the instructions), but cannot get themselves to act accordingly. By 5–6 years, they succeed on these tasks (Bell and Livesey, 1985; Livesey and Morgan, 1991).

Difficulty in holding two things in mind can also be seen in persons with frontal cortex damage. For example, they can have difficulty when asked to do two things (such as clean the windshield and change the oil). They are inclined to focus on only one aspect of a story, instead of on the story as a whole. Indeed, Goldstein (1936, 1944) considered the fundamental disorder caused by damage to the frontal lobe to be an "inability to grasp the entirety of a complex situation." Patients with frontal cortex damage also have a well-documented difficulty inhibiting a strong response tendency. For example, they are impaired on the Stroop task, which requires inhibiting the normal tendency to say the word one is reading; one is instructed instead to say the color of the ink in which the word is printed (Perret, 1974; Richer et al., 1993). They fail a perspective-taking task much like Piaget's, and make the same error as do the younger children (they give as their answer their current perspective, when the current answer is the scene as viewed from a different perspective; Price et al., 1990).

We have followed the developmental improvement in these abilities between $3\frac{1}{2}$–7 years of age using three tasks, the "day–night Stroop-like" task (Gerstadt et al., 1994), the tapping task (Diamond and Taylor, 1996), and the three pegs task (Diamond et al., 1997). These three tasks were also used in our research on the role of dopamine in prefrontal cortex function early in life in treated PKU children and so will be described briefly here.

For the day–night task, children must hold two rules in mind ("Say 'night' when you see a white card with a picture of the sun, and say 'day' when you see a black card with a picture of the moon and stars") and must inhibit the tendency to say what the stimuli really represent; instead they must say the opposite. Children of $3\frac{1}{2}$–$4\frac{1}{2}$ years find the task terribly difficult; by 6–7 years of age the task is trivially easy. Children younger than 6 years of age err often, whereas children of 6–7 years are correct on roughly 90 percent of the trials (see figure 22.4). Children of 3Ω and 4 years show long response latencies on the task (approximately 2 sec); older children take roughly half as long (1 sec). The age-related increase in the percentage of correct responses is relatively continuous from $3\frac{1}{2}$ to 7 years of age, but the decrease in speed of responding occurs primarily between $3\frac{1}{2}$ and $4\frac{1}{2}$ years. Passler, Isaac, and Hynd (1985) tested children on a similar, though slightly easier variant of this task, which required children to recognize the correct answer, whereas our task requires that they recall the correct answer. They found that children of 6 years were performing at ceiling on their task, which is consistent with the excellent performance that we found at 6–7 years of age.

To test whether the requirement to remember two rules alone is sufficient to cause the younger children difficulty, we tested a version of our day–night test where each card contained one of two abstract designs (Gerstadt et al., 1994). Children were instructed to say "day" to one design and "night" to the other. Here the children were still required to hold two rules in mind, but they did not also have to inhibit the tendency to say what the stimuli really represented because the stimuli were abstract designs. Even the youngest children performed superbly here. Thus, the requirement to learn and remember two rules is not in itself sufficient to account for the poor performance of the younger children on the day–night task.

Moreover, children's difficulty with the task depends critically on the correct responses being semantically related to the responses that must be inhibited. When we used the same

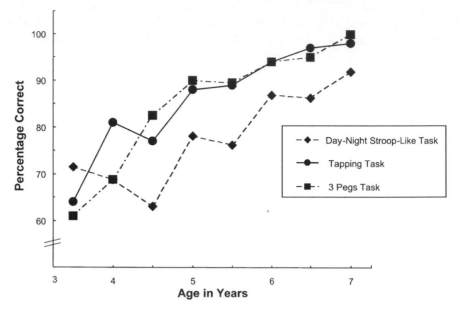

Figure 22.4 Performance of children, $3\frac{1}{2}$ through 7 years of age, on the day–night, tapping, and three pegs task. Note the close parallels in performance on all three tasks throughout this age range.

white/sun and black/moon cards, but instructed the children to say "dog" to one and "pig" to the other, even the youngest children again performed well (Diamond et al., submitted). The task of holding two rules in mind and inhibiting one's natural inclination is sufficiently hard for the younger children that they need a long time to formulate their answers in order to respond correctly. Although we gave children unlimited time, they tended to speed up their responses over the 16 test trials, and the accuracy of the youngest children correspondingly fell. When we made the children wait to respond, by singing a brief ditty to them on each trial after the stimulus was presented, the younger children were able to perform well, even though the period before their response was filled with potentially interfering verbal stimulation (Diamond et al., submitted). It is not simply that slowing down the testing helped, because when the children were made to wait before the start of each trial, they performed poorly. The day–night task is sufficiently difficult for young children that it takes them several seconds to compute the answer; often they do not take the needed time; when forced to take extra time they can perform well.

Luria's tapping test (Luria, 1966) also requires (a) remembering two rules and (b) inhibiting the response you were inclined to make, making the opposite response instead. Here, one needs to remember the rules, "Tap once when the experimenter taps twice, and tap twice when the experimenter taps once," and one needs to inhibit the tendency to mimic what the experimenter does. Children improve on this task over the same age period as they do on the day–night task (see figure 22.4). Over the period of $3\frac{1}{2}$–7 years, children improve in both speed and accuracy on the tapping task, with most of the improvement occurring by the age of 6 (Diamond and Taylor, 1996; Passler et al., 1985; Becker et al., 1987).

Adults with large frontal lobe lesions fail this same tapping task (Luria, 1966). They have similar problems when instructed to raise their finger in response to the experimenter making a fist and to make a fist in response to the experimenter raising a finger (Luria, 1966). The most common error by young children is to always tap once, or always tap twice, regardless of what the experimenter does. It may be that the young children are able to keep in mind only one of the two rules. Or, it may be that they lack the ability to flexibly switch between the two rules, although they remember both. (It cannot be because they do not understand what they should do because no child is tested who does not demonstrate understanding during training of what he or she should do when the experimenter taps once or twice.) This error is reminiscent of a characteristic error Luria (1966) observed in his patients. For example, when asked to alternately draw a circle and a cross, patients with extensive frontal lobe damage start out performing correctly (as do even the youngest children), but the patients soon deteriorate into following only one of the rules (i.e., drawing only circles or only crosses).

Other errors by the children seem more clearly to reflect inadequate inhibitory control. One common error among the younger children is to be unable to resist tapping many times, instead of just once or twice. Again, this error is reminiscent of behavior Luria noted in patients with excessive damage to the frontal lobe: "[When asked] to tap three times or to squeeze the doctor's hand three times . . . although the patient retains the verbal instruction and repeats it correctly, he taps many times or squeezes the doctor's hand five, six, or more times instead of three" (Luria, 1966: 252). Another error made by the younger children is to match what the experimenter does, instead of doing the reverse. Luria (1966; Luria and Homskaya, 1964) has extensively described such "echopractic" errors in frontal lobe patients. Indeed, on the tapping task itself, Luria found that although the patients could correctly comply with the instructions for a short while (like the younger children), they very soon began to imitate the experimenter's movements. Luria also found that the frontal patients could verbalize the rules even as they failed to act in accord with them.

Since Luria first introduced the tapping test over 30 years ago, it has been widely used in neurological assessments of frontal lobe damage in patients. However, much of the work with this test comes from old studies with patients with massive damage. It is not clear from such studies which regions within frontal cortex are critical for the task, or even whether the cortex, rather than the basal ganglia, is the critical site.

For the three pegs task (Balamore and Wozniak, 1984) a child is shown a pegboard containing three pegs arranged in the order: red, yellow, green. The child is asked to tap the pegs in the order: red, green, yellow. This task requires remembering a 3-item sequence and inhibiting the tendency to tap the pegs in their spatial order. The tapping and day–night tasks are more similar to one another than is the three pegs task. Although it, too, requires acting counter to one's initial tendency on the basis of information held in mind. Children show developmental improvements on the three pegs task during the same age period that they are improving on the tapping and day–night tasks (see figure 22.4; Diamond et al., 1997), and performance on the three tasks is correlated (tapping & three pegs tasks: r[144] = .53, p = .0001; tapping & day-night: r[144] = .35, p = .0001; day-night & three pegs: r[151] = .20, p = .01; Diamond et al., 1997).

Clearly, improvement in the performance of tasks requiring memory plus inhibition occurs between 3 and 6 years of age. Perhaps that improvement is made possible, in part, by maturational changes in DL-PFC, although that remains to be demonstrated. Perhaps one of those maturational changes in DL-PFC is in its dopamine system, although little is known about what is happening in the dopamine system in prefrontal cortex during this period. To begin to look at the role of the dopamine innervation of DL-PFC in helping to subserve cognitive functions during infancy and early childhood, we have been studying children who, we had good reason to believe, have reduced levels of dopamine in prefrontal cortex but otherwise remarkably normal brains – children treated early and continuously for phenylketonuria (PKU), whose phenylalanine (Phe) levels are 3–5 times normal (6–10 mg/dl [360–600 mmol/L]).

At the time we began this work, there were almost no data on the role of dopamine in prefrontal function *in humans*, and no data on the role of dopamine in aiding prefrontal function *early in development* in any species. As an initial way of beginning to look at the role of dopamine in prefrontal cortex function in humans early in development, we conducted a large, longitudinal study of children treated early and continuously for PKU (Diamond et al., 1997). We complemented that with work with an animal model of early- and continuously-treated PKU, where we could investigate the underlying biological mechanism (Diamond et al., 1994b). Additionally, we sought to obtain converging evidence from a study of visual contrast sensitivity in children treated early and continuously for PKU (Diamond and Herzberg, 1996), where we postulated that the same underlying mechanism was at work.

The Reasoning and Evidence Leading to the Hypothesis of a Selective Deficit in Dopamine in Prefrontal Cortex in Children Treated Early and Continuously for PKU

Phenylketonuria (PKU) defined

The core problem in PKU is a mutation of the gene on chromosome 12 (12q22 – 12q24.1) that codes for the enzyme phenylalanine hydroxylase. Phenylalanine hydroxylase is essential for hydroxylating (i.e., converting) the amino acid phenylalanine (Phe) into the amino acid tyrosine (Woo et al., 1983; Lidsky et al., 1985; DiLella et al., 1986; see figure 22.5). In the roughly 1 in every 10,000 people born with PKU, phenylalanine hydroxylase activity is either absent or markedly reduced. Hence, PKU is a member of the class of disorders called "inborn [i.e., genetic] errors of metabolism." In the case of PKU, the error is in the metabolism of Phe.

Since little, if any, Phe is metabolized, Phe levels in the bloodstream reach dangerously high levels. Indeed, when PKU is untreated, levels of Phe in the bloodstream rise to well over 10 times normal (>20 mg/dl [>1200 mmol/L]). Since little or no tyrosine is produced from Phe, the level of tyrosine in the bloodstream is low (e.g., Nord et al., 1988). (Tyrosine levels would be still lower were it not for the availability of tyrosine directly through the foods we eat.) This imbalance in blood levels of Phe and tyrosine, if not corrected early, causes widespread brain damage and severe mental retardation (Hsia, 1967; Cowie, 1971; Tourian and Sidbury, 1978; Koch et al., 1982; Krause et al., 1985). Indeed, PKU is the most common biochemical cause of mental retardation. The primary cause of the widespread brain damage is thought to be the toxic effects of grossly elevated levels of Phe in the brain.

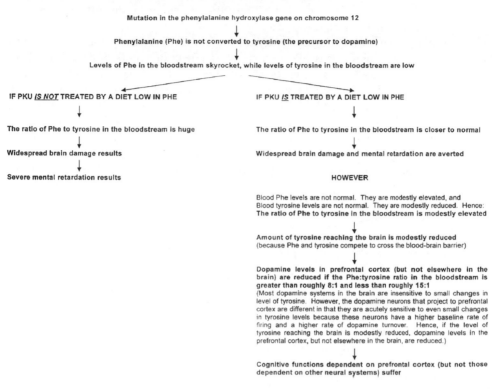

Figure 22.5 Diagram illustrating the reasoning leading to the hypothesis that children treated early and continuously for PKU, whose blood Phe levels are 6–10 mg/dl, would have a selective decrease of dopamine in prefrontal cortex and a selective deficit in the cognitive abilities dependent on prefrontal cortex.

The treatment for PKU: A diet low in phenylalanine

The treatment for PKU consists of a diet low in Phe. Since Phe is a constituent of protein, the low-Phe diet severely restricts the intake of milk and milk products (such as ice cream, butter, and cheese), and all meat and fish. When PKU is treated early and continuously by a diet low in Phe, gross brain damage and severe mental retardation are averted (e.g., Bickel et al., 1971; Holtzman et al., 1986). Note that here is an example of how a behavioral change (changing what you eat) can profoundly affect your biochemistry and your brain.

Limitations of the diet: Why problems might still exist when PKU is treated

The low-Phe diet rarely results in fully normal levels of Phe or tyrosine. This is because the need to minimize Phe intake must be balanced with the need for protein. Eliminating all Phe from the diet would require eliminating all protein. Phe is not present outside of protein in any naturally occurring food. Not only does the human body need to ingest protein, but the body needs a small quantity of Phe to produce its own protein. Hence, because persons with PKU need protein, blood Phe levels remain somewhat elevated in a person with PKU, even with conscientious adherence to the recommended diet, as an inevitable consequence of consuming even a small amount of protein. The advice of the U.S. National Collaborative Study of Treated PKU has been that as long as Phe levels in the bloodstream do not exceed 5 times normal (10 mg/dl [600 mmol/L]), persons with PKU are considered to be under adequate control (Williamson et al., 1981; Koch and Wenz, 1987). The diet has historically done little to correct the reduction in tyrosine, although recently the companies that manufacture the "formula" that persons with PKU drink instead of milk have added additional tyrosine to their formulas. Still, tyrosine levels are below normal in most children treated for PKU.

Even with a low-Phe diet, there is a moderate elevation in the ratio of Phe to tyrosine levels in the bloodstream and deficits in certain cognitive abilities

Thus, the consequence for PKU children of following a dietary regimen of reduced Phe intake and mild tyrosine supplementation is that they have moderately elevated levels of Phe and moderately reduced levels of tyrosine in their bloodstreams. (Were they not following this dietary regimen, the elevation in their Phe:tyrosine ratio would be huge, rather than moderate, and they would likely incur brain damage and become severely cognitively impaired.)

Given that the low-Phe diet does not return Phe and tyrosine levels fully to normal, one can see how the possibility for problems could still exist. Indeed, a number of studies have found significant cognitive deficits in PKU children on the low-Phe diet (e.g., Dobson et al., 1976; Williamson et al., 1981; Pennington et al., 1985; Faust et al., 1986; Smith and Beasley, 1989). For example, the IQs of these children are often significantly lower than the IQs of their siblings. Children with PKU, even when they have been on the special diet since shortly after birth, typically have IQs in the 80s or 90s – lower than the mean score of 100 of their same-age peers, though still within the normal range (e.g., Dobson et al., 1976; Berry et al., 1979; Williamson et al., 1981).

In the 1980s, studies reported problems in holding information in mind, problem-solving, and "executive functions" in children with PKU on the low-Phe diet (e.g., Krause et al., 1985; Pennington et al., 1985; Faust et al., 1986; Brunner et al., 1987; Smith and Beasley, 1989). These problems are reminiscent of the deficits seen after damage to prefrontal cortex, and that similarity did not escape the notice of others (see, especially, Welsh et al., 1990). Indeed, damage to prefrontal cortex typically results in IQs lowered to the 80s or 90s (Stuss and Benson, 1986, 1987), i.e., the same range as one sees in children treated for PKU. The impact of these findings was muted, however, because people were not sure how to make sense of them. No one had suggested a mechanism whereby the cognitive functions dependent on prefrontal cortex might be impaired in treated PKU children, while other cognitive functions appeared normal. Actually, the facts needed for understanding the underlying mechanism were already available. However, the neuroscientists working on the prefrontal dopamine system in the rat and the cognitive neuropsychologists and pediatricians working with PKU children did not know of one another's work, so no one had put the facts together.

Proposed mechanism: How a modest imbalance in the levels of Phe and Tyr in the bloodstream might produce deficits specific to the cognitive abilities dependent on prefrontal cortex

Children treated early and continuously for PKU have a moderate increase in the ratio of one amino acid (phenylalanine [Phe]) to another (tyrosine [Tyr]) in their bloodstreams. (Tyrosine is the precursor of dopamine.) We predicted that when the imbalance is moderate it would selectively affect the dopamine projection to prefrontal cortex.

Why should a modest imbalance in the levels of Phe and tyrosine in the bloodstream produce deficits in the cognitive abilities dependent on DL-PFC? And, why should deficits be confined to that neural system and not extend to other functions of the brain?

Modest reduction in the level of Tyrosine reaching the brain

The modest elevation in Phe relative to tyrosine in the bloodstream results in a modest reduction in the level of tyrosine reaching the brain. This is because Phe and tyrosine compete for the same limited supply of proteins to transport them across the blood-brain barrier (Chirigos et al., 1960; Oldendorf, 1973; Pardridge, 1977). Indeed, those transport proteins have a higher binding affinity for Phe than for tyrosine (Pardridge and Oldendorf, 1977; Miller et al., 1985). Thus, elevations in blood levels of Phe relative to tyrosine place tyrosine at a competitive disadvantage in finding transport into the brain. Because the ratio of Phe to tyrosine in the bloodstream is only modestly increased in those on dietary treatment for PKU, the decrease in the amount of tyrosine reaching the brain is correspondingly modest. In this way, the moderate plasma imbalance in Phe:tyrosine ratio results in modestly reduced tyrosine levels in the brain.

The dopamine neurons that project to prefrontal cortex are unusually sensitive to modest reductions

The special properties of the dopamine projection to prefrontal cortex make prefrontal cortex more sensitive to small changes in the level of tyrosine than other brain regions. The brain needs tyrosine to make dopamine (see figure 22.6). Indeed, the hydroxylation of tyrosine is the rate-limiting step in the synthesis of dopamine. Most dopamine systems in the brain are unaffected by small decreases in the amount of available tyrosine. Not so prefrontal cortex. The dopamine neurons that project to prefrontal cortex are unusual in that they have a higher firing rate and higher rate of dopamine turnover than other dopamine neurons (e.g., Thierry et al., 1977; Bannon et al., 1981; Roth, 1984). These unusual properties of the prefrontally-projecting dopamine neurons in the ventral tegmental area (VTA) make prefrontal cortex acutely sensitive to even a modest change in the supply of tyrosine (e.g., Wurtman et al., 1974; Tam et al., 1990). Reductions in the availability of tyrosine too small to have much effect on other dopamine systems in other neural regions (such as the striatum) have been shown to profoundly reduce dopamine levels in prefrontal cortex (Bradberry et al., 1989).

Reducing the level of dopamine in prefrontal cortex produces deficits in the cognitive abilities dependent on prefrontal cortex

As mentioned above, selectively depleting DL-PFC of dopamine can produce cognitive deficits as severe as those found when DL-PFC is removed altogether (Brozoski et al., 1979). Local injection of dopamine antagonists into DL-PFC impairs performance in a

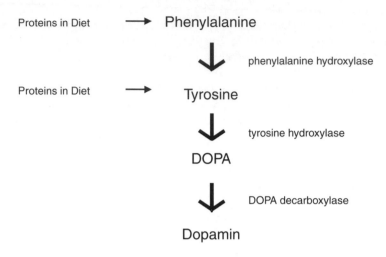

DOPA = dihydroxyphenylalanine

Figure 22.6 Diagram illustrating the mechanism by which the neurotransmitter, dopamine, is produced in the body. Persons with PKU either lack the enzyme phenylalanine hydroxylase, or have it in an inactive form. Note that the body acquires tyrosine via two routes, the hydroxylation of Phe and directly through diet. The hydroxylation of tyrosine is the rate-limiting step in the production of dopamine.

precise, dose–dependent manner (Sawaguchi and Goldman–Rakic, 1991). Destruction of the dopamine neurons in the VTA that project to prefrontal cortex also impairs performance on tasks dependent on DL-PFC (Simon et al., 1980). Similarly, injections of MPTP that disrupt the dopamine projection to prefrontal cortex, but are of sufficiently low dose that motor deficits are avoided, impair performance on the A-not-B/delayed response and object retrieval tasks (e.g., Schneider and Kovelowski, 1990; Taylor et al., 1990a, b).

Summary of the reasoning leading to the prefrontal dopamine hypothesis in treated PKU

For these reasons it seemed plausible that the moderate imbalance in the Phe:tyrosine ratio in the bloodstreams of children treated early and continuously for PKU might well result in deficits in the cognitive abilities dependent on prefrontal cortex (because of the unusual vulnerability of the dopamine projection to prefrontal cortex to a moderate reduction in the amount of available tyrosine) without significantly affecting other brain regions or other cognitive abilities. Hence, we hypothesized that here was a mechanism by which the modest elevation in the Phe:Tyr ratio in the bloodstream of some children treated for PKU, which results in moderate reductions in the level of tyrosine reaching the brain, might selectively affect prefrontal cortex (by modestly decreasing the level of tyrosine reaching the brain).

A 4-Year Longitudinal Study of Children Treated Early and Continuously for PKU

To investigate our prediction that children treated early and continuously for PKU have selective deficits in the cognitive functions dependent on prefrontal cortex we tested 148 children longitudinally and 364 children cross-sectionally (Diamond et al., 1997). Included were children treated early and continuously for PKU, siblings of the PKU children, matched controls, and children from the general population. Children from the general population were tested cross-sectionally; all other groups were tested longitudinally.

If a PKU child starts dietary treatment too late or discontinues it, the very high plasma Phe levels during those off-treatment periods can cause permanent, widespread brain damage. Therefore, we were careful to include in this study only those PKU children who started dietary treatment soon after birth (80 percent began the low-Phe diet within 14 days of age; all had been placed on a low-Phe diet within 1 month of birth) and who had been continuously maintained on the diet thereafter (i.e., children with early- and continuously-treated PKU).

Because no control group is perfect, we included three different control groups. Siblings provide a partial control for family background and genetic make-up. However, they are an imperfect control group because, except for twins, they are not matched on age or birth order, and are often not matched in gender or health status. Therefore, we also studied children unrelated to our PKU participants, but who matched them on a host of background and health variables such as gender, gestational age at birth, birthweight, ethnic background, religion, age at beginning of testing, community of residence, childcare arrangements, number of siblings, birth order, and the age, level of education, and occupational status of each parent. Selecting control subjects by matching on a list of variables is imperfect as well, however, because the children thus selected may not match on other critical variables that one had not considered. Therefore, we complemented the inclusion of siblings and matched controls with a normative sample of children from the general population. With this last group we attempted to get an estimate of the "normal" developmental progression on each of our tasks.

All children studied had normal birthweights, IQs within the normal range, and no known learning disabilities or serious medical problems. Almost all were full-term (100 percent of the children tested cross-sectionally; 96 percent of the children tested longitudinally). PKU is found primarily among Caucasians, so almost all of our participants were Caucasian (95 percent of the children tested cross-sectionally; 93 percent of the children tested longitudinally).

Because of the large age range studied (6 months–7 years), three different batteries of cognitive neuropsychological measures were used – one for infants (6–12 months of age), one for toddlers (15–30 months of age), and one for young children ($3\frac{1}{2}$–7 years old). A total of 19 cognitive neuropsychological measures were administered (see table 22.2). Infants were tested every month, toddlers every 3 months, and young children every 6 months. At each age, each child was tested on multiple tasks linked to prefrontal cortex and on multiple control tasks that were not linked to prefrontal cortex.

Findings

Deficits in the working memory and inhibitory control abilities dependent on DL-PFC in children treated early and continuously for PKU

We found that PKU children who had been on a low-Phe diet since the first month of life, but who had moderately elevated blood Phe levels (levels roughly 3–5 times normal [6–10 mg/dl; 360–600 mmol/L]), were impaired on all 6 tests that require both holding information in mind and overriding or resisting a dominant response, i.e., tasks dependent on DL-PFC. These six tasks were the A-not-B and the object retrieval tasks for infants; A-not-B with invisible displacement for toddlers; the day–night Stroop-like test, the tapping test, and the three pegs test for young children (see figure 22.7). The fact that even *infants* showed these impairments suggests that the dopaminergic innervation to prefrontal cortex is critical for the proper expression of these abilities even during the first year of life.

These deficits in the working memory and inhibitory control abilities dependent on DL-PFC were evident in all age groups (infants, toddlers, and young children), and remained significant even controlling for IQ, gender, health variables, and background characteristics. The deficits were clear whether the PKU children with blood Phe levels 3–5 times normal were compared to (a) other PKU children with lower Phe levels, (b) their own siblings, (c) matched controls, or (d) children from the general population.

One way to summarize the many comparisons across the 3 age groups and 19 tasks is to look at the results on one dependent measure for every task. For each task (the control tasks as well as those that required working memory plus inhibitory control) we selected the dependent measure that yielded the strongest between-group differences on that particular task. This gave each task the best possible opportunity to yield a difference between groups, whether we had predicted a group difference or not. Of the 24 comparisons between PKU children with blood Phe levels 3–5 times above normal and the 4 other groups of children (PKU children with Phe levels closer to normal [< 3× normal], siblings of PKU children, matched controls, and children from the general population) on the 6 tasks that require

Table 22.2   List of Tasks

TASKS USED WITH INFANTS (AGES 6–12 MONTHS)

Tests of WORKING MEMORY + INHIBITORY CONTROL, dependent on DORSOLATERAL PREFRONTAL CORTEX:

A-not-B: a hiding task requiring working memory & inhibition of a previously rewarded response. Subject sees reward hidden to left or right (2 identical hiding wells); after a delay subject is allowed to search one well. Linked to dorsolateral prefrontal cortex by work with rhesus monkeys (e.g., Diamond & Goldman-Rakic, 1989).

Object Retrieval: a transparent barrier detour task. Subject can see the reward through all sides of a transparent box, but can reach through only the one open side (Diamond, 1981, 1990). Linked to dorsolateral prefrontal cortex by work with rhesus monkeys (e.g., Diamond & Goldman-Rakic, 1985).

Tests that do NOT require WORKING MEMORY + INHIBITORY CONTROL:

Spatial Discrimination: an associative rule-learning & memory task. Hiding done unseen; subject must learn & remember that reward is always hidden to left or right (2 identical hiding places); after delay between trials, subject is allowed to reach. *Not* impaired by lesions to prefrontal cortex (e.g., Goldman & Rosvold, 1970).

Visual Paired Comparison: a recognition memory task where a sample is presented, a delay imposed, & then subject is given a choice of that stimulus or something new. Linked to the medial temporal lobe (Bachevalier, Brickson, & Hagger, 1993, McKee & Squire, 1992).

TASKS USED WITH TODDLERS (AGES 15–30 MONTHS)

Test of WORKING MEMORY + INHIBITORY CONTROL, dependent on DORSOLATERAL PREFRONTAL CORTEX:

A-Invisible Displacement: a hiding task requiring memory of where the container-with-reward was last moved & inhibition of a previously rewarded response. Similar to A for infants, but not independently, directly linked to prefrontal cortex.

Tests that do NOT require WORKING MEMORY + INHIBITORY CONTROL:

Three Boxes (boxes scrambled after each reach): a memory task where subjects are to try to open all boxes without repeating a choice; a delay is imposed between reaches. S must remember color/shape of the boxes; spatial location is irrelevant. Linked to dorsolateral prefrontal cortex by work with rhesus monkeys (Petrides, 1995).

Three Boxes (stationary): Here, uncovering the boxes in spatial order will suffice. Similar to a condition *not* impaired by damage to dorsolateral prefrontal cortex (Petrides & Milner, 1982).

Delayed Nonmatching to Sample: a recognition memory task where one is rewarded for reaching to the stimulus not matching the sample that was presented shortly before. Linked to the medial temporal lobe by work with rhesus monkeys & amnesic patients (e.g., Murray, Bachevalier, & Mishkin, 1989; Zola-Morgan, Squire, & Amaral, 1989; Squire, Zola-Morgan, & Chen, 1988).

Global–Local (preferential looking procedure): a visual–spatial attention task. Assesses attention to the global and the local features of composite stimuli (e.g., an H made up of S's). Similar to a task linked to parietal cortex by work with brain-damaged patients (e.g., Lamb, Robertson, & Knight, 1989; Robertson, Lamb, & Knight, 1988) and to a task linked to parietal cortex through functional magnetic imaging (fMRI) of neural activity in normal adults.

TASKS USED WITH YOUNG CHILDREN (AGES 3–7 YEARS)

Tests of WORKING MEMORY + INHIBITORY CONTROL, dependent on DORSOLATERAL PREFRONTAL CORTEX:

Day–Night Stroop-like Test: requires holding 2 rules in mind & exercising inhibitory control. S must say "night" when shown a white-sun card, and say "day" when shown a black-moon card. Hypothesized to require the functions of dorsolateral prefrontal cortex, but it has yet to be studied in relation to brain function.

Tapping: a conflict test requiring memory of 2 rules & inhibitory control. When E taps once, S must tap 2×; when E taps 2×, S must tap once. Linked to prefrontal cortex by work with brain-damaged patients (Luria, 1973).

Three Pegs: S is shown a board containing 3 colored pegs arranged in the order: red, yellow, green. S is instructed to tap the pegs in the order: red, GREEN, yellow. This requires remembering the instructed sequence & inhibiting the tendency to tap the pegs in their spatial order. It has yet to be studied in relation to brain function.

Tests that do NOT require WORKING MEMORY + INHIBITORY CONTROL:

Corsi–Milner Test of Temporal Order Memory: Subject is shown a series of stimuli one at a time, & is periodically shown 2 previously presented stimuli & asked, "Which of these two pictures did you see last?" Linked to prefrontal cortex by work with brain-damaged patients (Milner, Corsi, & Leonard, 1991).

Six Boxes (boxes scrambled after each reach): a memory task where S must try to open all boxes without repeating a choice; a delay is imposed between reaches. Similar to tasks linked to prefrontal cortex in rhesus monkeys (Petrides, 1995) & in brain-damaged human adults (Petrides & Milner, 1982).

Stroop control condition: requires learning & remembering 2 rules (as does Stroop above), but requires no inhibition (unlike Stroop above) – 2 arbitrary patterns used; to one, S must say "day," to other, S must say "night".

Corsi–Milner Test of Recognition Memory: S is shown a series of pictures and periodically asked, "Among the pictures I've shown you, which of these two have you already seen?" Linked to medical temporal lobe by work with brain-damaged patients (Milner, 1982; Milner et al.,1991).

Six Boxes (stationary): Here, uncovering the boxes in spatial order will suffice. Similar to a condition *not* impaired by damage to dorsolateral prefrontal cortex (Petrides & Milner 1982).

Global–Local (forced choice procedure): a visual–spatial attention task. Assesses attention to the global and the local features of composite stimuli (e.g., an H made up of S's). Linked to parietal cortex by work with brain-damaged patients (e.g., Lamb et al., 1989; Robertson et al., 1988) and by functional magnetic imaging (fMRI) of neural activity in normal adults.

Line Bisection: a spatial perception task. Subject is asked to indicate the middle of each line. Linked to parietal cortex by work with brain-damaged patients (e.g., Benton, 1969).

---

working memory + inhibitory control (6 tasks × 4 comparisons per task), PKU children with higher Phe levels performed significantly worse than the comparison groups on 79 percent of these comparisons using the stringent criterion of $p \leq .005$ for each test to correct for multiple comparisons (see table 22.3). This pattern of 19 out of 24 comparisons in the predicted direction would be very unlikely to occur by chance ($p < .004$ [binomial distribution]). In short, the impairment of the PKU children whose blood Phe levels were 3–5 times above normal, on the tasks that require the working memory and inhibitory control functions dependent on DL-PFC, was clear and consistent.

This finding of deficits in the working memory and inhibitory control abilities dependent on DL-PFC in PKU children whose blood Phe levels are mildly elevated (3–5× normal) is consistent with the results of a number of other studies. The most relevant are those by Welsh et al. (1990) and Smith et al. (1996), as these investigators used cognitive tasks tailored to the functions of DL-PFC.

The cognitive deficits documented in many studies of children treated for PKU could be explained away by saying that (a) the blood Phe levels of many of the children were outside the "safe" range (i.e., > 5 times normal), (b) even if current Phe levels were not excessively elevated, earlier Phe levels had been (during the years the children had been off diet), and/ or (c) the low-Phe diet had been started too late to avert early brain damage. Those disclaimers are not applicable to the Diamond et al. (1997) study.

A linear relationship between Phe level and performance

The higher a PKU child's current Phe level (the higher a child's Phe:tyrosine ratio), the worse that child's performance on the tasks that required the working memory and inhibitory control functions dependent on DL-PFC. PKU children whose blood Phe levels had been maintained between 2–6 mg/dl performed comparably to all control groups on our tasks. Thus, at least in this subgroup of PKU children, deficits in the ability to simultaneously exercise working memory and inhibitory control did not appear to be a necessary, unavoidable consequence of being born with PKU. The effect of elevated Phe

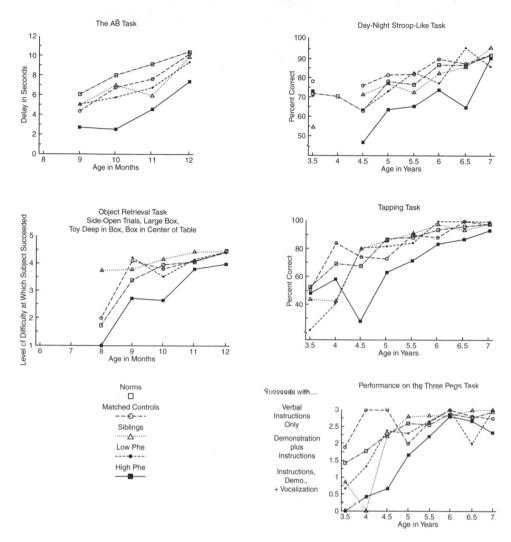

Figure 22.7 Performance of PKU children whose blood Phe levels are 6–10 mg/dl (3–5 times normal) on tasks requiring both working memory and inhibitory control. Note that they are significantly impaired compared to each comparison group: other PKU children with Phe levels closer to normal, siblings of the PKU children, control children matched to the PKU children on a large number of variables, and children from the general population. Note also that they are significantly impaired in the youngest age range investigated (as infants they are impaired on the A-not-B/delayed response and object retrieval tasks) and in the oldest age range investigated (as young children on the day–night, tapping, and three pegs tasks).

levels appeared to be acute, rather than chronic: Performance on these tasks was most strongly and consistently related to *current* blood Phe levels, rather than to mean Phe levels over a wide age range, during the first year of life, or during the first month of life. As current Phe levels varied so too, inversely, did behavioral performance on 5 of the 6 tasks that required acting counter to one's initial tendency on the basis of information held in

Table 22.3   Pairwise Comparisons between Subject Groups Significant at $p \leq .005$

	The 6 tasks that required the working memory & inhibitory control abilities dependent on dorsolateral prefrontal cortex	The 10 control tasks that did are not dependent on prefrontal cortex
PKU children whose plasma Phe levels were 3–5× normals performed significantly worse than the other groups of children on . . .	19 out of 24 comparisons (79%)	4 out of 40 comparisons (10%)
The other groups of children performed significantly differently from one another on . . .	2 out of 36 comparisons (5%)	3 out of 60 comparisons (5%)

The .005 significance level was chosen to correct for multiple comparisons. This is similar to what a Bonferroni correction would do.

mind (the exception being A-not-B with invisible displacement). Indeed, over time, changes in blood Phe levels *within the same child* were accompanied by concomitant, inverse changes in performance on these cognitive tasks.

The findings that performance is most closely tied to current blood Phe levels (rather than to Phe levels earlier in life) and that performance covaries with a child's current blood Phe levels is consistent with the biological mechanism outlined above concerning the cause of the cognitive deficits. That is, these findings are consistent with an effect of reduced dopamine on prefrontal cortex function, which would vary directly with changes in the Phe:Tyr ratio in the bloodstream, as opposed to structural, neuroanatomical changes, which might be more fixed.

Like us, Welsh et al. (1990) and Smith et al. (1996) found that performance on measures of DL-PFC function was significantly and negatively correlated with concurrent Phe levels and less so with lifetime Phe levels. Brunner et al. (1983) found that cognitive neuro-psychological performance was significantly correlated with concurrent Phe levels but not with Phe levels during infancy. Using IQ and school achievement as the outcome measures, Dobson et al. (1976) also found a significant, negative correlation with concurrent blood Phe levels, and a much weaker association with Phe levels earlier in life. Like us, Stemer-dink et al. (1995) found that when blood Phe levels were kept below 3 times normal from birth to the present, PKU children showed no cognitive deficits. The only contrary finding is the report of Sonneville et al. (1990) that Phe levels during the 2 years preceding cognitive testing were a better predictor of speed of responding on a continuous perform-ance test than were concurrent Phe levels.

The relationship found between blood Phe level and performance in Diamond et al. (1997), Welsh et al. (1990), and Smith and Beasley (1989) is particularly impressive considering the truncated range of Phe levels; all PKU children in those studies were on a dietary regimen and their Phe levels were generally within the "acceptable" range. Because participants in Diamond et al. (1997) were followed longitudinally, we are able to present evidence for the first time that performance on tasks requiring the working memory and inhibitory control functions of DL-PFC covaried inversely with Phe levels in the same child over time. Because of the evidence of cognitive deficits in PKU children whose blood Phe levels are 6–10 mg/dl, the national guidelines for the treatment of PKU have been changed in the United Kingdom, the Netherlands, and Denmark to say that Phe levels higher than 6 mg/dl are no longer considered acceptable, and several clinics in the United States have similarly revised their guidelines.

A developmental delay or absolute, lasting deficits?

Are the cognitive deficits in treated PKU children indicative of a developmental delay or of lasting deficits? On the one hand, all children, even PKU children with Phe levels 3–5 times above normal, improved over time on our tasks. On the other hand, the impression that PKU children may "catch up" to other children is probably misleading. In almost all cases this "catch up" was due to ceiling effects because the same tasks were administered over a wide age range, and these tasks were often too easy for children at the upper end of an age range. We have repeatedly found that the between-group differences reappeared on the next battery of tasks for the next age group. The impairment of the PKU children with higher Phe levels in simultaneously holding information in mind and inhibiting a prepotent response was as evident in our oldest age range (3Ω–7 year olds) as it was in our youngest age range (6–12 month olds). The deficit showed no evidence of subsiding within the age range we studied (6 months – 7 years).

The oldest children tested by Diamond et al. (1997) were 7 years old. One cannot tell from our study whether sometime after 7 years PKU children whose Phe levels remain only moderately elevated might no longer show the kinds of cognitive deficits we have documented. Many studies of elementary school-age PKU children on the low-Phe diet have found cognitive deficits (e.g., Smith and Beasley, 1988; Welsh et al., 1990; Weglage et al., 1995). Recent studies by Ris et al. (1994) and Smith et al. (1996) report deficits in the cognitive abilities dependent on prefrontal cortex in young adults with PKU. However, dietary compliance tends to become progressively more lax after children enter school so that these studies have included participants whose blood Phe levels were higher than 10 mg/dl. What would happen if blood Phe levels were maintained at 3–5 times normal; would the cognitive deficits eventually disappear? The data do not presently exist to answer that question. Amino acid uptake across the blood–brain barrier changes during development, offering more protection against blood Phe elevations as children get older (Greengard and Brass, 1984; Lajtha et al., 1987). Thus, it is quite possible that the blood Phe levels we found to be detrimental during infancy and early childhood might be more benign in later childhood or adolescence.

Early cognitive deficits or developmental delays – especially when they extend over a long period (such as the 6-year period we have documented) – are likely to have profound and enduring effects, even if the cognitive deficits themselves are subsequently resolved. They affect children's perceptions of, and expectations for, themselves and the perceptions and expectations of others for the children. Such perceptions and expectations can be inordinately difficult to change and can have major effects in shaping development and behavior.

Selective, rather than global, cognitive deficits

The same children, who were impaired on all 6 working memory + inhibitory control tasks, performed well on the 10 control tasks, which required other cognitive abilities dependent on other neural systems such as parietal cortex or the medial temporal lobe. Performance on the control tasks, moreover, was not related to current blood Phe levels. For each of the 10 control tasks, we compared the performance of PKU children with higher blood Phe levels (6–10 mg/dl; 3–5× normal) to that of the 4 comparison groups: other PKU children with lower blood Phe levels, siblings of the PKU children, matched controls, and children from the general population. This yielded a total of 40 pairwise comparisons (10 tasks × 4 comparisons per task). PKU children with higher Phe levels performed worse on only 10 percent of these comparisons (see table 22.3 above). This pattern of 36 out of 40 comparisons in the predicted direction would be extremely unlikely to occur by chance ($p < .001$ [z distribution]). The consistency of the deficits of the PKU children with Phe levels 3–5 times normal on the working-memory-plus-inhibitory-control tasks and the paucity of deficits on the control tasks is quite striking (55 out of 64 comparisons in the predicted direction [86 percent], $p < .0001$, z distribution).

Thus, the cognitive deficits in children treated early and continuously for PKU, whose blood Phe levels are 3–5 times normal, appear to be selective. The functions of parietal cortex and of the medial temporal lobe appear to be spared, even if the children's Phe levels go up to 6–10 mg/dl. This is consistent with reports by Welsh et al. (1990) and Smith et al. (1996) who found (a) greater impairments on tasks dependent on prefrontal cortex than on tasks dependent on parietal cortex or the medial temporal lobe in those treated early and continuously for PKU, and (b) an inverse relationship between Phe levels and performance on tasks dependent on prefrontal cortex function but no such relationship for tasks dependent on parietal cortex or the medial temporal lobe. This is an example of a very specific, selective effect resulting from a global insult (a moderate elevation in Phe and moderate reduction in tyrosine in the bloodstream that feeds the entire body, and moderately too little tyrosine in the entire brain). The reason for the specificity is the differential, unique sensitivity of prefrontally-projecting dopamine neurons to a mild reduction in the dopamine precursor, tyrosine.

This finding of a deficit in the working memory and inhibitory control functions of DL-PFC, but not in the cognitive functions dependent on other neural systems, is consistent with the mechanism I have hypothesized as the cause of the cognitive deficits: A moderate imbalance in the Phe:tyrosine ratio in blood (as when Phe levels are 3–5 times normal in PKU children) adversely affects the dopamine concentration in prefrontal cortex but not other dopamine systems in the brain because of the special properties of the prefrontally-projecting dopamine neurons, which makes them unusually vulnerable to modest reductions in the level of tyrosine reaching the brain. The specificity of the deficits observed suggests that the cause of those deficits is probably too little tyrosine reaching the brain, rather than too much Phe reaching the brain, because all neural regions would be equally vulnerable to the negative effects of too much Phe; the functions of DL-PFC would not be disproportionately affected. That is, if the cause of the cognitive deficits were too much Phe in the brain, the cognitive deficits should be global, rather than limited to the prefrontal neural system.

Findings we had NOT predicted: Preserved performance on self-ordered pointing and temporal order memory Tasks

The mechanism I have proposed to explain the cause of the cognitive deficits in children treated early and continuously for PKU whose Phe levels are 3–5 times normal, rests on the special properties of the dopamine neurons that project to prefrontal cortex. I had not hypothesized that only certain cognitive functions dependent on DL-PFC would be affected. I was surprised, therefore, that we found that PKU children with Phe levels

3–5 times normal performed normally on 3 tasks dependent on DL-PFC: the three- and six-boxes tasks ([boxes scrambled after each reach], which are adaptations of the Petrides and Milner self-ordered pointing task) and the Corsi–Milner test of temporal order memory. These tasks require working memory (remembering what choices one has already made or remembering the order in which stimuli have been presented) but not inhibitory control. Thus, the treated PKU children with moderately elevated Phe levels were only impaired on the subclass of prefrontal cortex tasks that required *both* working memory and resisting a prepotent action tendency.

These findings were puzzling since there had been nothing in my hypothesis to lead one to predict that certain cognitive functions dependent on dorsolateral PFC should be affected but not others. Although I have emphasized the conjunction of working memory plus inhibitory control as the hallmark of tasks dependent on DL-PFC, I had no explanation at the time for why performance on only certain cognitive tasks that require the functions of prefrontal cortex should be affected in PKU children. The evidence linking self-ordered pointing and temporal order memory to DL-PFC is strong, with converging evidence from lesion studies in rhesus macaques, human adult patients with damage to DL-PFC, and neuroimaging studies in normal human adults (e.g., Petrides and Milner, 1982; Milner et al., 1991; Petrides et al., 1993; Petrides, 1995a) – it was extremely unlikely that the failure to find a deficit on these tasks was due to their not requiring DL-PFC.

An excellent recent study by Collins et al. (1998) begins to make sense of what we found. They compared the effect of lesioning prefrontal cortex to the effect of depleting prefrontal cortex of dopamine. Their anatomical lesions were excitotoxic, which is a technique that destroys the cell bodies in the target region, but not the fibers of passage, so that one can have more confidence than with traditional lesioning methods that the observed effect is due to damage to the target region specifically. They depleted prefrontal cortex of dopamine by injecting it with 6-hydroxydopamine (6-OHDA). The concentrations of norepinephrine and serotonin in prefrontal cortex were not similarly reduced because the investigators pre-injected prefrontal cortex with a norepinephrine antagonist (talsupram) and a serotonin antagonist (citalopram). Although their work is in the marmoset, they replicated the findings of others in the rhesus macaque, plus they added one important new finding.

Replicating the work of others (e.g., Butters et al., 1969; Goldman and Rosvold, 1970; Diamond and Goldman-Rakic, 1989), Collins et al. (1998) found that their lesions of prefrontal cortex impaired performance on the delayed response task. Similarly, like others (e.g., Petrides and Milner, 1982; Petrides, 1995a) they found that their lesions of prefrontal cortex impaired performance on the self-ordered pointing task, and to the same degree as the same lesions impaired performance on delayed response. Finally, as others had reported (e.g., Sawaguchi and Goldman-Rakic, 1991), they found that depleting prefrontal cortex of dopamine impaired performance on delayed response. No one before had ever looked at the effect of dopamine depletion on self-ordered pointing. However, Collins et al. (1998) found that, when they depleted the same region of prefrontal cortex of dopamine, performance on the self-ordered pointing task was *not impaired*. (See table 22.4 for a summary of this set of results.)

Thus, even though prefrontal cortex is necessary for successful performance on self-ordered pointing (as can be seen from the lesion results), the dopamine innervation of prefrontal cortex is not necessary for successful performance of the task. Luciana and Collins (1997) found a dissociation that is perhaps similar in that performance on one of their working memory tasks appeared to rely critically on dopamine while performance of

Table 22.4 Summary of the results of the 1998 study by Collins, Roberts, Dias, Everitt, and Robbins

	Behavioral Task	
	Delayed Response	*Self-Ordered Pointing*
	requires working memory + inhibition	requires working memory
Type of Lesion to Frontal Cortex:		
Excitotoxic (cell bodies destroyed)	Performance IMPAIRED	Performance IMPAIRED
6-OHDA (dopamine depleted)	Performance IMPAIRED	Performance ***SPARED***

the other working memory task did not. They found that a dopamine agonist (bromocriptine) improved performance on delayed response and a dopamine antagonist (haloperidol) impaired performance on delayed response, but neither affected performance on a non-spatial working memory task. Unfortunately, though, there is no evidence that Luciana and Collins' non-spatial working memory task requires DL-PFC.

The effects we documented in children treated with PKU whose blood Phe levels were 6–10 mg/dl, is (we contend) due to reduced dopamine in prefrontal cortex. Consistent with the results that Collins et al. (1998) obtained after our study was completed, we found that these treated PKU children were impaired on our delayed response task (A-not-B) but not on our self-ordered pointing tasks (three- and six-boxes [boxes scrambled after each reach]). The results that had seemed puzzling at the time end up providing additional support for our hypothesis. It appears that the dopamine content of prefrontal cortex is critical for certain cognitive functions dependent on prefrontal cortex (working memory + inhibition) but not for others (when working memory is taxed alone). We still do not understand, however, why that is the case. Luciana and Collins (1997) suggested that dopamine might be critical when the information that must be held in mind is spatial. Such an explanation cannot account for our results, however, because not only were the prefrontal tasks on which we found sparing non-spatial, but we found impairments on the day–night and tapping tasks (neither of which require attending to, or holding in mind, spatial information).

An Animal Model of Mild, Chronic Plasma Phe Elevations

With children it was possible only to measure blood levels of Phe and tyrosine and cognitive performance. To more directly investigate the biological mechanism underlying the cognitive deficits of children treated for PKU, we developed and characterized the first animal model of treated PKU (Diamond et al., 1994b) and subsequently worked with the genetic mouse model of PKU (Zagreda et al., 1999). The animal model enabled us to study the effect of moderate, chronic plasma Phe elevations on neurotransmitter and metabolite levels in specific brain regions. Thus, we could directly investigate our hypothesis that the cognitive deficits associated with moderately elevated plasma Phe levels are produced by a selective reduction in dopamine synthesis in prefrontal cortex.

Building on work modeling the untreated PKU condition (Greengard et al., 1976; Brass and Greengard, 1982), Diamond et al. (1994) administered a phenylalanine hydroxylase inhibitor (a-methylphenylalanine) plus a small supplement of Phe to mildly and chronically elevate the blood Phe levels in rat pups. (The Phe supplement was needed because a-methylphenylalanine does not inhibit phenylalanine hydroxylase completely.) There were 2 experimental groups: (a) pups whose blood Phe levels were elevated postnatally, and (b) pups whose blood Phe levels were elevated pre- and postnatally. Control animals came from the same litters as the first group and received daily control injections of saline.

All were tested on delayed alteration, a task sensitive to prefrontal cortex dysfunction (e.g., Bättig et al., 1960; Kubota and Niki, 1971; Wikmark et al., 1973; Larsen and Divac, 1978; Bubser and Schmidt, 1990). Testers were blind to the group assignment of their animals. Each of the testers was assigned 4 animals in each group and the order of testing was randomized across experimental condition. Blood samples were collected at multiple time points to determine the animals' Phe levels. High performance liquid chromatographic (HPLC) analyses of the brain tissue assessed the distributions and concentrations of dopamine, serotonin, norepinephrine, and their metabolites in various brain regions (prefrontal cortex, caudate-putamen, and nucleus accumbens).[1]

The most dramatic neurochemical effects of the moderate elevation in blood Phe levels was the reduction in dopamine and in the dopamine metabolite, HVA, in prefrontal cortex in each of the PKU-model animals. There was almost no overlap between HVA levels in the prefrontal cortex of controls and that of either PKU-model group: All control animals but one had higher HVA levels in prefrontal cortex than *any* animal in either experimental group. In contrast, as predicted, the levels of dopamine and dopamine metabolites were not reduced elsewhere in the brain, and norepinephrine levels were not reduced elsewhere in the brain or in prefrontal cortex. We had predicted that norepinephrine levels would be unaffected (even though norepinephrine is made from dopamine) because previous work had shown that norepinephrine levels are relatively insensitive to alterations in precursor (Irie and Wurtman, 1987).

The PKU-model animals were impaired on delayed alternation in the same ways and under the same conditions as are animals with prefrontal cortex lesions. On the delayed alternation task, the animal is rewarded only for alternating goal arms (i.e., for selecting the goal arm *not* selected on the previous trial). Thus, the animal must remember which goal arm was last entered over the delay between trials and must inhibit repeating that response. The hallmark of performance after prefrontal cortex is removed is that subjects fail when a delay is imposed between trials, although they are unimpaired at learning the alternation rule or in performing the task when no delay is imposed (*in rats*: e.g., Wikmark et al., 1973; Larsen and Divac, 1978; Bubser and Schmidt, 1990; *in monkeys*: e.g., Jacobsen and Nissen, 1937; Bättig et al., 1960; Kubota and Niki, 1971). We found that the animals with moderately elevated plasma Phe levels learned the delayed alternation task normally and performed well when there was no delay, but failed when a delay was imposed between trials (see figure 22.8), just as do prefrontally-lesioned animals.

Moreover, we found that the lower an animal's prefrontal dopamine levels, the worse that animal performed on the delayed alternation task. The neurochemical variable most strongly and consistently related to performance on delayed alternation was the level of HVA in prefrontal cortex. This is consistent with previous work, which has demonstrated that delayed alternation performance is highly dependent on the level of dopamine in

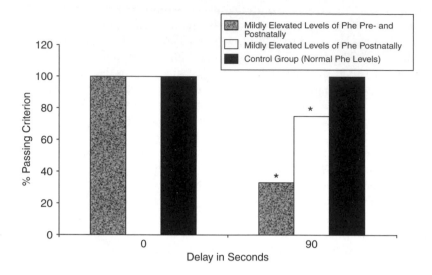

Figure 22.8 Rats with chronic, mild elevations in their blood Phe levels, to create an animal model of early- and continuously-treated PKU, show the same pattern of performance on the delayed alternation task, as do monkeys in whom dorsolateral prefrontal cortex has been lesioned and as do rats in whom the homologue to dorsolateral prefrontal cortex has been lesioned. That is, they can learn the delayed alternation rule and perform well when there is no delay, but are impaired when a delay is introduced.

prefrontal cortex, and is uncorrelated with serotonin or norepinephrine levels (Brozoski et al., 1979; Sahakian et al., 1985; Simon et al., 1980) or with dopamine elsewhere in the brain (Sahakian et al., 1985; Simon et al., 1980).

Thus, Diamond et al. (1994b) found the neurochemical changes (reduced levels dopamine and the dopamine metabolite, HVA, in prefrontal cortex) and the cognitive deficits (impaired performance on a behavioral task dependent on prefrontal cortex [delayed alternation]) predicted by our model in both groups of PKU-model animals with moderately elevated blood Phe levels. The only result that deviated from those predicted was an effect on the serotoninergic system in PKU-model animals. The lack of complete specificity may have been because blood Phe levels were a bit more elevated than intended ($6.5\times$ normal, rather than $\leq 5\times$ normal) or because the neurochemical effects of moderately elevated blood Phe levels are not quite as localized as I have hypothesized. We are investigating this further with the genetic mouse model of PKU created by McDonald and colleagues (McDonald et al., 1990; Shedlovsky et al., 1993).

What We Thought was Independent, Confirming Evidence from Visual Psychophysics for the Proposed Causal Mechanism

If it is the special properties of the dopamine neurons that project to prefrontal cortex that make the functions of prefrontal cortex particularly vulnerable to moderate increases in the ratio of Phe to tyrosine in the bloodstream, then any other dopamine neurons that share those special properties should also be affected by moderately elevated blood Phe:tyrosine ratios. It so happens that the dopamine neurons in the retina share all those same unusual properties. They, too, have unusually rapid firing and dopamine turnover rates (Iuvone et al., 1978; Fernstrom et al., 1986; Iuvone et al., 1989). Moreover, the competition between Phe and tyrosine at the blood–retinal barrier is fully comparable to their competitive uptake at the blood–brain barrier (Rapoport, 1976; Hjelle et al., 1978; Fernstrom et al., 1986; Tornquist and Alm, 1986). Indeed, it has been shown that a small reduction in the level of tyrosine reaching the retina dramatically reduces retinal dopamine synthesis (Fernstrom et al., 1986; Fernstrom and Fernstrom, 1988), mirroring the effect on dopamine synthesis in prefrontal cortex. Therefore, to be consistent, I had to predict that retinal function should also be affected in PKU children who have been on a low-Phe diet since the first month of life, but who have moderately elevated blood Phe levels (levels roughly 3–5 times normal [6–10 mg/dl; 360–600 mmol/L]) – even though no visual deficit had been reported in these children before.

The aspect of retinal function most firmly linked to the level of dopamine in the retina is contrast sensitivity. Contrast sensitivity refers to one's ability to detect differences in luminance (brightness) of adjacent regions in a pattern. Your contrast sensitivity threshold is the limit of how faint items printed in gray can become before you fail to perceive them at all. People with better contrast sensitivity can perceive fainter lines than can people who require more of a luminance difference between foreground and background. Patients with Parkinson's disease, who have greatly reduced levels of dopamine, have impaired contrast sensitivity (Kupersmith et al., 1982; Regan and Neima, 1984; Skrandies and Gottlob, 1986; Bodis-Wollner et al., 1987; Bodis-Wollner, 1990). It is thought that this occurs because dopamine is important for the center-surround organization of retinal receptive fields (Bodis-Wollner and Piccolino, 1988; Bodis-Wollner, 1990).

To investigate contrast sensitivity, we (Diamond and Herzberg, 1996) tested children between the ages of 5.4 and 9.8 years on the Vistech test (Ginsberg, 1984; Rogers et al., 1987; Mäntyjärvi et al., 1989; Tweten et al., 1990; Gilmore and Levy, 1991; Lederer and Bosse, 1992). We found that children treated early and continuously for PKU, whose blood Phe levels were 6–10 mg/dl (3–5× normal), were impaired in their sensitivity to contrast at each of the 5 spatial frequencies tested (1.5–18.0 cycles per degree; see figure 22.9). Even though all children had been tested under conditions of 20/20 acuity, the PKU children were significantly less sensitive to visual contrast than their same-aged peers across the entire range of spatial frequencies. These group differences remained robust even when the two PKU children whose IQs were below 90 were omitted from the analyses. Indeed, at the next to the highest spatial frequency (12 cycles per degree), the "group" variable accounted for 70 percent of the variance, controlling for acuity, gender, age, and testsite. At no spatial frequency was the contrast sensitivity of any PKU child better than that of his or her own sibling. Acuity was normal in the treated PKU children. Standard eye exams had never detected a problem in this population because acuity is normally tested under conditions of high contrast; an impairment in contrast sensitivity was not revealed before because no one had tested for it.

At the time, we interpreted these results as providing converging evidence in support of the biological mechanism I had proposed. I had predicted the contrast sensitivity deficit for the same reason I had predicted DL-PFC cognitive deficit. Both predictions had been based on the special sensitivity of dopamine neurons that fire rapidly and turn over dopamine rapidly to moderate reductions in the level of available tyrosine. We had found two superficially unrelated behavioral effects, a selective deficit in cognitive functions dependent on DL-PFC and a selective visual defect in contrast sensitivity, both of which had been predicted based on the same underlying hypothesis.

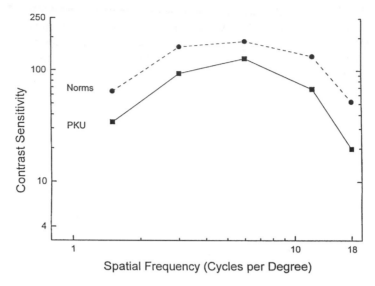

Figure 22.9 PKU children whose blood Phe levels are 6–10 mg/dl were found to be significantly impaired in contrast sensitivity compared to children of the same age at every spatial frequency investigated.

However, I was troubled by one lack of convergence. In the Diamond and Herzberg study (1996), we found that contrast sensitivity performance did not correlate with children's current blood Phe levels, but rather with their Phe levels during the first month of life. Whereas in the Diamond et al. (1997) study, we had found that, on the cognitive tasks that required the working memory and inhibitory control functions dependent on DL-PFC, performance had correlated with children's current blood Phe levels, not their Phe levels during the first month of life.

If contrast sensitivity were poor because the retina was low on "fuel" (i.e., low in dopamine) then contrast sensitivity performance should have covaried with current blood Phe levels. The failure to find such a relationship might have been due simply to the truncated range of concurrent Phe levels in the contrast sensitivity study. Only PKU children whose current Phe levels were 6–10 mg/dl had been included in that study; whereas the cognitive study had included PKU children with lower Phe levels as well as those with Phe levels of 6–10 mg/dl. On the other hand, the range in Phe levels during the first month of life was great and so included sufficient variability to find a relationship with contrast sensitivity performance. The possibility also existed, however, that long-lasting structural damage might occur to the visual system during the first weeks of life, when the visual system is maturing rapidly, and when the Phe levels of PKU infants are dramatically elevated. PKU infants are generally not placed on the low–Phe diet until they are about 2 weeks old; thus for the first 2 weeks of life, their Phe levels can easily reach 20–30 mg/dl. Might those extremely high Phe levels, at a time of very rapid maturation of the visual system, cause irreparable damage to the visual system? (In utero, the fetus's levels of Phe and tyrosine depend upon the mother's levels, so it is believed that the detrimental effects of PKU begin postnatally.)

One way to test for the latter possibility is to study pairs of siblings, both of whom have PKU. Since over 150 different mutations of the phenylalanine hydroxylase gene can cause

PKU, amniocentesis testing for PKU is extremely expensive. Therefore, fetuses are not usually tested for PKU unless there is already one child with PKU in the family. In the US, the older sibling with PKU (in whom it was detected postnatally) usually starts the low-Phe diet at about $1\frac{1}{2}$–2 weeks of age, while the younger sibling (in whom PKU was detected prenatally) usually starts the low-Phe diet by 2 or 3 days of age. For this study we have been flying in pairs of PKU siblings from all over the US and UK (Diamond et al., 1999a). Within each of these families, the earlier-born child (mean age at testing = 13 years, range = 7–16 years) was exposed to extremely high levels of Phe for a mean of 11 days (range = 8–14 days before initiation of diet), while the later-born sibling (mean age at testing = 10 years, range = 6–14 yrs) was exposed to extremely high levels of Phe for a mean of only 3 days (range = 1–5 days). All of the children began the low-Phe diet within the first month of life and have remained on it continuously ever since.

Our preliminary results indicate that the earlier-born PKU siblings show worse contrast sensitivity (as measured by the Regan low contrast letter acuity charts [Regan and Neima, 1983]) than their later-born siblings under conditions of low contrast (4 percent contrast; see figure 22.10). This is striking because contrast sensitivity usually improves with age. For example, among siblings pairs without PKU, older siblings performed significantly

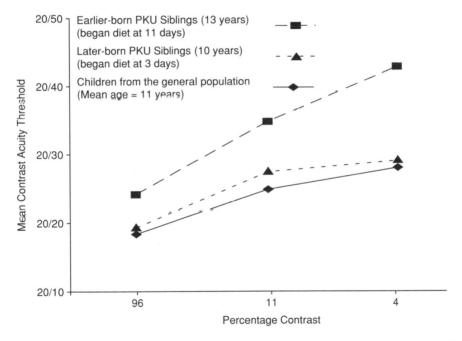

Figure 22.10 Discrimination performance for the PKU sibling pairs and a normal comparison group are shown for the three acuity charts, each chart was presented at a different level of contrast (96%, 11% and 4%). Thresholds were calculated by using the least squares error method to apply a linear curve fit to the obtained data and selecting the 75% correct discrimination value as the threshold. Earlier-born PKU children, who started on dietary treatment at roughly 11 days of age, showed impaired acuities compared to the other children, as can be seen by their elevated line on the graph. Since the charts differed only in contrast, the sharper drop-off in performance of the earlier-born PKU children when tested at lower contrast, indicates that these children have a deficit in contrast sensitivity.

better than their younger siblings, the reverse of the pattern seen in the PKU sibling pairs. The earlier-born PKU siblings (who started diet at $1\frac{1}{2}$–2 weeks of age) also showed worse contrast sensitivity than their same-age peers (see figure 22.10).

These results suggest that a short exposure, of only a couple of weeks, to high concentrations of Phe during the sensitive neonatal period can have long-lasting effects on the visual system, evident 13 years later, even if Phe levels are subsequently lowered and maintained at lower levels. This is significant because it suggests that the current practice of allowing up to 2 weeks to pass before beginning treatment for an infant born with PKU may be ill-advised. Since the blood sample to test for PKU is taken at birth, it would be feasible to start the diet earlier. These results also suggest that although we obtained the results I had predicted for contrast sensitivity in the Diamond and Herzberg (1996) study, we obtained those results for reasons *other* than the ones I had predicted. The deficits in the working memory and inhibitory control abilities dependent on DL-PFC do indeed appear to occur for the reason I had hypothesized (because of reduced levels of dopamine in DL-PFC due to elevated blood ratios of Phe to tyrosine). Those deficits covary with concurrent levels of Phe in the bloodstream. However, the retinal deficit in contrast sensitivity appears to be caused by the inordinately high levels of Phe in the first weeks of life, does not covary with current levels of Phe, and appears to be structural.

Conclusions

DL-PFC is recruited when one must concentrate, such as when one must both hold information in mind and inhibit a prepotent response. DL-PFC begins subserving these cognitive functions even during the first year of life. Even as infants, we are thinking problem-solvers. Prefrontal cortex continues to mature over the next 15–20 years of life, just as the child's cognitive development, while remarkable by 1 year, continues to unfold over the next 15–20 years.

Dopamine is a particularly important neurotransmitter in prefrontal cortex. The level of dopamine increases in the brain of rhesus macaques during the period when infant rhesus macaques are improving on the A-not-B/delayed response and object retrieval tasks, tasks linked to DL-PFC. To begin to look at the role of dopamine in prefrontal cortex function early in life in humans we studied children treated early and continuously for PKU because we predicted that they would have lower levels of dopamine in prefrontal cortex, but otherwise normal brains, a prediction we were able to confirm in an animal model. We predicted this because the children have moderately elevated levels of Phe (3–5 times normal [6–10 mg/dl]) and moderately reduced levels of tyrosine in their bloodstreams. Since Phe and tyrosine compete to cross from blood to brain, and since the transporter proteins have a higher affinity for Phe than for tyrosine, the upshot of a moderate increase in the Phe:tyrosine ratio in the bloodstream is a moderate reduction in the amount of tyrosine reaching the brain. Most dopamine systems in the brain are insensitive to modest decreases in the amount of precursor (i.e., tyrosine). However, the dopamine neurons that project to prefrontal cortex are different. They fire faster and turn over dopamine faster, and are acutely sensitive to even a modest change in the level of tyrosine. Because of the special properties of this dopamine projection, we predicted and found a specific, localized effect (prefrontal cortex affected but not other regions of the brain) even though the insult is global (a mildly increased Phe:tyrosine ratio throughout the bloodstream and mildly reduced tyrosine levels throughout the brain).

Cognitive deficits in children treated early and continuously for PKU whose blood Phe levels are 3–5 times normal went officially unrecognized for years, despite the protestations of parents and teachers that something was wrong, in part because the children performed within the normal range on IQ tests. Their IQ scores were in the 80s and the 90s, just as are the IQ scores of patients in whom prefrontal cortex has been damaged or removed. IQ tests, or any general tests of intellectual functioning, can easily miss specific deficits. The global cognitive measures that had been in use in clinics were too imprecise to detect the children's deficits. Global measures, such as overall IQ score, are poor indices of *specific* cognitive functions and poor indicators of what particular neural system might be affected if there is a problem. Developmental cognitive neuroscientists now have precise measures of specific cognitive functions, sensitive to the functions of particular neural subsystems. These measures can help in the study and treatment of diverse developmental disorders.

The other reason for the lack of official recognition of the cognitive deficits in children treated early and continuously for PKU was the lack of any hypothesized causal mechanism whereby a global insult might produce a selective effect on the functions of only one neural system (prefrontal cortex). The information on such a causal mechanism already existed in neuropharmacology through the work of Anne-Marie Thierry, Robert Roth, Michael Bannon, and colleagues, but the clinicians working on PKU and the neuroscientists working on the properties of the dopamine projection to prefrontal cortex did not know of one another's work.

Young children often fail to inhibit the prepotent response, despite their best intentions and despite knowing what they should do. It would be a shame to mistakenly label such a young child as "bad," "stupid," or "willful." It is not enough to know something or remember it, one must get that knowledge into one's behavior. Infants and young children, in whom prefrontal cortex is not yet mature, sometimes do the wrong thing even though they know what they should do and are trying to do it. Their attention is sometimes so captured by the desired goal object that they either cannot inhibit responding (as in delay of gratification or Go–No Go paradigms) or cannot override the strong tendency to go straight to that goal when an indirect route is required (as in the object retrieval and windows tasks). To sustain focused concentration one needs to be able to resist distraction; to relate multiple ideas to one another one needs to resist focusing exclusively on only one idea; when visual perception is misleading one needs to be able to resist acting in accord with what one sees; and to act in new ways one needs to resist falling back into one's usual way of acting or thinking. That is, one needs inhibitory control, dependent upon prefrontal cortex. The ability to exercise inhibitory control, which prefrontal cortex makes possible, frees us to act according to what we choose to do rather than being simply creatures of habit or immediate perception. The ability to hold information in mind, which also depends upon prefrontal cortex, enables us to remember what we are supposed to do, to consider alternatives, to remember the past and consider the future, and to use what we know and not just what we see to help guide our actions and choices. These abilities make it possible for us to solve new, undreamed-of challenges and make it possible for us to exercise free will and self-determination. This is not to say that it makes it easy, of course, but prefrontal cortex helps make it possible.

ACKNOWLEDGMENTS

The work summarized here was supported by grants from NIMH (R01-#MH41842, R01-#MH09007, R01-#MH00298, and R01-#MH38456), NICHD (R01-#HD35453, R01-#HD34346, R01-#HD10094, P30-#HD26979, P30-#HD04147), BRSG (S07-#RR07054-22,

S07-#RR07083-23, and S07-#RR07083-26), March of Dimes (#12-253 and #12-0554), NSF (Doctoral Dissertation Grant #BNS8013447), the Sloan Foundation, and the Arc Foundation. I would like to thank Natasha Kirkham and Kristin Shutts for their astute comments on an earlier draft.

NOTE

1   We had intended to include two regions of frontal cortex (prefrontal cortex and the anterior cingulate). However, it turned out the brain sections we sampled to assess the anterior cingulate were actually from prefrontal cortex.

REFERENCES

Akert, K. (1964). Comparative anatomy of frontal cortex and thalamofrontal connections. In J. M. Warren and K. Akert (ed.), *The Frontal Granular Cortex and Behavior* (372–6). NY: McGraw-Hill.

Akil, M., Pierri, J. N., Whitehead, R. E., Edgar, C. L., Mohila, C., Sampson, A. R., and Lewis, D. A. (1999). Lamina-specific alterations in the dopamine innervation of the prefrontal cortex in schizophrenic subjects. *American Journal of Psychiatry* 156, 1580–9.

Arikuni, T. and Kubota, K. (1986). The organization of prefrontocaudate projections and their laminar origin in the macaque monkey: A retrograde study using HRP-gel. *Journal of Comparative Neurology* 244, 492–510.

Bachevalier, J. and Mishkin, M. (1986). Visual recognition impairment follows ventromedial but not dorsolateral prefrontal lesions in monkeys. *Behavioral Brain Research* 20, 249–61.

Baddeley, A. (1992). Working memory. *Science* 255, 556–9.

Balamore, U. and Wozniak, R. H. (1984). Speech–action coordination in young children. *Developmental Psychology* 20, 850–8.

Barbas, H. and Mesulam, M. M. (1985). Cortical afferent input to the principalis region of the rhesus monkey. *Neuroscience* 15, 619–37.

Bannon, M. J., Bunney, E. B., and Roth, R. H. (1981). Mesocortical dopamine neurons: Rapid transmitter turnover compared to other brain catecholamine systems. *Brain Research* 218, 376–82.

Bättig, K., Rosvold, H. E., and Mishkin, M. (1960). Comparison of the effects of frontal and caudate lesions on delayed response and alternation in monkeys. *Journal of Comparative Physiology* 53, 400–4.

Bauer, R. H. and Fuster, J. M. (1976). Delayed-matching and delayed-response deficit from cooling dorsolateral prefrontal cortex in monkeys. *Journal of Comparative and Physiological Psychology* 90, 293–302.

Becker, M. G., Isaac, W., and Hynd, G. W. (1987). Neuropsychological development of nonverbal behaviors attributed to "frontal lobe" functioning. *Developmental Neuropsychology* 3, 275–98.

Bell, M. A. and Fox, N. A. (1992). The relations between frontal brain electrical activity and cognitive development during infancy. *Child Development* 63, 1142–63.

Bell, M. A. and Fox, N. A. (1997). Individual difference in object permanence performance at 8 months: Locomotor experience and brain electrical activity. *Developmental Psychobiology* 31, 287–97.

Bell, J. A. and Livesey, P. J. (1985). Cue significance and response regulation in 3- to 6-year old children's learning of multiple choice discrimination tasks. *Developmental Psychobiology* 18, 229–45.

Berns, G. S. and Cohen, J. D. (1998). Dissociating brain regions for novel learning from response competition using implicit sequence learning. *Society for Neuroscience Abstracts* #408.6.

Berry, H. K., O'Grady, D. J., Perlmutter, L. J., and Bofinger, M. K. (1979). Intellectual development and achievement of children treated early for phenylketonuria. *Developmental Medicine and Child Neurology* 21, 311–20.

Bickel, H., Hudson, F. P., and Woolf, L. I. (1971). *Phenylketonuria and some Other Inborn Errors of Metabolism.* Stuttgart: Georg Thiese Verlag.

Bjorklund, A., Divac, I., and Lindvall, O. (1978). Regional distribution of catecholamines in monkey cerebral cortex, evidence for a dopaminergic innervation of the primate prefrontal cortex. *Neuroscience Letters* 7, 115–19.

Bodis-Wollner, I. (1990). Visual deficits related to dopamine deficiency in experimental animals and Parkinson's disease patients. *Trends in Neural Science* 13, 296–302.

Bodis-Wollner, I. and Piccolino, M. (1988). *Dopaminergic Mechanisms in Vision.* New York: A. R. Liss.

Bradberry, C. W., Karasic, D. H., Deutsch, A. Y., and Roth, R. H. (1989). Regionally-specific alterations in mesotelencephalic dopamine synthesis in diabetic rats: Associations with precursor tyrosine. *Journal of Neural Transmission* 78, 221–9.

Brass, C. A. and Greengard, O. (1982). Modulation of cerebral catecholamine concentrations during hyperphenylalaninaemia. *Biochemical Journal* 208, 765–71.

Brodmann, K. (1912). Neue ergebnisse über die vergleichende histologische lokalisation der grosshirnrinde mit besonderer berücksichtigung des stirnhirns. *Anat. Anz. [Suppl.]* 41, 157–216.

Brown, R. M., Crane, A. M., and Goldman, P. S. (1976). Catecholamines in neocortex of rhesus monkeys: Regional distribution and ontogenetic development. *Brain Research* 124, 576–80.

Brown, R. M., Crane, A. M., and Goldman, P. S. (1979). Regional distribution of monoamines in the cerebral cortex and subcortical structures of the rhesus monkey: Concentrations and in vivo synthesis rates. *Brain Research* 168, 133–50.

Brown, R. M. and Goldman, P. S. (1977). Catecholamines in neocortex of rhesus monkeys: Regional distribution and ontogenetic development. *Brain Research* 127, 576–80.

Brozoski, T. J., Brown, R. M., Rosvold, H. E., and Goldman, P. S. (1979). Cognitive deficit caused by regional depletion of dopamine in prefrontal cortex of rhesus monkey. *Science* 205, 929–32.

Bruner, J. S. (1964). The course of cognitive growth. *American Psychologist* 19, 1–15.

Brunner, R. L., Berch, D. B., and Berry, H. (1987). Phenylketonuria and complex spatial visualization: An analysis of information processing. *Developmental Medicine and Child Neurology* 29, 460–8.

Brunner, R. L., Jordan, M. K., and Berry, H. K. (1983). Early-treated phenylketonuria: Neuropsychologic consequences. *Journal of Pediatrics* 102, 831–5.

Bubser, M. and Schmidt, W. J. (1990). 6-hydroxydopamine lesion of the rat prefrontal cortex increases locomotor activity, impairs acquisition of delayed alternation tasks, but does not affect uninterrupted tasks in the radial maze. *Behavioral Brain Research* 37, 157–68.

Bugbee, N. M. and Goldman-Rakic, P. S. (1981). Functional 2-deoxyglucose mapping in association cortex: Prefrontal activation in monkeys performing a cognitive task. *Society for Neuroscience Abstracts* 7, 239.

Burgess, P. W. and Shallice, T. (1996). Response suppression, initiation and strategy use following frontal lobe lesions. *Neuropsychologia* 34, 263–73.

Butters, N., Pandya, D., Sanders, K., and Dye, P. (1969). Behavioral deficits in monkeys after selective lesions within the middle third of sulcus principalis. *Journal of Comparative and Physiological Psychology* 76, 8–14.

Butterworth, G. (1976). Asymmetrical search errors in infancy. *Child Development* 47, 864–7.

Butterworth, G. (1977). Object disappearance and error in Piaget's stage IV task. *Journal of Experimental Child Psychology* 23, 391–401.

Butterworth, G. (1982). Structure of the mind in human infancy. In L. P. Lipsitt and C. K. Rovee-Collier (eds.), *Advances in Infancy Research*. Norwood, NJ: Ablex Publishing Corporation.

Butterworth, G., Jarrett, N., and Hicks, L. (1982). Spatiotemporal identity in infancy: Perceptual competence or conceptual deficit? *Developmental Psychology* 18, 435–49.

Carlson, S. M., Moses, L. J., and Hix, H. R. (1998). The role of inhibitory processes in young children's difficulties with deception and false belief. *Child Development* 69, 672–91.

Cavada, C. and Goldman-Rakic, P. S. (1989). Posterior parietal cortex in rhesus monkey: II. Evidence for segregated corticocortical networks linking sensory and limbic areas with frontal lobe. *Journal of Comparative Neurology* 287, 422–45.

Chen J. (1999). Effect of domain, delay, and information load on older adults' visuospatial working memory. *Cognitive Neuroscience Society, 1999 Annual Meeting, Abstract Program* 72.

Chirigos, M., Greengard, P., and Udenfriend, S. (1960). Uptake of tyrosine by rat brain in vivo. *Journal of Biological Chemistry* 235, 2075–9.

Clark, W. W. and Le Gros (1930). The thalamus of the tarsius. *Journal of Anatomy* 64, 371–414.

Collins, P. F., Roberts, A. C., Dias, R., Everitt, B. J., and Robbins, T. W. (1998). Perseveration and strategy in a novel spatial self-ordered task for nonhuman primates: Effect of excitotoxic lesions and dopamine depletions of the prefrontal cortex. *Journal of Cognitive Neuroscience* 10, 332–54.

Cornell, E. H. (1979). The effects of cue reliability on infants' manual search. *Journal of Experimental Child Psychology* 28, 81–91.

Cowie, V. A. (1971). Neurological and psychiatric aspects of phenylketonuria. In H. Bickel, F. P. Hudson, and L. I. Woolf (eds.), *Phenylketonuria and Some Other Inborn Errors of Amino Acid Metabolism*. Stuttgart: Georg Thiese Verlag.

Craft, J. L. and Simon, J. R. (1970). Processing symbolic information from a visual display: Interference from an irrelevant directional cue. *Journal of Experimental Psychology* 83, 415–20.

Crofts, H. S., Herrero, M. T., Del Vecchio, A., Wallis, J. D., Collins, P., Everitt, B. J., Robbins, T. W., and Roberts, A. C. (1999). Excitotoxic lesions of the caudate nucleus in the marmoset: Comparison with prefrontal lesions on discrimination learning, object retrieval and spatial delayed response. *Society for Neuroscience Abstracts* 25, 891.

D'Esposito, M. (1995). The neural basis of the central executive system of working memory. *Nature* 378: 279–81.

D'Esposito, M., Zarahn, E., Aguirre, G. K., and Rypma, B. (1999). The effect of normal aging on the coupling of neural activity to the bold hemodynamic response. *NeuroImage* 10, 6–14.

Diamond, A. (1981). Retrieval of an object from an open box: The development of visual-tactile control of reaching in the first year of life. *Society for Research in Child Development Abstracts* 3, 78.

Diamond, A. (1985). Development of the ability to use recall to guide action, as indicated by infants' performance on A not B. *Child Development* 56, 868–83.

Diamond, A. (1988). Differences between adult and infant cognition: Is the crucial variable presence or absence of language? In L. Weiskrantz (ed.), *Thought Without Language* (pp. 337–70). Oxford: Oxford University Press.

Diamond, A. (1990a). Developmental time course in human infants and infant monkeys, and the neural bases of inhibitory control in reaching. *Annals of the New York Academy of Sciences* 608, 637–76.

Diamond, A. (1990b). The development and neural bases of memory functions as indexed by the AB and delayed response tasks in human infants and infant monkeys. *Annals of the New York Academy of Sciences* 608, 267–317.

Diamond, A. (1991a). Neuropsychological insights into the meaning of object concept development. In S. Carey and R. Gelman (eds.), *The Epigenisis of Mind: Essays on Biology and Cognition* (pp. 67–110). Hillsdale, NJ: Lawrence Erlbaum Associates.

Diamond, A. (1991b). Frontal lobe involvement in cognitive changes during the first year of life. In K. R. Gibson and A. C. Peterson (eds.), *Brain Maturation and Cognitive Development: Comparative and cross-cultural perspectives* (pp. 127–80). NY: Aldine de Gruyter.

Diamond, A. (2000). Close interrelation of motor development and cognitive development and of the cerebellum and prefrontal cortex. *Child Development* 71, 44–56 (Special issue: New Directions for Child Development in the 21st Century).

Diamond, A. and Boyer, K. (1989). A version of the Wisconsin Card Sort Test for use with preschool children, and an exploration of their sources of error. *Journal of Clinical and Experimental Neuropsychology* 11, 83.

Diamond, A., Ciaramitaro, V., Donner, E., Djali, S., and Robinson, M. (1994b). An animal model of early-treated PKU. *Journal of Neuroscience* 14, 3072–82.

Diamond, A., Cruttenden, L., and Neiderman, D. (1994a). A-not-B with multiple wells: I. Why multiple wells are sometimes easier than two wells. II. Memory or memory + inhibition? *Developmental Psychology* 30, 192–205.

Diamond, A., Davidson, M., Cruess, L., Badali, S., Amso, D., and Oross, S. (1999a). Long-lasting, selective visual deficits from short-term exposure to high neonatal phenylalanine levels in humans. *Society for Neuroscience Abstracts* 25, 501.

Diamond, A. and Doar, B. (1989). The performance of human infants on a measure of frontal cortex function, the delayed response task. *Developmental Psychobiology* 22(3), 271–94.

Diamond, A. and Goldman-Rakic, P. S. (1985). Evidence for involvement of prefrontal cortex in cognitive changes during the first year of life: Comparison of performance of human infant and rhesus monkeys on a detour task with transparent barrier. *Society for Neuroscience Abstracts* 11, 832.

Diamond, A. and Goldman-Rakic, P. S. (1986). Comparative development in human infants and infant rhesus monkeys of cognitive functions that depend on prefrontal cortex. *Society for Neuroscience Abstracts* 12, 742.

Diamond, A. and Goldman-Rakic, P. S. (1986). Comparison of human infants and rhesus monkeys on Piaget's A-not-B task: Evidence for dependence on dorsolateral prefrontal cortex. *Experimental Brain Research* 74, 24–40.

Diamond, A. and Herzberg, C. (1996). Impaired sensitivity to visual contrast in children treated early and continuously for PKU. *Brain* 119, 101–16.

Diamond, A., Kirkham, N., and Amso, D. (submitted). Conditions under which young children CAN hold two rules in mind and inhibit a prepotent response.

Diamond, A., O'Craven, K. M., and Savoy, R. L. (1998a). Dorsolateral prefrontal cortex contributions to working memory and inhibition as revealed by fMRI. *Society for Neuroscience Abstracts* 24, 1251.

Diamond, A., O'Craven, K. M., Davidson, M., Cruess, C., Bergida, R., and Savoy, R. L. (1999b). Further fMRI-based studies of memory and inhibition in prefrontal cortex of adults. Presented at Cognitive Neuroscience Society Annual Meeting, Washington, DC, April.

Diamond, A., Prevor, M., Callender, G., and Druin, D. P. (1997). Prefrontal cortex cognitive deficits in children treated early and continuously for PKU. *Monographs of the Society for Research in Child Development* 62(4), Monograph # 252.

Diamond, A. and Taylor, C. (1996). Development of an aspect of executive control: Development of the abilities to remember what I said and to "Do as I say, not as I do." *Developmental Psychobiology* 29, 315–34.

Diamond, A., Zola-Morgan, S., and Squire, L. R. (1989). Successful performance by monkeys with lesions of the hippocampal formation on A-not-B and object retrieval, two tasks that mark developmental changes in human infants. *Behavioral Neuroscience* 103, 526–37.

DiLella, A. G., Marvit, J., Lidsky, A. S., Güttler, F., and Woo, S. L. C. (1986). Tight linkage between a splicing mutation and a specific DNA haplotype in phenylketonuria. *Nature* 322, 799–803.

Dobson, J. C., Kushida, E., Williamson, M. L., and Friedman, E. G. (1976). Intellectual performance of 36 phenylketonuric patients and their non-affected siblings. *Pediatrics* 58, 53–8.

Drewe, E. A. (1974). The effect of type and area of brain lesion on Wisconsin Card Sorting Test performance. *Cortex* 10, 159–70.

Faust, D., Libon, D., and Pueschel, S. (1986). Neuropsychological functioning in treated phenylketonuria. *International Journal of Psychiatry in Medicine* 16, 169–77.

Fernstrom, J. D. and Fernstrom, M. H. (1988). Tyrosine availability and dopamine synthesis in the retina. In I. Bodis-Wollner and M. Piccolino (eds.), *Dopaminergic Mechanisms in Vision* (pp. 59–70). New York: Alan Liss, Inc.

Fernstrom, M. H., Volk, E. A., and Fernstrom, J. D. (1986). In vivo inhibition of tyrosine uptake into rat retina by large neutral, but not acidic, amino acids. *American Journal of Physiology* 251, E393–E399.

Fitts, P. M. and Seger, C. M. (1953). S–R compatibility: Spatial characteristics of stimulus and response codes. *Journal of Experimental Psychology* 81, 174–6.

Flavell, J. H. (1986). The development of children's knowledge about the appearance–reality distinction. *American Psychologist* 41, 418–425.

Flavell, J. H. (1993). The development of children's understanding of false belief and the appearance–reality distinction. *International Journal of Psychology* 28, 595–604.

Fox, N. A. and Bell, M. A. (1990). Electrophysiological indices of frontal lobe development: Relations to cognitive and affective behavior in human infants over the first year of life. In A. Diamond (ed.), *The Development and Neural Bases of Higher Cognitive Functions* (Vol. 608, pp. 677–704). New York: Annals of the New York Academy of Sciences.

Fox, N. A., Kagan, J., and Weiskopf, S. (1979). The growth of memory during infancy. *Genetic Psychology Monographs* 99, 91–130.

Fritz, A. S. (1991, April). Is there a reality bias in young children's emergent theories of mind? Paper presented at the biennial meeting of the Society for Research in Child Development, Seattle.

Fuster, J. M. (1973). Unit activity in prefrontal cortex during delayed-response performance: Neuronal correlates of transient memory. *Journal of Neurophysiology* 36, 61–78.

Fuster, J. M. (1980). *The Prefrontal Cortex: Anatomy, physiology, and neuropsychology of the frontal lobe*. New York: Raven Press.

Fuster, J. M. and Alexander, G. E. (1970). Delayed response deficit by cryogenic depression of frontal cortex. *Brain Research* 61, 79–91.

Fuster, J. M. and Alexander, G. E. (1971). Neuron activity related to short-term memory. *Science* 173, 652–4.

Gaspar, P., Berger, B., Febvret, A., Vigny, A., and Henry, J. P. (1989). Catecholamine innervation of the human cerebral cortex as revealed by comparative immunohistochemistry of tyrosine hydroxylase and dopamine-beta-hydroxylase. *Journal of Comparative Neurology* 279, 249–71.

Gerstadt, C., Hong, Y., and Diamond, A. (1994). The relationship between cognition and action: Performance of 3.5–7 year old children on a Stroop-like day-night test. *Cognition* 53, 129–53.

Gilmore, G. C. and Levy, J. A. (1991). Spatial contrast sensitivity in Alzheimer's disease: A comparison of two methods. *Optometry and Vision Science* 68, 790–4.

Ginsberg, A. R. (1984). A new contrast sensitivity vision test chart. *American Journal of Optometry & Physiological Optics* 61, 403–7.

Goldman, P. S. and Nauta, W. J. H. (1977). An intricately patterned prefrontal-caudate projection in the rhesus monkey. *Journal of Comparative Neurology* 171, 369–85.

Goldman, P. S. and Rosvold, H. E. (1970). Localization of function within the dorsolateral prefrontal cortex of the rhesus monkey. *Experimental Neurology* 29, 291–304.

Goldman, P. S., Rosvold, H. E., and Mishkin, M. (1970). Evidence for behavioral impairment following prefrontal lobectomy in the infant monkey. *Journal of Comparative and Physiological Psychology* 70, 454–63.

Goldman-Rakic, P. S. (1987). Circuitry of primate prefrontal cortex and regulation of behavior by representational memory. In F. Plum (ed.), *Handbook of Physiology, the Nervous System, Higher Functions of the Brain* (Vol. V, pp. 373–417). Bethesda, MD: American Physiological Society.

Goldman-Rakic, P. S. and Porrino, L. J. (1985). The primate mediodorsal (MD) nucleus and its projection to the frontal lobe. *Journal of Comparative Neurology* 242, 535–60.

Goldman-Rakic, P. S. and Schwartz, M. L. (1982). Interdigitation of contralateral and ipsilateral columnar projections to frontal association cortex in primates. *Science* 216, 755–7.

Goldstein, K. (1936). The modifications of behavior consequent to cerebral lesions. *Psychiatric Quarterly* 10, 586–610.

Goldstein, K. (1944). The mental changes due to frontal lobe damage. *Journal of Psychology* 17, 187–208.

Grace, A. A. (1991). Phasic versus tonic dopamine release and the modulation of dopamine system responsivity. *Neuroscience* 41, 1–24.

Gratch, G., Appel, K. J., Evans, W. F., LeCompte, G. K., and Wright, N. A. (1974). Piaget's stage IV object concept error: Evidence for forgetting or object conception? *Child Development* 45, 71–7.

Gratch, G. and Landers, W. F. (1971). Stage IV of Piaget's theory of infants' object concepts: A longitudinal study. *Child Development* 42, 359–72.

Greengard, O. and Brass, C. A. (1984). Developmental changes of cerebral phenylalanine uptake from severely elevated blood levels. *Neurochemistry Research* 9, 837–48.

Greengard, O., Yoss, M. S., and DelValle, J. A. (1976). a-methylphenylalanine, a new inducer of chronic hyperphenylalaninemia in suckling rats. *Science* 192, 1007–8.

Harris, P. L. (1973) Perseverative errors in search by young infants. *Child Development* 44, 29–33.

Herberle, J. F., Clune, M., and Kelly, K. (1999, April). *Development of young children's understanding of the appearance–reality distinction*. Paper presented at the Biennial Meeting of the Society for Research in Child Development, Albuquerque, NM.

Hjelle, J. T., Baird-Lambert, J., Cardinale, G., Specor, S., and Udenfriend, S. (1978). Isolated microvessels: The blood–brain barrier in vitro. *Proceedings of the National Academy of Sciences (USA)* 75, 4544–8.

Hofstadter, M. and Reznick, J. S. (1996). Response modality affects human infant delayed-response performance. *Child Development* 67, 646–58.

Holtzman, N. A., Kronmal, R. A., van Doornink, W., Azen, C., and Koch, R. (1986). Effect of age at loss of dietary control on intellectual performance and behavior of children with phenylketonuria. *New England Journal of Medicine* 314, 593–8.

Hsia, D. Y. (1967). Phenylketonuria. *Developmental Medical Child Neurology* 9, 531–40.

Huttenlocher, P. R. (1979). Synaptic density in human frontal cortex – developmental changes and effects of aging. *Brain Research* 163, 195–205.

Huttenlocher, P. R. (1984). Synapse elimination and plasticity in developing human cerebral cortex. *American Journal of Mental Deficiency* 88, 488–96.

Huttenlocher, P. R. (1990). Morphometric study of human cerebral cortex development. *Neuropsychologia* 28, 517–27.

Huttenlocher, P. R., De Courten, C., Garey, L. J., and Van Der Loos, H. (1982). Synaptic development in human cerebral cortex. *International Journal of Neurology* 16–17, 144–54.

Irie, K. and Wurtman, R. J. (1987). Release of norepinephrine from rat hypothalamic slices: Effects of desipramine and tyrosine. *Brain Research* 432, 391–4.

Iuvone, P. M., Galli, C. L., Garrison-Gund, C. K., and Neff, N. H. (1978). Light stimulates tyrosine hydroxylase activity and dopamine synthesis in retinal amacrine neurons. *Science* 202, 901–2.

Iuvone, P. M., Tigges, M., Fernandes, A., and Tigges, J. (1989). Dopamine synthesis and metabolism in rhesus monkey retina: Development, aging, and the effects of monocular visual deprivation. *Visual Neuroscience* 2, 465–71.

Jacobsen, C. F. (1935). Functions of the frontal association areas in primates. *Archives of Neurology and Psychiatry* 33, 558–60.

Jacobsen, C. F. (1936). Studies of cerebral function in primates: I. The functions of the frontal association areas in monkeys. *Comparative Psychology Monographs* 13, 1–30.

Jacobsen, C. F. and Nissen, H. W. (1937). Studies of cerebral function in primates. The effects of frontal lobe lesions on the delayed alternation habit in monkeys. *Journal of Comparative Physiological Psychology* 23, 101–12.

Jacobson, S., Butters, N., and Tovsky, N. J. (1978). Afferent and efferent subcortical projections of behaviourally defined secotres of prefrontal granular cortex. *Brain Research* 159, 279–96.

Johnson, P. B., Angelucci, A., Ziparo, M., Minciacchi, D., Bentivoglio, M., and Caminti, R. (1989). Segregation and overlap of callosal and association neurons in frontal and parietal cortices of primates: A spectral and coherency analysis. *The Journal of Neuroscience* 9, 2313–26.

Kemp, J. M. and Powell, T. P. (1970). The cortico-striate projection in the monkey. *Brain* 93, 525–46.

Khokhryakova, M. (1979). Structural organization of the prefrontal cortex in cats and its differences from that in monkeys. *Neuroscience Behavioral Physiology* 9, 103–9.

Kievit, J. and Kuypers, H. G. J. M. (1977). Organization of the thalamo–cortical connexions to the frontal lobe in the rhesus monkey. *Experimental Brain Research* 29, 299–322.

Kirkham, N., Cruess, L., and Diamond, A. (submitted). Helping children apply their knowledge to their behavior on a dimension-switching task.

Kirkham, N. Z. and Diamond, A. (1999, April). *Integrating competing ideas in word and action.* Paper presented at the Biennial Meeting of the Society for Research in Child Development, Albuquerque, NM.

Koch, R., Azen, C., Friedman, E. G. and Williamson, E. L. (1982). Preliminary report on the effects of diet discontinuation in PKU. *Pediatrics* 100, 870–5.

Koch, R. and Wenz, E. (1987). Phenylketonuria. *Annual Review of Nutrition* 7, 117–35.

Krause, W. L., Helminski, M., McDonald, L., Dembure, P., Salvo, R., Freides, D., and Elsas, L. J. (1985). Biochemical and neuropsychological effects of elevated plasma phenylalanine in patients with treated phenylketonuria, a model for the study of phenylalanine in brain function in man. *Journal of Clinical Investigation* 75, 40–8.

Kubota, K. and Niki, H. (1971). Prefrontal cortical unit activity and delayed alternation performance in monkeys. *Journal of Neurophysiology* 34, 337–47.

Künzle, H. (1978). An autoradiographic analysis of the efferent connections from premotor and adjacent prefrontal regions (areas 6 and 9) in *Macaca fascicularis*. *Brain Behavior Evolution* 15, 185–234.

Kupersmith, M. J., Shakin, E., Siegel, I. M., and Lieberman, A. (1982). Visual system abnormalities in patients with Parkinson's disease. *Archives of Neurology* 39, 284–6.

Lajtha, A., Sershen, H., and Dunlop, D. (1987). Developmental changes in cerebral amino acids and protein metabolism. In G. Huether (ed.), *Amino Acid Availability and Brain Function in Health and Disease* (pp. 393–402). Berlin: Springer-Verlag.

Lamb, M. R., Robertson, L. C., and Knight, R. T. (1989). Effects of right and left temporal parietal lesions on the processing of global and local patterns in a selective attention task. *Neuropsychologia*, 27, 471–83.

Larsen, J. K. and Divac, I. (1978). Selective ablations within the prefrontal cortex of the rat and performance on delayed alternation. *Physiological Psychology* 6, 15–17.

Lederer, P. J. and Bosse, J. C. (1992). Clinical use of contrast sensitivity evaluation for general practice of optometry. *Practice of Optometry* 3, 34–40.

Leiner, H. C., Leiner, A. L., and Dow, R. S. (1989). Reappraising the cerebellum: What does the hindbrain contribute to the forebrain? *Behavioral Neuroscience* 103, 998–1008.

Levitt, M., Rakic, P., and Goldman-Rakic, P. S. (1984). Region-specific distribution of catecholamine afferents in primate cerebral cortex: A fluorescent histochemical analysis. *Journal of Comparative Neurology* 227, 23–36.

Lewis, D. A., Foote, S. L., Goldstein, M., and Morrison, J. H. (1988). The dopaminergic innervation of monkey prefrontal cortex: A tyrosine hydroxylase immunohistochemical study. *Brain Research* 565, 1–13.

Lewis, D. A. and Harris, H. W. (1991). Differential laminar distribution of tyrosine hydroxylase-immunoreactive axons in infant and adult monkey prefrontal cortex. *Neuroscience Letters* 125, 151–4.

Lewis, D. A., Sesack, S. R., Levey, A. I., and Rosenberg, D. R. (1998). Dopamine axons in primate prefrontal cortex: Specificity of distribution, synaptic targets, and development. *Advances in Pharmacology* 42, 703–6.

Lidow, M. S. and Rakic, P. (1992). Scheduling of monoaminergic neurotransmitter receptor expression in the primate neocortex during postnatal development. *Cerebral Cortex* 2, 401–16.

Lidsky, A. S., Law, M. L., Morse, H. G., Kao, F. T., and Woo, S. L. C. (1985). Regional mapping of the human phenylalanine hydroxylase gene and the PKU locus on chromosome 12. *Proceedings of the National Academy of Sciences (USA)* 82, 6221–5.

Livesey, D. J. and Morgan, G. A. (1991). The development of response inhibition in 4- and 5-year-old children. *Australian Journal of Psychology* 43, 133–7.

Luciana, M. and Collins, P. F. (1997). Dopaminergic modulation of working memory for spatial but not object cues in normal humans. *Journal of Cognitive Neuroscience* 9, 330–47.

Luciana, M., Depue, R. A., Arbisi, P., and Leon, A. (1992). Facilitation of working memory in humans by a D2 dopamine receptor agonist. *Journal of Cognitive Neuroscience* 4, 58–68.

Luria, A. R. and Homskaya, E. D. (1964). Disturbance in the regulative role of speech with frontal lobe lesions. In J. M. Warren and K. Akert (eds.), *The Frontal Granular Cortex and Behavior* (pp. 353–71). New York: McGraw-Hill.

Luria, A. R. (1966). *The Higher Cortical Functions in Man*. New York: Basic Books.

Mäntyjärvi, M. I., Autere, M.H., Silvennoinen, A.M., and Myöhänen, T. (1989). Observations of the use of three different contrast sensitivity tests in children and young adults. *Journal of Pediatric Ophthalmology and Strabismus* 26, 113–19.

McDonald, J. D., Bode, V. C., Dove, W. F., and Shedlovsky, A. (1990). Pahhph-5: A mouse mutant deficient in phenylalanine hydroxylase. *Proceedings of the National Academy of Science* 87, 1965–7.

McGuire, P. K., Bates, J. F., and Goldman-Rakic, P. S. (1991). Interhemispheric integration: I. Symmetry and convergence of the corticocortical connections of the left and the right principal sulcus (PS) and the left and the right supplementary motor area (SMA) in the rhesus monkey. *Cerebral Cortex* 1, 390–407.

McLardy, T. (1950). Thalamic projection to frontal cortex in man. *Journal of Neurological Neurosurgical Psychiatry* 13, 198–202.

Middleton, F. A. and Strick, P. L. (1994). Anatomical evidence for cerebellar and basal ganglia involvement in higher cognitive function. *Science* 266, 458–61.

Middleton, F. A. and Strick, P. L. (1997). Cerebellar output channels. In J. D. Schmahmann (ed.), *The Cerebellum and Cognition* (pp. 61–82). San Diego: Academic Press.

Miles, R. C. and Blomquist, A. J. (1960). Frontal lesions and behavioral deficits in monkey. *Journal of Neurophysiology* 23, 471–84.

Miller, L., Braun, L. D., Pardridge, W. M., and Oldendorf, W. H. (1985). Kinetic constants for blood–brain barrier amino acid transport in conscious rats. *Journal of Neurochemistry* 45, 1427–32.

Milner, B. (1963). Effects of different brain lesions on card sorting: The role of the frontal lobes. *Archives of Neurology* 9, 90–100.

Milner, B. (1964). Some effects of frontal lobectomy in man. In J. M. Warren and K. Akert (eds.), *The Frontal Granular Cortex and Behavior* (pp. 313–34). New York: McGraw Hill.

Milner, B., Corsi, P., and Leonard, G. (1991). Frontal-lobe contribution to recency judgments. *Neuropsychologia* 29, 601–18.

Mischel, H. N. and Mischel, W. (1983). The development of children's knowledge of self-control strategies. *Child Development* 54, 603–19.

Mishkin, M. and Manning, F. J. (1978). Nonspatial memory after selective prefrontal lesions in monkeys. *Brain Research* 143, 313–23.

Morris, R., Pandya, D. N., and Petrides, M. (1999). Fiber system linking the mid–dorsolateral frontal cortex with the retrosplenial/presubicular region in the rhesus monkey. *Journal of Comparative Neurology* 407, 183–92.

Morris, R., Petrides, M., and Pandya, D. N. (1999). Architecture and connections of retrosplenial area 30 in the rhesus monkey (*Macaca mulatta*). *European Journal of Neuroscience* 11, 2506–18.

Murray, E. A., Bachevalier, J., and Mishkin, M. (1989). Effects of rhinal cortical lesions on visual recognition memory in rhesus monkeys. *Society for Neuroscience Abstracts* 15, 342.

Niki, H. (1974). Differential activity of prefrontal units during right and left delayed response trials. *Brain Research* 70, 346–9.

Nord, A. M., McCabe, L., and McCabe, E. R. (1988). Biochemical and nutritional status of children with hyperphenylalaninaemia, *Journal of Inherited Metabolic Disorders* 11, 431–2.

Oldendorf, W. H. (1973). Stereospecificity of blood–brain barrier permeability to amino acids. *American Journal of Physiology* 224, 967–9.

Orzhekhovskaya, N. S. (1981). Fronto-striatal relationships in primate ontogeny. *Neuroscience Behavioral Physiology* 11, 379–85.

Owen, A. M., Morris, R. G., Sahakian, B. J., Polkey, C. E., and Robbins, T. W. (1996). Double dissociations of memory and executive functions in a self-ordered working memory task following frontal lobe excision, temporal lobe excisions or amygdalahippocampectomy in man. *Brain* 119, 1597–1615.

Owen, A. M., Herrod, N. J., Menon, D. K., Clark, J. C., Downey, S. P., Carpenter, T. A., Minhas, P. S., Turkheimer, F. E., Williams, E. J., Robbins, T. W., Sahakian, B. J., Petrides, M., and Pickard, J. D. (1999). Redefining the functional organization of working memory processes within human lateral prefrontal cortex. *European Journal of Neuroscience* 11(2), 567–74.

Pardridge, W. (1977). Regulation of amino acid availability to the brain. In R. J. Wurtman and J. J. Wurtman (eds.), *Nutrition and the Brain* (pp. 141–204). New York: Raven Press.

Pardridge, W. M. and Oldendorf, W. H. (1977). Transport of metabolic substrates through the blood–brain barrier. *Journal of Neurochemistry* 28, 5–12.

Passler, P. A., Isaac, W., and Hynd, G. W. (1985). Neuropsychological development of behavior attributed to frontal lobe functioning in children. *Developmental Neuropsychology* 4, 349–70.

Pelli, D. G., Robson, J. G., and Wilkins, A. J. (1988). The design of a new letter chart for measuring contrast sensitivity. *Clinical Vision Science* 2, 187–99.

Pennington, B. F., VanDoornick, W. J., McCabe, L. L., and McCabe, E. R. B. (1985). Neuropsychological deficits in early treated phenylketonuric children. *American Journal of Mental Deficiency* 89, 467–74.

Pennington, B. F. and Ozonoff, S. (1996). Executive function and developmental psychopathology. *Journal of Child Psychology and Psychiatry* 37, 51–87.

Perret, E. (1974). The left frontal lobe of man and the suppression of habitual responses in verbal categorical behaviour. *Neuropsychologia* 12, 527–37.

Petrides, M. (1994). Frontal lobes and working memory: Evidence from investigations of the effects of cortical excisions in nonhuman primates. In F. Boller and J. Grafman (eds.), *Handbook of Neuropsychology* (pp. 59–82). Amsterdam: Elsevier Science Publishers.

Petrides, M. (1995). Impairments on nonspatial self-ordered and externally ordered working memory tasks after lesions of the mid-dorsal part of the lateral frontal cortex in the monkey. *Journal of Neuroscience* 15, 359–75.

Petrides, M. (1995b). Functional organization of the human frontal cortex for mnemonic processing: Evidence from neuroimaging studies. *Annals of the New York Academy of Sciences* 769, 85–96.

Petrides, M. and Milner, B. (1982). Deficits in subject-ordered tasks after frontal- and temporal-lobe lesions in man. *Neuropsychologia* 20, 249–62.

Petrides, M. and Pandya, D. N. (1999). Dorsolateral prefrontal cortex: Comparative cytoarchitectonic analysis in the human and the macaque brain and corticocortical connection patterns. *European Journal of Neuroscience* 11, 1011–36.

Petrides, M. and Pandya, D. N. (1988). Association fiber pathways to the frontal cortex from the superior temporal region in the rhesus monkey. *Journal of Comparative Neurology* 273, 52–66.

Petrides, M. and Pandya, D. N. (1984). Projections to the frontal cortex from the posterior parietal region in the rhesus monkey. *Journal of Comparative Neurology* 228, 105–16.

Piaget, J. (1954 [1936]). *The Construction of Reality in the Child* (M. Cook, trans.). New York: Basic Books. (Original work published 1936).

Piaget, J. and Inhelder, B. (1941). *Le Développement des quantités chez l'enfant*. Neuchâtel: Delachaux et Niestlé.

Pines, J. L. (1927). Zur architektonik des thalamus opticus beim halbaffen (lemur catta). *J. of Psychol. Neurol.* 33, 31–72.

Pinsker, H. M. and French, G. M. (1967). Indirect delayed reactions under various testing conditions in normal and midlateral frontal monkeys. *Neuropsychologia* 5, 13–24.

Pohl, W. (1973). Dissociation of spatial discrimination deficits following frontal and parietal lesions in monkeys. *Journal of Comparative and Physiological Psychology* 82, 227–39.

Postle, B. R., Berger, J. S., and D'Esposito, M. (1999). Functional neuroanatomical double dissociation of mnemonic and executive control processes contributing to working memory performance. *Proceedings of the National Academy of Sciences* 96, 12959–64.

Postle, B. R. and D'Esposito, M. (1998). Homologous mechanisms underlie dissociable components of set-shifting and task-switching. The Psychonomic Society, 39th Annual Meeting, 43.

Price, B. H., Daffner, K. R., Stowe, R. M., and Mesulam, M. M. (1990). The comportmental learning disabilities of early frontal lobe damage. *Brain* 113, 1383–93.

Rapoport, S. I. (1976). Sites and functions of the blood–aqueous and blood–vitreous barriers of the eye. In S. I. Rapoport (ed.), *Blood–Brain Barrier in Physiology and Medicine* (pp. 207–32). New York: Raven Press.

Regan, D. and Neima, D. (1983). Low-contrast letter charts as a test of visual function. *Ophthalmology* 90, 1192–200.

Regan, D. and Neima, D. (1984). Low-contrast letter charts in early diabetic retinopathy, ocular hypertension, glaucoma, and Parkinson's disease. *British Journal of Ophthalmology* 68, 885–9.

Rice, C., Koinis, D., Sullivan, K., Tager-Flusberg, H., and Winner, E. (1997).When 3-year-olds pass the appearance–reality test. *Developmental Psychology* 33, 54–61.

Richer, F., Decary, A., Lapierre, M. F., Rouleau, I., and Bouvier, G. (1993). Target detection deficits in frontal lobotomy. *Brain and Cognition* 21, 203–11.

Ris, M. D., Williams, S. E., Hunt, M. M., Berry, H. K., and Leslie, N. (1994). Early-treated phenylketonuria: Adult neuropsychologic outcome. *Journal of Pediatrics* 124, 388–92.

Robertson, L. C., Lamb, M. R., and Knight, R. T. (1988). Effects of lesions of temporal–parietal junction on perceptual and attentional processing in humans. *Journal of Neuroscience* 8, 3757–69.

Rogers, G. L., Bremer, D. L., and Leguire, L. E. (1987). Contrast sensitivity functions in normal children with the Vistech method. *Journal of Pediatric Ophthalmology and Strabismus* 24, 216–19.

Rose, J. E. and Woolsey, C. N. (1948). The orbitofrontal cortex and its connections with the mediodorsal nucleus in rabbit, sheep and cat. *Research Publications of the Association for Research on Nervous and Mental Disorders* 27, 210–32.

Rosenberg, D. R. and Lewis, D. A. (1994). Changes in the dopaminergic innervation of monkey prefrontal cortex during late postnatal development: A tyrosine hydroxylase immunohisto-chemical study. *Biological Psychiatry* 15, 272–7.

Rosenberg, D. R. and Lewis, D. A. (1995). Postnatal maturation of the dopaminergic innerv-ation of monkey prefrontal and motor cortices: A tyrosine hydroxylase immunohistochemical analysis. *Journal of Comparative Neurology* 358, 383–400.

Roth, R. H. (1984). CNS dopamine autoreceptors: Distribution, pharmacology, and function. *Annals of the New York Academy of Sciences* 430, 27–53.

Russell, J., Mauthner, N., Sharpe, S., and Tidswell, T. (1991). The "windows task" as a measure of strategic deception in preschoolers and autistic subjects. *British Journal of Developmental Psychology* 9, 331–49.

Rypma, B. and D'Esposito, M. (1999). The roles of prefrontal brain regions in components of working memory: Effects of memory load and individual differences. *Proceedings of the National Academy of Sciences* 96, 6558–63.

Sahakian, B. J., Sarna, G. S., Kantamaneni, B. D., Jackson, A., Hutson, P. H., and Curzon, G. (1985). Association between learning and cortical catecholamines in non-drug-treated rats. *Psychopharmacology* 86, 339–43.

Saint-Cyr, J. A., Wan, R. O., Doudet, D., and Aigner, T. G. (1988). Impaired detour reaching in rhesus monkeys after MPTP lesions. *Society for Neuroscience Abstracts* 14, 389.

Sasaki, K., Jinnai, K., Gemba, H., Hashimoto, S., and Mizuno, N. (1979). Projection of the cerebellar dentate nucleus onto the frontal association cortex in monkeys. *Experimental Brain Research* 37, 193–8.

Savoy, R. L., O'Craven, K. M., Davidson, M., and Diamond, A. (1999). Memory load and inhibition in dorsolateral prefrontal cortex. Presented at the International Conference on Functional Mapping of the Human Brain, Dusseldorf, Germany.

Sawaguchi, T. and Goldman-Rakic, P. S. (1991). D1 dopamine receptors in prefrontal cortex: Involvement in working memory. *Science* 251, 947–50.

Sawaguchi, T., Matsumura, M., and Kubota, K. (1988). Dopamine enhances the neuronal activity of spatial short-term memory task in the primate prefrontal cortex. *Neuroscience Research* 5, 465–73.

Sawaguchi, T., Matsumura, M., and Kubota, K. (1990). Effects of dopamine antagonists on neuronal activity related to a delayed response task in monkey prefrontal cortex. *Journal of Neurophysiology* 63, 1401–12.

Schmahmann, J. D. and Pandya, D. N. (1995). Prefrontal cortex projections to the basilar pons in rhesus monkey: Implications for the cerebellar contribution to higher function. *Neuroscience Letters* 199, 175–8.

Schneider, J. S. and Kovelowski, C. J., II. (1990). Chronic exposure to low doses of MPTP: I. Cognitive deficits in motor asymptomatic monkeys. *Brain Research* 519, 122–8.

Schneider, J. S. and Roeltgen, D. P. (1993). Delayed matching-to-sample, object retrieval, and discrimination reversal deficits in chronic low dose MPTP-treated monkeys. *Brain Research* 615, 351–4.

Schwartz, M. L. and Golman-Rakic, P. S. (1984). Callosal and intrahemispheric connectivity of the prefrontal association cortex in rhesus monkey: Relation between intraparietal and principal sulcal cortex. *Journal of Comparative Neurology* 226, 403–20.

Selemon, L. D. and Goldman-Rakic, P. S. (1985). Longitudinal topography and interdigitation of corticostriatal projections in the rhesus monkey. *Journal of Neuroscience* 5, 776–94.

Selemon, L. D. and Goldman-Rakic, P. S. (1988). Common cortical and subcortical targets of the dorsolateral prefrontal and posterior parietal cortices in the rhesus monkey: Evidence for a distributed neural network subserving spatially guided behavior. *Journal of Neuroscience* 8, 4049–68.

Seltzer, B. and Pandya, D. N. (1989). Frontal lobe connections of the superior temporal sulcus in the rhesus monkey. *Journal of Comparative Neurology* 281, 97–113.

Shallice, T. (1988). *From Neuropsychology to Mental Structure*. Cambridge University Press, Cambridge.

Shedlovsky, A., McDonald, J. D., Symula, D., and Dove, W. F. (1993). Mouse models of human phenylketonuria. *Genetics* 134, 1205–10.

Simon, R. J. and Berbaum, K. (1990). Effect of conflicting cues on information processing: The "Stroop Effect" vs. the "Simon Effect." *Acta Psychologia* 73, 159–70.

Simon, H., Scatton, B., and LeMoal, M. (1980). Dopaminergic A10 neurons are involved in cognitive functions. *Nature* 286, 150–1.

Siwek, D. F. and Pandya, D. N. (1991). Prefrontal projections to the mediodorsal nucleus of the thalamus in the rhesus monkey. *Journal of Comparative Neurology* 312, 509–24.

Skrandies, W. and Gottlob, I. (1986). Alterations of visual contrast sensitivity in Parkinson's disease. *Human Neurobiology* 5, 255–9.

Smith, E. E., Jonides, J., Marshuetz, C., and Koeppe, R. A. (1998). Components of verbal working memory: Evidence from neuroimaging, *Proceedings of the National Academy of Sciences* 95(3), 876–82.

Smith, E. E. and Jonides, J. (1999). Storage and executive processes in the frontal lobes. *Science* 283, 1657–61.

Smith, I. and Beasley, M. (1989). Intelligence and behaviour in children with early treated phenylketonuria. *European Journal of Clinical Nutrition* 43, 1–5.

Smith, L. B., Thelen, E., Titzer, R., and McLin, D. (1999). Knowing in the context of acting: The task dynamics of the A-not-B error. *Psychol. Rev.* 106, 235–60.

Smith, M. L., Klim, P., Mallozzi, E., and Hanley, W. B. (1996). A test of the frontal-specificity hypothesis in the cognitive performance of adults with phenylketonuria. *Developmental Neuropsychology* 12, 327–41.

Sonneville, L. N. J. de., Schmidt, E., Michel, U., and Batzler, U. (1990). Preliminary neuropsychological test results. *European Journal of Pediatrics* 149 (supplement 1): S39–S44.

Sophian, C. and Wellman, H. M. (1983). Selective information use and perseveration in the search behavior of infants and young children. *Journal of Experimental Child Psychology* 35, 369–90.

Sowell, E. R., Thompson, P. M., Holmes, C. J., Jernigan, T. L., and Toga, A. W. (1999). In vivo evidence for post-adolescent brain maturation in frontal and striatal regions. *Nature Neuroscience* 2, 859–61.

Squire, L. R., Zola-Morgan, S., and Chen, K. S. (1988). Human amnesia and animal models of amnesia: Performance of amnesic patients on tests designed for the monkey. *Behavioral Neuroscience* 102, 210–21.

Stemerdink, B. A., van der Meere, J. J., van der Molen, M. W., Kalverboer, A. F., Hendrikx, M. M. T., Huisman, J., van der Schot, L. W. A., Slijper, F. M. E., van Spronsen, F. J., and Verkerk, P. H. (1995). Information processing in patients with early and continuously-treated phenylketonuria. *European Journal of Pediatrics* 154, 739–46.

Stuss, D. T. and Benson, D. F. (1986). *The Frontal Lobes.* New York: Raven Press.

Stuss, D. T. and Benson, D. F. (1987). The frontal lobes and control of cognition and memory. In E. Perecman (ed.), *The Frontal Lobes Revisited* (pp. 141–58). New York: IRBN Press.

Tam, S. Y., Elsworth, J. D., Bradberry, C. W., and Roth, R. H. (1990). Mesocortical dopamine neurons: High basal firing frequency predicts tyrosine dependence of dopamine synthesis. *Journal of Neural Transmission* 81, 97–110.

Taylor, J. R., Elsworth, J. D., Roth, R. H., Sladek, J. R., Jr., and Redmond, D. E., Jr. (1990a). Cognitive and motor deficits in the acquisition of an object retrieval detour task in MPTP-treated monkeys. *Brain* 113, 617–37.

Taylor, J. R., Roth, R. H., Sladek, J. R., Jr., and Redmond, D. E., Jr. (1990b). Cognitive and motor deficits in the performance of the object retrieval detour task in monkeys (*cercopithecus aethiops sabaeus*) treated with MPTP: Long-term performance and effect of transparency of the barrier. *Behavioral Neuroscience* 104, 564–76.

Thatcher, R. W., Walker, R. A., and Giudice, S. (1987). Human cerebral hemispheres develop at different rates and ages. *Science* 230, 1110–13.

Thierry, A. M., Tassin, J. P., Blanc, A., Stinus, L., Scatton, B., and Glowinski, J. (1977). Discovery of the mesocortical dopaminergic system: Some pharmacological and functional characteristics. *Advanced Biomedical Psychopharmacology* 16, 5–12.

Tobias, T. J. (1975). Afferents to prefrontal cortex from the thalamic mediodorsal nucleus in the rhesus monkey. *Brain Research* 83, 191–212.

Tornquist, P. and Alm, A. (1986). Carrier-mediated transport of amino acids through the blood–retinal and blood–brain barriers. *Graefe's Archive for Clinical and Experimental Ophthalmology* 224, 21–5.

Tourian, A. Y. and Sidbury, J. B. (1978). Phenylketonuria. In J. D. Stanbury, J. B. Wyngaarden, and D. Fredrickson (eds.), *The Metabolic Basis of Inherited Disease* (pp. 240–55). New York: McGraw-Hill.

Tweten, S., Wall, M., and Schwartz, B. D. (1990). A comparison of three clinical methods of spatial contrast-sensitivity testing in normal subjects. *Graefe's Archive for Clinical and Experimental Ophthalmology* 228, 24–7.

Vogt, B. A. and Pandya, D. N. (1987). Cingulate cortex of the rhesus monkey: II. Cortical afferents. *Journal of Comparative Neurology* 262, 271–89.

Vogt, B. A., Rosene, D. L., and Pandya, D. N. (1979). Thalamic and cortical afferents differentiate anterior from posterior cingulate cortex in the monkey. *Science* 204, 205–7.

Walker, A. E. (1940). A cytoarchitectural study of the prefrontal area of the macaque monkey. *Journal of Comparative Neurology* 73, 59–86.

Warren, J. M. and Akert, K. (1964). *The Frontal Granular Cortex and Behavior.* McGraw-Hill, New York.

Watanabe, M., Kodama, T., and Hikosaka, K. (1997). Increase of extracellular dopamine in primate prefrontal cortex during a working memory task. *Journal of Neurophysiology* 78, 2795–8.

Weglage, J., Pietsch, M., Funders, B., Koch, H. G., and Ullrich, K. (1995). Neurological findings in early treated phenylketonuria. *Acta Pædiatrica* 84, 411–15.

Welsh, M. C., Pennington, B. F., Ozonoff, S., Rouse, B., and McCabe, E. R. B. (1990). Neuropsychology of early-treated phenylketonuria: Specific executive function deficits. *Child Development* 61, 1697–1713.

Wiesendanger, M. (1981). Organization of the secondary motor areas of the cerebral cortex. In V. B. Brooks (ed.), *Handbook of Physiology: The Nervous System* (Vol. 2: *Motor Control*). Bethesda, MD: American Physiological Society.

Wikmark, R. G. E., Divac, I., and Weiss, R. (1973). Delayed alternation in rats with lesions in the frontal lobes: Implications for a comparative neuropsychology of the frontal system. *Brain, Behavior and Evolution* 8, 329–39.

Willats, P. (1985). Adjustment of means–ends coordination and the representation of spatial relations in the production of search errors by infants. *British Journal of Developmental Psychology* 3, 259–72.

Williams, S. M. and Goldman-Rakic, P. S. (1993). Characterization of the dopaminergic innervation of the primate frontal cortex using a dopamine-specific antibody. *Cerebral Cortex* 3, 199–222.

Williams, S. M. and Goldman-Rakic, P. S. (1995). Modulation of memory fields by dopamine D1 receptors in prefrontal cortex. *Nature* 376, 572–5.

Williamson, M. L., Koch, R., Azen, C., and Chang, C. (1981). Correlates of intelligence test results in treated phenylketonuric children. *Pediatrics* 68, 161–7.

Woo, S. L. C., Lidsky, A. S., Güttler, F., Chandra, T., and Robson, K. J. H. (1983). Cloned human phenylalanine hydroxylase gene allows prenatal diagnosis and carrier detection of classical phenylketonuria. *Nature* 306, 151–5.

Wurtman, R. J., Lorin, F., Mostafapour, S., and Fernstrom, J. D. (1974). Brain catechol synthesis: Control by brain tyrosine concentration. *Science* 185, 183–4.

Yakovlev, P. I. and Lecours, A. R. (1967). The myelogenetic cycles of regional maturation of the brain. In A. Minkowski (ed.), *Regional Development of the Brain in Early Life* (pp. 3–70). Oxford: Blackwell.

Yamamoto, T., Yoshida, K., Yoshikawa, H., Kishimoto, Y., and Oka, H. (1992). The medial dorsal nucleus is one of the thalamic relays of the cerebellocerebral responses to the frontal association cortex in the monkey: Horseradish peroxidase and florescent dye double staining study. *Brain Research* 579, 315–20.

Zagreda, L., Goodman, J., Druin, D. P., McDonald, D., and Diamond, A. (1999). Cognitive deficits in a genetic mouse model of the most common biochemical cause of human mental retardation. *Journal of Neuroscience* 19, 6175–82.

Zaitchik, D. (1991). Is only seeing really believing?: Sources of the true belief in the false belief task. *Cognitive Development* 6, 91–103.

Zelazo, P. D., Frye, D., and Rapus, T. (1996). An age-related dissociation between knowing rules and using them. *Cognitive Development* 11, 37–63.

Zelazo, P. D. and Reznick, J. S. (1991). Age-related asynchrony of knowledge and action. *Child Development* 62, 719–35.

Zelazo, P. D., Reznick, J. S., and Pinon, D. E. (1995). Response control and the execution of verbal rules. *Developmental Psychology* 31, 508–17.

Zola-Morgan, S., Squire, L. R., and Amaral, D. G. (1989). Lesions of the hippocampal formation but not lesions of the fornix or mammillary nuclei produce long-lasting memory impairment in monkeys. *Journal of Neuroscience*, 9, 897–912.

23

Genes and Brain: Individual Differences and Human Universals

Bruce F. Pennington

Developmental cognitive neuroscience has the ambitious goal of elucidating the neural mechanisms underlying both universals and individual differences in cognitive and behavioral development. In this chapter, I will review how genetic methods are relevant, indeed crucial, for achieving that goal. By adding the word developmental to the term cognitive neuroscience, we are committing ourselves to the proposition that brain–behavior relations in the mature organism cannot be understood without understanding how the brain develops and how the development of the brain mediates the development of cognition and behavior. I am also proposing that once we take development seriously, we must also take genetics seriously.

Genetics and Cognitive Neuroscience

In what follows, I will (1) consider general issues in the relation between genetics and cognitive neuroscience, (2) discuss two broad strategies for studying genetic effects on cognitive development, (3) provide an overview of behavioral and molecular genetic methods, and (4) consider the implications of these genetic methods for fundamental issues in developmental cognitive neuroscience.

On general principles, it should not be too surprising that there are genetic influences on cognitive and behavioral development. Of the roughly 30,000 structural genes in the human genome, approximately 40 percent are uniquely expressed in the central nervous system (Hahn, van Ness, and Maxwell, 1978), whereas many of the remaining 60 percent are expressed in the central nervous system as well as elsewhere in the body. We have no reason to suppose that the genes expressed uniquely in the central nervous system are less polymorphic than other genes. (Polymorphic means having alternate forms or "alleles," where an allele of a gene is a variant DNA sequence of that gene.) In fact, because of the relatively recent evolution of some human behaviors, there are good reasons for supposing they are more polymorphic. Since much of human evolution has involved rapid brain evolution, we should expect the genes expressed in the brain to be more polymorphic than those expressed in evolutionarily older organs. So, because of the large number of genes expressed in the human brain and its rapid, recent evolution, we expect individual differences in the genes that influence human brain and behavioral development. Consistent with this theoretical prediction, behavioral geneticists have documented moderate heritability for most human cognitive and personality traits (Plomin and McClearn, 1993). Because the heritability of these individual differences averages about .50, there are also substantial environmental influences on such individual differences.

Unfortunately, most studies of environmental influences on human development confound genetic and environmental influences. Such studies do not use genetically-sensitive designs and therefore their findings of a correlation between an environmental variable and a behavior in the developing child do not necessarily demonstrate an environmental influence on development (Scarr, 1992). Suppose we find a correlation between how emotion is regulated in the mother–infant relationship and the child's later emotion regulation in peer relations. It can seem straightforward to conclude that the earlier social experience shaped the later social behavior. However, if the study sample consisted only of biological mothers with their infants, then the design confounds genetic and environmental influences. Besides sharing early social experiences, such mother–infant pairs also share half their segregating genes (genes that vary across individual humans). Consequently, the observed correlation could be partly or totally mediated by genes. So, we need genetically-sensitive designs not only to study genetic influences on development, but also to study environmental influences as well.

Likewise, universals in human development are also a joint product of genes and environments, ones which do *not* vary across human individuals. It is likely that not all genes that influence brain development are polymorphic. Moreover, as Greenough, Black, and Wallace (1987; this volume) have discussed, there are very important environmental influences on brain development that do not vary across individuals in a species. As they demonstrate, synaptogenesis cannot proceed normally without these species-typical environmental influences. To understand the etiology of human universals, we need to identify these genes and environments that virtually all humans share. Cross-species studies can help with this identification.

The reader may wonder at this point, how exactly does a gene help build a neuron or a brain? These questions point to the central puzzle in developmental biology, which is how does a single cell become a differentiated multi-cellular organism. Although skin cells are different from blood cells, and both are different from neurons, all of these different kinds of cells have the same genes and chromosomes in their nuclei. So the differentiation of precursor cells (embryonic stem cells, which are derived from the single fertilized egg) into different kinds of cells, tissues, and organs has to reflect differences in gene expression across cells. At any one time, only a small fraction of the genes in a cell are actively being transcribed. Regulation of gene expression in development derives in part from local interactions among cells in different parts of the developing embryo. Although there is much still to be learned about how all this happens, considerable progress is being made (see Changeaux, 1985 for a very readable summary). So, in precursor cells that will become neurons, genes for neuronal functions, such as neurotransmission, are being transcribed and genes specific to skin and blood cells are not being transcribed. How interactions among immature neurons and glial cells under the influence of environmental input builds a brain is described in Changeaux (1985), Johnson (1997) and Shatz (1993; this volume).

Before proceeding, it is also important to address the long history of controversy about genetic studies in psychology. Some of this controversy derived from misleading claims about the implications of such studies, such as the view that the results of behavioral genetic studies support strict genetic determinism or provide a genetic explanation of group differences in behavior, neither of which is true. As Rende and Plomin (1995, p. 291) point out, it is important to "study nature AND nurture, rather than nature VERSUS nurture." Behavioral development is the emergent product of a complex process of probabilistic epigenesis (Gottlieb, 1991; 1998; this volume), to which both genes and environments contribute. But neither genes nor environments code for behavior directly. Both sides of the nature–nurture debate share the same erroneous assumption that the instructions for behavior are pre-existent either in the genome or the environment and are imposed from without on the developing organism (Oyama, 1985; this volume). Instead, genetic and environmental influences are inputs to a developmental process and their impact on behavioral outcome depends on their interactions with all the components of that process. Consequently, it is misleading to speak of the genome as a "blueprint" or to think that genes "code" for a behavior. Genes simply code for protein structure, and variations in the structure of a given protein, in a particular epigenetic context, may push behavioral outcomes in one direction or another. So, genetic and environmental factors are best conceptualized as acting as risk (or protective) factors in the development of individual differences in behavior; their effects are probabilistic rather than deterministic.

It is also useful to contrast this view of genetics and development with dominant views in both traditional neuropsychology and in some of contemporary cognitive neuroscience. Although the lesion study has been the central paradigm in traditional neuropsychology, a different paradigm is needed in developmental cognitive neuroscience for several reasons. An acquired lesion is rare in childhood, extrinsic to normal development, and essentially an irreproducible natural experiment. Indeed, since no two acquired lesions are exactly alike, some cognitive neuropsychologists have concluded that each single case should be treated separately. In contrast, genetic influences on development are common, are intrinsic to the neurobiological mechanisms underlying cognitive and social development, and are reproducible, thus permitting group studies.

At a deeper, theoretical level the central ideas implicit in the lesion paradigm do not fit well with emerging findings in developmental neurobiology. The lesion paradigm assumes a relatively invariant, modular, species-typical cognitive architecture which can be dissected into independent cognitive components through the method of double dissociation (Shallice, 1988). In contrast, brain development across the life span is turning out to be very plastic both within and across individuals (Changeaux, 1985). Moreover, the neural architecture may well be better characterized by recurrent, connectionist networks, whose activities are non-linear and interdependent, than as a set of independent, cognitive modules (Oliver et al., 2000; Van Orden, Pennington, and Stone, 2000).

The method of double dissociation has been applied to genetic disorders in an attempt to begin to relate genes to modules. For instance, children or adults with Down syndrome have a cognitive profile (language functions more impaired than spatial functions) that is opposite to the cognitive profile found in children and adults with Williams syndrome, hence a double dissociation. One could be tempted to conclude that the genetic etiologies of each of these syndromes have opposite effects on innate language modules. However, such a conclusion assumes that the double dissociation found in children and adults is also present in infants with these disorders. However, experiments with infants with Williams syndrome shows that their cognitive profile changes across development, even to the point of producing a within-syndrome double dissociation (Paterson et al., 1999). In particular, their strength in language is much less apparent in infancy. So, applying the lesion paradigm to genetic disorders can lead to erroneous conclusions.

Therefore, the central ideas of the lesion paradigm are all in question. Although the lesion method has been extremely useful in giving us a "first pass" mapping of structure–

function relations, other methods (and metaphors) are needed to tell us how the self-organizing system of the brain puts itself together in both normal and abnormal development.

Two Strategies for Relating Genes to Development

We now turn to a description of genetic designs which are useful for developmental cognitive neuroscience. Such designs may be grouped into two broad categories, representing two different strategies for tracing developmental pathways from genes to brain development to behavior. Genetic studies of cognitive and behavioral development may begin with a known gene or mutation and work "forwards" to understand its impact on development, or begin with a cognitive or behavioral phenotype and work "backwards" to uncover the main genetic and environmental influences on that phenotype.

Both the "forwards" and "backwards" strategies may be applied to understanding either universals or individual differences. So far, most of the human work has focused on the extreme individual differences that characterize different disorders of development. That is due in part to the obvious ethical requirement that human studies can only consider natural experiments. But as knowledge of the human and other mammalian genomes increases we will be able to identify which genes are unique to our species and which are shared with other mammals. Both some of the unique and some of the shared genes will contribute to human universals, and their role in normal brain and behavioral development can be at least partly elucidated through animal models.

Examples of the application of each strategy to extreme human individual differences are presented in different chapters of a recent edited volume on neurodevelopmental disorders (Tager-Flusberg, 1999). Examples of the first strategy are neurodevelopmental studies of Down syndrome, fragile X syndrome, PKU, and Williams syndrome, and other neurogenetic disorders. Examples of the second strategy are genetic studies of attention deficit hyperactivity disorder, autism, dyslexia, developmental speech and language disorders, schizophrenia, Tourette's syndrome, and other psychiatric disorders. Since the details of most of the discoveries using each strategy are reviewed elsewhere, this chapter will not review specific discoveries except in an illustrative way. Instead, the chapter will focus on methods and the general implications of what has already been discovered for developmental cognitive neuroscience.

It is important to remember that both strategies, when applied only to humans, suffer from some common weaknesses, one of which is the quasi-experimental nature of case-control designs. The genetic alteration is not randomly assigned by the experimenter, and so no matter how carefully comparison groups are matched, we can never be totally sure that the genetic alteration in question is the only factor that differs across groups. A second shared weakness is that both the genetic and environmental backgrounds of individuals with a given syndrome are obviously free to vary and this variance may mask the phenotypic effects of the genetic alteration in question.

A partial solution for both these problems is the use of animal models, in which the genetic alteration is randomly assigned and the genetic and environmental background is controlled. Complementary studies of humans and animals with the same genetic (or metabolic) alteration is a powerful strategy, which is now being applied to fragile X (Willems, Reyniers, and Oostra, 1995) and Down syndrome (Crnic and Pennington, 2000). Another important advantage of these animal models is they permit a clearer test of which brain correlates associated with a syndrome are directly caused by the genetic alteration in question.

In contrast, neuroimaging findings from humans with a given syndrome only provide correlates of the syndrome. Such findings could be a product of environmental differences associated with the syndrome, rather than a product of its genetic etiology. So, establishing a causal relations between a genetic alteration and a brain phenotype is difficult without an animal model.

In what follows, we will focus on the methods used in the "backwards" strategy, since those involved in the "forwards" strategy are already well described elsewhere. Then we will consider the implications of results from both strategies for fundamental issues in developmental cognitive neuroscience.

How to Go From Behavior to Genes

Until fairly recently, the main methods available for evaluating genetic influences on individual differences in human behavior were indirect ones that did not examine differences in DNA sequences. Instead, the influence of such differences on the development of individual differences in behavior was inferred through careful quantitative analyses of naturally occurring quasi-experiments, mainly twin births and adoptions. It is important to understand that both direct (molecular) and indirect (quantitative or biometric) genetic methods derive their power from a very strong theoretical constraint. This constraint is that while genotypes exert causal influences on phenotypes, phenotypes do not change genotypes, except in the unusual situation where the phenotype leads to a mutation through exposure to ionizing radiation. Our genome can alter our behavior, but our behavior cannot influence our genome (although behavior can influence gene expression). Therefore, if we find a non-artifactual relation between genotype and behavior, it means there is some causal pathway leading from that genotype to that behavior, no matter however torturous it is and no matter how many other causes also act on the behavior. Thus, genetic studies, unlike other non-experimental studies of human behavior, address causation.

One may organize the genetic analysis of any trait or phenotype into a series of four questions, one leading to the next, with each question answered by a different method. These questions are (1) Is the trait familial? (2) If so, is the familiality due in part to genetic influences? In other words, is the trait heritable? (3) If so, what is the mechanism of genetic transmission? and (4) What are the actual gene or genes responsible for that mechanism? Once such genes are discovered, additional questions of key relevance to developmental cognitive neuroscience may be addressed: (5) When and where are these genes expressed in the developing brain and how do they alter its development? (6) How do those alterations change developing neural networks, thus changing cognitive and behavioral development? and (7) How can the influences of other genes and environmental factors modify these developmental effects?

We will now briefly explain the methods used to answer each of the first four questions, and provide some illustrative findings. These methods are (1) family studies, (2) twin and adoption studies, (3) segregation analysis, and (4) linkage and association analysis. Tables 23.1 and 23.2 summarize these methods and some key issues involved in their interpretation.

The design of family studies is fairly straightforward; the goal is to measure the familiality of a trait, which can be quantified as the correlations among relatives for a

Table 23.1 Biometrical (indirect) methods

Method	Use	Issues
Family studies	Estimate familial risk (λ)	Ascertainment; familiality may be environmentally mediated
Twin and adoption studies	Estimate proportions of variance attributable to genes (h^2), shared environment (c^2), and non-shared environment (e^2)	Estimates are both population- and model-dependent
Segregation analysis	Model the mode of transmission	Familiality may be environmentally mediated. Results are limited to the range of models tested

Table 23.2 Molecular methods

Method	Use	Issues
Linkage		
Parametric	Find approximate location of a major locus influencing a phenotype	Transmission parameters of complex behavioral phenotypes are often unknown
Non-parametric	Find approximate location of genes influencing a phenotype	Less powerful
Association		
Case-Control	Identify an allele that influences a phenotype	Ethnic stratification; multiple mutations of the same gene
Family-Based		
Transmission Disequilibrium Test (TDT)	Same	Multiple mutations
Haplotype Relative Risk (HRR)	Same	Multiple mutations

continuous trait or as relative risk (the prevalence in relatives divided by the population prevalence) for a categorical trait. These correlations or relative risks are computed separately for different relationships in families, and tested for statistical significance. A very useful statistic for genetic studies is the relative risk to full siblings (λ), because the ease of finding genes that influence a trait is proportional to λ. For instance, an λ of 2 means that the relative risk to full siblings is twice the population risk.

It is now well established that many psychiatric disorders are familial. For instance, the value of λ is 9 for schizophrenia, 8 for bipolar disorder, and 3 for major depression (Plomin et al., 1997). Similar values have been found for childhood psychiatric disorders; λs are around 6 for attention deficit hyperactivity disorder (Faraone et al., 1992), about 8 for dyslexia (Gilger, Pennington, and DeFries, 1991), and as high as 100 for autism (Plomin et al., 1997). Although familiality does not prove genetic influence (since familial transmission may be environmentally mediated), data from twin and molecular studies have demonstrated that genetic influences make a large contribution to the familiality of psychiatric disorders.

Segregation analysis is a particular kind of family study, one which formally tests competing models for the mode of transmission of a trait in families. Segregation analysis is a computationally intensive modeling procedure and the results are limited to the range of modes of transmission that are modeled, which are mainly single locus, Mendelian modes. The transmission of a complex behavioral phenotype may well involve the interaction of several genes and several environmental risk factors. Obviously, segregation analysis only provides an indirect test of genetic mechanisms. Hence, if a major locus effect is found by segregation analysis, molecular methods are needed to confirm this result and to identify the location of the major locus in the genome.

The most widely used behavioral genetic methods have been twin and adoption studies, which mainly address question 2 concerning heritability. These methods provide a means of testing models of the etiology of a given behavior, or the relation between multiple behaviors, in a population. Such methods take the population variance in a behavioral trait and test which combination of genetic and environmental components best accounts for it. As in all of science, the meaning of the results naturally depends on the choice and validity of the models tested and their background assumptions. A good introduction to twin and adoption methods is provided by Plomin et al. (1997).

To study the etiology of developmental psychopathology, we need to apply twin and adoption methods to the analysis of extreme variations in behavior, rather than the analysis of variance across the whole distribution. Extreme variations may be treated as categories, in which case the appropriate method of analysis is non-parametric and involves comparing the rates of concordance for different degrees of relationship. Twin concordance studies have found genetic influences on most psychiatric disorders (Plomin et al., 1997; Plomin, Owen, and McGuffin, 1994).

However, if the trait in question is quantitative (can be measured using an ordinal or interval scale), then treating the trait as categorical does not use all the information contained in the data and is thus less statistically powerful. If we can measure not only whether someone has ADHD or reading disability, but also how severely they have it, then our data are quantitative rather than qualitative and can be analyzed with parametric statistics. A particularly powerful twin method for analyzing extreme variation in quantitative traits was developed by DeFries and Fulker (1988) and is now called the DF method in their honor. The DF method is based on the phenomenon of differential regression to the mean, first described by Francis Galton (1869).

The advantage of the DF method is that it provides a statistically powerful method of modeling these components of the etiology of the scores of an extreme group. Another advantage of this method is its flexibility; it can readily be extended to (1) the bivariate case, where we are interested in the etiologic basis of the phenotypic correlation between two extreme traits, (2) an evaluation of differential etiology (of subgroups, such as males and females, or extreme and normal variations) or (3) a test for linkage.

To answer the fourth question concerning gene locations, molecular methods are needed (table 23.2). In contrast to the methods discussed above, these methods can provide direct evidence of genetic influence on a trait or on the relation among traits. All of these methods test for a relation between DNA sequence variations and phenotypic variations, so these methods require precise measures in both domains and theoretically sound quantitative methods of relating genetic variation with phenotypic variation. As discussed earlier, it is important to understand that the relation being tested is not simply a correlation; rather, it is the hypothesis that sequence variation in a particular part of the genome causes, at least in part, the phenotypic variation.

We can divide molecular methods into tests of *linkage* and tests of *association*. Generally, we use linkage methods when we lack a hypothesis about which gene influences the trait in question, whereas tests of association have usually required such a hypothesis, although association methods are now being developed which can be used in a whole genome search.

The initial goal of linkage methods is to find the approximate locations of genes influencing a trait. The phenomenon of linkage depends on the fact that, as it were, the croupier in the genetic casino does not shuffle perfectly. The phenomenon of recombination shuffles genes (cards in this simile) in the process of forming gametes, but genes (cards) that are close together are less likely to be separated in a shuffle because they are physically close together: They are "linked." So, linkage represents a deviation from Mendel's second law of the independent assortment of genes.

Say we are searching the deck for a gene or genes whose location is unknown, such as a gene influencing a particular behavioral trait, such as dyslexia. As mentioned earlier, the deck in question, the genome, is vast since it contains approximately 30,000 genes in its coding regions and a much larger amount of non-coding DNA. Our job is to find sequence variations (particular cards) in this huge deck which influence the trait we are studying. Moreover, in this deck there are many, many other sequence variations influencing other traits and many more sequence variations in non-coding regions. A very few of these other sequence variations will happen to lie close enough to the sequence variations we are searching for so as to be linked to them. If we have a map of sequence variations or "markers" across the genome that are roughly evenly spaced and close enough together to detect linkage to most or all of the adjacent genes, then we can use these markers to search for the location of sequence variations that influence the trait we are interested in.

Somewhat more formally, we have a hypothesis that there are sequence variations somewhere in the genome that influence the trait in question. Presumably this hypothesis is based on studies of the trait with the indirect genetic methods discussed earlier, so that we already know that the trait is familial, heritable, and perhaps even subject to major gene influence. If our hypothesis is correct, then individuals with more of this trait will on average have more of these sequence variations than individuals with less of the trait. In other words, our hypothesis implies that these particular sequence variations are co-transmitted with levels of the trait across generations (in the case of a single gene and a categorical trait, we would say that they co-segregate). So, levels of the trait are a proxy for the unknown causative sequence variations, if our hypothesis is correct. Because of the phenomenon of linkage, nearby sequence variations, some of which are markers in our genomic map, are also co-transmitted within families along with levels of the trait and the unknown sequence variations. Hence, two out of the three co-transmitted things are known to us: levels of the trait and sequence variations in markers, and knowledge of these two things allows us to gain knowledge of the approximate location of the third unknown thing. Thus, a finding of linkage between particular markers and levels of the trait indicates that there is a gene near these markers which influences the trait we are studying.

In sum, co-transmission of genetic markers and a behavioral trait helps us to map the approximate location of genes whose alleles influence that trait.

Linkage methods are broadly divided into those that require specification of the mode of transmission and those that do not. The former, which require specification of these parameters of transmission are called "parametric" or "model-dependent" and the latter are called "non-parametric" or "model-free." Parametric linkage methods were developed first (Morton, 1955), partly because of the historical emphasis among geneticists on Mendelian traits. For a student of behavior, it is quickly apparent that parametric linkage analysis is testing a very strong hypothesis indeed, namely that there is a single Mendelian gene that has a major causal influence on the trait in question. If penetrance is modeled at a high value, then the finding of only a very few subjects in a family who have the relevant marker but not the trait (or the reverse), disconfirms this hypothesis.

For most behavioral traits, transmission is unlikely to be Mendelian because multiple genes and environmental risk factors will influence the trait and so the parameters of transmission will be unknown. Hence, to use parametric linkage methods we will have to make assumptions (specify parameters) which are likely to be incorrect. Parametric linkage methods do have the advantage of statistical power because they are testing such a strong hypothesis, namely of consistent co-transmission in an extended family between a marker and a trait. They can be useful in analyzing data from very large extended families, especially if these are considered one at a time. However, since there may be genetic heterogeneity across such families, combining their data may be misleading.

Non-parametric methods require fewer assumptions and are generally preferable in linkage studies of behavioral traits (Pauls, 1993; Rutter, 1994). They also do not require large extended families and often utilize sibling pairs from nuclear families. Sibling pair methods for analyzing quantitative traits utilizing multiple markers have been developed (e.g. Kruglyak and Lander, 1995). However, sibling pair methods are less powerful. The sample size necessary in a sib pair study to detect linkage increases considerably as the proportion of families linked to the same single locus goes down. In addition, nuclear families often do not provide enough genetic information to determine which markers are identical by descent in a sibling pair. So, applying model-free methods to extended pedigrees can be a useful compromise.

One sibling pair method which is useful for mapping genes that influence extreme, quantitative traits, is called "interval mapping." Interval mapping is an extension of the DF method discussed earlier; it was developed by David Fulker and colleagues at the Institute for Behavioral Genetics in Boulder, Colorado (Cardon and Fulker, 1994; Fulker, Cherny, and Cardon, 1995). Interval mapping is particularly useful in studies of cognitive and behavioral disorders because (1) it is appropriate for extreme traits that are measured quantitatively, (2) it is quite powerful statistically, (3) it readily tests whether the same chromosomal region is linked to different levels of the trait, even levels from either end of the distribution, and (4) it is quite flexible and can be readily extended to consider dominance, bivariate linkage (which is needed to find genes responsible for comorbidities), or interactions with other factors, such as gender. Interval mapping has been used successfully to identify the location of a QTL on the short arm of chromosome 6 which influences dyslexia (Cardon et al., 1994).

We now consider association analysis. Association analysis tests for a correlation between a particular allele of a candidate gene and a phenotype. To appreciate the difference between linkage and association analysis (Hodge, 1993), it is important to understand the difference between linkage and linkage disequilibrium. In the case of linkage, the particular allele of a given locus that is linked to a behavioral trait will vary across families because recombination will have sorted different alleles of the marker with the particular causative allele of the linked gene that influences the trait. Say we found linkage between dyslexia and the gene for the ABO blood type. In some families, most or all of the dyslexics would have type A blood, and the non-dyslexics would have types B or O. In other families, the dyslexics would have type B blood, and in still others they would have type O blood. So linkage between dyslexia and the ABO gene does *not* mean that all dyslexics have a particular blood type. In this case, the gene that influences dyslexia and the ABO gene are close enough together that recombination (shuffling) between is reduced but not eliminated. In the thousands of years since the mutation in the dyslexia gene occurred, recombination has shuffled that gene with different alleles of the ABO gene across families. But what if the dyslexia gene and the ABO gene are so close together that little or no reshuffling has occurred over those thousands of years? In this case, we would say the two genes are in linkage disequilibrium and, as a result, virtually all dyslexics across families would have a particular ABO blood type. In that case, there would be an association between dyslexia and the ABO allele that produces that particular blood type.

In sum, if there is allele sharing for a marker gene among individuals with a given trait (e.g. dyslexia) that is found within but not across families, we say there is linkage. If there is allele sharing both within and across families, we say there is association.

There are three possible reasons for a finding of association: (1) there is linkage disequilibrium between the candidate allele and a nearby causal allele, (2) the candidate allele *is* the causal allele (in which case, there would be no recombination), or (3) an artifact produces association but not linkage. One prominent artifact that has been identified in case-control association studies is ethnic stratification. Allele frequencies vary considerably in human populations, even within groups labeled as "Caucasian," "Hispanic," or "African American" (e.g. Seaman et al., 1999). Therefore, an ethnically-matched case-control association study may nonetheless confound allele frequencies with group, thus producing a spurious association.

To avoid this confound, within-family association methods are used, such as the transmission disequilibrium test (Ewens and Spielman, 1995) and the haplotype relative risk method (Falk and Rubenstein, 1987; Terwilliger and Ott, 1992). Both these methods test whether the candidate allele is more frequently transmitted to affected family members than to non-affected family members. These methods are now being generalized for use with continuous traits and covariates.

Nonetheless, even within-family association methods will fail to detect a causative gene in which there are multiple mutations across families, each of which produces the disorder. In this case, there would be linkage to markers close to this gene, but not association to a particular allele of the gene.

As stated previously, association analysis is usually appropriate only if one has a hypothesis about which particular gene is influencing a trait. That hypothesis could come from knowledge of the neurobiology of the trait (the trait involves dopamine transmission, therefore genes for dopamine receptors may be involved in its cause) or from previous linkage studies (there is a gene in this region influencing the trait and one of the known genes in this region has a function that makes it a possible candidate gene).

Obviously, the ultimate goals of both linkage and association methods are to identify the mutations which causally influence the trait in question, and to characterize how these mutations alter the function of their genes in the development of brain and behavior.

Linkage and association methods have begun to unravel part of the etiology of behaviorally defined developmental disorders. Linkage has been found between dyslexia and markers in a 2 centimorgan region of the short arm of chromosome 6 in five samples by three independent laboratories (Cardon et al., 1994; Grigorenko et al., 1997; Gayan et al., 1999; Fisher et al., 1999), although one study (Field and Kaplan, 1998) did not find this linkage. Association between an allele of the gene for dopamine 4 receptor (DRD4) and ADHD has now been found in several studies (e.g. Swanson et al., 1998; Faraone et al., 1999). This association makes theoretical sense because this particular allele causes a blunted response to dopamine.

Implications for Fundamental Issues

What we have already discovered from genetic studies of cognitive development has implications for fundamental issues in developmental cognitive neuroscience. I will discuss two such issues here: (1) How do conceptions of genetic influences fit with theories of development? (2) What have we already learned from genetic studies about brain mechanisms in atypical development?

With regard to the first issue, one can broadly distinguish two conceptions of development, each of which is compatible with a different view of how genes act in development. Nativism or neonativsm is compatible with genetic determinism whereas constructionism is compatible with probabilistic epigenesis (Gottlieb, 1991; 1998; this volume). As already discussed, it is misleading to think about the actions of genes in a deterministic way. In addition, individual genes frequently affect multiple phenotypes (pleiotropy) and complex behavioral phenotypes are almost undoubtedly affected by multiple genes (polygeny). The combination of these two notions of pleiotropy and polygeny means that the correspondence relations between genes and complex behavioral phenotypes are many-to-many, not one to one. Lying in between genes and behavioral outcomes are several levels of analysis and an undoubtedly very complicated set of developmental interactions.

So the nativist notion that there might be a gene that affects a very specific aspect of cognition, such as a particular aspect of grammar, is very unlikely. Support for this unlikely hypothesis seemed to be provided by an extended family (KE) that appeared to have an autosomal dominantly transmitted deficit in regular inflectional morphology, i.e. forming regular past tense and plural forms (Gopnik, 1990; Pinker, 1991). Further study revealed that although the KE family had an autosomal dominant disorder, the gene for which was localized to chromosome 7p (Fisher et al., 1998), their speech and language phenotype was actually much broader and included a severe oral facial dyspraxia, about a 20 point deficit in IQ, and deficits on a broad array of language measures (Varga-Khadem et al., 1995). So, instead of having a defective grammar gene, this family has a mutation which broadly disrupts cognitive and motor development but in such a way that speech and language development are more severely affected. So, this mutation produces a mix of general and specific deficits, which is characteristic of most genetic syndromes.

In thinking about the genetic contributions to human universals, like grammar, that are unique to our species, one is faced immediately with a severe constraint: the number of genes that are unique to humans must be quite small, since the genetic homology between humans and chimpanzees is about 99 percent. Since most of the base pair differences between humans and chimps are in genes that both species share, there are unlikely to be very many genes that are unique to humans, although the exact number is unknown. So, it is extremely unlikely that there are enough uniquely human genes to allocate each one to a unique human cognitive universal, even if it were biologically plausible for a gene to code for a specific aspect of cognition. A plausible alternative hypothesis is that the genetic basis of human uniqueness is partly due to changes in regulatory genes. Such changes would have increased the number of neurons produced in brain development and lengthened the time to maturity (Changeaux, 1985). These kind of general changes operating in a particular epigenetic and ecological context may go a long way towards explaining human uniqueness.

The second question concerns what have we already learned about different ways genes alter brain and cognitive development. One can already list three broad classes of genetic effects on brain development: (1) on brain size, by altering the number of neurons or synapses, (2) on neuronal migration, sometimes in a regionally-specific fashion, and on (3) neurotransmission, either by changing levels of neurotransmitter or by changing the binding properties of receptor proteins. There will undoubtedly be many other mechanisms, but just with these three, a fairly broad range of individual cognitive differences are being accounted for.

For instance, with regard to the first effect, it is well known that brain size is affected in many genetic syndromes. Thus, there is microcephaly in Down syndrome (Coyle, Oster-Granite, and Gearhart, 1986) and other mental retardation syndromes. In contrast, in about a quarter of individuals with autism (Bailey, Phillips, and Rutter, 1996) and in fragile X syndrome, there is macrocephaly. The mechanism in fragile X appears to be related to a gene that influences synaptic pruning (Willems et al., 1995). Neurocomputational models support the straightforward intuition that having too few or too many neurons or connections in brain networks would affect cognitive development in different ways. Having too few nodes or connections in a neural network would limit its representational capacity. Having too many would lead to a network that fails to generalize (see Oliver et al., 2000).

With regard to the second effect, there are well-studied genetic mutations in both mice and fruit flies that affect neuronal migration (Changeux, 1985), and there is evidence for migrational anomalies in several human syndromes. In the non-human cases it has sometimes been demonstrated that the migrational anomalies cause particular behavioral deficits.

The third kind of effect has been demonstrated in PKU, where an enzyme defect prevents the conversion of phenylalanine into tyrosine, which is the rate-limiting precursor for the synthesis of dopamine. So, even the mild elevations of phenylalanine found in treated PKU can produce dopamine depletion in prefrontal cortex (Diamond, this volume).

Another way neurotransmission can be affected is through alterations in the binding properties of receptors for neurotransmitters. These receptors are proteins coded for by genes. Their binding properties depend on their tertiary structure, which is determined by the way they fold up. Base pair differences in the gene for a receptor can cause differences in its tertiary structure and hence in its binding properties. These changes can in turn make a particular neurotransmitter more or less available at the synapse. As discussed earlier, ADHD has been found to be associated with an allele of the DRD4 gene. Evidence of allelic differences in other receptor genes in other psychiatric illnesses is beginning to emerge, so this third kind of effect could account for many of psychiatric disorders in which there are known neurotransmitter imbalances.

There are undoubtedly many other genetic mechanisms underlying brain development. Work is underway to identify candidate genes that affect brain development (Vicente et al., 1997) and to test whether these genes influence behavioral disorders.

In sum, the complex pathways that run from genes to brain development to behavioral development are beginning to be elucidated. The pace of such discoveries is now beginning to accelerate rapidly due to the success of the Human Genome Project, the increasing sophistication of the genetic methods applied to the analysis of cognition and behavior, and new methods and findings in other parts of cognitive neuroscience. It is fairly safe to say that these accelerating genetic discoveries will have a widening impact on the field of developmental cognitive neuroscience.

REFERENCES

Bailey, A., Phillips, W., and Rutter, M. (1996). Autism: Towards an integration of clinical, genetic, neuropsychological, and neurobiological perspectives. *J. of Child Psychology and Psych*. 37, 89–126.

Cardon, L. R., Smith, S. D., Fulker, D. W., Kimberling, W. J., Pennington, B. F., and DeFries, J. C. (1994). Quantitative trait locus for reading disability on chromosome 6. *Science* 266, 276–9.

Cardon, L. R. and Fulker, D. W. (1994). The power of interval mapping of quantitative trait loci, using selected sib pairs. *Am. J. Hum. Genet*. 55, 825–33.

Changeaux, J. P. (1985). *Neuronal Man*. New York: Oxford University Press.

Coyle, J. T., Oster-Granite, M. L., and Gearhart, J. D. (1986). The neurobiologic consequence of Down Syndrome. *Brain Res. Bul*. 16, 773–87.

Crnic, L. S., and Pennington, B. F. (2000). Down Syndrome: Neuropsychology and animal models. In C. Rovee-Collier, L. P. Lipsitt, and H. Hayne (eds.), *Progress in Infancy Research* (vol. I), pp. 69–111. Mahwah, NJ: Lawrence Erlbaum Associates.

DeFries, J. C. and Fulker, D. W. (1988). Multiple regression analysis of twin data: Etiology of deviant scores versus individual differences. *Acta Geneticae Medicae et Gemellolgiae* 37, 205–16.

Ewens, W. J. and Spielman, R. S. (1995). The transmission/disequilibrium test: history, subdivision, and admixture. *Am. J. Hum. Genet*. 98, 91–101.

Falk, C. T. and Rubenstein, P. (1987). Haplotype relative risks: an easy reliable way to construct a proper control sample for risk calculations. *Ann. Hum. Gen*. 51, 227–33.

Faraone, J. V., Biederman, J., Chen, W. J. et al. (1992). Segregation analysis of attention deficit hyperactivity disorder. *Psych. Gen*. 2, 257–75.

Faraone, J. V., Biedermann, J., Weiffenbach, B., Keith, T., Chu, M., Weaver, A., Spencer, T. J., Wilens, T. E., Frazier, J., Cleves, M., and Sakai, J. (1999). A family based association study of the dopamine D4 gene 7-repeat allele and attention deficit hyperactivity disorder in families ascertained through ADHD adults: A preliminary report. *Am. J. of Psychiatry* 156, 768–70.

Field, L. L. and Kaplan, B. J. (1998). Absence of linkage of phonological coding dyslexia to chromosome 6p23–p21.3 in a large family data set. *Am. J. Hum. Genet*. 63(5), 1448–56.

Fisher, S. E., Marlow, A. J., Lamb, J. M. E., Williams, D. F., Richardson, A. J., and Weeks, D. E. (1999). A quantitative-trait locus on chromosome 6p influences different aspects of developmental dyslexia. *Am. J. of Hum. Gen*. 64, 146–56.

Fisher, S. E., Varga-Khadem, F., Watkins, K. E., Monaco, A. P., and Pembrey, M. E. (1998). Localization of a gene implicated in a severe speech and language disorder. *Nature Genet*. 18, 168–70.

Fulker, D. W., Cherny, S. S., and Cardon, L. R. (1995). Multipoint interval mapping of quantitative trait loci using sib pairs. *Am. J. Hum. Genet*. 56, 1224–33.

Galton, F. (1869). *Hereditary genius: An inquiry into its laws and consequences*. London: Macmillan.

Gayan, J., Smith, S. D., Cherny, S. S., Cardon, L. R., Fulker, D. W., Brower, A. M., Olson, R. K., Pennington, B. F., and DeFries, J. C. (1999). Quantitative-trait locus for specific language and reading deficits on chromosome 6p. *Am. J. of Hum. Gen.* 64, 157–64.

Gilger, J. W., Pennington, B. F., and DeFries, J. C. (1991). Risk for reading disability as a function of parental history in three family studies. *Reading and Writing* 3, 205–17.

Gopnik, M. (1990). Feature-blind grammar and dysphasia. *Nature* 344 (6268), 715.

Gottlieb, G. (1991). Experiential canalization of behavioral development: Theory. *Dev. Psych.* 27, 4–13.

Gottlieb, G. (1998). Normally occurring environmental and behavioral influences on gene activity: From central dogma to probabilistic epigenesis. *Psych. Review.* 105, 792–802.

Greenough, W. T., Black, J. E., and Wallace, C. S. (1987). Experience and brain development. *Child Development* 58, 539–59.

Grigorenko, E. L., Wood, F. B., Meyer, M. S., Hart, L. A., Speed, W. C., Shuster, A., and Pauls, D. L. (1997). Susceptibility loci for distinct components of developmental dyslexia on chromosomes 6 and 15. *Am. J. of Hum. Gen.* 60, 27–39.

Hahn, W., van Ness, J., and Maxwell, I. (1978). Complex population of mRNA sequences in large polyadenylated nuclear RNA molecules. *Pro. Nat. Acad. of Sci. (USA)* 75, 5544–7.

Hodge, S. E. (1993). Linkage analysis versus association analysis: distinguishing between two models that explain disease-marker associations. *Am. J. Hum. Genet.* 53, 367–84.

Johnson, M. H. (1997). *Developmental cognitive neuroscience.* Oxford: Blackwell.

Kruglyak, L. and Lander, E. S. (1995). Complete multipoint sib-pair analysis of qualitative and quantitative traits. *Am. J. Hum. Genet.* 57, 439–54.

Morton, M. E. (1955). Sequential tests for the detection of linkage. *Am. J. Hum. Genet.* 7, 227–318.

Oliver, A., Johnson, M. H., Karmiloff-Smith, A. K., and Pennigton, B. F. (2000). Deviations in the emergence of representations: A neuroconstructionist framework for analyzing developmental disorders. *Dev. Sci.* 3, 1–40.

Oyama, S. (1985). *The ontogeny of information.* Cambridge: Cambridge University Press.

Pauls, D. L. (1993). Behavioral disorders: lessons in linkage. *Nature Genet.* 3, 4–5.

Paterson, S. J., Brown, J. H., Gsödl, M. K., Johnson, M. H., and Karmiloff-Smith, A. (1999). Cognitive modularity and genetic disorders. *Science* 286, 2355–8.

Pinker, S. (1991). Rules of language. *Science* 253, 530–5.

Plomin, R., Owen, M. J., and McGuffin, P. (1994). The genetic basis of complex human behaviors. *Science* 264, 1733–9.

Plomin, R. and McClearn, G. (1993). *Nature Nurture & Psychology.* Washington DC: American Psychological Association.

Plomin, R., McClearn, G. E., DeFries, J. C., and Rutter, M. (1997). *Behavioral Genetics.* New York: W. H. Freeman & Co.

Rende, R. and Plomin, R. (1995). Nature, nurture, and the development of psychopathology. In D. Cicchetti and D. J. Cohen (eds.). *Developmental Psychopathology* (vol. I), pp. 291–314. New York: John Wiley & Sons, Inc.

Rutter, M. (1994). Psychiatric genetics research challenges and pathways forward. *Am. J. Med. Genet. (Neuro. Genet.)* 54, 185–98.

Scarr, S. (1992). Developmental theories of the 1990s: Development and individual differences. *Child Dev.* 63, 1–19.

Seaman, M. I., Fisher, J. B., Chang, F. M., and Kidd, K. K. (1999). Tandem duplication polymorphism upstream of the dopamine D4 receptor gene (DRD4). *Am. J. of Med. Genet. (Neuro. Genet.)* 88.

Shallice, T. (1988). *From Neuropsychology to Mental Structure.* New York: Cambridge University Press.

Shatz, C. J. (1993). The developing brain. In *Mind and Brain. Scien. Am. Readings*, pp. 15–26. New York: W. H. Freeman and Co.

Swanson, J. M., Sunohara, G. A., Kennedy, J. L., Regino, R., Fineberg, E., Wigal, T., Lerner, M., Williams, L., LaHoste, G. J., and Wigal, S. (1998). Association of the dopamine receptor D4 (DRD4) gene with a refined phenotype of attention deficit hyperactivity disorder (ADHD): a family-based approach. *Mol. Psych.* 3, 38–41.

Tager-Flusberg, H. (1999). *Neurodevelopmental Disorders*. Cambridge, MA: MIT Press.

Terwilliger, J. D. and Ott, J. (1992). A haplotype-based "haplotype relative risk" approach to detecting allelic associations. *Hum. Heredity* 42, 337–46.

Van Orden, G. C., Pennington, B. F., and Stone, G. (2000). What do double dissociations prove? *Cog. Sci.* 25, 111–72.

Varga-Khadem, F., Watkins, K., Alcock, K., Fletcher, P., and Passingham, R. E. (1995). Praxic and nonverbal cognitive deficits in a large family with a genetically transmitted speech and language disorder. *Proc. Nat. Acad. Sciences USA* 92, 930–3.

Vicente, A. M., Macciardi, F., Verga, M., Bassett, A. S., Honer, W. E., Bean, G., and Kennedy, J. L. (1997). NCAM and schizophrenia: genetic studies. *Mol. Psychiatry* 2, 65–9.

Willems, P. J., Reyniers, E., and Oostra, B. A. (1995). An animal model for fragile X syndrome. *Mental Retard. and Dev. Dis. Res. Rev.* 1, 298–302.

Name Index

Subject Index